# NEW YORK BY THE NUMBERS

T0302982

# New York by the Numbers

## State and City in Perpetual Crisis

Raymond J. Keating

MADISON BOOKS
Lanham • New York • London

*Copyright © 1997 by Madison Books*

*All rights reserved.*
*No part of this book may be reproduced in any form or by any electronic or mechanical means, including information storage and retrieval systems, without written permission from the publisher, except by a reviewer who may quote passages in a review.*

*Published by Madison Books*
*4720 Boston Way*
*Lanham, Maryland 20706*

*3 Henrietta Street*
*London WC2E 8LU, England*

*Hardcover edition published by the University Press of America.*

*Library of Congress Cataloging-in-Publication Data*

*Keating, Raymond J.*
*New York by the numbers : state and city in perpetual crisis / Raymond J. Keating.*
*p. cm.*
*Includes bibliographical references and index.*
*ISBN 0-7618-0622-9 (cloth : alk. paper). — ISBN 1-56833-087-1 (pbk. : alk. paper)*
*1. New York (State)—Statistics. 2. New York (N. Y.)—Statistics. I. Title.*
*HA545.K43 1997*
*317.47—dc21 96-37327*

*ISBN 1–56833–087–1 (pbk : alk. paper)*

*Distributed by National Book Network*

*™ The paper used in this publication meets the minimum requirements of American National Standard for Information Sciences—Permanence of Paper for Printed Library Materials, ANSI Z39.48–1984.*
*Manufactured in the United States of America.*

For Beth and David

# TABLE OF CONTENTS

# Foreword

Burdensome taxes and regulations draining economic life and vitality. State and city government bureaucrats wasting billions of dollars annually. A public education monopoly failing our children while school property taxes skyrocket. Individual responsibility giving way to government dependency.

If a picture is worth a thousand words, then the charts, tables and graphs in the following pages are worth millions. Ray Keating's *New York by the Numbers: State and City in Perpetual Crisis* vividly illustrates the long and continuing decline of both New York State and New York City. Individuals concerned about New York must face reality by educating themselves about the facts and trends that have led to the decline of the once mighty Empire State. *New York by the Numbers* provides this reality check.

Keating's numbers tell a grim tale of social engineering run amok. Since the 1930s, faith in the individual and the marketplace in New York has been replaced by faith in the bureaucrat and government.

As is the case whenever false idols are worshiped, the price to be paid is heavy. Individuals, entrepreneurs, and businesses have fled the Empire State. New York State's job creation rate regularly lags far behind the national average. In the Big Apple over the past quarter century, job creation has been nonexistent. Indeed, in New York City today, fewer private-sector jobs exist than did in the late 1950s.

Don't get the wrong impression, though. Keating is no sour-puss conservative. For all of his sobering tables and graphs, he is optimistic about the possibility of revitalizing New York. Indeed, every New York elected official needs to read his opening chapter explaining why big government fails and markets succeed. If I can summarize: incentives matter and freedom works. Understanding this simple lesson would give New York a fighting chance.

Some positive movement has been detected recently. For example, New York's crime statistics are improving. State income tax rates have been slowly decreasing since the late 1970s. In the last two state budget years, the growth in total spending has slowed considerably. And efforts to restrain spending have been detected in New York City as well.

However, much more needs to be done. While crime numbers have been falling, they still remain above the crime rates of just thirty years ago. Government spending levels across the state of New York—particularly in New York City—far outpace the rest of the nation. The state budget, as Keating clearly shows, remains littered with thousands of pork expenditures amounting to billions of dollars wasted annually. State-level income tax rates continue to linger above the national average. The state's capital gains tax rate remains at a historically lofty level, and runs even higher in real terms as gains are not indexed for inflation. And in New York City, the combination of both state *and* city income taxes—personal income, non-indexed capital gains, corporate income, and unincorporated business taxes—keep the city's economy flat on its back. High property levies, regulations, failed public schools, and a bevy of other taxes add to the troubles.

Keating's pro-growth agenda of dramatic supply-side tax and regulatory cuts, school choice, and much smaller government stands as New York's only chance at rebirth. But we must not fool ourselves. Repairing decades of damage will be an arduous undertaking, subject to relapses along the way. In particular, as the numbers show, New York City faces the gravest challenge, with government spending, tax, and regulatory burdens far more crushing than in any other city in the country, only barring the District of Columbia.

Keating did his part in turning the public policy debate in a positive direction in Washington, D.C. with his first book, *D.C. by the Numbers: A State of Failure*. Instead of pushing new government programs, now the discussion is centered on a low flat tax for the District and downsizing government. Keating's *New York by the Numbers* will help to do the same thing for both the state and city of New York.

Keating may not get everything he calls for in his final chapter, "The Road to Revitalization." Given the nature of government and New York politicians, many wasteful programs will continue and some counterproductive taxes may live to see another day. But most of the goals set out in the final pages of this book—including the elimination of the state's personal income and capital gains taxes, dramatic regulatory reform, elimination of New York City's own income-based levies, the elimination of various state and city government programs, the implementation of state-level term limits, and the ending of the state's off-budget public authorities scams—generally must prevail if New York is to ever truly grow and prosper again.

Perhaps most critical, Keating understands that it takes more than merely slashing government programs to save New York. Taxes and regulations must be slashed as well so that real, private-sector opportunity can replace government dependency.

Indeed, throughout the nineteenth century and into the early twentieth century, New York was lush with opportunity. New York's was a landscape of hope and dreams, and to some extent it still is—but now far too many aspirations are crushed by big government. If the welfare state gives way to free markets, if bureaucrats step aside and let entrepreneurs create and take risks, if competition is allowed to shatter the public school monopoly, real opportunity will flourish in New York during the twenty-first century.

With *New York by the Numbers*, Ray Keating not only tracks New York's demise and the primary reasons for this dramatic fall, but he also plots a new course for the future. It is now up to the citizens and elected officials of New York to follow that course.

Steve Forbes
September 1996

# ACKNOWLEDGMENTS

This book would not have been possible without support from the following organizations:

The John M. Olin Foundation

The Small Business Survival Foundation

In addition, I thank my colleagues, Karen Kerrigan, Jim Slagter, and Matthew Carolan, and as always my wife, Beth Keating, for their support and understanding.

# Chapter One

# New York: Big Government vs. the Market

New York State and New York City always seem to be wrestling with major problems. A sagging economy, taxes, health care, budgets and deficits, jobs, education, homelessness, housing, crime, business flight, welfare, dwindling population—the list of woes is long and seemingly without end. Both state and city struggle year after year in perpetual crisis.

Unfortunately, few of New York's leaders seem to fully grasp the origins of these crises. In fact, New York officials continually brandish the very instrument of New York's destruction—excessive governmental action.

New York State and New York City suffer from an affliction that plagues much of the United States—big government—but to a far more severe degree. With the possible exception of the District of Columbia, New York's welfare state and its commensurate woes are more daunting than anywhere else in the nation.

Neither of the two major political parties can claim to have exerted much energy against the construction of New York's governmental leviathan. In New York, big government claims a long, unfortunate history of bipartisanship. Indeed, as we shall see, two Republicans probably carry the greatest guilt for New York's economic and fiscal troubles.

But the reader may ask—especially some lifelong New Yorkers—isn't government good and benevolent? Doesn't government action, for example, spur economic growth, provide housing to those who would not otherwise have it, help to educate our young, and alleviate poverty for the downtrodden? Such questions usually are followed by some kind of hopeful disclaimer wrapped in blissful ignorance: And besides, government in New York isn't that much bigger or more inefficient than other places across the country, right?

The following pages provide some answers to these and many other questions relating to the economy, tax and budget issues, education, crime, and societal trends in New York, through the use of numbers, rankings, charts, and graphs. But to help set the tone of this book, quick answers to the above-mentioned questions are in order here at the outset:

• Isn't government good and benevolent? More often than not, the answer is "no." As witnessed throughout the twentieth century, government is capable of great horror. Whether it be the countless murders carried out by totalitarian regimes around the globe, or the tax and regulatory strangleholds placed on entrepreneurs in New York, government is capable of varying degrees of destruction. At times, government purposely destroys, while at other times destruction is an unintended consequence.

• Doesn't government action, for example, spur economic growth, provide housing to those who would not otherwise have it, help educate our young, and alleviate poverty for the downtrodden? No. Governmental actions usually present substantial obstacles to economic growth, housing construction, and responsive and high-quality education, while doing more to perpetuate poverty than to alleviate it.

• Government in New York isn't that much bigger or inefficient than other places across the country, right? Wrong. Page after page of this book show that both New York State and New York City governments generally are far bigger and more burdensome than those in other states and cities.

In the end, big government creates far more problems than it solves. And since New York is a big government kind of place, we have big problems. A look at New York by the numbers tells much about the genesis and development of New York's many woes. However, before getting into the numbers and details of the economy, budgets, and life in both New York State and New York City, a general discussion of why the economics of expansive government fails is in order. Following is a discussion of why markets work best.

In numerous ways over the years, New York public-policy makers have subscribed to Keynesian economics and industrial policy, two prominent failures of twentieth-century economic thought. Both New Yorks grew to become international economic powerhouses throughout the nineteenth and early twentieth centuries largely because both state and city followed supply-side economic and fiscal policies. The demise of supply-side economic thought and policy contributed greatly to the demise of both New York State and City.

## The Problem with the Big Government Model

Government tends to be long on good intentions and short in terms of establishing sound economic incentives. Here lies one of the two basic problems with big government. The other, of course, is the question of government's infringement upon individual liberty.

Proponents of extensive governmental action in the economy and individuals' lives see problems everywhere they turn and propose government "solutions" for each and every one. The free marketplace, for example, is viewed as a source of exploitation, rather than a font of opportunity. The notion of exploitation, of course, implies that individuals lack the ability or wherewithal to make their own way in life. Indeed, paternalism deeply influences big-government advocates. The government must take care of individuals for they are not smart or wise enough to take care of themselves. The state has to step in and take over.

State action takes many forms. Income redistribution stands most prominent. New taxes are imposed, existing taxes increased, and myriad welfare programs created and expanded, all in order to transfer wealth and income. In addition, a regulatory web is spun to trap and control entire industries, businesses, and entrepreneurs. In turn, subsidies and loans are provided to industries or particular businesses deemed worthy by government bureaucrats (i.e., usually businesses exhibiting deft political skills or possessing close political allies). Most families are given no choice but to send children to government schools. The list goes on and on.

The possibility that dire consequences might result from governmental action rarely enters into consideration before such steps actually are taken, and once grim consequences materialize, they largely are ignored. But most of these outcomes are easily foreseeable when economics and incentives are considered and understood.

For example, lavish welfare programs skew incentives at both ends of the economic spectrum. Middle and upper income earners are heavily taxed in the name of income redistribution, thereby possessing few incentives to work harder, save, invest, and take economic risks. Meanwhile, government dependency is fostered among low-income individuals as incentives to undertake productive economic activity are diminished significantly. For many individuals, work, investment, and risk taking simply do not pay under a welfare regime.

Government support for teenage and single mothers sounds nice, but manages to inflict double damage. Single motherhood obviously is promoted through government subsidy, and the traditional male role as family provider is obliterated. The "daddy state" takes over the responsibilities of actual fathers. Individual responsibility trades at a deep discount under the welfare state.

Far-reaching regulation of entrepreneurs and businesses raises the costs of doing business significantly. Incentives for investment and entrepreneurship naturally suffer. Fewer jobs are created and many existing jobs destroyed. Consumers pay the burdens of higher prices and fewer choices.

Big-government advocates see so-called "market failure"—largely figments of their imaginations—all around them. They fail to consider the fact that government action may be the real source of woes, or that government action may only make matters far worse. Welfare serves as an example once again.

Government activists long ago deemed private charity as not being up to the job of helping the poor. But in fact, private charity works under an incentive structure that in the end does far more good for poor people than does government. Private charity must show its funders real, substantive results in order to continue being funded. Incentives are strong to quickly get people back on their feet, in a job, and self-sufficient. In addition, private charity tends to be local in nature. Recipients sit across a table from a neighbor, rather than merely filing a form with a faceless bureaucrat. Budgets also are usually quite tight in private charities, with dollars therefore spent carefully.

In contrast, government operates under no such incentives. Poor results generally translate into more funding. Incentives to get people off the dole are practically nonexistent. In fact, one can reasonably argue that public welfare bureaucrats possess every incentive to perpetuate poverty, thereby perpetuating their own programs and jobs. Government welfare advocates never claim that their goal is to make welfare unnecessary; instead, they assert their goal is to "help" as many people as possible. Lastly, government welfare budgets grow annually, and usually at a generous pace, so that incentives to spend wisely remain quite weak. Indeed, reported "cuts" in federal, state, and local welfare programs usually amount to nothing more than mere reductions in the projected rate of spending growth.

Additionally, the existence of a massive government welfare state has so supplanted private charity, and created such a tremendous underclass, that talk of whittling away government welfare and returning to a system of private charity even frightens today's private charity industry. Today, private charities tend to lobby hard against any kind of restraint or cuts in government welfare programs. It is perhaps most tragic to witness many priests, bishops, and pastors—who, in the past, would have been leaders of private charity efforts—leading the effort to preserve public welfare, one of the great destroyers of individual responsibility, morality, and the family structure. Many in the religious community succumb to government's perverse incentives—public welfare *seems* to make their jobs much easier—human nature being what it is. Also, a wide range of religious institutions receive their own pieces of silver courtesy of the taxpayers. The New York State budget is flush with line items directed at churches and various religious-based groups. Naturally, since these clerics fail to notice their own subjugation to perverse incentives, they forget that others will fall prey to such temptations as well.

For government in general, incentives to restrain or cut spending do not exist in any substantive way. After all, government officials and bureaucrats are spending someone else's—i.e., the taxpayers'—money. The market disciplines of ownership, profits, and losses do not factor into the government equation. In addition, influence and power in government remain largely tied to the size of budgets and the number of employees. Incentives lie in favor of expanding budgets and increasing staff. The government apparatus provides strong disincentives for productive activities.

Beyond incentives lies the second major problem with big government: its coercive nature. I am certainly not disputing the basic, *limited* role of government in helping to ensure a civil society and a productive economy. But this is accomplished through a government centered for the most part on the protection of life, limb, and property, guaranteeing contracts, and dispensing justice. When venturing far beyond these narrow functions, government infringes upon individual liberties.

Should individuals be forced by government to pay for ventures that are better left to the marketplace? This question applies to a wide range of activities undertaken and assets owned by government, including land purchases, golf courses, marinas, stadiums and arenas, business subsidies and loans, public housing, mass transit, energy production, higher education, as well as failed public schools and bloated welfare programs. Not only are such endeavors often counterproductive, with the political decisions of government bureaucrats holding sway, but liberty dictates that they be left to the private sector, where individuals are free to make their own decisions.

## The Supply-Side Model

Markets work. Unfortunately, this message sometimes seems to penetrate deeper into parts of the former Soviet Union than into parts of New York.

Markets fail to suffer from any of the woes that government action does. When unencumbered by high taxes and excessive government regulation, the free marketplace provides sound incentives for working, saving, investment, and risk taking—the very engines of economic growth.

Of course, individuals operating in the marketplace are subject to the disciplines of competition. Profits and losses, for example, are not merely some cold calculus of the marketplace, but signals as to where resources should be allocated, as well as measures of how well or poorly entrepreneurs and businesses are meeting and *creating* market demands. Indeed, *creating* new demands—that is, supplying new goods and services, along with new efficiencies and innovation—is the path to real prosperity.

Contrary to establishment economic thinking for more than the past half-century, since the time of John Maynard Keynes, the economy is not driven or guided by government attempts to manipulate aggregate demand. The Keynesian view of the economy certainly can be detected in both New York State's and New York City's government policies of the past several decades. Almost any government endeavor can be justified on the basis of the Keynesian economic model, that is, that increased government spending will boost aggregate demand and therefore boost the economy. But to the contrary, supply-side economics is correct to place supply ahead of demand in the economics pecking order.

Supply-side economics has been defined and ill-defined many times over the past two decades. Supply-siders—sometimes to their own detriment—often fail to agree on a definition. But at its core, supply-side economics is about relative prices. Economist Norman Ture blew away much of the supply-side fog by summarizing: "Supply-side economics is merely the application of price theory—so-called 'microeconomics'—in the analysis of problems concerning economic aggregates—so-called 'macroeconomics.'"[1]

Honing this definition a bit further: *Supply-side economics places supply over demand in the hierarchy of economics—therefore dealing with the enhancement of economic production, efficiency and growth within the context of the free market—working with the key understanding that economic decisions are impacted by relative prices, such as incentives for working, saving, investing, and risk taking.* The New York economy served as a shining model of supply-side success throughout much of the nineteenth century and during the very early years of the twentieth century.

## Say's Law

The phrase "supply creates its own demand" is known as Say's Law, after the nineteenth-century French economist Jean-Baptiste Say, and constitutes a central tenet of supply-side economics. The idea undergirding Say's Law is that supply comes before demand in the economic hierarchy. Indeed, nothing can be demanded before it is first offered, created, or invented—that is, before it has been supplied. The long-term well-being of any economy rests on an understanding that no one can *legitimately* demand something before first supplying a product or service of value to others.

Say, however, never actually wrote in his *Treatise on Political Economy* that "supply creates its own demand." He observed that "it is production which opens a demand for products,"[2] and that "products are always bought ultimately with products."[3]

Understanding that products are bought with products—that one must produce before one can demand—any economy that emphasizes demand over supply is destined to be confronted with stagnation and relative decline. Under demand-side economics, the size of government inevitably increases, the scope of wealth distribution efforts expand, and the economy slows as hard work, creativity, innovation, and risk taking diminish. This is what largely has occurred in New York throughout much of this century. Say himself asserted that "the encouragement of mere consumption is no benefit to commerce; for the difficulty lies in supplying the means, not in stimulating the desire of consumption; and we have seen that production alone furnishes those means. Thus, it is the aim of good government to stimulate production, of bad government to encourage consumption."[4] This is the anti-thesis of Keynesian economics. It is the anti-thesis of "New York economics" as it has stood for decades. In New York, policymakers have erected substantial obstacles to supply, and therefore to economic growth.

Indeed, Say's Law explains how economic growth occurs. George Gilder observed: "As the driving force of economic growth, Say's law exalts the creativity of suppliers over the wants and needs of demanders or consumers. As entrepreneurs invent new things and learn how to make them more efficiently, unit costs and prices drop and goods become more attractive. As goods become more affordable to a wider public, more people work to acquire them by creating goods to exchange. These new suppliers both provide and acquire new wealth at ever lower expense."[5] To summarize, supply—work, investment, entrepreneurship, and risk taking—drives economic growth.

Again, Ture identified the sheer absurdity of economic theory purporting to show otherwise, to show that government fine tuning or enhancement of aggregate demand fosters economic growth. Ture laid out a devastating supply-side criticism of Keynesian demand management:

> The prevailing view that government actions do directly affect aggregate income derives from perceiving these actions as impacting initially and directly on aggregate demand, via effects on disposable income, the changes in which are deemed to result directly in changes in total production. The supply side analysis, on the other hand, holds that government actions have no direct initial impact on real aggregate demand and, indeed, affect nominal aggregate demand only as a consequence of changes in the stock of money. Changes in real aggregate demand, to be sure, would elicit increases in total output. The pertinent question is how changes in real aggregate demand can occur without a preceding change in total output. By definition, aggregate demand is the sum of purchases of all types by all economic entities — governments, businesses, households, etc. Also, by definition, these outlays must exactly equal aggregate income which in turn, at every moment in

> time, must just equal the value of aggregate output. Changes in real income, therefore, occur only as changes in output occur. And changes in output occur only as a result of changes in the amount of production inputs or in the intensity or efficiency of their use. To have a first-order effect on income, therefore, government actions would have to alter directly the amount or effectiveness of production inputs committed to production. But government actions, in and of themselves, do not change the aggregate amount of production resources available in the economy or their productivity. Changes in the amount of production inputs committed to production will result only if the real rewards for their use, i.e., the real price received per unit of input, is changed.[6]

That is, products ultimately are purchased with products. Growth occurs when supply-oriented incentives are enhanced.

If, as Ture asserts, "changes in output occur only as a result of changes in the amount of production inputs or in the intensity or efficiency of their use," then entrepreneurs must take center stage as they are the agents of innovation and creativity that increase inputs and/or efficiency. Indeed, supply-side economics places the entrepreneur at the center of the economy.

## The Entrepreneur as Driving Force in the Economy

The modern-day Keynesian school's focus on government-attempted adjustments in aggregate demand naturally ignores the critical aspect of entrepreneurship in the economy. In addition, the increasing mathematical nature of economics as an academic discipline has left little room for the entrepreneur's roles as innovator and bearer of risk. The real world of risk taking and investing remains a messy place, far too untidy for economic fine tuners and neat econometric models. The models of Keynesians and econometricians relegate the entrepreneur—the agent of economic growth and dynamism—to exogenous status. Naturally, the officials and policymakers receiving advice from such economists lose sight of the entrepreneur as well. Such thinking surely guided mistaken, anti-entrepreneur policy initiatives in New York over the years.

Supply-sider Gilder has articulated the importance of returning the entrepreneur to the economist's center stage:

> Economic recovery depends on the resurrection of entrepreneurs.

> This resurrection cannot fully and durably occur until the ultimate arbiters of economic policy—the economists—resurrect entrepreneurship in their own influential theories. The contrary vision of capitalism without capitalists springs in part from a fundamental error of economic thought, drastically overrating the importance of physical capital formation and other quantitative measures of economic activity and drastically underestimating the decisive and controlling importance of entrepreneurial creativity.[7]

In addition, the entrepreneurship factor perhaps best illustrates the difference between supply-side economists and industrial policy economists. A free-market economy leaves most economic decisions to individuals operating in the private sector, rather than government bureaucrats or elected officials as is the case under industrial policy. While both supply-side and industrial policy economists generally concern themselves with supply-related issues (investment, production, etc.), *the supply-side school of economic thought operates within the wider framework of free-market economics. Production for the sake of production is fruitless. Production must meet current or create new demands. Value must be created.* Supply-side economics recognizes that government lacks the requisite experience, knowledge, and incentives to make resource allocation decisions or to create value.

Again, both New York State's and New York City's policies over the past several decades have leaned strongly toward industrial policy at the state and city levels. Government officials have played high profile roles in guiding investment and the New York economy. Indeed, the New York economic model—particularly the New York City model—calls for harshly taxing and regulating individuals, entrepreneurs, and businesses, and then providing subsidies, loans, and individualized tax breaks for particular firms deemed worthy by government bureaucrats. New York has subscribed to the notion that the bureaucrat can play the role of entrepreneur—a mistaken notion with grim and significant consequences.

The critical role of the entrepreneur in the economy is to see added value where others have failed to do so; to enhance production and efficiency; to fulfill the essence of Say's Law—supply creating demand. In turn, one can identify numerous levels of entrepreneurship. To economist Joseph Schumpeter, the entrepreneur served as the agent of "creative destruction," offering innovations or inventions transforming entire industries and economies. Other entrepreneurs offer improvements in the way particular firms perform through, perhaps, different management or production structures; while still others simply see better ways of doing things and undertake their own ventures. Additional entrepreneurs are at work in the investment community, perhaps seeing added value through mergers, takeovers, diversification, or downsizing. Meanwhile, venture capitalists stand ready to risk their own investment dollars supporting ideas, inventions, innovations, or new businesses.

New York economics amounts to a dismal mix of Keynesian fine tuning and industrial policy. Once a beacon for entrepreneurs around the world, New York either mistakenly tries to supplant the entrepreneur with the bureaucrat or simply treats the entrepreneur quite shabbily. Both the state and city have paid dearly for subscribing to this economic view of capitalism without capitalists.

The coming century promises great growth and opportunity through entrepreneurial dynamism. Leaps in computer, telecommunications, and other technologies are fostering substantial decentralization. As always, public policies matter in such an environment, particularly as they impact the costs of working, investing, and risk taking. Therefore, it remains essential that economists and public policymakers grasp the central role of entrepreneurship in the New York economy. Keynesian economics ignores the entrepreneur. Industrial policy economics believes that the government bureaucrat can take on the entrepreneur's role. In contrast, supply-side economics is entrepreneur-centered, that is, that private-sector entrepreneurs drive the economy. New York policymakers need to adopt entrepreneur-centered economics.

Of course, economics once stood as an entrepreneur-centered discipline. Keynes took economics astray to a discipline centered on aggregates and government fine tuning. Supply-side merely returns economics to its original roots. In this sense, it is somewhat inaccurate to refer to a supply-side "revolution" in economics, about which one often reads or hears. Instead, one should refer to a supply-side "reformation." In the sixteenth century, Martin Luther sparked Christianity's Reformation. Luther viewed the Church, with its emphasis on works, sales of indulgences, praying to saints, and a host of other issues, as going astray from its essence—faith in Christ. Luther sought to bring the Church back to its roots. To Luther, Christianity should obviously center on Christ. In the economics realm, supply-siders bring economics back to a "faith" in the entrepreneur. On the supply-side, economics once again centers on the entrepreneur.

## Back to Microeconomics

In the end, as noted, supply-side economic analysis is largely microeconomic in nature, in other words, supply-side in many ways equates to price theory. Price theory deals with the allocation of resources among different uses, the price of one item relative to another. In particular, supply-side economists focus on the relative prices of work versus leisure, saving and/or investment versus consumption, risk taking versus risk avoidance, and productive, market-based activities versus activities based on tax avoidance or government fiat. As a result, we see the great supply-side emphasis on marginal tax rates—or the tax on the next dollar earned—more so than on average tax rates.

Supply-side economists argue, for example, that high marginal income tax rates raise the cost of additional work or work effort as compared to leisure. Higher tax rates also make it cheaper for an individual to undertake nontaxable, do-it-yourself work, like fixing one's own roof in need of repair, rather than performing income-generating, taxable work, while hiring a roofer. Under these circumstances, the benefits of division of labor are lost to the economy. The returns of tax evasion also are enhanced under high tax rates.

A high marginal income tax rate regime creates a clear bias in favor of consumption over saving and investment. Real and human capital investments become relatively more expensive versus consumption. Particularly worrisome, high tax rates, as well as onerous regulations, raise the relative price of such critical, yet high-risk endeavors as entrepreneurship and venture capital investment. According to supply-side theory, the implications under such a regime can be severe. High-risk ventures require at least the opportunity for high returns. When such opportunities are diminished by governmental policies, a stultified economy results. The relative security of, for example, employment in government or in a large, mature corporation, and investment in government securities are enhanced versus the potential returns on more risky, and more productive, entrepreneurial endeavors. Risk taking, crucial to economic growth, is discouraged by high taxes and regulations.

Finally, relative prices influence decisions as to *where* to live, work, invest, and take risks. That is, relative costs of one state or city versus another state or city. As will be seen throughout this book, the relative price of economic activity in New York is quite high.

The full impact of relative prices on employment is illustrated by what supply-side economists refer to as the tax wedge. In essence, the tax wedge is the difference between the total cost to an employer for an employee, and the actual take-home pay of that employee. Taxes, regulations, and government mandates constitute the tax wedge. A large tax wedge significantly raises the price of labor relative to capital. Concurrently, the tax wedge can diminish incentives for employees to accept overtime; can boost employee compensation demands; and/or can narrow the gap between take-home pay and government benefits (e.g., welfare or unemployment compensation) for some workers. Indeed, as in the cases of both New York State and New York City, the tax wedge can do even more than narrow the gap between work and welfare; it can wash it completely away. As noted later, a recent CATO Institute study shows that the full welfare package in New York State stands as the equivalent of a pretax annual wage level of $27,300, or $13.13 per hour. In New York City, the welfare package equates to $30,700 in annual wages, or $14.76 per hour. Again, New York's sizeable tax wedge and lavish welfare system combine to create substantial disincentives to becoming a productive part of the economy.

## Substitution vs. Income Effects

These relative price/incentive arguments fall under the economists' label of "substitution effects." That is, as the costs of productive endeavors—such as working, investment, and risk taking—decline as marginal tax rates are reduced, incentives to substitute these activities for leisure, consumption, and tax avoidance are enhanced. The opportunity costs of *not* working, investing, or risk taking increase when tax rates fall.

Other economists have claimed that just the opposite occurs under a tax-cut scenario, that individuals will choose to paradoxically work or invest *less*. These economists claim that the income effect takes precedence over the substitution effect. The income-effect argument states that individuals have a targeted level of income, and a tax cut allows them to reach that target by working less. Substantive problems arise with such an argument.

First, the income-effect argument not only nullifies supply-side, relative-price arguments, but Keynesian demand-management policies as well. Keynesian arguments that more government spending increases aggregate demand and therefore economic growth, fall prey to the same income-effect argument. Individuals would work less, and gross domestic product (GDP) and income would fall. Second, if the income effect were to hold in general, that would mean that ever-higher marginal income tax rates should induce ever-increasing levels of work and investment. Or, under the contrary scenario of tax reductions, as the price of working, saving, or investing falls, individuals choose to work, save, and invest less. In essence, as supply-side economist Paul Craig Roberts has noted, income becomes an inferior good.

Roberts identified the full implication of the income effect argument: "In economics, any time the 'income effect' works counter to the 'substitution effect,' we have the relatively rare case of what is called an 'inferior good' (i.e., people purchase less of it as their income rises). Since income is command over all goods, [the income effect] argument implies that all goods are inferior goods: A tax cut will cause people to purchase only more leisure, not more income (i.e., goods)."[8]

In addition, the income effect in no way can explain away the widespread occurrence of individuals and businesses shifting economic activity away from states and cities offering high tax and burdensome regulatory environments to states and cities imposing lower costs. Relative prices and the substitution effect do explain such movements of capital and labor. Quite simply, low tax and light regulatory states and cities substitute for high cost ones.

## Low-Tax vs. High-Tax States

Indeed, research shows that the economies of low-tax states outperform high-tax states. In a December 1995 report for the Joint Economic Committee of the U.S. Congress, economist Richard Vedder found:[9]

• Relatively low tax states grew at almost a one-third faster rate than high-tax states over the period of 1960 to 1993.

• An increase in state and local tax burdens equal to 1 percent of personal income reduced income growth by more than 3.5 percent.

• Income taxes were particularly destructive. Indeed, if a state had kept its level of income taxation at the same share of personal income over this period, personal income in that state would be more than 30 percent higher today.

• And finally, states with flat income tax rate structures grew faster than states with progressive income tax regimes. Indeed, personal-income growth in flat tax states increased about 25 percent faster than in progressive income tax states.

### Incentives and Liberty Matter

In the end, with its emphasis on incentives, supply-side economics offers the clearest lens through which one can view how the economy works and how economic growth occurs.

The marketplace operates through voluntary transactions, as opposed to the more coercive nature of government. Individuals interact freely in the market—buying, selling, trading, offering charity, working, investing, and creating of their own accord. Liberty is advanced.

In the following pages, the economic and fiscal analysis will be shown to be supply-side in nature, and views on political decisions and on our society and culture will prove to be biased toward preserving and advancing liberty.

## New York State: Budget Issues

An examination of New York's state and local budget numbers reveals a state that relies heavily on government and generally treats entrepreneurship and private investment as givens that can be abused at will. Such a view lies in stark contrast to Say's warning that "encouragement of mere consumption is no benefit to commerce" and that problems arise in encouraging production. In New York, government spending rides high, as do taxes and borrowing.

For example, as noted in the following pages, New York's per capita state and local total expenditures topped the state and local average by 51.5 percent in 1993 (most recent complete comparative data), ranking third highest in the nation behind Alaska and the District of Columbia. Per capita state and local public welfare spending ranked second highest in the nation, just behind the District of Columbia, and outpaced the average by 88.2 percent. Indeed, of the categories ranking state and local or state-only government costs (e.g., expenditures, employment levels, salaries, etc.) in the following pages, New York landed in the top ten roughly three-quarters of the time.

New York also lays claim to a high rate of growth in government expenditures. For example, real per capita state and local general expenditures increased by 206 percent between 1962 and 1993. Over this same period, real per capita state and local public welfare spending jumped by 378.2 percent.

State-only numbers—excluding localities—also paint a picture of government expenditures careening out of control. As of 1994 (most recent comparative state numbers), New York's per capita total state spending ranked third highest in the nation, exceeding the average by 41.3 percent. Per capita state public welfare spending topped the state average by 85.8 percent, ranking highest among the 50 states.

While New York has long been a big spending state, the election of left-leaning Republican Nelson Rockefeller as governor in 1958 sparked one of the greatest state spending sprees in our nation's history. Rockefeller pushed state government action to previously unimaginable levels. During what essentially amounts to the Rockefeller era (after resigning as governor in 1973, Rockefeller's policies were carried on by his lieutenant governor, Malcolm Wilson)—1959 to 1975—real per capita state expenditures rose by 210 percent and welfare spending by 625 percent.

More than any other New York politician, Rockefeller suffered from the "edifice complex." Rockefeller built 55 state parks, 43 college campuses, 40 state office buildings, highways reportedly sizeable enough to stretch to Hawaii and back, as well as the infamous government mall in Albany, where state government office buildings span the size of 15 football fields.[10] To show that no expense is too great for the government bureaucrat, New York's state capital may be the only one in the nation where state employees have an express highway exit ramp leading directly into a parking garage for their convenience. In relative terms, the Rockefeller era makes the later high-spending reign of Governor Mario Cuomo seem almost frugal — relatively speaking, of course. Overall, since the beginning of the Rockefeller era in 1959 to 1994, New York State's real per capita spending skyrocketed by about 350 percent, and public welfare expenditures by more than 1,500 percent.

The first two years under Governor George Pataki have witnessed actual spending restraint at the state level. His first budget (1995-96) saw total state expenditures increase by only 2.3 percent. Pataki's second-year budget (1996-97), however, possessed a total projected spending increase of 3.9 percent, or $2.5 billion. It should be noted, though, that this spending hike was $2 billion more than the governor's original request. State legislators had a field day doling out more pork in an election year. Still, even with this 1996-97 spending splurge, New York has not seen such spending restraint in a half-century. In fact, Governor Cuomo's last two budgets saw spending increase by better than 8 percent in 1993-94 and better than 9 percent in 1994-95—far outpacing the rate of inflation. Even with *some* spending restraint now being exhibited, the total state budget still registered a whopping $66 billion in 1996-97.

The New York State budget has long been home to a host of ill-conceived and unnecessary programs and departments. Pork and waste run rampant. Beyond seemingly countless individual pork budget items, entire departments can be categorized under the headings of wasteful, duplicative, unnecessary, and counterproductive. In the concluding chapter of this book, I will specify where opportunities for savings lie in the New York State budget.

The reader should understand that when we refer to the total state budget equaling $63.5 billion in 1995-96 or $66 billion in 1996-97, for example, these numbers fail to capture the complete size of New York's state government. It does not represent the full measure of resources diverted from the private sector for use by the state. For example, another $12 billion or more in expenditures would have to be added from the state's public authorities—which are separated out from the state budget—to gain a more accurate measure of the size of state government in New York. These authorities were created over the years in order to expand state government with no input from the voters. In particular, state public authorities can incur long-term debt by eluding the state constitutional requirement for voter approval. These shady debt practices were perfected during Governor Rockefeller's tenure. Voter approval of long-term debt presented a serious drag on his plans for expanding state government, so Rockefeller stepped around the voters through the use of public authorities as well as debt arrangements with localities.

New York state-only debt has skyrocketed in recent decades. For example, according to the most recent U.S. Department of Commerce numbers, total per capita state-only debt in New York was more than double the U.S. state average in 1994. Since the mid-1960s, inflation-adjusted per capita state debt had leaped by better than 230 percent. Over the same period, real per capita interest paid on state debt jumped by almost 500 percent. Combined state *and* local per capita debt in New York tops the U.S. average by 70 percent (1993 is the most recent data available).

All of this spending and debt translates into higher taxes and fees for the average New Yorker. Per capita total state-only revenues in New York exceeded the state average by almost 40 percent in 1994, and state and local total revenues in 1993 outpaced the average by more than 45 percent. New York's state-only taxes surpassed the average by more than 25 percent, and state and local taxes by almost 60 percent, on a per capita basis.

The *growth* in government revenues also has been staggering. For example, state and local general revenues ballooned by more than 210 percent between 1962 and 1993, and state and local taxes by 145 percent, on a real, per capita basis. State-only real per capita general revenues increased by more than 260 percent between 1965 and 1994, and state taxes leaped by 143 percent.

Unfortunately, almost every tax imaginable to man is levied in New York. Government supplies no incentives to be frugal and efficient, but it supplies every incentive to find new revenue streams. Normally unimaginative government officials become quite creative when it comes to the issue of finding ways to tax. As Adam Smith wrote: "There is no art which one government sooner learns of another, than that of draining money from the pockets of the people."[11] New York has been both student and teacher over the years of this destructive art form.

Particularly destructive to working, saving, investing, and risk taking are income taxes. New York was one of the first seven states to levy a personal income tax. In 1919, state legislators claimed that the loss of liquor tax revenues due to Prohibition required the state to impose a personal income tax. This was done over the protestations of the state's comptroller at the time, Eugene Travis, who saw the new tax as unnecessary.[12] The personal income tax was imposed in 1919 with a top rate of 3 percent. In the 1930s, the top rate hit 8 percent—7 percent plus a separate 1 percent income tax designed to "help" the state through the Depression (in reality only making matters worse). Some temporary state personal income tax relief was provided in the 1940s, but the top rate stood at 7 percent once again by 1954.

An additional tax measure, which seemed specifically designed to further extinguish entrepreneurial activity in New York, was inflicted in February 1935. New York instituted a state unincorporated business tax—a tax on income from unincorporated enterprises, in addition to the personal income tax—along with an "emergency" tax on capital gains.

A glimpse of sanity flashed briefly in 1938, however, when state officials at least saw that capital gains were being taxed too heavily and provided for a 50 percent exclusion from taxation. By 1954, the effective top capital gains tax on individuals registered 3.5 percent.

New York State levied its own corporate income tax in 1917. By the time Nelson Rockefeller won the Governor's Mansion in 1958, the corporate tax rate stood at 5.5 percent, the personal income tax rate was 7 percent, the individual capital gains tax rate registered 3.5 percent, and the state imposed an unincorporated business income tax of 4 percent. At the close of the Rockefeller era in 1976, the corporate tax rate hit 12 percent, the top personal income tax rate was 15.375 percent, the capital gains tax rate topped 9 percent, and the unincorporated business tax was 5.5 percent.

Rockefeller also imposed a state sales tax of 2 percent in 1965, which doubled to 4 percent in 1971. Under Rockefeller's reign of economic terror, tax rates went from high and burdensome to utterly and completely destructive.

Rockefeller understood nothing about how the economy worked. He exhibited little, if any, regard for entrepreneurs and taxpayers. In his perverse view of the world, Rockefeller could not grasp that economic growth was the product of hard work, investment, and risk taking in the marketplace.

Rockefeller was pure politician, in the worst sense of the word. Political power was all that mattered. In his mistaken outlook, government bureaucrats and public works projects could guide the economy. If the voters or state constitution got in the way, he would simply find a way around such nuisances. New York had leaned clearly in favor of activist government since at least the 1930s; Rockefeller pushed the Empire State completely over the big-government cliff.

In the post-Rockefeller era, tax rates have come down at a painfully slow pace, but still remain far too high. The corporate rate has dropped to 9 percent and the top personal income tax rate is scheduled to decline to 6.85 percent in 1997. Numerous setbacks were suffered along the way to these lower tax rates. For example, the state eliminated the capital gains differential in 1987, which resulted in a 62 percent increase in the effective capital gains tax rate, from 5.4 percent to 8.75 percent. The rate has been coming down slowly since then, and is scheduled to register 6.85 percent in 1997 as well—still 27 percent higher than in the mid-1980s. In addition, state legislators and Governor Cuomo canceled already legislated tax cuts from 1990 through 1994.

Indeed, the tax rate cuts that did occur during Cuomo's reign originated in the state legislature and Cuomo largely had to be dragged along kicking and screaming. In his 1994 book *The New York Idea: An Experiment in Democracy*, Cuomo showed remorse for the rather smallish tax cuts he eventually signed on to: "In 1987 we cut the state's personal income tax rates deeper and faster than we should have."[13]

Like Rockefeller, Cuomo could not understand that millions of individuals interacting in the private marketplace—Adam Smith's invisible hand, if you will—could guide the economy better than a group of state bureaucrats in Albany. Indeed, Cuomo showed particular and regular distaste for supply-side economics. Perhaps it was because his opponent in the 1982 race for governor, which Cuomo won, was supply-sider Lew Lehrman. Until Cuomo's defeat in 1994, Lehrman gave Cuomo his most competitive race. In fact, if many of his fellow Republicans had not abandoned him, Lehrman may have defeated Cuomo. Twelve years later, Cuomo lost to then-State Senator George Pataki, who ran a mild supply-side tax-cut campaign. Interestingly, whatever very limited economic success Cuomo experienced during his time in the governor's mansion was largely the result of President Ronald Reagan's federal supply-side policies of lower taxes and restrained regulation, and state tax cuts forced upon or inherited by Cuomo. Mario Cuomo bit the supply-side hand that fed him.

The 1987 state tax cut bill was far too timid. As noted above, the capital gains tax rate actually rose, personal income tax rate cuts were too small, and besides, as of *1996* the *1987* tax cuts were yet to be fully implemented!

Finally, capital gains are not indexed for inflation. So the real capital gains tax rate actually reaches much higher. In fact, investors can wind up paying taxes on real capital *losses*. The negative impact of capital gains taxes cannot be overstated. Capital gains levies directly raise the costs of investment and entrepreneurship. I noted the importance of these activities earlier, namely, generating new products and services, efficiencies, innovations, inventions, economic opportunities, and jobs. Investment and entrepreneurship are high-risk endeavors, however, so the opportunity for high returns must be available. Capital gains taxes diminish potential returns, and therefore diminish the levels of investment and entrepreneurship. Naturally, the economy suffers.

Every tax raises costs for the private sector. Particularly burdensome are state and local income taxes, which directly raise the costs of living, working, saving, investing, and risk taking in New York, as well as incredibly high local property taxes, which make owning, maintaining, and improving a home or a business in New York quite costly.

The rankings, charts, graphs, and analyses in the pages ahead spell out many of the specifics of government spending, debt, and taxes in New York. In summary, they paint a depressing picture of a state plagued by government that spends too much and taxes too heavily.

## New York State: Education

Education provides one of the clearest examples of government failure in New York. In New York's public schools, costs have mounted while quality declines.

Per capita state and local expenditures on public schools in New York topped the national average by better than 35 percent in 1992-93, ranking third highest in the nation.

Per pupil *current* expenditures in New York exceeded the national average in 1993-94 by 59 percent. Between 1960 and 1994, real per pupil spending in New York increased by 228 percent.

Per pupil *total* spending hit almost $10,400 in 1993-94, topping the U.S. average by almost 60 percent. Within the state, average per pupil expenditures cleared the $10,000 mark in Hamilton, Rockland, Westchester (more than $12,000 per pupil), Nassau, Suffolk (more than $11,000 per pupil), and Putnam Counties. One school district (Kiryas Joel Village) spent almost $50,000 per student. Two districts (Bridgehampton and Newcomb) actually incurred costs in excess of $32,000 per pupil, an additional four districts saw per pupil spending register between $20,000 and $30,000, 59 districts spent more than $13,000 per student, and 197 districts spent more than $10,000 per pupil across the state. Only four districts spent less than $6,000 per pupil in 1993-94.

Of course, a significant part of this spending lies with teacher salaries. In 1995-96, the average public school teacher's salary in New York outpaced the national average by 27 percent, ranking fourth highest in the country. Between 1970 and 1996, the average teacher's salary in New York increased by 14 percent in inflation-adjusted terms. The pupil-teacher ratio has been declining steadily in New York as well — 20.0 in 1969-70 to 15.2 in 1994-95.

Over the past 25 years, enrollment in New York public schools is down while spending is up. Indeed, between 1970 and 1994, enrollment fell by 20.6 percent, but real expenditures increased by 35.7 percent.

As real per pupil costs have risen in New York, results have taken a nosedive. For example, in 1971-72, New York's average SAT score stood at 955, and topped the national average. By 1994-95, New York's SAT scores averaged 892, trailing well behind the national average. New York stands as a glaring example of the fact that higher levels of education spending in no way guarantee superior results.

## New York State: Crime

New York possesses a poor reputation on several fronts, such as burdensome taxes, high levels of government spending, and declining public schools (especially relative to costs). In addition, New York possesses a reputation as a high crime state. Interestingly, the overall numbers do not support the assertion that crime is far worse in New York than in other states, though a narrower focus on violent crime does spell trouble.

New York State actually falls in the middle on crime—ranking thirtieth out of the 50 states in terms of its total crime index, with the national total crime index actually exceeding New York's by 16 percent. Another bright spot, New York State's total crime index in 1995 was actually lower than it was in 1990 and in 1980. However, the 1995 rate still stood 16 percent higher than where it registered in 1970. So, overall, New Yorkers are still *less* safe in the mid-1990s than they were in 1970 or before.

Breaking the total crime numbers down a bit reveals that New York suffers from high rates of violent crime and lower rates of property crime when compared with the rest of the nation. New York State's 1995 property crime rate ranked thirty-ninth in the nation among the 50 states. In fact, the national property crime rate actually exceeded New York's by 23.5 percent. In contrast, New York State's violent crime rate ranked eighth highest in the nation, and topped the national average by 23 percent.

In the case of violent crime, justifiably the crimes that frighten individuals most, New York State deserves its reputation as a high crime state. Again, while the state's violent crime rate in 1995 was actually lower than in 1990 or in 1980, it still surpassed the 1970 rate by 25 percent.

A high crime rate stands as an example of two fundamental breakdowns in society: the first being a breakdown of morality and common decency, and the second being a fundamental failure of government. These breakdowns send clear signals to individuals that they would be wise to live, raise a family, and invest in a business elsewhere, in a location with a higher degree and feeling of safety.

## New York State: A Key Measure of Civility

As governor in 1988, Mario Cuomo called for initiating the "Decade of the Child." What this meant beyond pure political rhetoric was nothing more than a call for more government activity in the form of higher welfare expenditures, more public school spending, health programs, and sex education. One might consider it a prelude to the "it takes a village" idea. Unfortunately, this was simply more of the same in New York.

I've already noted some of the dismal results of such government endeavors pertaining to welfare and education. Other indicators point to grim failure as well. The "daddy state" translated into 37.2 percent of all births to unmarried women in 1993, sixth highest in the nation. The state's infant mortality rate tied for twentieth.

New York also stands out as a very dangerous place for unborn children. New York's 1992 rate of abortion per 1,000 women registered 46.2, outpacing every state in the nation and only trailing the District of Columbia. New York's ratio of abortions per 1,000 live births equaled 694 in 1992, again only behind the District of Columbia's even more horrifying number of 1,104 abortions per 1,000 live births. These numbers suggest that the "Decade of the Child" did not include unborn children. Efforts to change this situation will go nowhere under Republican Governor George Pataki, as he switched his position on abortion from pro-life to pro-choice.

## New York State: The Economy

The bright spot of the New York State economy lies with high income levels. New York ranks fifth in the nation in terms of both per capita personal income and per capita disposable income. Between 1980 and 1995, New York's real growth in these two measures topped U.S. growth. However, once past these indicators, the numbers that capture New York's economy deteriorate rather quickly. In fact, a longer term view of real per capita personal income growth—1960 through 1995—shows New York lagging the nation.

Median household income in New York ranked twenty-fourth in the nation in 1994, roughly equaling the U.S. median. Between 1989 and 1994, median household income in New York fell in real terms by 15.3 percent, compared with a U.S. real decline of 6.6 percent.

Gross state product (GSP) growth in New York has not grown at the same pace as the nation as a whole. GSP numbers are available for the period of 1977 to 1992, and during that time New York's real GSP grew by 33.8 percent versus U.S. GSP growth of 43.8 percent.

Other indicators clearly reveal a New York State economy not keeping up with the U.S. economy. In New York, new business formation, new business incorporations, population, domestic migration, and home ownership, all lag behind the nation as a whole.

Particularly glaring is New York's dismal rate of job creation—a reflection of a dearth of entrepreneurship. For example, between 1958 and 1995, U.S. private-sector employment expanded by 106 percent, while New York's grew by just 24.3 percent. Indeed, if New York's economy had generated jobs at the national annual rate over this period, New York would have laid claim to 4.26 million *more* jobs in 1995 than actually existed. In addition, New York's rates of labor force participation and employment have lagged well behind the U.S. rates for at least the past quarter century.

Burdensome taxes and regulations, and bloated government have taken a severe toll on the New York economy, chasing away investors, entrepreneurs, individuals, and jobs to more enterprising economic climates. No other explanation for New York's economic woes exists.

## New York City: Budget Issues

When combining state and city taxes, regulations, and expenditures, New York City is more weighed down by government than any other city in the entire nation. And the Big Apple is rotting accordingly. For at least the past three decades, entrepreneurship and job creation have been extinct and the city economy in relative decline.

In *every* category of spending, taxing, and borrowing, when compared with other large U.S. cities (population of 500,000 or more), New York City ranks among the very highest, that is to say, among the very worst. In fact, out of all the expenditure, tax, and debt categories comparing New York City versus other large cities, the Big Apple came in first, meaning the worst, two-thirds of the time.

For example, on the spending front, New York City's 1994 (most recent comparative data available) per capita total expenditures outpaced the large city average by more than 120 percent, and per capita welfare spending exceeded the average by an incredible 270 percent.

As one might imagine, growth in New York City spending has been mind boggling. Between 1965 and 1994, real per capita total spending jumped by 165 percent, with welfare expenditures skyrocketing by more than 300 percent in real per capita terms.

While New York City stood as a big-government city for quite some time, particularly since the beginning of the Great Depression, the period after 1965 marked a sharp acceleration in the expansion of government. In essence, New York City took a bad idea—"The Great Society" and the "War on Poverty"—and took it to its most absurd and destructive extremes. And the man at the New York City helm during this period was then-Republican John Lindsay. The resulting fiscal crisis of the mid-1970s—bringing both New York City and New York State to the brink of bankruptcy—now lives on in infamy. Indeed, the fiscal crisis of the 1970s never came to an end; it lives on into the late 1990s.

However, New York City government possesses a long history of excessive expenditures and problems paying its bills in the twentieth century. For example, New York City Mayor George B. McClellan, Jr., son of the Civil War general, had to turn to private bankers—namely J. P. Morgan—for a bailout when the city could not place its warrants in 1907.[14] Another fiscal crisis developed in the early 1930s. This crisis, however, served as the turning point for the entire New York City economy. As the Great Depression took hold between 1930 and 1932, New York City inflicted further economic harm by hiking taxes. During this period of tax hikes, the city's general revenues *declined* by $47 million while expenditures grew by almost $100 million. Bankers came to the rescue once again and essentially ran the city from 1934 to 1938.[15] Counterproductive tax hikes continued, including the imposition of a city sales tax at 2 percent and a business gross receipts tax of less than 1 percent.

It was during the early Depression that New York City greatly expanded its public welfare efforts. While the immediate threat of the early 1930s fiscal crisis eventually was resolved, the fate of the city's economy was sealed. Higher spending and taxes became New York City's governing model.

City government expanded for decades. Between 1930 and 1965, for example, real per capita city spending increased by almost 350 percent. The public assistance rolls in New York City grew from about 300,000 at the end of World War II to over 500,000 in 1965—a two-thirds jump while the city's population barely budged at all. At the same time, per capita property taxes—the city's prime source of revenues—doubled in real terms.

However, for all of New York City's tax and spending woes through the early 1960s, they soon would seem like frugal times compared with what was about to be unleashed. After winning the mayoralty race in 1965, Lindsay got out of the big-government starting gate quickly. As mayor-elect in late November 1965, he declared that imposing a city income tax was "definitely a last resort."[16] Just four months later, the income tax rested at the center of Lindsay's first budget proposal and was implemented by June 1966. The "last resort" quickly metamorphosed into the first resort. Both New York City and State elected officials approved several tax increases that year, including the imposition of city personal income and capital gains taxes with top rates of 2 percent, a city corporate income tax of 5.5 percent, and a city unincorporated business tax of 4 percent! By the mid-1970s, New York City's personal income and capital gains tax rates had more than doubled to 4.3 percent and the corporate rate rose to 10.05 percent.

In just the period of 1965 to 1976, on a real, per capita basis, city total expenditures more than doubled and public welfare expenditures increased by almost 335 percent. Real per capita city debt service jumped by 287 percent.

This massive ballooning of government spending, debt, and taxation led to New York City's 1970s fiscal crisis. By this time, sound economic incentives were obliterated at all income levels. The city's lucrative welfare system favored government dependency over individual responsibility. New York City's public welfare rolls topped 1.2 million by the mid-1970s.

In the meantime, the total New York City tax burden became prohibitive. The combined state and city marginal income tax rate reached 19.675 percent in 1976, up by 181 percent from the 1959 rate of 7 percent. For entrepreneurs operating enterprises not incorporated, the combined state and city unincorporated business tax registered 9.5 percent. This rate was added on top of the personal income tax—creating a top tax rate on New York City's entrepreneurs of just under 30 percent! The capital gains tax reached 13.525 percent, with an even higher real rate. On the corporate side, the state and city tax rate topped 22 percent. Of course, all these taxes came on top of federal taxes.

Sky-high tax rates destroyed incentives for working, investing, and entrepreneurship in New York City. Individuals and businesses were provided with every incentive to leave New York City and that is exactly what they did. And of course, city debt levels reached crisis levels as well. By the height of the budget crisis in fiscal year 1975-76, per capita city debt exceeded the large-city average by 126 percent.

The city could no longer float any short- or long-term debt. New York City managed to accomplish what few other governments in the history of mankind have done. Government had grown so large that it literally became impossible to finance. Far too burdensome taxes—not to mention regulations—fostered an exodus of labor and capital. The bond market knew that both taxes and debt levels in New York were much too high. In supply-side economics vernacular, the marginal cost of both taxes and borrowing in New York City reached prohibitive levels. Or, more simply, the marketplace signaled New York City that its government was far too big.

Today, people seem to think that New York City's fiscal crisis ended when the city was able to return unassisted to the debt markets in 1979. For a very brief time, some budget restraint actually was exhibited. From 1975-76 to 1980-81, for example, city spending *declined* on a real per capita basis by almost 25 percent, and city gross debt dropped by almost 60 percent. This was a fairly impressive accomplishment, though New York City's spending and debt levels still hovered at astronomical heights, far ahead, for example, of the average for large U.S. cities. And from 1981 into the early 1990s, under the mayoralties of Ed Koch and David Dinkins, spending resumed its high growth expansion.

On the tax side of the equation, the city's personal income and capital gains taxes actually rose to 4.73 percent by 1983, slowly declined to 3.4 percent by 1989, but then increased again to 4.46 percent by 1991. A small decline in the city's corporate tax rate to 8.85 percent occurred. The 4 percent unincorporated business tax still hampers entrepreneurship.

Today, the combined state and city income tax rate on entrepreneurs can top 15 percent and the combined corporate rate reaches higher than 19 percent. The individual capital gains tax exceeds 11 percent, and again, grows much higher when inflation is factored into the equation. And roughly 2 million New York City residents—about 1 in every 3.7 individuals—receive some kind of public assistance.

Since taking office in 1994, Mayor Rudolph Giuliani's spending proposals have only offered restraint or small cuts. In 1996, he announced somewhat tepid support for allowing the city's personal income tax surcharge to expire, dropping the top tax rate from 4.46 percent to 3.91 percent. Even this minor step was opposed by the speaker of the New York City Council. Giuliani reneged on his promise to allow the surcharge to expire by the time he proposed his 1996-97 budget and instead advocated a four-year extension. The severity of New York City's governmental costs on the private sector continues to elude *all* of the city's elected officials.

New York City's only chance at regaining economic greatness lies with restoring incentives to live, work, invest, and take risks in the city. That means throwing away New York's long-held big-government philosophy, opting instead for free markets, small government, and low taxes.

## New York City: Education

Perhaps more so than anywhere else in the state of New York, public education in New York City has proved to be an abysmal failure. In a state where education results are at best mediocre—especially when compared with costs—New York City's public schools perform among the very worst.

The dismal performance of New York City's public schools is not lost on the city's last two mayors—both Giuliani and Dinkins chose private schools for their own children—nor on the public. A recent poll conducted by the *New York Post* (April 28, 1996) found that only 6 percent of New Yorkers thought that city children were receiving an "excellent" education and 25 percent rated education as "good." In the meantime, 27 percent rated New York City public education as "fair" and a whopping 35 percent saw it as "poor." In addition, 27.9 percent of New York City public school teachers send their children to private schools.[17]

Student reading and math performance register at low levels. Only a little more than half of public high school students in New York City graduate on time. In addition, just 21 percent of New York City graduates earn Regents Diplomas, compared with 40 percent statewide.

New York City ranked among the very highest of the nation's largest cities in terms of per capita elementary and secondary public school spending. Between 1965 and 1994, real per capita school spending increased by 140 percent.

Among the 70 largest public school districts in the nation, New York City per pupil spending ranked second highest in the nation, with only the District of Columbia spending more per pupil. Within high-spending New York State, New York City ranked twenty-fourth out of 58 counties (the New York City number includes five counties), and 362 out of 688 school districts ranked.

In general, it remains difficult to find officials, policymakers, and commentators who believe, or at least will admit publicly, that education expenditures in New York State are too high. Such admissions verge on the impossible when it comes to New York City. When one sees crumbling school buildings, schools without libraries or librarians, and dismal results, it is difficult to say expenditures are too high. Practically everyone seems to agree that more needs to be spent on public education in New York City. In fact, education in New York City does not need to waste more tax dollars, it needs choice and competition.

## New York City: Crime

Contrary to the conventional wisdom, among large U.S. cities, New York City ranks as relatively safe when crime is measured according to the *rate* of crime per 100,000 population. For example, in 1995 New York City ranked forty-seventh out of 51 cities in terms of its total crime rate, forty-eighth out of 52 in terms of its rape rate, forty-seventh in terms of its burglary rate, fifty-first in the larceny-theft rate, thirty-ninth in terms of motor vehicle theft, and twenty-ninth (out of 49) in terms of the arson rate. New York City ranks highest in terms of its robbery rate (16th), the aggravated assault rate (24th), and the murder rate (28st).

In addition, in *every* major crime category, New York City's rates of crime in 1995 were lower than the 1990 rates, and most were lower than in 1980. This general decline continued in 1996 according to preliminary New York City numbers. Indeed, the decline may have accelerated. However, all of the 1995 crime rate numbers for New York City—but for burglary and motor vehicle theft—were still higher than 1970 rates.

The question remains: Does the average person or business owner think about crime in terms of rates or gross numbers? In terms of gross numbers, i.e. unadjusted for population, New York City obviously lays claim to more crimes in each category than any other U.S. city. Constantly hearing and reading about crime in New York City certainly takes a toll on how people think about crime.

The sheer gross number of crimes in a city the size of New York, combined with memories of far lower crime rates not too many years ago, present both real and public relations problems relating to crime in the Big Apple.

## New York City: Economy

In her 1969 book *The Economy of Cities*, city economics guru Jane Jacobs noted: "Beginning in about 1800, New York enjoyed tremendously high rates of development for twelve or thirteen decades."[18] In a 1984 book, Jacobs observed that the New York City economy "has been declining since at least the 1940s."[19] Jacobs is absolutely correct. In fact, I peg the beginning of New York City's economic demise with the aforementioned acceptance of the big-government model in the early 1930s. However, particularly since the late 1960s, the New York City economy has been in outright free fall.

The indicators of the city's steep economic decline are clear. For example, in the autumn 1992 issue of *The City Journal*, William Tucker reported that New York City had fewer small businesses in the early 1990s than it had in 1969. This absence of entrepreneurial activity, combined with an exodus of large firms as well, translates into economic stultification. Job creation simply does not exist. Between 1969 and 1995, total private sector employment in New York City *declined* by 14.5 percent.

In fact, between 1958 (as far back as the state's Department of Labor supplies numbers) and 1995, New York City has lost private sector jobs. From 1959 to 1995, New York City's annual rate of job creation topped the national average in only three years. Over those 36 years, if New York City had matched the national annual rate of job creation, the city would have had 3.56 million more jobs in 1995.

The incentives to live, work, and invest elsewhere are clear and individuals have responded accordingly. The last time New York City's population growth for a decade topped U.S. population growth was in the 1930s. During the 1950s and 1970s, and most recently, between 1990 and 1992, New York City's population declined.

New York City was built by the private sector—by entrepreneurs—and it has been slowly destroyed by government costs and bureaucrats.

Tinkering at the margin will, at best, only slow the city's continuing decline. But so many city officials seem content to be mere stewards of New York City's seemingly inevitable economic decline.

However, the economic demise of New York City can be reversed. An agenda of true revitalization and growth means a complete break with the big government model of the past six-plus decades. I outline such a plan at the close of this book. In essence, New York City must once again learn to treasure the entrepreneur and redeem its faith in the free market. It is time to encourage, rather than punish, risk taking. The building blocks of economic growth—working, investing, and entrepreneurship—must be rewarded.

# Part One: New York State

# Chapter Two

# New York State: Fiscal Issues

- Taxation
- Government Expenditures
- Debt
- Government Employment

Note:

• Expenditure numbers relating to education appear in the "New York State: Education" chapter, and numbers for spending on police protection and corrections appear in the "New York State: Crime" chapter.

• State and local and state-only fiscal numbers are both included so the reader can gauge the activities of all levels of government as well as state government alone in New York.

## PER CAPITA STATE AND LOCAL TOTAL REVENUES: STATE RANKINGS

In 1992-93, New York's per capita state and local total revenues ranked third highest in the nation, only topped by Alaska and the District of Columbia.

### Per Capita State and Local Total Revenues

| Rank | State | Per Capita Total Revenues |
|---|---|---|
| 1 | Alaska | $15,119.06 |
| 2 | District of Columbia | 10,373.41 |
| **3** | **New York** | **7,148.70** |
| 4 | Wyoming | 6,468.94 |
| 5 | Hawaii | 5,883.77 |
| 6 | Washington | 5,727.50 |
| 7 | Connecticut | 5,658.55 |
| 8 | Minnesota | 5,637.83 |
| 9 | New Jersey | 5,624.07 |
| 10 | California | 5,540.27 |
| 11 | Oregon | 5,365.82 |
| 12 | Wisconsin | 5,300.26 |
| 13 | Massachusetts | 5,231.04 |
| 14 | Delaware | 5,165.11 |
| 15 | Rhode Island | 5.096.77 |
| 16 | Ohio | 5,047.34 |
| 17 | Nebraska | 4,909.15 |
| 18 | Nevada | 4,846.38 |
| 19 | Colorado | 4,832.37 |
| 20 | Michigan | 4,790.69 |
| 21 | Vermont | 4,756.42 |
| 22 | Maryland | 4,723.90 |
| 23 | Pennsylvania | 4,713.84 |
| 24 | New Mexico | 4,713.76 |
| 25 | North Dakota | 4,648.29 |
| 26 | Montana | 4,605.96 |

*continued*

*continued*

| Rank | State | Per Capita Total Revenues |
|---|---|---|
| 27 | Louisiana | 4,501.25 |
| 28 | Illinois | 4,487.71 |
| 29 | Utah | 4,476.88 |
| 30 | Iowa | 4,474.94 |
| 31 | Arizona | 4,462.15 |
| 32 | Maine | 4,405.99 |
| 33 | Florida | 4,382.45 |
| 34 | Tennessee | 4,375.55 |
| 35 | Georgia | 4,306.32 |
| 36 | Kansas | 4,295.51 |
| 37 | South Carolina | 4,226.81 |
| 38 | North Carolina | 4,203.42 |
| 39 | New Hampshire | 4,203.07 |
| 40 | West Virginia | 4,183.72 |
| 41 | Idaho | 4,158.18 |
| 42 | Texas | 4,106.11 |
| 43 | South Dakota | 4,056.72 |
| 44 | Virginia | 4,040.46 |
| 45 | Alabama | 4,032.40 |
| 46 | Kentucky | 3,975.89 |
| 47 | Indiana | 3,957.68 |
| 48 | Mississippi | 3,867.49 |
| 49 | Oklahoma | 3,834.79 |
| 50 | Missouri | 3,690.84 |
| 51 | Arkansas | 3,522.98 |
| | U.S. Average | 4,918.41 |

Data Source: U.S. Department of Commerce

## PER CAPITA STATE AND LOCAL TOTAL REVENUES: NEW YORK VS. U.S.

In 1992-93, New York's per capita state and local total revenues exceeded the state and local average by 45.3 percent—$7,148.70 in New York versus the U.S. average of $4,918.41.

Between 1982 and 1993, real per capita state and local total revenues in New York grew by 45.2 percent, from $4,923.46 to $7,148.70 in 1993 dollars.

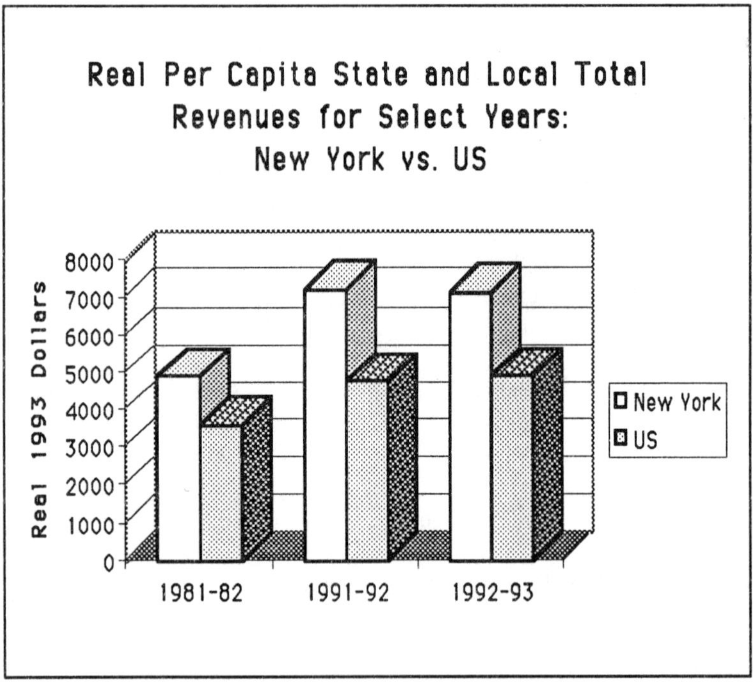


Data Source: U.S. Department of Commerce

## PER CAPITA STATE-ONLY TOTAL REVENUES: STATE RANKINGS

In 1994, New York's per capita state total revenues ranked fifth highest in the nation.

**Per Capita State Total Revenues**

| Rank | State | Per Capita Total Revenues |
|---|---|---|
| 1 | Alaska | $10,236.57 |
| 2 | Wyoming | 4,848.67 |
| 3 | Hawaii | 4,832.69 |
| 4 | Delaware | 4,584.68 |
| **5** | **New York** | **4,524.27** |
| 6 | Rhode Island | 4,143.26 |
| 7 | New Mexico | 4,055.93 |
| 8 | Wisconsin | 3,860.13 |
| 9 | New Jersey | 3,771.22 |
| 10 | Minnesota | 3,762.12 |
| 11 | Montana | 3,698.77 |
| 12 | Massachusetts | 3,691.16 |
| 13 | Ohio | 3,678.29 |
| 14 | California | 3,666.06 |
| 15 | Connecticut | 3,662.12 |
| 16 | Washington | 3,626.95 |
| 17 | North Dakota | 3,587.74 |
| 18 | Oregon | 3,527.66 |
| 19 | Vermont | 3,493.73 |
| 20 | West Virginia | 3,484.88 |
| 21 | Michigan | 3,350.28 |
| 22 | Maine | 3,304.78 |
| 23 | Nevada | 3,271.57 |
| 24 | Idaho | 3,202.55 |
| 25 | Pennsylvania | 3,173.94 |
| 26 | Iowa | 3,167.46 |
| 27 | Louisiana | 3,134.28 |

*continued*

*continued*

| Rank | State | Per Capita Total Revenues |
|---|---|---|
| 28 | Maryland | 3,112.52 |
| 29 | Utah | 3,096.02 |
| 30 | South Carolina | 3,075.43 |
| 31 | Kentucky | 3,064.94 |
| 32 | North Carolina | 2,977.50 |
| 33 | Kansas | 2,926.37 |
| 34 | Mississippi | 2,883.80 |
| 35 | Arizona | 2,883.08 |
| 36 | Colorado | 2,851.56 |
| 37 | South Dakota | 2,831.23 |
| 38 | Oklahoma | 2,818.93 |
| 39 | Arkansas | 2,800.48 |
| 40 | Indiana | 2,749.21 |
| 41 | Alabama | 2,748.32 |
| 42 | Nebraska | 2,739.60 |
| 43 | Illinois | 2,714.14 |
| 44 | New Hampshire | 2,709.83 |
| 45 | Virginia | 2,639.71 |
| 46 | Georgia | 2,588.89 |
| 47 | Missouri | 2,513.39 |
| 48 | Florida | 2,494.43 |
| 49 | Tennessee | 2,458.94 |
| 50 | Texas | 2,450.48 |
| | U.S. Average | 3,249.03 |

Data Source: U.S. Department of Commerce

## PER CAPITA STATE-ONLY TOTAL REVENUES: NEW YORK VS. U.S.

In 1994, New York's per capita state total revenues surpassed the state average by 39.3 percent—$4,524.27 in New York versus $3249.03 across the nation.

Between 1975 and 1994, New York's real per capita state total revenues increased by 100.3 percent. In 1994 dollars, New York's total revenues equaled $2,258.82 in 1975 versus $4,524.27 in 1994.

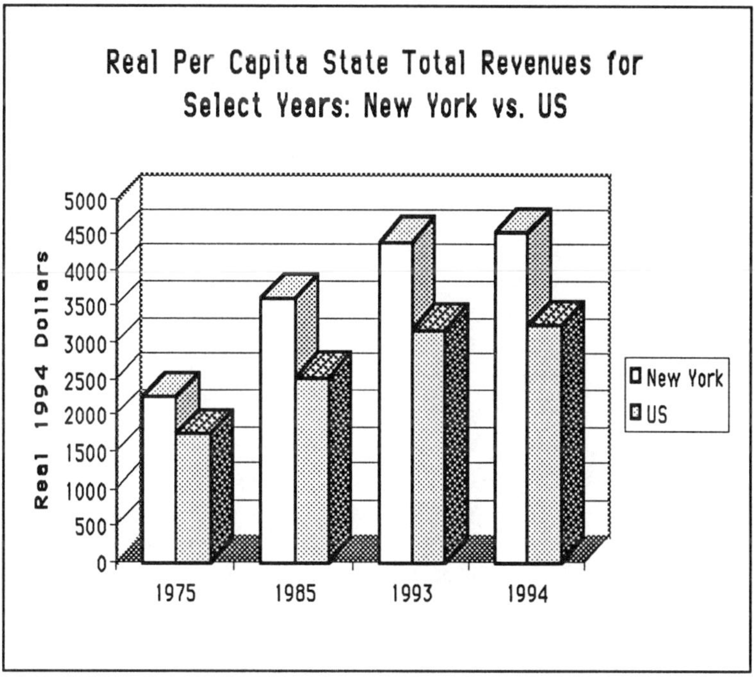


Data Source: U.S. Department of Commerce

# PER CAPITA STATE AND LOCAL GENERAL REVENUES: STATE RANKINGS

In 1992-93, New York's per capita state and local general revenues ranked third highest in the nation, only surpassed by Alaska and the District of Columbia.

**Per Capita State and Local General Revenues**

| Rank | State | Per Capita General Revenues |
|---|---|---|
| 1 | Alaska | $12,767.62 |
| 2 | District of Columbia | 8,621.26 |
| **3** | **New York** | **5,902.85** |
| 4 | Wyoming | 5,621.06 |
| 5 | Hawaii | 5,169.98 |
| 6 | Connecticut | 4,962.24 |
| 7 | New Jersey | 4,816.60 |
| 8 | Minnesota | 4,710.08 |
| 9 | Massachusetts | 4,497.94 |
| 10 | Delaware | 4,471.78 |
| 11 | California | 4,305.32 |
| 12 | Rhode Island | 4,249.91 |
| 13 | Vermont | 4,204.17 |
| 14 | Oregon | 4,158.30 |
| 15 | Washington | 4,155.72 |
| 16 | Michigan | 4,147.01 |
| 17 | Wisconsin | 4,123.61 |
| 18 | North Dakota | 4,122.19 |
| 19 | New Mexico | 4,013.55 |
| 20 | Maryland | 4,006.51 |
| 21 | Maine | 3,940.74 |
| 22 | Louisiana | 3,933.08 |
| 23 | Iowa | 3,906.00 |
| 24 | Colorado | 3,890.59 |
| 25 | New Hampshire | 3,868.84 |
| 26 | Pennsylvania | 3,842.71 |

*continued*

*continued*

| Rank | State | Per Capita General Revenues |
|---|---|---|
| 27 | Montana | 3,822.51 |
| 28 | Nevada | 3,779.62 |
| 29 | Kansas | 3,702.40 |
| 30 | Nebraska | 3,700.53 |
| 31 | Illinois | 3,700.16 |
| 32 | Florida | 3,678.60 |
| 33 | Ohio | 3,667.14 |
| 34 | Georgia | 3,628.84 |
| 35 | Indiana | 3,551.17 |
| 36 | West Virginia | 3,550.33 |
| 37 | Idaho | 3,480.95 |
| 38 | Texas | 3,479.20 |
| 39 | Arizona | 3,473.14 |
| 40 | Virginia | 3,469.34 |
| 41 | Utah | 3,441.40 |
| 42 | South Carolina | 3,409.50 |
| 43 | South Dakota | 3,399.87 |
| 44 | North Carolina | 3,396.98 |
| 45 | Kentucky | 3,372.37 |
| 46 | Alabama | 3,298.84 |
| 47 | Mississippi | 3,262.66 |
| 48 | Oklahoma | 3,239.39 |
| 49 | Tennessee | 3,230.57 |
| 50 | Arkansas | 3,046.59 |
| 51 | Missouri | 3,043.12 |
| | U.S. Average | 4,023.14 |

Data Source: U.S. Department of Commerce

## PER CAPITA STATE AND LOCAL GENERAL REVENUES: NEW YORK VS. U.S.

In 1992-93, New York's per capita state and local general revenues surpassed the U.S. state and local average by 46.7 percent—$5,902.85 in New York versus a national average of $4,023.14.

Between 1962 and 1993, real per capita state and local general revenues in New York increased by 213 percent—from $1,885.74 in 1962 to $5,902.85 in 1993 (1993 dollars).

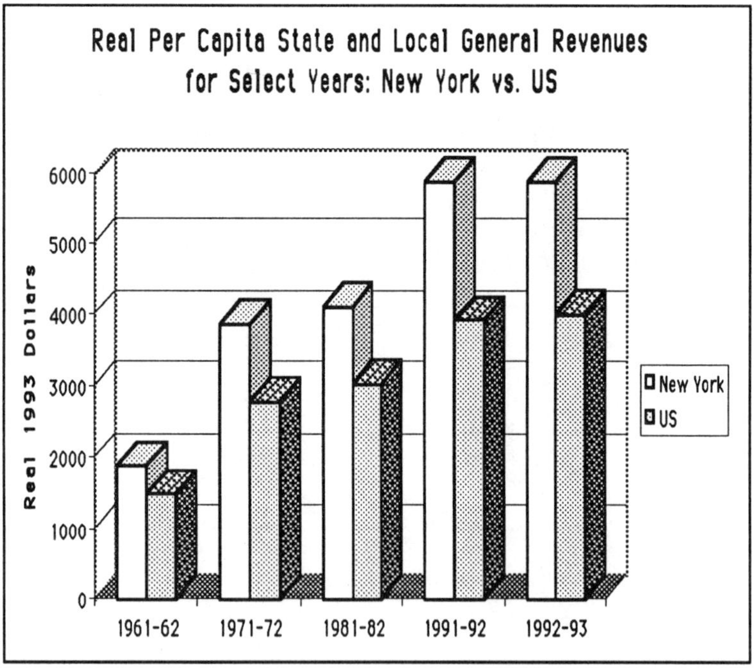


Data Source: U.S. Department of Commerce

## PER CAPITA STATE-ONLY GENERAL REVENUES: STATE RANKINGS

In 1994, New York's per capita state general revenues ranked fifth highest in the nation.

**Per Capita State General Revenues**

| Rank | State | Per Capita General Revenues |
|---|---|---|
| 1 | Alaska | $8,711.62 |
| 2 | Hawaii | 4,289.15 |
| 3 | Wyoming | 4,211.05 |
| 4 | Delaware | 3,999.67 |
| **5** | **New York** | **3,664.88** |
| 6 | New Mexico | 3,505.82 |
| 7 | Connecticut | 3,446.28 |
| 8 | Massachusetts | 3,367.91 |
| 9 | Rhode Island | 3,192.13 |
| 10 | North Dakota | 3,149.83 |
| 11 | Minnesota | 3,111.94 |
| 12 | Vermont | 3,072.34 |
| 13 | New Jersey | 3,040.50 |
| 14 | Montana | 2,941.86 |
| 15 | Washington | 2,931.27 |
| 16 | West Virginia | 2,926.99 |
| 17 | California | 2,855.52 |
| 18 | Maine | 2,850.37 |
| 19 | Michigan | 2,848.56 |
| 20 | Wisconsin | 2,846.69 |
| 21 | Oregon | 2,758.00 |
| 22 | Louisiana | 2,745.43 |
| 23 | Iowa | 2,693.31 |
| 24 | Kentucky | 2,638.84 |
| 25 | Maryland | 2,571.00 |
| 26 | North Carolina | 2,540.20 |
| 27 | Kansas | 2,530.38 |

*continued*

*continued*

| Rank | State | Per Capita General Revenues |
|---|---|---|
| 28 | Pennsylvania | 2,527.53 |
| 29 | Utah | 2,520.30 |
| 30 | Indiana | 2,518.46 |
| 31 | Idaho | 2,511.15 |
| 32 | Nebraska | 2,480.94 |
| 33 | Mississippi | 2,475.50 |
| 34 | South Carolina | 2,461.84 |
| 35 | Arkansas | 2,438.86 |
| 36 | Ohio | 2,436.67 |
| 37 | South Dakota | 2,414.93 |
| 38 | Arizona | 2,382.04 |
| 39 | Nevada | 2,374.92 |
| 40 | Alabama | 2,373.65 |
| 41 | New Hampshire | 2,330.08 |
| 42 | Oklahoma | 2,292.03 |
| 43 | Illinois | 2,263.02 |
| 44 | Virginia | 2,261.44 |
| 45 | Georgia | 2,201.25 |
| 46 | Colorado | 2,197.69 |
| 47 | Missouri | 2,134.53 |
| 48 | Tennessee | 2,113.94 |
| 49 | Florida | 2,113.09 |
| 50 | Texas | 2,069.37 |
| | U.S. Average | 2,662.53 |

Data Source: U.S. Department of Commerce

## PER CAPITA STATE-ONLY GENERAL REVENUES: NEW YORK VS. U.S.

In 1994, New York's per capita state general revenues exceeded the state average by 37.6 percent—$3,664.88 in New York versus a state average of $2,662.53.

Between 1965 and 1994, real per capita state general revenues increased by 260.6 percent. In 1994 dollars, New York's 1965 per capita general revenues equaled $1,016.29.

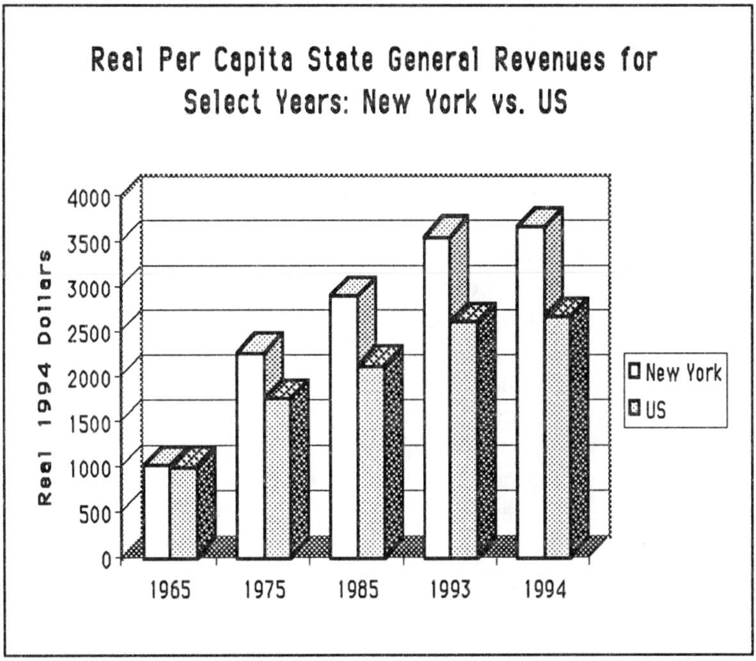


Data Source: U.S. Department of Commerce

## PER CAPITA STATE AND LOCAL REVENUES FROM THE FEDERAL GOVERNMENT (OR FEDERAL AID): STATE RANKINGS

In 1995, New York's per capita state and local revenues from the federal government, or federal aid, ranked fourth highest in the nation, only surpassed by the District of Columbia, Alaska, and Wyoming.

**Per Capita Federal Aid to State and Local Governments**

| Rank | State | Per Capita Aid |
|---|---|---|
| 1 | District of Columbia | $3,926 |
| 2 | Alaska | 1,856 |
| 3 | Wyoming | 1,571 |
| **4** | **New York** | **1,340** |
| 5 | Rhode Island | 1,280 |
| 6 | Louisiana | 1,226 |
| 7 | North Dakota | 1,204 |
| 8 | West Virginia | 1,138 |
| 9 | Massachusetts | 1,130 |
| 10(t) | New Mexico | 1,128 |
| 10(t) | South Dakota | 1,128 |
| 12 | Montana | 1,090 |
| 13 | Vermont | 1,078 |
| 14 | Maine | 1,060 |
| 15 | Mississippi | 1,026 |
| 16 | Hawaii | 986 |
| 17 | Connecticut | 976 |
| 18 | Kentucky | 898 |
| 19 | Oregon | 895 |
| 20 | Nebraska | 887 |
| 21 | Tennessee | 876 |
| 22 | Pennsylvania | 859 |
| 23 | California | 857 |
| 24 | Arkansas | 852 |
| 25 | New Jersey | 840 |

*continued*

*continued*

| Rank | State | Per Capita Aid |
|---|---|---|
| 26 | South Carolina | 826 |
| 27 | Ohio | 821 |
| 28 | Washington | 814 |
| 29 | Alabama | 810 |
| 30(t) | Illinois | 807 |
| 30(t) | Minnesota | 807 |
| 32 | Michigan | 799 |
| 33 | Delaware | 793 |
| 34 | Missouri | 788 |
| 35 | North Carolina | 776 |
| 36 | Georgia | 774 |
| 37 | Arizona | 773 |
| 38 | New Hampshire | 762 |
| 39 | Oklahoma | 759 |
| 40 | Idaho | 749 |
| 41 | Wisconsin | 734 |
| 42 | Iowa | 733 |
| 43 | Texas | 726 |
| 44 | Maryland | 718 |
| 45 | Utah | 691 |
| 46 | Colorado | 654 |
| 47 | Florida | 651 |
| 48 | Kansas | 646 |
| 49 | Indiana | 616 |
| 50 | Nevada | 605 |
| 51 | Virginia | 535 |
| | U.S. Average | 863 |

Data Source: U.S. Department of Commerce, *Statistical Abstract of the United States 1996*

## PER CAPITA STATE AND LOCAL REVENUES FROM THE FEDERAL GOVERNMENT: NEW YORK VS. US

In 1995, New York's per capita state and local federal aid outstripped the national average by 55.3 percent—$1,340 in New York versus a state and local average of $863.

Between 1962 and 1995, real (1993 dollars) per capita state and local revenues from the federal government in New York rose by 854.2 percent—$133.11 in 1962 versus $1,270.14 in 1995.

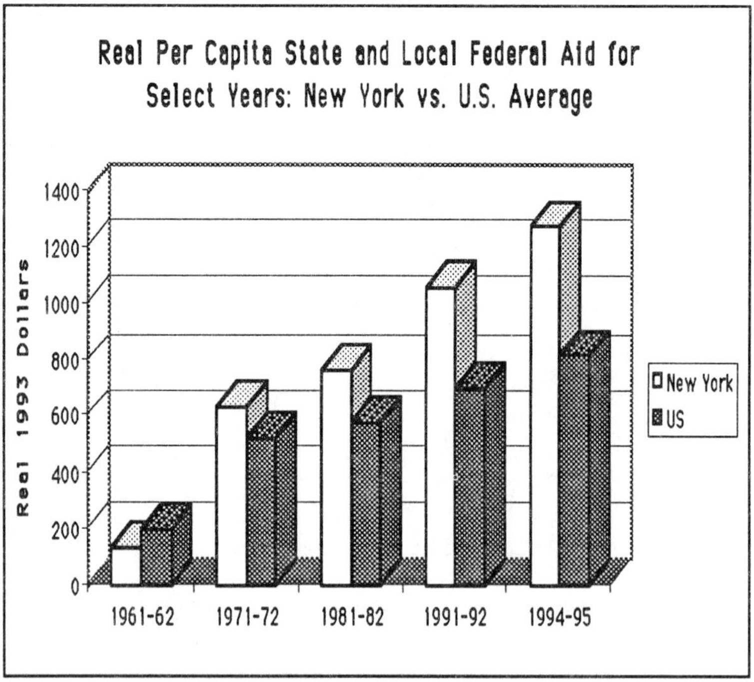


Data Sources: U.S. Department of Commerce, *1982 Census of Governments, Government Finances 1991-92 (Preliminary Data)*, and *Statistical Abstract of the United States 1996*

## PER CAPITA STATE-ONLY REVENUES FROM THE FEDERAL GOVERNMENT: STATE RANKINGS

In 1994, New York's per capita state revenues from the federal government ranked third highest in the nation.

**Per Capita State Revenues from the Federal Government**

| Rank | State | Per Capita Revenues |
|---|---|---|
| 1 | Wyoming | $1,663.87 |
| 2 | Alaska | 1,515.75 |
| **3** | **New York** | **1,128.52** |
| 4 | Louisiana | 1,083.17 |
| 5 | Vermont | 1,063.79 |
| 6 | West Virginia | 1,050.44 |
| 7 | Rhode Island | 991.95 |
| 8 | North Dakota | 985.91 |
| 9 | Montana | 962.62 |
| 10 | Hawaii | 927.84 |
| 11 | South Dakota | 903.18 |
| 12 | Mississippi | 896.63 |
| 13 | Maine | 882.97 |
| 14 | California | 859.94 |
| 15 | Oregon | 831.87 |
| 16 | Massachusetts | 831.32 |
| 17 | Connecticut | 800.92 |
| 18 | New Hampshire | 793.83 |
| 19 | New Mexico | 780.06 |
| 20 | Arkansas | 779.05 |
| 21 | South Carolina | 747.46 |
| 22 | Kentucky | 742.69 |
| 23 | Michigan | 723.35 |
| 24 | Alabama | 716.59 |
| 25 | Indiana | 714.68 |
| 26 | Ohio | 714.34 |
| 27 | Tennessee | 710.78 |
| 28 | Minnesota | 700.31 |

*continued*

*continued*

| Rank | State | Per Capita Revenues |
|---|---|---|
| 29 | Missouri | 697.86 |
| 30 | Wisconsin | 693.49 |
| 31 | Iowa | 691.63 |
| 32 | North Carolina | 688.40 |
| 33 | Utah | 688.32 |
| 34 | Delaware | 687.85 |
| 35 | Pennsylvania | 687.53 |
| 36 | Washington | 673.47 |
| 37 | Kansas | 662.49 |
| 38 | Nebraska | 649.01 |
| 39 | Georgia | 646.78 |
| 40 | New Jersey | 630.27 |
| 41 | Texas | 618.53 |
| 42 | Idaho | 616.40 |
| 43 | Arizona | 604.81 |
| 44 | Colorado | 590.93 |
| 45 | Oklahoma | 589.19 |
| 46 | Illinois | 583.13 |
| 47 | Maryland | 571.20 |
| 48 | Florida | 507.52 |
| 49 | Nevada | 461.70 |
| 50 | Virginia | 446.65 |
| | U.S. Average | 736.81 |

Data Source: U.S. Department of Commerce, *Statistical Abstract of the United States 1996.*

## PER CAPITA STATE-ONLY REVENUES FROM THE FEDERAL GOVERNMENT: NEW YORK VS. U.S.

In 1994, New York's per capita state revenues topped the state average by 53.2 percent—$1,128.52 in New York versus the national average of $736.81.

Between 1965 and 1994, New York's real per capita state revenues from the federal government (in 1994 dollars) increased from $171.60 in 1965 to $1,128.52 in 1994—a jump of 557.6 percent.

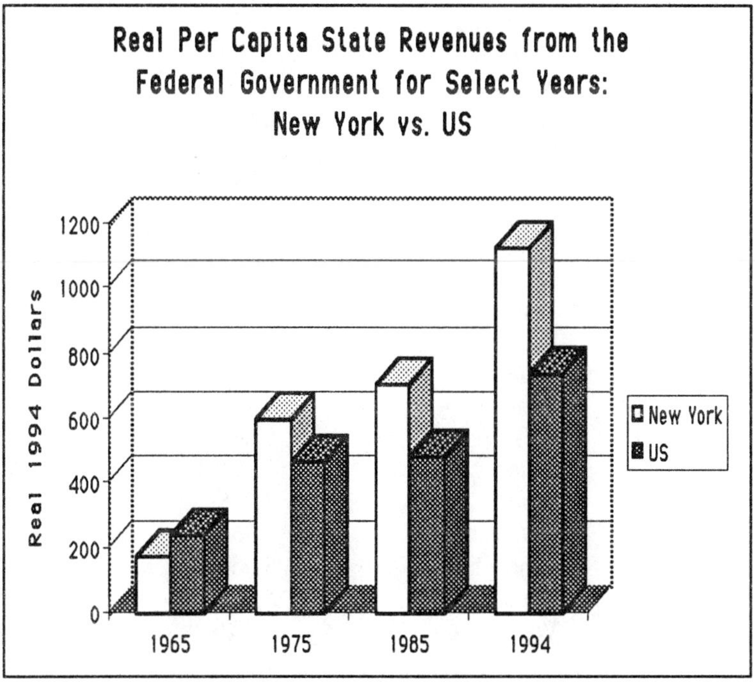


Data Sources: U.S. Department of Commerce, *State Government Finances*, annual, and *Statistical Abstract of the United States 1996*

## PER CAPITA FEDERAL FUNDS DISTRIBUTION: STATE RANKINGS

In 1994, New York's per capita federal funds distribution—or the amount of funds spent in the state by the federal government —ranked twenty-third in the nation.

**Per Capita Federal Funds Distribution**

| Rank | State | Per Capita Federal Funds |
|---|---|---|
| 1 | District of Columbia | $38,186 |
| 2 | Alaska | 7,656 |
| 3 | Maryland | 7,306 |
| 4 | Virginia | 7,004 |
| 5 | New Mexico | 6,816 |
| 6 | Hawaii | 6,449 |
| 7 | North Dakota | 6,127 |
| 8 | Missouri | 6,019 |
| 9 | Massachusetts | 5,856 |
| 10 | Rhode Island | 5,489 |
| 11 | Montana | 5,418 |
| 12 | Maine | 5,409 |
| 13 | South Dakota | 5,289 |
| 14 | Alabama | 5,281 |
| 15 | Mississippi | 5,272 |
| 16 | West Virginia | 5,242 |
| 17 | Colorado | 5,194 |
| 18 | Florida | 5,095 |
| 19 | Connecticut | 5,066 |
| 20 | Pennsylvania | 5,064 |
| 21 | Louisiana | 5,022 |
| 22 | Washington | 4,987 |
| **23** | **New York** | **4,973** |
| 24 | California | 4,944 |
| 25 | Wyoming | 4,924 |
| 26 | Kansas | 4,897 |

*continued*

*continued*

| Rank | State | Per Capita Federal Funds |
|---|---|---|
| 27 | Tennessee | 4,842 |
| 28 | Oklahoma | 4,824 |
| 29 | New Jersey | 4,723 |
| 30 | South Carolina | 4,666 |
| 31 | Arizona | 4,665 |
| 32 | Arkansas | 4,638 |
| 33 | Iowa | 4,588 |
| 34 | Nebraska | 4,584 |
| 35 | Kentucky | 4,574 |
| 36 | Georgia | 4,545 |
| 37 | Idaho | 4,382 |
| 38 | Ohio | 4,326 |
| 39 | Texas | 4,315 |
| 40 | Illinois | 4,249 |
| 41 | Oregon | 4,231 |
| 42 | Nevada | 4,189 |
| 43 | Delaware | 4,179 |
| 44 | Vermont | 4,157 |
| 45 | Minnesota | 4,116 |
| 46 | Michigan | 4,104 |
| 47 | North Carolina | 4,082 |
| 48 | New Hampshire | 4,078 |
| 49 | Utah | 3,980 |
| 50 | Wisconsin | 3,870 |
| 51 | Indiana | 3,843 |
| | U.S. Average | 4,996 |

Data Source: U.S. Department of Commerce, *Statistical Abstract of the United States 1995*

## PER CAPITA FEDERAL FUNDS DISTRIBUTION: NEW YORK VS. U.S.

In 1994, New York's per capita federal funds distribution actually registered just less than the national average—$4,973 in New York versus the U.S. average of $4,996.

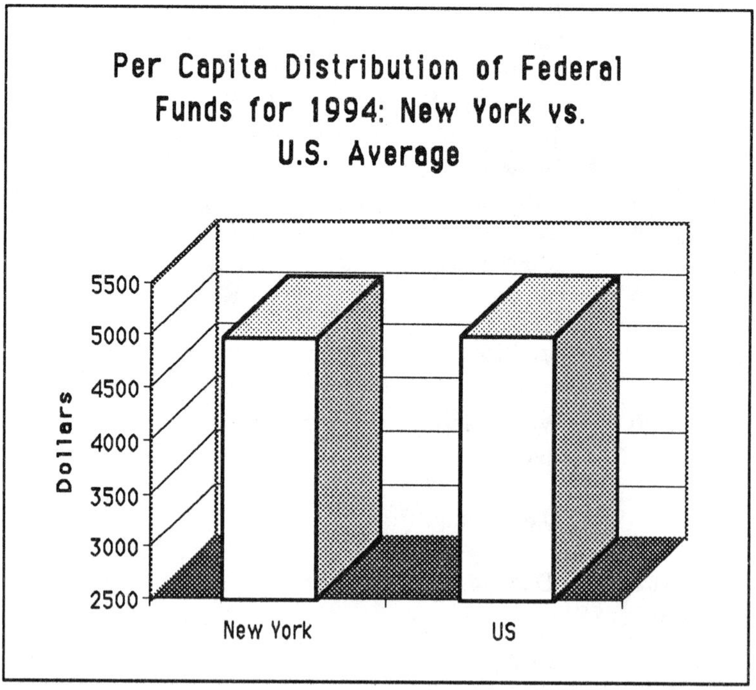


Data Source: U.S. Department of Commerce, *Statistical Abstract of the United States 1995*

## Per Capita State and Local Total Taxes: State Rankings

In 1992-93, New York's per capita state and local taxes ranked third highest in the nation, only exceeded by Alaska and the District of Columbia.

**Per Capita State and Local Total Taxes**

| Rank | State | Per Capita Total Taxes |
|---|---|---|
| 1 | Alaska | $4,930.07 |
| 2 | District of Columbia | 4,393.04 |
| **3** | **New York** | **3,654.90** |
| 4 | Connecticut | 3,333.95 |
| 5 | New Jersey | 3,050.91 |
| 6 | Hawaii | 2,983.58 |
| 7 | Minnesota | 2,672.47 |
| 8 | Massachusetts | 2,663.43 |
| 9 | Maryland | 2,565.64 |
| 10 | Wisconsin | 2,524.19 |
| 11 | Washington | 2,430.77 |
| 12 | California | 2,417.69 |
| 13 | Rhode Island | 2,404.72 |
| 14 | Vermont | 2,378.82 |
| 15 | Michigan | 2,371.14 |
| 16 | Delaware | 2,336.19 |
| 17 | Illinois | 2,332.35 |
| 18 | New Hampshire | 2,304.38 |
| 19 | Wyoming | 2,293.62 |
| 20 | Maine | 2,279.91 |
| 21 | Nevada | 2,269.77 |
| 22 | Pennsylvania | 2,260.48 |
| 23 | Iowa | 2,199.68 |
| 24 | Oregon | 2,167.16 |
| 25 | Nebraska | 2,128.17 |
| 26 | Kansas | 2,126.51 |
| 27 | Arizona | 2,107.68 |

*continued*

*continued*

| Rank | State | Per Capita Total Taxes |
|---|---|---|
| 28 | Colorado | 2,091.78 |
| 29 | Virginia | 2,073.42 |
| 30 | Ohio | 2,058.86 |
| 31 | Florida | 2,040.74 |
| 32 | Georgia | 1,998.48 |
| 33 | North Carolina | 1,974.51 |
| 34 | New Mexico | 1,952.64 |
| 35 | Texas | 1,932.69 |
| 36 | North Dakota | 1,922.45 |
| 37 | Indiana | 1,919.59 |
| 38 | Idaho | 1,909.90 |
| 39 | Montana | 1,853.51 |
| 40 | Kentucky | 1,816.54 |
| 41 | Utah | 1,802.69 |
| 42 | Oklahoma | 1,777.07 |
| 43 | West Virginia | 1,752.15 |
| 44 | South Carolina | 1,736.36 |
| 45 | Missouri | 1,720.88 |
| 46 | Tennessee | 1,706.37 |
| 47 | Louisiana | 1,684.53 |
| 48 | South Dakota | 1,667.29 |
| 49 | Arkansas | 1,590.25 |
| 50 | Alabama | 1,553.35 |
| 51 | Mississippi | 1,534.99 |
| | U.S. Average | 2,299.95 |

Data Source: U.S. Department of Commerce

## PER CAPITA STATE AND LOCAL TOTAL TAXES: NEW YORK VS. U.S.

In 1992-93, New York's per capita state and local taxes exceeded the state and local average by 58.9 percent—$3,654.90 in New York versus a national average of $2,299.95.

Between 1962 and 1993, real (1993 dollars) per capita state and local taxes in New York increased by 145.2 percent—from $1,490.67 in 1962 to $3,654.90 in 1993.

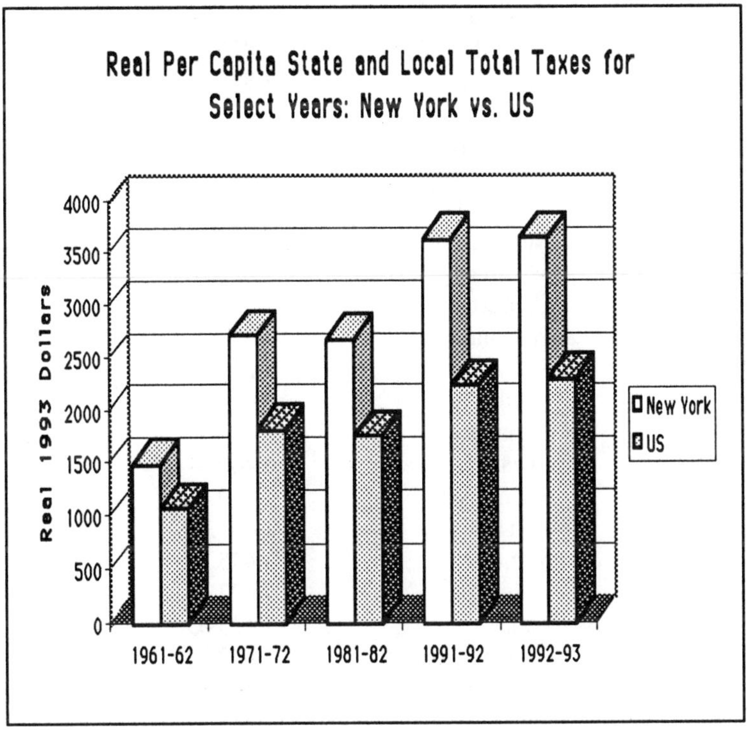


Data Source: U.S. Department of Commerce

## PER CAPITA STATE-ONLY TOTAL TAXES: STATE RANKINGS

In 1994, New York's per capita state total taxes ranked ninth highest in the nation.

**Per Capita State Total Taxes**

| Rank | State | Per Capita Total Taxes |
|---|---|---|
| 1 | Hawaii | $2,538.91 |
| 2 | Connecticut | 2,072.82 |
| 3 | Alaska | 2,046.66 |
| 4 | Delaware | 2,045.44 |
| 5 | Minnesota | 1,894.24 |
| 6 | New Mexico | 1,826.43 |
| 7 | Massachusetts | 1,823.62 |
| 8 | Washington | 1,815.62 |
| **9** | **New York** | **1,806.19** |
| 10 | New Jersey | 1,707.24 |
| 11 | Wisconsin | 1,658.34 |
| 12 | Nevada | 1,633.98 |
| 13 | Michigan | 1,623.78 |
| 14 | California | 1,581.09 |
| 15 | Wyoming | 1,553.35 |
| 16 | Maryland | 1,514.73 |
| 17 | North Carolina | 1,487.78 |
| 18 | Kentucky | 1,487.52 |
| 19 | Iowa | 1,460.04 |
| 20 | Rhode Island | 1,440.45 |
| 21 | Kansas | 1,438.35 |
| 22 | Vermont | 1,435.37 |
| 23 | Idaho | 1,427.10 |
| 24 | Maine | 1,423.05 |
| 25 | Pennsylvania | 1,422.34 |
| 26 | West Virginia | 1,401.86 |
| 27 | Arizona | 1,388.19 |
| 28 | North Dakota | 1,386.70 |
| 29 | Montana | 1,356.14 |

*continued*

*continued*

| Rank | State | Per Capita Total Taxes |
|---|---|---|
| 30 | Nebraska | 1,320.78 |
| 31 | Illinois | 1,316.52 |
| 32 | Oregon | 1,308.95 |
| 33 | Oklahoma | 1,308.47 |
| 34 | Arkansas | 1,294.73 |
| 35 | Ohio | 1,278.01 |
| 36 | Florida | 1,276.30 |
| 37 | Indiana | 1,266.25 |
| 38 | Utah | 1,266.18 |
| 39 | Mississippi | 1,245.93 |
| 40 | Georgia | 1,245.08 |
| 41 | South Carolina | 1,228.65 |
| 42 | Virginia | 1,226.66 |
| 43 | Colorado | 1,136.34 |
| 44 | Alabama | 1,129.91 |
| 45 | Missouri | 1,111.94 |
| 46 | Tennessee | 1,107.88 |
| 47 | Texas | 1,059.16 |
| 48 | Louisiana | 1,015.69 |
| 49 | South Dakota | 914.32 |
| 50 | New Hampshire | 736.15 |
| | U.S. Average | 1,435.85 |

Data Source: U.S. Department of Commerce

## PER CAPITA STATE-ONLY TOTAL TAXES: NEW YORK VS. U.S.

In 1994, New York's per capita state total taxes outpaced the state average by 25.8 percent—$1,806.19 in New York versus the state average of $1,435.85.

Between 1965 and 1994, real per capita state total taxes in New York grew by 142.9 percent. In 1994 dollars, New York's per capita total taxes equaled $743.47 in 1965.

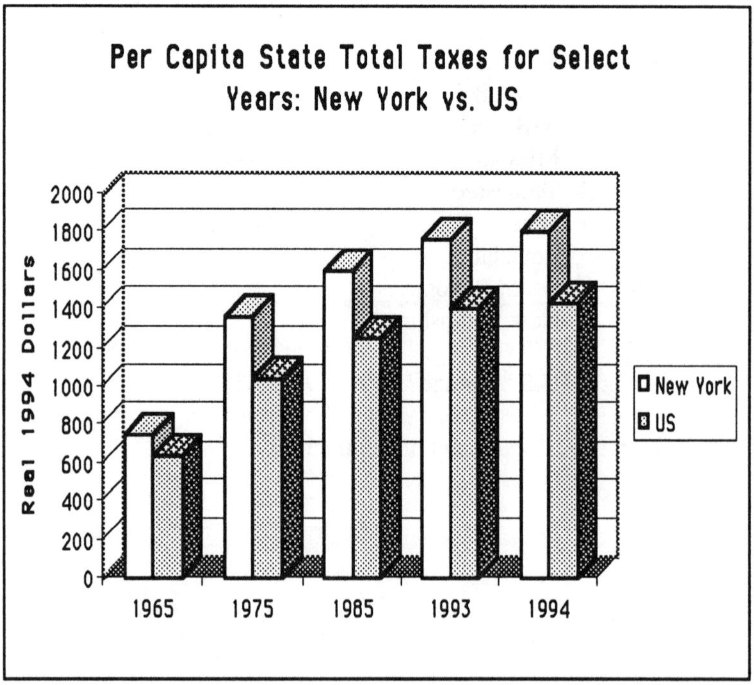


Data Source: U.S. Department of Commerce

## PER CAPITA STATE AND LOCAL PROPERTY TAXES: STATE RANKINGS

In 1992-93, New York's per capita state and local property taxes ranked fifth highest in the nation.

**Per Capita State and Local Property Taxes**

| Rank | State | Per Capita Property Taxes |
|---|---|---|
| 1 | District of Columbia | $1,750.28 |
| 2 | New Hampshire | 1,412.06 |
| 3 | New Jersey | 1,369.66 |
| 4 | Connecticut | 1,283.45 |
| **5** | **New York** | **1,191.32** |
| 6 | Alaska | 1,118.04 |
| 7 | Vermont | 1,010.42 |
| 8 | Michigan | 983.96 |
| 9 | Rhode Island | 968.33 |
| 10 | Wisconsin | 917.51 |
| 11 | Illinois | 913.57 |
| 12 | Massachusetts | 912.89 |
| 13 | Wyoming | 890.42 |
| 14 | Maine | 878.03 |
| 15 | Minnesota | 835.22 |
| 16 | Oregon | 834.19 |
| 17 | Nebraska | 783.83 |
| 18 | Iowa | 774.85 |
| 19 | Montana | 763.44 |
| 20 | Texas | 748.46 |
| 21 | Florida | 738.87 |
| 22 | Washington | 738.15 |
| 23 | Maryland | 727.50 |
| 24 | Kansas | 696.18 |
| 25 | California | 687.74 |
| 26 | Colorado | 685.26 |
| 27 | Arizona | 684.94 |
| 28 | South Dakota | 679.24 |

*continued*

*continued*

| Rank | State | Per Capita Property Taxes |
|---|---|---|
| 29 | Virginia | 656.37 |
| 30 | Pennsylvania | 637.71 |
| 31 | Indiana | 625.93 |
| 32 | Ohio | 622.66 |
| 33 | Georgia | 586.36 |
| 34 | North Dakota | 562.37 |
| 35 | Hawaii | 517.26 |
| 36 | Nevada | 509.87 |
| 37 | South Carolina | 506.96 |
| 38 | Idaho | 478.52 |
| 39 | Utah | 459.33 |
| 40 | North Carolina | 424.18 |
| 41 | Missouri | 389.73 |
| 42 | Mississippi | 388.64 |
| 43 | Tennessee | 371.04 |
| 44 | Delaware | 347.06 |
| 45 | West Virginia | 322.31 |
| 46 | Kentucky | 305.84 |
| 47 | Oklahoma | 291.50 |
| 48 | Louisiana | 274.10 |
| 49 | Arkansas | 260.42 |
| 50 | New Mexico | 237.51 |
| 51 | Alabama | 183.48 |
| | U.S. Average | 731.32 |

Data Source: U.S. Department of Commerce

## PER CAPITA STATE AND LOCAL PROPERTY TAXES: NEW YORK VS. U.S.

In 1992-93, New York's per capita state and local property taxes topped the state and local average by 62.9 percent—$1,191.32 in New York versus $731.32 across the nation.

Between 1962 and 1993, real per capita state and local property taxes in New York increased by 80.2 percent. In 1993 dollars, New York 1962 per capita property taxes equaled $661.20.

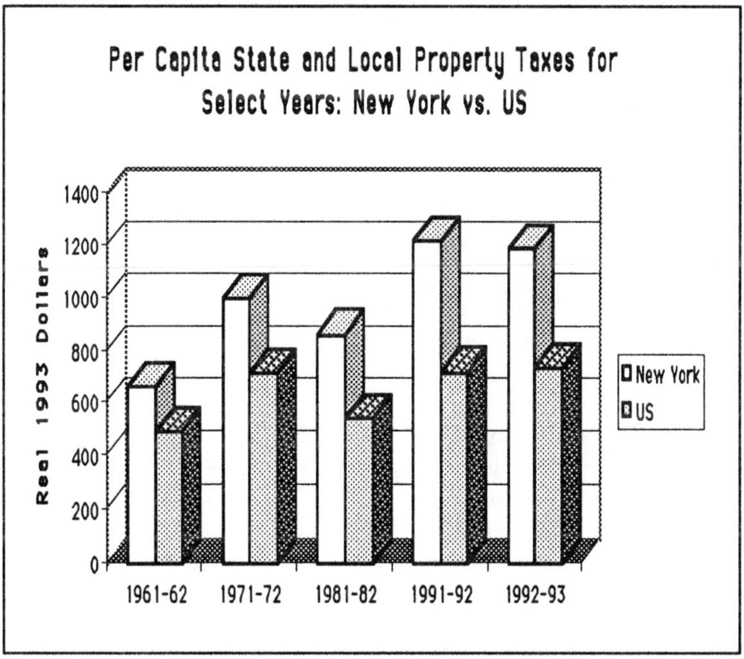


Data Source: U.S. Department of Commerce

# PER CAPITA STATE AND LOCAL SALES TAXES: STATE RANKINGS

In 1992-93, New York's per capita state and local sales and gross receipts taxes ranked eighth highest in the nation.

**Per Capita State and Local Sales and Gross Receipts Taxes**

| Rank | State | Per Capita Sales Taxes |
|---|---|---|
| 1 | Hawaii | $1,511.03 |
| 2 | Washington | 1,477.00 |
| 3 | Nevada | 1,429.22 |
| 4 | District of Columbia | 1,149.08 |
| 5 | Tennessee | 1,081.24 |
| 6 | Florida | 1,058.45 |
| 7 | New Mexico | 1,049.50 |
| **8** | **New York** | **999.67** |
| 9 | Texas | 951.24 |
| 10 | Connecticut | 944.78 |
| 11 | Arizona | 906.76 |
| 12 | Louisiana | 896.70 |
| 13 | California | 871.24 |
| 14 | New Jersey | 868.48 |
| 15 | Alabama | 812.92 |
| 16 | Minnesota | 810.91 |
| 17 | Illinois | 793.67 |
| 18 | South Dakota | 792.65 |
| 19 | Arkansas | 791.65 |
| 20 | Kansas | 783.15 |
| 21 | Utah | 767.74 |
| 22 | Georgia | 767.65 |
| 23 | Rhode Island | 764.67 |
| 24 | Mississippi | 760.11 |
| 25 | Colorado | 758.37 |
| 26 | North Carolina | 753.63 |
| 27 | West Virginia | 748.57 |
| 28 | North Dakota | 744.44 |

*continued*

*continued*

| Rank | State | Per Capita Sales Taxes |
|---|---|---|
| 29 | Maine | 736.76 |
| 30 | Nebraska | 733.44 |
| 31 | Missouri | 729.96 |
| 32 | Oklahoma | 720.62 |
| 33 | Wisconsin | 709.04 |
| 34 | Wyoming | 679.99 |
| 35 | Pennsylvania | 667.72 |
| 36 | Iowa | 664.40 |
| 37 | Kentucky | 662.92 |
| 38 | Maryland | 662.49 |
| 39 | Vermont | 653.72 |
| 40 | Ohio | 643.89 |
| 41 | Idaho | 639.53 |
| 42 | Virginia | 629.87 |
| 43 | South Carolina | 627.99 |
| 44 | New Hampshire | 599.60 |
| 45 | Indiana | 557.80 |
| 46 | Massachusetts | 556.61 |
| 47 | Michigan | 516.80 |
| 48 | Alaska | 343.59 |
| 49 | Delaware | 285.94 |
| 50 | Montana | 238.55 |
| 51 | Oregon | 195.67 |
| | U.S. Average | 812.82 |

Data Source: U.S. Department of Commerce

## PER CAPITA STATE AND LOCAL SALES TAXES: NEW YORK VS. U.S.

In 1992-93, New York's per capita state and local sales and gross receipts taxes outpaced the state and local average by 22.0 percent—$999.67 in New York versus a national average of $812.82.

Between 1962 and 1993, New York's real per capita state and local sales tax revenues grew by 452.6 percent. In 1993 dollars, New York's 1962 per capita state and local sales taxes registered $180.90.

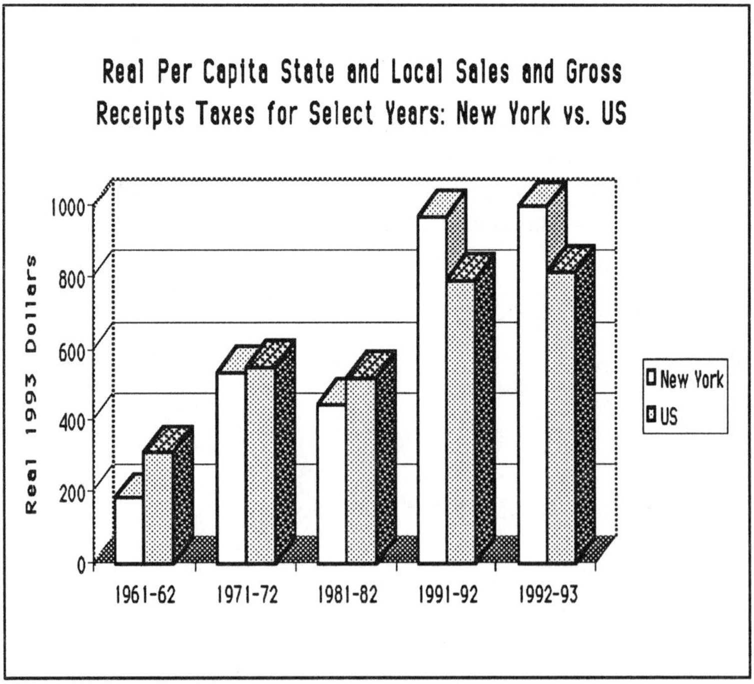


Data Source: U.S. Department of Commerce

## PER CAPITA STATE-ONLY SALES TAXES: STATE RANKINGS

In 1994, New York's per capita state sales and gross receipts taxes ranked thirty-fourth in the nation.

**Per Capita State Sales and Gross Receipts Taxes**

| Rank | State | Per Capita Sales Taxes |
|---|---|---|
| 1 | Hawaii | $1,570.65 |
| 2 | Washington | 1,354.74 |
| 3 | Nevada | 1,351.09 |
| 4 | New Mexico | 1,090.28 |
| 5 | Connecticut | 996.13 |
| 6 | Florida | 971.25 |
| 7 | New Jersey | 878.27 |
| 8 | Tennessee | 869.88 |
| 9 | Texas | 863.40 |
| 10 | Mississippi | 840.15 |
| 11 | Minnesota | 838.40 |
| 12 | Arizona | 802.31 |
| 13 | North Dakota | 778.58 |
| 14 | West Virginia | 760.51 |
| 15 | Arkansas | 727.95 |
| 16 | Rhode Island | 724.44 |
| 17 | Wisconsin | 720.70 |
| 18 | Maine | 718.31 |
| 19 | Kentucky | 710.87 |
| 20 | South Dakota | 710.36 |
| 21 | Kansas | 708.88 |
| 22 | Nebraska | 707.84 |
| 23 | Iowa | 694.63 |
| 24 | Vermont | 690.45 |
| 25 | Idaho | 684.77 |
| 26 | California | 682.94 |
| 27 | Pennsylvania | 673.75 |
| 28 | Illinois | 669.67 |
| 29 | Utah | 658.74 |

*continued*

*continued*

| Rank | State | Per Capita Sales Taxes |
|---|---|---|
| 30 | Maryland | 653.96 |
| 31 | North Carolina | 650.31 |
| 32 | Ohio | 644.13 |
| 33 | Michigan | 640.38 |
| **34** | **New York** | **638.22** |
| 35 | South Carolina | 633.76 |
| 36 | Alabama | 606.78 |
| 37 | Georgia | 588.44 |
| 38 | Massachusetts | 585.80 |
| 39 | Indiana | 583.06 |
| 40 | Missouri | 561.76 |
| 41 | Wyoming | 546.09 |
| 42 | Oklahoma | 544.47 |
| 43 | Louisiana | 528.71 |
| 44 | Virginia | 496.51 |
| 45 | Colorado | 485.67 |
| 46 | New Hampshire | 426.49 |
| 47 | Delaware | 299.03 |
| 48 | Montana | 282.97 |
| 49 | Oregon | 176.07 |
| 50 | Alaska | 164.45 |
| | U.S. Average | 713.85 |

Data Source: U.S. Department of Commerce

## PER CAPITA STATE-ONLY SALES TAXES: NEW YORK VS. U.S.

In 1994, the national state average per capita state sales and gross receipts taxes exceeded New York's by 11.9 percent—$638.22 in New York versus the state average of $713.85.

Between 1965 and 1994, real per capita state sales and gross receipts taxes in New York grew by 229.7 percent. In 1994 dollars, New York's per capita state sales and gross receipts taxes equaled $193.57.

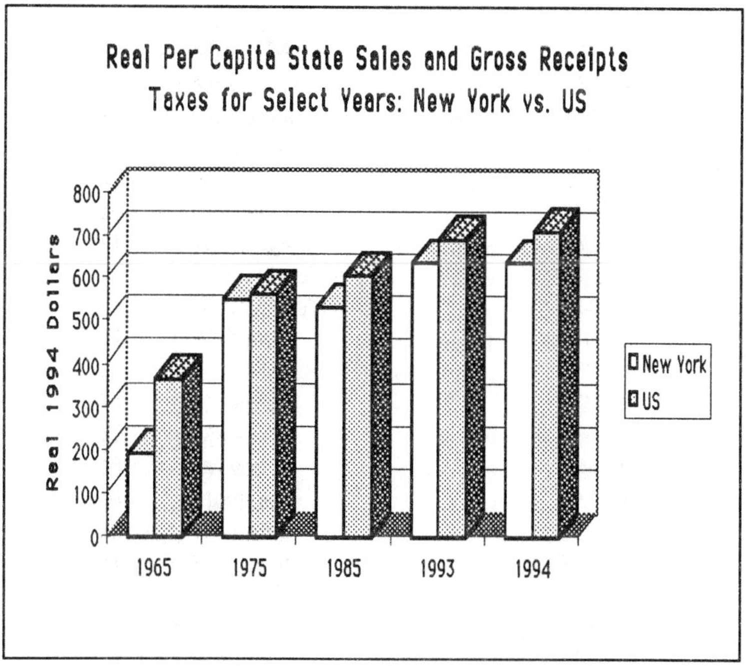


Data Source: U.S. Department of Commerce

## PER CAPITA STATE AND LOCAL INCOME TAXES: STATE RANKINGS

In 1992-93, New York's per capita state and local individual and corporate income taxes ranked second highest in the nation.

**Per Capita State and Local Income Taxes**

| Rank | State | Per Capita Income Taxes |
|---|---|---|
| 1 | Alaska | $1,458.63 |
| **2** | **New York** | **1,297.42** |
| 3 | District of Columbia | 1,263.87 |
| 4 | Massachusetts | 1,052.55 |
| 5 | Maryland | 986.02 |
| 6 | Delaware | 936.02 |
| 7 | Connecticut | 905.23 |
| 8 | Oregon | 852.80 |
| 9 | Minnesota | 846.93 |
| 10 | Hawaii | 837.08 |
| 11 | Wisconsin | 780.69 |
| 12 | Michigan | 748.07 |
| 13 | California | 702.37 |
| 14 | New Jersey | 676.93 |
| 15 | North Carolina | 676.35 |
| 16 | Ohio | 676.03 |
| 17 | Indiana | 673.54 |
| 18 | Pennsylvania | 667.07 |
| 19 | Idaho | 629.27 |
| 20 | Kentucky | 624.33 |
| 21 | Virginia | 610.06 |
| 22 | Iowa | 585.07 |
| 23 | Rhode Island | 567.65 |
| 24 | Georgia | 559.43 |
| 25 | Maine | 556.97 |
| 26 | Vermont | 552.80 |
| 27 | Colorado | 533.21 |
| 28 | Montana | 525.61 |

*continued*

*continued*

| Rank | State | Per Capita Income Taxes |
|---|---|---|
| 29 | Illinois | 505.74 |
| 30 | Utah | 497.87 |
| 31 | Kansas | 497.41 |
| 32 | Nebraska | 488.73 |
| 33 | Missouri | 463.82 |
| 34 | South Carolina | 460.75 |
| 35 | Oklahoma | 446.04 |
| 36 | West Virginia | 440.14 |
| 37 | Arkansas | 436.78 |
| 38 | Arizona | 412.14 |
| 39 | Alabama | 379.02 |
| 40 | New Mexico | 361.56 |
| 41 | Mississippi | 287.48 |
| 42 | North Dakota | 282.37 |
| 43 | Louisiana | 274.56 |
| 44 | New Hampshire | 144.21 |
| 45 | Tennessee | 90.36 |
| 46 | Florida | 55.09 |
| 47 | South Dakota | 39.29 |
| 48 | Texas | 0.07 |
| 49 | Nevada | 0.00 |
| 50 | Washington | 0.00 |
| 51 | Wyoming | 0.00 |
| | U.S. Average | 580.86 |

Data Source: U.S. Department of Commerce

## PER CAPITA STATE AND LOCAL INCOME TAXES: NEW YORK VS. U.S.

In 1992-93, New York's per capita state and local individual and corporate income taxes beat the state and local average by 123.4 percent—$1,297.42 in New York versus a national mean of $580.86.

Between 1962 and 1993, real per capita state and local income taxes increased by 268.3 percent. In 1993 dollars, New York's per capita state and local income taxes registered $352.30.

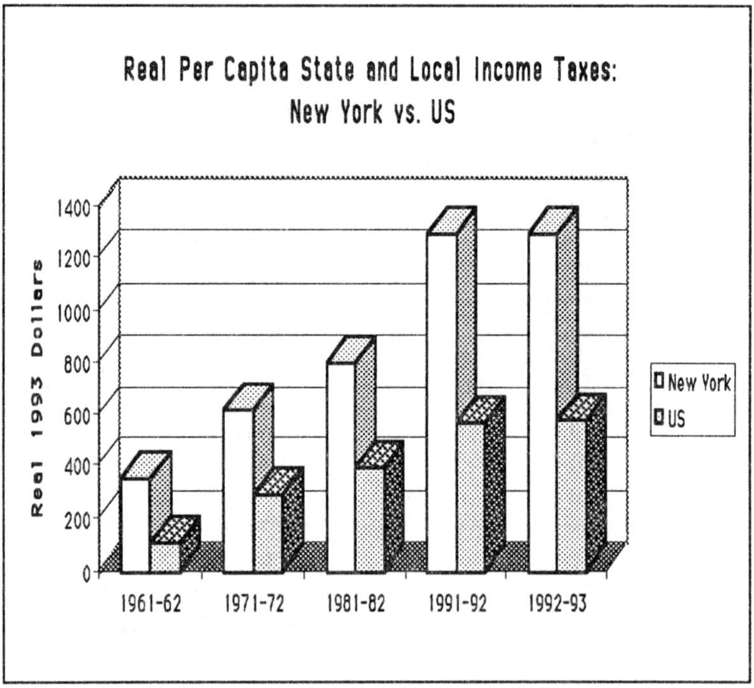


Data Source: U.S. Department of Commerce

# PER CAPITA STATE-ONLY INCOME TAXES: STATE RANKINGS

In 1994, New York's per capita state individual and corporate income taxes ranked second highest in the nation.

**Per Capita State Income Taxes**

| Rank | State | Per Capita Income Taxes |
|---|---|---|
| 1 | Massachusetts | $1,117.81 |
| **2** | **New York** | **1,054.19** |
| 3 | Delaware | 994.23 |
| 4 | Oregon | 922.62 |
| 5 | Connecticut | 897.30 |
| 6 | Minnesota | 876.10 |
| 7 | Hawaii | 874.17 |
| 8 | Wisconsin | 822.51 |
| 9 | Michigan | 813.82 |
| 10 | North Carolina | 710.81 |
| 11 | Maryland | 708.24 |
| 12 | California | 705.71 |
| 13 | New Jersey | 703.46 |
| 14 | Indiana | 629.67 |
| 15 | Virginia | 628.60 |
| 16 | Rhode Island | 609.24 |
| 17 | Iowa | 595.06 |
| 18 | Georgia | 581.44 |
| 19 | Idaho | 574.83 |
| 20 | Maine | 569.68 |
| 21 | Kansas | 567.43 |
| 22 | Colorado | 566.53 |
| 23 | Vermont | 553.52 |
| 24 | Utah | 550.41 |
| 25 | Illinois | 534.30 |
| 26 | Kentucky | 522.15 |
| 27 | Ohio | 519.06 |
| 28 | Pennsylvania | 516.27 |

*continued*

*continued*

| Rank | State | Per Capita Income Taxes |
|---|---|---|
| 29 | Nebraska | 510.62 |
| 30 | Montana | 484.25 |
| 31 | South Carolina | 477.63 |
| 32 | West Virginia | 468.89 |
| 33 | Arkansas | 465.79 |
| 34 | Oklahoma | 453.43 |
| 35 | Missouri | 450.41 |
| 36 | New Mexico | 422.97 |
| 37 | Arizona | 420.06 |
| 38 | Alabama | 375.86 |
| 39 | North Dakota | 326.66 |
| 40 | Mississippi | 301.80 |
| 41 | Alaska | 290.54 |
| 42 | Louisiana | 277.36 |
| 43 | New Hampshire | 158.43 |
| 44 | Tennessee | 100.69 |
| 45 | Florida | 68.10 |
| 46 | South Dakota | 50.68 |
| 47 | Nevada | 0.00 |
| 48 | Texas | 0.00 |
| 49 | Washington | 0.00 |
| 50 | Wyoming | 0.00 |
| | U.S. Average | 550.12 |

Data Source: U.S. Department of Commerce

## PER CAPITA STATE-ONLY INCOME TAXES: NEW YORK VS. U.S.

In 1994, New York's per capita state individual and corporate income taxes surpassed the state average by 91.6 percent—$1,054.19 in New York versus a national average of $550.12.

Between 1965 and 1994, real per capita state income taxes climbed by 144.6 percent. In 1994 dollars, New York's 1965 per capita state income taxes equaled $431.03.

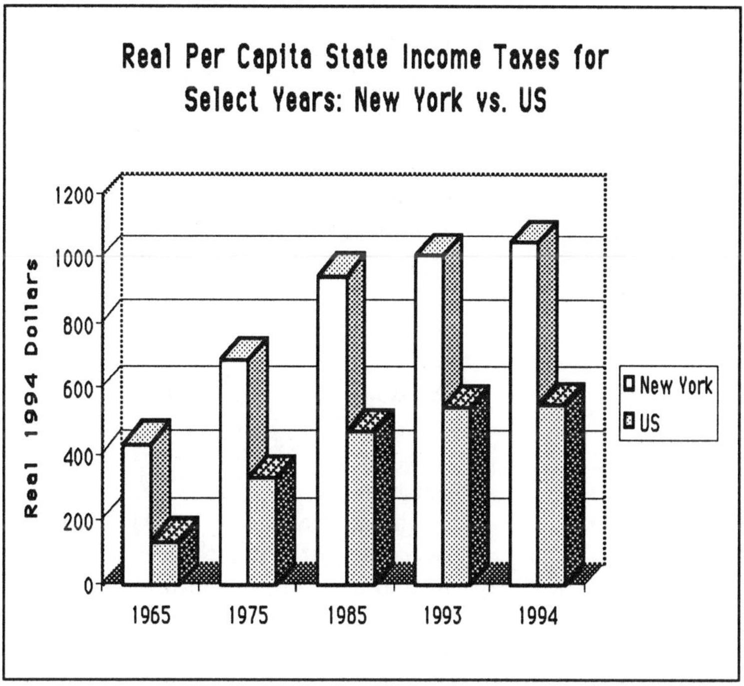


Data Source: U.S. Department of Commerce

## STATE PERSONAL INCOME TAX RATES: STATE RANKINGS

New York's top personal income tax rate of 6.85 percent (phased in during 1997) ranks twenty-third among the 50 states and the District of Columbia.

**State Top Personal Income Tax Rates**

| Rank | State | Top Rate |
|---|---|---|
| 1 | Montana | 11.00% |
| 2 | Rhode Island | 10.89 |
| 3 | Hawaii | 10.00 |
| 4 | Iowa | 9.98 |
| 5 | Vermont | 9.90 |
| 6 | District of Columbia | 9.50 |
| 7 | California | 9.30 |
| 8 | Oregon | 9.00 |
| 9(t) | Maine | 8.50 |
| 9(t) | Minnesota | 8.50 |
| 9(t) | New Mexico | 8.50 |
| 12 | Idaho | 8.20 |
| 13(t) | Kansas | 7.75 |
| 13(t) | North Carolina | 7.75 |
| 15 | Utah | 7.20 |
| 16 | Delaware | 7.10 |
| 17 | Ohio | 7.05 |
| 18(t) | Arkansas | 7.00 |
| 18(t) | Oklahoma | 7.00 |
| 18(t) | South Carolina | 7.00 |
| 21 | Nebraska | 6.99 |
| 22 | Wisconsin | 6.93 |
| **23** | **New York** | **6.85*** |
| 24 | West Virginia | 6.50 |
| 25 | New Jersey | 6.37 |
| 26(t) | Georgia | 6.00 |
| 26(t) | Kentucky | 6.00 |
| 26(t) | Louisiana | 6.00 |

*continued*

*continued*

| Rank | State | Top Rate |
|---|---|---|
| 26(t) | Missouri | 6.00 |
| 30 | Massachusetts | 5.95 |
| 31 | Virginia | 5.75 |
| 32 | Arizona | 5.60 |
| 33 | North Dakota | 5.54 |
| 34(t) | Alabama | 5.00 |
| 34(t) | Colorado | 5.00 |
| 34(t) | Maryland | 5.00 |
| 34(t) | Mississippi | 5.00 |
| 38 | Connecticut | 4.50 |
| 39 | Michigan | 4.40 |
| 40 | Indiana | 3.40 |
| 41 | Illinois | 3.00 |
| 42 | Pennsylvania | 2.80 |
| 43(t) | Alaska | 0.00 |
| 43(t) | Florida | 0.00 |
| 43(t) | Nevada | 0.00 |
| 43(t) | New Hampshire | 0.00 |
| 43(t) | South Dakota | 0.00 |
| 43(t) | Tennessee | 0.00 |
| 43(t) | Texas | 0.00 |
| 43(t) | Washington | 0.00 |
| 43(t) | Wyoming | 0.00 |
| | U.S. Average | 5.66 |

* Assumes final stage of tax cut is implemented in 1997.

Data Sources: CCH Incorporated, *State Tax Handbook* (as of December 31, 1995), National Conference of State Legislators, *State Tax Actions*, annual, and various state sources

## STATE PERSONAL INCOME TAX RATES: NEW YORK VS. U.S.

New York's top personal income tax rate of 6.85 percent (phased in by 1997) exceeds the average rate of 5.66 percent for the remaining 49 states and Washington, D.C. by 21 percent.

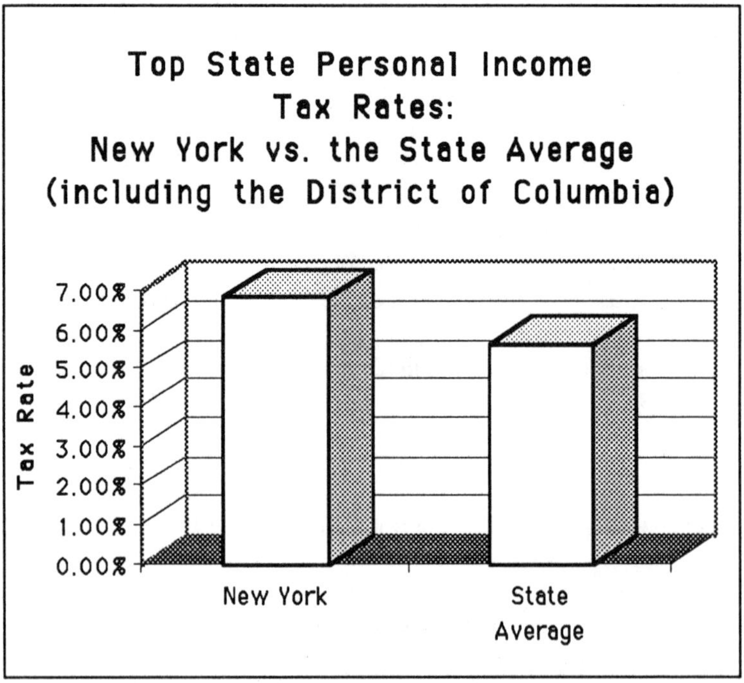


Data Sources: CCH Incorporated, *State Tax Handbook* (as of December 31, 1995), National Conference of State Legislators, *State Tax Actions*, annual, and various state sources

## TREND IN THE NEW YORK STATE PERSONAL INCOME TAX

New York was one of the earliest states to adopt an income tax. New York, along with North Dakota, implemented a personal income tax in 1919. Prior to that year, only seven other states had taken this dramatic step—Hawaii in 1901 (not then a state), Mississippi in 1912, Oklahoma in 1915, Massachusetts and Virginia in 1916, and Delaware and Missouri in 1917.

After being imposed with a top rate of 3 percent in 1919, the personal income tax rose considerably in the 1930s to a top rate of 8 percent—7 percent plus a separate 1 percent income tax designed to "help" the state through the Depression. The 1940s witnessed some temporary income tax relief, but reductions were limited and allowed to expire. By 1954, the top rate once again stood at 7 percent. Under the big-

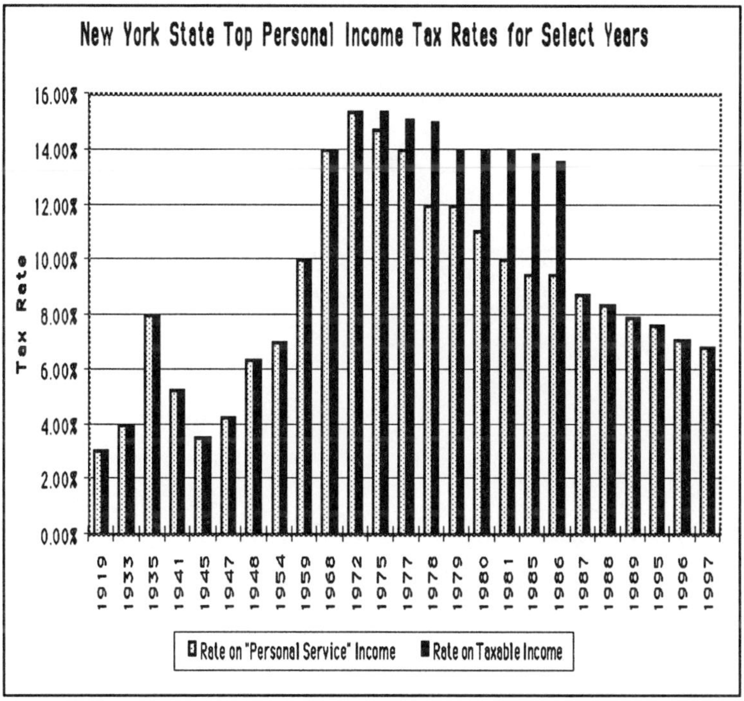


Data Sources: Variety of New York State budget documents and other state sources government reign of Governor Nelson Rockefeller, the top tax rate reached 15.38 percent. Since then, rates have come down slowly, with the help of Governor Hugh Carey in the 1970s and early 1980s, and largely to the chagrin of Governor Mario Cuomo during the rest of the 1980s.

However, the state top rate was supposed to be reduced to 7 percent by October 1990 according to legislation passed a few years earlier. But this tax cut was delayed from 1990 through 1994 by Governor Cuomo and the state legislature—leaving the top rate at 7.875 percent. In 1991, the governor and legislature actually raised the tax rate on income earners between $100,000 and $150,000. For these income levels, the state's top rate actually reached 9.3 percent.

Rates only began to decline again in 1995. Based on current legislation, the top tax rate is scheduled to decline to 6.85 percent in 1997 (though the rate will still be higher for the $100,000 to $150,000 income levels, actually topping 8 percent).

## NEW YORK STATE PERSONAL INCOME TAX AND INFLATION

New York State imposed a personal income tax in 1919. It was justified in part on typical class warfare grounds (i.e., soak the rich), and in part due to Prohibition.

State legislators at the time asserted that the loss of liquor tax revenues due to Prohibition made a personal income tax necessary, although the state comptroller, Eugene Travis, disputed such assertions and opposed the new income tax.[20] The state personal income tax in its original form is shown in the accompanying table.

**The Original 1919 New York State Personal Income Tax**

| Rate | Income Levels |
|---|---|
| 1% | up to $10,000 |
| 2% | $10,000-$50,000 |
| 3% | over $50,000 |

**The Original New York State Personal Income Tax in 1995 Dollars**

| Rate | Income Levels |
|---|---|
| 1% | up to $87,719 |
| 2% | $87,719-$438,596 |
| 3% | over $438,596 |

**1997 New York State Personal Income Tax**

| Rate | Income Levels |
|---|---|
| 4% | up to $16,000 |
| 4.5% | $16,000-$22,000 |
| 5.25% | $22,000-$26,000 |
| 5.9% | $26,000-$40,000 |
| 6.85% | over $40,000 |

Data Sources: New York State budgets

Translating the 1919 personal income tax to 1995 dollars makes clear that the higher tax rates of 2 percent and 3 percent were only meant to be levied on upper incomes. But as history has shown, the income tax turns out to be a very easy tax to increase. Even if the already legislated Pataki administration tax cuts are allowed to kick in in 1997 (see last table), rates will remain much higher and take hold at much lower levels of income than envisioned under the original state income tax. As always, envy makes for bad economics.

## STATE CAPITAL GAINS TAX RATES: STATE RANKINGS

New York's top individual capital gains tax rate of 6.85 percent (phased in during 1997) ranks twentieth among the 50 states and the District of Columbia.

**State Top Individual Capital Gains Tax Rates**

| Rank | State | Top Rate |
|---|---|---|
| 1 | Montana | 11.00% |
| 2 | Hawaii | 10.00 |
| 3 | Iowa | 9.98 |
| 4 | District of Columbia | 9.50 |
| 5 | California | 9.30 |
| 6 | Oregon | 9.00 |
| 7(t) | Maine | 8.50 |
| 7(t) | Minnesota | 8.50 |
| 7(t) | New Mexico | 8.50 |
| 10 | Idaho | 8.20 |
| 11(t) | Kansas | 7.75 |
| 11(t) | North Carolina | 7.75 |
| 13 | Rhode Island | 7.70 |
| 14 | Ohio | 7.50 |
| 15 | Utah | 7.20 |
| 16 | Delaware | 7.10 |
| 17(t) | Oklahoma | 7.00 |
| 17(t) | Vermont | 7.00 |
| 19 | Nebraska | 6.99 |
| **20** | **New York** | **6.85*** |
| 21 | West Virginia | 6.50 |
| 22 | New Jersey | 6.37 |
| 23(t) | Georgia | 6.00 |
| 23(t) | Kentucky | 6.00 |
| 23(t) | Louisiana | 6.00 |
| 23(t) | Missouri | 6.00 |
| 23(t) | Arkansas | 6.00 |
| 28 | Virginia | 5.75 |

*continued*

*continued*

| Rank | State | Top Rate |
|---|---|---|
| 29 | Arizona | 5.60 |
| 30 | North Dakota | 5.54 |
| 31(t) | Alabama | 5.00 |
| 31(t) | Colorado | 5.00 |
| 31(t) | Maryland | 5.00 |
| 34 | Connecticut | 4.50 |
| 35 | Michigan | 4.40 |
| 36 | South Carolina | 3.92 |
| 37 | Indiana | 3.40 |
| 38 | Illinois | 3.00 |
| 39 | Pennsylvania | 2.80 |
| 40 | Wisconsin | 2.77 |
| 41(t) | Alaska | 0.00 |
| 41(t) | Florida | 0.00 |
| 41(t) | Massachusetts | 0.00** |
| 41(t) | Mississippi | 0.00*** |
| 41(t) | Nevada | 0.00 |
| 41(t) | New Hampshire | 0.00 |
| 41(t) | South Dakota | 0.00 |
| 41(t) | Tennessee | 0.00 |
| 41(t) | Texas | 0.00 |
| 41(t) | Washington | 0.00 |
| 41(t) | Wyoming | 0.00 |
| | U.S. Average | 5.16 |

* Assumes final stage of tax cut is implemented in 1997.
** Zero percent rate applies to long-term (held at least six years) investments.
*** Zero percent rate applies to domestic (in-state) assets.

Data Sources: CCH Incorporated, *State Tax Handbook* (as of December 31, 1995), National Conference of State Legislators, *State Tax Actions*, annual, and various state sources

## STATE CAPITAL GAINS TAX RATES: NEW YORK VS. US

New York's top individual capital gains tax rate of 6.85 percent (phased in by 1997) exceeds the average rate for the remaining 49 states and Washington, D.C.—5.16 percent—by 32.8 percent.

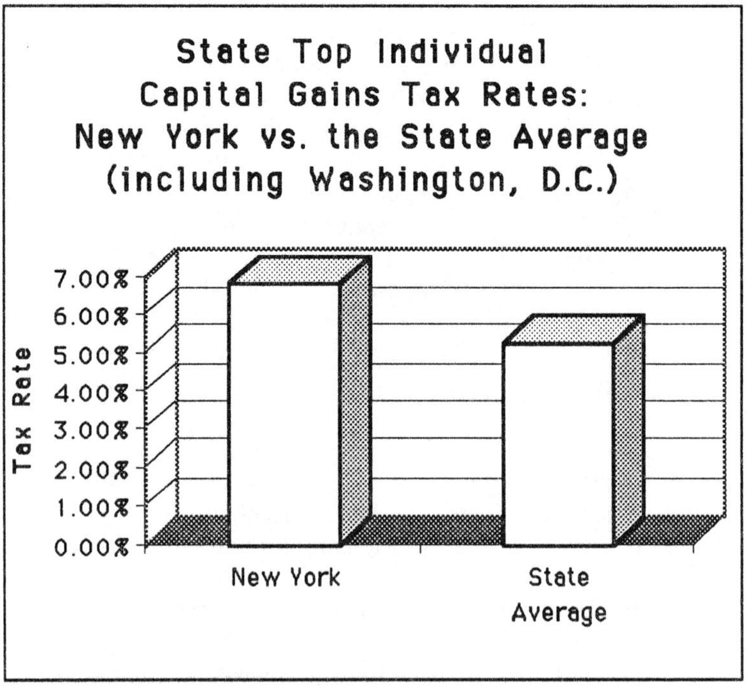


Data Sources: CCH Incorporated, *State Tax Handbook* (as of December 31, 1995), National Conference of State Legislators, *State Tax Actions*, annual, and various state sources

## TREND IN THE NEW YORK STATE CAPITAL GAINS TAX

In 1938, New York State recognized the importance of not taxing capital gains too heavily. After all, the capital gains tax—the tax on profits from the sale of assets—amounts to a direct tax on investment and entrepreneurship. These activities serve as the very engines of economic growth and job creation. New York instituted a capital gains differential compared with general personal income tax rates. At the time, a 50 percent exclusion was allowed, reducing the top capital gains tax rate from 8 percent to 4 percent. Over subsequent years, the capital gains rate had fluctuated with the state's personal income tax rate, but at some lower effective rate.

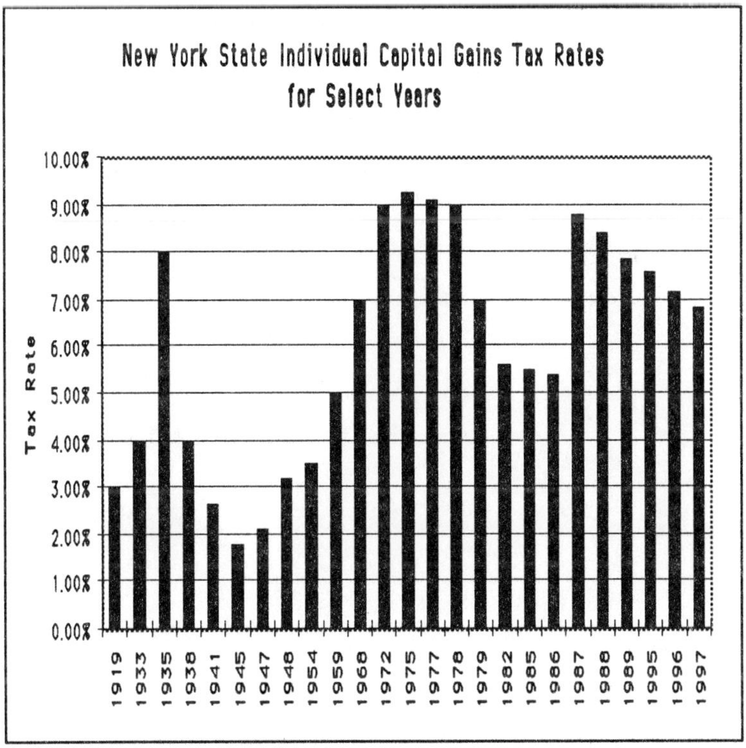


Data Sources: Variety of New York State budgets and other state sources

This changed in 1987, when the state eliminated any favorable treatment of capital gains income and increased the effective capital gains rate by a whopping 62 percent, from 5.4 percent to 8.75 percent. The rate has been coming down slowly since then and is scheduled to register 6.85 percent in 1997. At this level, New York's top capital gains tax rate will stand 26.9 percent higher than where it was in, for example, 1986.

## NEW YORK STATE'S CAPITAL GAINS TAX AND INFLATION

New York's capital gains tax on individuals is scheduled to be reduced to 6.85 percent in 1997. However, capital gains are not indexed for inflation. Therefore, the *real* capital gains tax actually reaches much higher than the stated 6.85 percent rate.

As noted in the table below, the inflation-adjusted capital gains tax rate can run quite high, depending on the rate of inflation. Indeed, under the worse case scenario, individuals can wind up paying taxes on a real capital loss.

**New York State Real Capital Gains Tax Rates at Various Investment Returns and Rates of Inflation**

| One-Year Rate of Return | Inflation Rate | Nominal Capital Gains Tax Rate | Real Capital Gains Tax Rate |
|---|---|---|---|
| 6% | 3% | 6.85% | 13.7% |
| 6% | 4% | 6.85% | 20.6% |
| 6% | 5% | 6.85% | 41.1% |
| 8% | 3% | 6.85% | 11.0% |
| 8% | 4% | 6.85% | 13.7% |
| 8% | 5% | 6.85% | 18.3% |
| 10% | 3% | 6.85% | 9.9% |
| 10% | 4% | 6.85% | 11.4% |
| 10% | 5% | 6.85% | 13.7% |

Data Source: Author's calculations

## STATE CORPORATE INCOME TAX RATES: STATE RANKINGS

New York's corporate income tax rate of 9 percent ties for ninth among the 50 states and the District of Columbia.

**State Top Corporate Income Tax Rates**

| Rank | State | Top Rate |
|---|---|---|
| 1 | Iowa | 12.00% |
| 2 | North Dakota | 10.50 |
| 3 | Pennsylvania | 9.99 |
| 4 | District of Columbia | 9.98 |
| 5 | Minnesota | 9.80 |
| 6 | Massachusetts | 9.50 |
| 7 | Alaska | 9.40 |
| 8 | California | 9.30 |
| 9(t) | Arizona | 9.00 |
| 9(t) | New Jersey | 9.00 |
| **9(t)** | **New York** | **9.00** |
| 9(t) | Rhode Island | 9.00 |
| 9(t) | West Virginia | 9.00 |
| 14 | Maine | 8.93 |
| 15 | Ohio | 8.90 |
| 16 | Delaware | 8.70 |
| 17 | Wisconsin | 8.33 |
| 18(t) | Kentucky | 8.25 |
| 18(t) | Vermont | 8.25 |
| 20(t) | Idaho | 8.00 |
| 20(t) | Louisiana | 8.00 |
| 22 | Indiana | 7.90 |
| 23 | Nebraska | 7.81 |
| 24 | North Carolina | 7.75 |
| 25 | New Mexico | 7.60 |
| 26 | Connecticut | 7.50 |
| 27 | Illinois | 7.30 |
| 28(t) | Maryland | 7.00 |
| 28(t) | New Hampshire | 7.00 |

*continued*

*continued*

| Rank | State | Top Rate |
|---|---|---|
| 30 | Montana | 6.75 |
| 31 | Oregon | 6.60 |
| 32 | Arkansas | 6.50 |
| 33 | Hawaii | 6.40 |
| 34 | Missouri | 6.25 |
| 35(t) | Georgia | 6.00 |
| 35(t) | Oklahoma | 6.00 |
| 35(t) | Tennessee | 6.00 |
| 35(t) | Virginia | 6.00 |
| 39 | Florida | 5.50 |
| 40(t) | Alabama | 5.00 |
| 40(t) | Colorado | 5.00 |
| 40(t) | Mississippi | 5.00 |
| 40(t) | South Carolina | 5.00 |
| 40(t) | Utah | 5.00 |
| 45 | Texas | 4.50 |
| 46 | Kansas | 4.13 |
| 47 | Michigan | 2.30 |
| 48(t) | Nevada | 0.00 |
| 48(t) | South Dakota | 0.00 |
| 48(t) | Washington | 0.00 |
| 48(t) | Wyoming | 0.00 |
| | U.S. Average | 6.83 |

Data Source: CCH Incorporated, *State Tax Handbook* (as of December 31, 1995), National Conference of State Legislators, *State Tax Actions*, annual, and various state sources

## STATE CORPORATE INCOME TAX RATES: NEW YORK VS. U.S.

New York's corporate income tax rate of 9 percent surpasses the average rate of 6.83 percent for the other 49 states and Washington, D.C. by 31.8 percent.

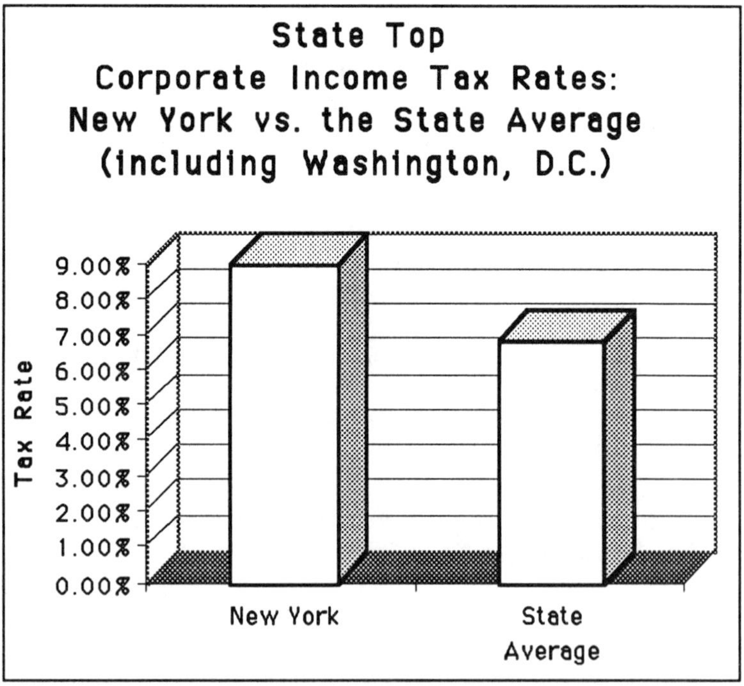


Data Sources: CCH Incorporated, *State Tax Handbook* (as of December 31, 1995), National Conference of State Legislators, *State Tax Actions*, annual, and various state sources

## TREND IN THE NEW YORK STATE CORPORATE INCOME TAX

New York's corporate income tax was instituted in 1917. By the late 1940s, the rate rested at 5.5 percent. During the Rockefeller era (generally, 1959 to 1976), the corporate rate rose by more than 118 percent to a peak of 12 percent in 1976. In 1978, the rate fell to 10 percent, and then to 9 percent in 1987. A new business tax surcharge raised the rate to 10.35 percent in 1990. The surcharge was phased out by mid-1996. The New York corporate tax rate again equals 9 percent.

New York State Corporate Income Tax Rate for Select Years

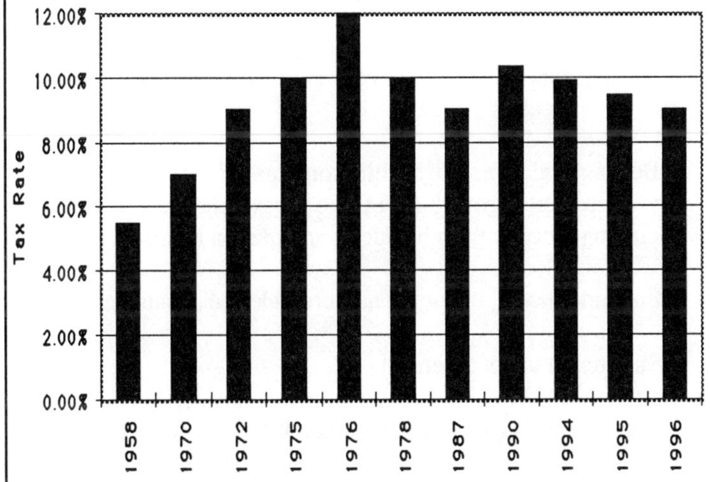


Note: Since December 1982, a 17 percent mass transit surcharge is added in the New York City area.

Data Source: New York State budgets

## NEW YORK STATE TAXES

In addition to a bevy of minor taxes and fees, New York State levies the following major taxes:

• Top personal income and capital gains tax rate of 6.85 percent as of 1997 (though for incomes between $100,000 and $150,000, the rate can top 8 percent).

• General corporate income tax rate of 9 percent as of mid-1996.

• Sales and use tax of 4 percent. Counties and cities add their own taxes.

• Estate tax with rates ranging between 2 percent and 21 percent.

• Racing admission charge of 4 percent to racetracks and simulcast theaters.

• Boxing and wrestling exhibitions tax of 5.5 percent on gross receipts from boxing and wrestling exhibitions, including receipts from broadcast and motion picture rights.

• Container tax of 1 cent per nonrefillable soda container.

• Auto rental tax of 5 percent.

• Highway use taxes, including a truck mileage tax based on weight and miles, a highway use vehicle permit of $15 paid triennially for an initial permit and $4 for a renewal, and a fuel use tax on fuel purchased outside, but used in New York.

• Additional insurance franchise tax of 0.8 percent on net premiums received from life, health, and accident insurance policies, and 1.3 percent on net premiums from property and casualty insurance.

• Motor fuel tax of 8 cents per gallon on gasoline and diesel fuel.

• Vehicle registration fees based primarily on vehicle weight.

• Annual driver's license fees ranging from $7.75 to $17.75.

• Petroleum business taxes: 13.4 cents per gallon of automotive-type fuel and aviation gasoline, 12.7 cents per gallon on nonautomotive middle distillate fuel, 11.2 cents per gallon of residual petroleum products, and 5.4 cents per gallon on kero-jet fuel.

• Pari-mutuel tax on horse race wagering.

• Real estate transfer tax of $2 per $500 of consideration.

• Liquor taxes: $1.70 per liter of liquor with over 24 percent alcohol, 67 cents per liter of all other liquor with more than 2 percent alcohol, 5 cents per liter on natural sparkling wine, 5 cents per liter on artificially carbonated sparkling wine, 5 cents per liter on still wine, 16 cents per gallon on beer with 0.5 percent alcohol or more, 1 cent per liter on liquor with not more than 2 percent alcohol, and 1 cent per liter on cider with more than 3.2 percent alcohol.

• Cigarette tax of 56 cents per package of 20 cigarettes.

• 20 percent of wholesale price on other tobacco products.

• Annual tobacco sales license fee of $100 per establishment.

• Tobacco vending machine tax of $25 per machine.

• Utility services tax of 3.5 percent of gross income.

• Public utilities franchise tax of 3/4 of 1 percent on gross earnings and 4.5 percent on the amount of dividends paid which exceed 4 percent of the amount of paid-in capital employed in New York State.

• Transportation and transmission companies franchise tax of 1.5 mills (a mill is one-tenth of a cent) on each dollar of net value of its issued capital stock allocated to New York State, or if dividends paid on its capital stock are 6 percent or more, the tax rate is 3/8 of a mill for each 1 percent of dividends.

• Additional transportation and transmission companies franchise tax of 3/4 of 1 percent of gross earnings.

• Newly incorporated or reincorporated domestic corporations tax of 1/20 of 1 percent of total par value of the stock the corporation is authorized to issue. Same tax applies to out-of-state corporations, plus a $300 annual maintenance fee.

• Importation of natural gas tax of 4.25 percent of the cost of the gas.

On top of these state levies, a plethora of taxes are levied at the local level in New York. Most prominent are local property taxes, sales taxes, hotel and motel taxes, and income taxes in New York City and Yonkers.

## SOURCES OF STATE AND LOCAL TAXES: NEW YORK VS. U.S.

In 1993, New York relied more heavily on income and property taxes, and less so on consumption-based taxes, when compared with the nation as a whole.

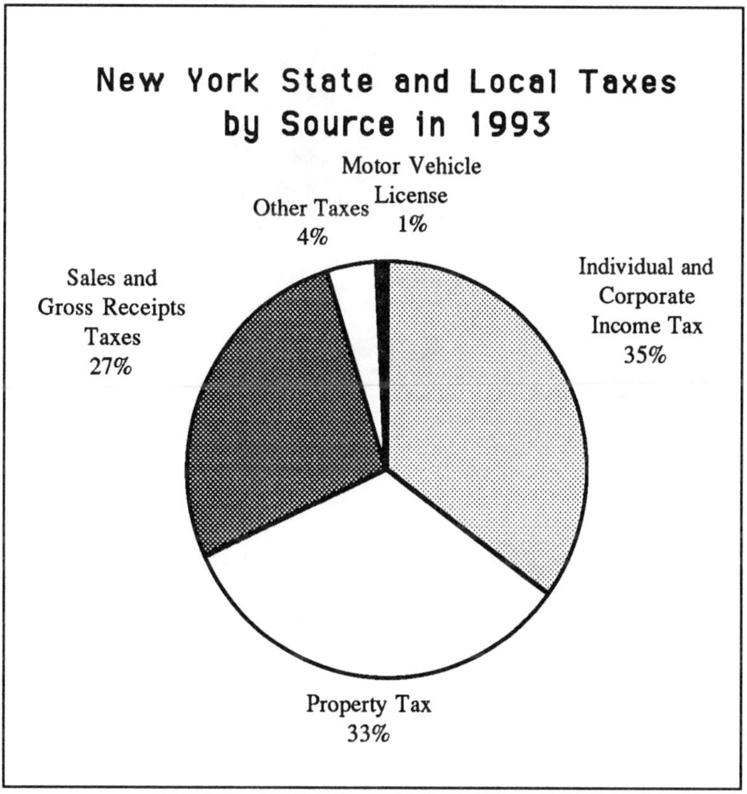


Data Source: U.S. Department of Commerce

*continued*

*continued*

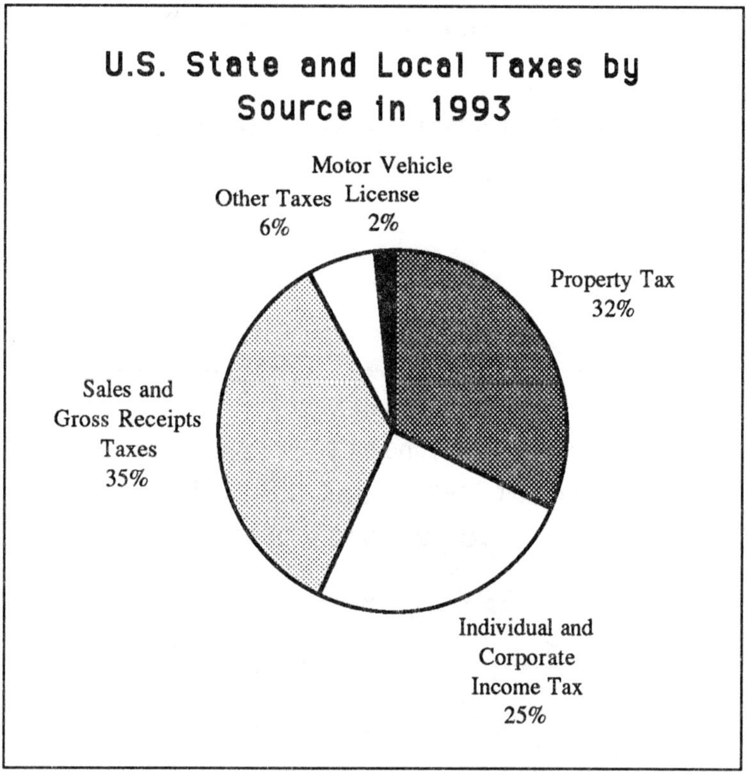


Data Source: U.S. Department of Commerce

## TAX FREEDOM DAY

In 1996, according to the Washington, D.C.-based Tax Foundation, New York claimed the second latest Tax Freedom Day in the nation—May 26—with only Connecticut suffering a later date (May 31). This compared with a U.S. Tax Freedom Day of May 7.

Tax Freedom Day is an estimate of the number of days one has to work in order to pay all taxes—federal, state, and local.

**Tax Freedom Day 1996**

| Rank | State | Tax Freedom Day |
|---|---|---|
| 1 | Connecticut | May 31 |
| **2** | **New York** | **May 26** |
| 3 | District of Columbia | May 22 |
| 4 | New Jersey | May 18 |
| 5 | Wisconsin | May 15 |
| 6 | Minnesota | May 14 |
| 7(t) | New Mexico | May 12 |
| 7(t) | Rhode Island | May 12 |
| 9(t) | Hawaii | May 11 |
| 9(t) | Vermont | May 11 |
| 11(t) | Washington | May 10 |
| 11(t) | New Hampshire | May 10 |
| 13(t) | Pennsylvania | May 9 |
| 13(t) | Michigan | May 9 |
| 13(t) | Massachusetts | May 9 |
| 16 | North Dakota | May 8 |
| 17 | Illinois | May 7 |
| 18 | Maryland | May 6 |
| 19(t) | Oregon | May 5 |
| 19(t) | California | May 5 |
| 19(t) | Kansas | May 5 |
| 22(t) | Maine | May 4 |
| 22(t) | Iowa | May 4 |
| 22(t) | Ohio | May 4 |
| 22(t) | Nebraska | May 4 |

*continued*

*continued*

| Rank | State | Tax Freedom Day |
|---|---|---|
| 26(t) | Arkansas | May 3 |
| 26(t) | Wyoming | May 3 |
| 26(t) | Nevada | May 3 |
| 26(t) | Texas | May 3 |
| 30(t) | Montana | May 2 |
| 30(t) | Idaho | May 2 |
| 30(t) | Alaska | May 2 |
| 30(t) | Colorado | May 2 |
| 30(t) | Florida | May 2 |
| 35(t) | North Carolina | May 1 |
| 35(t) | Indiana | May 1 |
| 35(t) | Kentucky | May 1 |
| 35(t) | Oklahoma | May 1 |
| 39(t) | Virginia | April 29 |
| 39(t) | Arizona | April 29 |
| 39(t) | Georgia | April 29 |
| 42(t) | Utah | April 28 |
| 42(t) | South Carolina | April 28 |
| 44 | Tennessee | April 27 |
| 45 | West Virginia | April 26 |
| 46(t) | South Dakota | April 25 |
| 46(t) | Delaware | April 25 |
| 46(t) | Louisiana | April 25 |
| 49(t) | Missouri | April 24 |
| 49(t) | Mississippi | April 24 |
| 51 | Alabama | April 23 |
| | U.S. Tax Freedom Day | May 7 |

Data Source: Stephen Gold, "Tax Freedom Day 1996 Not Until May 7," *Human Events*, April 26, 1996

## NEW YORK STATE AID TO LOCALITIES

Between 1960 and 1993, real state aid to New York localities increased by 220 percent, from approximately $5 billion (in 1993 dollars) in 1960 to $16 billion in 1993.

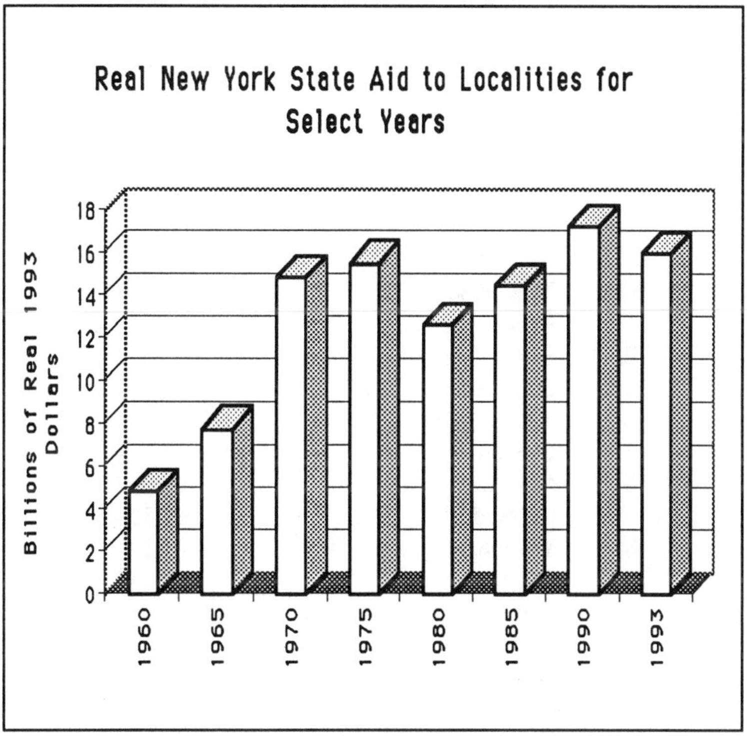


Data Source: The Nelson A. Rockefeller Institute of Government, *1995 New York State Statistical Yearbook*

# PER CAPITA STATE AND LOCAL TOTAL EXPENDITURES: STATE RANKINGS

In 1992-93, New York's per capita state and local total expenditures ranked the third highest in the nation, only trailing behind Alaska and the District of Columbia.

**Per Capita State and Local Total Expenditures**

| Rank | State | Per Capita Total Expenditures |
|---|---|---|
| 1 | Alaska | $11,577.69 |
| 2 | District of Columbia | 10,649.88 |
| **3** | **New York** | **7,115.79** |
| 4 | Hawaii | 6,130.10 |
| 5 | Washington | 5,932.25 |
| 6 | Wyoming | 5,753.19 |
| 7 | Connecticut | 5,543.37 |
| 8 | California | 5,387.29 |
| 9 | Minnesota | 5,360.45 |
| 10 | New Jersey | 5,344.93 |
| 11 | Massachusetts | 5,283.79 |
| 12 | Rhode Island | 5,255.02 |
| 13 | Delaware | 4,894.93 |
| 14 | Nevada | 4,849.43 |
| 15 | Oregon | 4,783.06 |
| 16 | Nebraska | 4,739.66 |
| 17 | Colorado | 4,732.42 |
| 18 | Wisconsin | 4,710.94 |
| 19 | Michigan | 4,527.71 |
| 20 | Vermont | 4,492.53 |
| 21 | Pennsylvania | 4,477.90 |
| 22 | North Dakota | 4,456.72 |
| 23 | New Mexico | 4,429.59 |
| 24 | Ohio | 4,366.63 |
| 25 | Maine | 4,346.23 |
| 26 | Louisiana | 4,311.09 |
| 27 | Illinois | 4,305.13 |

*continued*

*continued*

| Rank | State | Per Capita Total Expenditures |
|---|---|---|
| 28 | Maryland | 4,298.04 |
| 29 | Arizona | 4,270.30 |
| 30 | Iowa | 4,261.78 |
| 31 | Utah | 4,211.83 |
| 32 | Florida | 4,177.86 |
| 33 | West Virginia | 4,167.99 |
| 34 | New Hampshire | 4,114.34 |
| 35 | South Carolina | 4,091.73 |
| 36 | Georgia | 4,090.71 |
| 37 | Montana | 4,042.97 |
| 38 | Tennessee | 4,020.91 |
| 39 | Kansas | 4,006.06 |
| 40 | North Carolina | 3,941.28 |
| 41 | Alabama | 3,823.87 |
| 42 | Indiana | 3,820.57 |
| 43 | Kentucky | 3,807.96 |
| 44 | Virginia | 3,789.81 |
| 45 | Texas | 3,772.24 |
| 46 | Oklahoma | 3,700.19 |
| 47 | South Dakota | 3,675.32 |
| 48 | Idaho | 3,531.68 |
| 49 | Mississippi | 3,454.23 |
| 50 | Missouri | 3,311.31 |
| 51 | Arkansas | 3,306.80 |
| | U.S. Average | 4,696.57 |

Data Source: U.S. Department of Commerce

## PER CAPITA STATE AND LOCAL TOTAL EXPENDITURES: NEW YORK VS. U.S.

In 1992-93, New York's per capita state and local total expenditures outpaced the state and local average by 51.5 percent—$7,115.79 in New York versus the national average of $4,696.57.

Between 1982 and 1993, real (1993 dollars) per capita state and local total expenditures increased by 50.8 percent -- from $4,718.86 in 1982.

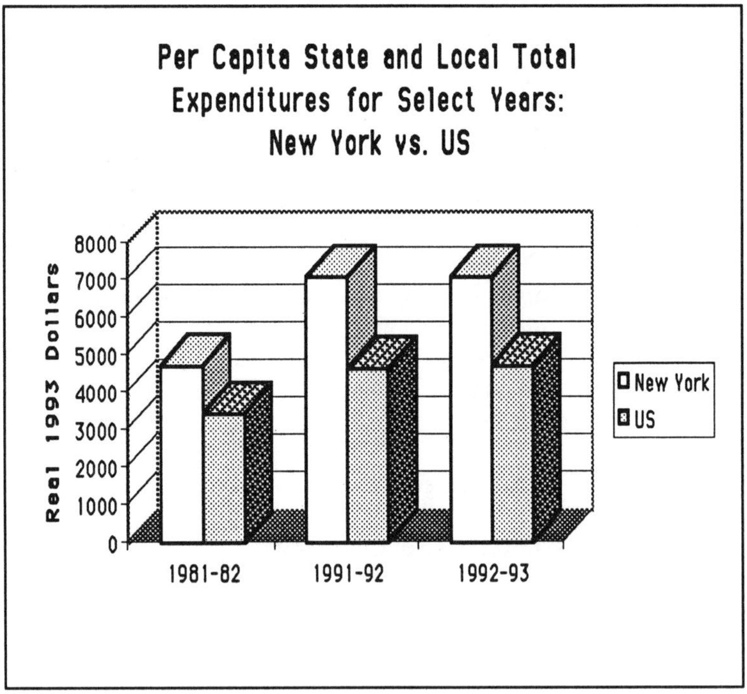


Data Source: U.S. Department of Commerce

## PER CAPITA STATE-ONLY TOTAL EXPENDITURES: STATE RANKINGS

In 1994, New York's per capita state total expenditures ranked third highest in the nation.

**Per Capita State Total Expenditures**

| Rank | State | Per Capita Total Expenditures |
|---|---|---|
| 1 | Alaska | $9,490.95 |
| 2 | Hawaii | 4,924.21 |
| **3** | **New York** | **4,230.92** |
| 4 | Wyoming | 4,148.94 |
| 5 | Connecticut | 3,958.46 |
| 6 | Rhode Island | 3,756.63 |
| 7 | New Jersey | 3,745.67 |
| 8 | Massachusetts | 3,716.94 |
| 9 | Delaware | 3,707.02 |
| 10 | Washington | 3,663.99 |
| 11 | New Mexico | 3,624.76 |
| 12 | West Virginia | 3,397.35 |
| 13 | California | 3,367.08 |
| 14 | Minnesota | 3,345.36 |
| 15 | Vermont | 3,298.11 |
| 16 | North Dakota | 3,265.56 |
| 17 | Montana | 3,244.95 |
| 18 | Maine | 3,146.58 |
| 19 | Pennsylvania | 3,137.90 |
| 20 | Michigan | 3,086.05 |
| 21 | South Carolina | 3,059.24 |
| 22 | Ohio | 3,010.41 |
| 23 | Wisconsin | 3,006.98 |
| 24 | Louisiana | 2,997.83 |
| 25 | Oregon | 2,950.20 |
| 26 | Nevada | 2,884.40 |
| 27 | Iowa | 2,863.58 |
| 28 | Maryland | 2,837.11 |

*continued*

*continued*

| Rank | State | Per Capita Total Expenditures |
|---|---|---|
| 29 | New Hampshire | 2,795.72 |
| 30 | Kentucky | 2,754.49 |
| 31 | North Carolina | 2,693.04 |
| 32 | Utah | 2,689.96 |
| 33 | Idaho | 2,638.41 |
| 34 | Indiana | 2,616.14 |
| 35 | Oklahoma | 2,606.68 |
| 36 | Kansas | 2,605.40 |
| 37 | Arizona | 2,582.16 |
| 38 | Alabama | 2,563.46 |
| 39 | Mississippi | 2,546.40 |
| 40 | South Dakota | 2,532.09 |
| 41 | Illinois | 2,505.83 |
| 42 | Arkansas | 2,477.68 |
| 43 | Nebraska | 2,458.98 |
| 44 | Colorado | 2,435.10 |
| 45 | Georgia | 2,384.53 |
| 46 | Virginia | 2,369.16 |
| 47 | Florida | 2,313.75 |
| 48 | Tennessee | 2,307.29 |
| 49 | Texas | 2,229.11 |
| 50 | Missouri | 2,172.91 |
| | U.S. Average | 2,993.90 |

Data Source: U.S. Department of Commerce

## PER CAPITA STATE-ONLY TOTAL EXPENDITURES: NEW YORK VS. U.S.

In 1994, New York's per capita state total expenditures surpassed the state average by 41.3 percent—$4,230.92 in New York versus the state average of $2,993.90.

Between 1985 and 1994, real per capita state total expenditures rose by 36.2 percent. In 1994 dollars, New York's 1985 per capita total spending registered $3,106.49.

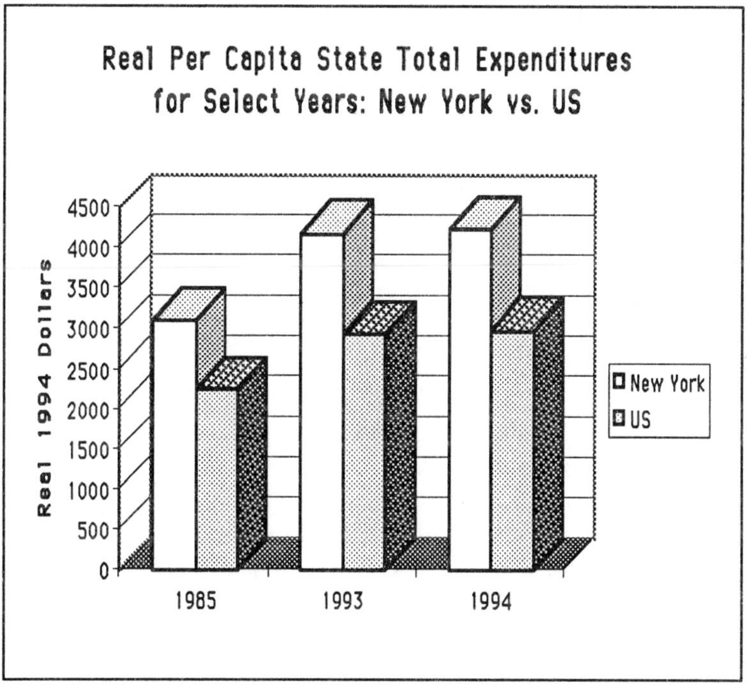


Data Source: U.S. Department of Commerce

## NEW YORK STATE-ONLY SPENDING BULGE

If New York real per capita state spending had merely grown at the 50-state annual rate of growth between 1980 and 1993, taxpayers would have saved $706 per capita in 1993—or a total of almost $13 billion in 1993 alone.

If New York real per capita state spending had merely grown at the same annual rate of growth as federal government spending grew between 1980 and 1993, taxpayers would have saved $1,302 per capita in 1993—or almost $24 billion.

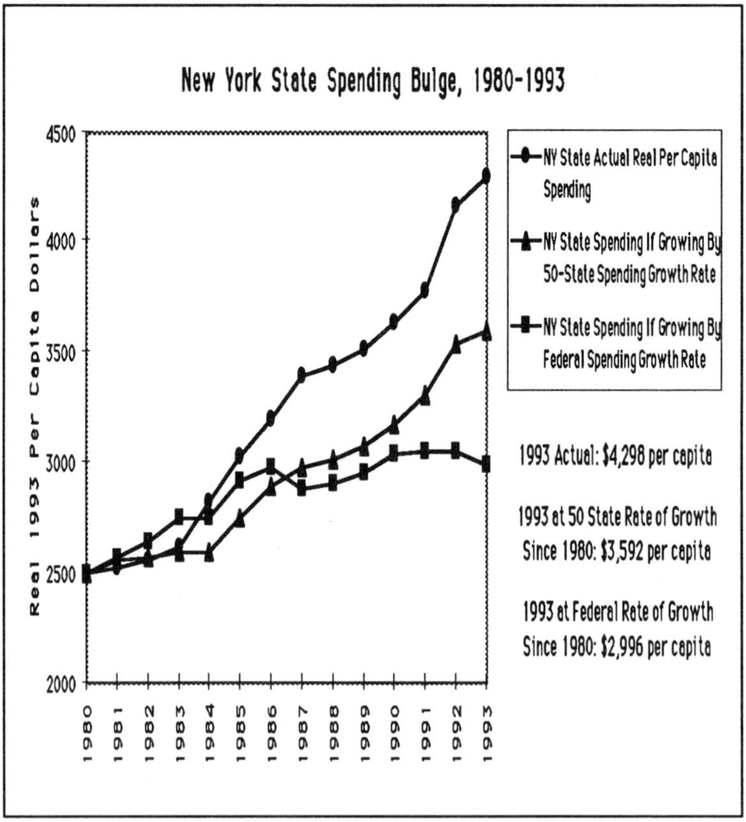


Data Source: U.S. Department of Commerce

# PER CAPITA STATE AND LOCAL GENERAL EXPENDITURES: STATE RANKINGS

In 1992-93, New York's per capita state and local general expenditures ranked the third highest in the nation, only trailing behind Alaska and the District of Columbia.

**Per Capita State and Local General Expenditures**

| Rank | State | Per Capita General Expenditures |
|---|---|---|
| 1 | Alaska | $10,092.05 |
| 2 | District of Columbia | 7,737.20 |
| **3** | **New York** | **5,891.71** |
| 4 | Hawaii | 5,463.41 |
| 5 | Wyoming | 5,126.38 |
| 6 | Connecticut | 4,803.12 |
| 7 | Minnesota | 4,769.38 |
| 8 | Washington | 4,717.20 |
| 9 | New Jersey | 4,588.18 |
| 10 | Rhode Island | 4,498.27 |
| 11 | Delaware | 4,375.33 |
| 12 | Massachusetts | 4,308.58 |
| 13 | California | 4,296.96 |
| 14 | Wisconsin | 4,235.05 |
| 15 | Oregon | 4,079.55 |
| 16 | Nevada | 4,056.96 |
| 17 | North Dakota | 4,040.88 |
| 18 | New Mexico | 4,035.96 |
| 19 | Vermont | 4,027.89 |
| 20 | Colorado | 4,014.85 |
| 21 | Michigan | 3,955.37 |
| 22 | Maine | 3,865.43 |
| 23 | Iowa | 3,858.05 |
| 24 | Louisiana | 3,845.18 |
| 25 | New Hampshire | 3,775.96 |
| 26 | Pennsylvania | 3,747.70 |
| 27 | Maryland | 3,734.49 |

*continued*

*continued*

| Rank | State | Per Capita General Expenditures |
|---|---|---|
| 28 | Florida | 3,664.02 |
| 29 | Illinois | 3,646.87 |
| 30 | Ohio | 3,598.13 |
| 31 | Arizona | 3,584.96 |
| 32 | Nebraska | 3,582.06 |
| 33 | Kansas | 3,563.78 |
| 34 | Montana | 3,538.28 |
| 35 | Georgia | 3,538.11 |
| 36 | Indiana | 3,486.53 |
| 37 | West Virginia | 3,476.79 |
| 38 | South Carolina | 3,437.57 |
| 39 | South Dakota | 3,403.72 |
| 40 | Virginia | 3,403.09 |
| 41 | Utah | 3,376.29 |
| 42 | North Carolina | 3,320.71 |
| 43 | Alabama | 3,283.26 |
| 44 | Kentucky | 3,266.82 |
| 45 | Texas | 3,240.03 |
| 46 | Oklahoma | 3,152.30 |
| 47 | Idaho | 3,141.86 |
| 48 | Tennessee | 3,087.18 |
| 49 | Mississippi | 3,057.06 |
| 50 | Arkansas | 2,983.96 |
| 51 | Missouri | 2,892.46 |
| | U.S. Average | 3,971.51 |

Data Source: U.S. Department of Commerce

## PER CAPITA STATE AND LOCAL GENERAL EXPENDITURES: NEW YORK VS. U.S.

In 1992-93, New York's per capita state and local general expenditures topped the state and local average by 48.3 percent—$5,891.71 in New York versus the national average of $3,971.51.

Between 1962 and 1993, New York's real (1993 dollars) per capita state and local general expenditures grew by 206 percent—from $1,926.79 in 1962.

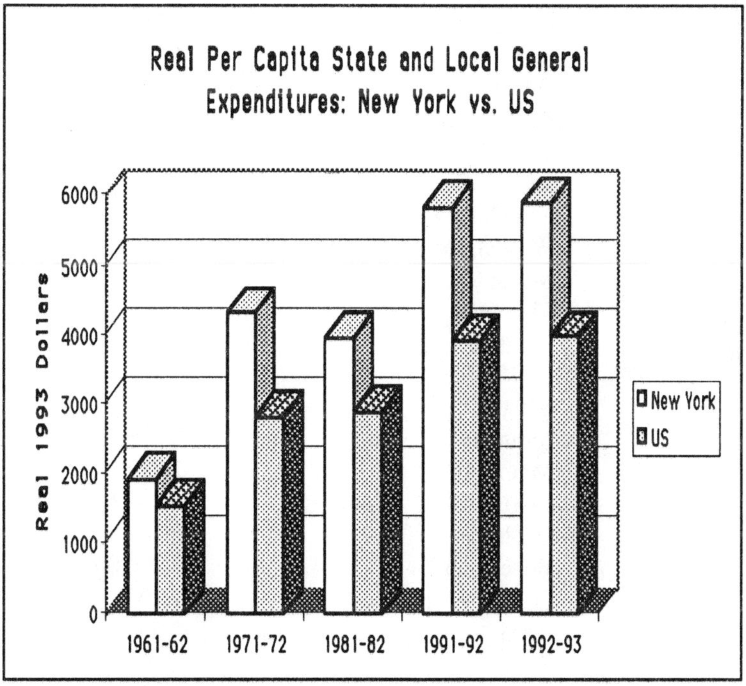


Data Source: U.S. Department of Commerce

## PER CAPITA STATE-ONLY GENERAL EXPENDITURES: STATE RANKINGS

In 1994, New York's per capita state general expenditures ranked fourth highest in the nation.

**Per Capita State General Expenditures**

| Rank | State | Per Capita General Expenditures |
|---|---|---|
| 1 | Alaska | $8,673.54 |
| 2 | Hawaii | 4,462.24 |
| 3 | Wyoming | 3,681.37 |
| **4** | **New York** | **3,556.65** |
| 5 | Connecticut | 3,422.03 |
| 6 | Delaware | 3,383.17 |
| 7 | Massachusetts | 3,381.49 |
| 8 | New Mexico | 3,367.41 |
| 9 | Rhode Island | 3,144.31 |
| 10 | New Jersey | 3,091.14 |
| 11 | Washington | 3,059.22 |
| 12 | Minnesota | 3,054.90 |
| 13 | Vermont | 3,052.14 |
| 14 | North Dakota | 2,955.66 |
| 15 | California | 2,907.23 |
| 16 | West Virginia | 2,881.56 |
| 17 | Montana | 2,795.57 |
| 18 | Maine | 2,782.20 |
| 19 | Louisiana | 2,731.42 |
| 20 | Michigan | 2,723.46 |
| 21 | Wisconsin | 2,720.00 |
| 22 | Pennsylvania | 2,703.22 |
| 23 | Iowa | 2,665.06 |
| 24 | South Carolina | 2,610.03 |
| 25 | Oregon | 2,533.14 |
| 26 | Kentucky | 2,497.74 |
| 27 | North Carolina | 2,495.40 |
| 28 | Indiana | 2,492.47 |

*continued*

*continued*

| Rank | State | Per Capita General Expenditures |
|---|---|---|
| 29 | New Hampshire | 2,460.38 |
| 30 | Utah | 2,457.59 |
| 31 | Ohio | 2,420.21 |
| 32 | South Dakota | 2,412.06 |
| 33 | Nebraska | 2,394.84 |
| 34 | Kansas | 2,385.26 |
| 35 | Maryland | 2,357.15 |
| 36 | Alabama | 2,351.83 |
| 37 | Idaho | 2,338.65 |
| 38 | Arizona | 2,338.64 |
| 39 | Nevada | 2,336.30 |
| 40 | Mississippi | 2,314.36 |
| 41 | Arkansas | 2,300.11 |
| 42 | Illinois | 2,217.32 |
| 43 | Georgia | 2,217.26 |
| 44 | Oklahoma | 2,216.46 |
| 45 | Virginia | 2,176.94 |
| 46 | Tennessee | 2,163.29 |
| 47 | Florida | 2,149.46 |
| 48 | Colorado | 2,093.03 |
| 49 | Texas | 2,030.90 |
| 50 | Missouri | 1,992.45 |
| | U.S. Average | 2,636.06 |

Data Source: U.S. Department of Commerce

## PER CAPITA STATE-ONLY GENERAL EXPENDITURES: NEW YORK VS. U.S.

In 1994, New York's per capita state general expenditures exceeded the state average by 34.9 percent—$3,556.65 in New York versus $2,636.06 for the state average.

Between 1965 and 1994, real per capita general expenditures in New York increased by 244.6 percent. In 1994 dollars, New York's 1965 per capita state general spending registered $1,035.16.

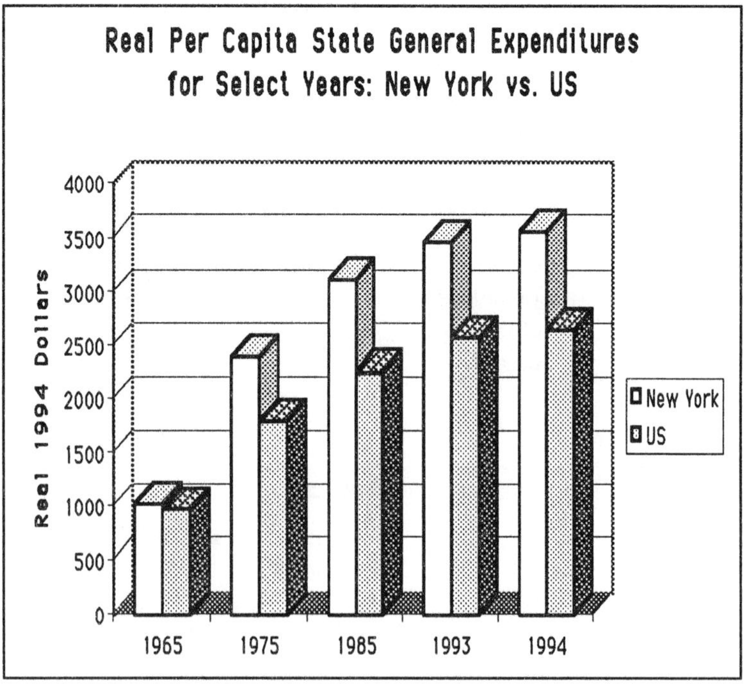


Data Source: U.S. Department of Commerce

# PER CAPITA STATE AND LOCAL PUBLIC WELFARE EXPENDITURES: STATE RANKINGS

In 1992-93, New York's per capita state and local public welfare expenditures ranked second highest in the nation, only trailing behind the District of Columbia.

**Per Capita State and Local Public Welfare Expenditures**

| Rank | State | Per Capita Public Welfare Expenditures |
|---|---|---|
| 1 | District of Columbia | $1,670.59 |
| **2** | **New York** | **1,219.36** |
| 3 | Maine | 902.02 |
| 4 | Rhode Island | 868.83 |
| 5 | New Hampshire | 866.11 |
| 6 | Massachusetts | 862.06 |
| 7 | Connecticut | 848.37 |
| 8 | Minnesota | 827.90 |
| 9 | Alaska | 789.41 |
| 10 | West Virginia | 767.49 |
| 11 | Pennsylvania | 729.28 |
| 12 | Louisiana | 719.64 |
| 13 | Wisconsin | 696.37 |
| 14 | North Dakota | 690.47 |
| 15 | Vermont | 683.70 |
| 16 | Kentucky | 682.88 |
| 17 | New Jersey | 682.01 |
| 18 | California | 681.00 |
| 19 | Ohio | 677.05 |
| 20 | Michigan | 654.67 |
| 21 | Indiana | 620.57 |
| 22 | Washington | 608.62 |
| 23 | Tennessee | 574.65 |
| 24 | Illinois | 568.78 |
| 25 | South Carolina | 567.96 |
| 26 | Arizona | 565.72 |

*continued*

*continued*

| Rank | State | Per Capita Public Welfare Expenditures |
|---|---|---|
| 27 | Iowa | 562.35 |
| 28 | Hawaii | 561.19 |
| 29 | Maryland | 549.39 |
| 30 | Arkansas | 543.72 |
| 31 | Georgia | 542.59 |
| 32 | Colorado | 540.03 |
| 33 | Nebraska | 514.16 |
| 34 | Montana | 507.16 |
| 35 | New Mexico | 496.69 |
| 36 | Texas | 494.99 |
| 37 | Oregon | 493.92 |
| 38 | Alabama | 491.21 |
| 39 | Missouri | 486.77 |
| 40 | Mississippi | 480.97 |
| 41 | North Carolina | 479.00 |
| 42 | South Dakota | 471.84 |
| 43 | Oklahoma | 470.05 |
| 44 | Delaware | 456.34 |
| 45 | Wyoming | 454.92 |
| 46 | Florida | 449.68 |
| 47 | Virginia | 419.32 |
| 48 | Idaho | 414.94 |
| 49 | Utah | 407.05 |
| 50 | Kansas | 401.50 |
| 51 | Nevada | 395.02 |
| | U.S. Average | 647.97 |

Data Source: U.S. Department of Commerce

## PER CAPITA STATE AND LOCAL PUBLIC WELFARE EXPENDITURES: NEW YORK VS. U.S.

In 1992-93, New York's per capita state and local public welfare expenditures surpassed the state and local average by 88.2 percent—$1,219.36 in New York versus a national average of $647.97.

Between 1962 and 1993, New York's real per capita state and local public welfare expenditures ballooned by 378.2 percent. In 1962, New York's per capita public welfare expenditures equaled $254.98 (in 1993 dollars), and reached $1,219.36 in 1993. Interestingly, though, in

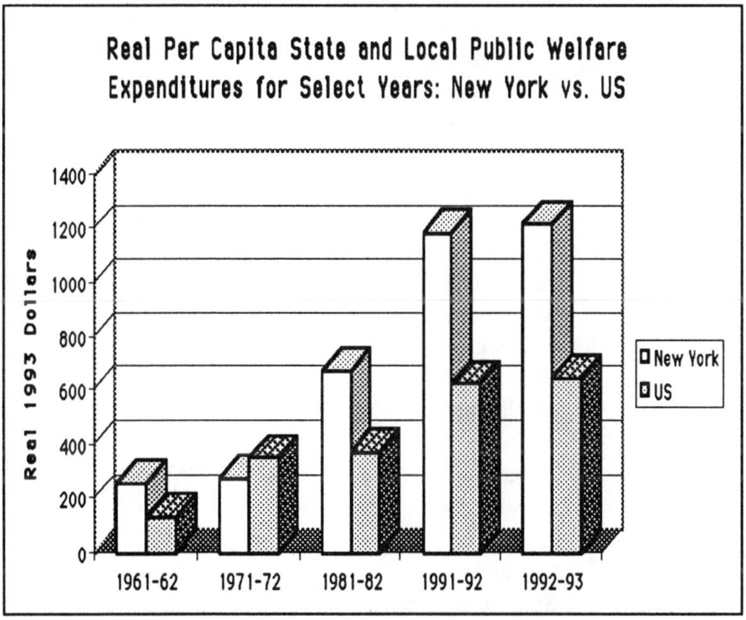


Data Source: U.S. Department of Commerce

1972, New York's per capita public welfare expenditures actually trailed the national average. So, between 1972 and 1993, New York witnessed a boost in real per capita public welfare expenditures of 339.5 percent versus national growth of 84.7 percent. New York's real public welfare spending grew at more than four times the U.S. rate.

## PER CAPITA STATE-ONLY PUBLIC WELFARE EXPENDITURES: STATE RANKINGS

In 1994, New York's per capita state public welfare expenditures ranked the very highest in the nation.

**Per Capita State Public Welfare Expenditures**

| Rank | State | Per Capita Public Welfare Expenditures |
|---|---|---|
| **1** | **New York** | **$1,321.40** |
| 2 | Alaska | 1,045.23 |
| 3 | Pennsylvania | 977.92 |
| 4 | Massachusetts | 970.86 |
| 5 | New Hampshire | 951.20 |
| 6 | Maine | 945.90 |
| 7 | Connecticut | 909.94 |
| 8 | California | 908.90 |
| 9 | West Virginia | 847.38 |
| 10 | Rhode Island | 797.59 |
| 11 | Minnesota | 792.70 |
| 12 | Vermont | 783.35 |
| 13 | New Jersey | 745.47 |
| 14 | Michigan | 722.78 |
| 15 | Ohio | 716.26 |
| 16 | Indiana | 679.88 |
| 17 | Washington | 677.45 |
| 18 | Louisiana | 662.85 |
| 19 | Kentucky | 657.88 |
| 20 | South Carolina | 639.73 |
| 21 | Tennessee | 633.67 |
| 22 | Illinois | 623.23 |
| 23 | Wisconsin | 620.71 |
| 24 | Hawaii | 608.63 |
| 25 | Mississippi | 597.08 |
| 26 | Georgia | 592.82 |
| 27 | North Dakota | 572.70 |

*continued*

*continued*

| Rank | State | Per Capita Public Welfare Expenditures |
|---|---|---|
| 28 | Arizona | 569.00 |
| 29 | Arkansas | 565.53 |
| 30 | Maryland | 549.52 |
| 31 | New Mexico | 549.37 |
| 32 | Iowa | 541.67 |
| 33 | Nebraska | 537.75 |
| 34 | Oregon | 533.03 |
| 35 | Texas | 515.49 |
| 36 | Alabama | 513.82 |
| 37 | Montana | 511.83 |
| 38 | North Carolina | 509.64 |
| 39 | Missouri | 501.58 |
| 40 | Delaware | 499.15 |
| 41 | South Dakota | 496.30 |
| 42 | Oklahoma | 482.95 |
| 43 | Florida | 481.98 |
| 44 | Wyoming | 472.57 |
| 45 | Colorado | 444.66 |
| 46 | Utah | 430.30 |
| 47 | Kansas | 428.82 |
| 48 | Idaho | 400.33 |
| 49 | Virginia | 388.16 |
| 50 | Nevada | 387.52 |
| | U.S. Average | 711.30 |

Data Source: U.S. Department of Commerce

## PER CAPITA STATE-ONLY PUBLIC WELFARE EXPENDITURES: NEW YORK VS. U.S.

In 1994, New York's per capita state public welfare expenditures outpaced the state average by 85.8 percent—$1,321.40 in New York versus the state average of $711.30.

Between 1965 and 1994, the 50-state average real per capita public welfare spending increased at a dizzying pace of 833.5 percent. Still, this was no match for New York, where real per capita public welfare spending rose by 1,556.5 percent. In 1994 dollars, New York's per capita state public welfare spending in 1965 equaled $79.77.

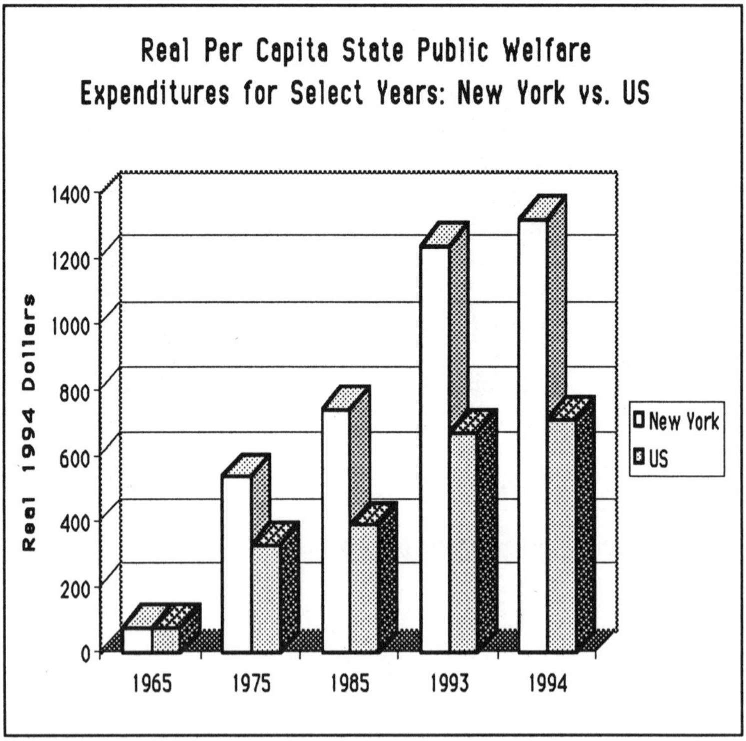


Data Source: U.S. Department of Commerce

## WAGE EQUIVALENT OF WELFARE: STATE RANKINGS

In a September 19, 1995, CATO Institute study ("The Work vs. Welfare Trade-Off: An Analysis of the Total Level of Welfare Benefits by State"), analysts Michael Tanner, Stephen Moore, and David Hartman calculated the pretax wage equivalent of total welfare benefits for each state. New York ranked sixth highest in the nation. The full welfare package in New York equals a pretax wage level of $27,300 annually, or $13.13 on an hourly basis (assuming a 2,080-hour work year).

**Wage Equivalent of Welfare**

| Rank | State | Pretax Wage Equivalent | Pretax Hourly Wage |
|---|---|---|---|
| 1 | Hawaii | $36,400 | $17.50 |
| 2 | Alaska | 32,200 | 15.48 |
| 3 | Massachusetts | 30,500 | 14.66 |
| 4 | Connecticut | 29,600 | 14.23 |
| 5 | District of Columbia | 29,100 | 13.99 |
| **6** | **New York** | **27,300** | **13.13** |
| 7 | New Jersey | 26,500 | 12.74 |
| 8 | Rhode Island | 26,100 | 12.55 |
| 9 | California | 24,100 | 11.59 |
| 10 | Virginia | 23,100 | 11.11 |
| 11(t) | Maryland | 22,800 | 10.96 |
| 11(t) | New Hampshire | 22,800 | 10.96 |
| 13 | Maine | 21,600 | 10.38 |
| 14 | Delaware | 21,500 | 10.34 |
| 15(t) | Colorado | 20,900 | 10.05 |
| 15(t) | Vermont | 20,900 | 10.05 |
| 17 | Minnesota | 20,800 | 10.00 |
| 18 | Washington | 20,700 | 9.95 |
| 19 | Nevada | 20,200 | 9.71 |
| 20 | Utah | 19,900 | 9.57 |
| 21(t) | Michigan | 19,700 | 9.47 |
| 21(t) | Pennsylvania | 19,700 | 9.47 |
| 23(t) | Illinois | 19,400 | 9.33 |

*continued*

*continued*

| Rank | State | Pretax Wage Equivalent | Pretax Hourly Wage |
|---|---|---|---|
| 23(t) | Wisconsin | 19,400 | 9.33 |
| 25 | Oregon | 19,200 | 9.23 |
| 26 | Wyoming | 19,100 | 9.18 |
| 27(t) | Indiana | 19,000 | 9.13 |
| 27(t) | Iowa | 19,000 | 9.13 |
| 29 | New Mexico | 18,600 | 8.94 |
| 30 | Florida | 18,200 | 8.75 |
| 31 | Idaho | 18,000 | 8.65 |
| 32 | Oklahoma | 17,700 | 8.51 |
| 33(t) | Kansas | 17,600 | 8.46 |
| 33(t) | North Dakota | 17,600 | 8.46 |
| 35(t) | Georgia | 17,400 | 8.37 |
| 35(t) | Ohio | 17,400 | 8.37 |
| 37 | South Dakota | 17,300 | 8.32 |
| 38 | Louisiana | 17,000 | 8.17 |
| 39(t) | Kentucky | 16,800 | 8.08 |
| 39(t) | North Carolina | 16,800 | 8.08 |
| 41 | Montana | 16,300 | 7.84 |
| 42 | South Carolina | 16,200 | 7.79 |
| 43 | Nebraska | 15,900 | 7.64 |
| 44(t) | Texas | 15,200 | 7.31 |
| 44(t) | West Virginia | 15,200 | 7.31 |
| 46 | Missouri | 14,900 | 7.16 |
| 47 | Arizona | 14,100 | 6.78 |
| 48 | Tennessee | 13,700 | 6.59 |
| 49 | Arkansas | 13,200 | 6.35 |
| 50 | Alabama | 13,000 | 6.25 |
| 51 | Mississippi | 11,500 | 5.53 |

Data Source: "The Work vs. Welfare Trade-Off: An Analysis of the Total Level of Welfare Benefits by State" by Michael Tanner, Stephen Moore, and David Hartman, CATO Institute, Washington, D.C., September 19, 1995

## PER CAPITA STATE AND LOCAL HOSPITALS EXPENDITURES: STATE RANKINGS

In 1992-93, New York's per capita state and local hospitals expenditures ranked fifth highest in the nation.

**Per Capita State and Local Hospitals Expenditures**

| Rank | State | Per Capita Hospitals Expenditures |
|---|---|---|
| 1 | District of Columbia | $611.82 |
| 2 | Wyoming | 472.34 |
| 3 | Georgia | 466.22 |
| 4 | Alabama | 459.10 |
| **5** | **New York** | **434.25** |
| 6 | Louisiana | 428.53 |
| 7 | South Carolina | 399.15 |
| 8 | Mississippi | 382.47 |
| 9 | Iowa | 330.26 |
| 10 | Tennessee | 314.65 |
| 11 | Minnesota | 312.08 |
| 12 | Indiana | 281.80 |
| 13 | North Carolina | 278.44 |
| 14 | California | 276.73 |
| 15 | Nebraska | 267.11 |
| 16 | Oklahoma | 256.65 |
| 17 | Texas | 254.60 |
| 18 | Connecticut | 250.65 |
| 19 | Kansas | 241.57 |
| 20 | Nevada | 238.04 |
| 21 | New Mexico | 236.17 |
| 22 | Idaho | 226.43 |
| 23 | Florida | 221.40 |
| 24 | Massachusetts | 213.38 |
| 25 | Arkansas | 211.91 |
| 26 | Washington | 207.50 |
| 27 | Oregon | 195.55 |
| 28 | Michigan | 191.60 |

*continued*

*continued*

| Rank | State | Per Capita Hospitals Expenditures |
|---|---|---|
| 29 | Virginia | 181.54 |
| 30 | Colorado | 181.50 |
| 31 | Hawaii | 174.36 |
| 32 | Ohio | 167.89 |
| 33 | Missouri | 156.58 |
| 34 | Wisconsin | 156.32 |
| 35 | Utah | 148.95 |
| 36 | New Jersey | 144.15 |
| 37 | West Virginia | 143.40 |
| 38 | Alaska | 135.78 |
| 39 | Kentucky | 133.11 |
| 40 | Illinois | 130.94 |
| 41 | Pennsylvania | 123.58 |
| 42 | North Dakota | 94.66 |
| 43 | South Dakota | 94.14 |
| 44 | Maine | 80.57 |
| 45 | Arizona | 77.48 |
| 46 | Montana | 77.17 |
| 47 | Rhode Island | 75.64 |
| 48 | Maryland | 65.18 |
| 49 | Delaware | 62.42 |
| 50 | Vermont | 35.87 |
| 51 | New Hampshire | 34.06 |
| | U.S. Average | 242.30 |

Data Source: U.S. Department of Commerce

## PER CAPITA STATE AND LOCAL HOSPITALS EXPENDITURES: NEW YORK VS. U.S.

In 1992-93, New York's per capita state and local hospitals expenditures surpassed the national average by 79.2 percent—$434.25 in New York versus $242.30 across the nation.

Between 1962 and 1993, real (1993 dollars) per capita state and local hospital expenditures in New York leaped by 167.0 percent—from $162.63 in 1962.

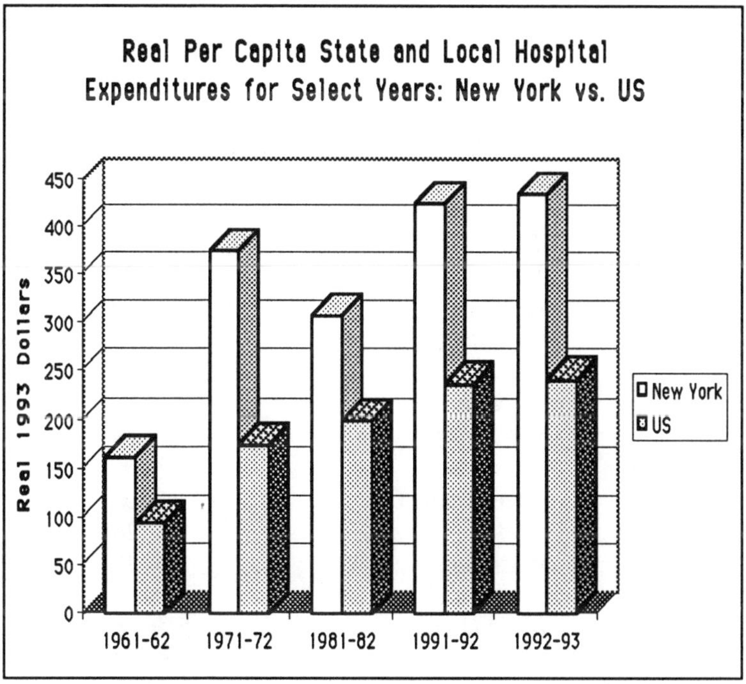


Data Source: U.S. Department of Commerce

## PER CAPITA STATE-ONLY HOSPITALS EXPENDITURES: STATE RANKINGS

In 1994, New York's per capita state hospitals expenditures ranked third in the nation.

**Per Capita State Hospitals Expenditures**

| Rank | State | Per Capita Hospitals Expenditures |
|---|---|---|
| 1 | Connecticut | $278.94 |
| 2 | Louisiana | 250.52 |
| **3** | **New York** | **198.95** |
| 4 | Alabama | 195.12 |
| 5 | Hawaii | 179.33 |
| 6 | Iowa | 173.95 |
| 7 | New Mexico | 173.26 |
| 8 | South Carolina | 168.14 |
| 9 | Virginia | 157.25 |
| 10 | Nebraska | 154.66 |
| 11 | Utah | 142.36 |
| 12 | Oregon | 131.39 |
| 13 | Michigan | 130.60 |
| 14 | Massachusetts | 129.78 |
| 15 | Kansas | 128.52 |
| 16 | Arkansas | 126.89 |
| 17 | New Jersey | 123.69 |
| 18 | Minnesota | 121.06 |
| 19 | Pennsylvania | 113.06 |
| 20 | Ohio | 112.26 |
| 21 | Mississippi | 104.19 |
| 22 | North Carolina | 100.81 |
| 23 | Washington | 96.86 |
| 24 | Texas | 93.67 |
| 25 | Oklahoma | 93.29 |
| 26 | Indiana | 92.15 |
| 27 | Tennessee | 89.92 |
| 28 | Kentucky | 87.84 |

*continued*

*continued*

| Rank | State | Per Capita Hospitals Expenditures |
|---|---|---|
| 29 | California | 86.11 |
| 30 | North Dakota | 85.05 |
| 31 | Georgia | 82.50 |
| 32 | Wisconsin | 81.74 |
| 33 | Missouri | 79.65 |
| 34 | Wyoming | 69.47 |
| 35 | Delaware | 66.84 |
| 36 | South Dakota | 64.14 |
| 37 | Illinois | 64.10 |
| 38 | Maryland | 63.10 |
| 39 | Rhode Island | 63.04 |
| 40 | Alaska | 53.98 |
| 41 | Maine | 45.99 |
| 42 | West Virginia | 43.69 |
| 43 | Colorado | 43.52 |
| 44 | Nevada | 36.89 |
| 45 | Montana | 35.59 |
| 46 | Florida | 34.89 |
| 47 | Idaho | 33.47 |
| 48 | New Hampshire | 32.32 |
| 49 | Vermont | 24.88 |
| 50 | Arizona | 21.86 |
| | U.S. Average | 109.06 |

Data Source: U.S. Department of Commerce

## PER CAPITA STATE-ONLY HOSPITALS EXPENDITURES: NEW YORK VS. U.S.

In 1994, New York's per capita state hospitals expenditures exceeded the state average by 82.4 percent—$198.95 in New York versus the state average of $109.06.

Between 1965 and 1994, New York's per capita state hospital spending (in 1993 dollars) increased from $88.64 to $198.95—a hike of 124.4 percent.

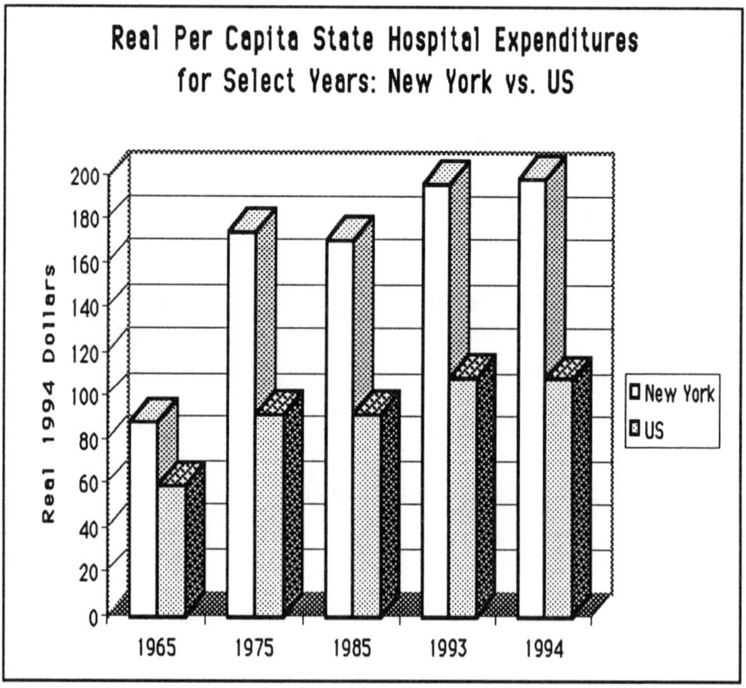


Data Source: U.S. Department of Commerce

## PER DAY COST AT A COMMUNITY HOSPITAL: STATE RANKINGS

In 1994, New York's per day costs at a community hospital ranked thirtieth in the nation.

**Per Day Cost at a Community Hospital**

| Rank | State | Per Day Hospital Cost |
|---|---|---|
| 1 | District of Columbia | $1,304 |
| 2 | California | 1,301 |
| 3 | Alaska | 1,263 |
| 4 | Washington | 1,206 |
| 5 | Massachusetts | 1,131 |
| 6 | Connecticut | 1,121 |
| 7 | Utah | 1,115 |
| 8 | Arizona | 1,091 |
| 9 | Oregon | 1,077 |
| 10 | Texas | 1,055 |
| 11 | New Mexico | 1,047 |
| 12 | Delaware | 1,042 |
| 13 | Nevada | 1,016 |
| 14 | Ohio | 1,008 |
| 15 | Colorado | 993 |
| 16 | Illinois | 988 |
| 17 | Maryland | 981 |
| 18 | Florida | 975 |
| 19 | Rhode Island | 970 |
| 20 | Hawaii | 958 |
| 21 | Indiana | 955 |
| 22 | New Jersey | 934 |
| 23(t) | Michigan | 929 |
| 23(t) | Louisiana | 929 |
| 25 | Missouri | 915 |
| 26 | Pennsylvania | 892 |
| 27 | Virginia | 885 |
| 28 | South Carolina | 876 |

*continued*

*continued*

| Rank | State | Per Day Hospital Cost |
|---|---|---|
| 29 | Tennessee | 870 |
| **30** | **New York** | **854** |
| 31 | Oklahoma | 848 |
| 32 | New Hampshire | 825 |
| 33 | North Carolina | 806 |
| 34(t) | Wisconsin | 802 |
| 34(t) | Maine | 802 |
| 36 | Georgia | 797 |
| 37 | Alabama | 781 |
| 38 | Kentucky | 748 |
| 39 | West Virginia | 727 |
| 40 | Arkansas | 724 |
| 41 | Kansas | 715 |
| 42 | Minnesota | 695 |
| 43 | Idaho | 679 |
| 44 | Iowa | 672 |
| 45 | Vermont | 651 |
| 46 | Nebraska | 606 |
| 47 | Mississippi | 584 |
| 48 | North Dakota | 515 |
| 49 | Wyoming | 504 |
| 50(t) | South Dakota | 470 |
| 50(t) | Montana | 470 |
| | U.S. Average | 931 |

Data Source: U.S. Department of Commerce, *Statistical Abstract of the United States 1996*

## PER DAY COST AT A COMMUNITY HOSPITAL: NEW YORK VS. U.S.

In 1994, the average U.S. per day cost at a community hospital surpassed the New York cost by 9 percent—$854 in New York versus the U.S. average of $931.

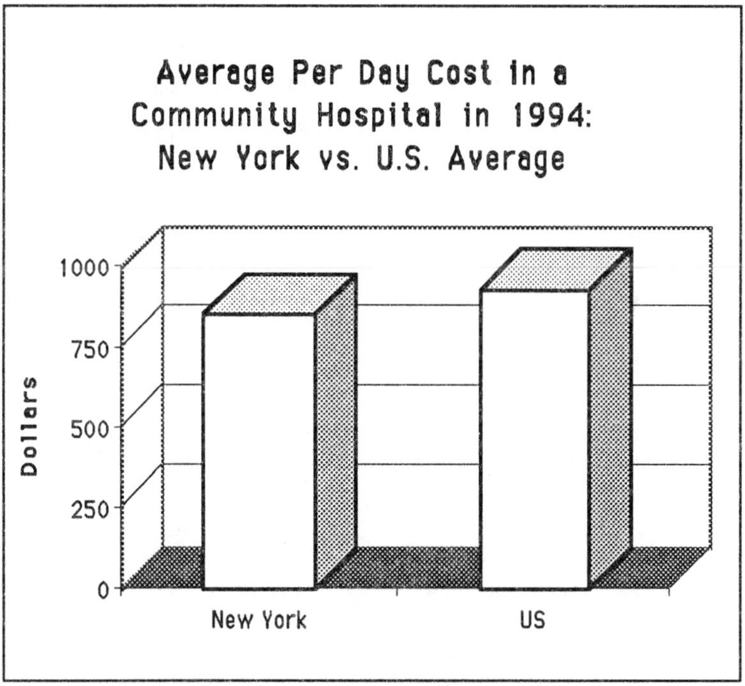


Data Source: U.S. Department of Commerce, *Statistical Abstract of the United States 1996*

# PER STAY COST AT A COMMUNITY HOSPITAL: STATE RANKINGS

In 1994, New York's per stay costs at a community hospital ranked fourth highest in the nation.

**Per Stay Cost at a Community Hospital**

| Rank | State | Per Stay Hospital Cost |
|---|---|---|
| 1 | District of Columbia | $9,021 |
| 2 | Hawaii | 8,428 |
| 3 | Alaska | 8,168 |
| **4** | **New York** | **8,127** |
| 5 | Connecticut | 7,835 |
| 6 | Delaware | 7,303 |
| 7 | California | 7,252 |
| 8 | Massachusetts | 7,018 |
| 9 | New Jersey | 6,933 |
| 10 | Nevada | 6,526 |
| 11 | Illinois | 6,372 |
| 12 | Pennsylvania | 6,332 |
| 13 | Missouri | 6,249 |
| 14 | Colorado | 6,241 |
| 15 | Michigan | 6,169 |
| 16 | Florida | 6,106 |
| 17 | Ohio | 6,103 |
| 18 | South Carolina | 6,056 |
| 19 | Texas | 6,051 |
| 20 | Minnesota | 6,029 |
| 21 | Nebraska | 6,006 |
| 22 | Rhode Island | 5,984 |
| 23 | New Hampshire | 5,978 |
| 24 | Louisiana | 5,916 |
| 25 | Washington | 5,909 |
| 26 | Alabama | 5,895 |
| 27 | Maryland | 5,833 |
| 28 | Indiana | 5,715 |

*continued*

*continued*

| Rank | State | Per Stay Hospital Cost |
|---|---|---|
| 29 | North Carolina | 5,701 |
| 30 | Maine | 5,685 |
| 31(t) | Tennessee | 5,621 |
| 31(t) | Georgia | 5,621 |
| 33 | New Mexico | 5,564 |
| 34 | North Dakota | 5,547 |
| 35 | Wisconsin | 5,536 |
| 36 | Virginia | 5,518 |
| 37 | Oregon | 5,492 |
| 38 | Vermont | 5,400 |
| 39 | Utah | 5,378 |
| 40 | Arizona | 5,375 |
| 41 | Oklahoma | 5,291 |
| 42 | Kansas | 5,240 |
| 43 | Iowa | 5,077 |
| 44 | Montana | 4,965 |
| 45 | Kentucky | 4,873 |
| 46 | West Virginia | 4,839 |
| 47 | South Dakota | 4,797 |
| 48 | Wyoming | 4,639 |
| 49 | Arkansas | 4,514 |
| 50 | Idaho | 4,448 |
| 51 | Mississippi | 4,235 |
| | U.S. Average | 6,230 |

Data Source: U.S. Department of Commerce, *Statistical Abstract of the United States 1996*

## PER STAY COST AT A COMMUNITY HOSPITAL: NEW YORK VS. U.S.

In 1994, New York's per stay costs at a community hospital of $8,127 topped the U.S. average of $6,230 by 30.4 percent.

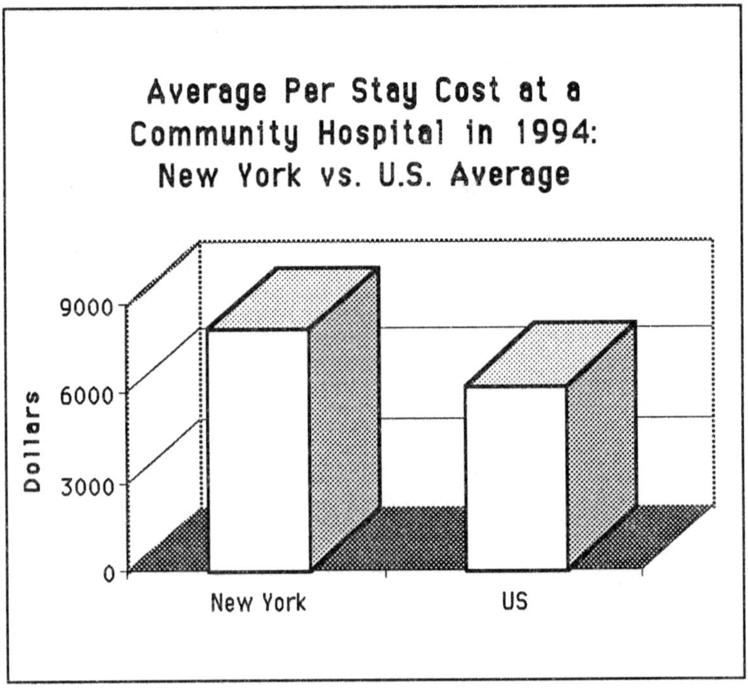


Data Source: U.S. Department of Commerce, *Statistical Abstract of the United States 1996*

# Per Capita State and Local Health Expenditures: State Rankings

In 1992-93, New York's per capita state and local health expenditures ranked ninth in the nation.

**Per Capita State and Local Health Expenditures**

| Rank | State | Per Capita Health Expenditures |
|---|---|---|
| 1 | District of Columbia | $316.01 |
| 2 | Alaska | 276.67 |
| 3 | Hawaii | 233.64 |
| 4 | Michigan | 189.41 |
| 5 | Rhode Island | 178.12 |
| 6 | Massachusetts | 172.25 |
| 7 | California | 169.97 |
| 8 | Delaware | 168.73 |
| **9** | **New York** | **154.30** |
| 10 | Florida | 153.54 |
| 11 | Washington | 150.83 |
| 12 | South Carolina | 146.91 |
| 13 | North Carolina | 144.46 |
| 14 | Alabama | 140.20 |
| 15 | New Mexico | 138.39 |
| 16 | Minnesota | 138.11 |
| 17 | Ohio | 134.73 |
| 18 | Oregon | 133.62 |
| 19 | Montana | 128.69 |
| 20 | Wyoming | 125.11 |
| 21 | Wisconsin | 124.25 |
| 22 | Connecticut | 119.48 |
| 23 | Arizona | 118.89 |
| 24 | Virginia | 111.83 |
| 25 | Maryland | 110.75 |
| 26 | Missouri | 110.11 |
| 27 | Illinois | 106.58 |
| 28 | New Hampshire | 105.54 |

*continued*

*continued*

| Rank | State | Per Capita Health Expenditures |
|---|---|---|
| 29 | Pennsylvania | 101.41 |
| 30 | Maine | 100.69 |
| 31 | Tennessee | 96.40 |
| 32 | Utah | 93.49 |
| 33 | Louisiana | 92.12 |
| 34 | Georgia | 89.51 |
| 35 | Colorado | 88.96 |
| 36 | Idaho | 87.78 |
| 37 | Kansas | 86.25 |
| 38 | South Dakota | 82.51 |
| 39 | Oklahoma | 82.21 |
| 40 | Iowa | 81.56 |
| 41 | Arkansas | 81.36 |
| 42 | New Jersey | 79.91 |
| 43 | West Virginia | 78.63 |
| 44 | Texas | 78.50 |
| 45 | Nevada | 73.13 |
| 46 | Kentucky | 71.15 |
| 47 | Mississippi | 68.60 |
| 48 | Indiana | 68.05 |
| 49 | Vermont | 67.83 |
| 50 | Nebraska | 56.47 |
| 51 | North Dakota | 51.85 |
| | U.S. Average | 124.84 |

Data Source: U.S. Department of Commerce

## PER CAPITA STATE AND LOCAL HEALTH EXPENDITURES: NEW YORK VS. U.S.

In 1992-93, New York's per capita state and local health expenditures surpassed the national average by 21.4 percent—$154.30 in New York versus a state and local average of $124.84.

Between 1962 and 1993, real (1993 dollars) per capita health expenditures in New York rose by 511.8 percent—from $25.22 in 1962 to $154.30 in 1993.

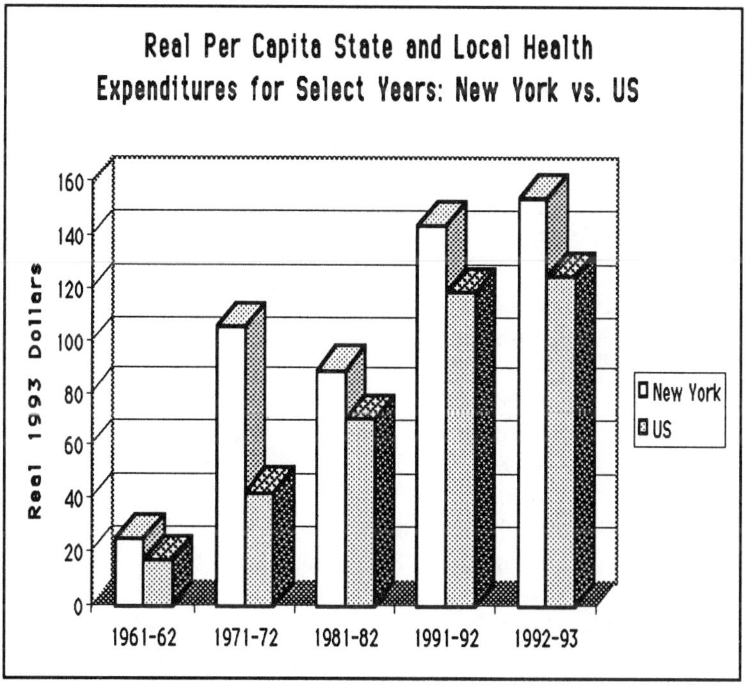


Data Source: U.S. Department of Commerce

# PER CAPITA STATE-ONLY HEALTH EXPENDITURES: STATE RANKINGS

In 1994, New York's per capita state health expenditures ranked fifteenth in the nation.

**Per Capita State Health Expenditures**

| Rank | State | Per Capita Health Expenditures |
|---|---|---|
| 1 | Alaska | $279.99 |
| 2 | Hawaii | 263.49 |
| 3 | Michigan | 203.82 |
| 4 | South Carolina | 201.87 |
| 5 | Delaware | 186.44 |
| 6 | Massachusetts | 180.43 |
| 7 | Rhode Island | 166.90 |
| 8 | Wyoming | 156.62 |
| 9 | California | 155.77 |
| 10 | New Mexico | 139.68 |
| 11 | Florida | 132.02 |
| 12 | Maryland | 128.61 |
| 13 | Montana | 127.11 |
| 14 | Washington | 123.36 |
| **15** | **New York** | **122.84** |
| 16 | Alabama | 115.44 |
| 17 | Arizona | 114.78 |
| 18 | Oregon | 107.24 |
| 19 | Maine | 104.72 |
| 20 | North Carolina | 99.12 |
| 21 | Nebraska | 98.73 |
| 22 | Pennsylvania | 94.66 |
| 23(t) | Wisconsin | 94.53 |
| 23(t) | New Hampshire | 94.53 |
| 25 | Illinois | 92.06 |
| 26 | Minnesota | 90.30 |
| 27 | Tennessee | 90.09 |
| 28 | Vermont | 87.74 |

*continued*

*continued*

| Rank | State | Per Capita Health Expenditures |
|---|---|---|
| 29 | Ohio | 86.63 |
| 30 | Arkansas | 86.31 |
| 31 | Oklahoma | 83.14 |
| 32 | Missouri | 82.02 |
| 33 | Louisiana | 81.33 |
| 34 | Connecticut | 80.00 |
| 35 | Virginia | 78.57 |
| 36 | Georgia | 77.32 |
| 37 | Utah | 77.02 |
| 38 | South Dakota | 76.34 |
| 39 | North Dakota | 74.52 |
| 40 | Kansas | 72.48 |
| 41 | New Jersey | 69.14 |
| 42 | Mississippi | 68.98 |
| 43 | West Virginia | 68.24 |
| 44 | Idaho | 65.83 |
| 45 | Texas | 64.33 |
| 46 | Colorado | 63.59 |
| 47 | Kentucky | 62.64 |
| 48 | Indiana | 60.32 |
| 49 | Iowa | 58.44 |
| 50 | Nevada | 42.54 |
| | U.S. Average | 109.06 |

Data Source: U.S. Department of Commerce

## PER CAPITA STATE-ONLY HEALTH EXPENDITURES: NEW YORK VS. U.S.

In 1994, New York's per capita state health expenditures exceeded the national average by 12.6 percent—$122.84 in New York versus a state average of $109.06.

Between 1965 and 1994, New York's real per capita state health spending increased by 544.5 percent. In 1994 dollars, New York's 1965 per capita health spending registered $19.06.

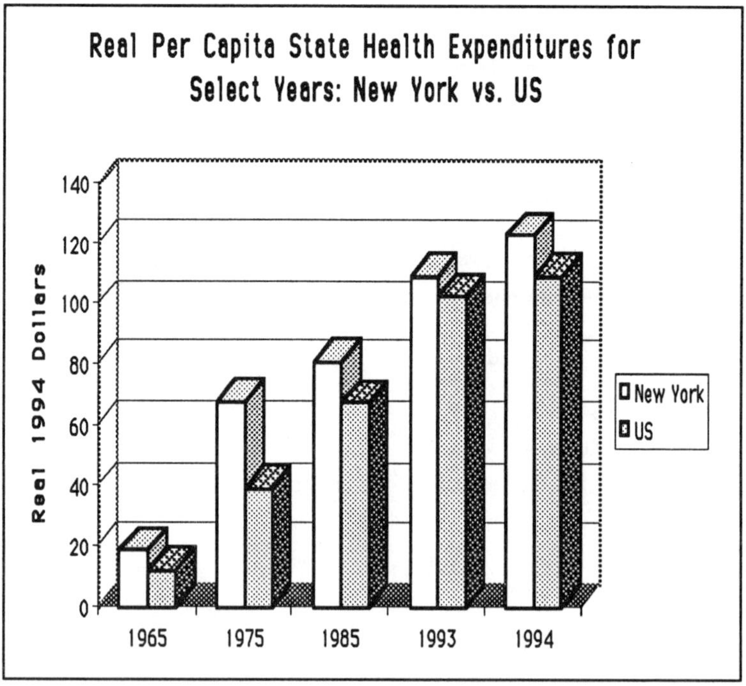


Data Source: U.S. Department of Commerce

## PER ENROLLEE MEDICARE PAYMENTS: STATE RANKINGS

In 1994, New York's per enrollee Medicare payments ranked eighth highest in the nation.

**Per Enrollee Medicare Payments**

| Rank | State | Per Enrollee Payments |
|---|---|---|
| 1 | District of Columbia | $14,367 |
| 2 | Florida | 5,377 |
| 3 | Massachusetts | 5,372 |
| 4 | California | 5,317 |
| 5 | Louisiana | 5,163 |
| 6 | Pennsylvania | 4,898 |
| 7 | Tennessee | 4,866 |
| **8** | **New York** | **4,799** |
| 9 | Nevada | 4,765 |
| 10 | Connecticut | 4,656 |
| 11 | Texas | 4,637 |
| 12 | Delaware | 4,612 |
| 13 | Maryland | 4,580 |
| 14 | New Jersey | 4,480 |
| 15 | Georgia | 4,475 |
| 16 | Alabama | 4,313 |
| 17 | Arizona | 4,303 |
| 18 | Michigan | 4,239 |
| 19 | Rhode Island | 4,235 |
| 20 | Illinois | 4,120 |
| 21 | Missouri | 4,073 |
| 22 | Kansas | 4,042 |
| 23 | Colorado | 3,998 |
| 24 | Ohio | 3,957 |
| 25 | Indiana | 3,878 |
| 26 | Mississippi | 3,787 |
| 27 | Kentucky | 3,786 |
| 28 | Oklahoma | 3,743 |
| 29 | North Carolina | 3,683 |

*continued*

*continued*

| Rank | State | Per Enrollee Payments |
|---|---|---|
| 30 | North Dakota | 3,657 |
| 31 | Hawaii | 3,644 |
| 32 | Arkansas | 3,498 |
| 33 | New Hampshire | 3,487 |
| 34 | Minnesota | 3,486 |
| 35 | Alaska | 3,469 |
| 36 | Utah | 3,462 |
| 37 | Oregon | 3,454 |
| 38 | South Carolina | 3,428 |
| 39 | Washington | 3,393 |
| 40 | West Virginia | 3,385 |
| 41 | Virginia | 3,384 |
| 42 | Wisconsin | 3,235 |
| 43 | Maine | 3,157 |
| 44 | Montana | 3,094 |
| 45 | Vermont | 3,086 |
| 46 | South Dakota | 3,078 |
| 47 | Nebraska | 3,069 |
| 48 | Iowa | 2,981 |
| 49 | New Mexico | 2,907 |
| 50 | Idaho | 2,747 |
| 51 | Wyoming | 2,695 |
| | U.S. Average | 4,391 |

Data Source: U.S. Department of Commerce, *Statistical Abstract of the United States 1996*

## PER ENROLLEE MEDICARE PAYMENTS: NEW YORK VS. U.S.

In 1994, New York's per enrollee Medicare payments of $4,799 outpaced the U.S. average of $4,391 by 9.3 percent.

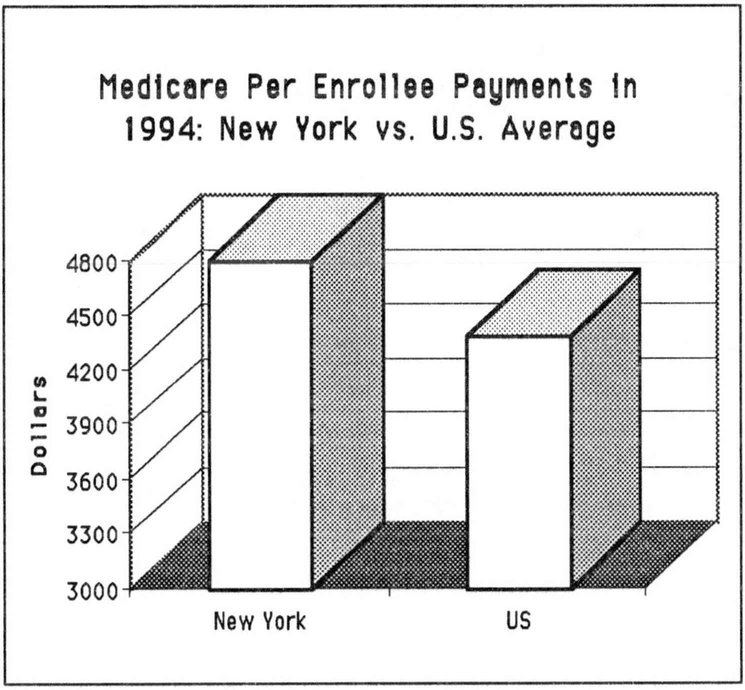


Data Source: U.S. Department of Commerce, *Statistical Abstract of the United States 1996*

## PER RECIPIENT MEDICAID PAYMENTS: STATE RANKINGS

In 1994, New York's per recipient Medicaid payments ranked the very highest in the nation.

**Per Recipient Medicaid Payments**

| Rank | State | Per Recipient Payments |
|---|---|---|
| **1** | **New York** | **$6,441** |
| 2 | Rhode Island | 5,957 |
| 3 | Connecticut | 5,489 |
| 4 | Minnesota | 4,653 |
| 5 | New Jersey | 4,572 |
| 6 | Maine | 4,559 |
| 7 | New Hampshire | 4,523 |
| 8 | Maryland | 4,518 |
| 9 | North Dakota | 4,508 |
| 10 | District of Columbia | 4,331 |
| 11 | Massachusetts | 4,299 |
| 12 | South Dakota | 3,944 |
| 13 | Wisconsin | 3,861 |
| 14 | Indiana | 3,719 |
| 15 | Delaware | 3,693 |
| 16 | Arkansas | 3,685 |
| 17 | Nebraska | 3,616 |
| 18 | Alaska | 3,522 |
| 19 | Louisiana | 3,450 |
| 20 | Pennsylvania | 3,366 |
| 21 | Illinois | 3,349 |
| 22 | Colorado | 3,294 |
| 23 | Ohio | 3,280 |
| 24 | Iowa | 3,241 |
| 25 | Nevada | 3,232 |
| 26 | Montana | 3,156 |
| 27 | Kansas | 3,103 |
| 28 | Wyoming | 3,078 |
| 29 | West Virginia | 3,016 |

*continued*

*continued*

| Rank | State | Per Recipient Payments |
|---|---|---|
| 30 | Idaho | 3,009 |
| 31 | Oklahoma | 2,991 |
| 32 | Utah | 2,873 |
| 33 | South Carolina | 2,872 |
| 34 | Hawaii | 2,793 |
| 35 | Kentucky | 2,788 |
| 36 | Michigan | 2,758 |
| 37 | Vermont | 2,755 |
| 38 | North Carolina | 2,726 |
| 39 | Missouri | 2,704 |
| 40 | Virginia | 2,680 |
| 41 | Georgia | 2,622 |
| 42 | Oregon | 2,521 |
| 43 | Texas | 2,493 |
| 44 | Florida | 2,470 |
| 45 | Alabama | 2,412 |
| 46 | New Mexico | 2,381 |
| 47 | Washington | 2,356 |
| 48 | Tennessee | 2,093 |
| 49 | Mississippi | 2,030 |
| 50 | California | 1,994 |
| 51 | Arizona | 390 |
| | U.S. Average | 3,167 |

Data Source: U.S. Department of Commerce, *Statistical Abstract of the United States 1996*

## PER RECIPIENT MEDICAID PAYMENTS: NEW YORK VS. U.S.

In 1994, New York's per recipient Medicaid payments of $6,441 outpaced the U.S. average of $3,167 by 103.4 percent.

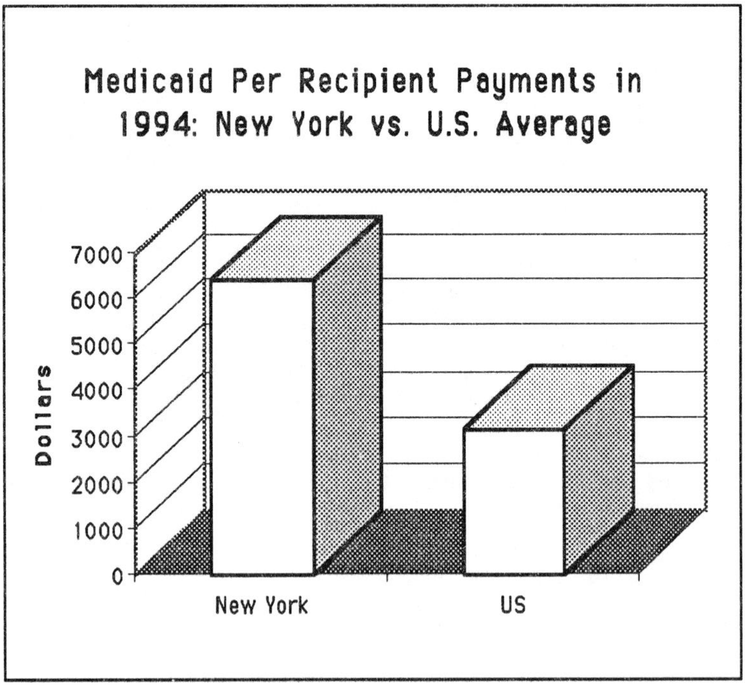


Data Source: U.S. Department of Commerce, *Statistical Abstract of the United States 1996*

## PER CAPITA STATE AND LOCAL HIGHWAYS EXPENDITURES: STATE RANKINGS

In 1992-93, New York's per capita state and local highways expenditures ranked twenty-ninth in the nation.

**Per Capita State and Local Highways Expenditures**

| Rank | State | Per Capita Highways Expenditures |
|---|---|---|
| 1 | Alaska | $1,113.74 |
| 2 | Wyoming | 603.80 |
| 3 | New Mexico | 595.82 |
| 4 | South Dakota | 460.51 |
| 5 | Vermont | 432.19 |
| 6 | Delaware | 431.37 |
| 7 | Iowa | 429.29 |
| 8 | North Dakota | 422.60 |
| 9 | Montana | 422.51 |
| 10 | Minnesota | 402.47 |
| 11 | Kansas | 385.37 |
| 12 | Hawaii | 372.61 |
| 13 | Nebraska | 370.38 |
| 14 | Nevada | 366.55 |
| 15 | Wisconsin | 349.86 |
| 16 | West Virginia | 339.85 |
| 17 | Maine | 312.24 |
| 18 | Connecticut | 309.69 |
| 19 | Idaho | 307.08 |
| 20 | Colorado | 288.32 |
| 21 | Oregon | 287.71 |
| 22 | New Jersey | 286.40 |
| 23 | Illinois | 286.10 |
| 24 | Arkansas | 280.34 |
| 25 | Washington | 275.74 |
| 26 | Kentucky | 274.98 |
| 27 | New Hampshire | 274.32 |
| 28 | Mississippi | 273.82 |

*continued*

*continued*

| Rank | State | Per Capita Highways Expenditures |
|---|---|---|
| **29** | **New York** | **273.18** |
| 30 | Massachusetts | 267.75 |
| 31 | Florida | 264.22 |
| 32 | Louisiana | 264.21 |
| 33 | Rhode Island | 255.62 |
| 34 | Alabama | 252.04 |
| 35 | Virginia | 249.99 |
| 36 | Tennessee | 246.38 |
| 37 | Texas | 245.72 |
| 38 | Utah | 244.97 |
| 39 | Oklahoma | 244.27 |
| 40 | Arizona | 242.44 |
| 41 | North Carolina | 239.61 |
| 42 | Indiana | 236.75 |
| 43 | Ohio | 232.49 |
| 44 | Pennsylvania | 227.97 |
| 45 | Missouri | 227.64 |
| 46 | Georgia | 226.47 |
| 47 | Maryland | 218.25 |
| 48 | Michigan | 211.06 |
| 49 | District of Columbia | 205.89 |
| 50 | California | 198.91 |
| 51 | South Carolina | 195.31 |
| | U.S. Average | 264.29 |

Data Source: U.S. Department of Commerce

## PER CAPITA STATE AND LOCAL HIGHWAYS EXPENDITURES: NEW YORK VS. U.S.

In 1992-93, New York's per capita state and local highways expenditures topped the national average by 3.4 percent—$273.18 in New York versus $264.29 across the nation.

Between 1962 and 1993, real per capita state and local highways expenditures grew by 85.5 percent—from $147.27 in 1962 to $273.18 in 1993. However, the striking fact from the chart below is the dramatic increase from 1962 to 1972—an incredible 324.5 percent increase over a ten-year period. In New York, the 1960s and early 1970s saw public works projects skyrocket, even as the state's population evened off and then began to decline.

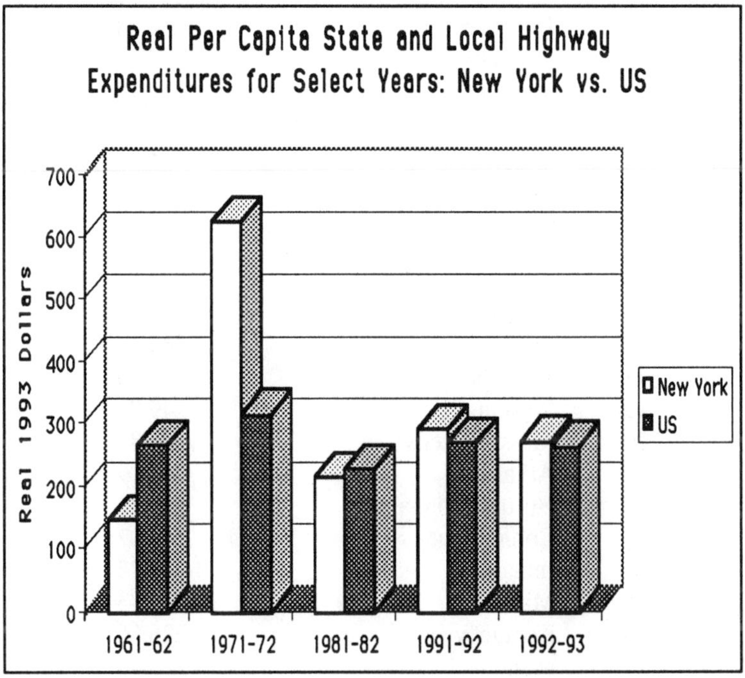


Data Source: U.S. Department of Commerce

## PER CAPITA STATE-ONLY HIGHWAYS EXPENDITURES: STATE RANKINGS

In 1994, New York's per capita state highways expenditures actually ranked forty-eighth in the nation.

**Per Capita State Highways Expenditures**

| Rank | State | Per Capita Highways Expenditures |
|---|---|---|
| 1 | Alaska | $931.94 |
| 2 | Wyoming | 578.58 |
| 3 | New Mexico | 434.88 |
| 4 | West Virginia | 385.61 |
| 5 | North Dakota | 370.40 |
| 6 | South Dakota | 369.59 |
| 7 | Delaware | 354.08 |
| 8 | Montana | 352.64 |
| 9 | Vermont | 335.48 |
| 10 | Iowa | 322.68 |
| 11 | Nebraska | 318.70 |
| 12 | Hawaii | 313.81 |
| 13 | Kansas | 298.99 |
| 14 | Idaho | 275.86 |
| 15 | Nevada | 273.95 |
| 16 | Arizona | 258.62 |
| 17 | Oregon | 254.26 |
| 18 | Virginia | 250.19 |
| 19 | Washington | 249.82 |
| 20 | Massachusetts | 245.83 |
| 21 | Arkansas | 244.09 |
| 22 | North Carolina | 242.36 |
| 23 | Connecticut | 242.07 |
| 24 | Indiana | 234.23 |
| 25 | Minnesota | 230.83 |
| 26 | Kentucky | 226.56 |
| 27 | Maine | 226.49 |
| 28 | New Jersey | 225.16 |

*continued*

*continued*

| Rank | State | Per Capita Highways Expenditures |
|---|---|---|
| 29 | Colorado | 224.55 |
| 30 | Wisconsin | 216.12 |
| 31 | Rhode Island | 212.59 |
| 32 | Tennessee | 212.07 |
| 33 | Illinois | 210.54 |
| 34 | Oklahoma | 210.28 |
| 35 | Mississippi | 209.92 |
| 36 | Alabama | 209.49 |
| 37 | Missouri | 208.95 |
| 38 | Ohio | 206.78 |
| 39 | Maryland | 205.43 |
| 40 | Louisiana | 199.54 |
| 41(t) | Pennsylvania | 194.29 |
| 41(t) | Florida | 194.29 |
| 43 | Utah | 192.41 |
| 44 | New Hampshire | 188.31 |
| 45 | Michigan | 180.63 |
| 46 | South Carolina | 164.58 |
| 47 | Texas | 158.96 |
| **48** | **New York** | **148.25** |
| 49 | California | 148.21 |
| 50 | Georgia | 138.62 |
| | U.S. Average | 206.83 |

Data Source: U.S. Department of Commerce

## PER CAPITA STATE-ONLY HIGHWAYS EXPENDITURES: NEW YORK VS. U.S.

In 1994, the national per capita state highways expenditures average actually outpaced New York by 39.5 percent—$148.25 in New York versus the state average of $206.83.

Between 1965 and 1994, New York's real per capita state highway spending declined by 9.8 percent. In 1994 dollars, New York spent $134.97 in 1965 in terms of per capita highway expenditures.

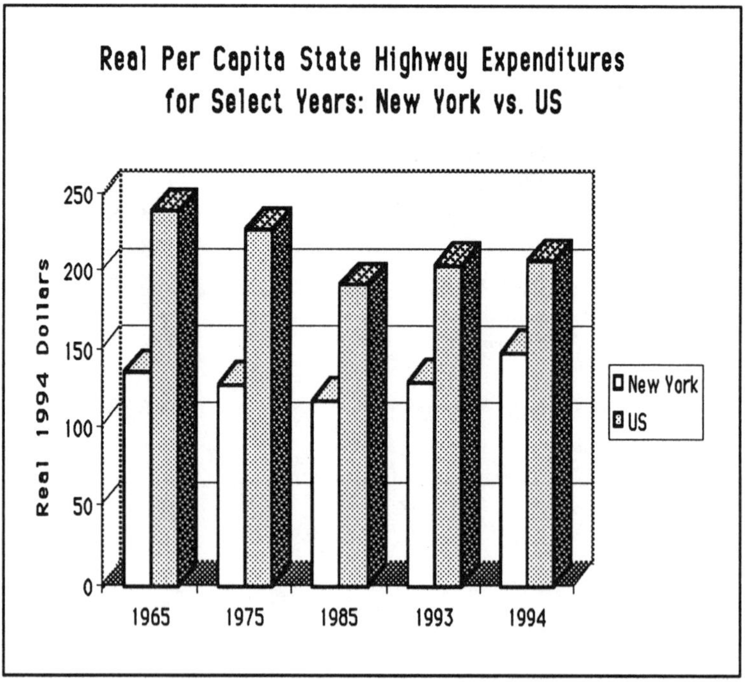


Data Source: U.S. Department of Commerce

## CONDITION OF NEW YORK BRIDGES

As of April 1994, 44 percent of New York's bridges were found to be deficient and 1.1 percent were closed. Out of 19,507 bridges, 8,585 were deficient and 208 were closed.

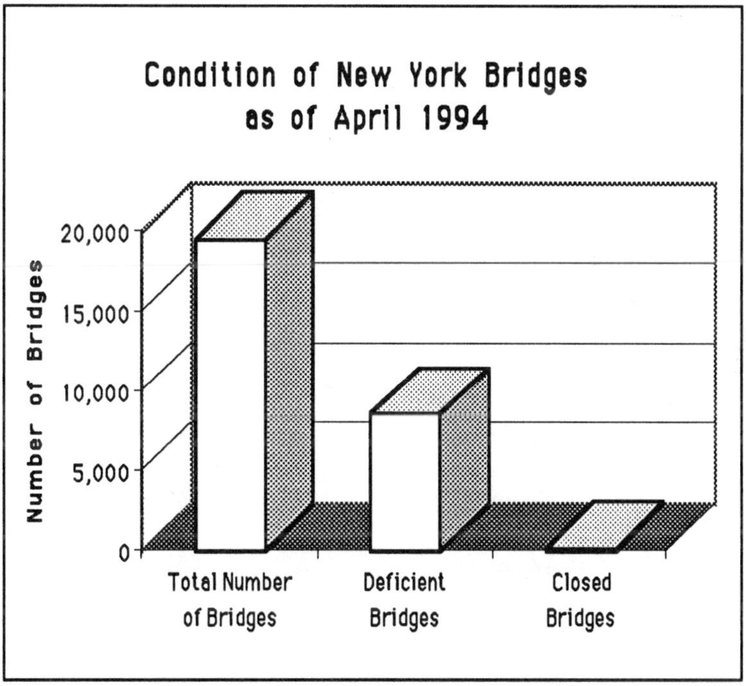


Data Source: The Nelson A. Rockefeller Institute of Government, *1995 New York State Statistical Yearbook*

# PER CAPITA STATE AND LOCAL FIRE PROTECTION EXPENDITURES: STATE RANKINGS

In 1992-93, New York's per capita state and local fire protection expenditures ranked tenth in the nation.

**Per Capita State and Local Fire Protection Expenditures**

| Rank | State | Per Capita Expenditures |
|---|---|---|
| 1 | District of Columbia | $173.39 |
| 2 | California | 108.91 |
| 3 | Rhode Island | 101.77 |
| 4 | Massachusetts | 91.40 |
| 5 | Alaska | 88.67 |
| 6 | Nevada | 86.60 |
| 7 | Connecticut | 85.98 |
| 8 | Oregon | 79.78 |
| 9 | Washington | 77.88 |
| **10** | **New York** | **76.30** |
| 11 | Florida | 69.81 |
| 12 | Maryland | 68.25 |
| 13 | Illinois | 67.10 |
| 14 | Ohio | 63.78 |
| 15 | Wisconsin | 63.41 |
| 16 | New Hampshire | 62.62 |
| 17 | Hawaii | 62.27 |
| 18 | Colorado | 61.40 |
| 19 | Virginia | 59.55 |
| 20 | New Jersey | 56.32 |
| 21 | Maine | 51.60 |
| 22 | Oklahoma | 50.78 |
| 23 | Georgia | 50.41 |
| 24 | New Mexico | 49.98 |
| 25 | Arizona | 49.05 |
| 26 | Kansas | 47.00 |
| 27 | Tennessee | 44.75 |
| 28 | Wyoming | 44.59 |

*continued*

*continued*

| Rank | State | Per Capita Expenditures |
|---|---|---|
| 29 | Louisiana | 44.49 |
| 30 | Texas | 44.09 |
| 31 | Indiana | 43.96 |
| 32 | Minnesota | 43.60 |
| 33 | Michigan | 42.31 |
| 34 | Missouri | 41.95 |
| 35 | Alabama | 39.52 |
| 36 | North Carolina | 38.34 |
| 37 | Idaho | 37.22 |
| 38 | Utah | 35.82 |
| 39 | Iowa | 35.64 |
| 40 | Nebraska | 34.32 |
| 41 | Vermont | 34.08 |
| 42 | North Dakota | 33.56 |
| 43 | Kentucky | 32.96 |
| 44 | Montana | 31.70 |
| 45 | South Carolina | 31.28 |
| 46 | Mississippi | 30.74 |
| 47 | Pennsylvania | 30.16 |
| 48 | South Dakota | 29.66 |
| 49 | Arkansas | 28.15 |
| 50 | West Virginia | 19.66 |
| 51 | Delaware | 18.65 |
| | U.S. Average | 61.27 |

Data Source: U.S. Department of Commerce

# PER CAPITA STATE AND LOCAL FIRE PROTECTION EXPENDITURES: NEW YORK VS. U.S.

In 1992-93, New York's per capita state and local fire protection expenditures exceeded the national average by 24.5 percent—$76.30 in New York versus a $61.27 state and local average.

Between 1962 and 1993, real per capita state and local fire protection spending grew by 69.8 percent. In 1962, New York spent $44.93 per capita (1993 dollars) on fire protection.

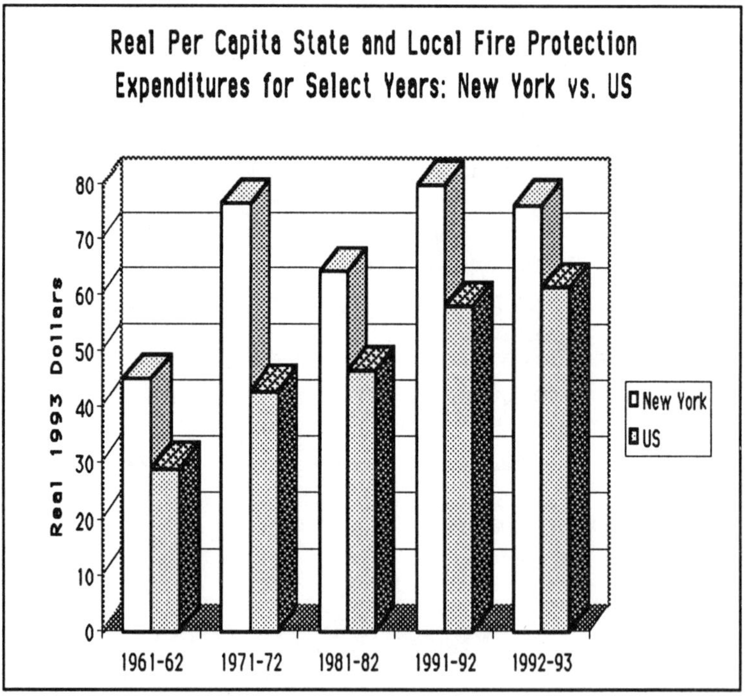


Data Source: U.S. Department of Commerce

## PER CAPITA STATE AND LOCAL PARKS AND RECREATION EXPENDITURES: STATE RANKINGS

In 1992-93, New York's per capita state and local parks and recreation expenditures ranked nineteenth among the 50 states and Washington, D.C.

**Per Capita State and Local Parks and Recreation Expenditures**

| Rank | State | Per Capita Expenditures |
|---|---|---|
| 1 | Hawaii | $165.22 |
| 2 | Nevada | 130.52 |
| 3 | Rhode Island | 119.63 |
| 4 | Illinois | 114.51 |
| 5 | Colorado | 112.68 |
| 6 | District of Columbia | 111.99 |
| 7 | Washington | 103.16 |
| 8 | Minnesota | 94.59 |
| 9 | Wyoming | 90.20 |
| 10 | Alaska | 83.55 |
| 11 | Florida | 78.62 |
| 12 | North Dakota | 75.34 |
| 13 | California | 75.18 |
| 14 | New Mexico | 74.92 |
| 15 | Maryland | 74.26 |
| 16 | Oregon | 71.84 |
| 17 | New Jersey | 71.45 |
| 18 | Utah | 70.24 |
| **19** | **New York** | **65.44** |
| 20 | Delaware | 65.18 |
| 21 | Wisconsin | 63.84 |
| 22 | Arizona | 63.24 |
| 23 | South Dakota | 60.76 |
| 24 | Iowa | 58.18 |
| 25 | Georgia | 54.88 |
| 26 | Oklahoma | 54.78 |
| 27 | Connecticut | 51.46 |

*continued*

*continued*

| Rank | State | Per Capita Expenditures |
|---|---|---|
| 28 | Virginia | 51.08 |
| 29 | Ohio | 51.05 |
| 30 | Tennessee | 49.58 |
| 31 | Louisiana | 49.06 |
| 32 | Missouri | 47.68 |
| 33 | Nebraska | 47.55 |
| 34 | Alabama | 47.01 |
| 35 | Indiana | 46.12 |
| 36 | Kansas | 46.02 |
| 37 | South Carolina | 45.78 |
| 38 | North Carolina | 45.75 |
| 39 | Texas | 43.41 |
| 40 | Michigan | 39.34 |
| 41 | New Hampshire | 38.60 |
| 42 | Pennsylvania | 37.80 |
| 43 | Idaho | 36.86 |
| 44 | Kentucky | 36.52 |
| 45 | Vermont | 34.02 |
| 46 | West Virginia | 33.52 |
| 47 | Maine | 32.12 |
| 48 | Arkansas | 30.67 |
| 49 | Montana | 28.19 |
| 50 | Massachusetts | 28.08 |
| 51 | Mississippi | 21.84 |
| | U.S. Average | 62.04 |

Data Source: U.S. Department of Commerce

## PER CAPITA STATE AND LOCAL PARKS AND RECREATION EXPENDITURES: NEW YORK VS. U.S.

In 1992-93, New York's per capita state and local parks and recreation expenditures exceeded the state and local average by 5.5 percent—$65.44 in New York versus a national average of $62.04.

Between 1962 and 1993, real (1993 dollars) per capita state and local parks and recreation expenditures increased by 100.9 percent—from $32.58 in 1962 to $65.44 in 1993.

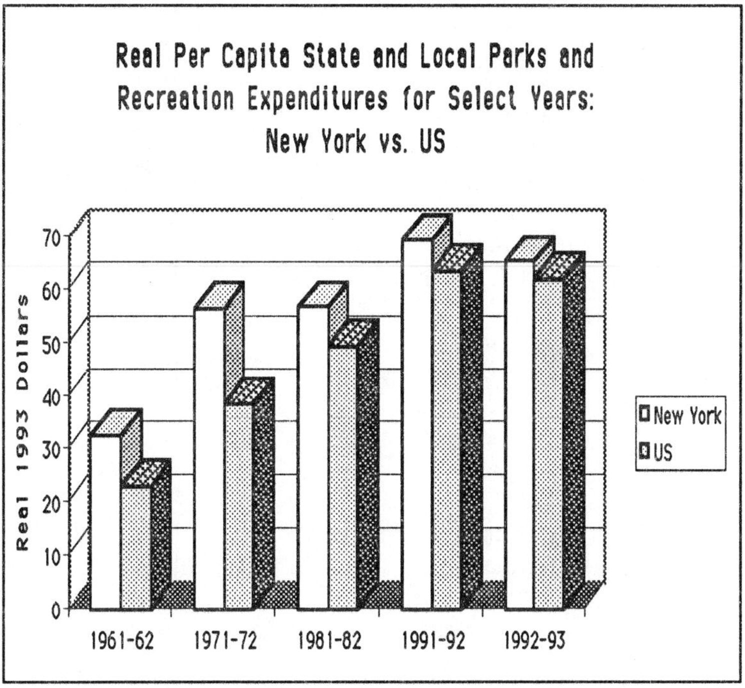


Data Source: U.S. Department of Commerce

# PER CAPITA STATE-ONLY PARKS AND RECREATION EXPENDITURES: STATE RANKINGS

In 1994, New York's per capita state parks and recreation expenditures ranked seventeenth among the 50 states.

**Per Capita State Parks and Recreation Expenditures**

| Rank | State | Per Capita Expenditures |
|---|---|---|
| 1 | Hawaii | $197.12 |
| 2 | Delaware | 39.90 |
| 3 | New Jersey | 35.39 |
| 4 | Wyoming | 27.83 |
| 5 | Montana | 26.85 |
| 6 | Alaska | 26.47 |
| 7 | Mississippi | 22.22 |
| 8 | Rhode Island | 21.95 |
| 9 | West Virginia | 21.82 |
| 10 | Georgia | 21.28 |
| 11 | Louisiana | 21.01 |
| 12 | South Dakota | 20.56 |
| 13 | Illinois | 20.08 |
| 14 | Kentucky | 19.66 |
| 15 | New Mexico | 18.44 |
| 16 | Minnesota | 16.03 |
| **17** | **New York** | **15.65** |
| 18 | Idaho | 15.62 |
| 19 | Utah | 14.93 |
| 20 | Arkansas | 14.61 |
| 21 | Vermont | 14.41 |
| 22 | Tennessee | 14.26 |
| 23 | Massachusetts | 14.15 |
| 24 | Oklahoma | 14.03 |
| 25 | New Hampshire | 12.77 |
| 26 | Washington | 12.00 |
| 27 | Nebraska | 11.21 |
| 28 | North Dakota | 11.12 |

*continued*

*continued*

| Rank | State | Per Capita Expenditures |
|---|---|---|
| 29 | South Carolina | 10.88 |
| 30 | Wisconsin | 10.43 |
| 31 | Nevada | 10.20 |
| 32 | Maryland | 10.14 |
| 33 | Connecticut | 9.86 |
| 34 | Maine | 9.82 |
| 35 | Michigan | 9.41 |
| 36 | Virginia | 9.32 |
| 37 | Colorado | 8.78 |
| 38 | North Carolina | 8.76 |
| 39 | Oregon | 7.70 |
| 40 | California | 7.64 |
| 41 | Pennsylvania | 7.63 |
| 42 | Arizona | 7.08 |
| 43 | Ohio | 6.41 |
| 44 | Iowa | 5.84 |
| 45 | Florida | 5.62 |
| 46 | Indiana | 5.24 |
| 47 | Missouri | 4.35 |
| 48 | Texas | 3.08 |
| 49 | Alabama | 2.86 |
| 50 | Kansas | 2.76 |
| | U.S. Average | 12.26 |

Data Source: U.S. Department of Commerce

## PER CAPITA STATE-ONLY PARKS AND RECREATION EXPENDITURES: NEW YORK VS. U.S.

In 1994, New York's per capita state parks and recreation expenditures surpassed the state average by 27.7 percent—$15.65 in New York versus $12.26 across the nation.

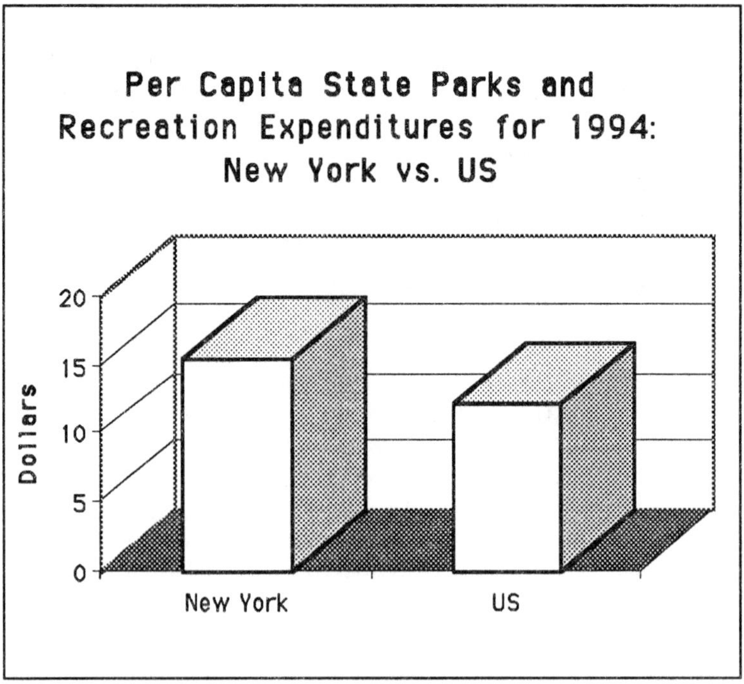


Data Source: U.S. Department of Commerce

# STATE PARKS AND RECREATION REVENUES AS A PERCENTAGE OF OPERATING EXPENDITURES: STATE RANKINGS

In 1992, New York's state parks and recreation revenues as a percentage of operating expenditures ranked thirty-fourth among the 50 states.

**State Parks and Recreation Revenues as a Percentage of Operating Expenditures**

| Rank | State | Percent |
|---|---|---|
| 1 | Colorado | 109.0% |
| 2 | Vermont | 96.2 |
| 3 | Alabama | 81.4 |
| 4 | Idaho | 79.8 |
| 5 | Michigan | 77.4 |
| 6 | Oklahoma | 76.7 |
| 7 | Indiana | 73.7 |
| 8 | Nebraska | 71.1 |
| 9 | Wisconsin | 70.0 |
| 10 | Massachusetts | 64.9 |
| 11 | West Virginia | 64.6 |
| 12 | South Dakota | 64.5 |
| 13 | Kentucky | 63.3 |
| 14 | South Carolina | 60.7 |
| 15 | Tennessee | 59.0 |
| 16 | Arkansas | 56.0 |
| 17 | New Hampshire | 51.5 |
| 18 | Texas | 49.8 |
| 19 | California | 49.3 |
| 20 | North Dakota | 49.1 |
| 21 | Montana | 48.6 |
| 22 | Mississippi | 48.0 |
| 23 | Connecticut | 47.9 |
| 24 | Kansas | 45.5 |
| 25 | Rhode Island | 44.8 |

*continued*

*continued*

| Rank | State | Percent |
|---|---|---|
| 26 | Delaware | 43.0 |
| 27 | Georgia | 42.5 |
| 28 | Minnesota | 41.6 |
| 29 | Florida | 38.9 |
| 30 | Oregon | 38.5 |
| 31 | Washington | 36.1 |
| 32 | Arizona | 35.9 |
| 33 | Maine | 34.9 |
| **34** | **New York** | **33.5** |
| 35 | Utah | 31.9 |
| 36 | Ohio | 30.8 |
| 37 | New Mexico | 29.0 |
| 38 | Virginia | 27.6 |
| 39 | Maryland | 26.0 |
| 40 | Louisiana | 25.0 |
| 41 | Iowa | 24.0 |
| 42 | New Jersey | 22.8 |
| 43 | Missouri | 22.4 |
| 44 | Alaska | 19.9 |
| 45 | North Carolina | 18.3 |
| 46 | Pennsylvania | 15.4 |
| 47 | Hawaii | 14.7 |
| 48 | Nevada | 14.5 |
| 49 | Illinois | 11.6 |
| 50 | Wyoming | 10.2 |

Data Source: U.S. Department of Commerce, *Statistical Abstract of the United States 1995*

## PER CAPITA STATE AND LOCAL HOUSING AND COMMUNITY DEVELOPMENT EXPENDITURES: STATE RANKINGS

In 1992-93, New York's per capita state and local housing and community development expenditures ranked third highest in the nation.

**Per Capita State and Local Housing and Community Development Expenditures**

| Rank | State | Per Capita Expenditures |
|---|---|---|
| 1 | District of Columbia | $354.08 |
| 2 | Hawaii | 250.78 |
| **3** | **New York** | **197.87** |
| 4 | Massachusetts | 127.88 |
| 5 | Alaska | 120.50 |
| 6 | California | 111.84 |
| 7 | Connecticut | 110.68 |
| 8 | Rhode Island | 110.64 |
| 9 | Minnesota | 101.85 |
| 10 | Maryland | 95.62 |
| 11 | Delaware | 93.97 |
| 12 | Vermont | 81.55 |
| 13 | Washington | 74.24 |
| 14 | Oregon | 73.55 |
| 15 | North Dakota | 73.29 |
| 16 | Maine | 71.45 |
| 17 | Illinois | 70.09 |
| 18 | Indiana | 63.75 |
| 19 | Pennsylvania | 62.90 |
| 20 | Georgia | 60.63 |
| 21 | Nevada | 60.30 |
| 22 | Montana | 58.90 |
| 23 | Alabama | 57.52 |
| 24 | Ohio | 54.25 |
| 25 | Virginia | 54.05 |
| 26 | Tennessee | 52.07 |

*continued*

*continued*

| Rank | State | Per Capita Expenditures |
|---|---|---|
| 27 | Colorado | 50.44 |
| 28 | New Jersey | 49.78 |
| 29 | Mississippi | 48.44 |
| 30 | Utah | 46.63 |
| 31 | Wisconsin | 45.38 |
| 32 | North Carolina | 44.17 |
| 33 | Florida | 42.65 |
| 34 | Louisiana | 40.97 |
| 35 | Arizona | 40.87 |
| 36 | New Hampshire | 39.85 |
| 37 | Nebraska | 38.70 |
| 38 | Missouri | 37.69 |
| 39 | Kentucky | 35.44 |
| 40 | South Carolina | 33.38 |
| 41 | Arkansas | 32.63 |
| 42 | Oklahoma | 31.02 |
| 43 | Iowa | 30.86 |
| 44 | Texas | 28.61 |
| 45 | West Virginia | 28.40 |
| 46 | South Dakota | 27.69 |
| 47 | New Mexico | 24.62 |
| 48 | Kansas | 19.53 |
| 49 | Wyoming | 17.45 |
| 50 | Michigan | 13.86 |
| 51 | Idaho | 12.51 |
| | U.S. Average | 71.91 |

Data Source: U.S. Department of Commerce

## PER CAPITA STATE AND LOCAL HOUSING AND COMMUNITY DEVELOPMENT EXPENDITURES: NEW YORK VS. U.S.

In 1992-93, New York's per capita state and local housing and community development expenditures outpaced the national average by 175.2 percent—$197.87 in New York versus a state and local average of $71.91.

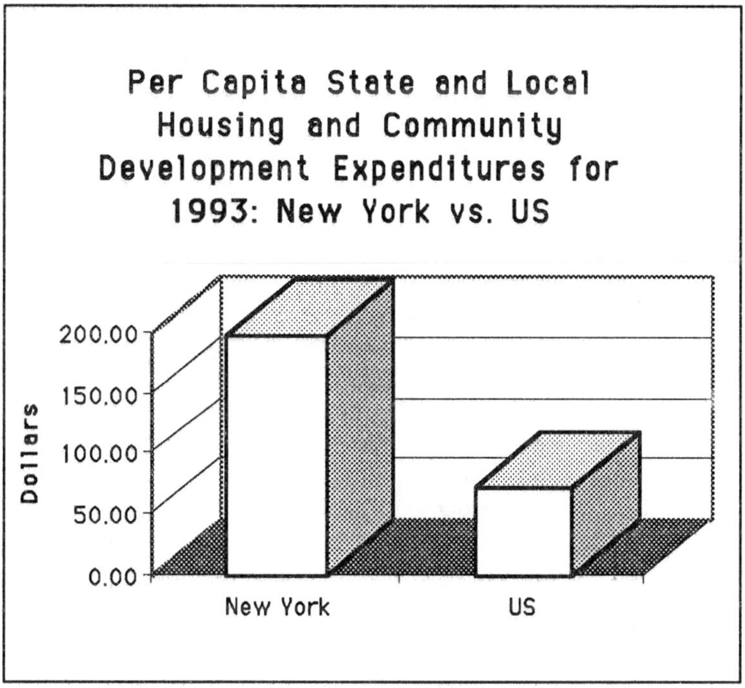


Data Source: U.S. Department of Commerce

# PER CAPITA STATE AND LOCAL SEWERAGE EXPENDITURES: STATE RANKINGS

In 1992-93, New York's per capita state and local sewerage expenditures ranked sixteenth highest in the nation.

**Per Capita State and Local Sewerage Expenditures**

| Rank | State | Per Capita Expenditures |
|---|---|---|
| 1 | Washington | $397.34 |
| 2 | District of Columbia | 274.32 |
| 3 | Massachusetts | 148.40 |
| 4 | Nevada | 137.42 |
| 5 | Alaska | 126.18 |
| 6 | Hawaii | 126.04 |
| 7 | Rhode Island | 120.67 |
| 8 | Wisconsin | 119.32 |
| 9 | Oregon | 116.75 |
| 10 | Delaware | 115.90 |
| 11 | New Jersey | 111.77 |
| 12 | California | 109.24 |
| 13 | Ohio | 104.99 |
| 14 | Michigan | 99.84 |
| 15 | Illinois | 96.95 |
| **16** | **New York** | **91.39** |
| 17 | Maryland | 86.69 |
| 18 | Virginia | 84.09 |
| 19 | Minnesota | 80.63 |
| 20 | Indiana | 77.61 |
| 21 | Maine | 76.97 |
| 22 | Pennsylvania | 76.54 |
| 23 | Connecticut | 74.24 |
| 24 | Texas | 68.79 |
| 25 | Iowa | 67.78 |
| 26 | Colorado | 63.38 |
| 27 | Vermont | 61.02 |
| 28 | Utah | 59.29 |

*continued*

*continued*

| Rank | State | Per Capita Expenditures |
|---|---|---|
| 29 | New Hampshire | 58.12 |
| 30 | Missouri | 57.89 |
| 31 | Arizona | 57.41 |
| 32 | Louisiana | 56.10 |
| 33 | North Carolina | 55.39 |
| 34 | Kentucky | 53.59 |
| 35 | Idaho | 52.93 |
| 36 | Oklahoma | 52.90 |
| 37 | Georgia | 51.71 |
| 38 | Florida | 51.53 |
| 39 | Tennessee | 50.81 |
| 40 | New Mexico | 50.80 |
| 41 | West Virginia | 48.48 |
| 42 | South Carolina | 47.48 |
| 43 | Wyoming | 47.23 |
| 44 | Arkansas | 46.22 |
| 45 | Montana | 44.98 |
| 46 | Nebraska | 44.56 |
| 47 | Kansas | 42.83 |
| 48 | South Dakota | 38.83 |
| 49 | Alabama | 34.69 |
| 50 | Mississippi | 34.27 |
| 51 | North Dakota | 24.41 |
| | U.S. Average | 88.02 |

Data Source: U.S. Department of Commerce

## PER CAPITA STATE AND LOCAL SEWERAGE EXPENDITURES: NEW YORK VS. U.S.

In 1992-93, New York's per capita state and local sewerage expenditures surpassed the state and local average by 3.8 percent—$91.39 in New York versus a national mean of $88.02.

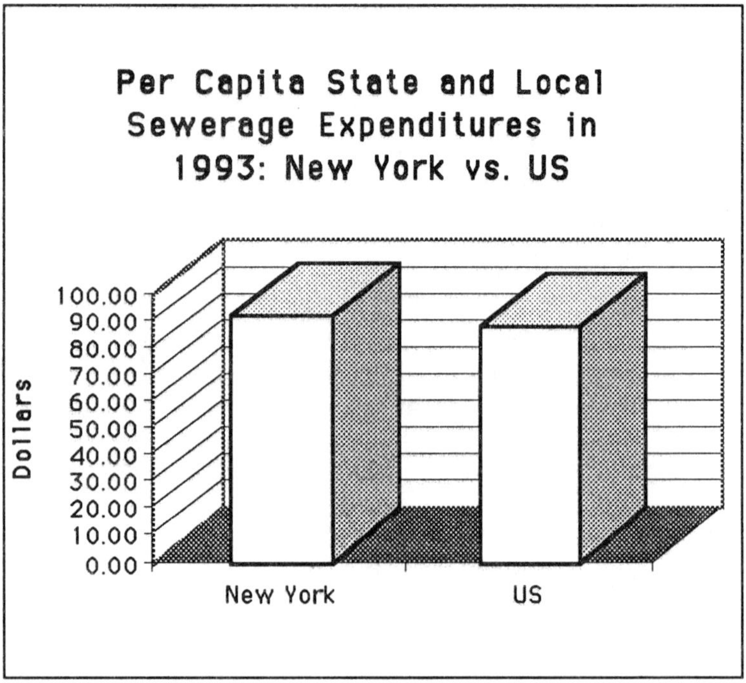


Data Source: U.S. Department of Commerce

## PER CAPITA STATE AND LOCAL SOLID WASTE MANAGEMENT EXPENDITURES: STATE RANKINGS

In 1992-93, New York's per capita state and local solid waste management expenditures ranked second highest in the nation.

**Per Capita State and Local Solid Waste Management Expenditures**

| Rank | State | Per Capita Expenditures |
|---|---|---|
| 1 | New Jersey | $109.93 |
| **2** | **New York** | **109.84** |
| 3 | Connecticut | 104.93 |
| 4 | Hawaii | 99.99 |
| 5 | Florida | 90.73 |
| 6 | Wyoming | 86.74 |
| 7 | Delaware | 82.26 |
| 8 | District of Columbia | 78.37 |
| 9 | Pennsylvania | 76.54 |
| 10 | Washington | 71.79 |
| 11 | Maryland | 71.60 |
| 12 | Alaska | 67.25 |
| 13 | Maine | 64.37 |
| 14 | North Carolina | 53.03 |
| 15 | New Mexico | 52.61 |
| 16 | Virginia | 51.95 |
| 17 | Minnesota | 50.57 |
| 18 | Vermont | 50.00 |
| 19 | California | 49.21 |
| 20 | Rhode Island | 47.62 |
| 21 | New Hampshire | 45.55 |
| 22 | Wisconsin | 43.45 |
| 23 | South Carolina | 39.45 |
| 24 | Oregon | 39.21 |
| 25 | Georgia | 38.93 |
| 26 | Massachusetts | 38.77 |
| 27 | Louisiana | 36.09 |

*continued*

*continued*

| Rank | State | Per Capita Expenditures |
|---|---|---|
| 28 | Tennessee | 34.34 |
| 29 | Iowa | 34.30 |
| 30 | Montana | 34.21 |
| 31 | Michigan | 33.29 |
| 32 | Arizona | 32.69 |
| 33 | Oklahoma | 32.31 |
| 34 | Idaho | 31.00 |
| 35 | Alabama | 30.75 |
| 36 | Texas | 29.20 |
| 37 | Ohio | 28.36 |
| 38 | Arkansas | 28.29 |
| 39 | Illinois | 27.69 |
| 40 | North Dakota | 27.20 |
| 41 | Kentucky | 26.05 |
| 42 | Utah | 25.61 |
| 43 | Indiana | 22.05 |
| 44 | Mississippi | 20.70 |
| 45 | Kansas | 19.65 |
| 46 | South Dakota | 17.94 |
| 47 | West Virginia | 17.81 |
| 48 | Nebraska | 17.35 |
| 49 | Colorado | 16.85 |
| 50 | Missouri | 13.44 |
| 51 | Nevada | 7.22 |
| | U.S. Average | 49.33 |

Data Source: U.S. Department of Commerce

## PER CAPITA STATE AND LOCAL SOLID WASTE MANAGEMENT EXPENDITURES: NEW YORK VS. U.S.

In 1992-93, New York's per capita state and local solid waste management expenditures outpaced the national average by 122.7 percent—$109.84 in New York versus $49.33 across the nation.

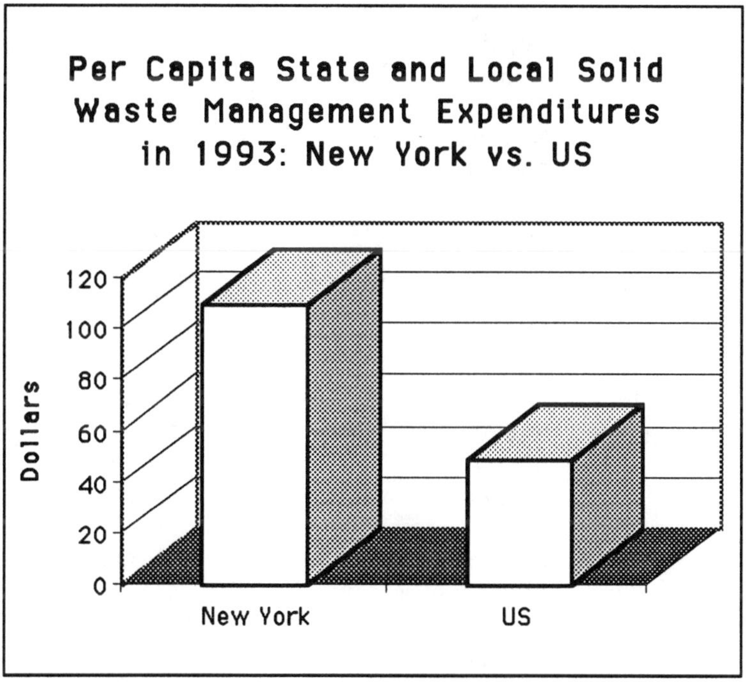


Data Source: U.S. Department of Commerce

# PER CAPITA STATE AND LOCAL TOTAL CAPITAL OUTLAYS: STATE RANKINGS

In 1992-93, New York's per capita state and local total capital outlays ranked the eighth highest in the nation.

**Per Capita State and Local Total Capital Outlays**

| Rank | State | Per Capita Capital Outlays |
|---|---|---|
| 1 | Alaska | $1,511.02 |
| 2 | Hawaii | 1,312.23 |
| 3 | Washington | 1,220.57 |
| 4 | District of Columbia | 1,007.02 |
| 5 | Nevada | 863.49 |
| 6 | Wyoming | 845.88 |
| 7 | Colorado | 785.82 |
| **8** | **New York** | **720.23** |
| 9 | Minnesota | 691.10 |
| 10 | Nebraska | 624.48 |
| 11 | Delaware | 604.17 |
| 12 | Arizona | 598.12 |
| 13 | Florida | 596.04 |
| 14 | Utah | 576.34 |
| 15 | Wisconsin | 570.86 |
| 16 | Texas | 557.43 |
| 17 | New Mexico | 553.75 |
| 18 | Illinois | 538.67 |
| 19 | Georgia | 535.89 |
| 20 | Iowa | 518.43 |
| 21 | Connecticut | 515.00 |
| 22 | South Carolina | 514.97 |
| 23 | Massachusetts | 512.13 |
| 24 | Rhode Island | 503.13 |
| 25 | California | 491.50 |
| 26 | Oregon | 488.63 |
| 27 | South Dakota | 485.97 |

*continued*

*continued*

| Rank | State | Per Capita Capital Outlays |
|---|---|---|
| 28 | Kentucky | 466.22 |
| 29 | Kansas | 463.35 |
| 30 | New Jersey | 456.67 |
| 31 | Montana | 453.39 |
| 32 | North Carolina | 451.38 |
| 33 | Tennessee | 444.35 |
| 34 | Ohio | 443.85 |
| 35 | Idaho | 436.52 |
| 36 | Indiana | 434.92 |
| 37 | Maryland | 432.18 |
| 38 | Virginia | 420.54 |
| 39 | Missouri | 413.65 |
| 40 | North Dakota | 411.14 |
| 41 | Alabama | 409.85 |
| 42 | Pennsylvania | 379.34 |
| 43 | Oklahoma | 367.28 |
| 44 | Maine | 364.33 |
| 45 | Louisiana | 363.85 |
| 46 | West Virginia | 363.53 |
| 47 | Michigan | 361.73 |
| 48 | Arkansas | 342.92 |
| 49 | Mississippi | 332.89 |
| 50 | Vermont | 326.07 |
| 51 | New Hampshire | 269.98 |
| | U.S. Average | 527.45 |

Data Source: U.S. Department of Commerce

## PER CAPITA STATE AND LOCAL TOTAL CAPITAL OUTLAYS: NEW YORK VS. U.S.

In 1992-93, New York's per capita state and local total capital outlays exceeded the state and local average by 40.8 percent—$720.23 in New York versus a $527.45 U.S. average.

Between 1972 and 1993, real (1993 dollars) per capita state and local capital outlays actually declined in New York by 6.3 percent—$768.89 in 1972 to $720.23 in 1993. However, the interesting dynamic, illustrated in the chart, is the dramatic drop in real per capita capital spending between 1972 and 1982 and then a dramatic rise from 1982 to 1993. Indeed, between 1982 and 1993, real per capita outlays grew by 78 percent.

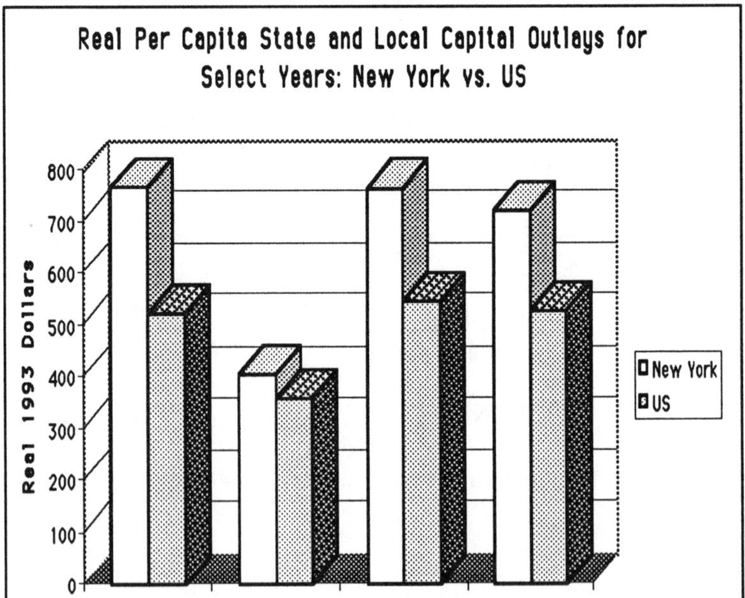


Data Source: U.S. Department of Commerce

# PER CAPITA STATE-ONLY TOTAL CAPITAL OUTLAYS: STATE RANKINGS

In 1994, New York's per capita state total capital outlays ranked fifteenth in the nation.

**Per Capita State Total Capital Outlays**

| Rank | State | Per Capita Capital Outlays |
|---|---|---|
| 1 | Hawaii | $939.15 |
| 2 | Alaska | 828.98 |
| 3 | Wyoming | 535.19 |
| 4 | Delaware | 361.42 |
| 5 | Massachusetts | 358.81 |
| 6 | Rhode Island | 334.28 |
| 7 | South Dakota | 327.72 |
| 8 | Montana | 326.00 |
| 9 | Connecticut | 304.18 |
| 10 | Washington | 299.94 |
| 11 | West Virginia | 295.80 |
| 12 | North Dakota | 295.14 |
| 13 | Nevada | 285.47 |
| 14 | Idaho | 285.15 |
| **15** | **New York** | **282.02** |
| 16 | South Carolina | 276.31 |
| 17 | New Jersey | 271.46 |
| 18 | Nebraska | 253.92 |
| 19 | Vermont | 240.98 |
| 20 | Iowa | 239.82 |
| 21 | Utah | 237.76 |
| 22 | Kentucky | 236.07 |
| 23 | Kansas | 222.30 |
| 24 | New Mexico | 217.19 |
| 25 | Tennessee | 208.32 |
| 26 | Georgia | 207.24 |
| 27 | Mississippi | 204.63 |
| 28 | Florida | 201.98 |

*continued*

*continued*

| Rank | State | Per Capita Capital Outlays |
|---|---|---|
| 29 | Louisiana | 200.91 |
| 30 | North Carolina | 195.38 |
| 31 | Arkansas | 191.71 |
| 32 | Ohio | 191.14 |
| 33 | Maryland | 183.34 |
| 34 | Alabama | 181.82 |
| 35 | Texas | 178.93 |
| 36 | Virginia | 174.04 |
| 37 | Colorado | 173.46 |
| 38 | Minnesota | 171.86 |
| 39 | Illinois | 171.17 |
| 40 | Oregon | 168.06 |
| 41 | Indiana | 166.39 |
| 42 | Wisconsin | 165.92 |
| 43 | Michigan | 160.48 |
| 44 | Maine | 159.59 |
| 45 | Arizona | 152.65 |
| 46 | Oklahoma | 152.08 |
| 47 | New Hampshire | 149.47 |
| 48 | Missouri | 140.68 |
| 49 | Pennsylvania | 131.80 |
| 50 | California | 126.71 |
| | U.S. Average | 203.29 |

Data Source: U.S. Department of Commerce

## PER CAPITA STATE-ONLY TOTAL CAPITAL OUTLAYS: NEW YORK VS. U.S.

In 1994, New York's per capita state total capital outlays outpaced the national average by 38.7 percent—$282.02 in New York versus $203.29 for the state average.

Between 1965 and 1994, real per capita state capital outlays grew by 66.5 percent. In 1994 dollars, New York's per capita state capital outlays equaled $169.39.

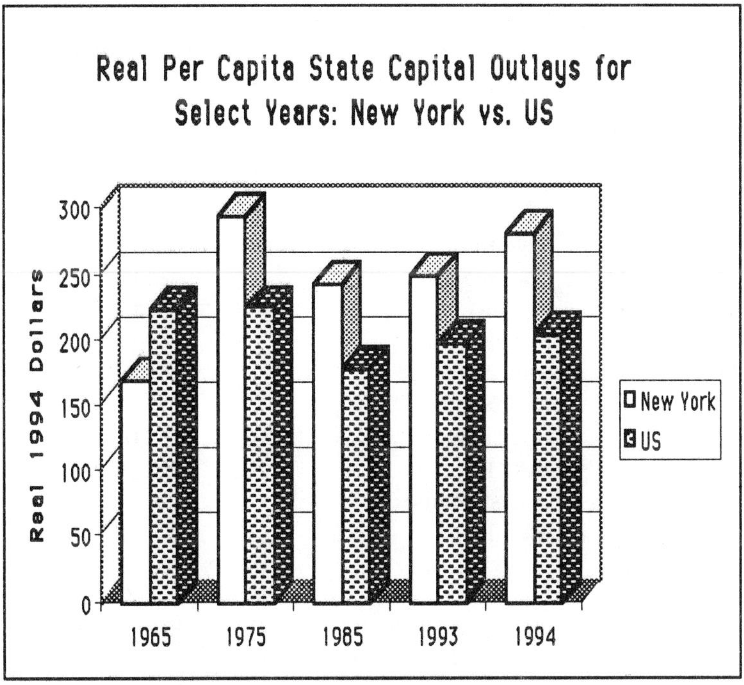


Data Source: U.S. Department of Commerce

# PER CAPITA STATE AND LOCAL INTEREST PAID ON DEBT: STATE RANKINGS

In 1992-93, New York's per capita state and local interest paid on debt ranked fourth highest in the nation.

**Per Capita State and Local Interest on Debt**

| Rank | State | Per Capita Interest on Debt |
|---|---|---|
| 1 | Alaska | $1,148.21 |
| 2 | District of Columbia | 629.29 |
| 3 | Delaware | 444.08 |
| **4** | **New York** | **426.94** |
| 5 | Utah | 370.27 |
| 6 | Rhode Island | 362.55 |
| 7 | New Hampshire | 351.15 |
| 8 | Massachusetts | 346.49 |
| 9 | Colorado | 345.31 |
| 10 | Hawaii | 322.60 |
| 11 | Wyoming | 322.08 |
| 12 | Washington | 315.05 |
| 13 | Arizona | 312.09 |
| 14 | Connecticut | 309.47 |
| 15 | Minnesota | 306.73 |
| 16 | Kentucky | 293.54 |
| 17 | Louisiana | 288.07 |
| 18 | New Jersey | 288.06 |
| 19 | Pennsylvania | 276.83 |
| 20 | Florida | 274.78 |
| 21 | Nevada | 257.02 |
| 22 | Texas | 255.75 |
| 23 | Nebraska | 253.03 |
| 24 | Maryland | 247.71 |
| 25 | Illinois | 234.42 |
| 26 | South Dakota | 230.49 |
| 27 | Vermont | 230.31 |
| 28 | California | 229.60 |

*continued*

*continued*

| Rank | State | Per Capita Interest on Debt |
|---|---|---|
| 29 | Montana | 226.34 |
| 30 | West Virginia | 225.39 |
| 31 | Oregon | 224.05 |
| 32 | Maine | 222.24 |
| 33 | North Dakota | 211.13 |
| 34 | Wisconsin | 210.29 |
| 35 | South Carolina | 204.29 |
| 36 | Georgia | 200.45 |
| 37 | Kansas | 199.46 |
| 38 | Virginia | 198.52 |
| 39 | New Mexico | 188.27 |
| 40 | Alabama | 181.73 |
| 41 | North Carolina | 177.78 |
| 42 | Oklahoma | 177.77 |
| 43 | Michigan | 167.73 |
| 44 | Ohio | 164.07 |
| 45 | Tennessee | 163.67 |
| 46 | Missouri | 152.08 |
| 47 | Indiana | 140.94 |
| 48 | Arkansas | 135.12 |
| 49 | Iowa | 133.00 |
| 50 | Mississippi | 130.54 |
| 51 | Idaho | 128.15 |
| | U.S. Average | 251.28 |

Source: U.S. Department of Commerce

## PER CAPITA STATE AND LOCAL INTEREST PAID ON DEBT: NEW YORK VS. U.S.

In 1992-93, New York's per capita state and local interest paid on debt surpassed the national average by 69.9 percent—$426.94 in New York versus a state and local average of $251.28.

Between 1962 and 1993, New York's real per capita state and local interest paid on debt increased by 365.2 percent. In 1962, New York's per capita interest paid on debt equaled $91.77, in 1993 dollars.

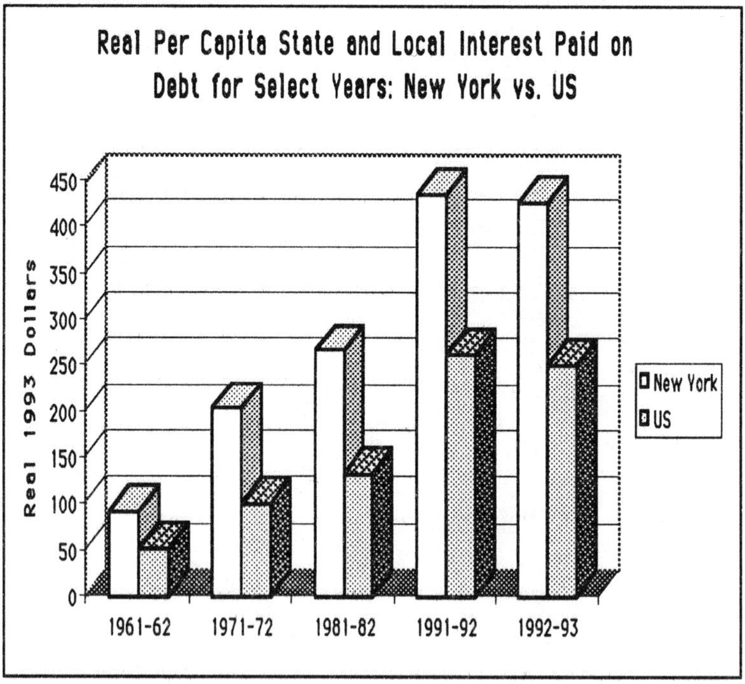


Data Source: U.S. Department of Commerce

## PER CAPITA STATE-ONLY INTEREST PAID ON DEBT: STATE RANKINGS

In 1994, New York's per capita state interest paid on debt ranked eighth in the nation.

**Per Capita State Interest on Debt**

| Rank | State | Per Capita Interest on Debt |
|---|---|---|
| 1 | Alaska | $581.61 |
| 2 | New Hampshire | 316.49 |
| 3 | Delaware | 316.46 |
| 4 | Rhode Island | 297.01 |
| 5 | Massachusetts | 241.06 |
| 6 | Hawaii | 234.56 |
| 7 | Connecticut | 231.07 |
| **8** | **New York** | **203.84** |
| 9 | New Jersey | 165.20 |
| 10 | Vermont | 159.73 |
| 11 | South Dakota | 158.47 |
| 12 | Maine | 148.62 |
| 13(t) | Montana | 120.78 |
| 13(t) | Oregon | 120.78 |
| 15 | Wyoming | 117.81 |
| 16 | Illinois | 110.83 |
| 17 | Wisconsin | 108.39 |
| 18 | Louisiana | 107.14 |
| 19 | Kentucky | 96.59 |
| 20 | Maryland | 95.79 |
| 21 | South Carolina | 95.16 |
| 22 | Pennsylvania | 94.97 |
| 23 | North Dakota | 90.45 |
| 24 | Washington | 84.85 |
| 25 | West Virginia | 83.94 |
| 26 | Idaho | 80.32 |
| 27 | California | 77.50 |
| 28 | Oklahoma | 76.34 |

*continued*

*continued*

| Rank | State | Per Capita Interest on Debt |
|---|---|---|
| 29 | Missouri | 73.80 |
| 30 | Virginia | 72.62 |
| 31 | Nevada | 71.14 |
| 32 | Colorado | 68.75 |
| 33 | Ohio | 68.47 |
| 34 | Utah | 66.91 |
| 35 | Nebraska | 66.04 |
| 36 | Michigan | 65.27 |
| 37 | Florida | 61.92 |
| 38 | New Mexico | 59.83 |
| 39 | Alabama | 59.41 |
| 40 | Minnesota | 58.62 |
| 41 | Georgia | 53.24 |
| 42 | Indiana | 52.80 |
| 43 | Arkansas | 47.18 |
| 44 | Arizona | 46.66 |
| 45 | Iowa | 45.30 |
| 46 | Mississippi | 44.95 |
| 47 | Tennessee | 35.78 |
| 48 | North Carolina | 34.13 |
| 49 | Texas | 28.96 |
| 50 | Kansas | 23.50 |
| | U.S. Average | 94.09 |

Data Source: U.S. Department of Commerce

## PER CAPITA STATE-ONLY INTEREST PAID ON DEBT: NEW YORK VS. U.S.

In 1994, New York's per capita state interest paid on debt exceeded the state average by 116.6 percent—$203.84 in New York versus $94.09 as the national average.

Between 1965 and 1994, New York's real per capita interest paid on state debt increased by 494.1 percent. In 1994 dollars, New York's 1965 real per capita interest equaled $34.31.

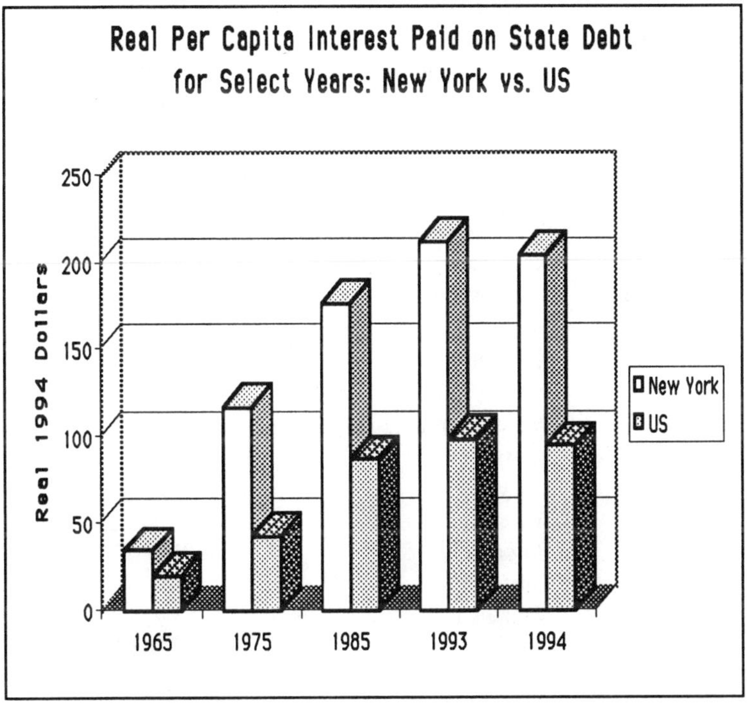


Data Source: U.S. Department of Commerce

## PER CAPITA STATE AND LOCAL DEBT: STATE RANKINGS

In 1992-93, New York's per capita state and local debt ranked third highest in the nation.

**Per Capita State and Local Debt**

| Rank | State | Per Capita Debt |
|---|---|---|
| 1 | Alaska | $13,803.75 |
| 2 | District of Columbia | 8,788.76 |
| **3** | **New York** | **6,766.71** |
| 4 | Delaware | 6,759.14 |
| 5 | Hawaii | 5,786.61 |
| 6 | Massachusetts | 5,730.88 |
| 7 | Rhode Island | 5,698.04 |
| 8 | Utah | 5,695.16 |
| 9 | Washington | 5,686.96 |
| 10 | New Hampshire | 5,571.22 |
| 11 | Connecticut | 5,130.80 |
| 12 | Arizona | 4,771.10 |
| 13 | Nevada | 4,735.81 |
| 14 | New Jersey | 4,725.42 |
| 15 | Minnesota | 4,642.85 |
| 16 | Kentucky | 4,572.90 |
| 17 | Florida | 4,309.14 |
| 18 | Pennsylvania | 4,228.23 |
| 19 | Louisiana | 4,163.73 |
| 20 | Maryland | 4,051.06 |
| 21 | Wyoming | 4,042.13 |
| 22 | Colorado | 4,036.75 |
| 23 | California | 3,950.11 |
| 24 | Nebraska | 3,838.30 |
| 25 | Texas | 3,801.26 |
| 26 | Illinois | 3,718.83 |
| 27 | Maine | 3,641.41 |
| 28 | Oregon | 3,526.71 |
| 29 | West Virginia | 3,505.39 |

*continued*

*continued*

| Rank | State | Per Capita Debt |
|---|---|---|
| 30 | South Dakota | 3,356.68 |
| 31 | Wisconsin | 3,305.15 |
| 32 | Vermont | 3,296.53 |
| 33 | Montana | 3,205.62 |
| 34 | Virginia | 3,182.70 |
| 35 | Kansas | 3,169.25 |
| 36 | South Carolina | 3,050.37 |
| 37 | Georgia | 2,912.87 |
| 38 | North Dakota | 2,797.23 |
| 39 | Michigan | 2,787.29 |
| 40 | New Mexico | 2,782.83 |
| 41 | Alabama | 2,734.06 |
| 42 | Oklahoma | 2,733.42 |
| 43 | North Carolina | 2,675.86 |
| 44 | Tennessee | 2,460.66 |
| 45 | Ohio | 2,392.04 |
| 46 | Missouri | 2,292.63 |
| 47 | Indiana | 2,239.50 |
| 48 | Arkansas | 2,049.58 |
| 49 | Iowa | 1,985.42 |
| 50 | Mississippi | 1,964.50 |
| 51 | Idaho | 1,825.43 |
| | U.S. Average | 3,941.69 |

Data Source: U.S. Department of Commerce

## PER CAPITA STATE AND LOCAL DEBT: NEW YORK VS. U.S.

In 1992-93, New York's per capita state and local debt surpassed the U.S. average by 71.7 percent—$6,766.71 in New York versus the national average of $3,941.69.

Between 1962 and 1993, New York's real per capita state and local debt grew by 77.3 percent. In 1993 dollars, New York state and local debt stood at $3,817.18 in 1962.

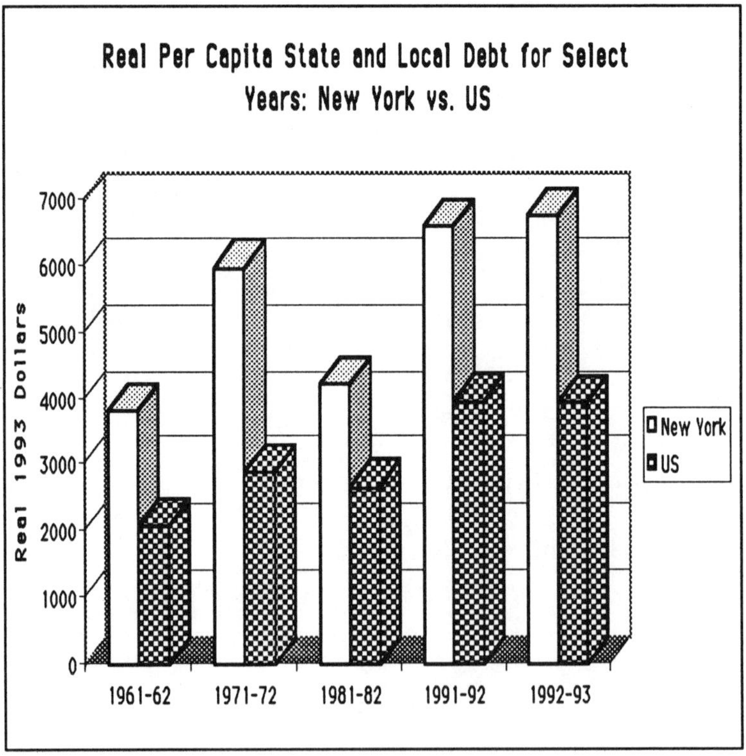


Data Source: U.S. Department of Commerce

## PER CAPITA STATE-ONLY DEBT: STATE RANKINGS

In 1994, New York's per capita state debt ranked eighth highest in the nation.

**Per Capita State Debt**

| Rank | State | Per Capita Debt |
|---|---|---|
| 1 | Alaska | $5,916.27 |
| 2 | Rhode Island | 5,560.53 |
| 3 | New Hampshire | 4,969.93 |
| 4 | Delaware | 4,812.29 |
| 5 | Massachusetts | 4,416.58 |
| 6 | Hawaii | 4,364.55 |
| 7 | Connecticut | 4,152.44 |
| **8** | **New York** | **3,581.69** |
| 9 | New Jersey | 2,896.53 |
| 10 | Vermont | 2,706.70 |
| 11 | Montana | 2,462.08 |
| 12 | Maine | 2,413.51 |
| 13 | South Dakota | 2,330.77 |
| 14 | Louisiana | 2,035.22 |
| 15 | Oregon | 1,829.28 |
| 16 | Maryland | 1,823.80 |
| 17 | Kentucky | 1,762.13 |
| 18 | Illinois | 1,732.07 |
| 19 | Washington | 1,547.00 |
| 20 | California | 1,530.99 |
| 21 | Wisconsin | 1,524.51 |
| 22 | Wyoming | 1,475.78 |
| 23 | West Virginia | 1,385.92 |
| 24 | South Carolina | 1,357.10 |
| 25 | Missouri | 1,225.13 |
| 26 | Michigan | 1,211.60 |
| 27 | Virginia | 1,207.57 |
| 28 | Oklahoma | 1,188.64 |
| 29 | North Dakota | 1,186.00 |

*continued*

*continued*

| Rank | State | Per Capita Debt |
|---|---|---|
| 30 | Nevada | 1,156.17 |
| 31 | Pennsylvania | 1,134.33 |
| 32 | Idaho | 1,130.40 |
| 33 | Utah | 1,102.11 |
| 34 | Ohio | 1,091.46 |
| 35 | New Mexico | 1,049.08 |
| 36 | Florida | 1,043.88 |
| 37 | Indiana | 968.79 |
| 38 | Minnesota | 952.81 |
| 39 | Alabama | 913.44 |
| 40 | Nebraska | 904.75 |
| 41 | Colorado | 892.48 |
| 42 | Arizona | 778.03 |
| 43 | Mississippi | 774.15 |
| 44 | Arkansas | 738.69 |
| 45 | Georgia | 733.38 |
| 46 | Iowa | 703.53 |
| 47 | North Carolina | 641.08 |
| 48 | Texas | 510.28 |
| 49 | Tennessee | 507.71 |
| 50 | Kansas | 431.98 |
| | U.S. Average | 1,578.64 |

Data Source: U.S. Department of Commerce

## PER CAPITA STATE-ONLY DEBT: NEW YORK VS. U.S.

In 1994, New York's per capita state debt exceeded the state average by 126.9 percent—$3,581.69 in New York versus the national average of $1,578.64.

Between 1965 and 1994, real per capita state debt increased by 234.1 percent. In 1994 dollars, New York's per capita state debt equaled $1,072.02.

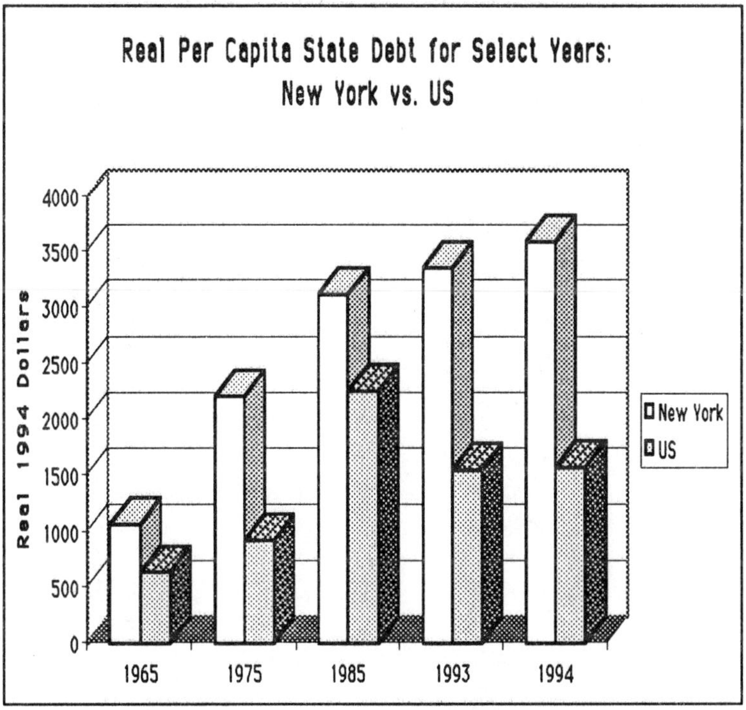


Data Source: U.S. Department of Commerce

# PER CAPITA STATE AND LOCAL EXPENDITURES ON SALARIES AND WAGES: STATE RANKINGS

In 1992-93, New York's per capita state and local expenditures on salaries and wages ranked third highest in the nation.

**Per Capita State and Local Salaries and Wages**

| Rank | State | Per Capita Salaries and Wages |
|---|---|---|
| 1 | District of Columbia | $3,479.43 |
| 2 | Alaska | 3,038.19 |
| **3** | **New York** | **2,275.38** |
| 4 | Wyoming | 2,142.55 |
| 5 | New Jersey | 1,828.35 |
| 6 | Connecticut | 1,766.85 |
| 7 | Washington | 1,754.39 |
| 8 | Hawaii | 1,705.55 |
| 9 | California | 1,700.94 |
| 10 | Minnesota | 1,689.80 |
| 11 | Nebraska | 1,651.14 |
| 12 | Delaware | 1,620.02 |
| 13 | Iowa | 1,611.59 |
| 14 | Colorado | 1,595.15 |
| 15 | Michigan | 1,584.06 |
| 16 | Vermont | 1,565.10 |
| 17 | Massachusetts | 1,562.48 |
| 18 | Nevada | 1,561.47 |
| 19 | Oregon | 1,560.27 |
| 20 | Kansas | 1,533.25 |
| 21 | Wisconsin | 1,525.44 |
| 22 | Maryland | 1,514.23 |
| 23 | South Carolina | 1,453.88 |
| 24 | Illinois | 1,453.68 |
| 25 | Rhode Island | 1,453.67 |
| 26 | Virginia | 1,447.20 |
| 27 | North Dakota | 1,445.47 |
| 28 | Louisiana | 1,442.43 |

*continued*

*continued*

| Rank | State | Per Capita Salaries and Wages |
|---|---|---|
| 29 | Ohio | 1,413.31 |
| 30 | New Mexico | 1,410.50 |
| 31 | Arizona | 1,392.52 |
| 32 | Georgia | 1,386.68 |
| 33 | Florida | 1,380.98 |
| 34 | Indiana | 1,368.24 |
| 35 | Oklahoma | 1,362.26 |
| 36 | Alabama | 1,338.97 |
| 37 | Montana | 1,330.78 |
| 38 | North Carolina | 1,324.77 |
| 39 | Texas | 1,323.01 |
| 40 | Pennsylvania | 1,310.71 |
| 41 | New Hampshire | 1,297.52 |
| 42 | Utah | 1,296.85 |
| 43 | Idaho | 1,287.58 |
| 44 | Maine | 1,282.70 |
| 45 | South Dakota | 1,247.56 |
| 46 | Kentucky | 1,240.82 |
| 47 | Tennessee | 1,211.66 |
| 48 | West Virginia | 1,202.48 |
| 49 | Arkansas | 1,200.44 |
| 50 | Mississippi | 1,179.19 |
| 51 | Missouri | 1,176.16 |
| | U.S. Average | 1,537.92 |

Data Source: U.S. Department of Commerce

## PER CAPITA STATE AND LOCAL EXPENDITURES ON SALARIES AND WAGES: NEW YORK VS. U.S.

In 1992-93, New York's per capita state and local expenditures on salaries and wages surpassed the national average by 48 percent—$2,275.38 in New York versus $1,537.92 as a state and local average.

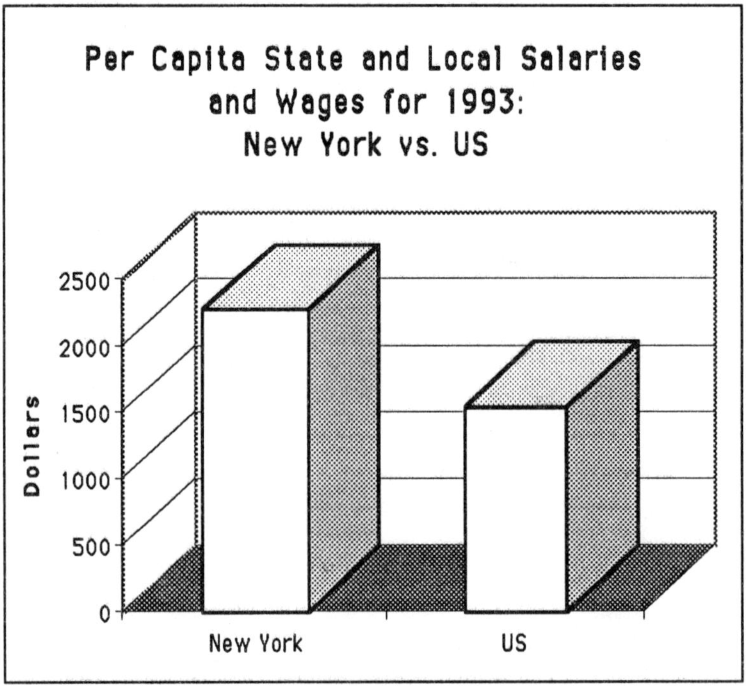


Data Source: U.S. Department of Commerce

## PER CAPITA STATE-ONLY EXPENDITURES ON SALARIES AND WAGES: STATE RANKINGS

In 1994, New York's per capita state expenditures on salaries and wages ranked eighteenth in the nation.

**Per Capita State Salaries and Wages**

| Rank | State | Per Capita Salaries and Wages |
|---|---|---|
| 1 | Alaska | $1,480.33 |
| 2 | Hawaii | 1,401.27 |
| 3 | Delaware | 888.89 |
| 4 | Connecticut | 729.09 |
| 5 | Rhode Island | 676.39 |
| 6 | Iowa | 662.36 |
| 7 | Wyoming | 649.95 |
| 8 | Vermont | 642.19 |
| 9 | North Dakota | 625.89 |
| 10 | Louisiana | 625.71 |
| 11 | South Carolina | 619.03 |
| 12 | Washington | 615.43 |
| 13 | New Mexico | 612.41 |
| 14 | Utah | 591.19 |
| 15 | Nebraska | 554.17 |
| 16 | Alabama | 553.38 |
| 17 | New Jersey | 552.28 |
| **18** | **New York** | **544.23** |
| 19 | Montana | 528.97 |
| 20 | Kentucky | 528.38 |
| 21 | Minnesota | 525.94 |
| 22 | Virginia | 513.90 |
| 23 | Kansas | 511.76 |
| 24 | Oregon | 511.08 |
| 25 | Arkansas | 505.01 |
| 26 | Massachusetts | 493.70 |
| 27 | South Dakota | 487.98 |
| 28 | Oklahoma | 486.33 |

*continued*

*continued*

| Rank | State | Per Capita Salaries and Wages |
|---|---|---|
| 29 | Michigan | 484.29 |
| 30 | Nevada | 481.11 |
| 31 | Colorado | 479.08 |
| 32 | Maine | 462.63 |
| 33 | Maryland | 457.27 |
| 34 | New Hampshire | 449.83 |
| 35 | West Virginia | 449.36 |
| 36 | Idaho | 443.97 |
| 37 | Ohio | 442.25 |
| 38 | Wisconsin | 441.04 |
| 39 | North Carolina | 422.30 |
| 40 | Florida | 402.94 |
| 41 | Tennessee | 399.47 |
| 42 | Indiana | 396.80 |
| 43 | Mississippi | 393.29 |
| 44 | California | 392.97 |
| 45 | Georgia | 385.89 |
| 46 | Pennsylvania | 384.55 |
| 47 | Missouri | 376.18 |
| 48 | Arizona | 371.78 |
| 49 | Illinois | 332.58 |
| 50 | Texas | 317.51 |
| | US Average | 462.18 |

Data Source: U.S. Department of Commerce

## Per Capita State-Only Expenditures on Salaries and Wages: New York vs. U.S.

In 1994, New York's per capita state expenditures on salaries and wages outpaced the U.S. average by 17.8 percent—$544.23 in New York versus the state average of $462.18.

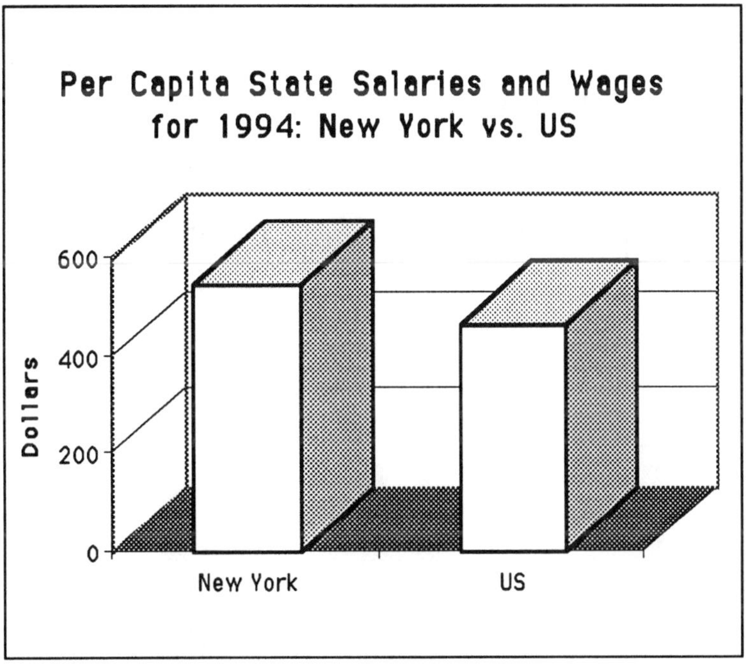


Data Source: U.S. Department of Commerce

## SALARIES OF TOP NEW YORK STATE OFFICIALS

New York State top officials are well paid. The state legislators' salary of $57,500 is a mere base, with most earning $6,500 to $30,000 more by serving on various committees. By the way, state legislator is a part-time job.

**Current Salaries of New York State Top Officials**

| | |
|---|---|
| • Governor: | $130,000 |
| • Lt. Governor: | $110,000 |
| • State Legislators | $ 57,500 |
| • Comptroller | $110,000 |

## Tardy State Budgets

The New York State fiscal year begins on April 1. Since 1980, the state budget has been passed on time in only three years. The budget has been late every year since 1985.

**Dates New York State Budget Was Passed—**
**Fiscal Year Starts on April 1**

| Year | Date Budget Passed | |
|---|---|---|
| 1980 | March 31 | |
| 1981 | May 12 | (42 days late) |
| 1982 | May 4 | (34 days late) |
| 1983 | March 28 | |
| 1984 | March 31 | |
| 1985 | April 5 | (5 days late) |
| 1986 | April 5 | (5 days late) |
| 1987 | April 11 | (11 days late) |
| 1988 | April 20 | (20 days late) |
| 1989 | April 19 | (19 days late) |
| 1990 | May 19 | (49 days late) |
| 1991 | July 4 | (94 days late) |
| 1992 | April 2 | (2 days late) |
| 1993 | April 5 | (5 days late) |
| 1994 | June 8 | (69 days late) |
| 1995 | June 7 | (68 days late) |
| 1996 | July 13 | (104 days late) |

## NEW YORK STATE BUDGET BY DEPARTMENT

The following is a list of the major departments in New York State government and their total 1995-96 budgets. (Source: New York State *1996-97 Executive Budget, Appendix I*)

| Department | Total Budget 1995-96 |
|---|---|
| Department of Health | $20,529,560,140 |
| State Education Department | 12,418,075,991 |
| Department of Social Services | 10,578,254,585 |
| Department of Transportation | 4,582,197,500 |
| Department of Labor | 4,424,795,220 |
| State University of New York (total) | 3,644,860,883 |
| City University of New York (total) | 2,358,522,475 |
| Office of Mental Retardation and Developmental Disabilities | 1,950,424,595 |
| Department of Correctional Services | 1,873,460,800 |
| Office of Mental Health | 1,870,522,200 |
| New York State Higher Education Services Corporation | 835,367,600 |
| Department of Environmental Conservation | 596,231,800 |
| Office of General Services | 432,592,100 |
| Office of Alcoholism and Substance Abuse | 418,619,500 |
| Division of Youth | 333,335,080 |
| Department of Taxation and Finance | 309,260,500 |
| State Insurance Fund | 291,615,800 |
| Division of State Police | 282,560,200 |
| Metropolitan Transit Authority | 238,700,000 |
| Department of Motor Vehicles | 198,476,500 |
| Office of Parks, Recreation and Historic Preservation | 181,739,720 |
| Division of Housing and Community Renewal | 180,734,950 |
| Division of Parole | 171,142,600 |
| Office of the Aging | 163,450,204 |
| Department of Criminal Justice Services | 133,483,406 |
| Department of Audit and Control | 128,413,400 |
| Department of Law | 115,824,100 |

*continued*

*continued*

| Department | Total Budget 1995-96 |
|---|---|
| Department of State | 98,764,583 |
| State of New York Mortgage Agency | 97,300,000 |
| Division of the Lottery | 96,282,000 |
| Empire State Development Corporation (formerly the Urban Development Corporation) | 92,347,276 |
| Division of Probation and Correctional Alternatives | 92,070,000 |
| Department of Agriculture and Markets | 87,810,800 |
| Insurance Department | 86,669,200 |
| Public Service Department | 65,281,500 |
| Division of Military and Naval Affairs | 64,471,300 |
| Banking Department | 51,072,400 |
| Department of Economic Development | 50,254,950 |
| Office of Real Property Services | 41,088,100 |
| Housing Trust Fund Corporation | 41,000,000 |
| New York State Energy Research and Development Authority | 36,421,000 |
| Council on the Arts | 36,048,600 |
| Division of the Budget | 34,491,213 |
| New York State Science and Technology Foundation | 34,150,000 |
| Crime Victims Board | 28,032,000 |
| Affordable Housing Corporation | 25,000,000 |
| Facilities Development Corporation | 20,052,000 |
| State Racing and Wagering Board | 13,627,700 |
| Division of Human Rights | 12,118,000 |
| Division of Alcoholic Beverage Control | 11,499,300 |
| Executive Chamber | 10,468,800 |
| Commission on Quality of Care for the Mentally Disabled | 9,805,700 |
| Olympic Regional Development Authority | 7,716,000 |
| Division of Veterans' Affairs | 6,984,100 |
| Office of Employee Relations | 6,301,100 |
| Development Disabilities Planning Council | 4,658,000 |
| Capital Defender Office | 4,500,000 |
| Adirondack Park Agency | 3,559,000 |
| Public Employment Relations Board | 3,373,000 |

*continued*

*continued*

| Department | Total Budget 1995-96 |
|---|---|
| Environmental Facilities Corporation | 3,322,700 |
| Division of Tax Appeal | 3,174,100 |
| Housing Finance Agency | 2,815,000 |
| State Board of Elections | 2,699,100 |
| State Consumer Protection Board | 2,610,600 |
| Governor's Office of Regulatory Reform | 2,367,900 |
| Commission of Correction | 2,216,100 |
| Office for the Prevention of Domestic Violence | 2,107,400 |
| New York State Thruway Authority | 2,000,000 |
| Temporary State Commission of Investigation | 1,941,000 |
| Office of Advocate for Persons with Disabilities | 1,873,000 |
| Judicial Commissions | 1,698,100 |
| Council on Children and Families | 1,679,600 |
| Office of the Inspector General | 1,496,000 |
| Harlem Community Development Corporation | 888,000 |
| Low-Level Radioactive Waste Siting Commission | 868,000 |
| Institute for Nonviolence | 500,000 |
| Temporary State Commission on Lobbying | 482,500 |
| Office of Lt. Governor | 340,600 |
| St. Lawrence-Eastern Ontario Commission | 79,100 |

## THE NEW YORK PORK BARREL

The following serves as a *very small* sample of pork items from the New York State budgets for 1993-94, 1994-95, 1995-96, and 1996-97. Remember the following list may seem lengthy, but it does not even come close to scratching the surface. In reality, each state budget contains hundreds of pages—in small print—filled with special-interest spending items that run into the billions of dollars annually.

**1993-94 New York State Budget Pork—A Small Sample**

• $100,000 for renovations to Murname Field, a baseball stadium in Utica.
• $250,000 for the National Soccer Hall of Fame in Oneonta.
• $100,000 for preliminary work on a swimming pool and diving center for the 1998 International Goodwill Games.
• $13 million for public television and radio in New York.
• $150,000 for the Utica Zoo.
• $610,000 to assist Long Island small businesses in reducing their dependency on defense contractors.
• $1,840 for the Leisure Club of Mineola, Long Island.
• $300,000 for the New York State Wine/Grape Foundation.
• $50,000 for a grape entomologist.
• $1 million for Finger Lakes Aquatic Vegetation Control program.
• $100,000 for New York/Long Island seafood promotion.
• $100,000 for the Nassau/Suffolk [Counties] School Superintendents Association.
• $5,000 for the Hempstead Hispanic Association.
• $25,000 for the Protection Animal Welfare Society (PAWS).
• $100,000 for the Lewis County Agricultural Society.
• $243,000 for the Small Business Innovation Research Matching Grants Program.
• $155,000 for Black Vets for Social Justice.
• $5,000 for 9 to 5, the National Association of Working Women.
• $100,000 for the New Berman Fire Hall.
• $50,000 for a feasibility study on an Adirondack Railroad.
• $20,000 for Long Island Railroad parking meters in the Village of Freeport.
• $10,000 for the Nassau County Girl Scouts of America and $10,000

for the Nassau County Boy Scouts of America.
• $15,000 for the South Shore YM-YWCA.
• $50,000 for the New York State Small Business Development Center at Corning Community College and $350,000 for the Small Business Development Center at the State University of New York.
• $75,000 for the Tilles Center—a concert hall—at Long Island University and $20,000 for LIU's Center on Aging.
• $65,000 for Hofstra University and $25,000 for Molloy College in 1993-94, and $220,000 for a communications network at Marist College.
• $150,000 for the Lower Great Lakes Information Center.
• $150,000 for the New York State/Latino Policy Institute.
• $228,920 for the Adirondack North Country Association.
• $147,500 for the Greenway Heritage Conservancy for the Hudson River Valley, along with $147,500 for the Hudson River Valley Greenway Communities Council.
• $500,000 for the Syracuse Symphony, $15,000 for the National Symphony, $3,000 for the Long Island Choral Society, $15,000 for the National Grand Opera, $250,000 for the Long Island Philharmonic, $200,000 for the Buffalo Philharmonic Orchestra, $100,000 for the National Actors Theater, $125,000 for the Friends of the Arts, $50,000 for the New York City Ballet, $100,000 for the New York City Philharmonic, and $50,000 for the Lincoln Center for the Performing Arts.
• $53 million for the state's Department of Economic Development—a 34 percent hike over the previous year's spending level—including $449,000 for "entrepreneurial assistance," $2.23 million for "economic development skills training," $250,000 for Hofstra University to develop a business development center, $50,000 to evaluate a plan for building an all-purpose sports arena in Nassau County, $500,000 for "assessing and improving the competitiveness of forest industry firms of fewer than 200 employees," and $15,000 for the Franklin Square Chamber of Commerce.

**1994-95 New York State Budget Pork—A Small Sample**

• More than $143 million for sports stadiums and facilities across the state.
• $350,000 for the World University Games, broken down between $100,000 for a pool on the Town of Tonawanda and $250,000 to the

Greater Buffalo Athletic Corporation.

• $17 million for public television and radio.

• $348,200 for the "Dairy Farm Productivity and Profitability" project.

• $100,000 for a study on the impact of real property taxes on agricultural profitability.

• $500,000 for the "design and implementation of a technology-based program to improve agricultural commodities production."

• Over $700,000 supporting local fairs.

• $500,000 for the New York State Wine/Grape Foundation.

• $50,000 for a grape entomologist.

• $1 million for Finger Lakes Aquatic Vegetation Control program.

• $100,000 for New York/Long Island seafood promotion.

• $5,000 for the Hempstead Hispanic Association.

• $4 million for the Small Business Technology Investment Program, designed to provide "seed, early stage, and working capital financing for small to medium-sized technology firms."

• Hofstra University received $750,000 for its Business Development Center.

• $935,000 for "parenting education programs."

• $130,000 for the construction of artificial dunes for the Village of Asharoken.

• $10 million for the acquisition of pine barrens land on Long Island.

• $150,000 for the Long Island Arborist Association's Oak Trees on Long Island program.

• The state Department of Economic Development's budget leaped by 20 percent to more than $64 million. The most fatty pork this year included more than $2 million for "entrepreneurial assistance," more than $3.2 million for "economic development skills training," $1.9 million for the Department of Economic Development/State University of New York/City University of New York Strategic Training Partnership for Industrial Modernization, $250,000 for Labor/Management Collaboration Assistance project, $250,000 for the Garment Industry Development Corporation (which received an additional $75,000 elsewhere in the state budget), $500,000 for the Forest Industry Development Program, $250,000 for the Office of Recycling and Market Development to establish the Empire State Center for Recycling Enterprise Development, $300,000 for a design and construction study for the Sports and Entertainment Center on Long Island, $50,000 for the United Auto Workers Retraining Program, more than $2 million for the Minority and Women-Owned Business

Development Program, and over $3.8 million for the Defense Diversification/Economic Adjustment Program.

• The state spent lavishly on local chambers of commerce, including $25,000 for the Canandaigua Chamber of Commerce, $110,000 for the Huntington Township Chamber of Commerce, $15,000 for the Jamaica Chamber of Commerce, and $50,000 for the Sullivan County Chamber of Commerce.

• $200,000 for AIDS education in elementary and secondary schools.

• $18.6 million for "family planning services."

• $2 million for magnetic levitation systems projects.

• $100,000 for left-turn traffic signals on Northern Blvd. in Queens County.

• $280,000 for the Amsterdam Local Waterfront Revitalization Project.

• $50,000 for the New York State National Abortion Rights Action League.

**1995-96 New York State Budget Pork—A Small Sample**

• $250,000 for the Brooklyn Sports Facility Commission.

• $3.6 million for the Olympic Facilities Operations Program.

• $13 million for public television and radio.

• $15,000 for asbestos removal for the Veterans of Foreign Wars Mineville Post 5802.

• $10,000 for the Korean War Veterans Association.

• $3,000 to the American Legion Continental Post 1424 for a Memorial Day Parade.

• $348,200 for the "Dairy Farm Productivity and Profitability" project.

• More than $500,000 supporting local fairs.

• $500,000 for the New York State Wine/Grape Foundation.

• $50,000 for the East End Economic and Environmental Institute Wine Symposium.

• $50,000 for a grape entomologist.

• $1 million for Finger Lakes Aquatic Vegetation Control program.

• $10,000 to the Beartown Ski Area.

• $50,000 for the New York Ski Educational Foundation.

• $375,000 for ski lift improvements and a new snow groomer at the state's Belleayre Mountain Ski Center.

• $4.1 million for "health and safety" projects at the state's Olympic venues and the Gore Mountain Ski Center.

• $1.3 million for "rehabilitation and improvements" to the Roosevelt

Island aerial tram stations.
• $480,000 for local planning grants related to canal developments.
• $225,000 for services and expenses of purchasing the Leatherstocking Railroad from Cooperstown Junction to Cooperstown.
• $42,000 for the Brooklyn Tenants Council.
• $13 million for the Centers for Advanced Technology.
• $700,000 for the Bio-Manufacturing Facility.
• $3.03 million for the operations of the Staten Island Ferry.
• $2,000 for the New York City Community Sailing Association.
• $506,400 for "parenting education programs."
• $258,000 for the Greenway Heritage Conservancy for the Hudson River Valley, along with $228,600 for the Hudson River Valley Greenway Communities Council.
• More than $22 million to orchestras, dance companies, museums and theater groups through the Council on the Arts.
• $21,500 for the Attica Rodeo and Show Association.
• $88,000 for the Society for the Preservation of Long Island Antiquities to buy the Cold Spring Harbor Methodist Church for the society's headquarters.
• $88,000 for the Ketcham Inn Foundation to restore an inn and former stagecoach stop in Center Moriches.
• $79,000 for Long Island's Nature Conservancy.
• $11,500 for operating expenses at the Cold Spring Harbor Fish Hatchery.
• $1.5 million to the Bronx Zoo from the state's Natural Heritage Trust.
• $10,000 for the Museum of Television and Radio.
• $1,500 for the Sacred Music Society of Our Lady Queen of Martyrs Church.
• $275,000 for the Nelson A. Rockefeller Empire State Plaza Performing Arts Center Corporation.
• $1.2 million for the New York State Theatre Institute Corporation.
• $5,000 for the Town of Carmel's summer concert series at Sycamore Park.
• $25,000 for park bleachers in the Town of Ohio.
• $25,000 for the Multigenerational Center in the Town of Yorktown.
• $12,500 for the Grand Island bike path.
• The Department of Economic Development budget actually declined by over 20 percent—a good sign—but it was still stuffed with pork. For example, expenditures included $2.5 million on "economic development skills training," $500,000 for "entrepreneurial assistance," $2.5

million for the Department of Economic Development/State University of New York/City University of New York Strategic Training Partnership for Industrial Modernization program, $200,000 each for operation of "Gateway Information Centers" in Beekmantown and Binghamton, and $32,500 for Alfred University's "Ceramic Collaboration."

• State Economic Development dollars going to local Chambers of Commerce totaled more than $180,000.

• $990,000 for AIDS education in elementary and secondary schools.

• $80,000 for the Rural Education Advisory Committee.

• $80,000 for the International Education Task Force at Cornell University.

• $80,000 for the Hispanic Information and Telecommunications Network, Inc.

• $140,000 for the Schomburg Center for Research in Black Culture.

• $18.3 million for "family planning services."

• $40,000 for the Correctional Association's study regarding the mental health needs of women in state prison.

• $64,000 for police cars for the city of Poughkeepsie, $70,000 for a surveillance vehicle for the Utica police, $16,000 for police cars for the City of Beacon, and $10,000 for canine unit vehicles and equipment in Kingston.

• $50,000 for the New York City Police Foundation.

**1996-97 New York State Budget Pork—A Small Sample**

• $38.1 million for the Council on the Arts.

• $7,500 for the CUNY Dominican Studies Institute.

• $1.9 million for the Effective Schools Consortia Network.

• $13.7 million for Teacher Resource and Computer Training Centers.

• $506,400 for parenting education.

• More than $870,000 for the Institute for Community Development.

• $50,000 for the Western New York Regional Education Center for Economic Development.

• $100,000 for the Environmental Education Empowerment Program.

• More than $41 million for independent colleges and universities.

• $100,000 for the International Education Task Force at Cornell University.

• $25,000 for the New York State Collectibles Series.

• More than $12 million for public television and radio.

- $5,000 for the American Chess Foundation.
- $2,500 for the Bay Ridge Festival of the Arts.
- $5,000 for the Boy Scouts of America/Suffolk County Council.
- $2,000 for Christ the King Seminary.
- $5,000 for the New York State Envirothon Committee.
- $5,000 for the Staten Island historian.
- $40,000 for St. Joseph's College.
- $5,000 for the Brooklyn Women's Martial Arts Organization.
- $66,000 for the Federation of Italian-American Organization of Queens.
- $10,000 for New Yorkers for Inclusive Educational Curricula.
- More than $30,000 for Nontraditional Employment for Women.
- $5,000 for the Carpenters Local Union 964.
- $16,000 for the New York State Association of Black Women Owned Enterprises, Inc.
- $50,000 for the Homeless Action Committee.
- $5,000 for Planned Parenthood of New York City and $3,000 for Planned Parenthood of Westchester.
- $1.9 million for the Earthquake Center.
- $507,400 for the Rockefeller Institute.
- More than $1 million for Small Business Development Centers.
- $1.9 million for the Strategic Partnership for Industrial Resurgence.
- $100,000 for the Monroe County Vietnam Memorial.
- $11,000 for the Intrepid Sea, Air and Space Museum.
- $125,000 for the Stony Brook Center for Regional Policy Analysis.
- $100,000 for the Stony Brook Center for Waste Reduction and Management Institute.
- $37,500 for the Brooklyn Tenants Council.
- $15,000 for Historic Hudson Valley.
- $20,000 for the Rye Historical Society.
- $5,000 for the St. Patrick's Day Parade and Cultural Committee.
- $40,000 study regarding the mental health needs of women in state prison.
- $13,000 for the New York State National Abortion Rights Action League Foundation.
- $10,000 for the Utica Boxing Association, Inc.
- $400,000 for the New York State Wine/Grape Foundation.
- $100,000 for the East End Economic and Environmental Task Force of Long Island.
- $54 million for the Department of Economic Development, including

$200,000 for the Thousand Island Visitor Center, $16,000 for the Hudson Valley Film and Video Office, $84,000 for the Patchogue Village Waterfront Revitalization, $115,000 for the St. Lawrence County Aquarium and Ecological Center, and tens of thousands of dollars for various Chambers of Commerce across the state.

- $450,000 to the Altmar Fish Hatchery.
- $10,000 to the New York Ski Foundation.
- $125,000 for fixing up ski lifts at the Belleayre Mountain Ski Center.
- $172.6 million for the Division of Housing and Community Renewal, including $52,750 for the Long Island Housing Partnership, $50,000 for the New Perspectives Development Corporation, and more than $40 million for local public housing subsidies.
- $10.8 million for the Olympic Regional Development Authority.
- $150,000 for the Albany Symphony Orchestra.
- $1.25 million for the Albany Institute of History and Art.
- $125,000 to the National Actors Theater.
- $120,000 for the Buffalo Philharmonic.
- $150,000 for the Rochester Philharmonic.
- $200,000 for the Syracuse Symphony.
- $255,000 for the Lincoln Center.
- $5,000 for the American Craft Museum.
- $110,000 for the Double "H" Hole in the Woods Ranch.
- $54,000 for the Irish American Heritage Museum.
- $20,000 for the Manhattan Theatre Club.
- $150,000 for the National Warplane Museum.
- $10,000 for the Troy Flag Day Celebration.
- $17,000 for Shakespeare in Delaware Park.
- $22.6 million for the New York State Science and Technology Foundation.
- $290,000 for the Adirondack Railway Preservation Society.
- $1.9 million for the Minority- and Women-Owned Business Development and Lending Program.
- $500,000 for the UAW/Ford Return to Work Project.
- $165,000 for the Brooklyn Sports Facility Commission.
- $500,000 for the Hofstra University Business Development Centers.
- $750,000 for the Long Island Aquarium in Bay Shore.
- $30,000 to the Seneca Chamber of Commerce for "Agri-Tourism."
- $3,000 for the Center for Lesbian and Gay Studies.
- $800,000 for the Greenway Heritage Conservancy for the Hudson Valley and the Hudson River Valley Greenway Communities Council.

In addition, tens of thousands of state taxpayer dollars are spent annually for various little league baseball, basketball, midget football, softball, tennis and soccer programs across the state. Millions of dollars go to local fire departments. Hundreds of thousands of dollars annually find their way to local senior citizens clubs across the state. And millions of dollars go for local curbs, sidewalks, and road pavings. The list of pork items in the New York State budget seems virtually endless.

Among the most bizarre of the countless bizarre pork entries in the state budget in recent years has been state dollars going to the North Amityville *Taxpayers* Association (emphasis added) on Long Island—$25,000 from the state's Division of Youth in 1993-94, $7,500 in 1995-96 from the state's Natural Heritage Trust, and $5,000 in 1996-97 from the Department of Parks, Recreation and Historic Preservation. You know New York is in trouble when a taxpayers' group takes state government money!

But perhaps the absurd state of New York's budget was best exemplified by a single line item in the 1995-96 state budget. On June 12, 1995, the *New York Post* reported that a $30,000 spending entry for the "Department of Biology—Students Using Corroborated Knowledge Satisfactorily" turned out to be a fake. In fact, the acronym for this group spells out "DOB SUCKS." DOB stands for the state's Department of the Budget.

One need only sit down with and page through the New York State budget each year (a favorite pastime of mine) to realize that any politician claiming that government spending has been cut to the bone in New York is a liar or an idiot.

## AVERAGE WEEKLY UNEMPLOYMENT BENEFITS: STATE RANKINGS

In 1994, New York's average weekly unemployment benefits ranked eleventh highest in the nation.

**Average Weekly Unemployment Benefits**

| Rank | State | Avg. Weekly Benefits |
|---|---|---|
| 1 | Hawaii | $266 |
| 2 | New Jersey | 246 |
| 3 | Massachusetts | 237 |
| 4 | Connecticut | 222 |
| 5(t) | District of Columbia | 220 |
| 5(t) | Rhode Island | 220 |
| 7 | Minnesota | 217 |
| 8 | Michigan | 213 |
| 9 | Pennsylvania | 212 |
| 10 | Washington | 206 |
| **11** | **New York** | **203** |
| 12 | Illinois | 199 |
| 13 | Colorado | 195 |
| 14 | Kansas | 192 |
| 15 | Ohio | 191 |
| 16 | Wisconsin | 188 |
| 17 | Utah | 187 |
| 18(t) | Nevada | 185 |
| 18(t) | Texas | 185 |
| 20(t) | Delaware | 183 |
| 20(t) | Iowa | 183 |
| 22 | Maryland | 180 |
| 23 | Oregon | 179 |
| 24 | North Carolina | 175 |
| 25 | Wyoming | 173 |
| 26 | Alaska | 170 |
| 27 | Virginia | 169 |
| 28(t) | Florida | 168 |

*continued*

*continued*

| Rank | State | Avg. Weekly Benefits |
|---|---|---|
| 28(t) | Oklahoma | 168 |
| 30(t) | Idaho | 167 |
| 30(t) | West Virginia | 167 |
| 32 | Vermont | 164 |
| 33(t) | Maine | 161 |
| 33(t) | Arkansas | 161 |
| 35 | North Dakota | 160 |
| 36 | Kentucky | 159 |
| 37 | Indiana | 158 |
| 38 | Montana | 156 |
| 39(t) | California | 154 |
| 39(t) | South Carolina | 154 |
| 41 | Georgia | 153 |
| 42 | Missouri | 150 |
| 43 | Arizona | 148 |
| 44 | New Hampshire | 146 |
| 45 | Tennessee | 142 |
| 46(t) | New Mexico | 140 |
| 46(t) | Nebraska | 140 |
| 48 | South Dakota | 138 |
| 49 | Alabama | 131 |
| 50 | Mississippi | 129 |
| 51 | Louisiana | 118 |
| | U.S. Average | 182 |

Data Source: U.S. Department of Commerce, *Statistical Abstract of the United States 1996*

## AVERAGE WEEKLY UNEMPLOYMENT BENEFITS: NEW YORK VS. US

In 1994, New York's average weekly unemployment benefits of $203 outpaced the national average of $182 by 11.5 percent.

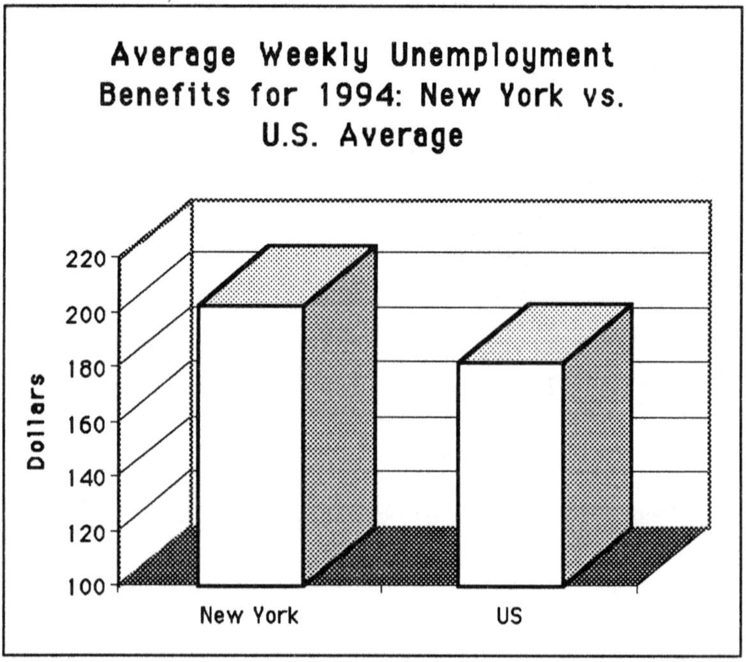


Data Source: U.S. Department of Commerce, *Statistical Abstract of the United States 1996*

## PUBLIC AID RECIPIENTS: STATE RANKINGS

In 1994, New York tied for fourth highest in the nation in terms of the percentage of its population receiving public aid (i.e., Aid to Families with Dependent Children and Federal Supplemental Security Income).

**Percentage of Population Receiving Public Aid**

| Rank | State | Percent |
|---|---|---|
| 1 | District of Columbia | 16.7% |
| 2 | California | 11.7 |
| 3 | Mississippi | 10.9 |
| **4** | **New York** | **10.0** |
| 5 | Louisiana | 9.7 |
| 6 | West Virginia | 9.6 |
| 7 | Kentucky | 9.3 |
| 8 | Michigan | 9.1 |
| 9 | Tennessee | 9.0 |
| 10 | New Mexico | 8.7 |
| 11 | Rhode Island | 8.6 |
| 12 | Illinois | 8.3 |
| 13 | Georgia | 8.2 |
| 14 | Ohio | 8.1 |
| 15 | Massachusetts | 7.5 |
| 16(t) | Maine | 7.4 |
| 16(t) | Alaska | 7.4 |
| 18(t) | North Carolina | 7.2 |
| 18(t) | Pennsylvania | 7.2 |
| 20 | Washington | 7.1 |
| 21(t) | Vermont | 7.0 |
| 21(t) | Missouri | 7.0 |
| 23 | Hawaii | 6.9 |
| 24(t) | Alabama | 6.8 |
| 24(t) | Florida | 6.8 |
| 26 | South Carolina | 6.7 |
| 27 | Arkansas | 6.6 |

*continued*

*continued*

| Rank | State | Percent |
|---|---|---|
| 28(t) | Wisconsin | 6.5 |
| 28(t) | Arizona | 6.5 |
| 30 | Connecticut | 6.4 |
| 31 | Texas | 6.3 |
| 32 | Oklahoma | 6.2 |
| 33 | New Jersey | 6.0 |
| 34 | Maryland | 5.9 |
| 35 | Montana | 5.6 |
| 36(t) | Minnesota | 5.4 |
| 36(t) | Iowa | 5.4 |
| 38(t) | Delaware | 5.2 |
| 38(t) | Indiana | 5.2 |
| 40 | Oregon | 5.1 |
| 41 | Virginia | 4.8 |
| 42(t) | Kansas | 4.7 |
| 42(t) | Colorado | 4.7 |
| 44 | Wyoming | 4.5 |
| 45 | South Dakota | 4.4 |
| 46 | Nebraska | 4.0 |
| 47 | North Dakota | 3.9 |
| 48 | Nevada | 3.8 |
| 49 | Utah | 3.6 |
| 50 | New Hampshire | 3.5 |
| 51 | Idaho | 3.4 |
| | U.S. Average | 7.7 |

Data Source: U.S. Department of Commerce, *Statistical Abstract of the United States 1996*

## PUBLIC AID RECIPIENTS: NEW YORK VS. U.S.

In 1994, New York's percentage of population receiving public aid (i.e., Aid to Families with Dependent Children and Federal Supplemental Security Income) outpaced the U.S. average by 29.9 percent—10 percent in New York versus 7.7 percent across the United States. The New York rate has risen from 7.7 percent in 1990 and 8.4 percent in 1980.

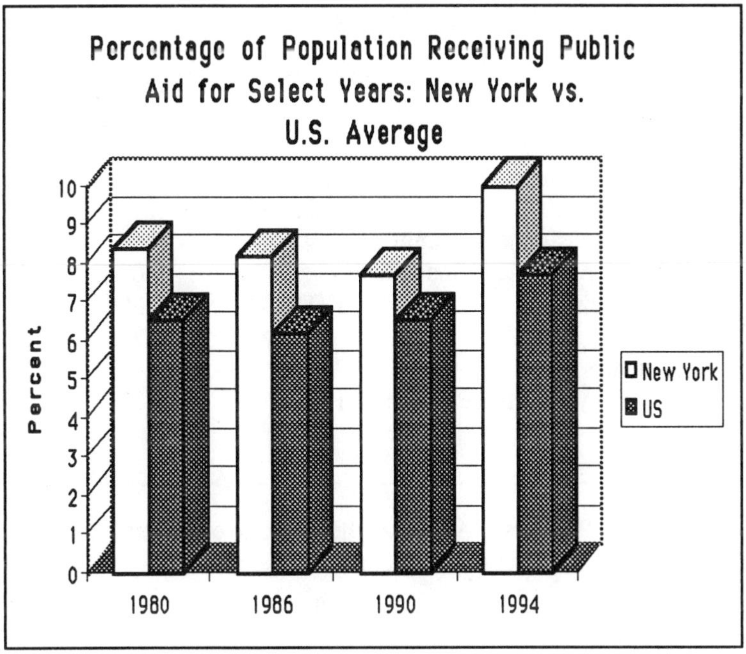


Data Source: U.S. Department of Commerce, *Statistical Abstract of the United States 1996*

## INDIVIDUALS RECEIVING PUBLIC ASSISTANCE IN NEW YORK

The following chart breaks down the number of persons receiving public assistance by program type in New York during 1993.

**Individuals Receiving Public Assistance in New York for 1993**

| Program | Persons | Percent of N.Y. Population |
|---|---|---|
| Aid to Families with Dependent Children | 1,215,527 | 6.7% |
| Home Relief | 388,088 | 2.1% |
| Emergency Assistance—Families | 45,684 | 0.3% |
| Emergency Assistance—Individuals | 2,856 | 0.02% |
| Medical Assistance | 1,688,975 | 9.3% |
| Services | 401,482 | 2.2% |
| Food Stamps | 2,076,598 | 11.4% |
| Home Energy Assistance Program | 1,262,480 | 7.0% |

Data Source: The Nelson A. Rockefeller Institute of Government, *1995 New York State Statistical Yearbook*

## TOTAL NUMBER OF GOVERNMENTAL UNITS: STATE RANKINGS

In 1992, the number of governmental units in New York ranked ninth in the nation.

**Number of Governmental Units**

| Rank | State | Governmental Units |
|---|---|---|
| 1 | Illinois | 6,810 |
| 2 | Pennsylvania | 5,397 |
| 3 | Texas | 4,919 |
| 4 | California | 4,495 |
| 5 | Kansas | 3,918 |
| 6 | Minnesota | 3,616 |
| 7 | Ohio | 3,534 |
| 8 | Missouri | 3,368 |
| **9** | **New York** | **3,319** |
| 10 | Nebraska | 2,997 |
| 11 | Indiana | 2,976 |
| 12 | North Dakota | 2,795 |
| 13 | Wisconsin | 2,752 |
| 14 | Michigan | 2,727 |
| 15 | Iowa | 1,904 |
| 16 | Colorado | 1,826 |
| 17 | Oklahoma | 1,822 |
| 18 | South Dakota | 1,803 |
| 19 | Washington | 1,796 |
| 20 | New Jersey | 1,625 |
| 21 | Oregon | 1,487 |
| 22 | Arkansas | 1,473 |
| 23 | Kentucky | 1,345 |
| 24 | Georgia | 1,321 |
| 25 | Montana | 1,305 |
| 26 | Alabama | 1,134 |
| 27 | Idaho | 1,105 |
| 28 | Florida | 1,041 |

*continued*

*continued*

| Rank | State | Governmental Units |
|---|---|---|
| 29 | Tennessee | 960 |
| 30 | North Carolina | 954 |
| 31 | Mississippi | 898 |
| 32 | Massachusetts | 851 |
| 33 | Maine | 799 |
| 34 | West Virginia | 708 |
| 35 | South Carolina | 705 |
| 36 | Vermont | 690 |
| 37 | Utah | 635 |
| 38 | Arizona | 598 |
| 39(t) | Connecticut | 576 |
| 39(t) | Wyoming | 576 |
| 41 | New Hampshire | 531 |
| 42 | New Mexico | 494 |
| 43(t) | Louisiana | 461 |
| 43(t) | Virginia | 461 |
| 45 | Maryland | 416 |
| 46 | Delaware | 281 |
| 47 | Nevada | 212 |
| 48 | Alaska | 176 |
| 49 | Rhode Island | 128 |
| 50 | Hawaii | 21 |
| 51 | District of Columbia | 2 |

Data Source: U.S. Department of Commerce, *Statistical Abstract of the United States 1995*

## STATE AND LOCAL GOVERNMENT EMPLOYMENT: STATE RANKINGS

In 1993, New York ranked seventh in the nation in terms of the number of full-time equivalent state and local government employees per 10,000 population.

**State and Local Government Employees per 10,000 Population**

| Rank | State | Employees per 10,000 pop. |
|---|---|---|
| 1 | Wyoming | 761.3 |
| 2 | Alaska | 733.5 |
| 3 | New Mexico | 653.7 |
| 4 | Kansas | 642.2 |
| 5 | Montana | 621.0 |
| 6 | Nebraska | 618.5 |
| **7** | **New York** | **618.2** |
| 8 | Vermont | 602.4 |
| 9 | North Dakota | 601.4 |
| 10 | Georgia | 596.1 |
| 11 | Oklahoma | 587.1 |
| 12 | Mississippi | 585.4 |
| 13 | Louisiana | 583.4 |
| 14 | Iowa | 579.8 |
| 15 | Alabama | 572.8 |
| 16 | Hawaii | 567.1 |
| 17 | Texas | 562.4 |
| 18 | North Carolina | 559.9 |
| 19 | Idaho | 559.1 |
| 20 | South Dakota | 558.6 |
| 21 | South Carolina | 558.3 |
| 22 | Delaware | 543.7 |
| 23 | Virginia | 543.6 |
| 24 | Arkansas | 540.5 |
| 25 | Minnesota | 538.4 |
| 26 | New Jersey | 526.6 |
| 27 | Utah | 526.3 |

*continued*

*continued*

| Rank | State | Employees per 10,000 pop. |
|---|---|---|
| 28 | Colorado | 524.4 |
| 29 | Arizona | 520.8 |
| 30 | Wisconsin | 514.4 |
| 31 | Maine | 513.3 |
| 32 | Kentucky | 510.9 |
| 33 | Indiana | 510.4 |
| 34 | Oregon | 510.2 |
| 35 | Washington | 509.8 |
| 36 | Tennessee | 508.1 |
| 37 | West Virginia | 498.2 |
| 38 | Maryland | 494.1 |
| 39 | Michigan | 488.6 |
| 40 | Missouri | 487.8 |
| 41 | Florida | 484.7 |
| 42 | Illinois | 481.2 |
| 43 | Ohio | 479.9 |
| 44 | Rhode Island | 475.3 |
| 45 | Connecticut | 472.7 |
| 46 | Nevada | 470.4 |
| 47 | Massachusetts | 469.7 |
| 48 | New Hampshire | 462.1 |
| 49 | California | 457.6 |
| 50 | Pennsylvania | 425.8 |
| | U.S. Average | 521.4 |

Note: Data for District of Columbia unavailable.

Data Source: U.S. Department of Commerce

## STATE AND LOCAL GOVERNMENT EMPLOYMENT: NEW YORK VS. U.S.

In 1993, New York's number of full-time equivalent state and local government employees per 10,000 population outpaced the U.S. average. The chart below shows various New York state and local employment rates versus the U.S. averages.

**State & Local Government Employees Per 10,000 Population in 1993 for Select Categories: New York vs. U.S. Averages**

| Category | New York | U.S. Average | Percent by Which New York Exceeds the U.S. Average |
|---|---|---|---|
| **Total** | **618.2** | **521.4** | **18.6%** |
| Education—Total | 251.2 | 258.5 | -2.8 |
| Education—Elem. & Secondary | 212.4 | 196.9 | 7.9 |
| Public Welfare | 36.3 | 18.7 | 94.1 |
| Hospitals | 68.9 | 40.3 | 71.0 |
| Health | 15.1 | 13.6 | 11.0 |
| Highways | 25.6 | 21.0 | 21.9 |
| Police Protection | 38.3 | 28.1 | 36.3 |
| Fire Protection | 11.1 | 9.9 | 12.1 |
| Correction | 32.9 | 21.4 | 53.7 |
| Natural Resources | 2.1 | 7.0 | -70.0 |
| Parks & Recreation | 8.1 | 9.0 | -10.0 |
| Public Transit | 32.8 | 7.5 | 337.3 |
| Libraries | 3.8 | 3.7 | 2.7 |
| Judicial & Legal | 15.6 | 11.9 | 31.1 |
| Solid Waste Mgmt. | 9.5 | 4.2 | 126.2 |
| Sewerage | 4.1 | 4.7 | -12.8 |

Data Source: U.S. Department of Commerce

# CIVILIAN EMPLOYMENT IN FEDERAL GOVERNMENT: STATE RANKINGS

In 1994, the number of federal government civilian employees in New York ranked fifth in the nation.

**Civilian Employment in Federal Government**

| Rank | State | Employees (in thousands) |
|---|---|---|
| 1 | California | 295 |
| 2 | District of Columbia | 204 |
| 3 | Texas | 175 |
| 4 | Virginia | 160 |
| **5** | **New York** | **145** |
| 6 | Maryland | 133 |
| 7 | Pennsylvania | 127 |
| 8 | Florida | 114 |
| 9 | Illinois | 106 |
| 10(t) | Ohio | 92 |
| 10(t) | Georgia | 92 |
| 12 | New Jersey | 72 |
| 13 | Washington | 66 |
| 14 | Missouri | 64 |
| 15(t) | Massachusetts | 60 |
| 15(t) | Michigan | 60 |
| 17 | Colorado | 57 |
| 18 | Alabama | 55 |
| 19 | North Carolina | 54 |
| 20 | Tennessee | 53 |
| 21(t) | Oklahoma | 42 |
| 21(t) | Indiana | 42 |
| 23 | Arizona | 40 |
| 24 | Kentucky | 36 |
| 25 | Louisiana | 35 |
| 26 | Minnesota | 34 |
| 27 | Utah | 31 |
| 28(t) | South Carolina | 30 |

*continued*

*continued*

| Rank | State | Employees (in thousands) |
|---|---|---|
| 28(t) | Oregon | 30 |
| 28(t) | Wisconsin | 30 |
| 31 | New Mexico | 27 |
| 32 | Kansas | 26 |
| 33(t) | Mississippi | 25 |
| 33(t) | Hawaii | 25 |
| 33(t) | Connecticut | 25 |
| 36 | Iowa | 21 |
| 37 | Arkansas | 20 |
| 38 | West Virginia | 18 |
| 39 | Nebraska | 16 |
| 40 | Alaska | 15 |
| 41 | Maine | 14 |
| 42 | Montana | 13 |
| 43 | Nevada | 12 |
| 44(t) | Idaho | 11 |
| 44(t) | Rhode Island | 11 |
| 46 | South Dakota | 10 |
| 47 | New Hampshire | 9 |
| 48 | North Dakota | 8 |
| 49 | Wyoming | 7 |
| 50(t) | Vermont | 6 |
| 50(t) | Delaware | 6 |

Data Source: U.S. Department of Commerce

## GOVERNMENT EMPLOYMENT AS A SHARE OF TOTAL EMPLOYMENT: NEW YORK VS. U.S.

In 1995, government employees accounted for 17.7 percent of total nonagricultural employment in New York, compared with a national rate of 16.5 percent.

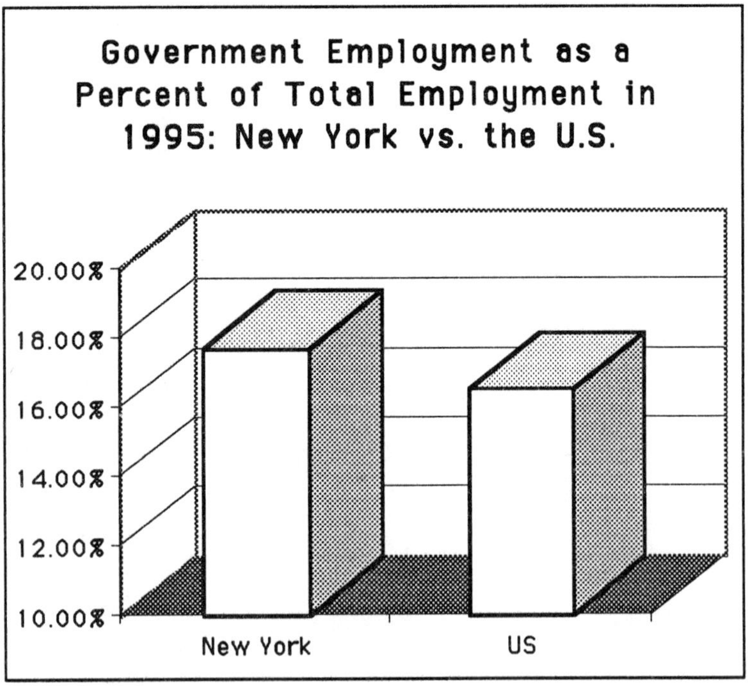


Data Sources: U.S. Department of Labor and the New York State Department of Labor

# STATE EMPLOYER UNEMPLOYMENT TAX RATES: STATE RANKINGS

In the fourth quarter of 1995, New York levied the third highest unemployment tax rate on taxable wages in the nation.

**Employer-Paid Unemployment Tax Rate on Taxable Wages**

| Rank | State | Top Rate |
|---|---|---|
| 1 | District of Columbia | 7.40% |
| 2 | Pennsylvania | 4.90 |
| **3** | **New York** | **4.50** |
| 4(t) | Connecticut | 4.40 |
| 4(t) | Michigan | 4.40 |
| 6 | Massachusetts | 3.80 |
| 7(t) | California | 3.60 |
| 7(t) | Maine | 3.60 |
| 7(t) | Rhode Island | 3.60 |
| 10 | Illinois | 3.40 |
| 11 | Maryland | 3.20 |
| 12 | West Virginia | 3.10 |
| 13 | Delaware | 2.90 |
| 14 | Ohio | 2.80 |
| 15 | Vermont | 2.50 |
| 16(t) | Arkansas | 2.20 |
| 16(t) | Mississippi | 2.20 |
| 16(t) | Wisconsin | 2.20 |
| 19 | Kentucky | 2.10 |
| 20(t) | Alaska | 2.00 |
| 20(t) | Missouri | 2.00 |
| 20(t) | Washington | 2.00 |
| 23(t) | Arizona | 1.90 |
| 23(t) | Hawaii | 1.90 |
| 23(t) | New Jersey | 1.90 |
| 23(t) | South Carolina | 1.90 |
| 23(t) | Tennessee | 1.90 |
| 28(t) | Florida | 1.80 |

*continued*

*continued*

| Rank | State | Top Rate |
|---|---|---|
| 28(t) | Louisiana | 1.80 |
| 28(t) | New Hampshire | 1.80 |
| 31(t) | Minnesota | 1.60 |
| 31(t) | New Mexico | 1.60 |
| 33(t) | Nevada | 1.50 |
| 33(t) | Wyoming | 1.50 |
| 35(t) | Georgia | 1.40 |
| 35(t) | Idaho | 1.40 |
| 35(t) | Indiana | 1.40 |
| 35(t) | Oregon | 1.40 |
| 35(t) | Virginia | 1.40 |
| 40(t) | Montana | 1.30 |
| 40(t) | Texas | 1.30 |
| 42 | Colorado | 1.20 |
| 43(t) | Alabama | 1.10 |
| 43(t) | North Dakota | 1.10 |
| 43(t) | Oklahoma | 1.10 |
| 46 | Iowa | 1.00 |
| 47 | Utah | 0.90 |
| 48 | Nebraska | 0.80 |
| 49 | Kansas | 0.70 |
| 50(t) | North Carolina | 0.60 |
| 50(t) | South Dakota | 0.60 |

Data Sources: National Conference of State Legislators and the U.S. Department of Labor

## WORKERS' COMPENSATION: STATE RANKINGS

In a March 1996 report, the New York Public Policy Institute and Actuarial & Technical Solutions ranked the states according to workers' compensation net insurance costs. New York ranked second highest in the nation.

The U.S. average index number is 1.00. Therefore, New York's workers' compensation costs, with an index of 1.57, are estimated to be 57 percent higher than the average.

**Workers' Compensation Net Insurance Costs**

| Rank | State | Index |
|---|---|---|
| 1 | Maine | 1.861 |
| **2** | **New York** | **1.570** |
| 3 | Louisiana | 1.481 |
| 4 | Rhode Island | 1.460 |
| 5 | Hawaii | 1.456 |
| 6 | Montana | 1.390 |
| 7 | Oklahoma | 1.304 |
| 8 | New Mexico | 1.269 |
| 9 | Colorado | 1.224 |
| 10 | Michigan | 1.206 |
| 11 | New Hampshire | 1.204 |
| 12 | Kentucky | 1.202 |
| 13 | Pennsylvania | 1.189 |
| 14 | Florida | 1.178 |
| 15 | Texas | 1.174 |
| 16 | California | 1.108 |
| 17 | Alabama | 1.098 |
| 18 | Missouri | 1.083 |
| 19 | Massachusetts | 1.028 |
| 20 | Illinois | 1.020 |
| 21 | Vermont | 0.994 |
| 22 | Kansas | 0.993 |
| 23 | Connecticut | 0.987 |
| 24 | Georgia | 0.961 |

*continued*

*continued*

| Rank | State | Index |
|---|---|---|
| 25 | Delaware | 0.886 |
| 26 | Minnesota | 0.861 |
| 27 | New Jersey | 0.848 |
| 28 | South Dakota | 0.840 |
| 29 | Alaska | 0.833 |
| 30 | Tennessee | 0.826 |
| 31 | Nebraska | 0.822 |
| 32 | Arizona | 0.813 |
| 33 | Wisconsin | 0.764 |
| 34 | Mississippi | 0.763 |
| 35 | Utah | 0.757 |
| 36 | Arkansas | 0.729 |
| 37 | North Carolina | 0.692 |
| 38 | Idaho | 0.677 |
| 39 | Oregon | 0.662 |
| 40 | Iowa | 0.655 |
| 41 | Maryland | 0.640 |
| 42 | South Carolina | 0.603 |
| 43 | Indiana | 0.456 |
| 44 | Virginia | 0.445 |

Note: Six states not included provide workers' compensation insurance exclusively through state funds.

Data Source: The Public Policy Institute of New York State, Inc., "The Cost of Comp," March 1996.

## TOP SPENDERS ON NEW YORK STATE LOBBYING IN 1995

The following organizations ranked highest in terms of dollars spent on lobbying New York in 1995.

**New York State Lobbying Expenditures**

| Rank | Organization | Amount |
|---|---|---|
| 1 | United Federation of Teachers (total) | $1,565,966 |
| 2 | Greater New York Hospital Association | 1,181,706 |
| 3 | AT&T and its companies | 1,157,667 |
| 4 | Health Care Association | 1,038,404 |
| 5 | Civil Service Employees Association and the CSEA PAC | 994,577 |
| 6 | Local 1199 of the National Health and Human Services Employees Union | 976,640 |
| 7 | Public Employees Federation | 546,357 |
| 8 | City of New York | 487,090 |
| 9 | A.F.L.-C.I.O. | 430,266 |

Data Source: "Huge Rise in Spending on State Lobbying," *The New York Times*, March 14, 1996

## SOME ADDITIONAL FISCAL FACTS ON NEW YORK

• The Washington, D.C.-based Tax Foundation reported in the July 1996 issue of *Tax Features* that New York's per capita federal tax burden for fiscal year 1996 ranked fifth highest among the 50 states and Washington, D.C. New York's per capita burden ($6,352) topped the U.S. average ($5,225) by 21.6 percent.

• As of late December 1995, Standard & Poor credit agency gave New York the worst credit rating of any state in the nation.

• According to the Citizens Budget Commission, there are 3,179 taxing entities in New York.

• In New York State, Medicaid coverage includes sex-change operations. In early January 1996, the Albany *Times Union* (January 6, 1996) reported that the Pataki Administration sought to put an end to this practice.

• In 1994, per family monthly AFDC payments in New York ($543) topped the U.S. average ($382) by 42.1 percent.

• In 1994, 15 percent of all households in New York participated in the food stamp program, compared with a national rate of 11.6 percent.

• Lastly, perhaps some hope flickers on the New York fiscal front. In "A Fiscal Policy Report Card on America's Governors: 1996" from Stephen Moore and Dean Stansel (CATO Institute, Washington, D.C.), Governor George Pataki registered as one of only three governors to receive a grade of "A"—along with Steve Merrill in New Hampshire and Fife Symington in Arizona. The grades are based on fiscal performance. As Moore and Stansel summarize: "Governors who have cut spending and taxes the most get the highest grades; governors who have raised spending and taxes the most get the lowest grades."

Pataki's performance should be commended as far as it goes. Much, much more needs to be done.

## Chapter Three

# New York State: Education

- Expenditure levels by state, county, and district
- Teacher salaries
- Staff and school trends
- Student performance measures
- Various higher education expenditure amounts

## PER CAPITA STATE AND LOCAL TOTAL EDUCATION EXPENDITURES: STATE RANKINGS

New York ranked fifth in the nation in 1992-93 in terms of per capita state and local total education expenditures.

**Per Capita State and Local Total Education Expenditures**

| Rank | State | Per Capita Education Expenditures |
|---|---|---|
| 1 | Alaska | $2,492.65 |
| 2 | Wyoming | 1,868.02 |
| 3 | Vermont | 1,655.76 |
| 4 | Delaware | 1,648.58 |
| **5** | **New York** | **1,638.86** |
| 6 | Washington | 1,631.72 |
| 7 | New Jersey | 1,619.00 |
| 8 | Wisconsin | 1,590.01 |
| 9 | Minnesota | 1,574.48 |
| 10 | Michigan | 1,572.82 |
| 11 | North Dakota | 1,533.39 |
| 12 | Iowa | 1,495.51 |
| 13 | Oregon | 1,468.88 |
| 14 | Nebraska | 1,464.34 |
| 15 | Connecticut | 1,445.82 |
| 16 | Utah | 1,429.63 |
| 17 | Kansas | 1,425.39 |
| 18 | New Mexico | 1,403.06 |
| 19 | Colorado | 1,372.99 |
| 20 | Pennsylvania | 1,340.75 |
| 21 | Texas | 1,339.74 |
| 22 | Rhode Island | 1,337.97 |
| 23 | Maryland | 1,335.36 |
| 24 | Arizona | 1,320.13 |
| 25 | West Virginia | 1,318.32 |
| 26 | Maine | 1,311.68 |
| 27 | Indiana | 1,310.02 |

*continued*

*continued*

| Rank | State | Per Capita Education Expenditures |
|---|---|---|
| 28 | Ohio | 1,304.26 |
| 29 | Virginia | 1,290.46 |
| 30 | California | 1,290.26 |
| 31 | District of Columbia | 1,246.20 |
| 32 | Hawaii | 1,241.03 |
| 33 | North Carolina | 1,234.48 |
| 34 | South Dakota | 1,231.48 |
| 35 | New Hampshire | 1,229.04 |
| 36 | Montana | 1,226.68 |
| 37 | Illinois | 1,220.51 |
| 38 | Oklahoma | 1,214.76 |
| 39 | South Carolina | 1,207.41 |
| 40 | Nevada | 1,203.15 |
| 41 | Arkansas | 1,170.63 |
| 42 | Idaho | 1,169.96 |
| 43 | Georgia | 1,153.62 |
| 44 | Louisiana | 1,140.53 |
| 45 | Massachusetts | 1,127.86 |
| 46 | Kentucky | 1,103.19 |
| 47 | Mississippi | 1,095.50 |
| 48 | Florida | 1,085.15 |
| 49 | Alabama | 1,065.87 |
| 50 | Missouri | 1,049.69 |
| 51 | Tennessee | 954.94 |
| | U.S. Average | 1,328.92 |

Data Source: U.S. Department of Commerce

## PER CAPITA STATE AND LOCAL TOTAL EDUCATION EXPENDITURES: NEW YORK VS. U.S.

New York's 1992-93 per capita state and local total education expenditures surpassed the national average by 23.3 percent—$1,638.86 in New York versus a national average of $1,328.92.

Between 1962 and 1993, real per capita state and local total education spending increased by 177.5 percent. In 1962, New York's per capita total education expenditures equaled $590.62 (in 1993 dollars).

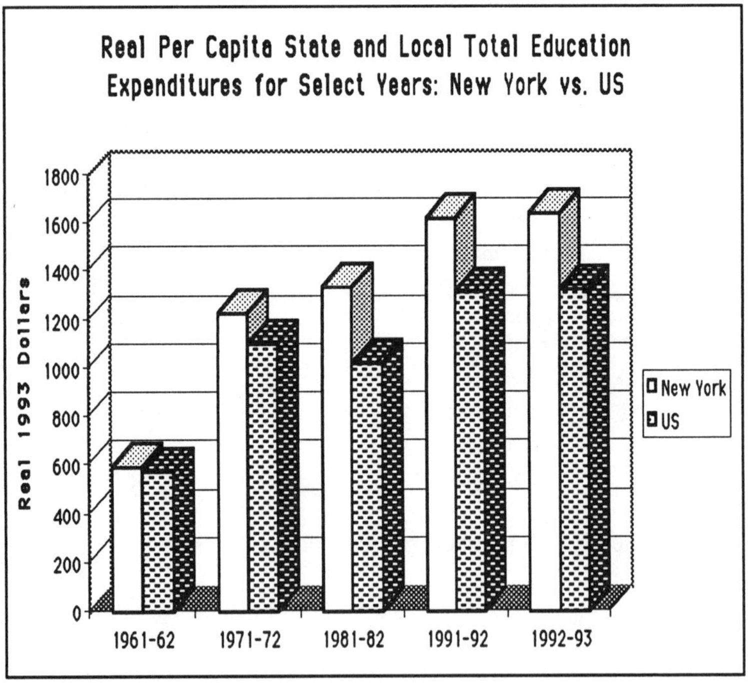


Data Source: U.S. Department of Commerce

# PER CAPITA STATE-ONLY TOTAL EDUCATION EXPENDITURES: STATE RANKINGS

New York ranked twentieth in the nation in 1994 in terms of per capita state-only total education expenditures.

**Per Capita State Total Education Expenditures**

| Rank | State | Per Capita Education Expenditures |
|---|---|---|
| 1 | Alaska | $2,109.02 |
| 2 | Wyoming | 1,375.04 |
| 3 | Washington | 1,313.49 |
| 4 | New Mexico | 1,304.99 |
| 5 | Hawaii | 1,268.87 |
| 6 | Utah | 1,179.90 |
| 7 | Delaware | 1,173.18 |
| 8 | Minnesota | 1,145.41 |
| 9 | North Dakota | 1,132.22 |
| 10 | North Carolina | 1,084.90 |
| 11 | Iowa | 1,070.43 |
| 12 | Kansas | 1,070.35 |
| 13 | West Virginia | 1,058.91 |
| 14 | Montana | 1,046.62 |
| 15 | Kentucky | 1,004.87 |
| 16 | Oklahoma | 987.03 |
| 17 | Vermont | 981.43 |
| 18 | Idaho | 981.20 |
| 19 | New Jersey | 963.34 |
| **20** | **New York** | **950.55** |
| 21 | Indiana | 947.39 |
| 22 | Alabama | 940.81 |
| 23 | Michigan | 920.47 |
| 24 | Louisiana | 919.61 |
| 25 | Georgia | 918.91 |
| 26 | Colorado | 918.42 |
| 27 | Wisconsin | 916.96 |
| 28 | South Carolina | 905.79 |

*continued*

*continued*

| Rank | State | Per Capita Education Expenditures |
|---|---|---|
| 29 | Arkansas | 903.77 |
| 30 | California | 894.48 |
| 31 | Mississippi | 856.09 |
| 32 | Nevada | 851.09 |
| 33 | Virginia | 849.34 |
| 34 | Oregon | 848.08 |
| 35 | Texas | 843.70 |
| 36 | Maine | 839.53 |
| 37 | Nebraska | 834.01 |
| 38 | Rhode Island | 817.32 |
| 39 | Connecticut | 813.71 |
| 40 | Arizona | 811.47 |
| 41 | Ohio | 798.71 |
| 42 | Pennsylvania | 760.88 |
| 43 | Tennessee | 751.84 |
| 44 | Maryland | 750.84 |
| 45 | Missouri | 741.80 |
| 46 | Florida | 733.26 |
| 47 | South Dakota | 716.74 |
| 48 | Illinois | 677.98 |
| 49 | Massachusetts | 615.15 |
| 50 | New Hampshire | 470.75 |
| | U.S. Average | 886.47 |

Data Source: U.S. Department of Commerce

## PER CAPITA STATE-ONLY TOTAL EDUCATION EXPENDITURES: NEW YORK VS. U.S.

New York's 1994 per capita state total education expenditures surpassed the state average by 7.2 percent—$950.55 for New York and a national average of $886.47.

Between 1965 and 1994, real per capita state total education expenditures grew by 129.3 percent. In 1994 dollars, per capita state total education expenditures registered at $414.51.

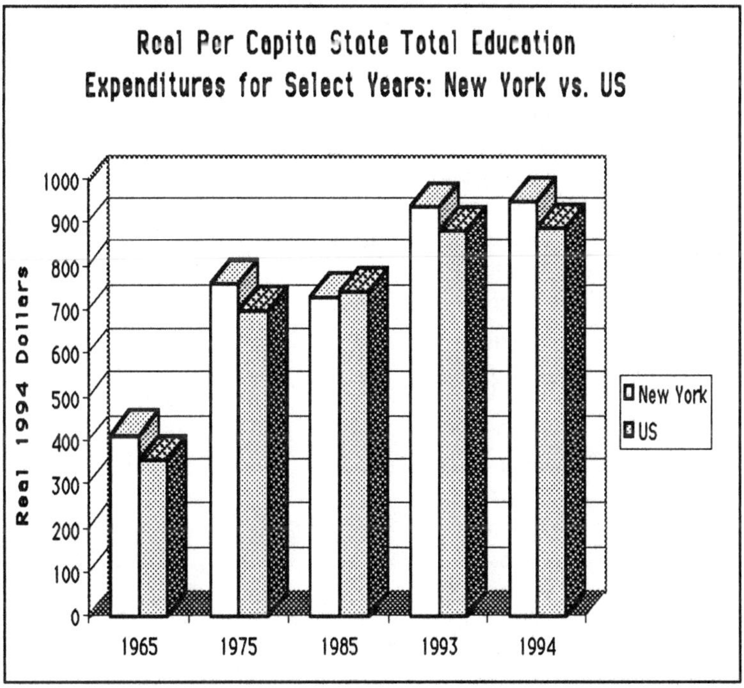


Data Source: U.S. Department of Commerce

## PER CAPITA STATE AND LOCAL PRIMARY AND SECONDARY EDUCATION EXPENDITURES: STATE RANKINGS

New York ranked third highest in the nation in 1992-93 in terms of per capita state and local primary and secondary education expenditures.

**Per Capita Primary and Secondary Education Expenditures**

| Rank | State | Per Capita Education Expenditures |
|---|---|---|
| 1 | Alaska | $1,865.48 |
| 2 | New Jersey | 1,281.67 |
| **3** | **New York** | **1,262.66** |
| 4 | Wyoming | 1,258.95 |
| 5 | Connecticut | 1,150.11 |
| 6 | Washington | 1,133.40 |
| 7 | Minnesota | 1,102.98 |
| 8 | Michigan | 1,090.84 |
| 9 | Wisconsin | 1,078.39 |
| 10 | District of Columbia | 1,073.48 |
| 11 | Vermont | 1,070.77 |
| 12 | Oregon | 1,012.26 |
| 13 | Nebraska | 992.14 |
| 14 | Pennsylvania | 969.47 |
| 15 | Maine | 965.70 |
| 16 | Delaware | 963.27 |
| 17 | Iowa | 955.39 |
| 18 | Texas | 952.74 |
| 19 | Kansas | 942.35 |
| 20 | Ohio | 937.22 |
| 21 | Rhode Island | 928.59 |
| 22 | West Virginia | 927.50 |
| 23 | Colorado | 912.22 |
| 24 | Maryland | 904.71 |
| 25 | New Hampshire | 903.74 |
| 26 | Arizona | 895.39 |
| 27 | Virginia | 889.29 |

*continued*

*continued*

| Rank | State | Per Capita Education Expenditures |
|---|---|---|
| 28 | Nevada | 888.75 |
| 29 | North Dakota | 881.58 |
| 30 | California | 877.21 |
| 31 | South Dakota | 875.36 |
| 32 | Utah | 874.25 |
| 33 | Indiana | 862.26 |
| 34 | Georgia | 854.72 |
| 35 | Illinois | 854.51 |
| 36 | New Mexico | 850.73 |
| 37 | Massachusetts | 848.21 |
| 38 | Oklahoma | 832.89 |
| 39 | Montana | 822.34 |
| 40 | Florida | 814.14 |
| 41 | South Carolina | 809.46 |
| 42 | Missouri | 781.65 |
| 43 | Louisiana | 774.67 |
| 44 | North Carolina | 774.03 |
| 45 | Idaho | 767.01 |
| 46 | Arkansas | 726.11 |
| 47 | Mississippi | 723.88 |
| 48 | Hawaii | 715.35 |
| 49 | Kentucky | 688.14 |
| 50 | Tennessee | 620.71 |
| 51 | Alabama | 608.84 |
| | U.S. Average | 933.24 |

Data Source: U.S. Department of Commerce

## PER CAPITA STATE AND LOCAL PRIMARY AND SECONDARY EDUCATION EXPENDITURES: NEW YORK VS. U.S.

In 1992-93, New York's per capita state and local primary and secondary education expenditures exceeded the national average by 35.3 percent—$1,262.66 in New York versus a national average of $933.24.

From 1962 to 1993, real per capita state and local school spending increased by 142.8 percent. In 1993 dollars, New York's 1962 expenditures equaled $520.00.

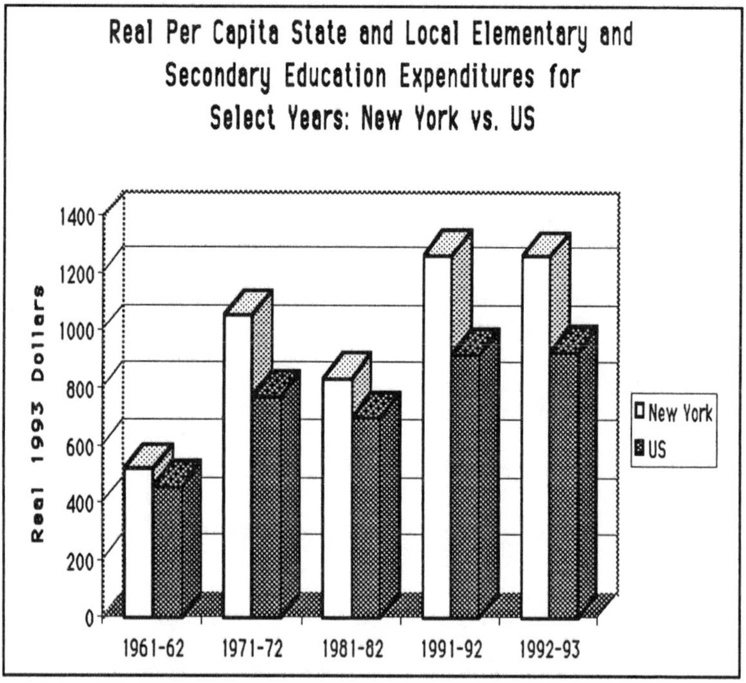


Data Source: U.S. Department of Commerce

## PER PUPIL EXPENDITURES: STATE RANKINGS

New York ranked third in the nation in 1993-94 in terms of per pupil current expenditures in public schools, trailing only Washington, D.C. and New Jersey.

**Per Pupil Current Expenditures**

| Rank | State | Per Pupil Current Expenditures |
|---|---|---|
| 1 | District of Columbia | $10,180 |
| 2 | New Jersey | 9,677 |
| **3** | **New York** | **9,175** |
| 4 | Alaska | 8,882 |
| 5 | Connecticut | 8,473 |
| 6 | Rhode Island | 7,333 |
| 7 | Pennsylvania | 6,983 |
| 8 | Massachusetts | 6,959 |
| 9 | Maryland | 6,958 |
| 10 | Wisconsin | 6,717 |
| 11 | Michigan | 6,658 |
| 12 | Delaware | 6,621 |
| 13 | Vermont | 6,600 |
| 14 | Oregon | 6,263 |
| 15 | Maine | 6,069 |
| 16 | Ohio | 5,971 |
| 17 | Wyoming | 5,899 |
| 18 | Illinois | 5,893 |
| 19 | Hawaii | 5,879 |
| 20 | Washington | 5,751 |
| 21 | New Hampshire | 5,723 |
| 22 | Minnesota | 5,720 |
| 23 | West Virginia | 5,713 |
| 24 | Kansas | 5,659 |
| 25 | Nebraska | 5,651 |
| 26 | Indiana | 5,630 |
| 27 | Montana | 5,598 |
| 28 | Florida | 5,516 |

*continued*

*continued*

| Rank | State | Per Pupil Current Expenditures |
|---|---|---|
| 29 | Iowa | 5,288 |
| 30 | Missouri | 5,114 |
| 31 | Virginia | 5,109 |
| 32 | Kentucky | 5,107 |
| 33 | Colorado | 5,097 |
| 34 | Nevada | 5,049 |
| 35 | California | 4,921 |
| 36 | Georgia | 4,915 |
| 37 | Texas | 4,898 |
| 38 | North Carolina | 4,894 |
| 39 | South Carolina | 4,761 |
| 40 | Oklahoma | 4,697 |
| 41 | North Dakota | 4,674 |
| 42 | Arizona | 4,611 |
| 43 | South Dakota | 4,586 |
| 44 | Louisiana | 4,519 |
| 45 | Arkansas | 4,280 |
| 46 | New Mexico | 4,261 |
| 47 | Tennessee | 4,149 |
| 48 | Alabama | 4,037 |
| 49 | Idaho | 3,844 |
| 50 | Mississippi | 3,660 |
| 51 | Utah | 3,439 |
| | U.S. Average | 5,767 |

Source: U.S. Department of Education

## PER PUPIL EXPENDITURES: NEW YORK VS. U.S.

Average per pupil public school current expenditures in New York State far outpace the U.S. average on a regular basis.

• In 1994, New York's per pupil current expenditures average of $9,175 surpassed the national average of $5,767 by 59.1 percent.

• Between 1960 and 1994, real per pupil expenditures in New York increased by 228.3 percent.

• Per pupil *total* education expenditures in New York State in 1994 registered $10,389.54, as compared with the national average of $6,604.82.

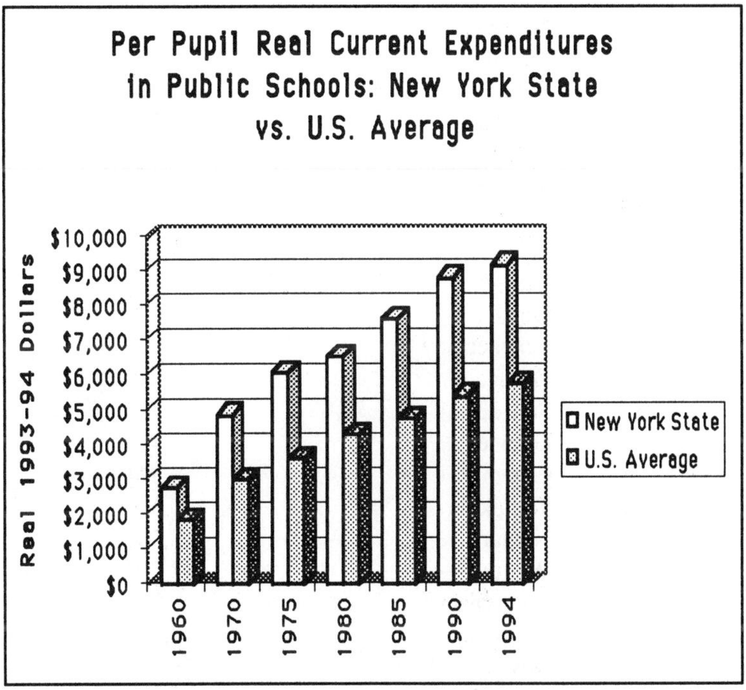


Data Source: U.S. Department of Education

## RANKING PER PUPIL EXPENDITURES BY NEW YORK COUNTY

Among New York counties in 1993-94, the top per pupil public school expenditures were registered in Hamilton, Rockland, Westchester, Nassau, Suffolk, and Putnam counties—all over $10,000 per pupil. The five New York City counties averaged $8,205 per pupil, ranking twenty-fourth out of 58.

**Per Pupil Total Expenditures**

| Rank | County | Per Pupil Total Expenditures |
|---|---|---|
| 1 | Hamilton | $12,559 |
| 2 | Rockland | 12,431 |
| 3 | Westchester | 12,364 |
| 4 | Nassau | 11,774 |
| 5 | Suffolk | 11,136 |
| 6 | Putnam | 10,297 |
| 7 | Sullivan | 9,377 |
| 8 | Ulster | 9,143 |
| 9 | Monroe | 9,052 |
| 10 | Essex | 8,865 |
| 11 | Albany | 8,737 |
| 12 | Otsego | 8,690 |
| 13 | Dutchess | 8,684 |
| 14 | Schenectady | 8,590 |
| 15 | Orange | 8,548 |
| 16 | Schoharie | 8,487 |
| 17 | Greene | 8,419 |
| 18 | Columbia | 8,374 |
| 19 | Tompkins | 8,311 |
| 20 | Niagara | 8,302 |
| 21 | Warren | 8,278 |
| 22 | Rennsalaer | 8,273 |
| 23 | Onondaga | 8,254 |
| **24** | **New York City** | **8,205** |
| 25 | Schuyler | 8,169 |

*continued*

*continued*

| Rank | County | Per Pupil Total Expenditures |
|---|---|---|
| 26 | Saratoga | 8,160 |
| 27(t) | Steuben | 8,155 |
| 27(t) | Chenango | 8,155 |
| 29 | Seneca | 8,085 |
| 30 | Erie | 8,084 |
| 31 | Wayne | 8,075 |
| 32 | Montgomery | 8,045 |
| 33 | Ontario | 8,012 |
| 34 | Delaware | 7,956 |
| 35 | Franklin | 7,954 |
| 36 | Oneida | 7,853 |
| 37 | Genesee | 7,818 |
| 38(t) | Fulton | 7,730 |
| 38(t) | Oswego | 7,730 |
| 40 | St. Lawrence | 7,625 |
| 41 | Washington | 7,610 |
| 42 | Chemung | 7,608 |
| 43 | Broome | 7,551 |
| 44 | Clinton | 7,504 |
| 45(t) | Livingston | 7,421 |
| 45(t) | Madison | 7,421 |
| 47 | Jefferson | 7,401 |
| 48 | Chautauqua | 7,260 |
| 49 | Yates | 7,224 |
| 50 | Allegany | 7,206 |
| 51 | Cayuga | 7,162 |
| 52 | Wyoming | 7,126 |
| 53 | Herkimer | 7,125 |
| 54 | Cattaraugus | 7,090 |
| 55(t) | Cortland | 6,996 |
| 55(t) | Orleans | 6,996 |
| 57 | Lewis | 6,726 |
| 58 | Tioga | 6,542 |

Note: New York City includes five counties.
Data Source: New York State Education Department, *Seventh Annual School District Fiscal Profile Report, 1989-90—1993-94*

## RANKING PER PUPIL EXPENDITURES BY NEW YORK SCHOOL DISTRICT

When looking at per pupil total expenditures by public school district, the results in 1993-94 were staggering. Out of the 688 districts for which the state supplies data:

- one district spent almost $50,000 per pupil,
- a total of seven districts spent more than $20,000 per pupil,
- 59 districts spent more than $13,000 per pupil,
- 197 districts—over 28 percent of all New York School districts—spent more than $10,000 per pupil,
- 411 districts—almost 60 percent of all districts—spent more than $8,000 per pupil per year,
- and only four districts spent less than $6,000 per pupil.

**Per Pupil Total Expenditures**

| Rank | School District | Per Pupil Total Expenditures |
|---|---|---|
| 1 | Kiryas Joel Village UFSD | $49,806 |
| 2 | Newcomb CSD | 33,471 |
| 3 | Bridgehampton UFSD | 32,218 |
| 4 | Fire Island UFSD | 27,398 |
| 5 | Fishers Island UFSD | 25,392 |
| 6 | Gilbertsville-Mount Upton CSD | 24,900 |
| 7 | Pocantico Hills CSD | 24,432 |
| 8 | Shelter Island UFSD | 18,920 |
| 9 | Shoreham-Wading River CSD | 17,854 |
| 10 | Port Jefferson UFSD | 17,353 |
| 11 | Great Neck UFSD | 16,926 |
| 12 | Long Lake CSD | 16,918 |
| 13 | Jericho UFSD | 16,279 |
| 14 | Minerva CSD | 16,165 |
| 15 | Manhasset UFSD | 16,138 |
| 16 | Greenburgh CSD | 16,053 |
| 17 | White Plains City SD | 15,922 |
| 18 | South Orangetown CSD | 15,516 |

*continued*

*continued*

| Rank | School District | Per Pupil Total Expenditures |
|---|---|---|
| 19 | Elmsford UFSD | 15,331 |
| 20 | Bedford CSD | 15,195 |
| 21 | Roslyn UFSD | 15,154 |
| 22 | North Shore CSD | 15,140 |
| 23 | Oyster Bay-East Norwich CSD | 14,927 |
| 24 | Quogue UFSD | 14,853 |
| 25 | Somers CSD | 14,773 |
| 26 | Southampton UFSD | 14,751 |
| 27 | Tuckahoe Comn SD | 14,678 |
| 28 | Lawrence UFSD | 14,531 |
| 29 | Tuxedo UFSD | 14,505 |
| 30 | Port Washington UFSD | 14,494 |
| 31 | East Williston UFSD | 14,377 |
| 32 | Bronxville UFSD | 14,303 |
| 33 | Amagansett UFSD | 14,291 |
| 34 | Harrison CSD | 14,196 |
| 35 | Bolton CSD | 14,116 |
| 36 | UFSD—Tarrytowns | 13,933 |
| 37 | Croton—Harmon UFSD | 13,871 |
| 38 | Mamaroneck CSD | 13,811 |
| 39 | Mineola UFSD | 13,806 |
| 40 | East Hampton UFSD | 13,789 |
| 41 | Bayport-Blue Point UFSD | 13,665 |
| 42 | Briarcliff Manor UFSD | 13,659 |
| 43 | East Ramapo CSD (Spring Valley) | 13,641 |
| 44 | Sag Harbor UFSD | 13,634 |
| 45 | Hendrick Hudson CSD | 13,600 |
| 46 | Locust Valley CSD | 13,575 |
| 47 | Pearl River UFSD | 13,445 |
| 48 | Rye City SD | 13,421 |
| 49 | Valhalla UFSD | 13,318 |
| 50(t) | Greenport UFSD | 13,301 |
| 50(t) | Scarsdale UFSD | 13,301 |
| 52 | Irvington UFSD | 13,275 |
| 53 | Chappaqua CSD | 13,262 |

*continued*

*continued*

| Rank | School District | Per Pupil Total Expenditures |
|---|---|---|
| 54 | Nyack UFSD | 13,257 |
| 55 | Nanuet UFSD | 13,096 |
| 56 | Hewlett-Woodmere UFSD | 13,080 |
| 57 | Blind Brook—Rye UFSD | 13,069 |
| 58 | Peekskill City SD | 13,053 |
| 59 | Lake Pleasant CSD | 13,023 |
| 60 | North Salem CSD | 12,976 |
| 61 | Long Beach City SD | 12,975 |
| 62 | Cold Spring Harbor CSD | 12,970 |
| 63 | Ossining UFSD | 12,961 |
| 64 | Katonah-Lewisboro UFSD | 12,941 |
| 65 | Island Park UFSD | 12,916 |
| 66 | Edgemont UFSD | 12,890 |
| 67 | Westbury UFSD | 12,838 |
| 68 | Eastchester UFSD | 12,818 |
| 69 | Hicksville UFSD | 12,810 |
| 70 | Hauppauge UFSD | 12,777 |
| 71 | Ramapo CSD | 12,710 |
| 72 | Garden City UFSD | 12,638 |
| 73(t) | Bethpage UFSD | 12,603 |
| 73(t) | Northport-East Northport UFSD | 12,603 |
| 75 | Keene CSD | 12,577 |
| 76 | Campbell-Savona CSD | 12,574 |
| 77 | Huntington UFSD | 12,523 |
| 78 | Half Hollow Hills CSD | 12,382 |
| 79 | Smithtown CSD | 12,346 |
| 80 | Downsville CSD | 12,212 |
| 81 | Central Islip UFSD | 12,170 |
| 82 | Montauk UFSD | 12,149 |
| 83 | Uniondale UFSD | 12,136 |
| 84 | Pelham UFSD | 12,118 |
| 85 | New Rochelle City SD | 12,104 |
| 86 | Bellmore UFSD | 12,094 |
| 87 | Herricks UFSD | 12,072 |
| 88 | Glen Cove City SD | 12,064 |

*continued*

*continued*

| Rank | School District | Per Pupil Total Expenditures |
|---|---|---|
| 89 | Dobbs Ferry UFSD | 12,061 |
| 90 | Hempstead UFSD | 12,049 |
| 91 | Connetquot CSD | 11,996 |
| 92 | Afton CSD | 11,958 |
| 93 | Elwood UFSD | 11,912 |
| 94 | Westhampton Beach UFSD | 11,906 |
| 95 | Lakeland CSD | 11,895 |
| 96 | Ardsley UFSD | 11,866 |
| 97 | Fallsburg CSD | 11,837 |
| 98 | Valley Stream Central HS District | 11,817 |
| 99 | Oysterponds UFSD | 11,803 |
| 100(t) | Carle Place UFSD | 11,740 |
| 100(t) | Bay Shore UFSD | 11,740 |
| 102 | East Islip UFSD | 11,731 |
| 103 | Syosset CSD | 11,698 |
| 104 | Kings Park CSD | 11,680 |
| 105 | Rye Neck UFSD | 11,679 |
| 106 | Harborfields CSD | 11,672 |
| 107 | Seaford UFSD | 11,644 |
| 108 | Hastings-on-Hudson UFSD | 11,619 |
| 109 | Rockville Centre UFSD | 11,597 |
| 110 | Remsenberg-Speonk UFSD | 11,582 |
| 111 | Bellmore-Merrick Central HS Dist | 11,536 |
| 112 | Indian Lake CSD | 11,531 |
| 113 | Malverne UFSD | 11,490 |
| 114 | Haverstraw-Stony Point CSD | 11,470 |
| 115 | Wyandanch UFSD | 11,468 |
| 116 | Wantagh UFSD | 11,462 |
| 117 | Plainedge UFSD | 11,454 |
| 118 | Jasper-Troupsburg CSD | 11,427 |
| 119 | Byram Hills CSD | 11,384 |
| 120 | South Country CSD | 11,362 |
| 121 | Lynbrook UFSD | 11,357 |
| 122 | South Huntington UFSD | 11,331 |
| 123 | Mt Pleasant CSD | 11,323 |

*continued*

*continued*

| Rank | School District | Per Pupil Total Expenditures |
|---|---|---|
| 124 | Center Moriches UFSD | 11,282 |
| 125(t) | Amityville UFSD | 11,264 |
| 125(t) | Brookhaven-Comsewogue UFSD | 11,264 |
| 127 | Island Trees UFSD | 11,236 |
| 128 | Mt Vernon City SD | 11,226 |
| 129 | Southold UFSD | 11,195 |
| 130 | Plainview-Old Bethpage CSD | 11,188 |
| 131 | Poughkeepsie City SD | 11,180 |
| 132 | Andes CSD | 11,164 |
| 133 | Mt Sinai UFSD | 11,152 |
| 134 | West Hempstead UFSD | 11,148 |
| 135 | Farmingdale UFSD | 11,145 |
| 136 | Islip UFSD | 11,128 |
| 137 | Commack UFSD | 11,071 |
| 138 | Sayville UFSD | 11,017 |
| 139 | East Rockaway UFSD | 11,011 |
| 140 | Deer Park UFSD | 10,982 |
| 141 | Tuckahoe UFSD | 10,947 |
| 142 | East Moriches UFSD | 10,940 |
| 143 | Hunter—Tannersville CSD | 10,931 |
| 144 | Longwood CSD | 10,930 |
| 145 | Pleasantville | 10,838 |
| 146 | Brighton CSD | 10,835 |
| 147 | Massapequa UFSD | 10,824 |
| 148 | Wells CSD | 10,821 |
| 149 | Levittown UFSD | 10,807 |
| 150 | Riverhead CSD | 10,780 |
| 151(t) | Middle Country CSD | 10,708 |
| 151(t) | Onteora CSD | 10,708 |
| 153 | Gilboa-Conesville CSD | 10,658 |
| 154 | Town of Webb UFSD | 10,645 |
| 155 | Garrison UFSD | 10,643 |
| 156 | Putnam CSD | 10,623 |
| 157 | North Babylon UFSD | 10,602 |
| 158 | Three Village CSD | 10,598 |

*continued*

*continued*

| Rank | School District | Per Pupil Total Expenditures |
|---|---|---|
| 159 | South Seneca CSD | 10,566 |
| 160 | Chester CSD | 10,552 |
| 161 | Ellenville CSD | 10,541 |
| 162 | Johnsburg CSD | 10,505 |
| 163 | Mattituck—Cutchogue UFSD | 10,503 |
| 164 | Valley Stream 24 UFSD | 10,488 |
| 165 | Sewanhaka Central HS District | 10,483 |
| 166 | Oceanside UFSD | 10,481 |
| 167 | Carmel CSD | 10,469 |
| 168 | Brewster CSD | 10,430 |
| 169 | Colton-Pierrepont CSD | 10,410 |
| 170 | Rochester City SD | 10,403 |
| 171 | Brentwood UFSD | 10,398 |
| 172 | Haldane CSD | 10,390 |
| 173 | West Islip UFSD | 10,370 |
| 174 | Clarkstown CSD | 10,360 |
| 175 | Millbrook CSD | 10,353 |
| 176 | Yorktown CSD | 10,328 |
| 177 | Sachem CSD | 10,307 |
| 178 | West Babylon UFSD | 10,299 |
| 179 | East Quogue UFSD | 10,265 |
| 180 | Baldwin UFSD | 10,224 |
| 181 | Roosevelt UFSD | 10,201 |
| 182 | Liberty CSD | 10,199 |
| 183 | Albany City SD | 10,193 |
| 184 | Merrick UFSD | 10,179 |
| 185 | Mahopac CSD | 10,178 |
| 186 | Spackenkill UFSD | 10,176 |
| 187 | Springs UFSD | 10,153 |
| 188 | Valley Stream 30 UFSD | 10,117 |
| 189 | Yonkers City SD | 10,104 |
| 190 | Rush-Henrietta CSD | 10,102 |
| 191 | Florida UFSD | 10,055 |
| 192 | Freeport UFSD | 10,049 |
| 193 | Hampton Bays UFSD | 10,045 |

*continued*

*continued*

| Rank | School District | Per Pupil Total Expenditures |
|---|---|---|
| 194 | Goshen CSD | 10,022 |
| 195 | Chautauqua CSD | 10,017 |
| 196(t) | Schroon Lake CSD | 10,011 |
| 196(t) | Roscoe CSD | 10,011 |
| 198 | Scheneyus CSD | 9,998 |
| 199 | Jeffersonville-Youngsville CSD | 9,924 |
| 200 | East Meadow UFSD | 9,915 |
| 201 | Patchogue-Medford UFSD | 9,861 |
| 202 | Cheektowaga-Maryvale UFSD | 9,851 |
| 203 | Livingston Manor CSD | 9,849 |
| 204 | Amherst CSD | 9,806 |
| 205(t) | Eastport UFSD | 9,789 |
| 205(t) | Milford CSD | 9,789 |
| 207(t) | Clifton-Fine CSD | 9,771 |
| 207(t) | Tri-Valley CSD | 9,771 |
| 209 | Lake George CSD | 9,760 |
| 210 | Putnam Valley CSD | 9,749 |
| 211 | Deposit CSD | 9,724 |
| 212 | Marlboro CSD | 9,688 |
| 213 | Pittsford CSD | 9,682 |
| 214 | Van Hornesville-Owen Young CSD | 9,673 |
| 215 | Babylon UFSD | 9,668 |
| 216 | Tory City SD | 9,660 |
| 217 | Jamesville-DeWitt CSD | 9,657 |
| 218 | Highland Falls CSD | 9,656 |
| 219 | Copiague UFSD | 9,629 |
| 220 | Monroe Woodbury CSD | 9,620 |
| 221 | Kingston City SD | 9,597 |
| 222 | Fort Edward UFSD | 9,544 |
| 223 | Niagara Falls City SD | 9,528 |
| 224 | Middletown City SD | 9,494 |
| 225 | Port Chester-Rye UFSD | 9,462 |
| 226 | Menands UFSD | 9,460 |
| 227 | Rocky Point UFSD | 9,451 |
| 228 | Edinburg Comn SD | 9,412 |

*continued*

*continued*

| Rank | School District | Per Pupil Total Expenditures |
|---|---|---|
| 229 | Warrensburg CSD | 9,407 |
| 230 | Lansing CSD | 9,405 |
| 231 | William Floyd UFSD | 9,376 |
| 232 | Wheelerville UFSD | 9,336 |
| 233 | Oswego City SD | 9,331 |
| 234 | Rensselaer City SD | 9,330 |
| 235 | Brookfield CSD | 9,292 |
| 236 | Cincinnatus CSD | 9,287 |
| 237 | Catskill CSD | 9,261 |
| 238 | Franklin Square UFSD | 9,256 |
| 239 | Ballston Spa CSD | 9,250 |
| 240 | Belmont CSD | 9,229 |
| 241 | Voorheesville CSD | 9,221 |
| 242 | Rotterdam—Mohonasen CSD | 9,215 |
| 243 | Northeast CSD | 9,199 |
| 244 | Morristown CSD | 9,162 |
| 245 | Honeoye Falls-Lima CSD | 9,146 |
| 246 | La Fayette CSD | 9,144 |
| 247 | Syracuse City SD | 9,120 |
| 248 | South Manor UFSD | 9,111 |
| 249 | Barker CSD | 9,098 |
| 250 | Dunkirk City SD | 9,096 |
| 251 | Schnectady City SD | 9,076 |
| 252 | North Collins CSD | 9,053 |
| 253 | North Bellmore UFSD | 9,046 |
| 254 | Sweet Home CSD | 9,020 |
| 255 | North Merrick UFSD | 9,017 |
| 256 | Pawling CSD | 9,006 |
| 257 | Berlin CSD | 8,985 |
| 258 | Kenmore—Tonawanda UFSD | 8,976 |
| 259 | Hadley-Luzerne CSD | 8,973 |
| 260 | Lindenhurst UFSD | 8,967 |
| 261 | Germantown CSD | 8,966 |
| 262 | Rondout Valley CSD | 8,956 |
| 263 | Miller Place UFSD | 8,952 |

*continued*

*continued*

| Rank | School District | Per Pupil Total Expenditures |
|---|---|---|
| 264 | Sodus CSD | 8,936 |
| 265 | Westport CSD | 8,927 |
| 266 | Lackawanna City SD | 8,917 |
| 267 | Wappingers CSD | 8,913 |
| 268 | Cobleskill-Richmondville CSD | 8,911 |
| 269 | Ithaca City SD | 8,906 |
| 270 | Roxbury CSD | 8,892 |
| 271 | Chatham CSD | 8,888 |
| 272 | East Bloomfield CSD | 8,874 |
| 273 | East Syracuse-Minoa CSD | 8,855 |
| 274 | East Irondequoit CSD | 8,831 |
| 275 | Madrid-Waddington CSD | 8,823 |
| 276 | Crown Point CSD | 8,819 |
| 277 | Onondaga CSD | 8,809 |
| 278 | Whitehall CSD | 8,805 |
| 279 | Salamanca City SD | 8,803 |
| 280(t) | Lewiston-Porter CSD | 8,800 |
| 280(t) | Schuylerville CSD | 8,800 |
| 282 | Windham-Ashland-Jewett CSD | 8,796 |
| 283(t) | East Rochester UFSD | 8,788 |
| 283(t) | North Rose—Wolcott CSD | 8,788 |
| 285 | Morris CSD | 8,786 |
| 286(t) | Canaseraga CSD | 8,781 |
| 286(t) | Penfield CSD | 8,781 |
| 288 | Greenwood lake UFSD | 8,773 |
| 289 | Green Island UFSD | 8,761 |
| 290 | Laurel Comn SD | 8,741 |
| 291 | Chateaugay CSD | 8,739 |
| 292 | St Johnsville CSD | 8,714 |
| 293 | Saranac Lake CSD | 8,710 |
| 294 | Greenville CSD | 8,692 |
| 295 | Guilderland CSD | 8,687 |
| 296(t) | Cheektowaga—Sloan UFSD | 8,678 |
| 296(t) | New Lebanon CSD | 8,678 |
| 296(t) | Ravena-Coeymans-Selkirk CSD | 8,678 |

*continued*

*continued*

| Rank | School District | Per Pupil Total Expenditures |
|---|---|---|
| 299 | Niagara-Wheatfield CSD | 8,661 |
| 300 | Utica City SD | 8,655 |
| 301 | Geneva City SD | 8,653 |
| 302 | Narrowsburg CSD | 8,649 |
| 303 | Beacon City SD | 8,640 |
| 304 | New Hyde Pk-Garden City UFSD | 8,626 |
| 305 | St Regis Falls CSD | 8,608 |
| 306 | Gates-Chili CSD | 8,607 |
| 307 | Highland CSD | 8,591 |
| 308 | Batavia City SD | 8,573 |
| 309 | Waterford-Halfmoon UFSD | 8,561 |
| 310 | Georgetown-So Otselic CSD | 8,560 |
| 311 | Wallkill CSD | 8,554 |
| 312 | Niskayuna CSD | 8,549 |
| 313 | Alexandria CSD | 8,534 |
| 314 | Salmon River CSD | 8,528 |
| 315 | NY Mills UFSD | 8,504 |
| 316 | Harrisville CSD | 8,501 |
| 317 | Hudson City SD | 8,487 |
| 318(t) | Hancock CSD | 8,467 |
| 318(t) | Delaware Valley CSD | 8,467 |
| 320 | Oriskany CSD | 8,462 |
| 321(t) | Northville CSD | 8,460 |
| 321(t) | Fairport CSD | 8,460 |
| 323 | Oneida City SD | 8,455 |
| 324(t) | Remsen CSD | 8,453 |
| 324(t) | Warwick Valley CSD | 8,453 |
| 326 | Geneseo CSD | 8,449 |
| 327 | South Kortright CSD | 8,448 |
| 328 | Copake—Taconic Hills CSD | 8,445 |
| 329 | Romulus CSD | 8,430 |
| 330(t) | Brunswick CSD (Brittonkill) | 8,427 |
| 330(t) | Ticonderoga CSD | 8,427 |
| 332 | Iroquois CSD | 8,413 |
| 333 | Canajoharie CSD | 8,409 |

*continued*

*continued*

| Rank | School District | Per Pupil Total Expenditures |
|---|---|---|
| 334 | Jefferson CSD | 8,400 |
| 335 | North Warren CSD | 8,386 |
| 336(t) | Corning City SD | 8,381 |
| 336(t) | Cohoes City SD | 8,381 |
| 338 | Bethlehem CSD | 8,372 |
| 339 | Williamsville CSD | 8,369 |
| 340 | Newburgh City SD | 8,364 |
| 341 | Depew UFSD | 8,360 |
| 342 | Johnson City SD | 8,356 |
| 343 | Wheatland-Chili CSD | 8,355 |
| 344 | Lyons CSD | 8,343 |
| 345 | Eldred CSD | 8,335 |
| 346 | Lansingburgh CSD | 8,332 |
| 347 | Cherry Valley-Springfield CSD | 8,330 |
| 348 | South Colonie CSD | 8,329 |
| 349 | Wayne CSD | 8,326 |
| 350 | Rhinebeck CSD | 8,309 |
| 351(t) | Cheektowaga CSD | 8,292 |
| 351(t) | New Paltz CSD | 8,292 |
| 353 | Warsaw CSD | 8,289 |
| 354 | Waterville CSD | 8,282 |
| 355 | Odessa-Montour CSD | 8,280 |
| 356 | Stamford CSD | 8,267 |
| 357 | Wayland-Cohocton CSD | 8,236 |
| 358 | Gananda CSD | 8,219 |
| 359 | West Irondequoit CSD | 8,217 |
| 360 | Evans-Brant CSD (Lake Shore) | 8,207 |
| 361 | Middleburgh CSD | 8,206 |
| **362** | **New York City** | **8,205** |
| 363 | Sharon Springs CSD | 8,193 |
| 364 | Canandaigua City SD | 8,179 |
| 365(t) | Lancaster CSD | 8,175 |
| 365(t) | Willsboro CSD | 8,175 |
| 367 | Schodack CSD | 8,171 |
| 368 | Victor CSD | 8,167 |

*continued*

*continued*

| Rank | School District | Per Pupil Total Expenditures |
|---|---|---|
| 369 | Alden CSD | 8,157 |
| 370 | Burnt Hills-Balston Lake CSD | 8,152 |
| 371 | Johnstown City SD | 8,150 |
| 372 | Palmyra-Macedon CSD | 8,149 |
| 373 | De Ruyter CSD | 8,135 |
| 374 | Bradford CSD | 8,132 |
| 375 | Parishville-Hopkinton CSD | 8,121 |
| 376 | Orchard Park CSD | 8,120 |
| 377 | Galway CSD | 8,110 |
| 378 | New Hartford CSD | 8,103 |
| 379 | North Tonawanda City SD | 8,101 |
| 380 | Avon CSD | 8,093 |
| 381 | Watkins Glen CSD | 8,092 |
| 382 | Cleveland Hill UFSD | 8,080 |
| 383 | Fort Plain CSD | 8,079 |
| 384 | Carthage CSD | 8,074 |
| 385 | North Syracuse CSD | 8,071 |
| 386 | Stillwater CSD | 8,067 |
| 387(t) | Elizabethtown-Lewis CSD | 8,066 |
| 387(t) | Plattsburgh City SD | 8,066 |
| 389 | West Valley CSD | 8,062 |
| 390 | Maine-Endwell CSD | 8,061 |
| 391 | Laurens CSD | 8,042 |
| 392 | Dover UFSD | 8,036 |
| 393 | Red Hook CSD | 8,032 |
| 394 | Norwich City SD | 8,022 |
| 395 | Fayetteville—Manlius CSD | 8,020 |
| 396 | Mayville CSD | 8,016 |
| 397 | Clarence CSD | 8,010 |
| 398 | Monticello CSD | 8,006 |
| 399 | Shenendehowa CSD | 8,005 |
| 400 | Sherburne—Earlville CSD | 8,003 |
| 401 | Hyde Park CSD | 8,001 |
| 402 | Spencer-Van Etten CSD | 8,000 |
| 403 | Webster CSD | 7,983 |

*continued*

*continued*

| Rank | School District | Per Pupil Total Expenditures |
|---|---|---|
| 404 | Williamson CSD | 7,981 |
| 405 | East Greenbush CSD | 7,975 |
| 406 | Hilton CSD | 7,973 |
| 407(t) | Greece CSD | 7,957 |
| 407(t) | Trumansburg CSD | 7,957 |
| 409 | Schalmont CSD | 7,949 |
| 410(t) | Margaretville CSD | 7,947 |
| 410(t) | Valley Stream 13 UFSD | 7,947 |
| 412 | Fulton City SD | 7,942 |
| 413 | Elba CSD | 7,937 |
| 414 | Pine Plains CSD | 7,936 |
| 415 | Newfane CSD | 7,933 |
| 416 | Mechanicville City SD | 7,928 |
| 417 | Saratoga Springs City SD | 7,927 |
| 418 | Lyme CSD | 7,922 |
| 419 | Corinth CSD | 7,912 |
| 420 | Amsterdam City SD | 7,908 |
| 421(t) | Hartford CSD | 7,906 |
| 421(t) | Mayfield CSD | 7,906 |
| 423 | Hamburg CSD | 7,903 |
| 424 | Starpoint CSD | 7,897 |
| 425 | Whitesboro CSD | 7,893 |
| 426 | New Berlin CSD | 7,890 |
| 427(t) | Frontier CSD | 7,881 |
| 427(t) | Rome City SD | 7,881 |
| 429 | Belleville Henderson CSD | 7,876 |
| 430 | Andover | 7,870 |
| 431 | Elmont UFSD | 7,861 |
| 432 | Fonda-Fultonville CSD | 7,849 |
| 433 | Minisink Valley CSD | 7,842 |
| 434(t) | Heuvelton CSD | 7,841 |
| 434(t) | Liverpool CSD | 7,841 |
| 436 | Greenwood CSD | 7,827 |
| 437 | Washingtonville CSD | 7,814 |
| 438 | Skaneateles CSD | 7,811 |

*continued*

*continued*

| Rank | School District | Per Pupil Total Expenditures |
|---|---|---|
| 439 | Elmira City SD | 7,806 |
| 440 | Bainbridge-Guilford CSD | 7,803 |
| 441 | Addison CSD | 7,793 |
| 442 | Westmoreland CSD | 7,792 |
| 443 | Dryden CSD | 7,791 |
| 444 | Le Roy CSD | 7,786 |
| 445 | West Seneca CSD | 7,771 |
| 446 | Poland CSD | 7,768 |
| 447 | Edwards-Knox CSD | 7,765 |
| 448 | Northeastern Clinton CSD | 7,762 |
| 449 | North Colonie CSD | 7,750 |
| 450 | Brocton CSD | 7,748 |
| 451 | Buffalo City SD | 7,746 |
| 452 | Binghamton City SD | 7,743 |
| 453 | Potsdam CSD | 7,733 |
| 454 | Marion CSD | 7,729 |
| 455 | Hammondsport CSD | 7,714 |
| 456(t) | Dundee CSD | 7,700 |
| 456(t) | La Fargeville CSD | 7,700 |
| 458 | Union Springs CSD | 7,696 |
| 459 | Pine Bush CSD | 7,693 |
| 460 | Wilson CSD | 7,691 |
| 461 | Naples CSD | 7,683 |
| 462 | Altmar Parish-Williamstown CSD | 7,677 |
| 463 | Eden CSD | 7,676 |
| 464 | Alexander CSD | 7,673 |
| 465 | Sackets Harbor CSD | 7,672 |
| 466 | Oneonta City SD | 7,670 |
| 467 | Hoosic Valley CSD | 7,668 |
| 468 | Manchester-Shortsville CSD (Red) | 7,656 |
| 469 | Churchville—Chili CSD | 7,652 |
| 470 | Ausable Valley CSD | 7,635 |
| 471(t) | Whitesville CSD | 7,632 |
| 471(t) | Gloversville City SD | 7,632 |
| 473(t) | Saranac CSD | 7,631 |

*continued*

*continued*

| Rank | School District | Per Pupil Total Expenditures |
|---|---|---|
| 473(t) | Kinderhook CSD | 7,631 |
| 475 | Duanesburg CSD | 7,629 |
| 476 | Pembroke CSD | 7,623 |
| 477 | Union-Endicott CSD | 7,616 |
| 478 | Berne-Knox-Westerlo CSD | 7,612 |
| 479 | Ogdensburg City SD | 7,608 |
| 480 | Vestal CSD | 7,605 |
| 481 | Greene CSD | 7,604 |
| 482 | Grand Island CSD | 7,597 |
| 483 | Worcester CSD | 7,588 |
| 484(t) | Cazenovia CSD | 7,586 |
| 484(t) | South Glens Falls CSD | 7,586 |
| 486 | Auburn City SD | 7,583 |
| 487 | Chenango Valley CSD | 7,570 |
| 488(t) | Newark CSD | 7,558 |
| 488(t) | Malone CSD | 7,558 |
| 490 | Springville—Griffith Inst CSD | 7,553 |
| 491 | Solvay UFSD | 7,552 |
| 492 | Floral Park-Bellrose UFSD | 7,536 |
| 493 | Olean City SD | 7,532 |
| 494 | Ripley CSD | 7,530 |
| 495 | Byron-Bergen CSD | 7,529 |
| 496 | Glens Falls City SD | 7,527 |
| 497 | Scotia—Glenville CSD | 7,525 |
| 498(t) | Gowanda CSD | 7,520 |
| 498(t) | Scio CSD | 7,520 |
| 500 | Fort Ann CSD | 7,519 |
| 501 | Lake Placid CSD | 7,514 |
| 502 | Honeoye CSD | 7,513 |
| 503 | Thousand Islands CSD | 7,512 |
| 504 | Westhill CSD | 7,510 |
| 505 | Granville CSD | 7,508 |
| 506 | Canton CSD | 7,507 |
| 507 | South New Berlin CSD | 7,503 |
| 508 | Delhi CSD | 7,498 |

*continued*

*continued*

| Rank | School District | Per Pupil Total Expenditures |
|---|---|---|
| 509 | Jordan—Elbridge CSD | 7,495 |
| 510 | Clyde-Savannah CSD | 7,491 |
| 511 | McGraw CSD | 7,482 |
| 512 | Indian River CSD | 7,478 |
| 513 | Cairo—Durham CSD | 7,468 |
| 514 | Beekmantown CSD | 7,464 |
| 515 | Holland Patent CSD | 7,459 |
| 516 | Walton CSD | 7,449 |
| 517 | Phelps—Clifton Springs CSD | 7,431 |
| 518(t) | Franklin CSD | 7,427 |
| 518(t) | Tonawanda City SD | 7,427 |
| 520 | Saugerties CSD | 7,426 |
| 521 | Dalton—Nunda CSD (Keshequa) | 7,423 |
| 522 | Mt Morris CSD | 7,419 |
| 523 | Cuba—Rushford CSD | 7,416 |
| 524 | Lisbon CSD | 7,413 |
| 525 | Livonia CSD | 7,412 |
| 526 | Argyle CSD | 7,411 |
| 527 | Horseheads CSD | 7,407 |
| 528 | Arlington CSD | 7,396 |
| 529 | Perry CSD | 7,392 |
| 530 | East Aurora UFSD | 7,391 |
| 531 | Lyndonville CSD | 7,387 |
| 532 | Spencerport CSD | 7,375 |
| 533 | West Genesee CSD | 7,373 |
| 534 | Tupper Lake CSD | 7,369 |
| 535 | Cornwall CSD | 7,362 |
| 536 | Mexico CSD | 7,360 |
| 537 | Richfield Springs CSD | 7,359 |
| 538 | Hudson Falls CSD | 7,356 |
| 539 | Fabius-Pompey CSD | 7,355 |
| 540 | Chazy UFSD | 7,353 |
| 541 | Prattsburgh CSD | 7,351 |
| 542 | Port Byron CSD | 7,348 |
| 543 | Arkport CSD | 7,346 |

*continued*

*continued*

| Rank | School District | Per Pupil Total Expenditures |
|---|---|---|
| 544 | Bath CSD | 7,343 |
| 545 | Pine Valley CSD (South Dayton) | 7,339 |
| 546 | Valley CSD (Montgomery) | 7,338 |
| 547 | York CSD | 7,333 |
| 548 | Schoharie CSD | 7,328 |
| 549 | Copenhagen CSD | 7,326 |
| 550 | Port Jervis City SD | 7,325 |
| 551 | Ellicottville CSD | 7,323 |
| 552 | Hermon—Dekalb CSD | 7,322 |
| 553 | West Canada Valley CSD | 7,321 |
| 554 | Central Square CSD | 7,317 |
| 555 | Peru CSD | 7,309 |
| 556 | Southwestern CSD (Jamestown) | 7,298 |
| 557(t) | Bridgewater-West Winfield CSD | 7,295 |
| 557(t) | Maplewood Comn SD | 7,295 |
| 559 | Waterville City SD | 7,285 |
| 560 | Sherman CSD | 7,281 |
| 561(t) | Pulaski CSD | 7,280 |
| 561(t) | Waterloo CSD | 7,280 |
| 563 | Windsor CSD | 7,278 |
| 564(t) | Edmeston CSD | 7,277 |
| 564(t) | Wynantskill UFSD | 7,277 |
| 566 | Susquehanna Valley CSD | 7,266 |
| 567(t) | Canastota CSD | 7,264 |
| 567(t) | Gorham-Middlesex CSD (Whitman) | 7,264 |
| 569 | Madison CSD | 7,262 |
| 570 | Fredonia CSD | 7,255 |
| 571 | Queensbury UFSD | 7,254 |
| 572 | Little Valley CSD | 7,237 |
| 573 | Seneca Falls CSD | 7,218 |
| 574 | Marcellus CSD | 7,215 |
| 575 | Medina CSD | 7,206 |
| 576 | Oakfield-Alabama CSD | 7,201 |
| 577 | Sidney CSD | 7,197 |
| 578 | Hammond CSD | 7,190 |

*continued*

*continued*

| Rank | School District | Per Pupil Total Expenditures |
|---|---|---|
| 579 | Coxsackie—Athens CSD | 7,187 |
| 580 | Baldwinsville CSD | 7,185 |
| 581 | Massena CSD | 7,178 |
| 582 | Brasher Falls CSD | 7,175 |
| 583 | Pavilion CSD | 7,167 |
| 584 | Cortland City SD | 7,161 |
| 585 | Brockport CSD | 7,160 |
| 586 | Sherrill City SD | 7,156 |
| 587 | Clinton CSD | 7,148 |
| 588 | Greenwich CSD | 7,143 |
| 589 | Chittenango CSD | 7,133 |
| 590 | Herkimer CSD | 7,121 |
| 591 | Averill Park CSD | 7,108 |
| 592 | Charlotte Valley CSD | 7,107 |
| 593 | Watertown City SD | 7,105 |
| 594 | Moriah CSD | 7,099 |
| 595 | Elmira Hts CSD | 7,096 |
| 596 | Jamestown City SD | 7,095 |
| 597 | Wyoming CSD | 7,089 |
| 598(t) | Broadalbin—Perth CSD | 7,086 |
| 598(t) | Lockport City SD | 7,086 |
| 600 | Newfield CSD | 7,085 |
| 601(t) | Dolgeville CSD | 7,079 |
| 601(t) | Stockbridge Valley CSD | 7,079 |
| 603 | Franklinville CSD | 7,078 |
| 604 | Oxford Acad & CSD | 7,075 |
| 605 | Belfast CSD | 7,068 |
| 606 | Weedsport CSD | 7,057 |
| 607 | Wellsville CSD | 7,055 |
| 608 | Gouverneur CSD | 7,051 |
| 609 | Bemus Point CSD | 7,048 |
| 610 | Mohawk CSD | 7,019 |
| 611 | Cambridge CSD | 7,017 |
| 612 | Red Creek CSD | 7,014 |
| 613(t) | Clymer CSD | 7,012 |

*continued*

*continued*

| Rank | School District | Per Pupil Total Expenditures |
|---|---|---|
| 613(t) | PennYan CSD | 7,012 |
| 615 | Salem CSD | 6,988 |
| 616 | Hornell City SD | 6,977 |
| 617 | Holley CSD | 6,957 |
| 618 | Avoca CSD | 6,950 |
| 619 | Camden CSD | 6,946 |
| 620 | Chenango Forks CSD | 6,939 |
| 621 | Dansville CSD | 6,926 |
| 622 | Cattaraugus CSD | 6,917 |
| 623 | Holland CSD | 6,890 |
| 624 | Harpursville CSD | 6,888 |
| 625 | Tully CSD | 6,880 |
| 626 | Akron CSD | 6,849 |
| 627 | Norwood—Norfolk CSD | 6,844 |
| 628 | Sauquoit Valley CSD | 6,840 |
| 629 | Albion CSD | 6,828 |
| 630 | South Jefferson CSD | 6,827 |
| 631 | Friendship CSD | 6,826 |
| 632(t) | Phoenix CSD | 6,814 |
| 632(t) | Caledonia–Mumford CSD | 6,814 |
| 634 | Frankfort—Schuyler CSD | 6,813 |
| 635 | Angelica CSD | 6,805 |
| 636 | Alfred—Almond CSD | 6,801 |
| 637 | Letchworth CSD | 6,795 |
| 638 | Sandy Creek CSD | 6,791 |
| 639 | Randolph CSD | 6,785 |
| 640 | Limestone UFSD | 6,778 |
| 641 | Cooperstown CSD | 6,774 |
| 642 | Groton CSD | 6,772 |
| 643 | Marathon CSD | 6,766 |
| 644 | Oppenheim-Ephratah CSD | 6,763 |
| 645 | Hannibal CSD | 6,757 |
| 646 | Westfield CSD | 6,748 |
| 647 | Cassadaga Valley CSD | 6,733 |
| 648 | Silver Creek CSD | 6,729 |

*continued*

*continued*

| Rank | School District | Per Pupil Total Expenditures |
|---|---|---|
| 649 | Brushton—Moira CSD | 6,715 |
| 650 | Falconer CSD | 6,692 |
| 651 | Kendall CSD | 6,690 |
| 652 | Hamilton CSD | 6,672 |
| 653 | Royalton—Hartland CSD | 6,667 |
| 654 | Morrisville–Eaton CSD | 6,662 |
| 655 | Canisteo CSD | 6,656 |
| 656 | Yorkshire—Pioneer CSD | 6,650 |
| 657 | South Lewis CSD | 6,644 |
| 658 | Owego—Apalachin CSD | 6,636 |
| 659 | Little Falls City SD | 6,628 |
| 660 | Brunswick Comn SD | 6,588 |
| 661 | Frewsburg CSD | 6,564 |
| 662 | Glens Falls Comn SD | 6,557 |
| 663 | General Brown CSD | 6,539 |
| 664 | Adirondack CSD | 6,528 |
| 665 | Bolivar—Richburg CSD | 6,520 |
| 666 | Fillmore CSD | 6,503 |
| 667 | Beaver River CSD | 6,496 |
| 668 | Attica CSD | 6,489 |
| 669 | Cato—Meridian CSD | 6,459 |
| 670 | Northern Adirondack CSD | 6,454 |
| 671 | Moravia CSD | 6,428 |
| 672 | Allegany CSD | 6,406 |
| 673 | Newark Valley CSD | 6,384 |
| 674 | Hinsdale CSD | 6,375 |
| 675 | Waverly CSD | 6,358 |
| 676 | Otego—Unadilla CSD | 6,332 |
| 677 | Forestville CSD | 6,306 |
| 678 | Southern Cayuga CSD | 6,289 |
| 679 | Ilion CSD | 6,258 |
| 680 | Hoosick Falls CSD | 6,242 |
| 681 | Lowville Acad & CSD | 6,177 |
| 682 | Homer CSD | 6,100 |
| 683 | Panama CSD | 6,064 |

*continued*

*continued*

| Rank | School District | Per Pupil Total Expenditures |
|---|---|---|
| 684 | Candor CSD | 6,055 |
| 685 | Tioga CSD | 5,946 |
| 686 | Whitney Point CSD | 5,932 |
| 687 | Lyncourt UFSD | 5,783 |
| 688 | Portville CSD | 5,616 |

Source: New York State Education Department, *Seventh Annual School District Fiscal Profile Report, 1989-90—1993-94*

## RANKINGS OF TEACHER SALARIES BY STATE

The average public school teacher salary in New York ranked fourth highest in the nation in 1995-96, only trailing Connecticut, Alaska, and Michigan.

**Average Teacher Salaries**

| Rank | State | Average Teacher Salary |
|---|---|---|
| 1 | Connecticut | $50,400 |
| 2 | Alaska | 49,620 |
| 3 | Michigan | 49,168 |
| **4** | **New York** | **48,115** |
| 5 | New Jersey | 47,910 |
| 6 | Pennsylvania | 46,916 |
| 7 | Massachusetts | 43,756 |
| 8 | District of Columbia | 43,700 |
| 9 | California | 42,516 |
| 10 | Rhode Island | 42,160 |
| 11 | Maryland | 41,215 |
| 12 | Illinois | 41,008 |
| 13 | Delaware | 40,533 |
| 14 | Oregon | 39,650 |
| 15 | Wisconsin | 38,571 |
| 16 | Washington | 38,025 |
| 17 | Ohio | 37,835 |
| 18 | Indiana | 37,805 |
| 19 | Minnesota | 36,937 |
| 20 | Vermont | 36,295 |
| 21 | Nebraska | 36,167 |
| 22 | Nevada | 36,167 |
| 23 | Hawaii | 35,807 |
| 24 | New Hampshire | 35,792 |
| 25 | Kansas | 35,518 |
| 26 | Colorado | 35,364 |
| 27 | Virginia | 34,687 |
| 28 | Georgia | 34,307 |

*continued*

*continued*

| Rank | School District | Average Teacher Salary |
|---|---|---|
| 29 | Tennessee | 33,451 |
| 30 | Missouri | 33,341 |
| 31 | Florida | 33,320 |
| 32 | Kentucky | 33,018 |
| 33 | Maine | 32,869 |
| 34 | Arizona | 32,484 |
| 35 | Iowa | 32,376 |
| 36 | West Virginia | 32,155 |
| 37 | Texas | 32,000 |
| 38 | Wyoming | 31,571 |
| 39 | South Carolina | 31,568 |
| 40 | Alabama | 31,307 |
| 41 | Idaho | 30,891 |
| 42 | North Carolina | 30,564 |
| 43 | Utah | 30,452 |
| 44 | Montana | 29,364 |
| 45 | New Mexico | 29,349 |
| 46 | Arkansas | 29,322 |
| 47 | Oklahoma | 28,909 |
| 48 | Mississippi | 27,689 |
| 49 | North Dakota | 26,969 |
| 50 | Louisiana | 26,800 |
| 51 | South Dakota | 26,346 |
| | U.S. Average | 37,846 |

Data Source: U.S. Department of Education, *Digest of Education Statistics 1996*

## TEACHER SALARIES: NEW YORK VS. U.S.

The average public school teacher salary in New York State consistently outpaces the U.S. average teacher salary.

• In 1995-96, the average public school teacher salary in New York State of $48,115 exceeded the national average of $37,846 by 27.1 percent.

• Between 1970 and 1996, the real average public school teacher salary in New York State grew by 13.6 percent. However, between 1980 and 1995, the real average teacher salary rose by better than 21.8 percent.

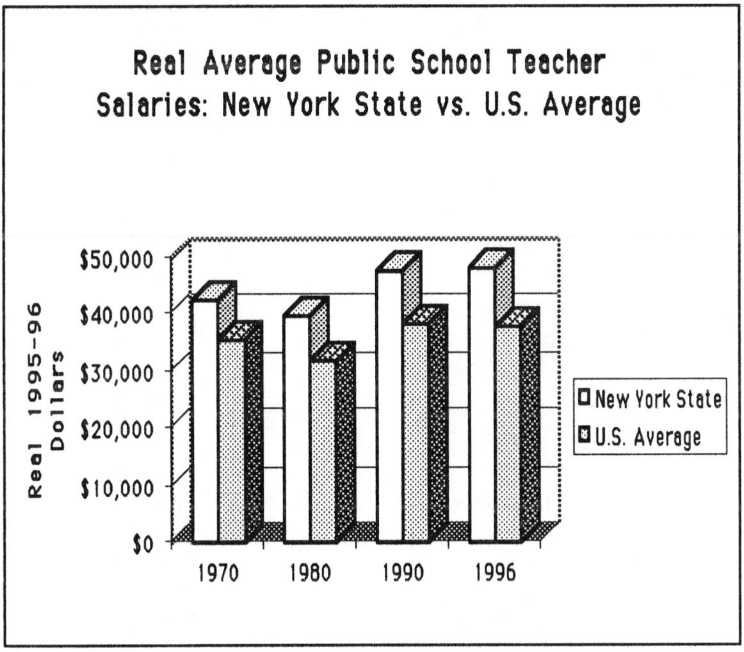


Data Source: U.S. Department of Education, *Digest of Education Statistics 1996*

## TEACHER BEGINNING SALARIES: STATE RANKINGS

The beginning public school teacher salary in New York ranked fifth highest in the nation in 1994-95.

**Beginning Teacher Salaries**

| Rank | State | Beginning Teacher Salary |
|---|---|---|
| 1 | Alaska | $31,709 |
| 2 | New Jersey | 30,226 |
| 3 | Pennsylvania | 29,416 |
| 4 | Connecticut | 28,549 |
| **5** | **New York** | **28,298** |
| 6 | Maryland | 26,813 |
| 7 | District of Columbia | 25,937 |
| 8 | Illinois | 25,616 |
| 9 | California | 25,500 |
| 10 | Hawaii | 25,436 |
| 11 | Michigan | 25,132 |
| 12 | Alabama | 24,818 |
| 13 | Nevada | 24,640 |
| 14 | Oregon | 24,366 |
| 15 | Wisconsin | 24,293 |
| 16 | Massachusetts | 24,150 |
| 17 | Rhode Island | 24,095 |
| 18 | Oklahoma | 24,015 |
| 19 | Virginia | 23,971 |
| 20 | Florida | 23,941 |
| 21 | Delaware | 23,746 |
| 22 | Georgia | 23,486 |
| 23 | Vermont | 23,442 |
| 24 | Minnesota | 23,413 |
| 25 | New Hampshire | 22,803 |
| 26 | New Mexico | 22,731 |
| 27 | Indiana | 22,680 |
| 28 | Texas | 22,510 |
| 29 | Arizona | 22,152 |

*continued*

*continued*

| Rank | State | Beginning Teacher Salary |
|---|---|---|
| 30 | West Virginia | 21,960 |
| 31 | Washington | 21,814 |
| 32 | Iowa | 21,803 |
| 33 | Kentucky | 21,682 |
| 34 | Missouri | 21,653 |
| 35 | Kansas | 21,325 |
| 36 | Tennessee | 21,115 |
| 37 | Nebraska | 20,958 |
| 38 | Colorado | 20,888 |
| 39 | South Carolina | 20,878 |
| 40 | Arkansas | 20,876 |
| 41 | Wyoming | 20,722 |
| 42 | North Carolina | 20,620 |
| 43 | Ohio | 20,059 |
| 44 | Maine | 20,001 |
| 45 | Mississippi | 19,650 |
| 46 | Utah | 19,605 |
| 47 | Montana | 19,589 |
| 48 | Idaho | 19,411 |
| 49 | South Dakota | 19,328 |
| 50 | Louisiana | 18,551 |
| 51 | North Dakota | 17,933 |
| | U.S. Average | 23,915 |

Data Source: U.S. Department of Education, *Digest of Education Statistics 1996*

## RANKINGS OF INSTRUCTIONAL STAFF SALARIES BY STATE

New York's average annual salary for public school instructional staff (including supervisors, principals, teachers, and other instructional staff) ranked sixth highest in the nation in 1995-96.

**Instructional Staff Salaries**

| Rank | State | Staff Salary |
|---|---|---|
| 1 | Massachusetts | $53,033 |
| 2 | Connecticut | 52,200 |
| 3 | Michigan | 50,764 |
| 4 | Alaska | 50,516 |
| 5 | New Jersey | 50,435 |
| **6** | **New York** | **49,690** |
| 7 | Pennsylvania | 47,911 |
| 8 | California | 44,027 |
| 9 | Rhode Island | 42,900 |
| 10 | Arizona | 42,870 |
| 11 | Maryland | 42,702 |
| 12 | Illinois | 42,489 |
| 13 | New Hampshire | 42,188 |
| 14 | Delaware | 42,177 |
| 15 | Oregon | 40,900 |
| 16 | Washington | 39,741 |
| 17 | District of Columbia | 39,663 |
| 18 | Wisconsin | 39,498 |
| 19 | Ohio | 39,038 |
| 20 | Indiana | 38,294 |
| 21 | Nevada | 37,879 |
| 22 | Minnesota | 37,680 |
| 23 | Kansas | 37,626 |
| 24 | Georgia | 37,102 |
| 25 | Hawaii | 37,057 |
| 26 | Vermont | 37,054 |
| 27 | Colorado | 36,430 |
| 28 | Virginia | 35,535 |

*continued*

*continued*

| Rank | State | Staff Salary |
|---|---|---|
| 29 | Kentucky | 35,324 |
| 30 | Tennessee | 34,735 |
| 31 | Florida | 34,365 |
| 32 | Nebraska | 34,023 |
| 33 | Maine | 33,994 |
| 34 | Missouri | 33,870 |
| 35 | Texas | 33,861 |
| 36 | Iowa | 33,534 |
| 37 | West Virginia | 33,296 |
| 38 | South Carolina | 33,100 |
| 39 | Wyoming | 32,493 |
| 40 | Alabama | 32,453 |
| 41 | Idaho | 32,285 |
| 42 | North Carolina | 31,778 |
| 43 | Utah | 31,565 |
| 44 | Montana | 30,908 |
| 45 | Arkansas | 30,607 |
| 46 | Oklahoma | 29,894 |
| 47 | New Mexico | 29,389 |
| 48 | Mississippi | 28,710 |
| 49 | Louisiana | 28,167 |
| 50 | South Dakota | 27,354 |
| 51 | North Dakota | 27,153 |
| | U.S. Average | 39,662 |

Source: U.S. Department of Education, *Digest of Education Statistics 1996*

## INSTRUCTIONAL STAFF SALARIES: NEW YORK VS. U.S.

New York's average annual salary for public school instructional staff increased by 44.4 percent, in inflation-adjusted 1995-96 dollars, between 1960 and 1996—from $34,405 to $49,690.

In 1995-96, the New York average salary outpaced the national average by 25.3 percent—New York equaling $49,690 versus the national average of $39,662.

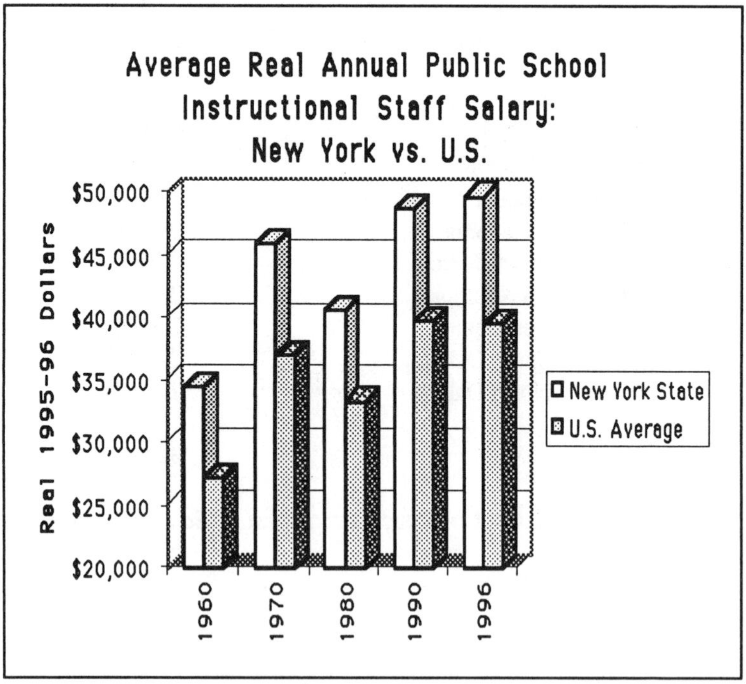


Data Source: U.S. Department of Education, *Digest of Education Statistics 1996*

# RANKINGS OF TEACHER SALARIES BY NEW YORK COUNTY: 21-25 YEARS EXPERIENCE

For public school teachers with 21-25 years of experience in New York, the average 1993-94 salary topped $60,000 in five counties (Rockland, Suffolk, Nassau, Westchester, and Putnam). The average for New York City's five counties equaled $53,805, ranking twelfth out of 58. The state average equaled $53,805.

**Average Teacher Salary with 21-25 Years Experience**

| Rank | County | Average Teacher Salary |
|---|---|---|
| 1 | Rockland | $72,317 |
| 2 | Suffolk | 69,198 |
| 3 | Nassau | 68,500 |
| 4 | Westchester | 66,245 |
| 5 | Putnam | 64,844 |
| 6 | Erie | 59,029 |
| 7 | Monroe | 57,905 |
| 8 | Niagara | 57,000 |
| 9 | Dutchess | 55,706 |
| 10 | Saratoga | 54,645 |
| 11 | Albany | 54,065 |
| **12** | **New York City** | **53,805** |
| 13 | Ulster | 53,304 |
| 14 | Rennsalaer | 52,767 |
| 15 | Schenectady | 52,304 |
| 16 | Warren | 52,210 |
| 17 | Orange | 52,000 |
| 18 | Columbia | 51,544 |
| 19 | Genesee | 51,010 |
| 20 | Orleans | 50,814 |
| 21 | Wyoming | 50,700 |
| 22 | Sullivan | 50,095 |
| 23 | Washington | 49,280 |
| 24 | Oswego | 48,828 |
| 25 | Wayne | 48,217 |

*continued*

*continued*

| Rank | County | Average Teacher Salary |
|---|---|---|
| 26 | Jefferson | 48,147 |
| 27 | Chautauqua | 48,084 |
| 28 | Ontario | 47,699 |
| 29 | Oneida | 47,500 |
| 30 | Livingston | 47,325 |
| 31 | Clinton | 47,217 |
| 32 | St. Lawrence | 46,768 |
| 33 | Greene | 46,639 |
| 34 | Onondaga | 46,322 |
| 35 | Montgomery | 46,157 |
| 36 | Schuyler | 45,963 |
| 37 | Lewis | 45,410 |
| 38 | Madison | 45,330 |
| 39 | Tompkins | 45,098 |
| 40 | Schoharie | 45,092 |
| 41 | Yates | 45,056 |
| 42 | Fulton | 44,880 |
| 43 | Essex | 44,872 |
| 44 | Franklin | 44,581 |
| 45 | Broome | 44,035 |
| 46 | Hamilton | 43,361 |
| 47 | Steuben | 43,326 |
| 48 | Chemung | 43,306 |
| 49 | Cattagaugus | 43,240 |
| 50 | Seneca | 43,144 |
| 51 | Cortland | 43,033 |
| 52 | Herkimer | 42,599 |
| 53 | Allegany | 41,724 |
| 54 | Cayuga | 41,550 |
| 55 | Tioga | 41,474 |
| 56 | Otsego | 41,258 |
| 57 | Delaware | 40,923 |
| 58 | Chenango | 39,868 |

Note: New York City includes five counties.
Data Source: New York State Education Department, *Seventh Annual School District Fiscal Profile Report, 1989-90—1993-94*

# RANKINGS OF TEACHER SALARIES BY NEW YORK COUNTY: 11-15 YEARS EXPERIENCE

For public school teachers with 11-15 years of experience in New York, the average 1993-94 salary topped $50,000 in five counties (Westchester, Nassau, Rockland, Putnam, and Suffolk). The average for New York City's five counties equaled $43,014, ranking seventh out of 58. The state average also equaled $43,014.

**Average Teacher Salary with 11-15 Years Experience**

| Rank | County | Average Teacher Salary |
|---|---|---|
| 1 | Westchester | $56,859 |
| 2 | Nassau | 56,124 |
| 3 | Rockland | 55,375 |
| 4 | Putnam | 54,288 |
| 5 | Suffolk | 53,750 |
| 6 | Ulster | 43,587 |
| **7** | **New York City** | **43,014** |
| 8 | Orange | 42,848 |
| 9 | Albany | 42,821 |
| 10 | Monroe | 42,310 |
| 11 | Schenectady | 41,592 |
| 12 | Saratoga | 41,000 |
| 13 | Rennsalaer | 40,726 |
| 14 | Niagara | 40,722 |
| 15 | Columbia | 40,545 |
| 16 | Dutchess | 40,082 |
| 17 | Erie | 39,830 |
| 18 | Sullivan | 39,757 |
| 19 | Jefferson | 39,467 |
| 20 | Warren | 39,238 |
| 21 | Clinton | 38,767 |
| 22 | Greene | 38,542 |
| 23 | Oswego | 37,945 |
| 24 | Ontario | 37,905 |
| 25 | Livingston | 37,896 |

*continued*

*continued*

| Rank | County | Average Teacher Salary |
|---|---|---|
| 26 | Genesee | 37,596 |
| 27 | Montgomery | 37,512 |
| 28 | Washington | 37,285 |
| 29 | Essex | 37,098 |
| 30 | Wyoming | 36,812 |
| 31 | Schoharie | 36,648 |
| 32 | St. Lawrence | 36,195 |
| 33 | Hamilton | 35,798 |
| 34 | Chautauqua | 35,778 |
| 35 | Orleans | 35,700 |
| 36 | Franklin | 35,608 |
| 37 | Onondaga | 35,487 |
| 38 | Lewis | 35,478 |
| 39 | Yates | 35,443 |
| 40 | Oneida | 35,201 |
| 41 | Wayne | 35,073 |
| 42 | Madison | 35,000 |
| 43 | Cortland | 34,999 |
| 44 | Tompkins | 34,737 |
| 45 | Broome | 34,531 |
| 46 | Fulton | 34,452 |
| 47 | Seneca | 34,150 |
| 48 | Schuyler | 33,681 |
| 49 | Allegany | 33,663 |
| 50 | Cattagaugus | 33,415 |
| 51 | Steuben | 33,376 |
| 52 | Herkimer | 33,291 |
| 53 | Tioga | 33,052 |
| 54 | Chenango | 33,043 |
| 55 | Cayuga | 32,993 |
| 56 | Delaware | 32,810 |
| 57 | Otsego | 32,248 |
| 58 | Chemung | 32,113 |

Note: New York City includes five counties.
Source: New York State Education Department, *Seventh Annual School District Fiscal Profile Report, 1989-90—1993-94*

# RANKINGS OF TEACHER SALARIES BY NEW YORK COUNTY: FIVE YEARS EXPERIENCE

For public school teachers with five years of experience in New York, the average 1993-94 salary topped $40,000 in three counties (Nassau, Putnam, and Westchester). The average for New York City's five counties equaled $31,465, ranking twenty-first out of 58. The state average equaled $32,004.

**Average Teacher Salary with Five Years Experience**

| Rank | County | Average Teacher Salary |
|---|---|---|
| 1 | Nassau | $41,539 |
| 2 | Putnam | 41,092 |
| 3 | Westchester | 41,012 |
| 4 | Suffolk | 39,675 |
| 5 | Rockland | 39,185 |
| 6 | Ulster | 36,281 |
| 7 | Albany | 34,500 |
| 8 | Dutchess | 34,000 |
| 9 | Monroe | 33,500 |
| 10 | Orange | 33,423 |
| 11 | Oswego | 33,391 |
| 12 | Jefferson | 33,105 |
| 13 | Greene | 32,867 |
| 14 | Schnectady | 32,717 |
| 15 | Saratoga | 32,350 |
| 16 | Clinton | 32,040 |
| 17 | Niagara | 31,996 |
| 18 | Sullivan | 31,725 |
| 19 | Erie | 31,702 |
| 20 | Ontario | 31,575 |
| **21** | **New York City** | **31,465** |
| 22 | Onondaga | 31,370 |
| 23 | Lewis | 31,154 |
| 24 | St. Lawrence | 31,015 |
| 25 | Genesee | 31,002 |

continued

continued

| Rank | County | Average Teacher Salary |
|---|---|---|
| 26 | Washington | 30,980 |
| 27 | Franklin | 30,580 |
| 28 | Cayuga | 30,335 |
| 29 | Livingston | 30,327 |
| 30 | Cortland | 30,314 |
| 31 | Columbia | 30,081 |
| 32 | Montgomery | 30,068 |
| 33 | Schuyler | 30,051 |
| 34 | Tompkins | 30,050 |
| 35 | Schoharie | 29,899 |
| 36 | Yates (for 1992-93) | 29,818 |
| 37 | Warren | 29,743 |
| 38 | Orleans | 29,609 |
| 39 | Rensselaer | 29,600 |
| 40 | Steuben | 29,526 |
| 41 | Essex | 29,452 |
| 42 | Fulton | 29,392 |
| 43 | Hamilton | 29,329 |
| 44 | Broome | 29,298 |
| 45 | Chemung | 29,211 |
| 46 | Wayne | 29,062 |
| 47 | Seneca | 29,000 |
| 48 | Tioga | 28,914 |
| 49 | Chautauqua | 28,573 |
| 50 | Chenango | 28,220 |
| 51 | Cattaraugus | 28,019 |
| 52 | Madison | 27,905 |
| 53 | Wyoming | 27,776 |
| 54 | Delaware | 27,653 |
| 55 | Otsego | 27,608 |
| 56 | Allegany | 27,514 |
| 57 | Oneida | 27,230 |
| 58 | Herkimer | 26,919 |

Note: New York City includes five counties.
Source: New York State Education Department, *Seventh Annual School District Fiscal Profile Report, 1989-90—1993-94*

# PUPIL-TEACHER RATIO: STATE RANKINGS

New York State ranked fourteenth in terms of the public-school pupil-teacher ratio in the nation in the fall 1994.

**Pupil-Teacher Ratio**

| Rank | State | Ratio |
|---|---|---|
| 1 | District of Columbia | 13.2 |
| 2(t) | Vermont | 13.8 |
| 2(t) | New Jersey | 13.8 |
| 2(t) | Maine | 13.8 |
| 5(t) | Connecticut | 14.4 |
| 5(t) | South Dakota | 14.4 |
| 7 | Nebraska | 14.5 |
| 8 | Virginia | 14.6 |
| 9 | Rhode Island | 14.7 |
| 10(t) | Massachusetts | 14.8 |
| 10(t) | West Virginia | 14.8 |
| 12 | Wyoming | 15.0 |
| 13 | Kansas | 15.1 |
| **14** | **New York** | **15.2** |
| 15 | North Dakota | 15.3 |
| 16(t) | Missouri | 15.5 |
| 16(t) | Oklahoma | 15.5 |
| 18 | New Hampshire | 15.6 |
| 19(t) | Iowa | 15.7 |
| 19(t) | Texas | 15.7 |
| 21 | Wisconsin | 15.9 |
| 22 | North Carolina | 16.2 |
| 23(t) | Georgia | 16.3 |
| 23(t) | Montana | 16.3 |
| 25 | South Carolina | 16.4 |
| 26(t) | Delaware | 16.6 |
| 26(t) | Louisiana | 16.6 |
| 26(t) | Ohio | 16.6 |
| 29(t) | Kentucky | 17.0 |

*continued*

*continued*

| Rank | State | Ratio |
|---|---|---|
| 29(t) | Maryland | 17.0 |
| 31(t) | Arkansas | 17.1 |
| 31(t) | Pennsylvania | 17.1 |
| 33(t) | Alabama | 17.2 |
| 33(t) | New Mexico | 17.2 |
| 35 | Illinois | 17.3 |
| 36(t) | Minnesota | 17.5 |
| 36(t) | Indiana | 17.5 |
| 36(t) | Mississippi | 17.5 |
| 39 | Alaska | 17.6 |
| 40 | Hawaii | 17.9 |
| 41 | Colorado | 18.4 |
| 42 | Tennessee | 18.6 |
| 43 | Nevada | 18.7 |
| 44(t) | Florida | 19.1 |
| 44(t) | Idaho | 19.1 |
| 46 | Arizona | 19.3 |
| 47 | Oregon | 19.9 |
| 48 | Michigan | 20.1 |
| 49 | Washington | 20.2 |
| 50 | California | 24.0 |
| 51 | Utah | 24.3 |
| | U.S. Average | 17.4 |

Source: U.S. Department of Education, *Digest of Education Statistics 1996*

## PUPIL-TEACHER RATIO: NEW YORK VS. U.S. FOR BOTH PUBLIC AND PRIVATE SCHOOLS

In the fall 1993, New York's pupil-teacher ratio in public schools of 15.2 compared with a U.S. pupil-teacher ratio in public schools of 17.4. The pupil-teacher ratio in New York's private schools stood at 13.6, and for private schools across the nation the pupil-teacher ratio was 14.3.

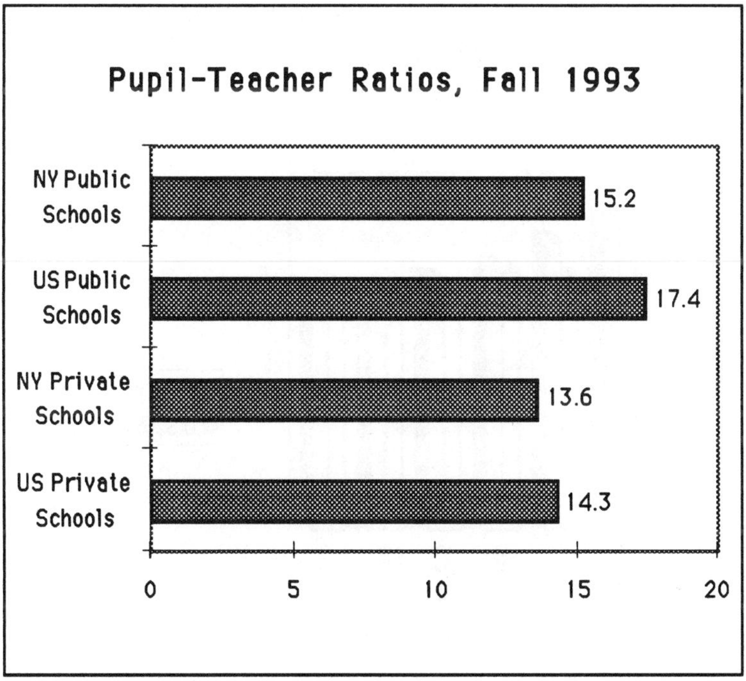


Data Source: U.S. Department of Education, *Digest of Education Statistics 1995*

## TREND IN THE PUPIL-TEACHER RATIO

Both in New York and nationally, the trend over the past two-and-a-half decades has been toward fewer pupils per teacher in public schools. New York's pupil-teacher ratio went from 20.0 in 1969-70 to 15.2 in 1994-95, while at the national level, the pupil-teacher ratio stood at 22.6 in 1969-70 and at 17.3 in 1994-95.

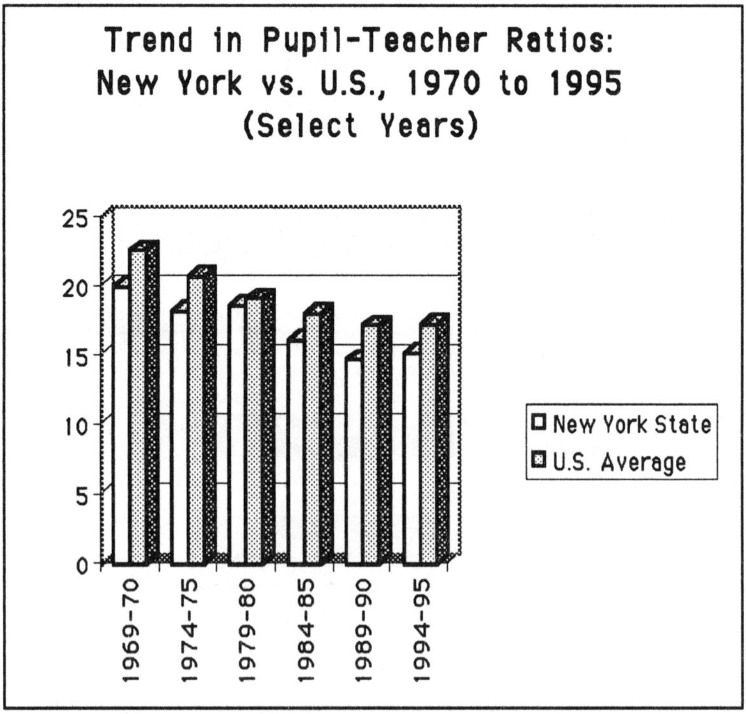


Data Source: U.S. Department of Education, *Digest of Education Statistics* , annual

# PUPIL-STAFF RATIO: STATE RANKINGS

New York State tied for eighth with regard to public-school pupil-teacher ratio in the nation in the fall 1994.

**Pupil-Staff Ratio**

| Rank | State | Ratio |
|---|---|---|
| 1 | Vermont | 6.8 |
| 2(t) | New Jersey | 7.3 |
| 2(t) | Maine | 7.3 |
| 4 | Missouri | 7.5 |
| 5(t) | District of Columbia | 7.7 |
| 5(t) | Nebraska | 7.7 |
| 5(t) | Wyoming | 7.7 |
| 8(t) | Oklahoma | 7.8 |
| 8(t) | Connecticut | 7.8 |
| **8(t)** | **New York** | **7.8** |
| 11 | Georgia | 7.9 |
| 12(t) | Kentucky | 8.0 |
| 12(t) | South Dakota | 8.0 |
| 12(t) | Virginia | 8.0 |
| 15(t) | Kansas | 8.1 |
| 15(t) | West Virginia | 8.1 |
| 17 | Texas | 8.2 |
| 18(t) | Massachusetts | 8.3 |
| 18(t) | Mississippi | 8.3 |
| 18(t) | Iowa | 8.3 |
| 18(t) | Louisiana | 8.3 |
| 22(t) | Alaska | 8.4 |
| 22(t) | Indiana | 8.4 |
| 22(t) | North Carolina | 8.4 |
| 25(t) | New Hampshire | 8.5 |
| 25(t) | New Mexico | 8.5 |
| 25(t) | Wisconsin | 8.5 |
| 28 | North Dakota | 8.6 |
| 29 | South Carolina | 8.7 |

*continued*

*continued*

| Rank | State | Ratio |
|---|---|---|
| 30(t) | Arkansas | 8.9 |
| 30(t) | Montana | 8.9 |
| 30(t) | Ohio | 8.9 |
| 33 | Alabama | 9.0 |
| 34(t) | Delaware | 9.1 |
| 34(t) | Pennsylvania | 9.1 |
| 36 | Tennessee | 9.2 |
| 37(t) | Florida | 9.3 |
| 37(t) | Maryland | 9.3 |
| 39 | Illinois | 9.4 |
| 40 | Rhode Island | 9.6 |
| 41 | Michigan | 9.8 |
| 42(t) | Arizona | 9.9 |
| 42(t) | Colorado | 9.9 |
| 44(t) | Oregon | 10.4 |
| 44(t) | Washington | 10.4 |
| 46 | Nevada | 10.9 |
| 47 | Minnesota | 11.0 |
| 48 | Hawaii | 11.1 |
| 49 | Idaho | 11.3 |
| 50 | California | 12.4 |
| 51 | Utah | 13.1 |
| | U.S. Average | 9.0 |

Data Source: U.S. Department of Education, *Digest of Education Statistics 1996*

## PUPIL-STAFF RATIO: NEW YORK VS. U.S.

In fall 1994, New York's public-school pupil-staff ratio exceeded the U.S. average—7.8 in New York versus 9.0 for the U.S. The trend over the past 25 years has been toward fewer pupils per staff member. In the fall 1969, New York's pupil-staff ratio stood at 11.8 versus the U.S. pupil-staff ratio of 13.6.

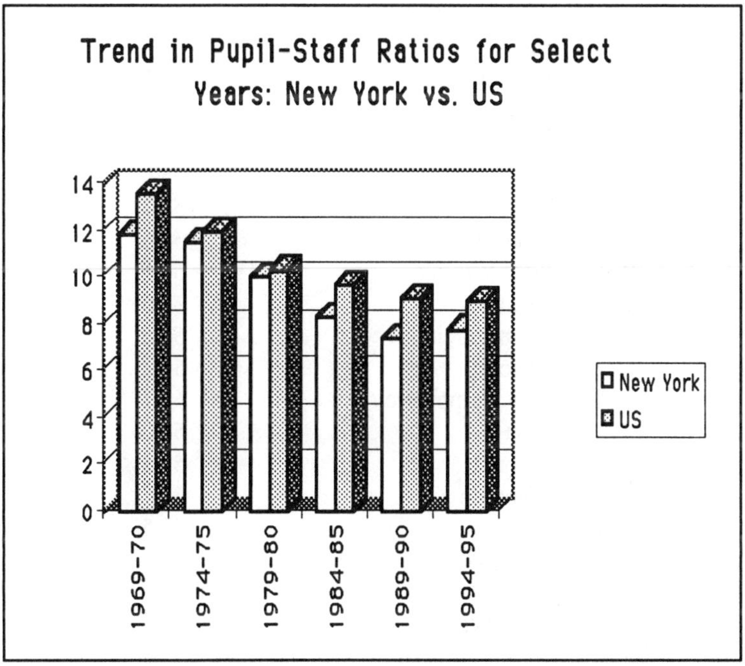


Data Sources: U.S. Department of Education, *Digest of Education Statistics 1996* and *State Comparisons of Education Statistics: 1969-70 to 1993-94*.

## TEACHERS AS A PERCENTAGE OF STAFF: STATE RANKINGS

In the fall 1994, New York State ranked thirty-eighth in the nation in terms of public school teachers as a percent of total staff.

**Teachers as a Percentage of Staff**

| Rank | State | Percent |
|---|---|---|
| 1 | Rhode Island | 65.2% |
| 2 | Minnesota | 62.7 |
| 3 | Hawaii | 61.8 |
| 4 | Idaho | 59.4 |
| 5 | District of Columbia | 58.2 |
| 6 | Nevada | 58.1 |
| 7 | North Dakota | 56.0 |
| 8 | Massachusetts | 55.9 |
| 9 | South Dakota | 55.5 |
| 10 | Maryland | 55.0 |
| 11 | Virginia | 54.7 |
| 12(t) | Delaware | 54.6 |
| 12(t) | West Virginia | 54.6 |
| 12(t) | Montana | 54.6 |
| 15 | Connecticut | 54.5 |
| 16(t) | Illinois | 54.2 |
| 16(t) | New Hampshire | 54.2 |
| 18 | Utah | 54.0 |
| 19 | Kansas | 53.8 |
| 20 | Colorado | 53.7 |
| 21(t) | Ohio | 53.5 |
| 21(t) | Wisconsin | 53.5 |
| 23(t) | Pennsylvania | 53.2 |
| 23(t) | Nebraska | 53.2 |
| 23(t) | South Carolina | 53.2 |
| 26 | New Jersey | 52.8 |
| 27 | Maine | 52.6 |
| 28(t) | Alabama | 52.5 |
| 28(t) | Iowa | 52.5 |

*continued*

*continued*

| Rank | State | Percent |
|---|---|---|
| 30 | Arkansas | 52.2 |
| 31(t) | North Carolina | 52.0 |
| 31(t) | Texas | 52.0 |
| 31(t) | Oregon | 52.0 |
| 34(t) | California | 51.6 |
| 34(t) | Wyoming | 51.6 |
| 36 | Washington | 51.3 |
| 37 | Arizona | 51.2 |
| **38** | **New York** | **51.1** |
| 39 | Oklahoma | 50.3 |
| 40 | Louisiana | 49.5 |
| 41 | Vermont | 49.3 |
| 42(t) | New Mexico | 49.2 |
| 42(t) | Tennessee | 49.2 |
| 44 | Michigan | 48.9 |
| 45 | Florida | 48.8 |
| 46 | Missouri | 48.4 |
| 47 | Georgia | 48.3 |
| 48 | Indiana | 48.1 |
| 49 | Alaska | 47.6 |
| 50(t) | Mississippi | 47.5 |
| 50(t) | Kentucky | 47.5 |
| | U.S. Average | 52.0 |

Data Source: U.S. Department of Education, *Digest of Education Statistics 1996*

## TEACHERS AS A PERCENT OF STAFF: NEW YORK VS. U.S.

In New York public schools in the Fall of 1994, 51.1 percent of staff were teachers, versus the national average of 52 percent.

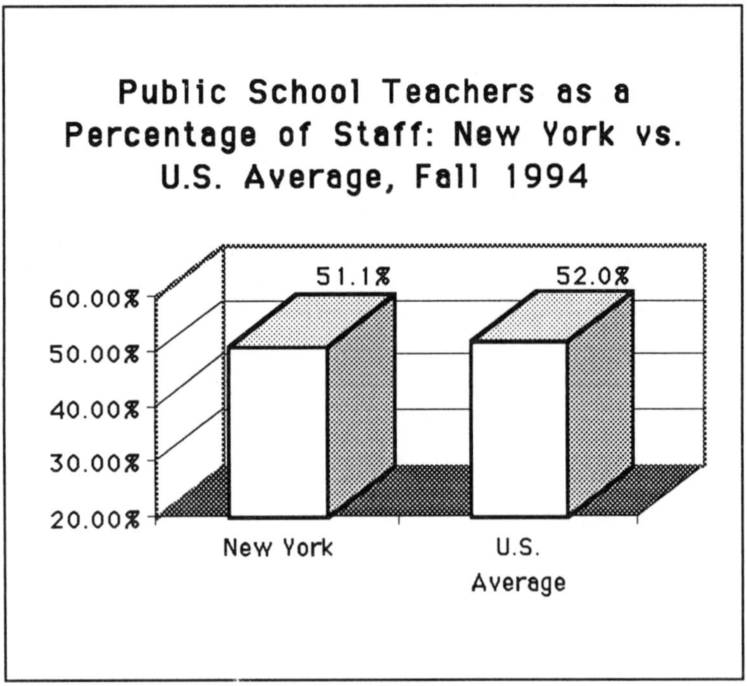


Data Source: U.S. Department of Education, *Digest of Education Statistics 1996*

## TREND IN EXPENDITURES AND ENROLLMENT

Since 1970, student enrollment in New York State public schools generally has been on the decline; in the mean time real expenditures have increased. Though not perfectly smooth, these trends are unmistakable. Between 1970 and 1994, enrollment *fell* by 20.6 percent—from 3.4 million to 2.7 million—and inflation-adjusted expenditures (1991-92 dollars) *rose* by 35.7 percent—from about $16.3 billion to $22.1 billion.

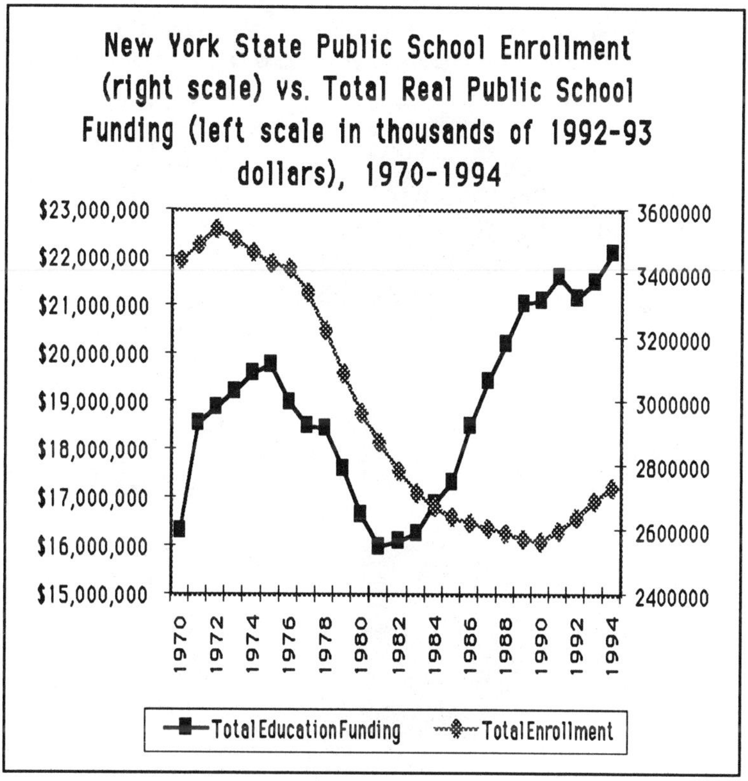


Data Source: New York State Education Department

## BREAKDOWN OF NEW YORK PUBLIC SCHOOL FINANCING

In 1994, public schools in New York received 56 percent of their total revenues from local sources, 39 percent from the state, and 5 percent from the federal government. This composition has changed over the past 25 years. In 1969, local revenues accounted for 49 percent, state revenues 48 percent, and federal revenues 3 percent. One should not misunderstand the origins of this change. Over these 25 years, real per pupil state education revenues increased by more than 40 percent, but local schools allowed total spending to increase even more.

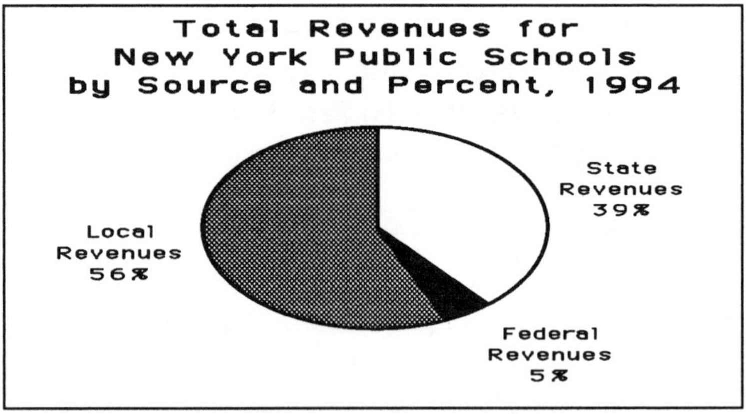


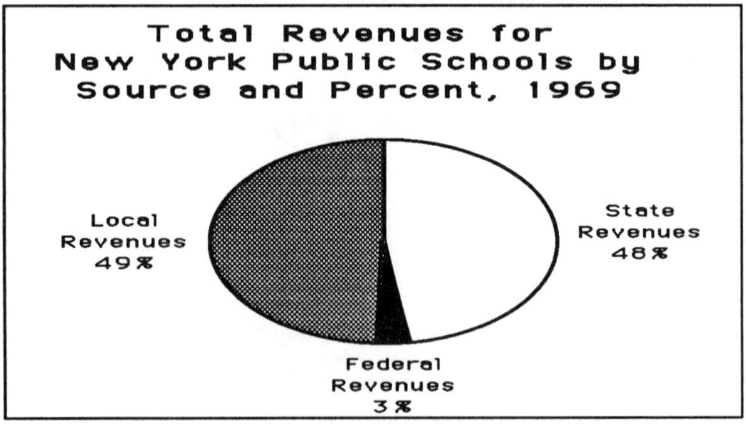


Data Source: New York State Education Department

## CONSOLIDATION TREND

Consolidation in New York's public school system has been going on throughout most of this century. In the very early 1900s, the state had over 10,000 public school districts. In 1930, the number of districts already had fallen to 9,118. By 1960, the number of districts was down to 1,292. In 1993, New York claimed 715 public school districts.

The chart below shows the changes in public school districts, enrollment, professional staff, and per pupil costs. The assumption is regularly made today that school district consolidations will save taxpayer dollars in public education. However, as the chart shows, between 1960 and 1993, the number of school districts declined and enrollment remained fairly steady (just a small decline). Meanwhile, the professional staff jumped by more than 64 percent and per pupil costs leaped by more than 226 percent in real terms.

In the end, larger public schools and school districts merely are used to justify larger bureaucracies.

**New York Public School Trends, 1960 vs. 1993**

| | 1960 | 1993 | Percent Change |
|---|---|---|---|
| Public School Districts | 1,292 | 715 | -44.7% |
| Public School Enrollment | 2.8 million | 2.7 million | -3.6% |
| Professional Staff | 135,915 | 223,423 | +64.4% |
| Real Per Pupil Current Expenditures (in real 1992-93 dollars) | $2,728 | $8,902 | +226.3% |

Data Source: The Nelson A. Rockefeller Institute of Government, *1995 New York State Statistical Yearbook*

# AVERAGE NUMBER OF STUDENTS PER PUBLIC ELEMENTARY SCHOOL: STATE RANKINGS

New York State ranked fifth in the nation in terms of the average number of students enrolled per public elementary school in 1994-95.

**Average Number of Students Per Public Elementary School**

| Rank | State | Average Number of Students |
|---|---|---|
| 1 | Florida | 769 |
| 2 | Georgia | 634 |
| 3 | Hawaii | 621 |
| 4 | California | 611 |
| **5** | **New York** | **603** |
| 6 | Arizona | 579 |
| 7 | Delaware | 553 |
| 8(t) | Nevada | 552 |
| 8(t) | Utah | 552 |
| 10 | Texas | 551 |
| 11 | South Carolina | 548 |
| 12 | Maryland | 543 |
| 13 | North Carolina | 525 |
| 14 | Virginia | 523 |
| 15 | Mississippi | 511 |
| 16 | Louisiana | 504 |
| 17 | Tennessee | 503 |
| 18 | Alabama | 487 |
| 19 | Pennsylvania | 474 |
| 20 | Connecticut | 450 |
| 21 | Washington | 449 |
| 22(t) | Minnesota | 445 |
| 22(t) | New Jersey | 445 |
| 24 | Indiana | 439 |
| 25 | District of Columbia | 437 |
| 26(t) | Michigan | 425 |
| 26(t) | Massachusetts | 425 |
| 28(t) | Colorado | 424 |

*continued*

*continued*

| Rank | State | Average Number of Students |
|---|---|---|
| 28(t) | Kentucky | 424 |
| 28(t) | Ohio | 424 |
| 31 | Illinois | 416 |
| 32 | New Mexico | 406 |
| 33 | Rhode Island | 401 |
| 34 | Arkansas | 393 |
| 35 | Missouri | 384 |
| 36 | Wisconsin | 375 |
| 37 | Idaho | 371 |
| 38 | Oregon | 370 |
| 39 | Alaska | 367 |
| 40 | New Hampshire | 366 |
| 41 | Oklahoma | 340 |
| 42 | West Virginia | 295 |
| 43 | Iowa | 287 |
| 44 | Kansas | 286 |
| 45 | Maine | 260 |
| 46 | Vermont | 218 |
| 47 | Wyoming | 212 |
| 48 | North Dakota | 193 |
| 49 | Montana | 187 |
| 50 | South Dakota | 182 |
| 51 | Nebraska | 168 |
| | U.S. Average | 471 |

Source: U.S. Department of Education, *Digest of Education Statistics 1996*

## AVERAGE NUMBER OF STUDENTS PER PUBLIC ELEMENTARY SCHOOL: NEW YORK VS. U.S.

New York State's average number of students enrolled per public elementary school of 603 in 1994-95 outpaced the national average of 471 by 28 percent.

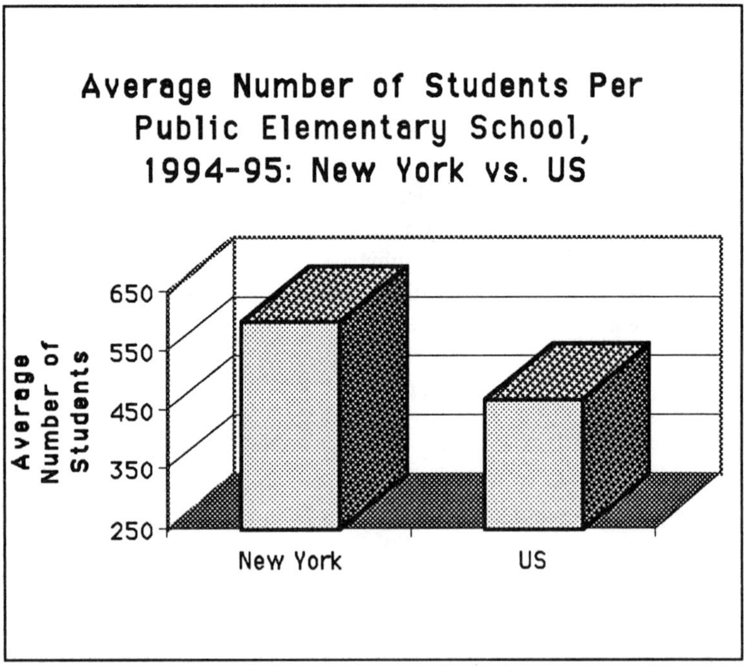


Data Source: U.S. Department of Education, *Digest of Education Statistics 1996*

# AVERAGE NUMBER OF STUDENTS PER PUBLIC SECONDARY SCHOOL: STATE RANKINGS

New York State ranked seventh in the nation in terms of the average number of students enrolled per public secondary school in 1994-95.

**Average Number of Students Per Public Secondary School**

| Rank | State | Average Number of Students |
|---|---|---|
| 1 | Hawaii | 1,333 |
| 2 | Florida | 1,108 |
| 3 | Georgia | 1,097 |
| 4 | Maryland | 1,057 |
| 5 | Virginia | 981 |
| 6 | Arizona | 973 |
| **7** | **New York** | **943** |
| 8 | California | 939 |
| 9 | Utah | 932 |
| 10 | New Jersey | 909 |
| 11 | Delaware | 898 |
| 12 | North Carolina | 872 |
| 13 | Tennessee | 864 |
| 14 | Rhode Island | 853 |
| 15 | Pennsylvania | 850 |
| 16 | South Carolina | 825 |
| 17 | Nevada | 803 |
| 18 | Indiana | 792 |
| 19 | Massachusetts | 777 |
| 20 | Louisiana | 762 |
| 21 | Ohio | 708 |
| 22(t) | Connecticut | 700 |
| 22(t) | Illinois | 700 |
| 24 | Texas | 699 |
| 25 | Alabama | 697 |
| 26 | Oregon | 675 |
| 27 | Michigan | 672 |
| 28 | Mississippi | 667 |

*continued*

*continued*

| Rank | State | Average Number of Students |
|---|---|---|
| 29 | Kentucky | 647 |
| 30 | District of Columbia | 643 |
| 31 | New Mexico | 640 |
| 32 | West Virginia | 636 |
| 33 | Washington | 634 |
| 34 | Vermont | 601 |
| 35 | Colorado | 579 |
| 36(t) | New Hampshire | 563 |
| 36(t) | Wisconsin | 563 |
| 38 | Missouri | 528 |
| 39 | Maine | 499 |
| 40 | Idaho | 477 |
| 41 | Minnesota | 465 |
| 42 | Alaska | 463 |
| 43 | Arkansas | 440 |
| 44 | Iowa | 406 |
| 45 | Kansas | 368 |
| 46 | Wyoming | 339 |
| 47 | Oklahoma | 327 |
| 48 | Nebraska | 320 |
| 49 | North Dakota | 233 |
| 50 | Montana | 177 |
| 51 | South Dakota | 168 |
| | U.S. Average | 697 |

Source: U.S. Department of Education, *Digest of Education Statistics 1996*

## AVERAGE NUMBER OF STUDENTS PER PUBLIC SECONDARY SCHOOL: NEW YORK VS. U.S.

New York State's average number of students enrolled per public secondary school of 943 in 1994-95 outpaced the national average of 697 by 35.3 percent.

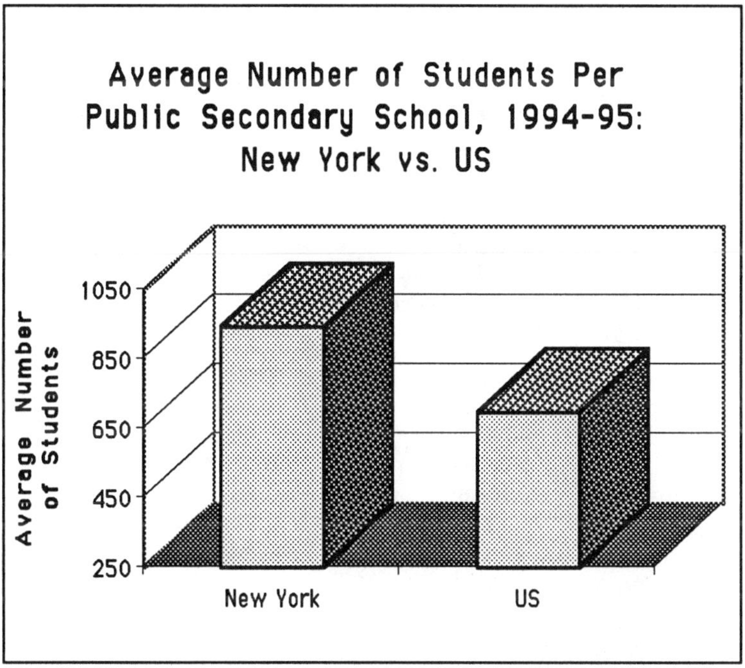


Data Source: U.S. Department of Education, *Digest of Education Statistics 1996*

## PERCENTAGE OF 8TH-GRADERS WATCHING 6 OR MORE HOURS OF TV EACH DAY: STATE RANKINGS

In 1992, New York State tied for twelfth out of the 42 states supplying data in terms of the percentage of eighth-grade public school students watching at least 6 hours of television each day.

**Percentage of 8th-Graders Watching 6 or More Hours of TV Per Day**

| Rank | State | Percent |
|---|---|---|
| 1 | District of Columbia | 31% |
| 2 | Hawaii | 22 |
| 3 | Mississippi | 21 |
| 4(t) | Alabama | 20 |
| 4(t) | Arkansas | 20 |
| 4(t) | Louisiana | 20 |
| 7 | Georgia | 18 |
| 8(t) | Delaware | 17 |
| 8(t) | Maryland | 17 |
| 8(t) | South Carolina | 17 |
| 11 | North Carolina | 16 |
| 12(t) | Florida | 15 |
| **12(t)** | **New York** | **15** |
| 12(t) | Virginia | 15 |
| 15 | Tennessee | 14 |
| 16(t) | Kentucky | 13 |
| 16(t) | Michigan | 13 |
| 16(t) | New Jersey | 13 |
| 16(t) | West Virginia | 13 |
| 20(t) | Missouri | 12 |
| 20(t) | Ohio | 12 |
| 20(t) | Texas | 12 |
| 23(t) | Connecticut | 11 |
| 23(t) | New Mexico | 11 |
| 23(t) | Oklahoma | 11 |
| 26 | California | 10 |

*continued*

*continued*

| Rank | State | Percent |
|---|---|---|
| 27(t) | Arizona | 9 |
| 27(t) | Indiana | 9 |
| 27(t) | Pennsylvania | 9 |
| 27(t) | Rhode Island | 9 |
| 31(t) | Maine | 8 |
| 31(t) | Massachusetts | 8 |
| 31(t) | Nebraska | 8 |
| 31(t) | Wisconsin | 8 |
| 31(t) | Wyoming | 8 |
| 36(t) | Colorado | 7 |
| 36(t) | Idaho | 7 |
| 36(t) | Iowa | 7 |
| 36(t) | New Hampshire | 7 |
| 40(t) | Minnesota | 5 |
| 40(t) | North Dakota | 5 |
| 40(t) | Utah | 5 |
| | U.S. Average | 13 |

Data Source: U.S. Department of Education, *Digest of Education Statistics 1995*

## PERCENTAGE OF 8TH-GRADERS WATCHING 6 OR MORE HOURS OF TV EACH DAY: NEW YORK VS. U.S.

New York State exceeded the national average in terms of the percentage of eighth-grade public school students watching at least 6 hours of television each day in 1992. New York registered 15 percent versus the national average of 13 percent.

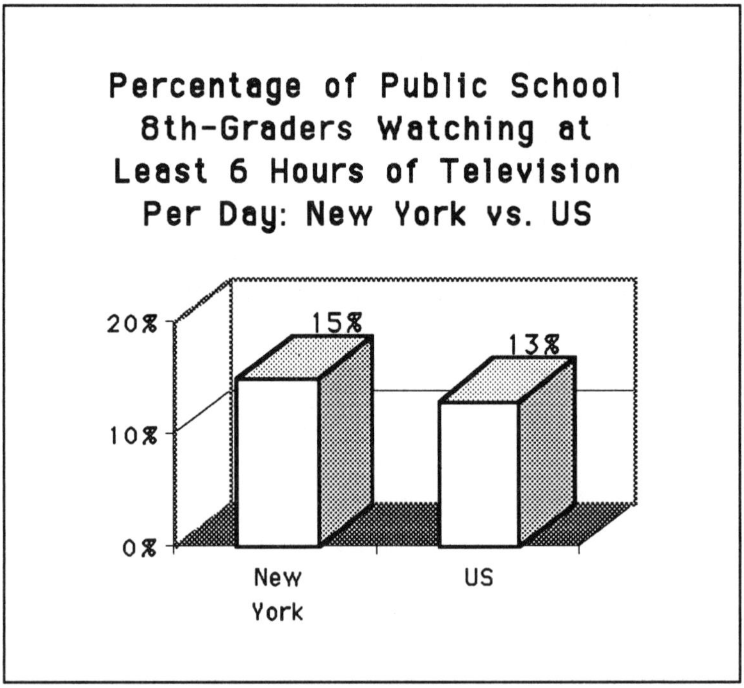


Data Source: U.S. Department of Education, *Digest of Education Statistics 1995*

# PRIVATE ELEMENTARY AND SECONDARY ENROLLMENT: STATE RANKINGS

In fall 1991, New York State tied for fifth among the states in terms of private elementary and secondary school enrollment as a percentage of total enrollment.

**Private School Enrollment as a Percentage of Total Enrollment**

| Rank | State | Percent |
|---|---|---|
| 1 | District of Columbia | 18.9% |
| 2 | Delaware | 18.3 |
| 3 | Pennsylvania | 17.5 |
| 4 | Hawaii | 17.2 |
| 5(t) | New Jersey | 16.0 |
| **5(t)** | **New York** | **16.0** |
| 7(t) | Louisiana | 15.1 |
| 7(t) | Wisconsin | 15.1 |
| 9 | Illinois | 14.3 |
| 10 | Maryland | 13.6 |
| 11 | Ohio | 13.2 |
| 12(t) | Massachusetts | 13.0 |
| 12(t) | Rhode Island | 13.0 |
| 14 | Nebraska | 12.5 |
| 15 | Connecticut | 12.4 |
| 16 | Missouri | 12.3 |
| 17 | Minnesota | 10.8 |
| 18 | California | 10.7 |
| 19 | Michigan | 10.6 |
| 20 | Mississippi | 10.5 |
| 21 | Florida | 9.7 |
| 22(t) | Iowa | 9.6 |
| 22(t) | New Hampshire | 9.6 |
| 24(t) | Indiana | 9.4 |
| 24(t) | Kentucky | 9.4 |
| 26 | Tennessee | 9.1 |
| 27 | Colorado | 8.9 |

*continued*

*continued*

| Rank | State | Percent |
|---|---|---|
| 28 | Alabama | 8.8 |
| 29 | Vermont | 8.0 |
| 30 | Georgia | 7.6 |
| 31(t) | South Dakota | 7.4 |
| 31(t) | Virginia | 7.4 |
| 33 | Kansas | 7.3 |
| 34 | Washington | 7.1 |
| 35 | New Mexico | 7.0 |
| 36 | South Carolina | 6.8 |
| 37 | Maine | 6.5 |
| 38 | North Dakota | 6.0 |
| 39 | Oregon | 5.9 |
| 40 | Montana | 5.8 |
| 41 | Arizona | 5.7 |
| 42(t) | North Carolina | 5.5 |
| 42(t) | Oklahoma | 5.5 |
| 44 | Arkansas | 4.9 |
| 45 | Texas | 4.8 |
| 46 | Alaska | 4.5 |
| 47(t) | Nevada | 3.9 |
| 47(t) | West Virginia | 3.9 |
| 49 | Idaho | 2.9 |
| 50 | Utah | 2.1 |
| 51 | Wyoming | 1.8 |
| | U.S. Average | 10.5 |

Data Source: U.S. Department of Education, *Digest of Education Statistics 1995*

## PRIVATE ELEMENTARY AND SECONDARY ENROLLMENT: NEW YORK VS. U.S.

In fall 1991, New York State's private elementary and secondary school enrollment as a percentage of total enrollment stood at 16 percent, 52.4 percent higher than the nationwide rate of 10.5 percent.

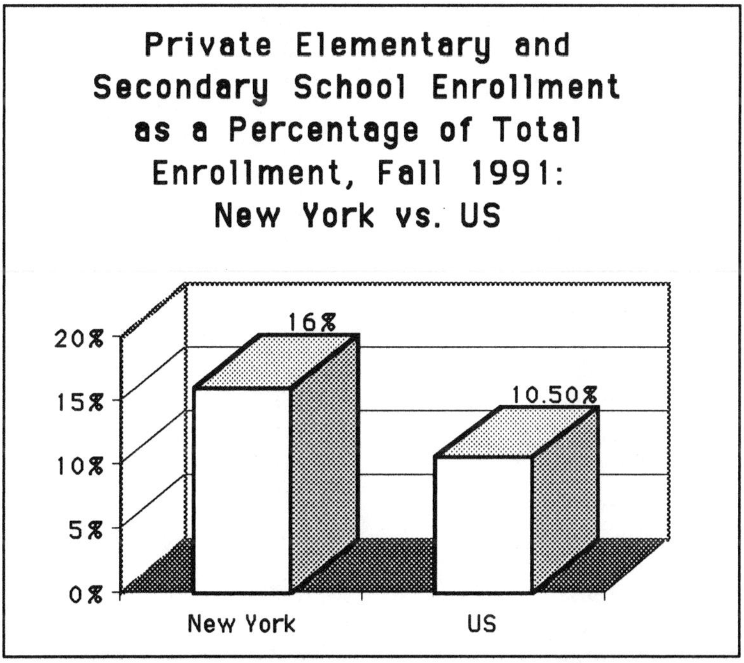


Data Source: U.S. Department of Education, *Digest of Education Statistics 1995*

# SCHOLASTIC ASSESSMENT TEST (SAT): STATE RANKINGS

Among the 50 states and the District of Columbia, New York ranked forty-second in the nation in terms of average 1994-95 SAT scores.

Narrowing the list of states to only those where at least 25 percent of graduates took the SATs, New York ranked eighteenth out of 27.

**Average SAT Scores**

| Rank | State | Average SAT | % of Graduates Taking SAT |
|---|---|---|---|
| 1 | North Dakota | 1,107 | 5% |
| 2 | Iowa | 1,099 | 5 |
| 3 | Minnesota | 1,085 | 9 |
| 4 | Utah | 1,076 | 4 |
| 5 | Wisconsin | 1,073 | 9 |
| 6 | South Dakota | 1,068 | 5 |
| 7 | Kansas | 1,060 | 9 |
| 8 | Nebraska | 1,050 | 9 |
| 9 | Illinois | 1,048 | 13 |
| 10 | Missouri | 1,045 | 9 |
| 11 | Tennessee | 1,040 | 12 |
| 12 | Mississippi | 1,038 | 4 |
| 13 | Michigan | 1,033 | 11 |
| 14 | Alabama | 1,029 | 8 |
| 15 | Oklahoma | 1,027 | 9 |
| 16 | Louisiana | 1,021 | 9 |
| 17 | New Mexico | 1,015 | 11 |
| 18 | Montana | 1,009 | 21 |
| 19 | Arkansas | 1,005 | 6 |
| 20 | Wyoming | 1,001 | 10 |
| 21 | Kentucky | 999 | 11 |
| 22 | Colorado | 980 | 29 |
| 23 | Idaho | 979 | 15 |
| 24 | Ohio | 975 | 23 |
| 25 | Oregon | 947 | 51 |

*continued*

*continued*

| Rank | State | Average SAT | % of Graduates Taking SAT |
|---|---|---|---|
| 26 | Arizona | 944 | 27 |
| 27 | Washington | 937 | 48 |
| 28 | New Hampshire | 935 | 70 |
| 29 | Alaska | 934 | 47 |
| 30 | West Virginia | 932 | 17 |
| 31 | Nevada | 917 | 30 |
| 32 | Maryland | 909 | 64 |
| 33 | Connecticut | 908 | 81 |
| 34 | Massachusetts | 907 | 80 |
| 35 | California | 902 | 46 |
| 36 | Vermont | 901 | 66 |
| 37 | New Jersey | 898 | 70 |
| 38 | Delaware | 897 | 68 |
| 39(t) | Maine | 896 | 68 |
| 39(t) | Virginia | 896 | 65 |
| 41 | Texas | 893 | 47 |
| **42** | **New York** | **892** | **74** |
| 43(t) | Hawaii | 889 | 57 |
| 43(t) | Florida | 889 | 48 |
| 45 | Rhode Island | 888 | 70 |
| 46 | Indiana | 882 | 58 |
| 47 | Pennsylvania | 880 | 70 |
| 48 | North Carolina | 865 | 60 |
| 49 | District of Columbia | 857 | 53 |
| 50 | Georgia | 854 | 65 |
| 51 | South Carolina | 844 | 56 |
| | U.S. Average | 910 | 41 |

Data Source: The College Board

## THE SAT TREND

SAT scores in New York State plunged in the 1970s, and have remained at this substantially lower level ever since, drifting to its lowest point in 1990-91 (total SAT average of 881). A similar trend appeared in national SAT scores, though not as severe a drop as in New York and the national average has since recovered somewhat. The lowest point for the U.S. average total SAT score was hit in 1979-80 and 1980-81 with a score of 890.

In 1971-72 (earliest data supplied by the College Board), New York's average total SAT score of 955 exceeded the national average of 937. New York has not surpassed or matched the U.S. average since 1981-82. In 1994-95, New York's average total SAT score equaled 892 versus a U.S. average of 910.

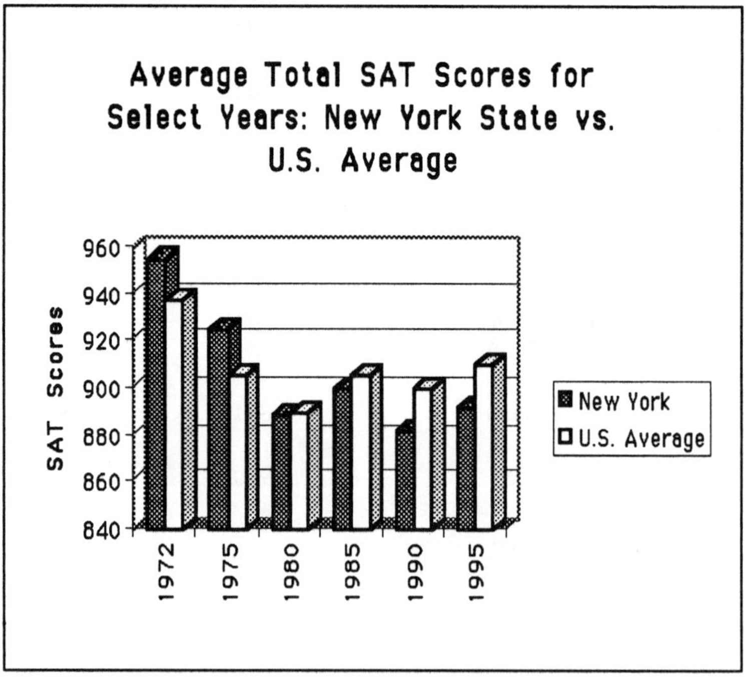


Data Source: The College Board

## AVERAGE READING PROFICIENCY FOR PUBLIC SCHOOL 4TH-GRADERS: STATE RANKINGS

Among the 39 states participating in the National Assessment of Education Progress testing in 1994, New York tied for twenty-fourth out of 39 states in terms of average reading proficiency scores for public school fourth-graders.

**Average Reading Proficiency Scores —Public School 4th-Graders**

| Rank | State | Average Score |
|---|---|---|
| 1 | Maine | 229 |
| 2 | North Dakota | 226 |
| 3 | Wisconsin | 225 |
| 4(t) | Iowa | 224 |
| 4(t) | Massachusetts | 224 |
| 4(t) | New Hampshire | 224 |
| 7(t) | Connecticut | 223 |
| 7(t) | Montana | 223 |
| 9 | Wyoming | 222 |
| 10(t) | Indiana | 221 |
| 10(t) | Nebraska | 221 |
| 10(t) | Rhode Island | 221 |
| 13 | New Jersey | 220 |
| 14 | Minnesota | 219 |
| 15(t) | Missouri | 218 |
| 15(t) | Utah | 218 |
| 17 | Pennsylvania | 216 |
| 18 | North Carolina | 215 |
| 19(t) | Colorado | 214 |
| 19(t) | Tennessee | 214 |
| 19(t) | Virginia | 214 |
| 19(t) | Washington | 214 |
| 19(t) | West Virginia | 214 |
| 24(t) | Kentucky | 213 |
| **24(t)** | **New York** | **213** |
| 24(t) | Texas | 213 |

*continued*

*continued*

| Rank | State | Average Score |
|---|---|---|
| 27 | Maryland | 211 |
| 28 | Arkansas | 210 |
| 29 | Alabama | 209 |
| 30 | Georgia | 208 |
| 31(t) | Arizona | 207 |
| 31(t) | Delaware | 207 |
| 33(t) | Florida | 206 |
| 33(t) | New Mexico | 206 |
| 35 | South Carolina | 205 |
| 36 | Mississippi | 203 |
| 37 | Hawaii | 202 |
| 38(t) | California | 198 |
| 38(t) | Louisiana | 198 |
| | U.S. Average | 213 |

Note: Numbers for Delaware, Maine, Nebraska, New Hampshire, New Jersey, and New York may be subject to "appreciable nonresponse bias," according to the U.S. Department of Education.

Data Source: U.S Department of Education, *Digest of Education Statistics 1995*

## AVERAGE READING PROFICIENCY FOR PUBLIC SCHOOL 4TH GRADERS: NEW YORK VS. U.S.

In 1994, New York equaled the national average in terms of average reading proficiency scores (National Assessment of Education Progress testing) for public school fourth-graders.

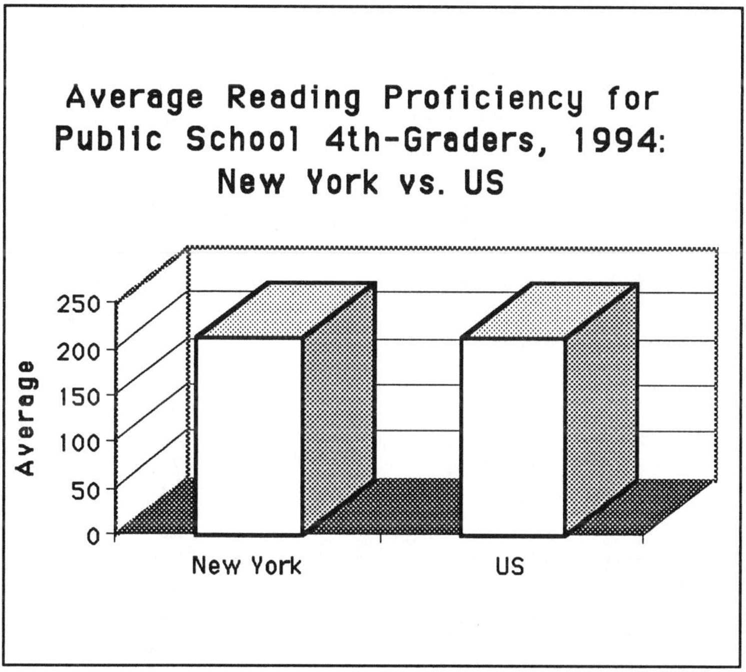


Data Source: U.S Department of Education, *Digest of Education Statistics 1995*

## AVERAGE MATHEMATICS PROFICIENCY FOR PUBLIC SCHOOL 4TH-GRADERS: STATE RANKINGS

Among the 42 states participating in the National Assessment of Education Progress testing in 1992, New York tied for twenty-first in terms of average mathematics proficiency scores for public school fourth-graders.

### Average Mathematics Proficiency Scores—Public School 4th-Graders

| Rank | State | Average Score |
|---|---|---|
| 1 | Maine | 231 |
| 2(t) | Iowa | 229 |
| 2(t) | New Hampshire | 229 |
| 4(t) | North Dakota | 228 |
| 4(t) | Wisconsin | 228 |
| 6 | Minnesota | 227 |
| 7(t) | Connecticut | 226 |
| 7(t) | Massachusetts | 226 |
| 7(t) | New Jersey | 226 |
| 10(t) | Nebraska | 224 |
| 10(t) | Wyoming | 224 |
| 12(t) | Pennsylvania | 223 |
| 12(t) | Utah | 223 |
| 14 | Missouri | 221 |
| 15(t) | Colorado | 220 |
| 15(t) | Idaho | 220 |
| 15(t) | Indiana | 220 |
| 15(t) | Virginia | 220 |
| 19(t) | Michigan | 219 |
| 19(t) | Oklahoma | 219 |
| 21(t) | Delaware | 217 |
| **21(t)** | **New York** | **217** |
| 21(t) | Ohio | 217 |
| 21(t) | Texas | 217 |
| 25 | Maryland | 216 |

*continued*

*continued*

| Rank | State | Average Score |
|---|---|---|
| 26(t) | Arizona | 214 |
| 26(t) | Georgia | 214 |
| 26(t) | Kentucky | 214 |
| 26(t) | Rhode Island | 214 |
| 26(t) | West Virginia | 214 |
| 31 | Hawaii | 213 |
| 32(t) | Florida | 212 |
| 32(t) | New Mexico | 212 |
| 34(t) | North Carolina | 211 |
| 34(t) | South Carolina | 211 |
| 36(t) | Arkansas | 209 |
| 36(t) | Tennessee | 209 |
| 38(t) | Alabama | 207 |
| 38(t) | California | 207 |
| 40 | Louisiana | 203 |
| 41 | Mississippi | 200 |
| 42 | District of Columbia | 191 |
| | U.S. Average | 217 |

Data Source: U.S Department of Education, *Digest of Education Statistics 1995*

## AVERAGE MATHEMATICS PROFICIENCY FOR PUBLIC SCHOOL 4TH-GRADERS: NEW YORK VS. U.S.

In 1992, New York equaled the national average in terms of average mathematics proficiency scores (National Assessment of Education Progress testing) for public school fourth-graders.

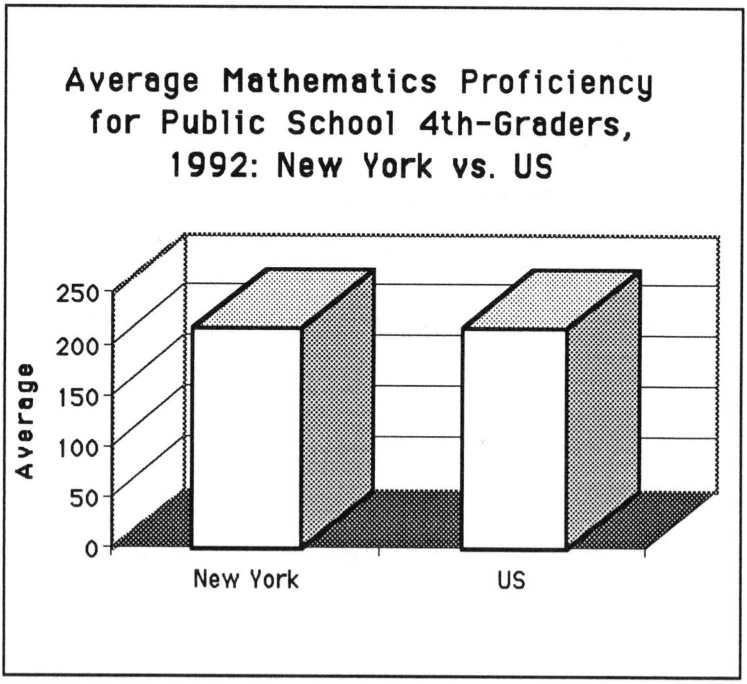


Data Source: U.S Department of Education, *Digest of Education Statistics 1995*

# AVERAGE MATHEMATICS PROFICIENCY FOR PUBLIC SCHOOL 8TH-GRADERS: STATE RANKINGS

Among the 42 states participating in the National Assessment of Education Progress testing in 1992, New York ranked twenty-second in terms of average mathematics proficiency scores for public school eighth-graders.

**Average Mathematics Proficiency Scores—Public School 8th-Graders**

| Rank | State | Average Score |
|---|---|---|
| 1(t) | Iowa | 283 |
| 1(t) | North Dakota | 283 |
| 3 | Minnesota | 282 |
| 4(t) | Maine | 278 |
| 4(t) | New Hampshire | 278 |
| 6(t) | Nebraska | 277 |
| 6(t) | Wisconsin | 277 |
| 8(t) | Idaho | 274 |
| 8(t) | Utah | 274 |
| 8(t) | Wyoming | 274 |
| 11 | Connecticut | 273 |
| 12(t) | Colorado | 272 |
| 12(t) | Massachusetts | 272 |
| 14(t) | New Jersey | 271 |
| 14(t) | Pennsylvania | 271 |
| 16 | Missouri | 270 |
| 17 | Indiana | 269 |
| 18(t) | Michigan | 267 |
| 18(t) | Ohio | 267 |
| 18(t) | Oklahoma | 267 |
| 18(t) | Virginia | 267 |
| **22** | **New York** | **266** |
| 23(t) | Alaska | 265 |
| 23(t) | Rhode Island | 265 |
| 25(t) | Maryland | 264 |

*continued*

*continued*

| Rank | State | Average Score |
|---|---|---|
| 25(t) | Texas | 264 |
| 27 | Delaware | 262 |
| 28 | Kentucky | 261 |
| 29(t) | California | 260 |
| 29(t) | South Carolina | 260 |
| 31(t) | Florida | 259 |
| 31(t) | Georgia | 259 |
| 31(t) | New Mexico | 259 |
| 34(t) | North Carolina | 258 |
| 34(t) | Tennessee | 258 |
| 34(t) | West Virginia | 258 |
| 37 | Hawaii | 257 |
| 38 | Arkansas | 255 |
| 39 | Alabama | 251 |
| 40 | Louisiana | 249 |
| 41 | Mississippi | 246 |
| 42 | District of Columbia | 234 |
| | U.S. Average | 266 |

Data Source: U.S Department of Education, *Digest of Education Statistics 1995*

## AVERAGE MATHEMATICS PROFICIENCY FOR PUBLIC SCHOOL 8TH-GRADERS: NEW YORK VS. U.S.

In 1992, New York equaled the national average in terms of average mathematics proficiency scores (National Assessment of Education Progress testing) for public school eighth-graders.

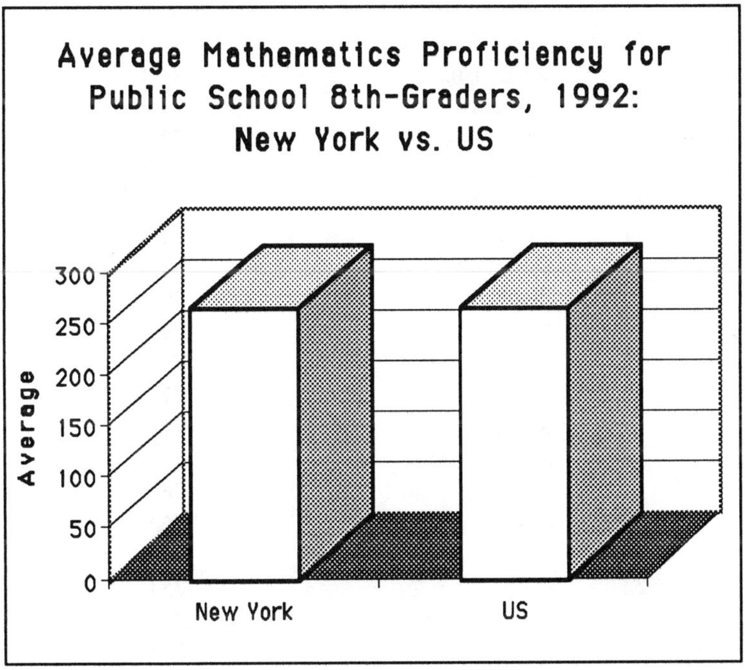


Data Source: U.S Department of Education, *Digest of Education Statistics 1995*

## GRADUATION RATES: STATE RANKINGS

In 1995, New York ranked forty-third among the 50 states and District of Columbia in terms of its estimated public high school graduation rate.

**Graduation Rates**

| Rank | State | Graduation Rate* |
|---|---|---|
| 1 | Nebraska | 93.2% |
| 2 | Minnesota | 89.5 |
| 3 | South Dakota | 88.9 |
| 4 | Vermont | 86.4 |
| 5 | Iowa | 86.2 |
| 6 | Wisconsin | 84.4 |
| 7 | Montana | 84.2 |
| 8 | North Dakota | 83.5 |
| 9 | Utah | 83.4 |
| 10 | Wyoming | 83.0 |
| 11 | Maine | 81.7 |
| 12 | New Jersey | 81.6 |
| 13 | Pennsylvania | 79.6 |
| 14 | Hawaii | 79.2 |
| 15 | West Virginia | 77.9 |
| 16 | Idaho | 77.8 |
| 17 | Kansas | 77.3 |
| 18 | Massachusetts | 77.0 |
| 19 | Arkansas | 76.5 |
| 20(t) | Connecticut | 76.0 |
| 20(t) | Illinois | 76.0 |
| 22 | Ohio | 75.0 |
| 23 | Colorado | 74.6 |
| 24 | Maryland | 74.0 |
| 25(t) | Indiana | 73.8 |
| 25(t) | Washington | 73.8 |
| 27 | Virginia | 72.3 |
| 28(t) | Michigan | 72.1 |

*continued*

*continued*

| Rank | State | Graduation Rate* |
|---|---|---|
| 28(t) | Rhode Island | 72.1 |
| 30 | Oregon | 70.9 |
| 31 | Oklahoma | 70.8 |
| 32 | Alaska | 70.4 |
| 33 | Missouri | 69.8 |
| 34 | New Hampshire | 68.5 |
| 35 | Kentucky | 68.1 |
| 36 | Tennessee | 66.5 |
| 37(t) | California | 65.7 |
| 37(t) | North Carolina | 65.7 |
| 39 | New Mexico | 65.0 |
| 40 | Nevada | 64.7 |
| 41 | Delaware | 64.5 |
| 42 | Arizona | 63.6 |
| **43** | **New York** | **63.3** |
| 44 | District of Columbia | 63.1 |
| 45 | Alabama | 61.6 |
| 46 | South Carolina | 60.9 |
| 47 | Florida | 59.4 |
| 48 | Mississippi | 58.2 |
| 49 | Louisiana | 58.0 |
| 50 | Georgia | 57.7 |
| 51 | Texas | 57.0 |
| | U.S. Average | 69.4 |

* Graduation rate equals estimated high school graduates for 1994-95 divided by ninth-grade enrollment for 1991-92.

Data Source: U.S. Department of Education, *Digest of Education Statistics*, annual

## GRADUATION RATES: NEW YORK VS. U.S.

In 1995, New York's estimated public high school graduation rate of 63.3 percent trailed behind the total U.S. rate of 69.4 percent.

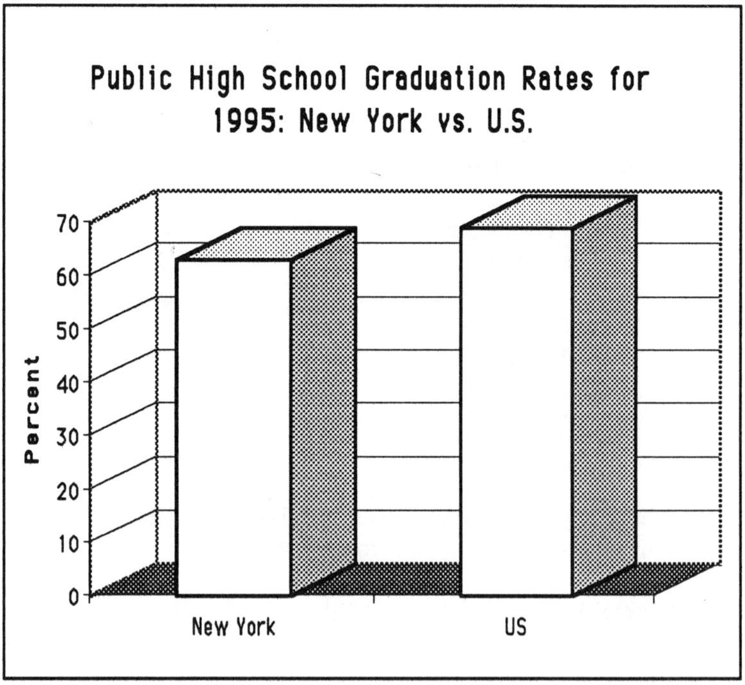


Data Source: U.S. Department of Education, *Digest of Education Statistics*, annual

## EDUCATIONAL ATTAINMENT: DROPOUTS—STATE RANKINGS

New York ranked thirty-first in the nation in 1990 in terms of the number of dropouts (i.e., 16- to 19-year-olds not in regular school and have not completed twelfth grade).

**Dropouts—16 to 19 Years of Age**

| Rank | State | Percent of Population |
|---|---|---|
| 1 | Nevada | 15.2% |
| 2 | Arizona | 14.4 |
| 3 | Florida | 14.3 |
| 4 | California | 14.2 |
| 5 | Georgia | 14.1 |
| 6 | District of Columbia | 13.9 |
| 7 | Tennessee | 13.4 |
| 8 | Kentucky | 13.3 |
| 9 | Texas | 12.9 |
| 10 | Alabama | 12.6 |
| 11(t) | Louisiana | 12.5 |
| 11(t) | North Carolina | 12.5 |
| 13(t) | Mississippi | 11.8 |
| 13(t) | Oregon | 11.8 |
| 15(t) | New Mexico | 11.7 |
| 15(t) | South Carolina | 11.7 |
| 17(t) | Arkansas | 11.4 |
| 17(t) | Indiana | 11.4 |
| 17(t) | Missouri | 11.4 |
| 20 | Rhode Island | 11.1 |
| 21(t) | Alaska | 10.9 |
| 21(t) | Maryland | 10.9 |
| 21(t) | West Virginia | 10.9 |
| 24(t) | Illinois | 10.6 |
| 24(t) | Washington | 10.6 |
| 26(t) | Delaware | 10.4 |
| 26(t) | Idaho | 10.4 |

*continued*

*continued*

| Rank | State | Percent of Population |
|---|---|---|
| 26(t) | Oklahoma | 10.4 |
| 29(t) | Michigan | 10.0 |
| 29(t) | Virginia | 10.0 |
| **31** | **New York** | **9.9** |
| 32 | Colorado | 9.8 |
| 33 | New Jersey | 9.6 |
| 34 | New Hampshire | 9.4 |
| 35 | Pennsylvania | 9.1 |
| 36 | Connecticut | 9.0 |
| 37 | Ohio | 8.9 |
| 38(t) | Kansas | 8.7 |
| 38(t) | Utah | 8.7 |
| 40 | Massachusetts | 8.5 |
| 41 | Maine | 8.3 |
| 42 | Montana | 8.1 |
| 43 | Vermont | 8.0 |
| 44 | South Dakota | 7.7 |
| 45 | Hawaii | 7.5 |
| 46 | Wisconsin | 7.1 |
| 47 | Nebraska | 7.0 |
| 48 | Wyoming | 6.9 |
| 49 | Iowa | 6.6 |
| 50 | Minnesota | 6.4 |
| 51 | North Dakota | 4.6 |
| | U.S. Average | 11.2 |

Data Source: U.S. Department of Commerce, *Statistical Abstract of the United States 1995*

## EDUCATIONAL ATTAINMENT: DROPOUTS—NEW YORK VS. U.S.

New York's dropout rate (i.e., 16- to 19-year-olds not in regular school and have not completed twelfth grade) in 1990 was better than the U.S. average -- New York's 9.9 percent versus the national average of 11.2 percent.

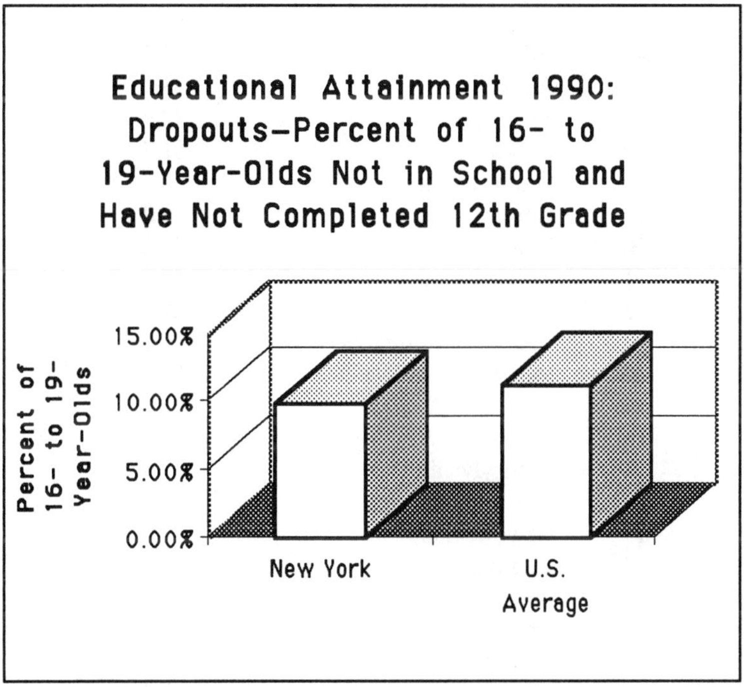


Data Source: U.S. Department of Commerce, *Statistical Abstract of the United States 1995*

## EDUCATIONAL ATTAINMENT: NO HIGH SCHOOL DIPLOMA—STATE RANKINGS

New York ranked eighteenth in the nation in 1990 in terms of the percentage of individuals 25 years of age and older without a high school diploma.

**No High School Diploma—25 Years of Age and Older**

| Rank | State | Percent of Population |
|---|---|---|
| 1 | Mississippi | 35.7% |
| 2 | Kentucky | 35.4 |
| 3 | West Virginia | 34.0 |
| 4 | Arkansas | 33.7 |
| 5 | Alabama | 33.1 |
| 6 | Tennessee | 32.9 |
| 7(t) | Louisiana | 31.7 |
| 7(t) | South Carolina | 31.7 |
| 9 | North Carolina | 30.0 |
| 10 | Georgia | 29.1 |
| 11 | Rhode Island | 28.0 |
| 12 | Texas | 27.9 |
| 13 | District of Columbia | 26.9 |
| 14 | Missouri | 26.1 |
| 15 | Florida | 25.6 |
| 16 | Oklahoma | 25.4 |
| 17 | Pennsylvania | 25.3 |
| **18** | **New York** | **25.2** |
| 19 | New Mexico | 24.9 |
| 20 | Virginia | 24.8 |
| 21 | Indiana | 24.4 |
| 22 | Ohio | 24.3 |
| 23(t) | California | 23.8 |
| 23(t) | Illinois | 23.8 |
| 25(t) | New Jersey | 23.3 |
| 25(t) | North Dakota | 23.3 |
| 27 | Michigan | 23.2 |

*continued*

*continued*

| Rank | State | Percent of Population |
|---|---|---|
| 28 | South Dakota | 22.9 |
| 29 | Delaware | 22.5 |
| 30 | Maryland | 21.6 |
| 31 | Wisconsin | 21.4 |
| 32 | Arizona | 21.3 |
| 33(t) | Maine | 21.2 |
| 33(t) | Nevada | 21.2 |
| 35 | Connecticut | 20.8 |
| 36 | Idaho | 20.3 |
| 37 | Massachusetts | 20.0 |
| 38(t) | Hawaii | 19.9 |
| 38(t) | Iowa | 19.9 |
| 40 | Vermont | 19.2 |
| 41 | Montana | 19.0 |
| 42 | Kansas | 18.7 |
| 43 | Oregon | 18.5 |
| 44 | Nebraska | 18.2 |
| 45 | New Hampshire | 17.8 |
| 46 | Minnesota | 17.6 |
| 47 | Wyoming | 17.0 |
| 48 | Washington | 16.2 |
| 49 | Colorado | 15.6 |
| 50 | Utah | 14.9 |
| 51 | Alaska | 13.4 |
| | U.S. Average | 24.8 |

Data Source: U.S. Department of Commerce, *Statistical Abstract of the United States 1995*

## EDUCATIONAL ATTAINMENT: NO HIGH SCHOOL DIPLOMA—NEW YORK VS. U.S.

The share of New Yorkers, 25 years of age and older, without a high school diploma exceeded the national average in 1990—25.2 percent in New York versus 24.8 percent nationwide.

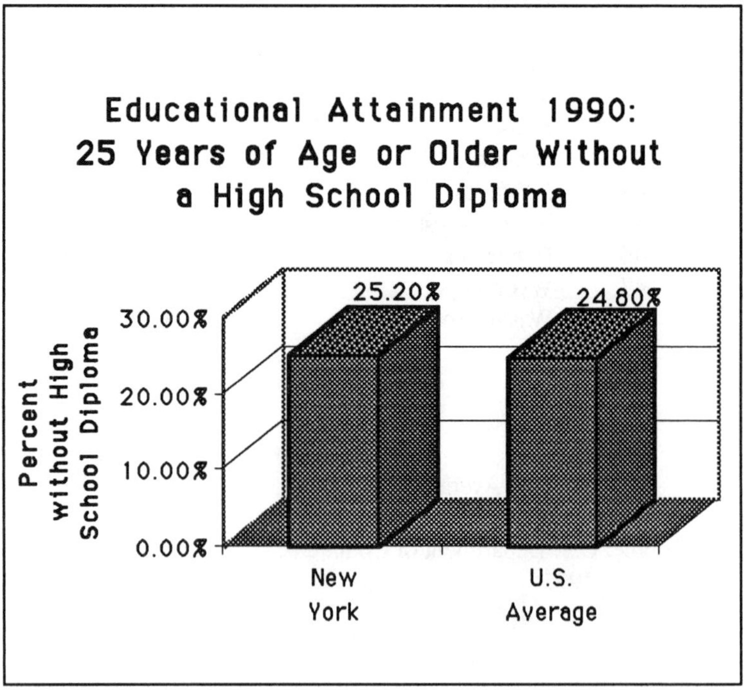


Data Source: U.S. Department of Commerce, *Statistical Abstract of the United States 1995*

## EDUCATIONAL ATTAINMENT: ASSOCIATE'S DEGREE OR HIGHER—STATE RANKINGS

New York ranked sixteenth in the nation in 1990 in terms of the percentage of individuals 25 years of age and older with an associate's degree or higher.

**Associate's Degree or Higher—25 Years of Age and Older**

| Rank | State | Percent of Population |
|---|---|---|
| 1 | District of Columbia | 36.4% |
| 2 | Massachusetts | 34.4 |
| 3 | Colorado | 33.9 |
| 4 | Connecticut | 33.8 |
| 5 | New Hampshire | 32.4 |
| 6 | Maryland | 31.7 |
| 7 | Vermont | 31.5 |
| 8 | California | 31.3 |
| 9 | Hawaii | 31.2 |
| 10 | Washington | 30.8 |
| 11 | Minnesota | 30.5 |
| 12 | Alaska | 30.2 |
| 13(t) | New Jersey | 30.0 |
| 13(t) | Utah | 30.0 |
| 13(t) | Virginia | 30.0 |
| **16** | **New York** | **29.6** |
| 17 | North Dakota | 28.0 |
| 18 | Delaware | 27.9 |
| 19 | Rhode Island | 27.6 |
| 20 | Oregon | 27.5 |
| 21 | Arizona | 27.1 |
| 22 | Illinois | 26.9 |
| 23 | Kansas | 26.5 |
| 24 | Nebraska | 26.1 |
| 25(t) | Maine | 25.7 |
| 25(t) | Wyoming | 25.7 |
| 27 | Texas | 25.6 |

*continued*

*continued*

| Rank | State | Percent of Population |
|---|---|---|
| 28(t) | Montana | 25.4 |
| 28(t) | New Mexico | 25.4 |
| 30 | Idaho | 25.2 |
| 31 | Florida | 24.9 |
| 32 | Wisconsin | 24.8 |
| 33(t) | Iowa | 24.6 |
| 33(t) | South Dakota | 24.6 |
| 35 | Georgia | 24.3 |
| 36 | North Carolina | 24.2 |
| 37 | Michigan | 24.0 |
| 38 | Pennsylvania | 23.1 |
| 39 | South Carolina | 22.9 |
| 40 | Oklahoma | 22.8 |
| 41(t) | Missouri | 22.3 |
| 41(t) | Ohio | 22.3 |
| 43 | Nevada | 21.5 |
| 44 | Indiana | 20.9 |
| 45 | Alabama | 20.6 |
| 46 | Tennessee | 20.1 |
| 47 | Mississippi | 20.0 |
| 48 | Louisiana | 19.4 |
| 49 | Kentucky | 17.7 |
| 50 | Arkansas | 17.1 |
| 51 | West Virginia | 16.1 |
| | U.S. Average | 26.5 |

Data Source: U.S. Department of Commerce, *Statistical Abstract of the United States 1995*

## EDUCATIONAL ATTAINMENT: ASSOCIATE'S DEGREE OR HIGHER—NEW YORK VS. U.S.

New York outpaced the national average in 1990 in terms of the percentage of individuals 25 years of age and older with an associate's degree or higher—New York's 29.6 percent versus the U.S. average 26.5 percent.

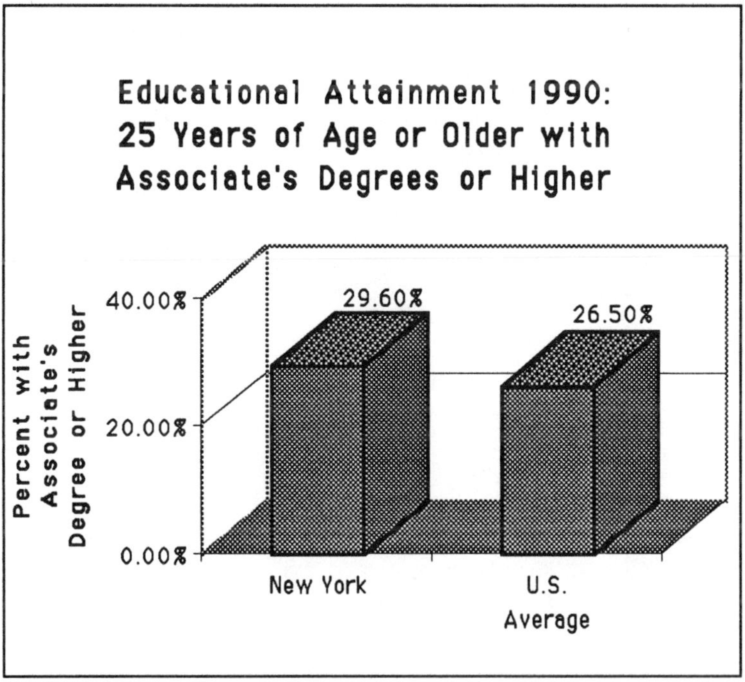


Data Source: U.S. Department of Commerce, *Statistical Abstract of the United States 1995*

# PER STUDENT CURRENT EDUCATIONAL AND GENERAL EXPENDITURES AT 4-YEAR PUBLIC INSTITUTIONS OF HIGHER LEARNING: STATE RANKINGS

New York State ranked eighteenth in the nation in 1991-92 in terms of per full-time-equivalent student current educational and general expenditures at four-year public institutions of higher learning.

**Per Student Current Expenditures at 4-Year Public Institutions of Higher Learning**

| Rank | State | Per Student Expenditures |
|---|---|---|
| 1 | Hawaii | $23,376 |
| 2 | Washington | 18,522 |
| 3 | Vermont | 17,270 |
| 4 | District of Columbia | 16,749 |
| 5 | California | 15,945 |
| 6 | Alaska | 15,905 |
| 7 | Iowa | 15,241 |
| 8 | New Mexico | 15,212 |
| 9 | New Jersey | 15,102 |
| 10 | North Carolina | 14,842 |
| 11 | Utah | 14,769 |
| 12 | Delaware | 14,593 |
| 13 | Minnesota | 14,156 |
| 14 | Wyoming | 14,054 |
| 15 | Oregon | 14,019 |
| 16 | Arizona | 13,735 |
| 17 | Michigan | 13,731 |
| **18** | **New York** | **13,489** |
| 19 | Connecticut | 13,017 |
| 20 | Wisconsin | 13,004 |
| 21 | Illinois | 12,988 |
| 22 | Florida | 12,947 |
| 23 | Pennsylvania | 12,927 |
| 24 | Nevada | 12,561 |

*continued*

*continued*

| Rank | State | Per Student Expenditures |
|---|---|---|
| 25 | Texas | 12,537 |
| 26 | South Carolina | 12,447 |
| 27 | Maryland | 12,388 |
| 28 | Kentucky | 12,344 |
| 29 | North Dakota | 11,880 |
| 30 | Indiana | 11,747 |
| 31 | Virginia | 11,705 |
| 32 | Alabama | 11,513 |
| 33 | Ohio | 11,430 |
| 34 | Massachusetts | 11,425 |
| 35 | Colorado | 11,311 |
| 36 | Georgia | 11,260 |
| 37 | Maine | 11,082 |
| 38 | Nebraska | 11,080 |
| 39 | Tennessee | 11,061 |
| 40 | Mississippi | 10,973 |
| 41 | Rhode Island | 10,906 |
| 42 | Kansas | 10,850 |
| 43 | New Hampshire | 10,435 |
| 44 | Arkansas | 10,187 |
| 45 | Idaho | 10,120 |
| 46 | Missouri | 9,677 |
| 47 | Louisiana | 9,472 |
| 48 | Oklahoma | 9,311 |
| 49 | Montana | 8,821 |
| 50 | West Virginia | 8,318 |
| 51 | South Dakota | 8,090 |
| | U.S. Average | 12,988 |

Data Source: U.S. Department of Education, *State Comparisons of Education Statistics: 1969-70 to 1993-94*

## PER STUDENT CURRENT EDUCATIONAL AND GENERAL EXPENDITURES AT 4-YEAR PUBLIC INSTITUTIONS OF HIGHER LEARNING: NEW YORK VS. U.S.

In 1991-92, New York State's per full-time-equivalent student current educational and general expenditures at 4-year public institutions of higher learning exceeded the national average by 3.9 percent—New York's $13,489 versus the U.S. average of $12,988.

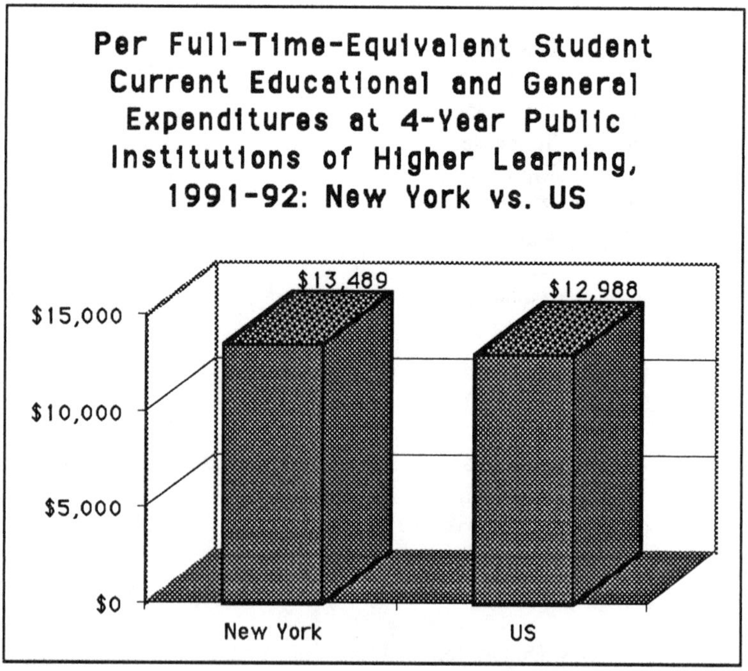


Data Source: U.S. Department of Education, *State Comparisons of Education Statistics: 1969-70 to 1993-94*

## FULL-TIME INSTRUCTIONAL FACULTY SALARIES AT 4-YEAR PUBLIC INSTITUTIONS OF HIGHER LEARNING: STATE RANKINGS

In 1994-95, the average full-time instructional faculty salary—based on nine-month contracts—at a four-year public institution of higher learning in New York ranked fifth highest in the nation.

**Average Instructional Faculty Salary at Public Institutions of Higher Learning**

| Rank | State | Average Salary |
|---|---|---|
| 1 | New Jersey | $65,540 |
| 2 | Connecticut | 58,443 |
| 3 | California | 58,335 |
| 4 | Hawaii | 57,481 |
| **5** | **New York** | **57,273** |
| 6 | Pennsylvania | 54,748 |
| 7 | Delaware | 54,684 |
| 8 | Rhode Island | 54,102 |
| 9 | Michigan | 53,641 |
| 10 | Iowa | 53,226 |
| 11 | Massachusetts | 52,787 |
| 12 | Arizona | 51,903 |
| 13 | Ohio | 51,520 |
| 14 | Wisconsin | 51,171 |
| 15 | District of Columbia | 50,764 |
| 16 | Minnesota | 50,685 |
| 17 | Virginia | 49,811 |
| 18 | Alaska | 49,554 |
| 19 | Maryland | 49,333 |
| 20 | New Hampshire | 49,267 |
| 21 | Colorado | 49,137 |
| 22 | Washington | 49,086 |
| 23 | Nevada | 48,957 |
| 24 | Florida | 48,581 |

*continued*

*continued*

| Rank | State | Average Salary |
|---|---|---|
| 25 | Illinois | 48,312 |
| 26 | North Carolina | 47,884 |
| 27 | Tennessee | 47,601 |
| 28 | Indiana | 47,206 |
| 29 | Wyoming | 46,418 |
| 30 | Nebraska | 46,341 |
| 31 | Texas | 45,785 |
| 32 | New Mexico | 45,575 |
| 33 | Missouri | 45,199 |
| 34 | Kansas | 45,166 |
| 35 | Kentucky | 44,860 |
| 36 | Georgia | 44,833 |
| 37 | South Carolina | 44,821 |
| 38 | Oregon | 44,533 |
| 39 | Utah | 44,454 |
| 40 | Alabama | 43,457 |
| 41 | Vermont | 43,336 |
| 42 | Maine | 42,268 |
| 43 | Oklahoma | 41,622 |
| 44 | Idaho | 41,418 |
| 45 | Mississippi | 41,109 |
| 46 | Arkansas | 40,073 |
| 47 | West Virginia | 39,226 |
| 48 | Louisiana | 39,029 |
| 49 | Montana | 38,522 |
| 50 | North Dakota | 37,229 |
| 51 | South Dakota | 36,324 |
| | U.S. Average | 49,738 |

Data Source: U.S. Department of Education, *Digest of Education Statistics 1996*

## FULL-TIME INSTRUCTIONAL FACULTY SALARIES AT 4-YEAR PUBLIC INSTITUTIONS OF HIGHER LEARNING: NEW YORK VS. U.S.

In 1994-95, the average full-time instructional faculty salary—based on 9-month contracts—at a four-year public university or college in New York outpaced the national average by 15.1 percent—$57,273 in New York versus the national average of $49,738.

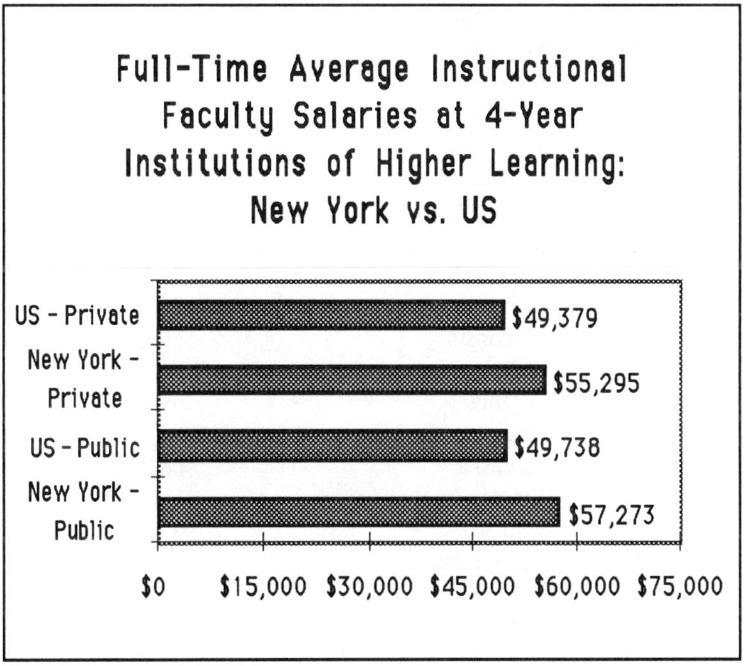


Data Source: U.S. Department of Education, *Digest of Education Statistics 1996*

# FULL-TIME PROFESSOR SALARIES AT PUBLIC UNIVERSITIES: STATE RANKINGS

In 1994-95, the average full-time professor salary—based on nine-month contracts—at a public university in New York ranked fourth highest in the nation.

**Average Professor Salary at a Public University**

| Rank | State | Average Salary |
|---|---|---|
| 1 | New Jersey | $92,907 |
| 2 | California | 79,866 |
| 3 | Connecticut | 78,326 |
| **4** | **New York** | **77,256** |
| 5 | Pennsylvania | 76,390 |
| 6 | Delaware | 75,506 |
| 7 | Michigan | 73,515 |
| 8 | Hawaii | 73,450 |
| 9 | Minnesota | 71,786 |
| 10 | North Carolina | 71,748 |
| 11 | Maryland | 71,645 |
| 12 | Iowa | 71,033 |
| 13 | Wisconsin | 70,553 |
| 14 | Massachusetts | 70,551 |
| 15 | Virginia | 69,653 |
| 16 | Texas | 68,359 |
| 17 | Nebraska | 68,242 |
| 18 | Illinois | 67,068 |
| 19 | Ohio | 67,041 |
| 20 | Rhode Island | 66,974 |
| 21 | Arizona | 66,703 |
| 22 | Nevada | 66,395 |
| 23 | Colorado | 66,061 |
| 24 | Georgia | 65,381 |
| 25 | Washington | 65,346 |
| 26 | New Hampshire | 65,286 |
| 27 | Missouri | 64,582 |

continued

*continued*

| Rank | State | Average Salary |
|---|---|---|
| 28 | Alaska | 64,525 |
| 29 | Indiana | 64,414 |
| 30 | Tennessee | 64,114 |
| 31 | Kentucky | 63,819 |
| 32 | South Carolina | 63,596 |
| 33 | Florida | 63,138 |
| 34 | Alabama | 62,540 |
| 35 | Utah | 61,493 |
| 36 | Louisiana | 61,197 |
| 37 | Vermont | 60,942 |
| 38 | New Mexico | 60,566 |
| 39 | Kansas | 59,503 |
| 40 | Oregon | 58,766 |
| 41 | Oklahoma | 57,936 |
| 42 | Arkansas | 57,623 |
| 43 | Wyoming | 57,025 |
| 44 | Maine | 56,652 |
| 45 | West Virginia | 54,984 |
| 46 | Mississippi | 52,972 |
| 47 | Idaho | 52,388 |
| 48 | North Dakota | 47,360 |
| 49 | Montana | 47,208 |
| 50 | South Dakota | 46,861 |
| | U.S. Average | 67,853 |

Data Source: U.S. Department of Education, *Digest of Education Statistics 1996*

## FULL-TIME PROFESSOR SALARIES AT PUBLIC UNIVERSITIES: NEW YORK VS. U.S.

In 1994-95, the average full-time professor salary—based on nine-month contracts—at a public university in New York outpaced the national average by 13.9 percent—$77,256 in New York versus the national average of $67,853.

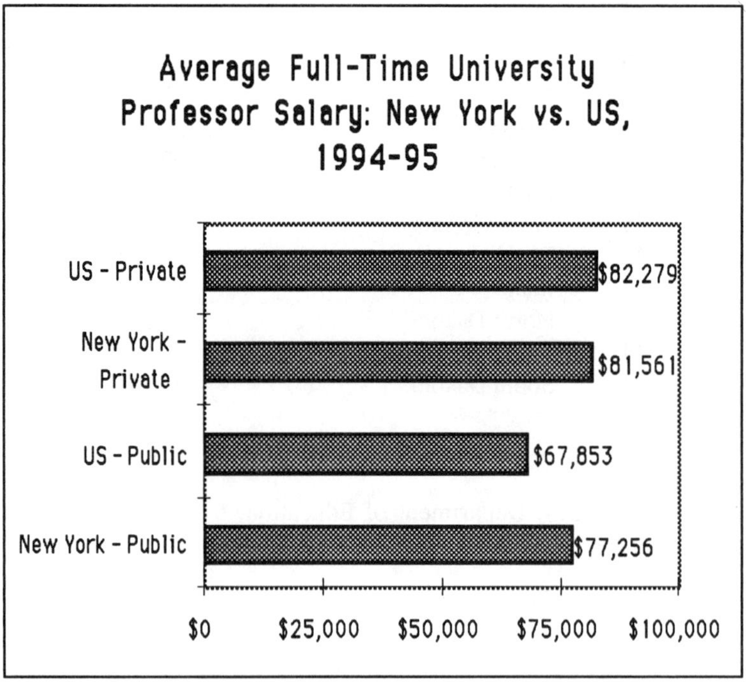


Data Source: U.S. Department of Education, *Digest of Education Statistics 1996*

# PER CAPITA COST OF STATE UNDERGRADUATE SCHOLARSHIP AND GRANT PROGRAMS BASED ON "NEED": STATE RANKINGS

In 1993-94, the per capita cost of state scholarship and grant programs in New York ranked the very highest in the nation.

**State Undergraduate Scholarship and Grant Programs**

| Rank | State | Per Capita Cost |
|---|---|---|
| **1** | **New York** | **$34.06** |
| 2 | Minnesota | 22.54 |
| 3 | Vermont | 19.25 |
| 4 | Illinois | 18.28 |
| 5 | New Jersey | 17.11 |
| 6 | Pennsylvania | 15.66 |
| 7 | Iowa | 12.27 |
| 8 | Indiana | 9.70 |
| 9 | Wisconsin | 9.24 |
| 10 | Washington | 8.72 |
| 11 | Michigan | 8.40 |
| 12 | Massachusetts | 7.46 |
| 13 | Ohio | 7.02 |
| 14 | California | 6.62 |
| 15 | Rhode Island | 6.52 |
| 16 | Connecticut | 6.30 |
| 17 | New Mexico | 5.60 |
| 18 | Kentucky | 5.39 |
| 19 | Maryland | 4.74 |
| 20 | South Carolina | 4.58 |
| 21 | Colorado | 4.51 |
| 22 | Oregon | 4.18 |
| 23 | Maine | 4.17 |
| 24 | Oklahoma | 4.11 |
| 25 | Georgia | 3.81 |
| 26 | Kansas | 3.55 |

*continued*

*continued*

| Rank | State | Per Capita Cost |
|---|---|---|
| 27 | Tennessee | 3.24 |
| 28 | North Dakota | 3.19 |
| 29 | West Virginia | 3.18 |
| 30 | Arkansas | 3.14 |
| 31 | Florida | 2.24 |
| 32 | Missouri | 2.11 |
| 33 | North Carolina | 2.04 |
| 34 | Delaware | 1.80 |
| 35 | District of Columbia | 1.79 |
| 36 | Nebraska | 1.65 |
| 37 | Texas | 1.58 |
| 38 | Louisiana | 1.48 |
| 39 | Virginia | 0.98 |
| 40 | Arizona | 0.85 |
| 41 | South Dakota | 0.82 |
| 42 | Alaska | 0.75 |
| 43 | New Hampshire | 0.74 |
| 44 | Hawaii | 0.63 |
| 45 | Utah | 0.59 |
| 46 | Idaho | 0.56 |
| 47 | Alabama | 0.54 |
| 48 | Wyoming | 0.53 |
| 49(t) | Mississippi | 0.47 |
| 49(t) | Montana | 0.47 |
| 51 | Nevada | 0.23 |
| | U.S. Average | 8.04 |

Data Source: U.S. Department of Education, *Digest of Education Statistics 1995*

## PER CAPITA COST OF STATE UNDERGRADUATE SCHOLARSHIP AND GRANT PROGRAMS BASED ON "NEED": NEW YORK VS. U.S.

In 1993-94, the per capita cost of state scholarship and grant programs in New York exceeded the national average by 303.6 percent—New York's $34.06 versus the national average of $8.04.

However, New York State accounts for such a significant portion of total U.S. funding in this area that if you exclude New York State, per capita U.S. costs drop to $6.51. New York's $34.06 surpasses this excluding-New York national average by 423.2 percent.

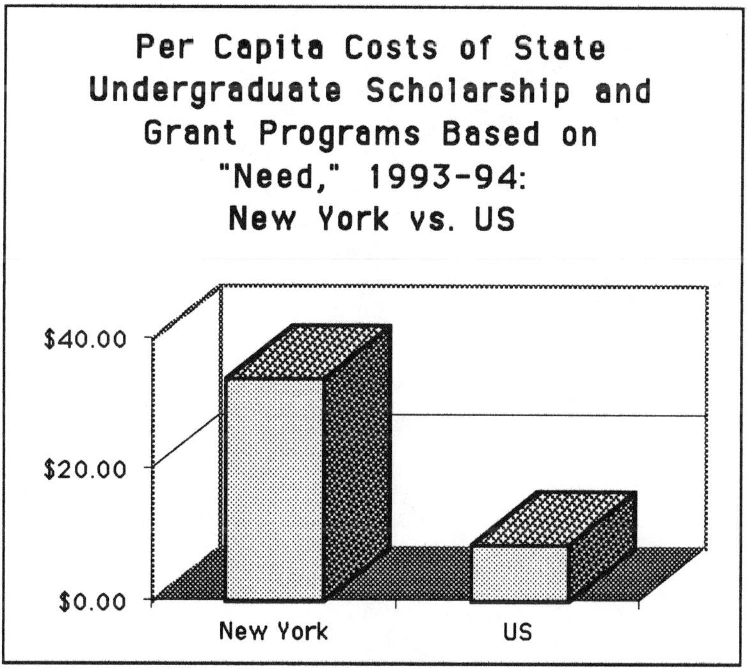


Data Source: U.S. Department of Education, *Digest of Education Statistics 1995*

# Chapter Four

# New York State: Crime

- Total Crime
- Violent Crime
- Property Crime
- Murder
- Rape
- Robbery
- Aggravated Assault
- Burglary
- Larceny-Theft
- Motor Vehicle Theft
- Police Protection Employees
- Police Protection and Corrections Spending

# TOTAL CRIME: STATE RANKINGS

In 1995, New York ranked thirtieth among the 50 states in terms of the total number of crimes per 100,000 inhabitants.

Total crime index takes into account the violent crimes of murder and non-negligent manslaughter, forcible rape, robbery, and aggravated assault, and the property crimes of burglary, larceny-theft, motor vehicle theft, and arson.

**Total Crime Index (Per 100,000 Inhabitants)**

| Rank | State | Total Crime Index |
|---|---|---|
| 1 | Arizona | 8,213.6 |
| 2 | Florida | 7,701.5 |
| 3 | Hawaii | 7,198.6 |
| 4 | Louisiana | 6,676.0 |
| 5 | Nevada | 6,579.3 |
| 6 | Oregon | 6,563.9 |
| 7 | New Mexico | 6,428.0 |
| 8 | Maryland | 6,294.8 |
| 9 | Washington | 6,269.8 |
| 10 | Utah | 6,090.8 |
| 11 | South Carolina | 6,063.8 |
| 12 | Georgia | 6,003.6 |
| 13 | California | 5,831.1 |
| 14 | Alaska | 5,753.8 |
| 15 | Texas | 5,684.3 |
| 16 | North Carolina | 5,639.5 |
| 17 | Oklahoma | 5,596.8 |
| 18 | Illinois | 5,455.7 |
| 19 | Colorado | 5,396.3 |
| 20 | Tennessee | 5,362.5 |
| 21 | Montana | 5,304.9 |
| 22 | Michigan | 5,182.8 |
| 23 | Delaware | 5,158.7 |
| 24 | Missouri | 5,120.5 |
| 25 | Kansas | 4,886.9 |

*continued*

*continued*

| Rank | State | Total Crime Index |
|---|---|---|
| 26 | Alabama | 4,848.1 |
| 27 | New Jersey | 4,703.7 |
| 28 | Arkansas | 4,690.0 |
| 29 | Indiana | 4,631.5 |
| **30** | **New York** | **4,560.1** |
| 31 | Nebraska | 4,544.5 |
| 32 | Mississippi | 4,514.5 |
| 33 | Connecticut | 4,503.2 |
| 34 | Minnesota | 4,497.3 |
| 35 | Ohio | 4,405.2 |
| 36 | Idaho | 4,401.5 |
| 37 | Massachusetts | 4,341.6 |
| 38 | Wyoming | 4,320.2 |
| 39 | Rhode Island | 4,244.5 |
| 40 | Iowa | 4,101.9 |
| 41 | Virginia | 3,989.2 |
| 42 | Wisconsin | 3,885.7 |
| 43 | Vermont | 3,433.7 |
| 44 | Pennsylvania | 3,364.9 |
| 45 | Kentucky | 3,351.7 |
| 46 | Maine | 3,284.7 |
| 47 | South Dakota | 3,060.6 |
| 48 | North Dakota | 2,866.3 |
| 49 | New Hampshire | 2,655.4 |
| 50 | West Virginia | 2,458.2 |
| | U.S. Average | 5,277.6 |

Data Source: Federal Bureau of Investigation, *Crime in the United States 1995*

## TOTAL CRIME: NEW YORK VS. U.S.

In 1995, the total crime rate in New York registered below the national average. The national rate exceeded New York's by 15.7 percent—4,560.1 (per 100,000 population) in New York versus the national rate of 5,277.6.

New York's 1995 rate still exceeded the 1970 rate of 3,922.1 by 16.3 percent, for example, but was less than the 1980 rate of 6,911.6 and the 1990 rate of 6,364.

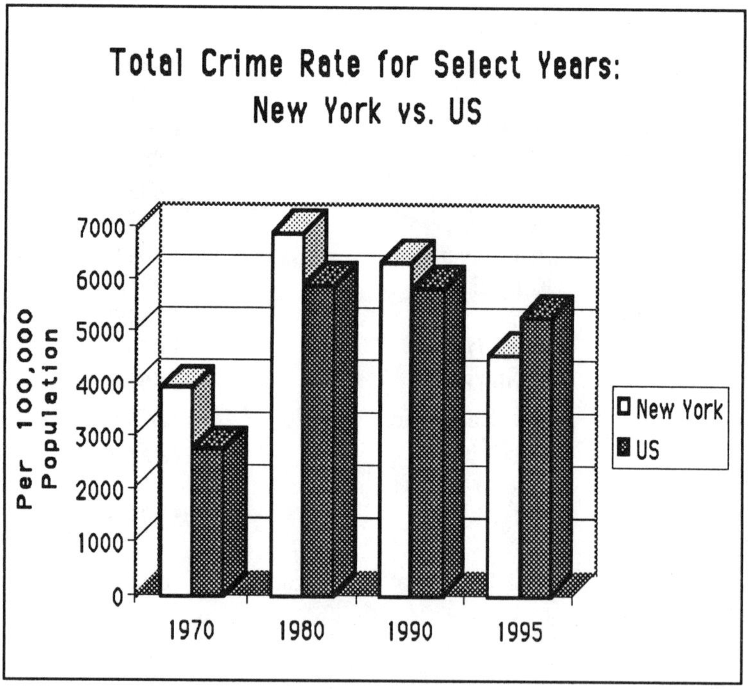


Data Source: Federal Bureau of Investigation, *Crime in the United States*, annual

## VIOLENT CRIME: STATE RANKINGS

In 1995, New York ranked eighth among the 50 states in terms of the number of violent crimes per 100,000 inhabitants.

As defined by the FBI, violent crime is composed of four offenses: murder and non-negligent manslaughter, forcible rape, robbery, and aggravated assault.

### Violent Crime Index (Per 100,000 Inhabitants)

| Rank | State | Violent Crime Index |
|---|---|---|
| 1 | Florida | 1,071.0 |
| 2 | Louisiana | 1,007.4 |
| 3 | Illinois | 996.1 |
| 4 | Maryland | 986.9 |
| 5 | South Carolina | 981.9 |
| 6 | California | 966.0 |
| 7 | Nevada | 945.2 |
| **8** | **New York** | **841.9** |
| 9 | New Mexico | 819.2 |
| 10 | Tennessee | 771.5 |
| 11 | Alaska | 770.9 |
| 12 | Delaware | 725.0 |
| 13 | Arizona | 713.5 |
| 14 | Michigan | 687.8 |
| 15 | Massachusetts | 687.2 |
| 16 | Oklahoma | 664.2 |
| 17 | Texas | 663.9 |
| 18 | Missouri | 663.8 |
| 19 | Georgia | 657.1 |
| 20 | North Carolina | 646.4 |
| 21 | Alabama | 632.4 |
| 22 | New Jersey | 599.8 |
| 23 | Arkansas | 553.2 |
| 24 | Indiana | 524.7 |
| 25 | Oregon | 522.4 |
| 26 | Mississippi | 502.8 |

*continued*

*continued*

| Rank | State | Violent Crime Index |
|---|---|---|
| 27 | Washington | 484.3 |
| 28 | Ohio | 482.5 |
| 29 | Colorado | 440.2 |
| 30 | Pennsylvania | 427.3 |
| 31 | Kansas | 420.7 |
| 32 | Connecticut | 405.9 |
| 33 | Nebraska | 382.0 |
| 34 | Rhode Island | 368.0 |
| 35 | Kentucky | 364.7 |
| 36 | Virginia | 361.5 |
| 37 | Minnesota | 356.1 |
| 38 | Iowa | 354.4 |
| 39 | Utah | 328.8 |
| 40 | Idaho | 322.0 |
| 41 | Hawaii | 295.6 |
| 42 | Wisconsin | 281.1 |
| 43 | Wyoming | 254.2 |
| 44 | West Virginia | 210.2 |
| 45 | South Dakota | 207.5 |
| 46 | Montana | 170.6 |
| 47 | Maine | 131.4 |
| 48 | Vermont | 118.3 |
| 49 | New Hampshire | 114.5 |
| 50 | North Dakota | 86.7 |
| | U.S. Average | 684.6 |

Data Source: Federal Bureau of Investigation, *Crime in the United States 1995*

# VIOLENT CRIME: NEW YORK VS. U.S.

In 1995, the violent crime rate in New York exceeded the U.S. average by 23 percent—841.9 (per 100,000 population) in New York versus the national rate of 684.6.

New York's 1995 rate surpassed the state's 1970 rate of 676 by 24.5 percent, for example, but was less than the 1980 rate of 1,029.5 and the 1990 rate of 1,181.

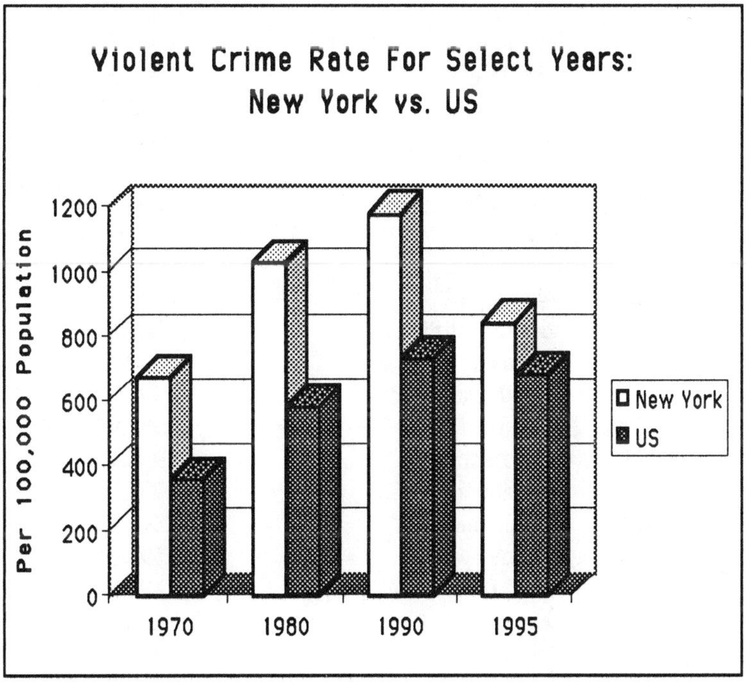


Data Source: Federal Bureau of Investigation, *Crime in the United States*, annual

## PROPERTY CRIME: STATE RANKINGS

In 1995, New York ranked thirty-ninth among the 50 states in terms of the rate of property crime per 100,000 population.

As defined by the FBI, property crime consists of burglary, larceny-theft, motor vehicle theft, and arson.

**Property Crime Index (Per 100,000 Inhabitants)**

| Rank | State | Property Crime Index |
|---|---|---|
| 1 | Arizona | 7,500.1 |
| 2 | Hawaii | 6,902.9 |
| 3 | Florida | 6,630.6 |
| 4 | Oregon | 6,041.5 |
| 5 | Washington | 5,785.5 |
| 6 | Utah | 5,762.0 |
| 7 | Louisiana | 5,668.6 |
| 8 | Nevada | 5,634.2 |
| 9 | New Mexico | 5,608.8 |
| 10 | Georgia | 5,346.5 |
| 11 | Maryland | 5,307.9 |
| 12 | Montana | 5,134.4 |
| 13 | South Carolina | 5,081.8 |
| 14 | Texas | 5,020.5 |
| 15 | North Carolina | 4,993.1 |
| 16 | Alaska | 4,982.9 |
| 17 | Colorado | 4,956.1 |
| 18 | Oklahoma | 4,932.7 |
| 19 | California | 4,865.1 |
| 20 | Tennessee | 4,591.2 |
| 21 | Michigan | 4,495.0 |
| 22 | Kansas | 4,466.2 |
| 23 | Illinois | 4,459.6 |
| 24 | Missouri | 4,456.8 |
| 25 | Delaware | 4,433.8 |
| 26 | Alabama | 4,215.7 |
| 27 | Nebraska | 4,162.5 |

*continued*

*continued*

| Rank | State | Property Crime Index |
|---|---|---|
| 28 | Minnesota | 4,141.2 |
| 29 | Arkansas | 4,137.7 |
| 30 | Indiana | 4,106.8 |
| 31 | New Jersey | 4,103.9 |
| 32 | Connecticut | 4,097.3 |
| 33 | Idaho | 4,079.4 |
| 34 | Wyoming | 4,066.8 |
| 35 | Mississippi | 4,011.7 |
| 36 | Ohio | 3,922.7 |
| 37 | Rhode Island | 3,876.6 |
| 38 | Iowa | 3,747.5 |
| **39** | **New York** | **3,718.3** |
| 40 | Massachusetts | 3,654.4 |
| 41 | Virginia | 3,627.7 |
| 42 | Wisconsin | 3,604.6 |
| 43 | Vermont | 3,315.4 |
| 44 | Maine | 3,153.3 |
| 45 | Kentucky | 2,987.0 |
| 46 | Pennsylvania | 2,937.6 |
| 47 | South Dakota | 2,853.1 |
| 48 | North Dakota | 2,779.6 |
| 49 | New Hampshire | 2,540.9 |
| 50 | West Virginia | 2,248.0 |
| | U.S. Average | 4,593.0 |

Data Source: Federal Bureau of Investigation, *Crime in the United States 1995*

## PROPERTY CRIME: NEW YORK VS. U.S.

In 1995, New York's property crime rate actually registered less than the U.S. average. The U.S. average rate of 4,593 (per 100,000 population) surpassed the New York rate of 3,718.3 by 23.5 percent.

New York's 1995 property crime rate was down from the 1980 rate of 5,882, down from the 1990 rate of 5,183, but still surpassed the 1970 rate of 3,246 by 14.6 percent.

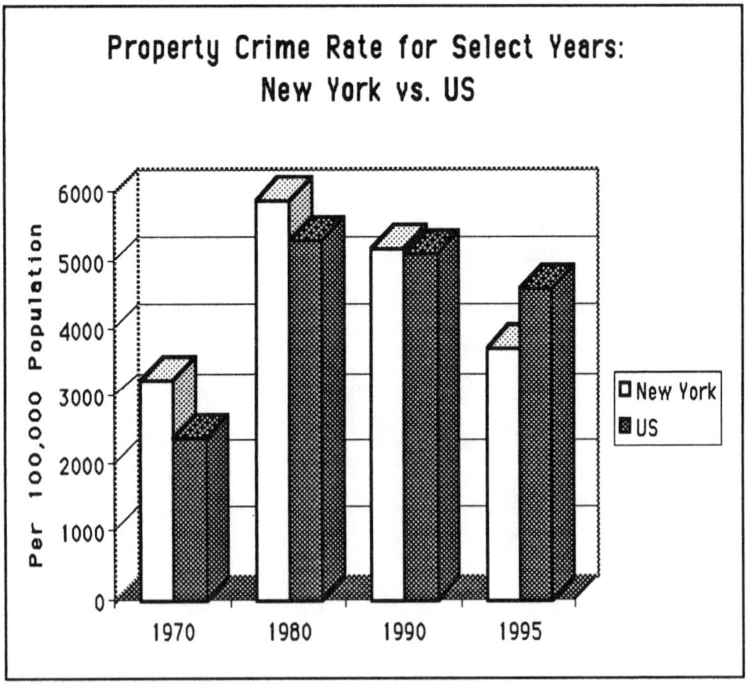


Data Source: Federal Bureau of Investigation, *Crime in the United States*, annual

# MURDER RATE: STATE RANKINGS

In 1995, New York tied for eighteenth among the 50 states in terms of its murder rate per 100,000 residents.

The murder index includes murder and non-negligent manslaughter. According to the FBI, murder and non-negligent manslaughter is defined as the willful (non-negligent) killing of one human being by another.

**Murder Index (Per 100,000 Inhabitants)**

| Rank | State | Murder Index |
|---|---|---|
| 1 | Louisiana | 17.0 |
| 2 | Mississippi | 12.9 |
| 3 | Oklahoma | 12.2 |
| 4 | Maryland | 11.8 |
| 5(t) | Alabama | 11.2 |
| 5(t) | California | 11.2 |
| 7 | Nevada | 10.7 |
| 8 | Tennessee | 10.6 |
| 9(t) | Arkansas | 10.4 |
| 9(t) | Arizona | 10.4 |
| 11 | Illinois | 10.3 |
| 12 | Georgia | 9.5 |
| 13 | North Carolina | 9.4 |
| 14 | Alaska | 9.1 |
| 15 | Texas | 9.0 |
| 16(t) | New Mexico | 8.8 |
| 16(t) | Missouri | 8.8 |
| **18(t)** | **New York** | **8.5** |
| 18(t) | Michigan | 8.5 |
| 20 | Indiana | 8.0 |
| 21 | South Carolina | 7.9 |
| 22 | Virginia | 7.6 |
| 23 | Florida | 7.3 |
| 24 | Kentucky | 7.2 |
| 25 | Pennsylvania | 6.3 |

*continued*

*continued*

| Rank | State | Murder Index |
|---|---|---|
| 26 | Kansas | 6.2 |
| 27 | Colorado | 5.8 |
| 28 | Ohio | 5.4 |
| 29(t) | New Jersey | 5.1 |
| 29(t) | Washington | 5.1 |
| 31 | West Virginia | 4.9 |
| 32 | Hawaii | 4.7 |
| 33 | Connecticut | 4.6 |
| 34 | Wisconsin | 4.3 |
| 35(t) | Idaho | 4.1 |
| 35(t) | Oregon | 4.1 |
| 37(t) | Minnesota | 3.9 |
| 37(t) | Utah | 3.9 |
| 39 | Massachusetts | 3.6 |
| 40 | Delaware | 3.5 |
| 41 | Rhode Island | 3.3 |
| 42 | Montana | 3.0 |
| 43 | Nebraska | 2.9 |
| 44 | Vermont | 2.2 |
| 45 | Wyoming | 2.1 |
| 46 | Maine | 2.0 |
| 47(t) | Iowa | 1.8 |
| 47(t) | New Hampshire | 1.8 |
| 47(t) | South Dakota | 1.8 |
| 50 | North Dakota | 0.9 |
| | U.S. Average | 8.2 |

Data Source: Federal Bureau of Investigation, *Crime in the United States 1995*

## MURDER RATE: NEW YORK VS. U.S.

In 1995, New York's murder rate (per 100,000 population) topped the U.S. average by just 3.7 percent—8.5 in New York versus the national average of 8.2.

New York's 1995 murder rate of 8.5 compares with 14.5 in 1990, 12.7 in 1980, and 7.9 in 1970. Between 1970 and 1995, New York's murder rate increased by 7.6 percent.

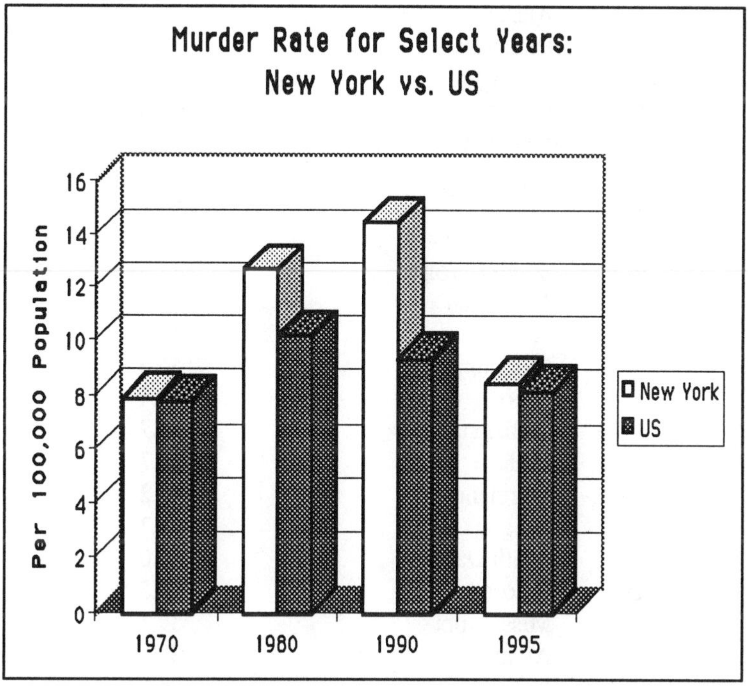


Data Source: Federal Bureau of Investigation, *Crime in the United States*, annual

## RAPES: STATE RANKINGS

In 1995, New York tied for forty-third out of the 50 states in terms of rapes per 100,000 inhabitants.

As defined by the FBI, forcible rape is the carnal knowledge of a female forcibly and against her will. Assaults and attempts to commit rape also are included, but statutory rape without force and other sex offenses are not included.

**Forcible Rape Index (Per 100,000 Inhabitants)**

| Rank | State | Rape Index |
|---|---|---|
| 1 | Alaska | 80.3 |
| 2 | Delaware | 80.2 |
| 3 | Michigan | 62.0 |
| 4 | Nevada | 61.2 |
| 5 | Washington | 59.2 |
| 6 | New Mexico | 56.6 |
| 7 | Minnesota | 56.2 |
| 8 | Florida | 48.6 |
| 9 | South Carolina | 47.3 |
| 10 | Tennessee | 47.1 |
| 11 | Texas | 45.7 |
| 12 | Oklahoma | 44.6 |
| 13 | Ohio | 43.4 |
| 14(t) | Louisiana | 42.7 |
| 14(t) | Utah | 42.7 |
| 16 | Maryland | 42.2 |
| 17 | Oregon | 41.7 |
| 18 | South Dakota | 41.0 |
| 19 | Colorado | 39.5 |
| 20 | Mississippi | 39.1 |
| 21 | Arkansas | 37.2 |
| 22 | Kansas | 36.6 |
| 23 | Illinois | 36.5 |
| 24 | Georgia | 35.3 |
| 25 | Wyoming | 34.4 |

*continued*

*continued*

| Rank | State | Rape Index |
|---|---|---|
| 26 | Arizona | 33.6 |
| 27 | California | 33.4 |
| 28 | Indiana | 33.3 |
| 29 | North Carolina | 32.2 |
| 30 | Missouri | 32.1 |
| 31 | Kentucky | 31.9 |
| 32 | Alabama | 31.7 |
| 33(t) | New Hampshire | 29.0 |
| 33(t) | Massachusetts | 29.0 |
| 35 | Idaho | 28.4 |
| 36 | Hawaii | 28.3 |
| 37 | Vermont | 28.2 |
| 38 | Virginia | 27.2 |
| 39 | Rhode Island | 27.0 |
| 40 | Montana | 25.9 |
| 41 | Pennsylvania | 25.2 |
| 42 | New Jersey | 24.3 |
| 43(t) | Connecticut | 23.7 |
| **43(t)** | **New York** | **23.7** |
| 45 | Wisconsin | 23.3 |
| 46 | North Dakota | 22.8 |
| 47 | Iowa | 21.8 |
| 48 | Maine | 21.4 |
| 49 | West Virginia | 21.2 |
| 50 | Nebraska | 19.4 |
| | U.S. Average | 37.1 |

Data Source: Federal Bureau of Investigation, *Crime in the United States 1995*

## RAPES: NEW YORK VS. U.S.

In 1995, New York's rape index (per 100,000 population) registered lower than the U.S. average. The national average rate of 37.1 exceeded New York's rate of 23.7 by 56.5 percent.

New York's 1995 rape rate of 23.7 compared favorably with the 1990 rate of 30, the 1980 rate of 30.9, but still surpassed the 1970 rate of 15.5 by 52.9 percent.

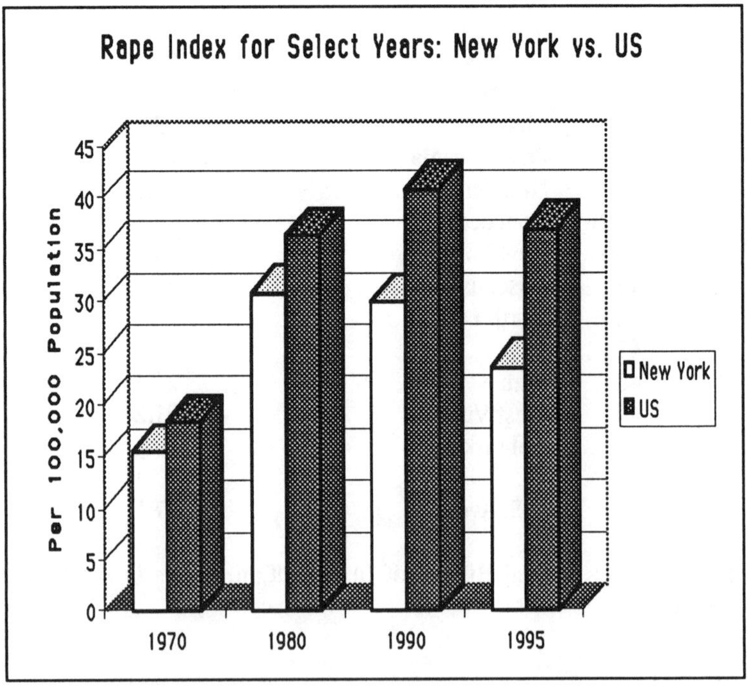


Data Source: Federal Bureau of Investigation, *Crime in the United States*, annual

## ROBBERIES: STATE RANKINGS

In 1995, New York carried the second heaviest burden of robberies per 100,000 inhabitants among the 50 states.

As defined by the FBI, robbery is the taking or attempted taking of value from the care, custody, or control of a person or persons by force or threat of force or violence and/or by putting the victim in fear.

**Robbery Index (Per 100,000 Inhabitants)**

| Rank | State | Robbery Index |
|---|---|---|
| 1 | Maryland | 423.1 |
| **2** | **New York** | **399.7** |
| 3 | California | 331.2 |
| 4 | Illinois | 330.8 |
| 5 | Nevada | 324.6 |
| 6 | Florida | 299.9 |
| 7 | New Jersey | 283.0 |
| 8 | Louisiana | 268.6 |
| 9 | Tennessee | 223.2 |
| 10 | Georgia | 205.2 |
| 11 | Missouri | 204.0 |
| 12 | Delaware | 198.7 |
| 13 | Pennsylvania | 189.3 |
| 14 | Michigan | 187.3 |
| 15 | Alabama | 185.8 |
| 16 | Texas | 179.8 |
| 17 | North Carolina | 179.2 |
| 18 | Ohio | 178.7 |
| 19 | South Carolina | 175.9 |
| 20 | Arizona | 173.8 |
| 21 | Connecticut | 163.2 |
| 22 | Alaska | 155.1 |
| 23 | New Mexico | 154.5 |
| 24 | Massachusetts | 150.4 |
| 25 | Oregon | 137.9 |
| 26 | Indiana | 135.2 |

*continued*

*continued*

| Rank | State | Robbery Index |
|---|---|---|
| 27 | Washington | 132.7 |
| 28 | Virginia | 131.7 |
| 29 | Mississippi | 130.9 |
| 30 | Hawaii | 130.8 |
| 31 | Arkansas | 125.7 |
| 32 | Minnesota | 123.7 |
| 33 | Oklahoma | 115.6 |
| 34 | Kansas | 108.2 |
| 35 | Wisconsin | 105.1 |
| 36 | Kentucky | 103.7 |
| 37 | Colorado | 96.2 |
| 38 | Rhode Island | 92.3 |
| 39 | Utah | 67.1 |
| 40 | Nebraska | 65.2 |
| 41 | Iowa | 53.0 |
| 42 | West Virginia | 42.7 |
| 43 | Montana | 33.2 |
| 44 | New Hampshire | 27.4 |
| 45 | Maine | 26.9 |
| 46 | South Dakota | 25.9 |
| 47 | Idaho | 24.0 |
| 48 | Wyoming | 17.9 |
| 49 | Vermont | 10.9 |
| 50 | North Dakota | 10.0 |
| | U.S. Average | 220.9 |

Data Source: Federal Bureau of Investigation, *Crime in the United States 1995*

## ROBBERIES: NEW YORK VS. U.S.

In 1995, the rate of robberies (per 100,000 population) in New York topped the national average by 80.9 percent -- 399.7 in New York versus 220.9 across the U.S.

New York's 1995 robbery rate compared favorably with the state's 1990 rate of 625, the 1980 rate of 641.3, and the 1970 rate of 443.3.

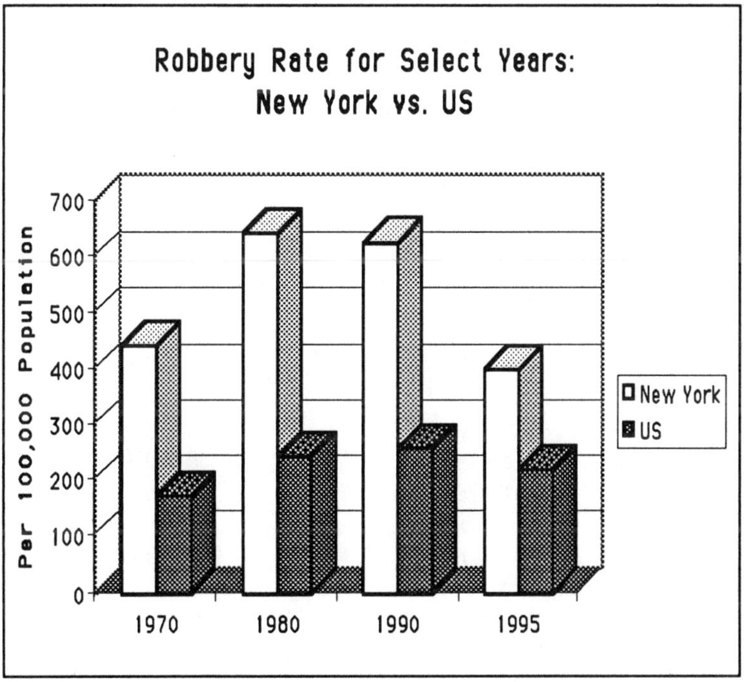


Source: Federal Bureau of Investigation, *Crime in the United States*, annual

## AGGRAVATED ASSAULTS: STATE RANKINGS

In 1995, New York ranked nineteenth out of the 50 states in terms of aggravated assaults per 100,000 residents.

As defined by the FBI, aggravated assault is an unlawful attack by one person upon another for the purpose of inflicting severe or aggravated bodily injury.

**Aggravated Assault Index (Per 100,000 Inhabitants)**

| Rank | State | Aggravated Assault Index |
|---|---|---|
| 1 | South Carolina | 750.8 |
| 2 | Florida | 715.1 |
| 3 | Louisiana | 679.0 |
| 4 | Illinois | 618.5 |
| 5 | New Mexico | 599.3 |
| 6 | California | 590.3 |
| 7 | Nevada | 548.7 |
| 8 | Alaska | 526.3 |
| 9 | Maryland | 509.7 |
| 10 | Massachusetts | 504.2 |
| 11 | Arizona | 495.7 |
| 12 | Oklahoma | 491.8 |
| 13 | Tennessee | 490.5 |
| 14 | Delaware | 442.5 |
| 15 | Michigan | 430.1 |
| 16 | Texas | 429.3 |
| 17 | North Carolina | 425.5 |
| 18 | Missouri | 418.8 |
| **19** | **New York** | **410.0** |
| 20 | Georgia | 407.1 |
| 21 | Alabama | 403.7 |
| 22 | Arkansas | 379.8 |
| 23 | Indiana | 348.3 |
| 24 | Oregon | 338.7 |
| 25 | Mississippi | 319.9 |
| 26 | Colorado | 298.7 |

*continued*

*continued*

| Rank | State | Aggravated Assault Index |
|---|---|---|
| 27 | Nebraska | 294.5 |
| 28 | New Jersey | 287.4 |
| 29 | Washington | 287.3 |
| 30 | Iowa | 277.8 |
| 31 | Kansas | 269.8 |
| 32 | Idaho | 265.5 |
| 33 | Ohio | 255.0 |
| 34 | Rhode Island | 245.4 |
| 35 | Kentucky | 222.0 |
| 36 | Utah | 215.1 |
| 37 | Connecticut | 214.4 |
| 38 | Pennsylvania | 206.5 |
| 39 | Wyoming | 199.8 |
| 40 | Virginia | 194.9 |
| 41 | Minnesota | 172.2 |
| 42 | Wisconsin | 148.4 |
| 43 | West Virginia | 141.1 |
| 44 | South Dakota | 138.8 |
| 45 | Hawaii | 131.8 |
| 46 | Montana | 108.5 |
| 47 | Maine | 81.1 |
| 48 | Vermont | 76.9 |
| 49 | New Hampshire | 56.3 |
| 50 | North Dakota | 53.0 |
| | U.S. Average | 418.3 |

Data Source: Federal Bureau of Investigation, *Crime in the United States 1995*

## AGGRAVATED ASSAULTS: NEW YORK VS. U.S.

In 1995, the U.S. aggravated assault rate (per 100,000 population) outpaced New York's by 2 percent—410 in New York versus the national average rate of 418.3.

New York's 1995 rate of 410 compared with 512 in 1990, 344.6 in 1980, and 209.3 in 1970. Between 1970 and 1995, the state's aggravated assault rate grew by 95.9 percent.

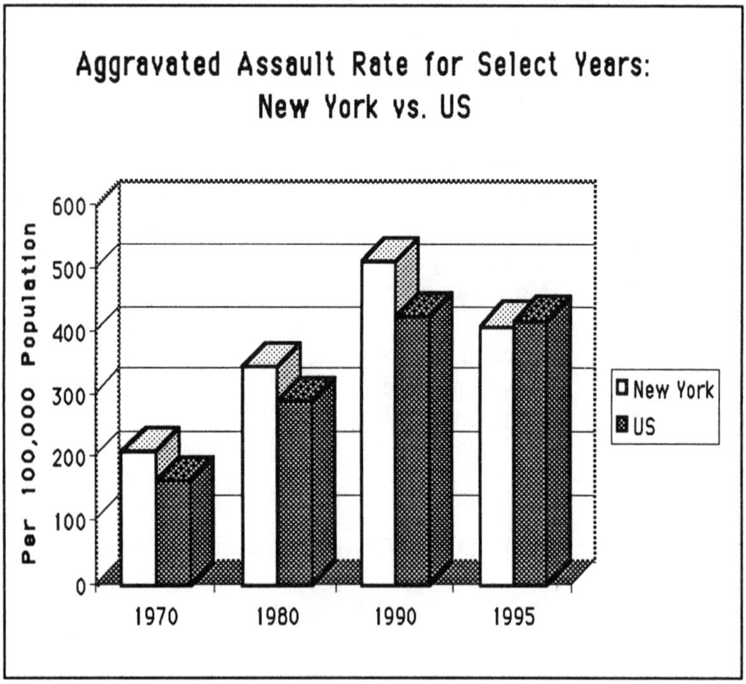


Data Source: Federal Bureau of Investigation, *Crime in the United States*, annual

## BURGLARIES: STATE RANKINGS

In 1995, New York ranked thirty-third out of the 50 states in terms of the number of burglaries per 100,000 residents.

As defined by the FBI, burglary is the unlawful entry of a structure to commit a felony or a theft.

**Burglary Index (Per 100,000 Inhabitants)**

| Rank | State | Burglary Index |
|---|---|---|
| 1 | Florida | 1,522.4 |
| 2 | New Mexico | 1,447.1 |
| 3 | North Carolina | 1,417.6 |
| 4 | Arizona | 1,416.8 |
| 5 | Nevada | 1,322.5 |
| 6 | Oklahoma | 1,271.9 |
| 7 | South Carolina | 1,254.6 |
| 8 | Louisiana | 1,231.7 |
| 9 | Hawaii | 1,165.3 |
| 10 | Tennessee | 1,143.2 |
| 11 | Mississippi | 1,131.1 |
| 12 | California | 1,120.3 |
| 13 | Oregon | 1,102.8 |
| 14 | Washington | 1,091.2 |
| 15 | Texas | 1,082.3 |
| 16 | Kansas | 1,068.4 |
| 17 | Georgia | 1,059.9 |
| 18 | Maryland | 1,057.5 |
| 19 | Alabama | 1,024.8 |
| 20 | Arkansas | 996.9 |
| 21 | Colorado | 934.1 |
| 22 | Rhode Island | 932.7 |
| 23 | Missouri | 932.6 |
| 24 | Illinois | 917.6 |
| 25 | Michigan | 909.7 |
| 26 | Delaware | 905.3 |
| 27 | Connecticut | 888.4 |

*continued*

*continued*

| Rank | State | Burglary Index |
|---|---|---|
| 28 | New Jersey | 875.2 |
| 29 | Ohio | 838.8 |
| 30 | Alaska | 836.9 |
| 31 | Indiana | 821.6 |
| 32 | Massachusetts | 817.7 |
| **33** | **New York** | **808.1** |
| 34 | Utah | 800.8 |
| 35 | Minnesota | 797.3 |
| 36 | Idaho | 779.8 |
| 37 | Vermont | 760.9 |
| 38 | Iowa | 757.5 |
| 39 | Kentucky | 735.5 |
| 40 | Maine | 726.4 |
| 41 | Montana | 720.8 |
| 42 | Nebraska | 631.9 |
| 43 | Wisconsin | 613.2 |
| 44 | Wyoming | 612.1 |
| 45 | Virginia | 595.2 |
| 46 | West Virginia | 565.0 |
| 47 | Pennsylvania | 561.8 |
| 48 | South Dakota | 540.7 |
| 49 | New Hampshire | 418.6 |
| 50 | North Dakota | 350.7 |
| | U.S. Average | 987.6 |

Data Source: Federal Bureau of Investigation, *Crime in the United States 1995*

## BURGLARIES: NEW YORK VS. U.S.

In 1995, the U.S. average burglary rate (per 100,000 population) surpassed the New York rate by 22.2 percent—808.1 in New York compared with the national average of 987.6.

The 1995 New York rate compared favorably with the 1990 rate of 1,161, the 1980 rate of 2,061.1, and the 1970 rate of 1,414.2. Indeed, between 1980 and 1995, New York's burglary rate has plummeted by 60.8 percent.

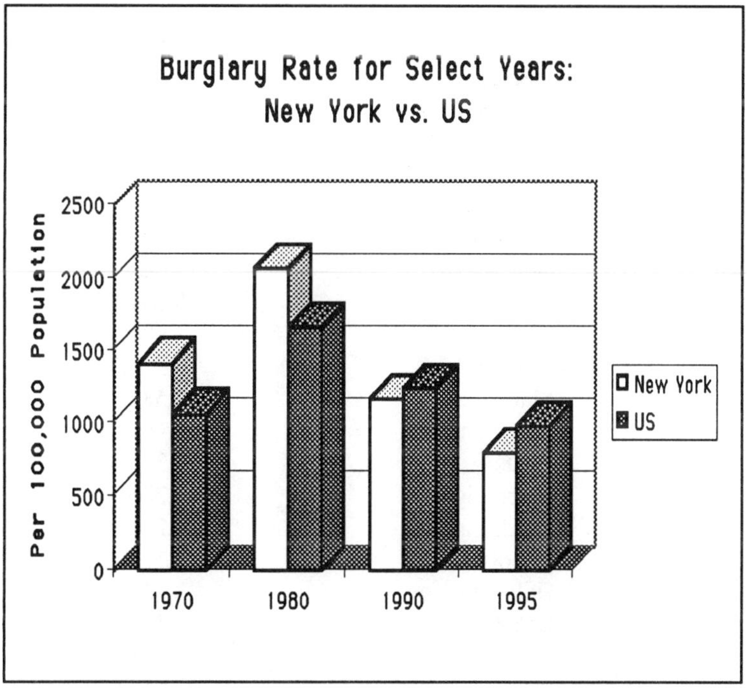


Data Source: Federal Bureau of Investigation, *Crime in the United States*, annual

## LARCENY-THEFT: STATE RANKINGS

In 1995, New York ranked forty-second out of the 50 states in terms of its larceny-theft rate per 100,000 inhabitants.

As defined by the FBI, larceny-theft is the unlawful taking, carrying, leading, or riding away of property from the possession or constructive possession of another.

**Larceny-Theft Index (Per 100,000 Inhabitants)**

| Rank | State | Larceny-Theft Index |
|---|---|---|
| 1 | Hawaii | 5,046.9 |
| 2 | Arizona | 4,925.6 |
| 3 | Utah | 4,572.1 |
| 4 | Florida | 4,322.4 |
| 5 | Oregon | 4,236.7 |
| 6 | Washington | 4,140.3 |
| 7 | Montana | 4,105.5 |
| 8 | Louisiana | 3,838.5 |
| 9 | Georgia | 3,678.3 |
| 10 | New Mexico | 3,648.5 |
| 11 | Colorado | 3,634.5 |
| 12 | Alaska | 3,624.3 |
| 13 | Nevada | 3,566.2 |
| 14 | Maryland | 3,532.8 |
| 15 | South Carolina | 3,441.8 |
| 16 | Texas | 3,377.8 |
| 17 | Wyoming | 3,286.3 |
| 18 | North Carolina | 3,264.9 |
| 19 | Nebraska | 3,179.2 |
| 20 | Oklahoma | 3,164.3 |
| 21 | Delaware | 3,114.2 |
| 22 | Kansas | 3,074.3 |
| 23 | Idaho | 3,057.6 |
| 24 | Missouri | 3,050.9 |
| 25 | Illinois | 3,019.0 |
| 26 | Minnesota | 3,002.5 |

*continued*

*continued*

| Rank | State | Larceny-Theft Index |
|---|---|---|
| 27 | Michigan | 2,939.7 |
| 28 | California | 2,856.9 |
| 29 | Alabama | 2,844.3 |
| 30 | Indiana | 2,819.5 |
| 31 | Arkansas | 2,815.4 |
| 32 | Tennessee | 2,799.5 |
| 33 | Iowa | 2,767.2 |
| 34 | Virginia | 2,740.0 |
| 35 | Connecticut | 2,688.7 |
| 36 | Ohio | 2,669.0 |
| 37 | Wisconsin | 2,627.8 |
| 38 | New Jersey | 2,597.1 |
| 39 | Mississippi | 2,520.1 |
| 40 | Rhode Island | 2,503.0 |
| 41 | Vermont | 2,418.8 |
| **42** | **New York** | **2,344.4** |
| 43 | Maine | 2,292.0 |
| 44 | North Dakota | 2,249.8 |
| 45 | Massachusetts | 2,232.2 |
| 46 | South Dakota | 2,191.5 |
| 47 | Kentucky | 1,992.4 |
| 48 | New Hampshire | 1,977.2 |
| 49 | Pennsylvania | 1,963.1 |
| 50 | West Virginia | 1,516.6 |
| | U.S. Average | 3,044.9 |

Data Source: Federal Bureau of Investigation, *Crime in the United States 1995*

## LARCENY-THEFT: NEW YORK VS. U.S.

In 1995, the U.S. average larceny-theft rate (per 100,000 population) outpaced the New York rate by 29.9 percent—2,344.4 in New York versus the national average rate of 3,044.9.

New York's 1995 larceny-theft rate of 2,344.4 was down from 2,979 in 1990 and from 3,060.4 in 1980. However, it was still far above the 1970 rate of 1,149.6. Indeed, between 1970 and 1995, the larceny-theft rate increased by 103.9 percent.

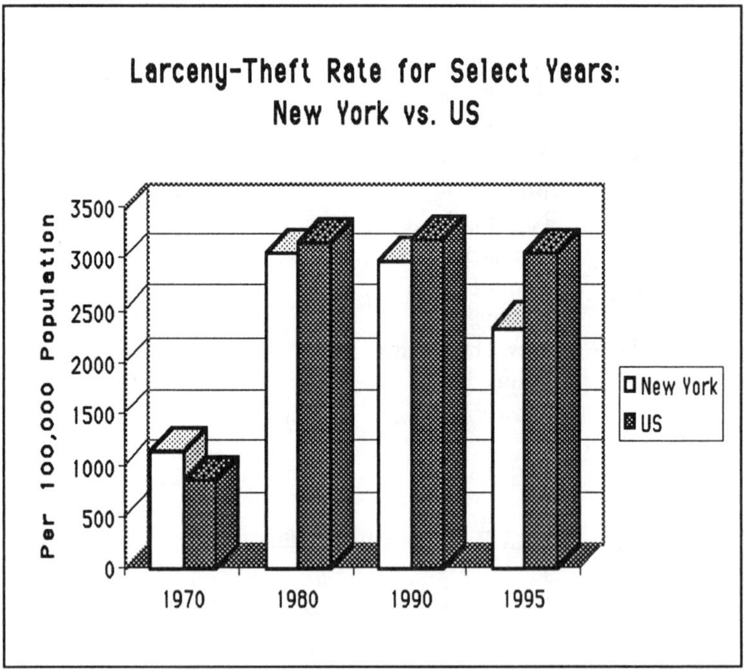


Data Source: Federal Bureau of Investigation, *Crime in the United States*, annual

# MOTOR VEHICLE THEFT: STATE RANKINGS

In 1995, New York ranked fourteenth in the nation in terms of its motor vehicle theft rate per 100,000 inhabitants.

As defined by the FBI, obviously, motor vehicle theft is the theft or attempted theft of a motor vehicle.

**Motor Vehicle Theft Index (Per 100,000 Inhabitants)**

| Rank | State | Motor Vehicle Theft Index |
|---|---|---|
| 1 | Arizona | 1,157.7 |
| 2 | California | 887.9 |
| 3 | Florida | 785.8 |
| 4 | Nevada | 745.4 |
| 5 | Maryland | 717.6 |
| 6 | Oregon | 702.0 |
| 7 | Hawaii | 690.7 |
| 8 | Tennessee | 648.5 |
| 9 | Michigan | 645.5 |
| 10 | New Jersey | 631.6 |
| 11 | Georgia | 608.4 |
| 12 | Massachusetts | 604.5 |
| 13 | Louisiana | 598.4 |
| **14** | **New York** | **565.7** |
| 15 | Texas | 560.4 |
| 16 | Washington | 554.0 |
| 17 | Connecticut | 540.2 |
| 18 | Illinois | 523.0 |
| 19 | Alaska | 521.7 |
| 20 | New Mexico | 513.2 |
| 21 | Oklahoma | 496.4 |
| 22 | Missouri | 473.3 |
| 23 | Indiana | 465.7 |
| 24 | Rhode Island | 440.8 |
| 25 | Ohio | 414.9 |
| 26 | Delaware | 414.2 |
| 27 | Pennsylvania | 412.7 |

*continued*

*continued*

| Rank | State | Motor Vehicle Theft Index |
|---|---|---|
| 28 | Utah | 389.1 |
| 29 | Colorado | 387.5 |
| 30 | South Carolina | 385.4 |
| 31 | Wisconsin | 363.6 |
| 32 | Mississippi | 360.5 |
| 33 | Nebraska | 351.4 |
| 34 | Alabama | 346.6 |
| 35 | Minnesota | 341.5 |
| 36 | Arkansas | 325.4 |
| 37 | Kansas | 323.5 |
| 38 | North Carolina | 310.6 |
| 39 | Montana | 308.0 |
| 40 | Virginia | 292.6 |
| 41 | Kentucky | 259.1 |
| 42 | Idaho | 242.0 |
| 43 | Iowa | 222.8 |
| 44 | North Dakota | 179.1 |
| 45 | Wyoming | 167.7 |
| 46 | West Virginia | 166.3 |
| 47 | New Hampshire | 145.1 |
| 48 | Vermont | 135.7 |
| 49 | Maine | 134.8 |
| 50 | South Dakota | 120.9 |
| | U.S. Average | 560.5 |

Data Source: Federal Bureau of Investigation, *Crime in the United States 1995*

## TREND IN MOTOR VEHICLE THEFT

New York's 1995 motor vehicle theft rate (per 100,000 population) topped the U.S. average by 0.9 percent—565.7 in New York versus a U.S. average of 560.5.

New York's 1995 rate compared with 1,043 in 1990, 759.9 in 1980, and 682.2 in 1970. Between 1990 and 1995, New York's motor vehicle theft rate dropped by a dramatic 45.8 percent.

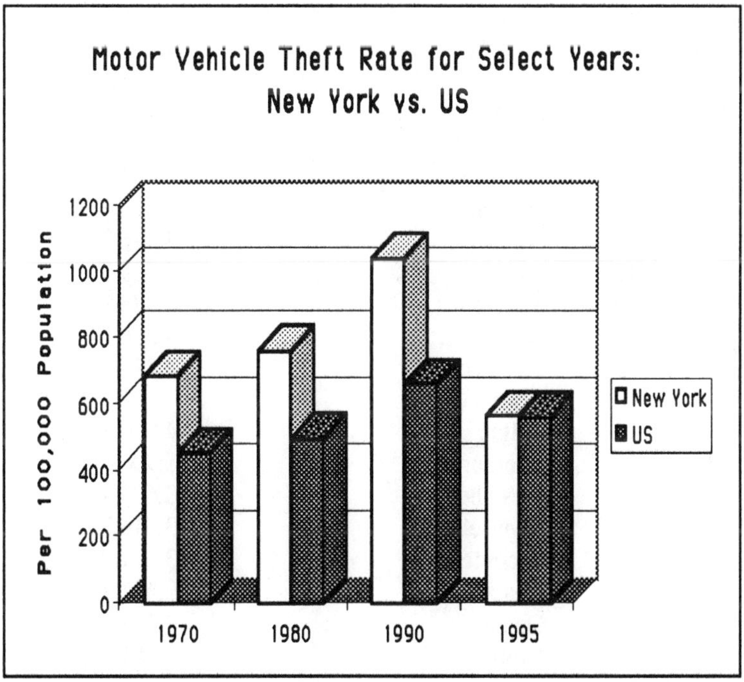


Data Source: Federal Bureau of Investigation, *Crime in the United States*, annual

## TOTAL CRIME RATES BY NEW YORK COUNTIES

In 1993, New York County (i.e., Manhattan) laid claim to the highest crime rate in the state, followed by the Bronx, Queens, and Kings Counties.

**Total Crime Index (Per 100,000 Inhabitants)**

| Rank | County | Total Crime Index |
|---|---|---|
| 1 | New York | 11,533.5 |
| 2 | Bronx | 7,629.1 |
| 3 | Queens | 7,596.2 |
| 4 | Kings | 7,335.6 |
| 5 | Monroe | 5,830.1 |
| 6 | Erie | 5,465.5 |
| 7 | Albany | 5,144.0 |
| 8 | Tompkins | 5,082.4 |
| 9 | Richmond | 4,764.5 |
| 10 | Warren | 4,523.2 |
| 11 | Niagara | 4,446.2 |
| 12 | Suffolk | 4,405.5 |
| 13 | Sullivan | 4,378.9 |
| 14 | Onondaga | 4,256.1 |
| 15 | Schenectady | 4,247.0 |
| 16 | Cortland | 4,212.5 |
| 17 | Fulton | 4,050.4 |
| 18 | Chemung | 3,906.4 |
| 19 | Westchester | 3,693.4 |
| 20 | Rennselaer | 3,614.3 |
| 21 | Broome | 3,571.9 |
| 22 | Chautauqua | 3,491.7 |
| 23 | Oneida | 3,251.7 |
| 24 | Orange | 3,181.2 |
| 25 | Cattaraugus | 3,130.0 |
| 26 | Wayne | 3,094.2 |
| 27 | St. Lawrence | 3,013.9 |
| 28 | Greene | 3,007.9 |

*continued*

*continued*

| Rank | County | Total Crime Index |
|---|---|---|
| 29 | Dutchess | 2,994.0 |
| 30 | Steuben | 2,985.6 |
| 31 | Nassau | 2,978.1 |
| 32 | Ulster | 2,969.3 |
| 33 | Rockland | 2,810.1 |
| 34 | Orleans | 2,783.0 |
| 35 | Columbia | 2,778.5 |
| 36 | Oswego | 2,751.0 |
| 37 | Genessee | 2,726.9 |
| 38 | Wyoming | 2,693.9 |
| 39 | Livingston | 2,672.2 |
| 40 | Cayuga | 2,652.4 |
| 41 | Ontario | 2,611.7 |
| 42 | Jefferson | 2,523.5 |
| 43 | Franklin | 2,506.3 |
| 44 | Allegany | 2,448.8 |
| 45 | Delaware | 2,408.7 |
| 46 | Yates | 2,369.4 |
| 47 | Hamilton | 2,368.8 |
| 48 | Saratoga | 2,259.4 |
| 49 | Schuyler | 2,254.1 |
| 50 | Chenango | 2,240.1 |
| 51 | Otsego | 2,212.8 |
| 52 | Herkimer | 2,209.6 |
| 53 | Clinton | 2,200.1 |
| 54 | Washington | 2,153.2 |
| 55 | Madison | 2,128.9 |
| 56 | Tioga | 2,080.7 |
| 57 | Essex | 2,047.4 |
| 58 | Seneca | 1,946.5 |
| 59 | Montgomery | 1,936.3 |
| 60 | Schoharie | 1,797.5 |
| 61 | Putnam | 1,761.2 |
| 62 | Lewis | 1,150.0 |

Data Source: The Nelson A. Rockefeller Institute of Government, *1995 New York State Statistical Yearbook*

# PER CAPITA STATE AND LOCAL POLICE PROTECTION EXPENDITURES: STATE RANKINGS

In 1992-93, New York ranked third highest in the nation in terms of its per capita state and local police protection expenditures.

**Per Capita State and Local Police Protection Expenditures**

| Rank | State | Per Capita Expenditures |
|---|---|---|
| 1 | District of Columbia | $461.28 |
| 2 | Alaska | 231.06 |
| **3** | **New York** | **208.56** |
| 4 | Nevada | 193.99 |
| 5 | California | 192.09 |
| 6 | Florida | 184.26 |
| 7 | New Jersey | 179.47 |
| 8 | Hawaii | 155.82 |
| 9 | Illinois | 154.05 |
| 10 | Wisconsin | 150.35 |
| 11 | Wyoming | 148.37 |
| 12 | Arizona | 147.74 |
| 13 | Delaware | 144.01 |
| 14 | Connecticut | 142.53 |
| 15 | Maryland | 142.17 |
| 16 | Massachusetts | 138.73 |
| 17 | New Mexico | 138.32 |
| 18 | Louisiana | 136.74 |
| 19 | Rhode Island | 136.27 |
| 20 | Colorado | 132.99 |
| 21 | Washington | 132.96 |
| 22 | Oregon | 129.20 |
| 23 | Michigan | 127.04 |
| 24 | Virginia | 124.69 |
| 25 | Minnesota | 124.38 |
| 26 | Ohio | 122.18 |
| 27 | Texas | 117.85 |
| 28 | Georgia | 117.52 |

*continued*

*continued*

| Rank | State | Per Capita Expenditures |
|---|---|---|
| 29 | New Hampshire | 117.40 |
| 30 | Kansas | 114.64 |
| 31 | North Carolina | 109.81 |
| 32 | Idaho | 109.42 |
| 33 | Missouri | 104.69 |
| 34 | Pennsylvania | 103.80 |
| 35 | Utah | 100.96 |
| 36 | Nebraska | 100.03 |
| 37 | Oklahoma | 97.91 |
| 38 | Iowa | 97.88 |
| 39 | Montana | 97.79 |
| 40 | Alabama | 96.43 |
| 41 | Vermont | 95.29 |
| 42 | Tennessee | 95.12 |
| 43 | South Carolina | 92.36 |
| 44 | South Dakota | 84.22 |
| 45 | Kentucky | 83.92 |
| 46 | Indiana | 83.84 |
| 47 | Maine | 81.75 |
| 48 | Arkansas | 74.85 |
| 49 | Mississippi | 73.34 |
| 50 | North Dakota | 68.93 |
| 51 | West Virginia | 52.91 |
| | U.S. Average | 140.21 |

Data Source: U.S. Department of Commerce

## PER CAPITA STATE AND LOCAL POLICE PROTECTION EXPENDITURES: NEW YORK VS. U.S.

In 1992-93, New York's per capita state and local police protection expenditures outpaced the national average by 48.7 percent—$208.56 in New York versus $140.21 across the nation.

Between 1962 and 1993, real per capita state and local police protection expenditures grew by 135.2 percent. In 1962, per capita police spending in 1993 dollars equaled $88.66.

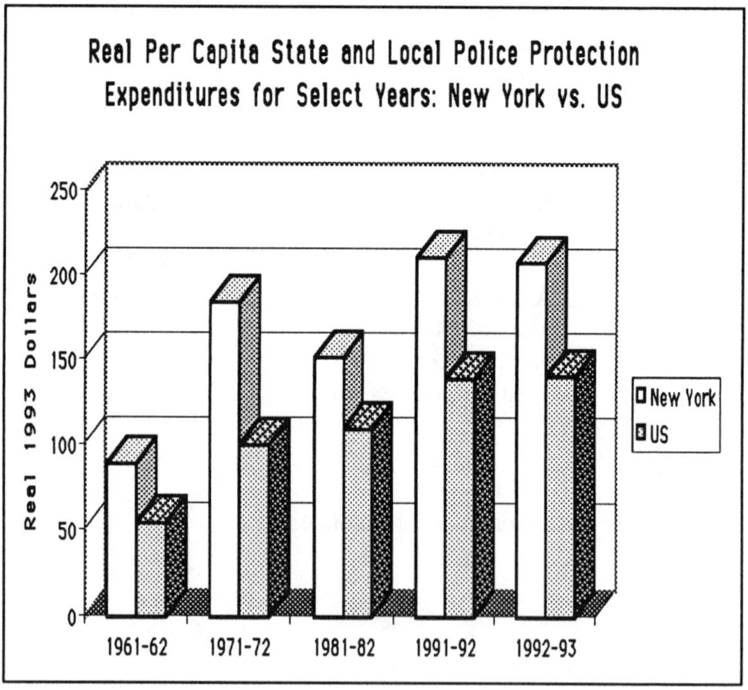


Data Source: U.S. Department of Commerce

# PER CAPITA STATE-ONLY POLICE PROTECTION EXPENDITURES: STATE RANKINGS

In 1994, New York ranked thirty-fifth in the nation in terms of its per capita state-only police protection expenditures.

**Per Capita State Police Protection Expenditures**

| Rank | State | Per Capita Expenditures |
|---|---|---|
| 1 | Alaska | $90.67 |
| 2 | Delaware | 53.30 |
| 3 | Vermont | 42.86 |
| 4 | Virginia | 42.85 |
| 5 | Maryland | 40.71 |
| 6 | New Jersey | 35.27 |
| 7 | Massachusetts | 32.89 |
| 8 | Oregon | 32.68 |
| 9 | Idaho | 31.06 |
| 10 | Montana | 31.01 |
| 11 | New Mexico | 30.84 |
| 12 | Connecticut | 30.49 |
| 13 | Washington | 30.09 |
| 14 | South Carolina | 28.98 |
| 15 | Louisiana | 28.15 |
| 16 | California | 27.63 |
| 17 | Kentucky | 27.39 |
| 18 | North Carolina | 26.78 |
| 19 | Pennsylvania | 26.55 |
| 20 | Rhode Island | 26.01 |
| 21 | Wyoming | 25.17 |
| 22 | Arizona | 24.16 |
| 23 | Minnesota | 24.10 |
| 24 | Nebraska | 24.08 |
| 25 | Nevada | 22.54 |
| 26 | Michigan | 22.30 |
| 27 | New Hampshire | 22.21 |
| 28 | Missouri | 21.87 |

*continued*

*continued*

| Rank | State | Per Capita Expenditures |
|---|---|---|
| 29 | Maine | 21.86 |
| 30 | South Dakota | 21.85 |
| 31 | Illinois | 20.86 |
| 32 | Alabama | 20.58 |
| 33 | Indiana | 20.03 |
| 34 | Utah | 19.97 |
| **35** | **New York** | **18.51** |
| 36 | West Virginia | 18.36 |
| 37 | Arkansas | 18.14 |
| 38 | Iowa | 18.10 |
| 39 | Georgia | 16.60 |
| 40 | Kansas | 15.93 |
| 41 | Florida | 15.76 |
| 42 | Mississippi | 15.74 |
| 43 | Ohio | 15.52 |
| 44 | Tennessee | 15.13 |
| 45 | Oklahoma | 14.68 |
| 46 | Colorado | 13.75 |
| 47 | Texas | 12.61 |
| 48(t) | North Dakota | 10.45 |
| 48(t) | Wisconsin | 10.45 |
| 50 | Hawaii | 9.44 |
| | U.S. Average | 23.05 |

Data Source: U.S. Department of Commerce

## PER CAPITA STATE-ONLY POLICE PROTECTION EXPENDITURES: NEW YORK VS. U.S.

In 1994, New York's per capita state-only police protection expenditures ranked below the national average. The state average of $23.05 outpaced New York's $18.51 by 24.5 percent.

Between 1985 and 1994, real per capita state police protection spending in New York fell by 8.5 percent. In 1994 dollars, New York spent $20.23 per capita on police protection in 1985.

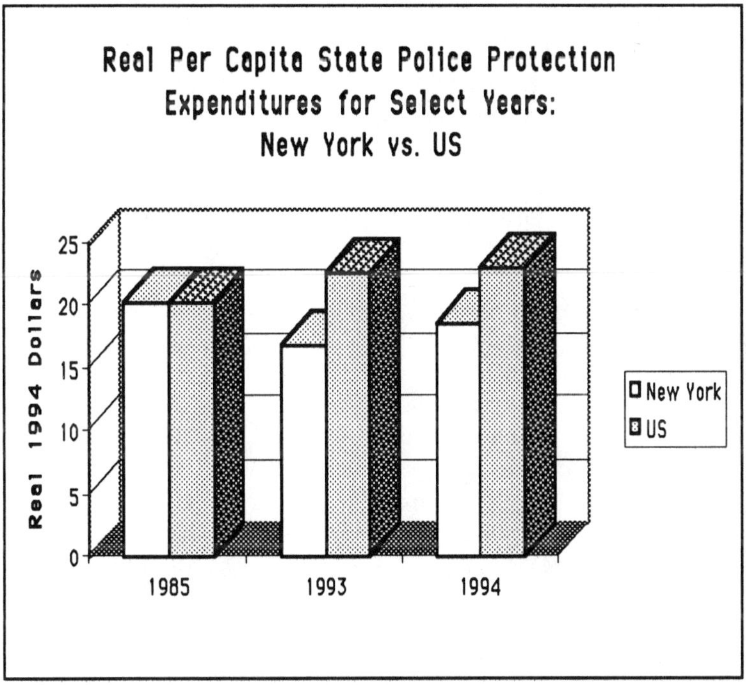


Data Source: U.S. Department of Commerce

## PER CAPITA STATE AND LOCAL CORRECTION EXPENDITURES: STATE RANKINGS

In 1992-93, New York ranked third highest in the nation in terms of its per capita state and local correction expenditures.

**Per Capita State and Local Correction Expenditures**

| Rank | State | Per Capita Expenditures |
|---|---|---|
| 1 | District of Columbia | $550.22 |
| 2 | Alaska | 219.94 |
| **3** | **New York** | **191.32** |
| 4 | Nevada | 177.14 |
| 5 | California | 154.80 |
| 6 | Maryland | 140.00 |
| 7 | Connecticut | 135.44 |
| 8 | Florida | 133.89 |
| 9 | Georgia | 131.79 |
| 10 | Washington | 129.29 |
| 11 | Delaware | 128.62 |
| 12 | Arizona | 124.28 |
| 13 | Michigan | 123.52 |
| 14 | New Mexico | 123.10 |
| 15 | New Jersey | 119.25 |
| 16 | Massachusetts | 115.27 |
| 17 | South Carolina | 114.38 |
| 18 | Texas | 111.70 |
| 19 | North Carolina | 111.03 |
| 20 | Virginia | 109.32 |
| 21 | Colorado | 107.72 |
| 22 | Rhode Island | 107.32 |
| 23 | Wisconsin | 105.29 |
| 24 | Oregon | 100.84 |
| 25 | Hawaii | 96.52 |
| 26 | Pennsylvania | 90.86 |
| 27 | Ohio | 90.35 |
| 28 | Tennessee | 90.10 |

*continued*

*continued*

| Rank | State | Per Capita Expenditures |
|---|---|---|
| 29 | Louisiana | 88.66 |
| 30 | Illinois | 83.91 |
| 31 | Wyoming | 83.84 |
| 32 | Kansas | 82.14 |
| 33 | Minnesota | 79.30 |
| 34 | Utah | 76.65 |
| 35 | Indiana | 72.89 |
| 36 | Vermont | 72.59 |
| 37 | Kentucky | 72.23 |
| 38 | Idaho | 71.69 |
| 39 | Maine | 71.44 |
| 40 | Nebraska | 70.33 |
| 41 | Oklahoma | 66.41 |
| 42 | Arkansas | 65.33 |
| 43 | New Hampshire | 64.67 |
| 44 | Alabama | 61.70 |
| 45 | South Dakota | 60.87 |
| 46 | Missouri | 59.42 |
| 47 | Montana | 58.49 |
| 48 | Iowa | 53.88 |
| 49 | Mississippi | 40.21 |
| 50 | North Dakota | 38.16 |
| 51 | West Virginia | 32.31 |
| | U.S. Average | 114.87 |

Data Source: U.S. Department of Commerce

## PER CAPITA STATE AND LOCAL CORRECTION EXPENDITURES: NEW YORK VS. U.S.

In 1992-93, New York's per capita state and local correction expenditures outpaced the national average by 66.6 percent—$191.32 in New York versus $114.87 across the nation.

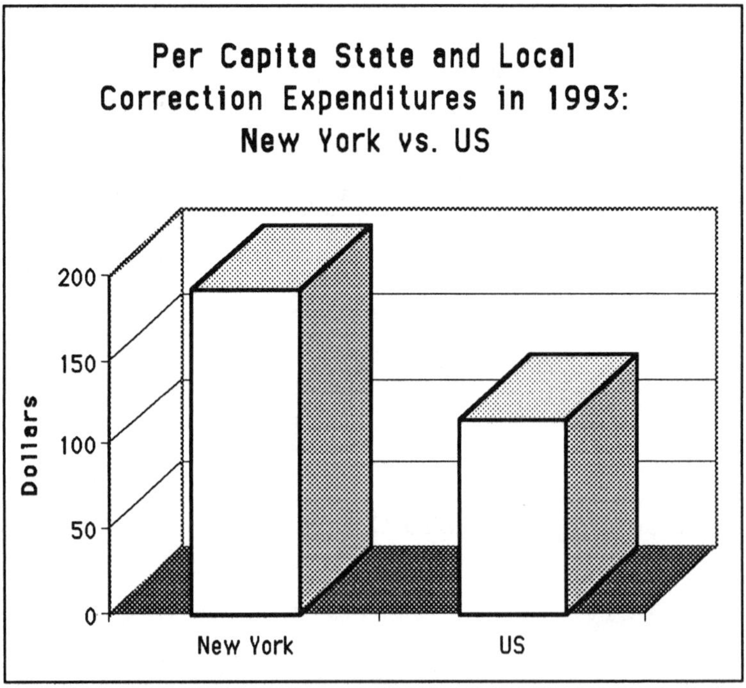


Data Source: U.S. Department of Commerce

# PER CAPITA STATE-ONLY CORRECTION EXPENDITURES: STATE RANKINGS

In 1994, New York ranked sixth in the nation in terms of its per capita state-only correction expenditures.

**Per Capita State Correction Expenditures**

| Rank | State | Per Capita Expenditures |
|---|---|---|
| 1 | Alaska | $234.61 |
| 2 | Connecticut | 142.07 |
| 3 | Maryland | 137.70 |
| 4 | Texas | 122.03 |
| 5 | Delaware | 119.47 |
| **6** | **New York** | **113.38** |
| 7 | California | 111.33 |
| 8 | Michigan | 108.38 |
| 9 | Massachusetts | 104.76 |
| 10 | Rhode Island | 104.47 |
| 11 | Virginia | 104.41 |
| 12 | North Carolina | 101.90 |
| 13 | Georgia | 95.03 |
| 14 | Arizona | 94.23 |
| 15 | Nevada | 93.27 |
| 16 | Hawaii | 92.63 |
| 17 | Florida | 89.34 |
| 18 | New Jersey | 88.84 |
| 19 | New Mexico | 86.69 |
| 20 | South Carolina | 83.88 |
| 21 | Washington | 82.74 |
| 22 | Ohio | 79.72 |
| 23 | Colorado | 79.15 |
| 24 | Wisconsin | 77.45 |
| 25 | Tennessee | 76.61 |
| 26 | Louisiana | 75.71 |
| 27 | Kansas | 70.91 |
| 28 | Oregon | 70.57 |

*continued*

*continued*

| Rank | State | Per Capita Expenditures |
|---|---|---|
| 29 | Pennsylvania | 66.35 |
| 30 | Oklahoma | 65.12 |
| 31 | Wyoming | 64.65 |
| 32 | Illinois | 62.95 |
| 33 | Idaho | 61.63 |
| 34 | Utah | 59.94 |
| 35 | South Dakota | 58.07 |
| 36 | Iowa | 57.68 |
| 37 | Indiana | 57.31 |
| 38 | Kentucky | 54.04 |
| 39 | Arkansas | 53.93 |
| 40 | Vermont | 52.14 |
| 41 | Alabama | 51.36 |
| 42 | Minnesota | 51.26 |
| 43 | Nebraska | 48.69 |
| 44 | Montana | 47.41 |
| 45 | New Hampshire | 47.04 |
| 46 | Maine | 44.91 |
| 47 | Missouri | 41.71 |
| 48 | Mississippi | 38.73 |
| 49 | West Virginia | 31.18 |
| 50 | North Dakota | 27.26 |
| | U.S. Average | 88.85 |

Data Source: U.S. Department of Commerce

## PER CAPITA STATE-ONLY CORRECTION EXPENDITURES: NEW YORK VS. U.S.

In 1994, New York's per capita state correction expenditures exceeded the U.S. average by 27.6 percent—$113.38 in New York versus a state average of $88.85.

Between 1965 and 1994, real per capita state corrections spending grew by 493.3 percent. In 1994 dollars, New York's 1965 per capita state corrections spending equaled $19.11.

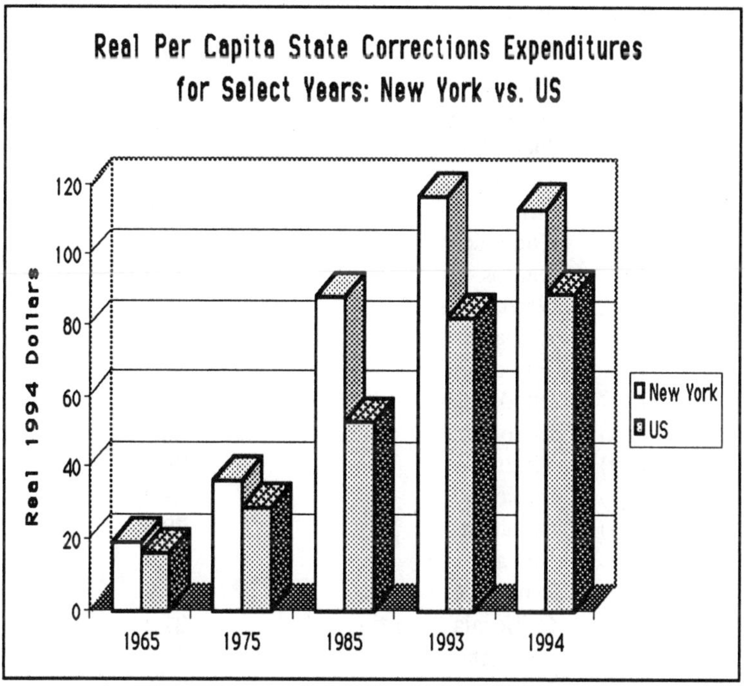


Data Source: U.S. Department of Commerce

## LAW ENFORCEMENT EMPLOYEES: STATE RANKINGS

In 1994, New York ranked eighth in the nation in terms of the number of full-time law-enforcement employees per 10,000 inhabitants.

**Full-time Law-Enforcement Employees (Per 10,000 Inhabitants)**

| Rank | State | Employees per 10,000 pop. |
|---|---|---|
| 1 | New Jersey | 43.5 |
| 2 | Florida | 41.8 |
| 3 | Louisiana | 39.1 |
| 4(t) | Georgia | 35.7 |
| 4(t) | Texas | 35.7 |
| 6 | Nevada | 35.3 |
| 7 | Illinois | 34.8 |
| **8** | **New York** | **34.5** |
| 9 | Maryland | 34.4 |
| 10 | Wyoming | 33.8 |
| 11 | Arizona | 33.6 |
| 12 | Colorado | 33.3 |
| 13 | Kansas | 31.6 |
| 14 | North Carolina | 30.7 |
| 15 | Alabama | 30.1 |
| 16 | Wisconsin | 29.5 |
| 17 | Rhode Island | 29.0 |
| 18(t) | Delaware | 28.5 |
| 18(t) | Virginia | 28.5 |
| 20(t) | Missouri | 28.0 |
| 20(t) | Oklahoma | 28.0 |
| 22(t) | Hawaii | 27.9 |
| 22(t) | Tennessee | 27.9 |
| 24(t) | California | 27.7 |
| 24(t) | Massachusetts | 27.7 |
| 26 | New Mexico | 27.5 |
| 27(t) | Connecticut | 27.4 |
| 27(t) | South Carolina | 27.4 |
| 29 | Michigan | 26.4 |

*continued*

*continued*

| Rank | State | Employees per 10,000 pop. |
|---|---|---|
| 30 | Alaska | 26.2 |
| 31 | Arkansas | 25.8 |
| 32 | Nebraska | 25.2 |
| 33 | Ohio | 25.1 |
| 34 | Montana | 24.1 |
| 35 | Idaho | 24.0 |
| 36 | Indiana | 23.6 |
| 37 | Kentucky | 23.3 |
| 38 | Mississippi | 22.9 |
| 39 | Utah | 22.8 |
| 40(t) | Iowa | 22.2 |
| 40(t) | Washington | 22.2 |
| 42 | New Hampshire | 21.9 |
| 43 | Oregon | 21.4 |
| 44 | Pennsylvania | 21.3 |
| 45(t) | North Dakota | 21.2 |
| 45(t) | South Dakota | 21.2 |
| 47 | Maine | 20.9 |
| 48 | West Virginia | 20.7 |
| 49 | Vermont | 19.9 |
| 50 | Minnesota | 19.3 |
| | U.S. Average | 32.0 |

Data Source: Federal Bureau of Investigation, *Crime in the United States 1994*

## LAW ENFORCEMENT EMPLOYEES: NEW YORK VS. U.S.

In 1994, New York's full-time law-enforcement employees per 10,000 inhabitants edged out the national average by 7.8 percent—34.5 in New York versus 32.0 across the nation.

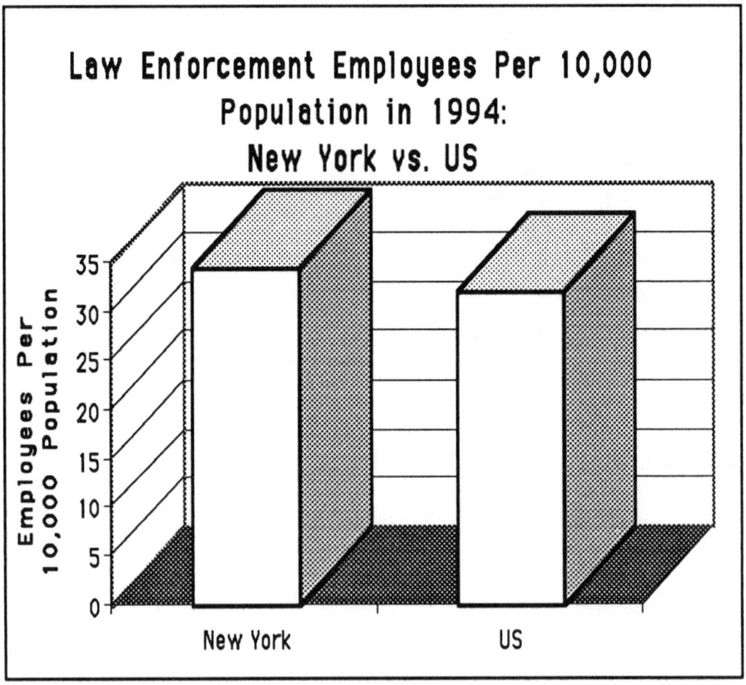


Data Source: Federal Bureau of Investigation, *Crime in the United States 1994*

# Chapter Five

# New York State: Societal Indicators

- Low Birth Weight Babies
- Births to Teenage Mothers
- Births to Unmarried Women
- Abortions
- Infant Mortality

## LOW BIRTH WEIGHT BABIES: STATE RANKINGS

New York ranked fourteenth in the nation in terms of the percentage of low birth weight babies in 1993.

**Percentage of Low Birth Weight Babies**

| Rank | State | Percent |
|---|---|---|
| 1 | District of Columbia | 14.6% |
| 2 | Mississippi | 10.1 |
| 3(t) | Louisiana | 9.3 |
| 3(t) | South Carolina | 9.3 |
| 5 | Tennessee | 8.8 |
| 6(t) | Alabama | 8.7 |
| 6(t) | Georgia | 8.7 |
| 8 | North Carolina | 8.6 |
| 9 | Maryland | 8.5 |
| 10 | Colorado | 8.4 |
| 11 | Arkansas | 8.2 |
| 12 | Illinois | 8.1 |
| 13 | Delaware | 7.8 |
| **14** | **New York** | **7.7** |
| 15(t) | Michigan | 7.6 |
| 15(t) | New Jersey | 7.6 |
| 17(t) | Florida | 7.5 |
| 17(t) | Missouri | 7.5 |
| 17(t) | Ohio | 7.5 |
| 20(t) | Nevada | 7.4 |
| 20(t) | Pennsylvania | 7.4 |
| 22(t) | New Mexico | 7.3 |
| 22(t) | Virginia | 7.3 |
| 22(t) | Wyoming | 7.3 |
| 25 | West Virginia | 7.2 |
| 26(t) | Kentucky | 7.1 |
| 26(t) | Texas | 7.1 |
| 28 | Indiana | 7.0 |
| 29 | Connecticut | 6.9 |

*continued*

*continued*

| Rank | State | Percent |
|---|---|---|
| 30 | Hawaii | 6.8 |
| 31(t) | Oklahoma | 6.7 |
| 31(t) | Arizona | 6.7 |
| 33 | Kansas | 6.6 |
| 34 | Rhode Island | 6.5 |
| 35 | Massachusetts | 6.2 |
| 36 | Wisconsin | 6.1 |
| 37(t) | Montana | 6.0 |
| 37(t) | California | 6.0 |
| 39(t) | Nebraska | 5.9 |
| 39(t) | Utah | 5.9 |
| 41(t) | Iowa | 5.7 |
| 41(t) | Vermont | 5.7 |
| 43(t) | Minnesota | 5.5 |
| 43(t) | South Dakota | 5.5 |
| 45 | Maine | 5.4 |
| 46(t) | Idaho | 5.3 |
| 46(t) | North Dakota | 5.3 |
| 48(t) | Washington | 5.2 |
| 48(t) | Oregon | 5.2 |
| 50 | New Hampshire | 5.0 |
| 51 | Alaska | 4.9 |
| | U.S. Average | 7.2 |

Data Source: U.S. Department of Commerce, *Statistical Abstract of the United States 1996*

## LOW BIRTH WEIGHT BABIES: NEW YORK VS. US

In 1993, the percentage of low birth weight babies in New York equaled 7.7 percent versus the U.S. average of 7.2 percent. New York's 7.7 percent was up from 7.0 percent in 1985 and 7.4 percent in 1980.

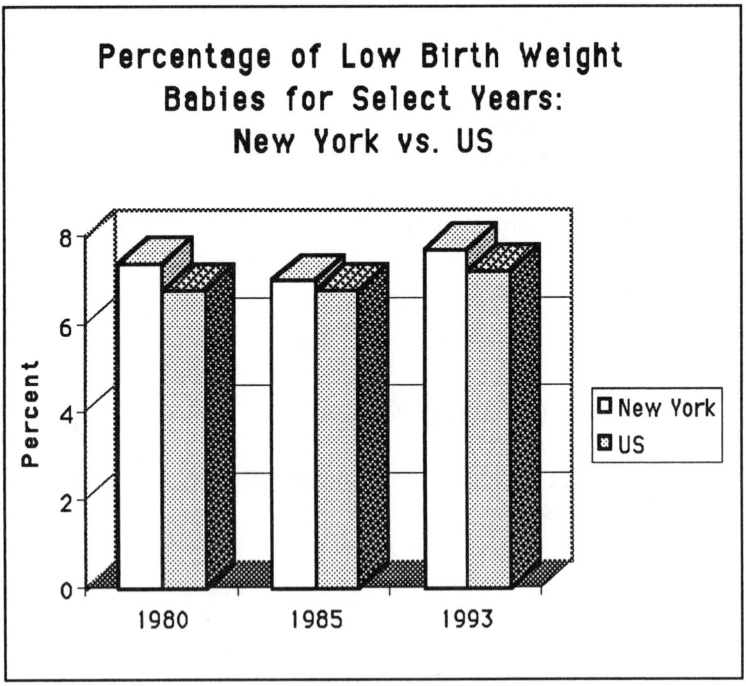


Data Source: U.S. Department of Commerce, *Statistical Abstract of the United States*, annual

## BIRTHS TO TEENAGE MOTHERS: STATE RANKINGS

In 1993, New York ranked forty-fifth in the nation in terms of the percentage of births to teenage mothers.

**Percentage of Births to Teenage Mothers**

| Rank | State | Percent |
|---|---|---|
| 1 | Mississippi | 21.7% |
| 2 | Arkansas | 19.4 |
| 3 | Louisiana | 18.7 |
| 4(t) | Alabama | 17.8 |
| 4(t) | New Mexico | 17.8 |
| 6 | West Virginia | 17.6 |
| 7 | District of Columbia | 17.4 |
| 8 | Oklahoma | 17.2 |
| 9 | Tennessee | 16.9 |
| 10 | Kentucky | 16.8 |
| 11 | South Carolina | 16.2 |
| 12(t) | Georgia | 16.1 |
| 12(t) | Texas | 16.1 |
| 14 | North Carolina | 15.3 |
| 15 | Arizona | 15.1 |
| 16 | Missouri | 14.2 |
| 17 | Indiana | 14.1 |
| 18 | Wyoming | 14.0 |
| 19 | Ohio | 13.6 |
| 20(t) | Florida | 13.4 |
| 20(t) | Idaho | 13.4 |
| 22 | Nevada | 13.3 |
| 23 | Kansas | 12.9 |
| 24 | Illinois | 12.8 |
| 25 | Michigan | 12.6 |
| 26(t) | Delaware | 12.5 |
| 26(t) | Montana | 12.5 |
| 28 | Oregon | 12.4 |
| 29 | California | 12.0 |

*continued*

*continued*

| Rank | State | Percent |
|---|---|---|
| 30 | Colorado | 11.9 |
| 31 | South Dakota | 11.1 |
| 32 | Washington | 11.0 |
| 33 | Virginia | 10.9 |
| 34(t) | Alaska | 10.8 |
| 34(t) | Utah | 10.8 |
| 36 | Iowa | 10.7 |
| 37 | Pennsylvania | 10.5 |
| 38(t) | Wisconsin | 10.4 |
| 38(t) | Rhode Island | 10.4 |
| 40(t) | Maine | 10.1 |
| 40(t) | Hawaii | 10.1 |
| 40(t) | Nebraska | 10.1 |
| 43 | Maryland | 10.0 |
| 44 | North Dakota | 9.6 |
| **45** | **New York** | **9.3** |
| 46 | Vermont | 8.7 |
| 47 | Minnesota | 8.2 |
| 48 | Connecticut | 8.0 |
| 49 | New Jersey | 7.9 |
| 50 | Massachusetts | 7.8 |
| 51 | New Hampshire | 6.8 |
| | | |
| | U.S. Average | 12.8 |

Data Source: U.S. Department of Commerce, *Statistical Abstract of the United States 1996*

## BIRTHS TO TEENAGE MOTHERS: NEW YORK VS. U.S.

In 1993, the percentage of births to teenage mothers in New York registered 9.3 percent, down from 10 percent in 1985 and 11.8 percent in 1980. New York's 1993 rate trailed the percentage for the U.S. which was 12.8 percent.

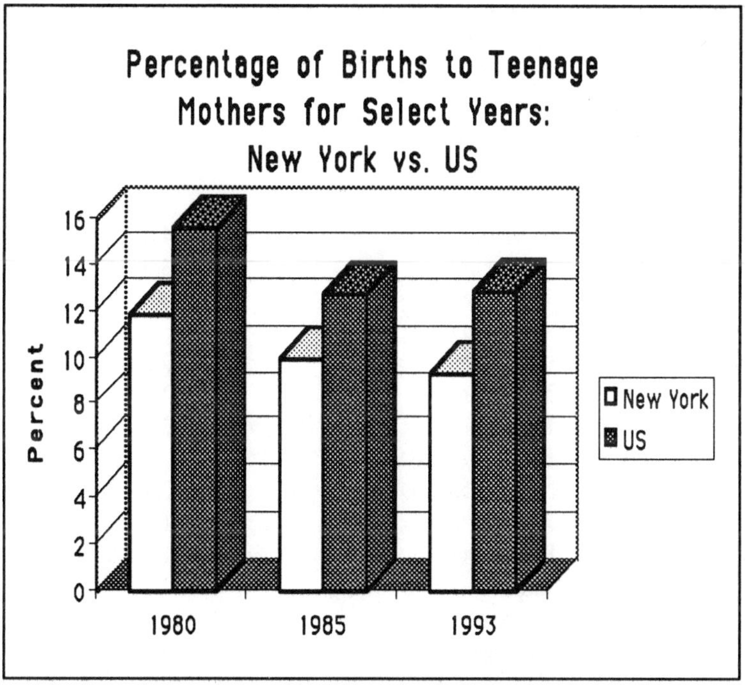


Data Source: U.S. Department of Commerce, *Statistical Abstract of the United States*, annual

## BIRTHS TO UNMARRIED WOMEN: STATE RANKINGS

In 1993, New York ranked sixth in the nation in terms of the percentage of births to unmarried women.

**Percentage of Births to Unmarried Women**

| Rank | State | Percent |
|---|---|---|
| 1 | District of Columbia | 67.8% |
| 2 | Mississippi | 44.4 |
| 3 | Louisiana | 42.0 |
| 4 | New Mexico | 41.4 |
| 5 | Arizona | 37.9 |
| **6** | **New York** | **37.2** |
| 7 | South Carolina | 36.0 |
| 8 | Georgia | 35.8 |
| 9 | California | 35.3 |
| 10 | Florida | 35.0 |
| 11 | Illinois | 34.1 |
| 12 | Nevada | 34.0 |
| 13 | Delaware | 33.8 |
| 14 | Tennessee | 33.6 |
| 15 | Alabama | 33.5 |
| 16 | Ohio | 33.0 |
| 17 | Maryland | 32.5 |
| 18 | Missouri | 32.4 |
| 19 | Pennsylvania | 32.2 |
| 20 | North Carolina | 32.1 |
| 21(t) | Arkansas | 31.7 |
| 21(t) | Rhode Island | 31.7 |
| 23 | Indiana | 30.8 |
| 24 | Connecticut | 29.8 |
| 25 | Oklahoma | 29.1 |
| 26(t) | Virginia | 29.0 |
| 26(t) | West Virginia | 29.0 |
| 28 | Oregon | 28.2 |
| 29 | Alaska | 28.0 |

*continued*

*continued*

| Rank | State | Percent |
|---|---|---|
| 30 | South Dakota | 27.7 |
| 31 | Montana | 27.3 |
| 32(t) | Kentucky | 27.2 |
| 32(t) | Hawaii | 27.2 |
| 34(t) | New Jersey | 27.1 |
| 34(t) | Wisconsin | 27.1 |
| 36 | Maine | 27.0 |
| 37 | Massachusetts | 26.4 |
| 38 | Washington | 26.3 |
| 39 | Michigan | 26.0 |
| 40 | Kansas | 25.9 |
| 41 | Wyoming | 25.8 |
| 42 | Colorado | 24.8 |
| 43 | Iowa | 24.6 |
| 44 | Vermont | 24.2 |
| 45 | Nebraska | 23.5 |
| 46 | Minnesota | 23.4 |
| 47 | North Dakota | 23.0 |
| 48 | New Hampshire | 20.6 |
| 49 | Idaho | 18.7 |
| 50 | Texas | 17.0 |
| 51 | Utah | 15.5 |
| | U.S. Average | 31.0 |

Data Source: U.S. Department of Commerce, *Statistical Abstract of the United State 1996*

## BIRTHS TO UNMARRIED WOMEN: NEW YORK VS. U.S.

In 1993, the percentage of births to unmarried women registered 37.2 percent versus the U.S. rate of 31.0 percent. New York's percentage was up from 28.1 percent in 1985 and 23.8 percent in 1980.

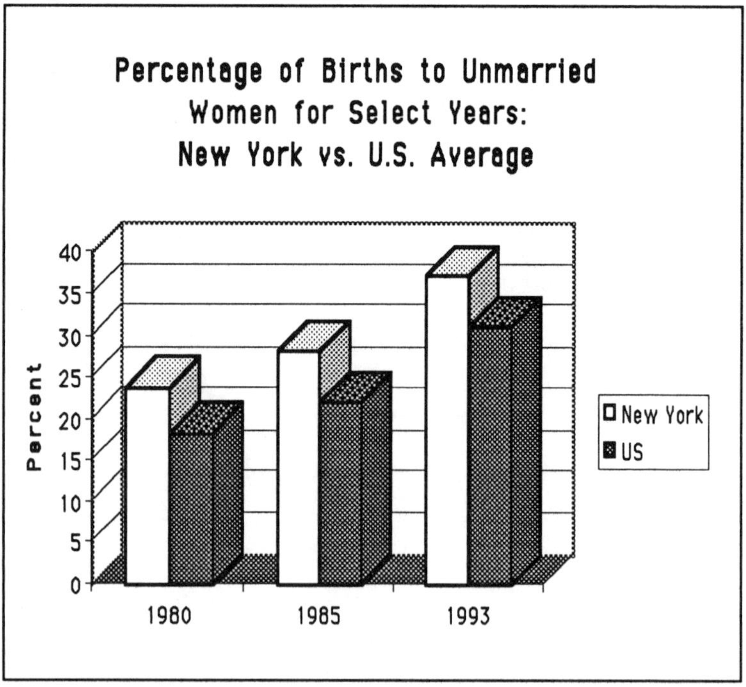


Data Source: U.S. Department of Commerce, *Statistical Abstract of the United States*, annual

## ABORTION RATE: STATE RANKINGS

In 1992, New York ranked second highest in the nation in terms of the rate of abortions per 1,000 women (15 to 44 years old), only outpaced by the even more tragic number in the District of Columbia.

**Rate of Abortions Per 1,000 Women**

| Rank | State | Rate |
|---|---|---|
| 1 | District of Columbia | 138.4 |
| **2** | **New York** | **46.2** |
| 3 | Hawaii | 46.0 |
| 4 | Nevada | 44.2 |
| 5 | California | 42.1 |
| 6 | Delaware | 35.2 |
| 7 | New Jersey | 31.0 |
| 8(t) | Florida | 30.0 |
| 8(t) | Rhode Island | 30.0 |
| 10 | Massachusetts | 28.4 |
| 11 | Washington | 27.7 |
| 12 | Maryland | 26.4 |
| 13 | Connecticut | 26.2 |
| 14 | Illinois | 25.4 |
| 15 | Michigan | 25.2 |
| 16 | Arizona | 24.1 |
| 17 | Georgia | 24.0 |
| 18 | Oregon | 23.9 |
| 19 | Colorado | 23.6 |
| 20 | Texas | 23.1 |
| 21 | Virginia | 22.7 |
| 22(t) | Kansas | 22.4 |
| 22(t) | North Carolina | 22.4 |
| 24 | Vermont | 21.2 |
| 25 | Ohio | 19.5 |
| 26 | Pennsylvania | 18.6 |
| 27(t) | Alabama | 18.2 |
| 27(t) | Montana | 18.2 |

*continued*

*continued*

| Rank | State | Rate |
|---|---|---|
| 29 | New Mexico | 17.7 |
| 30 | Alaska | 16.5 |
| 31 | Tennessee | 16.2 |
| 32 | Nebraska | 15.7 |
| 33 | Minnesota | 15.6 |
| 34 | Maine | 14.7 |
| 35 | New Hampshire | 14.6 |
| 36 | South Carolina | 14.2 |
| 37 | Wisconsin | 13.6 |
| 38 | Arkansas | 13.5 |
| 39 | Louisiana | 13.4 |
| 40 | Oklahoma | 12.5 |
| 41 | Mississippi | 12.4 |
| 42 | Indiana | 12.0 |
| 43 | Missouri | 11.6 |
| 44(t) | Iowa | 11.4 |
| 44(t) | Kentucky | 11.4 |
| 46 | North Dakota | 10.7 |
| 47 | Utah | 9.3 |
| 48 | West Virginia | 7.7 |
| 49 | Idaho | 7.2 |
| 50 | South Dakota | 6.8 |
| 51 | Wyoming | 4.3 |
| | U.S. Average | 25.9 |

Data Source: U.S. Department of Commerce, *Statistical Abstract of the United States*, annual

## ABORTION RATE: NEW YORK VS. U.S.

In 1992, New York's abortions per 1,000 women (ages 15 to 44) equaled 46.2, 78.4 percent higher than the U.S. average of 25.9. The New York rate was down from 54.5 in 1973.

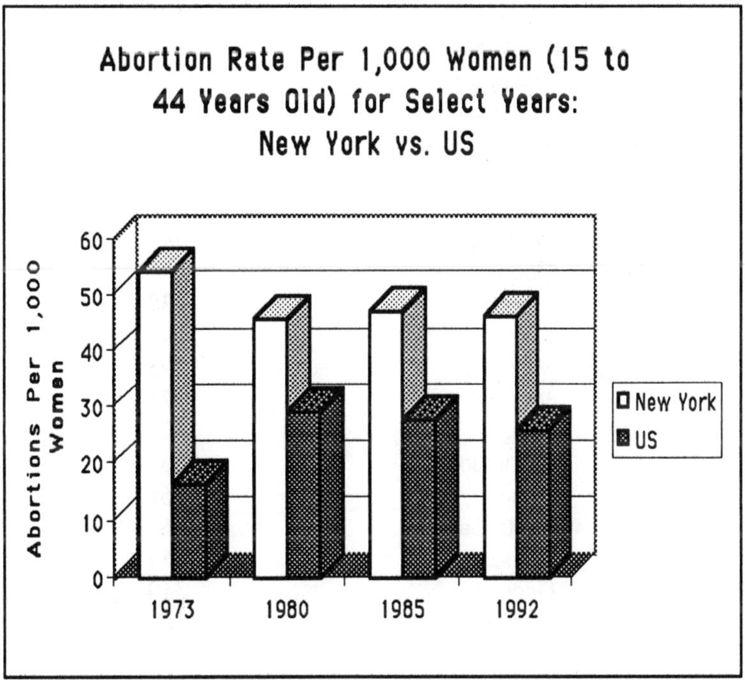


Data Source: U.S. Department of Commerce, *Statistical Abstract of the United States*, annual

## ABORTION RATIO PER LIVE BIRTHS: STATE RANKINGS

In 1992, New York ranked second highest in the nation in terms of the number of abortions per 1,000 live births, only outpaced by the even more tragic number in the District of Columbia.

**Abortions Per 1,000 Live Births**

| Rank | State | Ratio |
|---|---|---|
| 1 | District of Columbia | 1,104 |
| **2** | **New York** | **694** |
| 3 | Hawaii | 617 |
| 4 | Nevada | 591 |
| 5 | California | 519 |
| 6 | Delaware | 502 |
| 7 | Massachusetts | 472 |
| 8 | Rhode Island | 461 |
| 9 | New Jersey | 460 |
| 10 | Maryland | 454 |
| 11 | Washington | 447 |
| 12 | Connecticut | 444 |
| 13 | Florida | 438 |
| 14(t) | Michigan | 393 |
| 14(t) | Vermont | 393 |
| 16 | Virginia | 373 |
| 17 | Oregon | 372 |
| 18 | Colorado | 362 |
| 19 | Illinois | 361 |
| 20 | North Carolina | 357 |
| 21 | Kansas | 353 |
| 22 | Georgia | 350 |
| 23 | Pennsylvania | 302 |
| 24 | Montana | 298 |
| 25 | Texas | 297 |
| 26 | Arizona | 295 |
| 27 | Ohio | 294 |
| 28 | Maine | 282 |

*continued*

*continued*

| Rank | State | Ratio |
|---|---|---|
| 29 | Alabama | 277 |
| 30 | New Hampshire | 269 |
| 31 | Minnesota | 251 |
| 32 | Nebraska | 246 |
| 33 | Tennessee | 243 |
| 34 | South Carolina | 229 |
| 35 | New Mexico | 228 |
| 36 | Wisconsin | 223 |
| 37 | Alaska | 222 |
| 38 | Arkansas | 213 |
| 39 | Louisiana | 195 |
| 40 | Oklahoma | 193 |
| 41 | Kentucky | 191 |
| 42(t) | Indiana | 185 |
| 42(t) | Iowa | 185 |
| 44 | Mississippi | 176 |
| 45 | Missouri | 175 |
| 46 | North Dakota | 149 |
| 47 | West Virginia | 134 |
| 48 | Utah | 104 |
| 49 | Idaho | 97 |
| 50 | South Dakota | 92 |
| 51 | Wyoming | 74 |
| | U.S. Average | 379 |

Data Source: U.S. Department of Commerce, *Statistical Abstract of the United States 1995*

## ABORTION RATIO PER LIVE BIRTHS: NEW YORK VS. U.S.

In 1992, the number of abortions per 1,000 live births outpaced the U.S. average by 83.1 percent—694 in New York versus 379 across the nation. The New York ratio has declined from 904 in 1973.

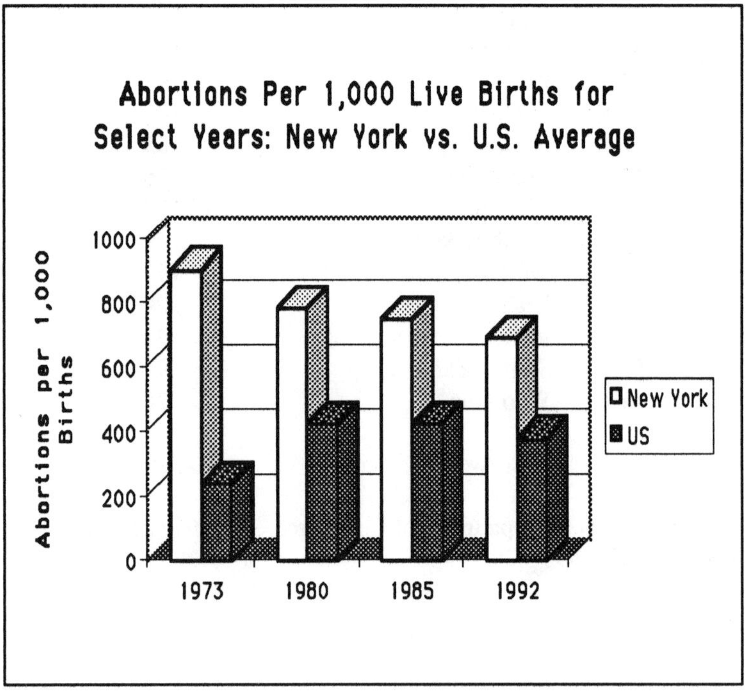


Data Source: U.S. Department of Commerce, *Statistical Abstract of the United States*, annual

## INFANT MORTALITY RATES: STATE RANKINGS

In 1992, New York tied for twentieth in the nation in terms of its infant mortality rate (per 1,000 live births).

**Infant Mortality Rate Per 1,000 Live Births**

| Rank | State | Rate |
|---|---|---|
| 1 | District of Columbia | 19.6 |
| 2 | Mississippi | 11.9 |
| 3 | Alabama | 10.5 |
| 4 | South Carolina | 10.4 |
| 5(t) | Arkansas | 10.3 |
| 5(t) | Georgia | 10.3 |
| 7 | Michigan | 10.2 |
| 8 | Illinois | 10.1 |
| 9 | North Carolina | 10.0 |
| 10 | Maryland | 9.8 |
| 11 | Virginia | 9.5 |
| 12(t) | Indiana | 9.4 |
| 12(t) | Louisiana | 9.4 |
| 12(t) | Ohio | 9.4 |
| 12(t) | Tennessee | 9.4 |
| 16 | South Dakota | 9.3 |
| 17 | West Virginia | 9.2 |
| 18 | Pennsylvania | 9.0 |
| 19 | Wyoming | 8.9 |
| 20(t) | Florida | 8.8 |
| 20(t) | Idaho | 8.8 |
| **20(t)** | **New York** | **8.8** |
| 20(t) | Oklahoma | 8.8 |
| 24 | Kansas | 8.7 |
| 25(t) | Alaska | 8.6 |
| 25(t) | Delaware | 8.6 |
| 27 | Missouri | 8.5 |
| 28(t) | Arizona | 8.4 |
| 28(t) | New Jersey | 8.4 |

*continued*

*continued*

| Rank | State | Rate |
|---|---|---|
| 30 | Kentucky | 8.3 |
| 31 | Iowa | 8.0 |
| 32(t) | North Dakota | 7.8 |
| 32(t) | Texas | 7.8 |
| 34(t) | Colorado | 7.6 |
| 34(t) | Connecticut | 7.6 |
| 34(t) | New Mexico | 7.6 |
| 37 | Montana | 7.5 |
| 38(t) | Nebraska | 7.4 |
| 38(t) | Rhode Island | 7.4 |
| 40(t) | Vermont | 7.2 |
| 40(t) | Wisconsin | 7.2 |
| 42(t) | Minnesota | 7.1 |
| 42(t) | Oregon | 7.1 |
| 44 | California | 7.0 |
| 45 | Washington | 6.8 |
| 46 | Nevada | 6.7 |
| 47 | Massachusetts | 6.5 |
| 48 | Hawaii | 6.3 |
| 49(t) | New Hampshire | 5.9 |
| 49(t) | Utah | 5.9 |
| 51 | Maine | 5.6 |
| | U.S. Average | 8.5 |

Data Source: U.S. Department of Commerce, *Statistical Abstract of the United States 1995*

## INFANT MORTALITY RATES: NEW YORK VS. U.S.

In 1992, New York's infant mortality rate (per 1,000 live births) equaled 8.8 versus the U.S. rate of 8.5. The New York rate is down from 12.5 in 1980.

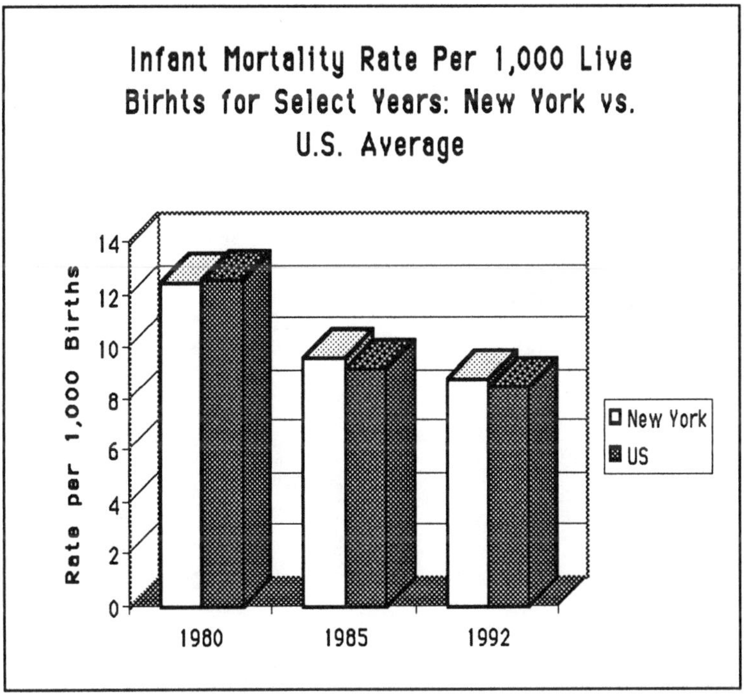


Data Source: U.S. Department of Commerce, *Statistical Abstract of the United States*, annual

# CHAPTER SIX

# NEW YORK STATE: THE ECONOMY

- Gross State Product
- Income
- New Firms and New Business Incorporations
- Employment
- Poverty
- Exports
- Climate for Entrepreneurship
- Home Ownership
- Population
- Union Membership

## GROSS STATE PRODUCT GROWTH: NEW YORK VS. U.S.

Between 1982 and 1992, New York's real gross state product grew by 25.9 percent versus total U.S. gross state product growth of 33.7 percent. That is, U.S. real gross state product growth surpassed New York's by 30.1 percent.

From the first year for which gross state product data is available—1977—to the latest year available—1992—total U.S. real gross state product increased by 43.8 percent, outpacing New York's increase of 33.8 percent by 29.6 percent.

Gross state product is the market value of the goods and services produced by labor and property located in a state. Gross state product has been calculated by Richard M. Beemiller and Ann E. Dunbar and published in various issues of the *Survey of Current Business* (U.S. Department of Commerce).

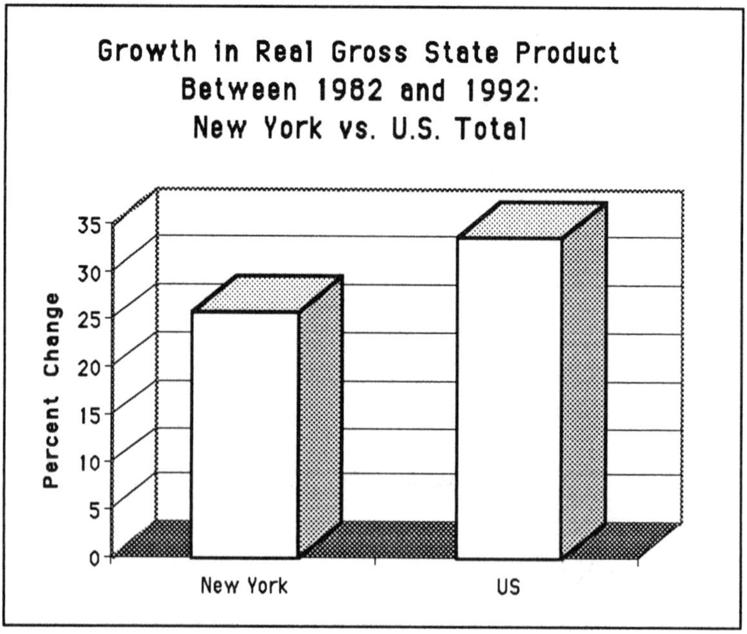

## PERSONAL INCOME: STATE RANKINGS

In 1995, New York ranked fifth highest in the nation in terms of per capita personal income.

**Per Capita Personal Income**

| Rank | State | Per Capita Personal Income |
|---|---|---|
| 1 | District of Columbia | $32,274 |
| 2 | Connecticut | 30,303 |
| 3 | New Jersey | 28,858 |
| 4 | Massachusetts | 26,994 |
| **5** | **New York** | **26,782** |
| 6 | Maryland | 25,927 |
| 7 | New Hampshire | 25,151 |
| 8 | Nevada | 25,013 |
| 9 | Illinois | 24,763 |
| 10 | Hawaii | 24,738 |
| 11 | Alaska | 24,182 |
| 12 | Delaware | 24,124 |
| 13 | California | 23,699 |
| 14 | Washington | 23,639 |
| 15 | Virginia | 23,597 |
| 16 | Michigan | 23,551 |
| 17 | Colorado | 23,449 |
| 18 | Rhode Island | 23,310 |
| 19 | Pennsylvania | 23,279 |
| 20 | Minnesota | 23,118 |
| 21 | Florida | 22,916 |
| 22 | Ohio | 22,021 |
| 23 | Wisconsin | 21,839 |
| 24 | Kansas | 21,825 |
| 25 | Oregon | 21,736 |
| 26 | Nebraska | 21,703 |
| 27 | Missouri | 21,627 |
| 28 | Wyoming | 21,321 |
| 29 | Georgia | 21,278 |

*continued*

*continued*

| Rank | State | Per Capita Personal Income |
|---|---|---|
| 30 | Indiana | 21,273 |
| 31 | Iowa | 21,012 |
| 32 | Vermont | 20,927 |
| 33 | Texas | 20,654 |
| 34 | North Carolina | 20,604 |
| 35 | Maine | 20,527 |
| 36 | Arizona | 20,421 |
| 37 | Tennessee | 20,376 |
| 38 | South Dakota | 19,506 |
| 39 | Idaho | 19,264 |
| 40 | Louisiana | 18,827 |
| 41 | South Carolina | 18,788 |
| 42 | Alabama | 18,781 |
| 43 | North Dakota | 18,663 |
| 44 | Kentucky | 18,612 |
| 45 | Montana | 18,482 |
| 46 | Utah | 18,223 |
| 47 | Oklahoma | 18,152 |
| 48 | New Mexico | 18,055 |
| 49 | West Virginia | 17,915 |
| 50 | Arkansas | 17,429 |
| 51 | Mississippi | 16,531 |
| | U.S. Average | 22,788 |

Data Sources: U.S. Department of Commerce, *Survey of Current Business August 1995* and *Statistical Abstract of the United States 1996*

## PERSONAL INCOME: NEW YORK VS. U.S.

In 1995, New York's per capita personal income of $26,782 surpassed the U.S. per capita personal income amount of $22,788 by 17.5 percent.

Between 1980 and 1995, New York's real per capita personal income grew by 32.9 percent, from $20,159 to $26,782 in 1995 dollars. This compares to a U.S. increase of 24 percent over the same period. From 1970 to 1995, New York's growth in real per capita personal income registered 40.5 percent versus U.S. growth of 43.6 percent, and between 1960 and 1995, New York's grew by 94.9 percent versus U.S. growth of 95.8 percent.

In summary, New York's relative growth in real per capita personal income was slower than the United States in general during the 1960s and 1970s, and faster during the 1980s and 1990s.

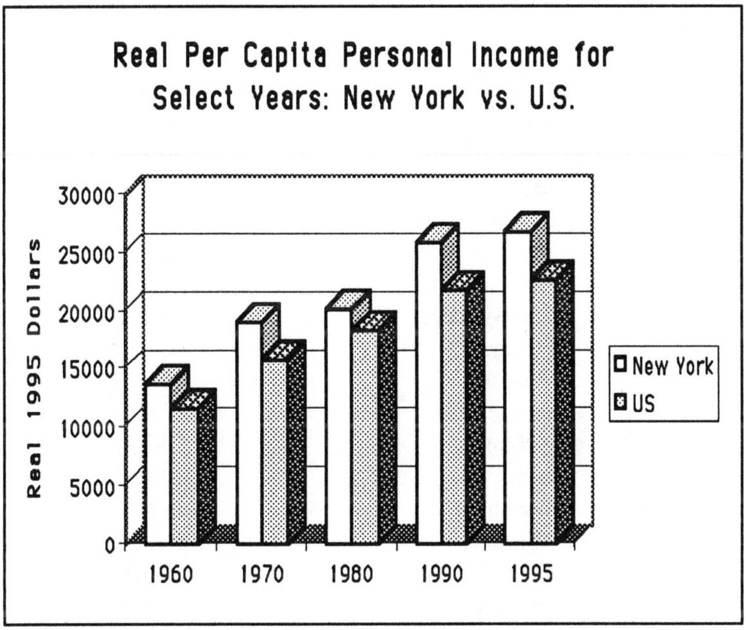


Data Sources: U.S. Department of Commerce, *Survey of Current Business August 1995* and *Statistical Abstract of the United States 1996*

## DISPOSABLE PERSONAL INCOME: STATE RANKINGS

In 1995, New York ranked fifth highest in the nation in terms of per capita disposable personal income.

**State Per Capita Disposable Personal Income**

| Rank | State | Per Capita Income |
|---|---|---|
| 1 | District of Columbia | $27,012 |
| 2 | Connecticut | 25,130 |
| 3 | New Jersey | 24,554 |
| 4 | Massachusetts | 22,764 |
| **5** | **New York** | **22,603** |
| 6 | New Hampshire | 22,209 |
| 7 | Maryland | 21,852 |
| 8 | Nevada | 21,648 |
| 9 | Alaska | 21,417 |
| 10 | Illinois | 21,371 |
| 11 | Hawaii | 21,157 |
| 12 | Washington | 20,808 |
| 13 | California | 20,560 |
| 14 | Michigan | 20,393 |
| 15 | Delaware | 20,333 |
| 16 | Virginia | 20,288 |
| 17 | Rhode Island | 20,263 |
| 18 | Pennsylvania | 20,260 |
| 19 | Florida | 20,074 |
| 20 | Colorado | 19,788 |
| 21 | Minnesota | 19,427 |
| 22 | Nebraska | 19,250 |
| 23 | Ohio | 19,123 |
| 24 | Wyoming | 19,021 |
| 25 | Missouri | 18,931 |
| 26 | Kansas | 18,920 |
| 27 | Vermont | 18,839 |
| 28 | Wisconsin | 18,725 |
| 29 | Indiana | 18,438 |

*continued*

*continued*

| Rank | State | Per Capita Income |
|---|---|---|
| 30 | Georgia | 18,404 |
| 31 | Oregon | 18,392 |
| 32 | Texas | 18,332 |
| 33 | Maine | 18,282 |
| 34 | Iowa | 18,270 |
| 35 | Tennessee | 18,105 |
| 36 | Arizona | 17,850 |
| 37 | North Carolina | 17,772 |
| 38 | South Dakota | 17,434 |
| 39 | Idaho | 17,122 |
| 40 | Louisiana | 16,725 |
| 41 | Alabama | 16,657 |
| 42 | North Dakota | 16,636 |
| 43 | South Carolina | 16,617 |
| 44 | Montana | 16,218 |
| 45 | New Mexico | 16,145 |
| 46 | West Virginia | 16,090 |
| 47 | Kentucky | 16,060 |
| 48 | Oklahoma | 15,827 |
| 49 | Utah | 15,692 |
| 50 | Arkansas | 15,349 |
| 51 | Mississippi | 14,948 |
| | U.S. Average | 19,729 |

Data Source: U.S. Department of Commerce, *Statistical Abstract of the United States 1996*

## DISPOSABLE PERSONAL INCOME: NEW YORK VS. U.S.

In 1995, New York's per capita disposable income of $22,603 exceeded the U.S. per capita amount of $19,729 by 14.6 percent.

From 1990 to 1995, New York's real per capita disposable personal income increased by 3.5 percent, versus a national increase of 4.7 percent. Between 1980 and 1995, New York's real per capita disposable income rose by 32.2 percent, as compared with an increase of 24.6 percent for the U.S. average. From 1970 to 1995, New York increased by 39.7 percent, versus a 43.1 percent rise across the nation. Since 1960, New York witnessed an 85.9 percent rise, as opposed to a 92.5 percent boost in real per capita disposable personal income country wide.

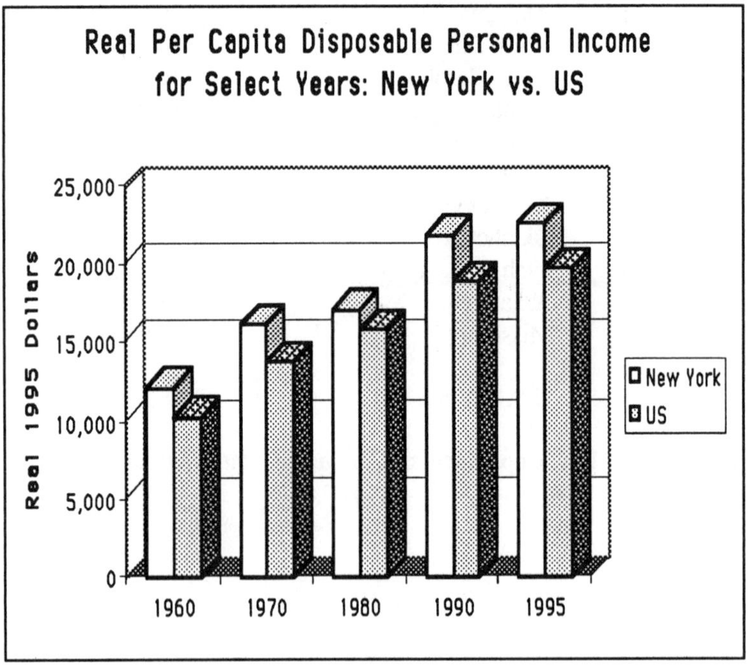


Data Source: U.S. Department of Commerce, *Survey of Current Business August 1995* and *Statistical Abstract of the United States 1996*

# MEDIAN HOUSEHOLD INCOMES: STATE RANKINGS

In 1994, New York ranked twenty-fourth in the nation in terms of median household income.

**Median Household Income**

| Rank | State | Median Household Income |
|---|---|---|
| 1 | Alaska | $45,367 |
| 2 | New Jersey | 42,280 |
| 3 | Hawaii | 42,255 |
| 4 | Connecticut | 41,097 |
| 5 | Massachusetts | 40,500 |
| 6 | Maryland | 39,198 |
| 7 | Colorado | 37,833 |
| 8 | Virginia | 37,647 |
| 9 | Delaware | 35,873 |
| 10 | Nevada | 35,871 |
| 11 | Vermont | 35,802 |
| 12 | Utah | 35,716 |
| 13 | Wisconsin | 35,388 |
| 14 | California | 35,331 |
| 15 | Michigan | 35,284 |
| 16 | New Hampshire | 35,245 |
| 17 | Illinois | 35,081 |
| 18 | Minnesota | 33,644 |
| 19 | Washington | 33,533 |
| 20 | Wyoming | 33,140 |
| 21 | Iowa | 33,079 |
| 22 | Pennsylvania | 32,066 |
| 23 | Rhode Island | 31,928 |
| **24** | **New York** | **31,899** |
| 25 | Ohio | 31,855 |
| 26 | Nebraska | 31,794 |
| 27 | Idaho | 31,536 |
| 28 | Georgia | 31,467 |
| 29 | Oregon | 31,456 |

*continued*

*continued*

| Rank | State | Median Household Income |
|---|---|---|
| 30 | Arizona | 31,293 |
| 31 | Texas | 30,755 |
| 32 | Maine | 30,316 |
| 33 | Missouri | 30,190 |
| 34 | District of Columbia | 30,116 |
| 35 | North Carolina | 30,114 |
| 36 | South Carolina | 29,846 |
| 37 | South Dakota | 29,733 |
| 38 | Florida | 29,294 |
| 39 | Tennessee | 28,639 |
| 40 | Kansas | 28,322 |
| 41 | North Dakota | 28,278 |
| 42 | Indiana | 27,858 |
| 43 | Montana | 27,631 |
| 44 | Alabama | 27,196 |
| 45 | Oklahoma | 26,991 |
| 46 | New Mexico | 26,905 |
| 47 | Kentucky | 26,595 |
| 48 | Louisiana | 25,676 |
| 49 | Arkansas | 25,565 |
| 50 | Mississippi | 25,400 |
| 51 | West Virginia | 23,564 |
| | U.S. Average | 32,264 |

Data Source: U.S. Department of Commerce, *Statistical Abstract of the United States 1996*

## MEDIAN HOUSEHOLD INCOMES: NEW YORK VS. U.S.

In 1994, the U.S. median household income of $32,264 topped the New York median household income of $31,899 by just 1.1 percent.

Between 1984 and 1994, New York's real median household income increased by only 1.5 percent, and between 1989 and 1994, real median household income fell by 15.3 percent. These numbers compare with a 0.9 percent increase in U.S. real median household income between 1984 and 1994, and a 6.6 percent decline between 1989 and 1994.

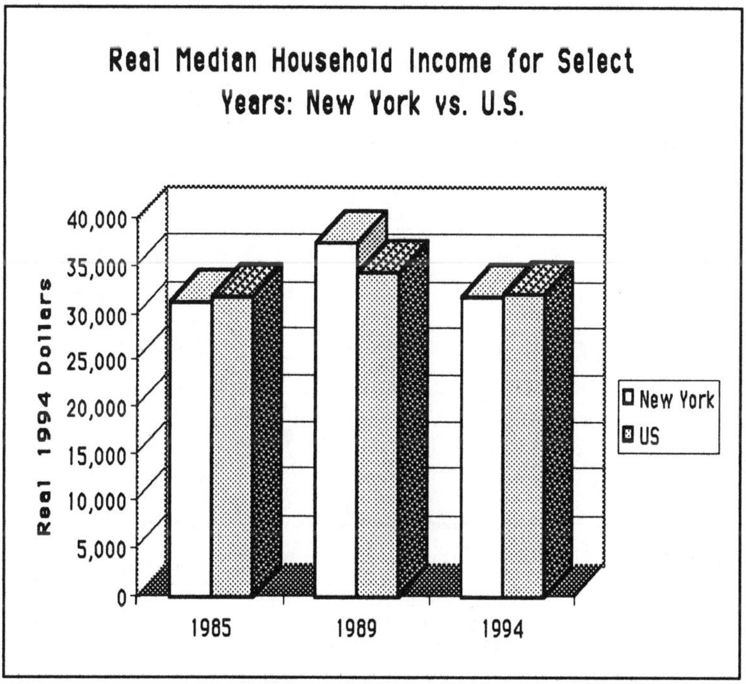


Data Source: U.S. Department of Commerce, *Statistical Abstract of the United States 1996*

# NEW FIRMS: NEW YORK VS. U.S.

In 1995, new business firms established in New York equaled 54,620, a figure 9.1 percent higher than 1983's 50,049. This 1995 number represented a decline of 9.8 percent from the New York high of 60,588 in 1987. Meanwhile, nationwide, new firms registered 819,477 in 1995 (a U.S. high), 29.5 percent higher than 1983's 632,922.

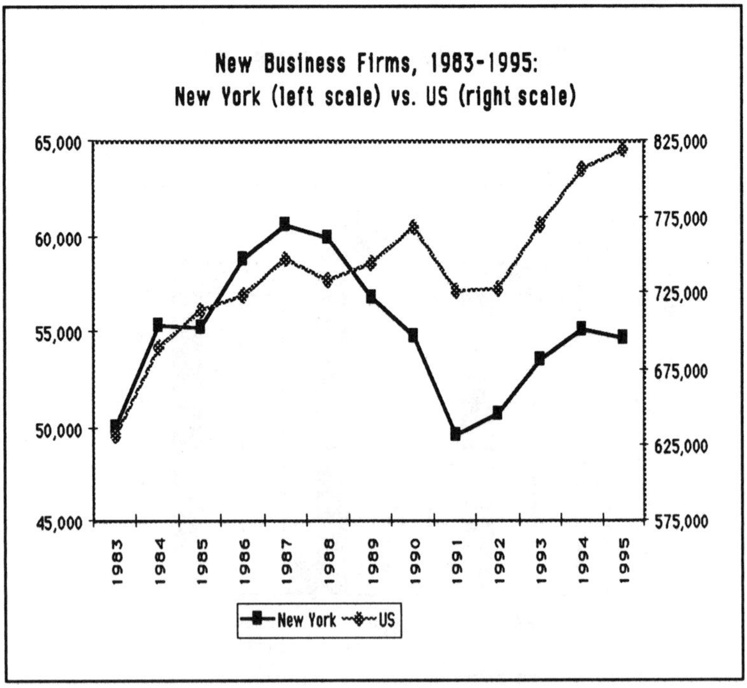


Data Source: U.S. Small Business Administration

## NEW BUSINESS INCORPORATIONS: NEW YORK VS. U.S.

In 1995, new business incorporations in New York equaled 72,437—31.2 percent higher than 1979's 55,210. This 1995 number represented a decline of 6.8 percent from the New York high of 77,687 in 1988. Meanwhile, nationwide, new business incorporations registered 770,324 in 1993 (a U.S. high), 46.9 percent higher than 1979's 524,565.

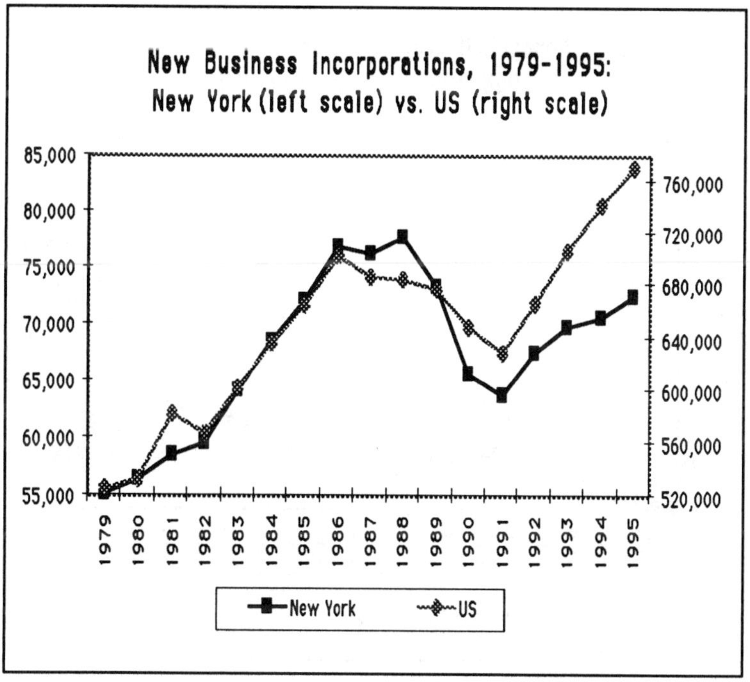


Data Source: The Dun & Bradstreet Corporation

## TOTAL EMPLOYMENT: NEW YORK VS. U.S.

From 1959 to 1995, New York's annual rate of job creation exceeded the U.S. rate in only two years—1982 and 1985. In all other years, New York's job creation rate lagged the U.S. rate. Between 1958 and 1995, total U.S. employment increased by 111.4 percent, while total employment in New York grew by just 30.7 percent. Between 1989 and 1995, total New York employment *declined* by 4.5 percent, while U.S. employment *grew* by 6.4 percent.

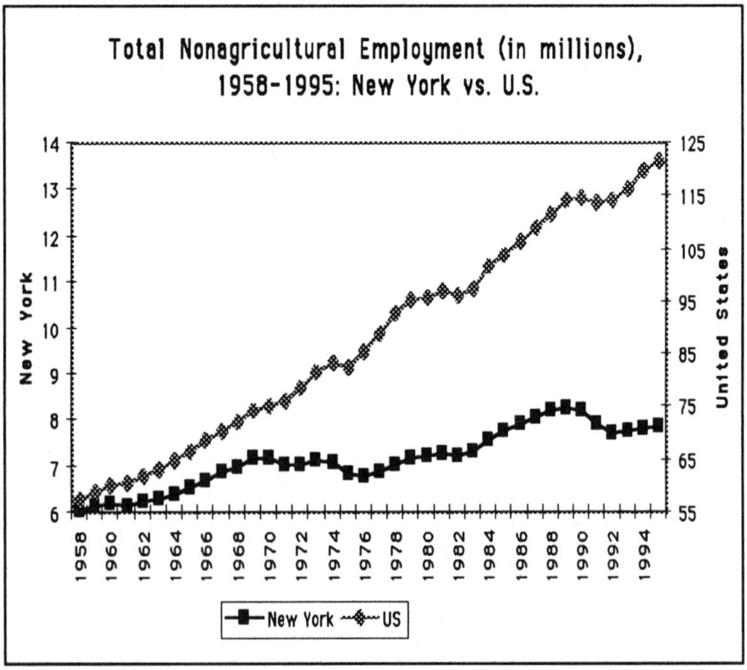


Data Sources: U.S. Department of Labor and the New York State Department of Labor

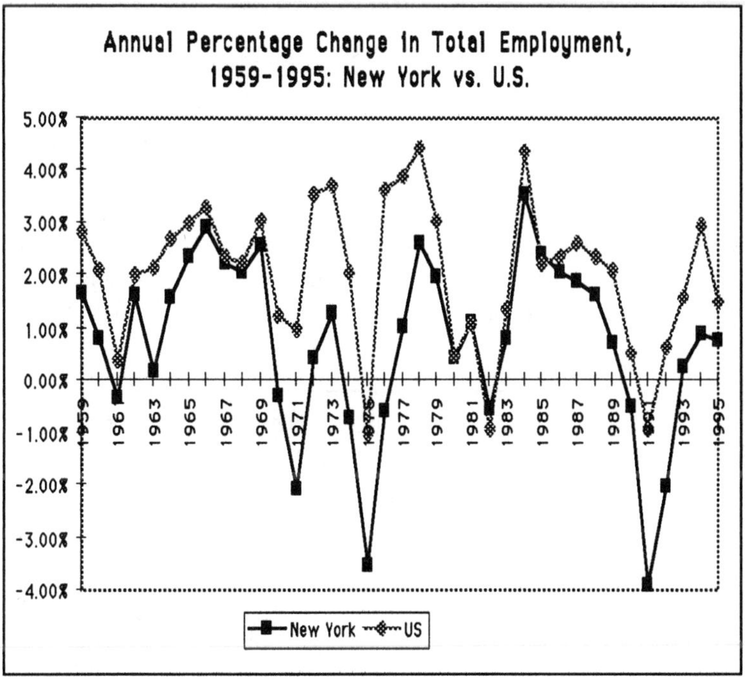


Data Sources: U.S. Department of Labor and the New York State Department of Labor

# TOTAL PRIVATE SECTOR EMPLOYMENT: NEW YORK VS. U.S.

From 1959 to 1995, New York's annual rate of private-sector job creation exceeded the U.S. rate in only three years—1980, 1982, and 1985. In all other years, New York's private-sector job creation rate lagged the U.S. rate. Between 1958 and 1995, total U.S. private sector employment increased by 106 percent, while New York's grew by just 24.3 percent. Between 1989 and 1995, U.S. private sector employment *grew* by 6 percent compared with New York's *decline* of 4.6 percent.

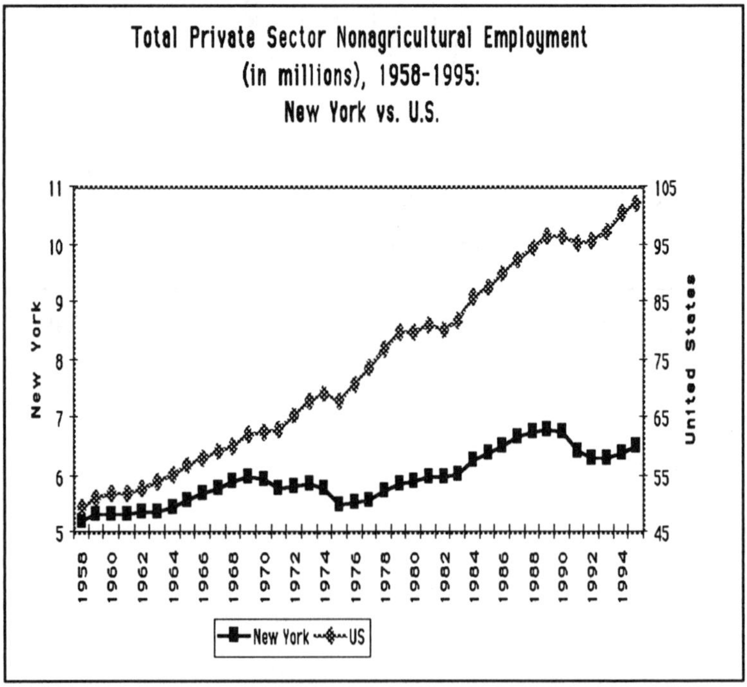


Data Sources: U.S. Department of Labor and the New York State Department of Labor

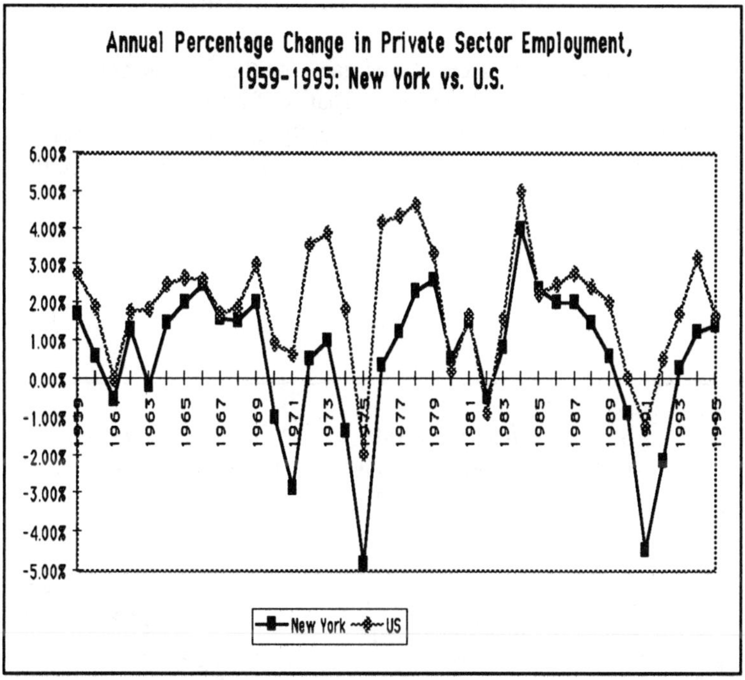


Data Sources: U.S. Department of Labor and the New York State Department of Labor

## NEW YORK PRIVATE SECTOR JOBS GAP

New York's private sector "jobs gap" for the 36-year period from 1958 to 1995 reached 4.26 million. That is, if New York's annual rate of job creation in the private sector merely matched the national rate over this period, 4.26 million more jobs would have been created than actually were.

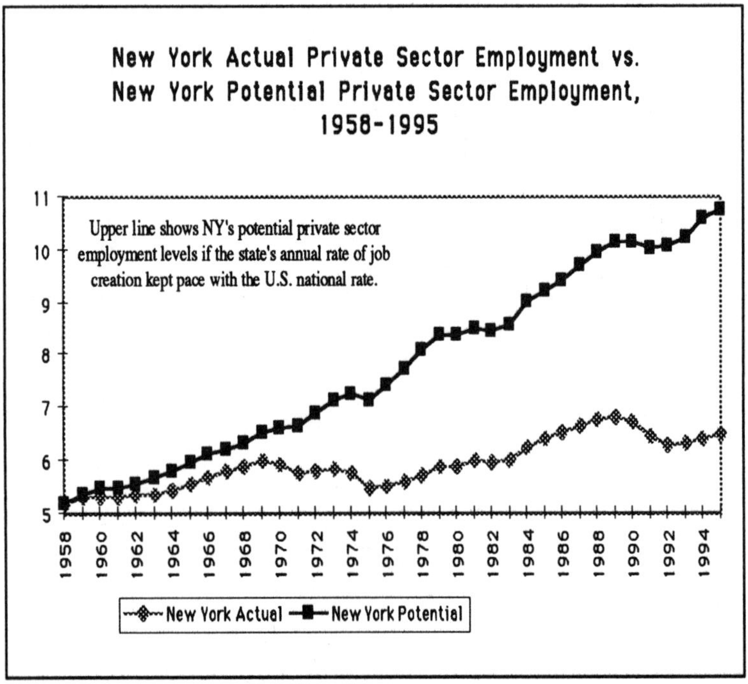

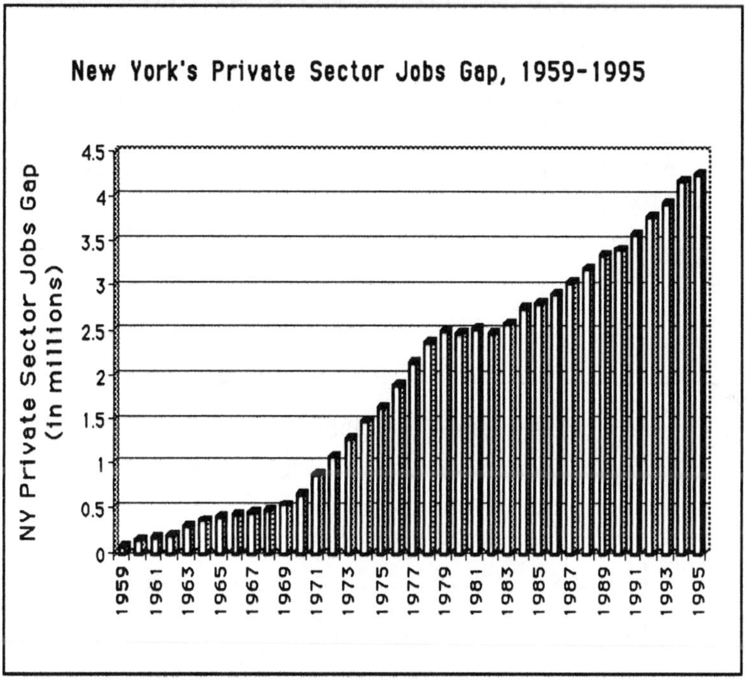
New York's Private Sector Jobs Gap, 1959-1995
NY Private Sector Jobs Gap
(in millions)
4.5
4
3.5
3
2.5
2
1.5
1
0.5
0
1959
1961
1963
1965
1967
1969
1971
1973
1975
1977
1979
1981
1983
1985
1987
1989
1991
1993
1995

## LABOR FORCE PARTICIPATION RATES: NEW YORK VS. U.S.

In 1995, New York's labor force participation rate (civilian labor force as a percentage of civilian noninstitutional population) equaled 60.9 percent, compared with the U.S. rate of 66.6 percent. New York's labor force participation rate has consistently lagged the U.S. rate over at least the past 25 years.

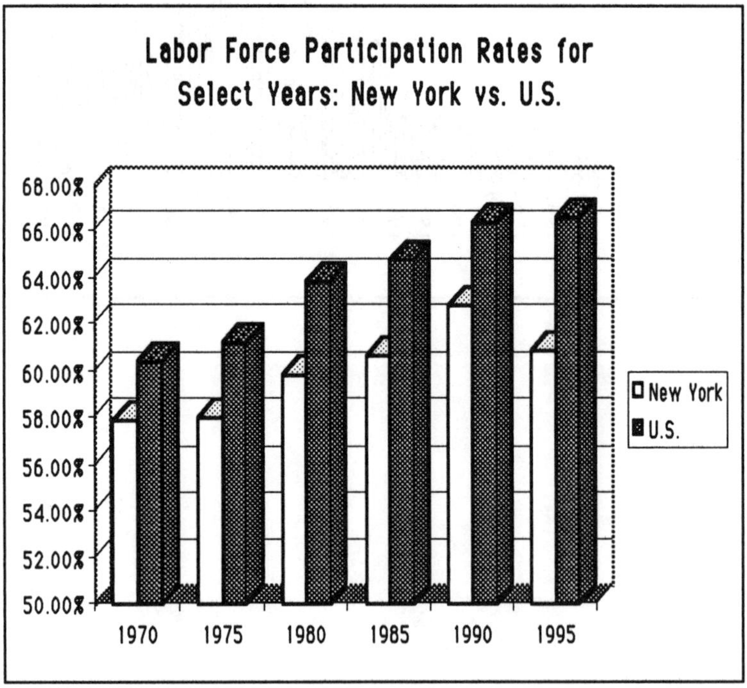


Data Source: U.S. Department of Labor

## EMPLOYMENT RATES: NEW YORK VS. U.S.

In 1995, New York's employment rate (employment as a percent of civilian noninstitutional population) equaled 57 percentage, compared with the U.S. rate of 62.9 percent. New York's employment rate has consistently lagged the U.S. rate over at least the past 25 years.

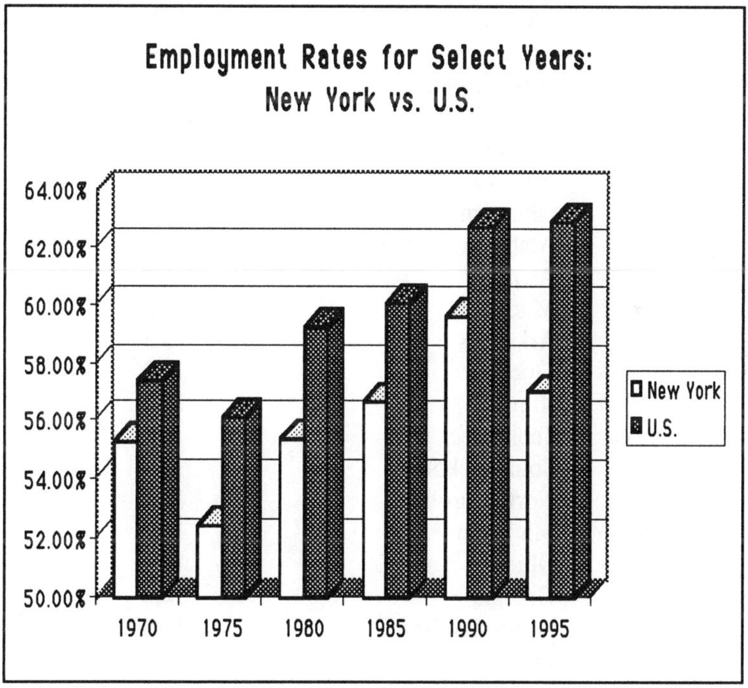


Data Source: U.S. Department of Labor

# INDIVIDUALS BELOW THE POVERTY LINE: STATE RANKINGS

In 1994, New York ranked ninth in the nation in terms of the percentage of individuals falling below the poverty level.

**Percentage Below the Poverty Level**

| Rank | State | Percent |
|---|---|---|
| 1 | Louisiana | 25.7% |
| 2 | District of Columbia | 21.2 |
| 3 | New Mexico | 21.1 |
| 4 | Mississippi | 19.9 |
| 5 | Texas | 19.1 |
| 6 | West Virginia | 18.6 |
| 7 | Kentucky | 18.5 |
| 8 | California | 17.9 |
| **9** | **New York** | **17.0** |
| 10 | Oklahoma | 16.7 |
| 11 | Alabama | 16.4 |
| 12 | Arizona | 15.9 |
| 13 | Missouri | 15.6 |
| 14 | Arkansas | 15.3 |
| 15(t) | Florida | 14.9 |
| 15(t) | Kansas | 14.9 |
| 17 | Tennessee | 14.6 |
| 18 | South Dakota | 14.5 |
| 19 | North Carolina | 14.2 |
| 20(t) | Michigan | 14.1 |
| 20(t) | Ohio | 14.1 |
| 22 | Georgia | 14.0 |
| 23 | South Carolina | 13.8 |
| 24 | Indiana | 13.7 |
| 25 | Pennsylvania | 12.5 |
| 26 | Illinois | 12.4 |
| 27 | Idaho | 12.0 |
| 28 | Oregon | 11.8 |

*continued*

*continued*

| Rank | State | Percent |
|---|---|---|
| 29(t) | Minnesota | 11.7 |
| 29(t) | Washington | 11.7 |
| 31 | Montana | 11.5 |
| 32 | Nevada | 11.1 |
| 33 | Connecticut | 10.8 |
| 34(t) | Iowa | 10.7 |
| 34(t) | Maryland | 10.7 |
| 34(t) | Virginia | 10.7 |
| 37 | North Dakota | 10.4 |
| 38 | Rhode Island | 10.3 |
| 39 | Alaska | 10.2 |
| 40 | Massachusetts | 9.7 |
| 41 | Maine | 9.4 |
| 42 | Wyoming | 9.3 |
| 43 | New Jersey | 9.2 |
| 44(t) | Colorado | 9.0 |
| 44(t) | Wisconsin | 9.0 |
| 46 | Nebraska | 8.8 |
| 47 | Hawaii | 8.7 |
| 48 | Delaware | 8.3 |
| 49 | Utah | 8.0 |
| 50 | New Hampshire | 7.7 |
| 51 | Vermont | 7.6 |
| | U.S. Average | 14.5 |

Data Source: U.S. Department of Commerce, *Statistical Abstract of the United States 1996*

## INDIVIDUALS BELOW THE POVERTY LINE: NEW YORK VS. US

In 1994, the percentage of New Yorkers below the poverty line registered 17.0 percent, exceeding the U.S. rate of 14.5 percent by 17.2 percent.

Between 1980 and 1994, New York's percentage of individuals below the poverty line increased from 13.8 percent to 17.0 percent, a rise of 23.1 percent.

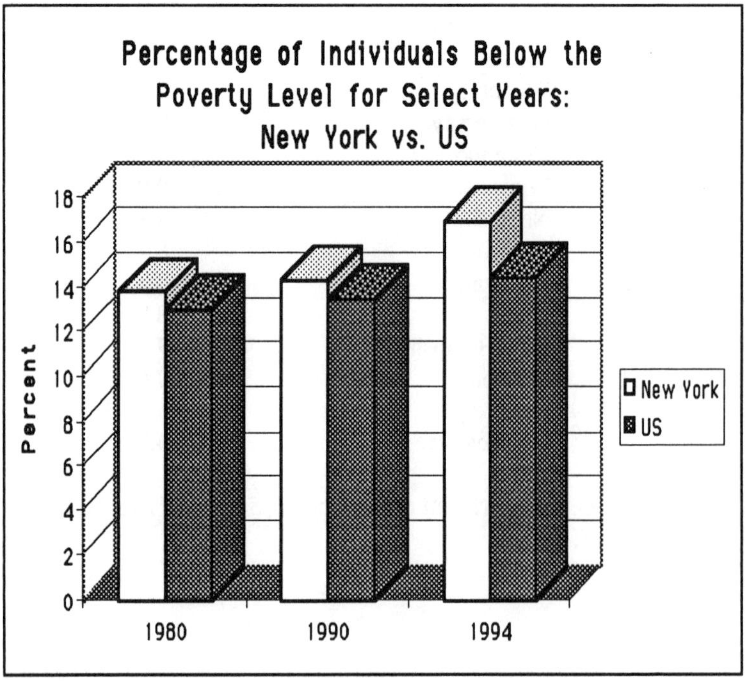


Data Source: U.S. Department of Commerce, *Statistical Abstract of the United States 1996*

## EXPORTS: STATE RANKINGS

In 1995, New York ranked third in the nation in terms of total exports.

**Total Exports (in millions of dollars)**

| Rank | State | Exports |
|---|---|---|
| 1 | California | $77,529 |
| 2 | Texas | 59,116 |
| **3** | **New York** | **28,095** |
| 4 | Michigan | 25,275 |
| 5 | Illinois | 22,163 |
| 6 | Washington | 21,879 |
| 7 | Ohio | 20,967 |
| 8 | Louisiana | 19,793 |
| 9 | Florida | 18,909 |
| 10 | North Carolina | 14,313 |
| 11 | Pennsylvania | 13,031 |
| 12 | Massachusetts | 12,946 |
| 13 | Virginia | 11,512 |
| 14 | New Jersey | 11,071 |
| 15 | Indiana | 10,383 |
| 16 | Georgia | 10,291 |
| 17 | Wisconsin | 8,931 |
| 18 | Tennessee | 7,778 |
| 19 | Minnesota | 7,747 |
| 20 | Oregon | 7,667 |
| 21 | Arizona | 7,327 |
| 22 | South Carolina | 6,423 |
| 23 | Connecticut | 5,666 |
| 24 | Kentucky | 5,253 |
| 25 | Maryland | 5,223 |
| 26 | Alabama | 4,764 |
| 27 | Colorado | 4,460 |
| 28 | Missouri | 3,876 |
| 29 | Iowa | 3,842 |

*continued*

*continued*

| Rank | State | Exports |
|---|---|---|
| 30 | Kansas | 3,433 |
| 31 | Utah | 3,282 |
| 32 | Alaska | 2,772 |
| 33 | Mississippi | 2,592 |
| 34 | Oklahoma | 2,079 |
| 35 | West Virginia | 2,040 |
| 36 | Arkansas | 1,994 |
| 37 | Idaho | 1,804 |
| 38 | Nebraska | 1,759 |
| 39 | Vermont | 1,620 |
| 40 | Delaware | 1,402 |
| 41 | Maine | 1,357 |
| 42 | New Hampshire | 1,253 |
| 43 | Rhode Island | 897 |
| 44 | Nevada | 665 |
| 45 | North Dakota | 526 |
| 46 | New Mexico | 432 |
| 47 | Wyoming | 411 |
| 48 | South Dakota | 388 |
| 49 | Montana | 358 |
| 50 | Hawaii | 241 |
| 51 | District of Columbia | 231 |

Data Source: U.S. Department of Commerce, *Statistical Abstract of the United States 1996*

## MANUFACTURING EXPORTS: STATE RANKINGS

In 1991, New York ranked twenty-second in the nation in terms of its export-related manufactures as a share of all manufacture shipments.

**Export-Related Manufactures as a Percentage of Total Manufacture Shipments**

| Rank | State | Percent |
|---|---|---|
| 1 | Alaska | 49.7% |
| 2 | Washington | 43.6 |
| 3 | Idaho | 28.8 |
| 4 | West Virginia | 26.2 |
| 5 | Connecticut | 25.9 |
| 6 | Massachusetts | 23.4 |
| 7 | Oregon | 23.1 |
| 8 | Arizona | 23.0 |
| 9 | New Hampshire | 22.1 |
| 10 | South Carolina | 21.4 |
| 11 | California | 21.3 |
| 12 | Texas | 21.1 |
| 13 | Maine | 20.9 |
| 14 | New Mexico | 20.7 |
| 15 | Vermont | 20.6 |
| 16 | Ohio | 20.5 |
| 17 | Florida | 20.0 |
| 18 | Rhode Island | 19.4 |
| 19 | Louisiana | 19.2 |
| 20(t) | Alabama | 19.1 |
| 20(t) | Michigan | 19.1 |
| **22** | **New York** | **18.6** |
| 23 | Indiana | 18.1 |
| 24 | Illinois | 18.0 |
| 25 | North Carolina | 17.5 |
| 26 | Kentucky | 17.4 |
| 27(t) | Tennessee | 17.2 |
| 27(t) | Utah | 17.2 |

*continued*

*continued*

| Rank | State | Percent |
|---|---|---|
| 27(t) | Virginia | 17.2 |
| 30 | Delaware | 17.1 |
| 31 | Colorado | 16.9 |
| 32 | Pennsylvania | 16.8 |
| 33 | Maryland | 16.7 |
| 34 | Mississippi | 16.6 |
| 35 | Minnesota | 16.4 |
| 36 | Hawaii | 16.3 |
| 37 | Wisconsin | 16.2 |
| 38 | Arkansas | 16.0 |
| 39 | Georgia | 15.7 |
| 40 | Nevada | 15.6 |
| 41 | New Jersey | 15.2 |
| 42(t) | Missouri | 15.1 |
| 42(t) | Montana | 15.1 |
| 44 | Oklahoma | 14.9 |
| 45 | Iowa | 14.6 |
| 46 | North Dakota | 14.4 |
| 47 | Kansas | 14.3 |
| 48 | South Dakota | 13.7 |
| 49 | Wyoming | 13.3 |
| 50 | Nebraska | 13.1 |
| 51 | District of Columbia | 10.4 |
| | U.S. Average | 19.4 |

Data Source: U.S. Department of Commerce, *Statistical Abstract of the United States 1995*

## MANUFACTURING EXPORTS: NEW YORK VS. U.S.

In 1991, U.S. export-related manufactures as a share of all manufacture shipments equaled 19.4 percent, exceeding New York's rate of 18.6 percent.

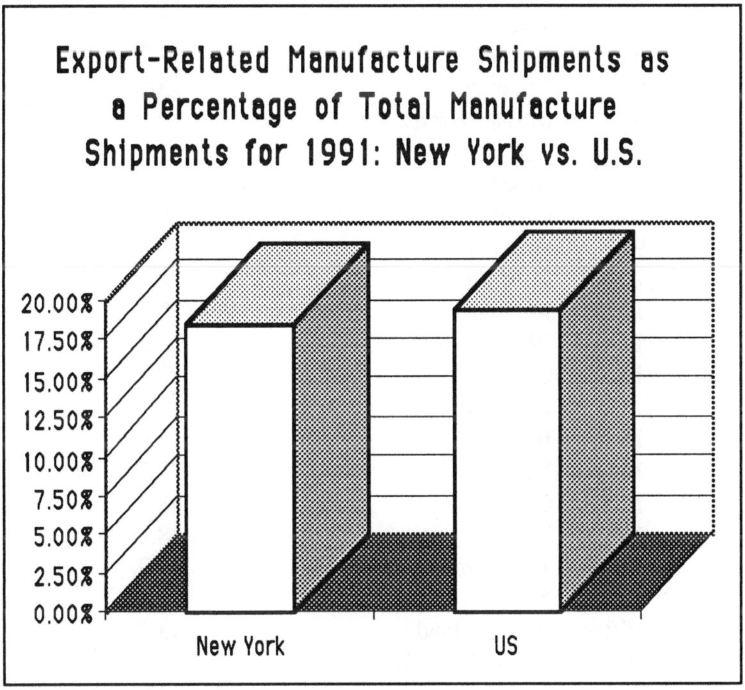


Data Source: U.S. Department of Commerce, *Statistical Abstract of the United States 1995*

# MANUFACTURING EXPORT-RELATED EMPLOYMENT: STATE RANKINGS

In 1991, New York tied for nineteenth in the nation in terms of its export-related manufacturing employment as a share of all manufacturing employment.

**Export-Related Manufacturing Employment as a Percentage of Total Manufacturing Employment**

| Rank | State | Percent |
|---|---|---|
| 1 | Alaska | 49.3% |
| 2 | Washington | 31.2 |
| 3 | Connecticut | 24.2 |
| 4 | Texas | 23.9 |
| 5 | Massachusetts | 22.7 |
| 6 | Idaho | 22.0 |
| 7 | New Hampshire | 21.2 |
| 8 | Oregon | 20.9 |
| 9 | Arizona | 20.8 |
| 10 | California | 20.5 |
| 11 | Michigan | 20.4 |
| 12 | West Virginia | 20.2 |
| 13 | Ohio | 20.0 |
| 14 | Delaware | 19.9 |
| 15 | Illinois | 18.6 |
| 16 | Vermont | 18.5 |
| 17 | Colorado | 18.2 |
| 18 | Maine | 18.1 |
| 19(t) | Minnesota | 18.0 |
| **19(t)** | **New York** | **18.0** |
| 19(t) | Rhode Island | 18.0 |
| 19(t) | South Carolina | 18.0 |
| 23 | Florida | 17.9 |
| 24 | Indiana | 17.8 |
| 25(t) | Pennsylvania | 17.7 |
| 25(t) | Utah | 17.7 |

*continued*

*continued*

| Rank | State | Percent |
|---|---|---|
| 27(t) | New Jersey | 17.3 |
| 27(t) | Wisconsin | 17.3 |
| 29 | Louisiana | 17.0 |
| 30 | Kentucky | 16.6 |
| 31 | South Dakota | 16.5 |
| 32 | Oklahoma | 16.0 |
| 33(t) | Kansas | 15.7 |
| 33(t) | Tennessee | 15.7 |
| 35(t) | Alabama | 15.6 |
| 35(t) | Maryland | 15.6 |
| 37 | Missouri | 15.3 |
| 38(t) | Nevada | 15.2 |
| 38(t) | North Carolina | 15.2 |
| 40 | Iowa | 14.9 |
| 41 | Georgia | 14.8 |
| 42 | Arkansas | 14.7 |
| 43 | New Mexico | 14.5 |
| 44 | Wyoming | 14.3 |
| 45 | Montana | 14.1 |
| 46(t) | Hawaii | 14.0 |
| 46(t) | Virginia | 14.0 |
| 48 | Nebraska | 13.7 |
| 49 | Mississippi | 12.9 |
| 50 | North Dakota | 12.2 |
| 51 | District of Columbia | 9.0 |
| | U.S. Average | 18.6 |

Data Source: U.S. Department of Commerce, *Statistical Abstract of the United States 1995*

## MANUFACTURING EXPORT-RELATED EMPLOYMENT: NEW YORK VS. U.S.

In 1991, U.S. export-related manufacturing employment as a share of all manufacturing employment equaled 18.6 percent, exceeding New York's rate of 18.0 percent.

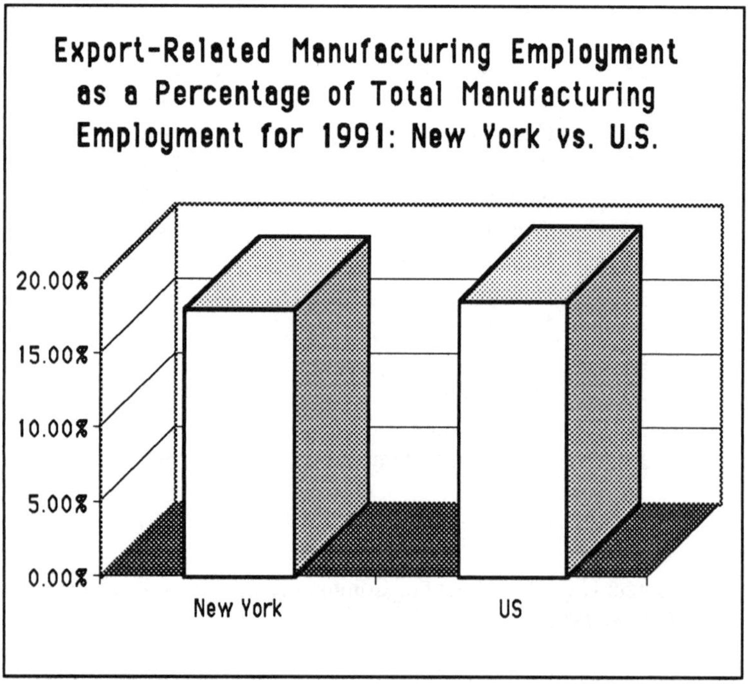


Data Source: U.S. Department of Commerce, *Statistical Abstract of the United States 1995*

## Small Business Survival Index

In June 1996, the Small Business Survival Foundation published a study of mine called "The Small Business Survival Index: Ranking the Environment for Entrepreneurship Across the Nation." I assembled nine indicators of government-imposed or government-related costs on entrepreneurs—personal income tax rate, capital gains tax rate, corporate income tax rate, property taxes, sales taxes, workers' compensation insurance, employer unemployment tax rates, estate taxes, and the crime rate—into one index—the Small Business Survival Index. Unfortunately, no reliable, comparable indicator of state regulations is available. The lower the index number, the better the environment for entrepreneurship in that state.

New York ranked a dismal forty-sixth out of the 50 states. The Small Business Survival Index also was estimated for New York City, which scored far worse than any state or Washington, D.C.

**Small Business Survival Index**

| Rank | State | Survival Index |
|---|---|---|
| 1 | South Dakota | 14.140 |
| 2 | Wyoming | 15.510 |
| 3 | Nevada | 17.390 |
| 4 | Washington | 19.130 |
| 5 | Texas | 22.584 |
| 6 | New Hampshire | 22.844 |
| 7 | Tennessee | 22.876 |
| 8 | Alaska | 24.793 |
| 9 | Florida | 25.838 |
| 10 | Mississippi | 26.453 |
| 11 | Alabama | 27.998 |
| 12 | Indiana | 29.056 |
| 13 | Michigan | 30.166 |
| 14 | Colorado | 30.184 |
| 15 | Virginia | 30.745 |
| 16 | Massachusetts | 30.808 |
| 17 | South Carolina | 31.203 |

*continued*

*continued*

| Rank | State | Survival Index |
|---|---|---|
| 18 | Illinois | 31.210 |
| 19 | Pennsylvania | 32.309 |
| 20 | Missouri | 32.803 |
| 21 | North Dakota | 33.198 |
| 22 | Wisconsin | 33.331 |
| 23 | Maryland | 33.690 |
| 24 | Georgia | 33.701 |
| 25 | Kentucky | 34.022 |
| 26 | Arkansas | 34.149 |
| 27 | Utah | 34.397 |
| 28 | West Virginia | 34.540 |
| 29 | Delaware | 34.836 |
| 30 | Kansas | 35.007 |
| 31 | Oklahoma | 35.114 |
| 32 | Connecticut | 35.617 |
| 33 | Nebraska | 36.862 |
| 34 | North Carolina | 37.662 |
| 35 | Idaho | 37.717 |
| 36 | New Jersey | 38.648 |
| 37 | Louisiana | 38.661 |
| 38 | Ohio | 38.840 |
| 39 | Oregon | 39.032 |
| 40 | Arizona | 40.373 |
| 41 | Vermont | 40.864 |
| 42 | Minnesota | 41.771 |
| 43 | New Mexico | 42.039 |
| 44 | Maine | 43.381 |
| 45 | Montana | 43.650 |
| **46** | **New York** | **44.300** |
| 47 | Rhode Island | 45.120 |
| 48 | Iowa | 45.765 |
| 49 | Hawaii | 45.966 |
| 50 | California | 46.028 |
| 51 | District of Columbia | 58.375 |
| | **New York City** | **73.760** |

## HOME OWNERSHIP RATES: STATE RANKINGS

In 1995, New York ranked forty-ninth in the nation in terms of its home ownership rate, with only Hawaii and the District of Columbia faring worse.

**Home Ownership Rates**

| Rank | State | Rate |
|---|---|---|
| 1 | Maine | 76.7% |
| 2 | Minnesota | 73.3 |
| 3 | West Virginia | 73.1 |
| 4 | Michigan | 72.2 |
| 5 | Idaho | 72.0 |
| 6 | Delaware | 71.7 |
| 7(t) | Pennsylvania | 71.5 |
| 7(t) | Utah | 71.5 |
| 9 | Iowa | 71.4 |
| 10 | South Carolina | 71.3 |
| 11 | Kentucky | 71.2 |
| 12 | Mississippi | 71.1 |
| 13 | Indiana | 71.0 |
| 14 | Vermont | 70.4 |
| 15(t) | North Carolina | 70.1 |
| 15(t) | Alabama | 70.1 |
| 17 | Oklahoma | 69.8 |
| 18 | Missouri | 69.4 |
| 19 | Wyoming | 69.0 |
| 20 | Montana | 68.7 |
| 21 | Connecticut | 68.2 |
| 22 | Virginia | 68.1 |
| 23 | Ohio | 67.9 |
| 24(t) | Wisconsin | 67.5 |
| 24(t) | Kansas | 67.5 |
| 24(t) | South Dakota | 67.5 |
| 27 | North Dakota | 67.3 |
| 28 | Arkansas | 67.2 |

*continued*

*continued*

| Rank | State | Rate |
|---|---|---|
| 29 | Nebraska | 67.1 |
| 30(t) | Tennessee | 67.0 |
| 30(t) | New Mexico | 67.0 |
| 32(t) | Florida | 66.6 |
| 32(t) | Georgia | 66.6 |
| 34 | Illinois | 66.4 |
| 35 | New Hampshire | 66.0 |
| 36 | Maryland | 65.8 |
| 37 | Louisiana | 65.3 |
| 38 | New Jersey | 64.9 |
| 39 | Colorado | 64.6 |
| 40 | Oregon | 63.2 |
| 41 | Arizona | 62.9 |
| 42 | Washington | 61.6 |
| 43 | Texas | 61.4 |
| 44 | Alaska | 60.9 |
| 45 | Massachusetts | 60.2 |
| 46 | Nevada | 58.6 |
| 47 | Rhode Island | 57.9 |
| 48 | California | 55.4 |
| **49** | **New York** | **52.7** |
| 50 | Hawaii | 50.2 |
| 51 | District of Columbia | 38.2 |
| | U.S. Average | 64.7 |

Data Source: U.S. Department of Commerce, *Statistical Abstract of the United States 1996*

## HOME OWNERSHIP RATES: NEW YORK VS. US

In 1995, the U.S. home ownership rate of 64.7 percent outpaced New York's rate of 52.7 percent by 22.8 percent.

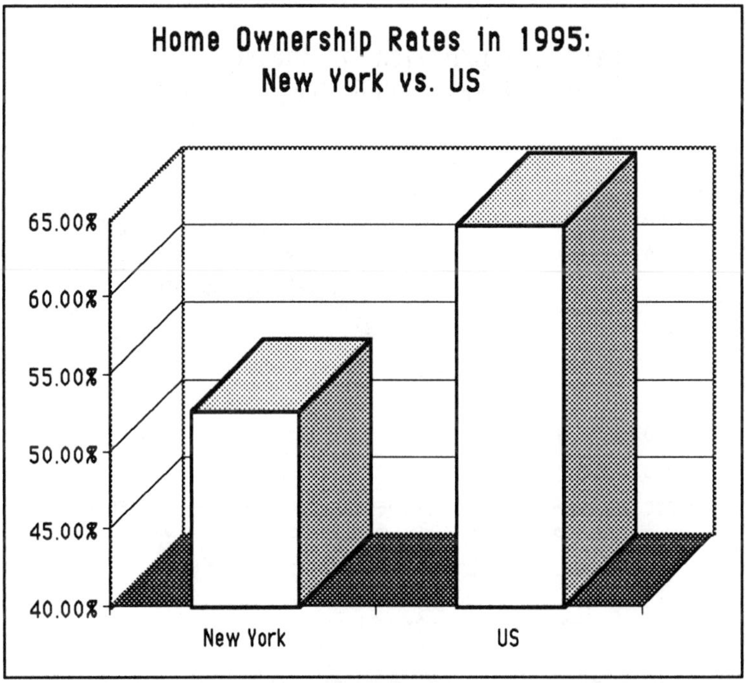


Data Source: U.S. Department of Commerce, *Statistical Abstract of the United States 1996*

## POPULATION TREND: NEW YORK VS. U.S.

New York's population grew at respectable rates throughout most of the first six decades of the twentieth century. In the 1960s, growth slowed somewhat as compared to the United States as a whole, and New York's population actually declined in the 1970s—a drop of 3.7 percent in 1980 versus 1970 levels. The 1980s and the early 1990s witnessed anemic population growth. And, the state's population in 1995 actually *declined* versus 1994 levels—18.136 million in 1995 compared to 18.153 million in 1994. Only Rhode Island and Washington, D.C. also lost population in 1995.

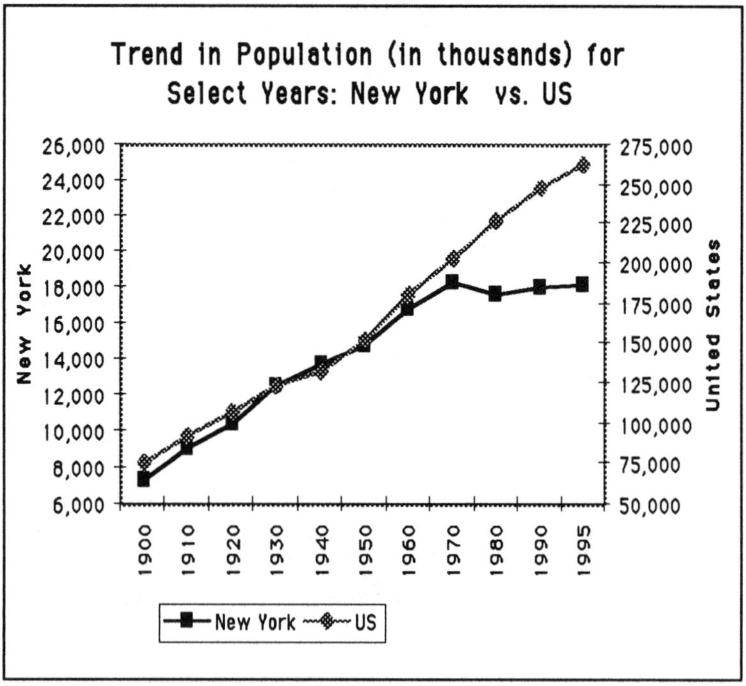


Data Source: U.S. Department of Commerce

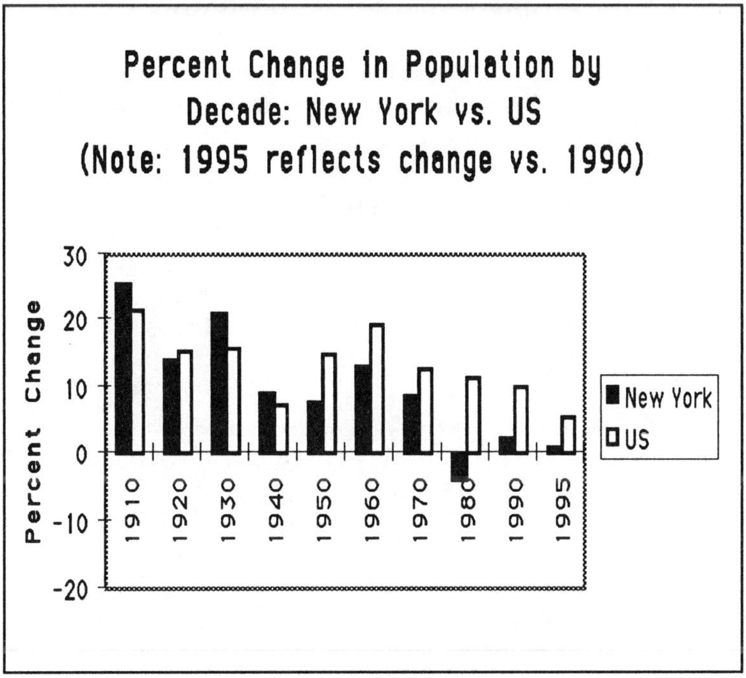


Data Source: U.S. Department of Commerce

# IMMIGRATION: STATE RANKINGS

In 1994, New York admitted the second highest number of immigrants among the 50 states and Washington, D.C., trailing well behind number one California and well outpacing number three Texas.

**Immigrants**

| Rank | State | Immigrants |
|---|---|---|
| 1 | California | 208,498 |
| **2** | **New York** | **144,354** |
| 3 | Florida | 58,093 |
| 4 | Texas | 56,158 |
| 5 | New Jersey | 44,083 |
| 6 | Illinois | 42,400 |
| 7 | Massachusetts | 22,882 |
| 8 | Washington | 18,180 |
| 9 | Pennsylvania | 15,971 |
| 10 | Maryland | 15,937 |
| 11 | Virginia | 15,342 |
| 12 | Michigan | 12,728 |
| 13 | Georgia | 10,032 |
| 14 | Connecticut | 9,537 |
| 15 | Ohio | 9,184 |
| 16 | Arizona | 9,141 |
| 17 | Hawaii | 7,746 |
| 18 | Minnesota | 7,098 |
| 19 | Colorado | 6,825 |
| 20 | Oregon | 6,784 |
| 21 | North Carolina | 6,204 |
| 22 | Wisconsin | 5,328 |
| 23 | Missouri | 4,362 |
| 24 | Nevada | 4,051 |
| 25 | Indiana | 3,725 |
| 26 | Tennessee | 3,608 |
| 27 | Louisiana | 3,366 |
| 28 | District of Columbia | 3,204 |

*continued*

*continued*

| Rank | State | Immigrants |
|---|---|---|
| 29 | Utah | 2,951 |
| 30 | New Mexico | 2,936 |
| 31 | Rhode Island | 2,907 |
| 32 | Kansas | 2,902 |
| 33 | Oklahoma | 2,728 |
| 34 | Iowa | 2,163 |
| 35 | South Carolina | 2,110 |
| 36 | Kentucky | 2,036 |
| 37 | Alabama | 1,837 |
| 38 | Nebraska | 1,595 |
| 39 | Idaho | 1,559 |
| 40 | New Hampshire | 1,144 |
| 41 | Alaska | 1,129 |
| 42 | Arkansas | 1,031 |
| 43 | Delaware | 984 |
| 44 | Maine | 829 |
| 45 | Mississippi | 815 |
| 46 | West Virginia | 663 |
| 47 | Vermont | 658 |
| 48 | North Dakota | 635 |
| 49 | South Dakota | 570 |
| 50 | Montana | 447 |
| 51 | Wyoming | 217 |

Data Source: U.S. Department of Commerce, *Statistical Abstract of the United States 1996*

## NET DOMESTIC MIGRATION 1990-1995: STATE RANKINGS

New York ranked fiftieth out of 51 in terms of the state's net domestic migration between 1990 and 1995. Only California fared worse.

**Net Domestic Migration 1990 to 1995 (in thousands)**

| Rank | State | Net Migration |
|---|---|---|
| 1 | Florida | 672 |
| 2 | Georgia | 357 |
| 3 | Texas | 321 |
| 4 | Arizona | 293 |
| 5 | North Carolina | 283 |
| 6 | Washington | 277 |
| 7 | Colorado | 245 |
| 8 | Nevada | 240 |
| 9 | Tennessee | 223 |
| 10 | Oregon | 187 |
| 11 | Idaho | 99 |
| 12 | Alabama | 84 |
| 13 | Arkansas | 79 |
| 14(t) | Wisconsin | 71 |
| 14(t) | Utah | 71 |
| 16 | Indiana | 66 |
| 17 | Kentucky | 63 |
| 18 | Virginia | 61 |
| 19 | New Mexico | 60 |
| 20 | Missouri | 57 |
| 21 | Minnesota | 53 |
| 22 | Montana | 46 |
| 23 | South Carolina | 35 |
| 24 | Oklahoma | 27 |
| 25 | Mississippi | 24 |
| 26(t) | West Virginia | 20 |
| 26(t) | Delaware | 20 |
| 28 | South Dakota | 8 |
| 29 | Wyoming | 6 |

*continued*

*continued*

| Rank | State | Net Migration |
|---|---|---|
| 30(t) | Nebraska | 3 |
| 30(t) | Vermont | 3 |
| 32 | Iowa | 1 |
| 33 | New Hampshire | -5 |
| 34 | Alaska | -7 |
| 35 | Kansas | -10 |
| 36 | Maryland | -14 |
| 37 | Maine | -15 |
| 38 | North Dakota | -18 |
| 39 | Hawaii | -38 |
| 40 | Rhode Island | -46 |
| 41 | Ohio | -52 |
| 42 | Louisiana | -68 |
| 43 | Pennsylvania | -75 |
| 44 | District of Columbia | -89 |
| 45 | Michigan | -139 |
| 46 | Connecticut | -149 |
| 47 | Massachusetts | -194 |
| 48 | New Jersey | -235 |
| 49 | Illinois | -298 |
| **50** | **New York** | **-1,053** |
| 51 | California | -1,548 |

Data Source: U.S. Department of Commerce, *Statistical Abstract of the United States 1996*

## POPULATION MAGNETS: STATE RANKINGS

New York ranked forty-eighth out of the 50 states in terms of the state's percentage of American-born residents who are natives of other states. Essentially, New York ranks poorly in terms of being a population magnet.

**Percentage of American-Born Residents Who Are Natives of Other States**

| Rank | State | Percent |
|---|---|---|
| 1 | Nevada | 76.1% |
| 2 | Florida | 65.1 |
| 3 | Alaska | 64.4 |
| 4 | Arizona | 63.0 |
| 5 | Wyoming | 56.6 |
| 6 | Colorado | 54.7 |
| 7 | New Hampshire | 54.2 |
| 8 | Oregon | 51.0 |
| 9 | Washington | 48.4 |
| 10 | Delaware | 48.1 |
| 11 | Idaho | 47.9 |
| 12 | Maryland | 46.7 |
| 13 | New Mexico | 45.4 |
| 14 | Virginia | 42.9 |
| 15 | Vermont | 41.0 |
| 16 | California | 40.8 |
| 17 | Montana | 40.0 |
| 18 | Connecticut | 37.7 |
| 19 | New Jersey | 37.4 |
| 20 | Kansas | 37.1 |
| 21 | Oklahoma | 35.2 |
| 22 | Hawaii | 34.2 |
| 23 | Georgia | 33.7 |
| 24 | Arkansas | 32.2 |
| 25 | South Carolina | 30.6 |
| 26 | Utah | 30.4 |

*continued*

*continued*

| Rank | State | Percent |
|---|---|---|
| 27(t) | Rhode Island | 30.0 |
| 27(t) | Tennessee | 30.0 |
| 29 | Maine | 29.4 |
| 30 | Missouri | 29.2 |
| 31 | South Dakota | 29.0 |
| 32 | Texas | 28.9 |
| 33 | Nebraska | 28.6 |
| 34 | North Carolina | 28.3 |
| 35 | Indiana | 27.7 |
| 36 | North Dakota | 25.7 |
| 37 | Illinois | 24.6 |
| 38 | Minnesota | 24.4 |
| 39 | Ohio | 24.1 |
| 40 | Massachusetts | 24.0 |
| 41 | Alabama | 23.3 |
| 42 | Michigan | 22.2 |
| 43 | Mississippi | 22.1 |
| 44 | West Virginia | 22.0 |
| 45 | Kentucky | 21.9 |
| 46 | Wisconsin | 21.6 |
| 47 | Iowa | 21.2 |
| **48** | **New York** | **19.8** |
| 49 | Louisiana | 19.4 |
| 50 | Pennsylvania | 17.2 |

Data Source: G. Scott Thomas; *The Rating Guide to Life in America's Fifty States*, Prometheus Books, Amherst, N.Y., 1994.

## UNION MEMBERSHIP: STATE RANKINGS

In 1995, New York ranked the very highest among the 50 states and District of Columbia in terms of the percentage of workers that are union members.

**Percentage of Workers Union Members**

| Rank | State | Percent |
|---|---|---|
| **1** | **New York** | **27.7%** |
| 2 | Hawaii | 24.6 |
| 3 | Michigan | 23.7 |
| 4 | Alaska | 23.1 |
| 5 | New Jersey | 21.9 |
| 6 | Washington | 21.0 |
| 7 | Minnesota | 20.3 |
| 8(t) | Connecticut | 20.2 |
| 8(t) | Illinois | 20.2 |
| 8(t) | Nevada | 20.2 |
| 11 | Oregon | 20.1 |
| 12 | Rhode Island | 19.4 |
| 13 | Pennsylvania | 18.9 |
| 14 | Ohio | 18.5 |
| 15(t) | Wisconsin | 17.7 |
| 15(t) | California | 17.7 |
| 17 | Indiana | 16.5 |
| 18 | West Virginia | 16.3 |
| 19 | Massachusetts | 16.2 |
| 20 | Montana | 15.8 |
| 21 | Maine | 15.6 |
| 22 | District of Columbia | 15.1 |
| 23 | Maryland | 14.9 |
| 24 | Missouri | 14.6 |
| 25 | Alabama | 13.6 |
| 26 | Delaware | 13.0 |
| 27(t) | Kentucky | 12.6 |
| 27(t) | New Hampshire | 12.6 |

*continued*

*continued*

| Rank | State | Percent |
|---|---|---|
| 29 | Iowa | 12.1 |
| 30 | Wyoming | 11.2 |
| 31 | Kansas | 10.2 |
| 32 | North Dakota | 10.0 |
| 33 | Colorado | 9.9 |
| 34 | Tennessee | 9.5 |
| 35 | New Mexico | 9.4 |
| 36(t) | Oklahoma | 9.3 |
| 36(t) | Vermont | 9.3 |
| 38 | Nebraska | 9.1 |
| 39 | Utah | 9.0 |
| 40 | Idaho | 8.1 |
| 41 | Arizona | 8.0 |
| 42 | Arkansas | 7.8 |
| 43 | South Dakota | 7.7 |
| 44 | Florida | 7.3 |
| 45 | Louisiana | 7.0 |
| 46 | Georgia | 6.8 |
| 47 | Virginia | 6.7 |
| 48 | Texas | 6.5 |
| 49 | Mississippi | 5.2 |
| 50 | North Carolina | 4.2 |
| 51 | South Carolina | 3.3 |
| | U.S. Average | 14.9 |

Data Source: U.S. Department of Commerce, *Statistical Abstract of the United States 1996*

## UNION MEMBERSHIP: NEW YORK VS. US

In 1995, New York's percentage of workers that are union members surpassed the U.S. percent by 85.9 percent—27.7 percent in New York versus 14.9 percent across the nation. Between 1983 and 1995, union membership declined as a share of the New York workforce from 32.5 percent to 27.7 percent, compared with a national drop from 20.1 percent to 14.9 percent.

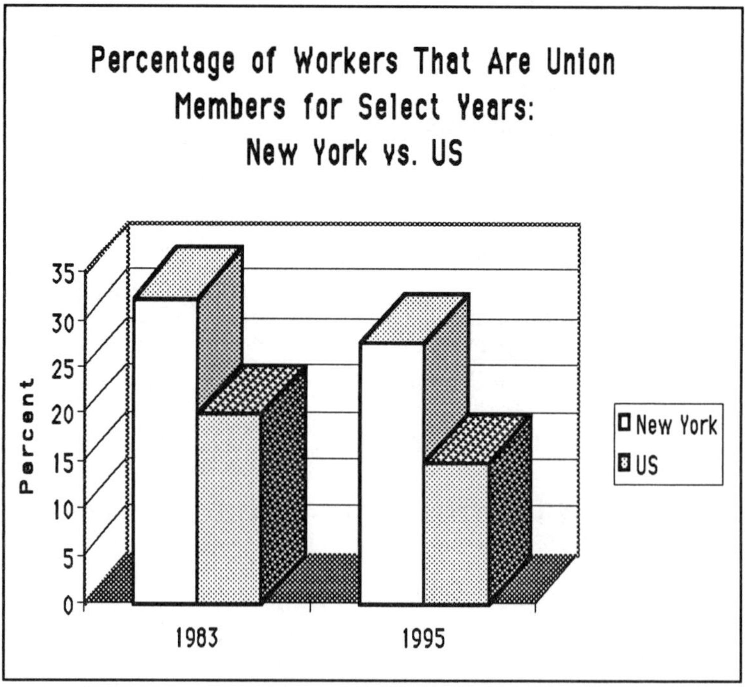


Data Source: U.S. Department of Commerce, *Statistical Abstract of the United States 1996*

# Part Two: New York City

## CHAPTER SEVEN

# NEW YORK CITY: FISCAL ISSUES

- Taxation
- Government Expenditures
- Debt
- Government Employment

## CITY TOTAL REVENUES: CITY RANKINGS

New York City ranked highest among the largest cities (500,000+ population) in the nation in terms of per capita city total revenues in 1994.

**Per Capita City Total Revenues**

| Rank | City | Per Capita Total Revenues |
|---|---|---|
| 1 | **New York City** | **$6,144.73** |
| 2 | San Francisco | 5,138.14 |
| 3 | Boston | 3,711.71 |
| 4 | Memphis | 3,448.16 |
| 5 | Baltimore | 2,940.52 |
| 6 | Philadelphia | 2,562.59 |
| 7 | Jacksonville | 2,527.64 |
| 8 | Seattle | 2,435.42 |
| 9 | Los Angeles | 2,139.55 |
| 10 | Detroit | 2,112.72 |
| 11 | San Antonio | 1,736.22 |
| 12 | Cleveland | 1,584.35 |
| 13 | Chicago | 1,583.71 |
| 14 | Dallas | 1,528.18 |
| 15 | Milwaukee | 1,450.99 |
| 16 | Indianapolis | 1,430.50 |
| 17 | Honolulu | 1,290.41 |
| 18 | San Diego | 1,285.11 |
| 19 | Phoenix | 1,263.59 |
| 20 | Houston | 1,196.57 |
| 21 | San Jose | 1,105.38 |
| 22 | Columbus | 1,094.71 |
| 23 | El Paso | 947.32 |
| | Large City Average | 2,946.39 |

Note: See Part One of this book for District of Columbia.

Data Source: U.S. Department of Commerce

## CITY TOTAL REVENUES: NEW YORK CITY VS. LARGE CITY AVERAGE

In 1994, New York City's per capita city total revenues topped the large city (500,000+ population) average by 108.6 percent—$6,144.73 in New York City versus a large city average of $2,946.39.

Between 1965 and 1994, real per capita New York City total revenues jumped by 141.2 percent. In real 1994 dollars, the city's 1965 total revenues equaled $2,547.93.

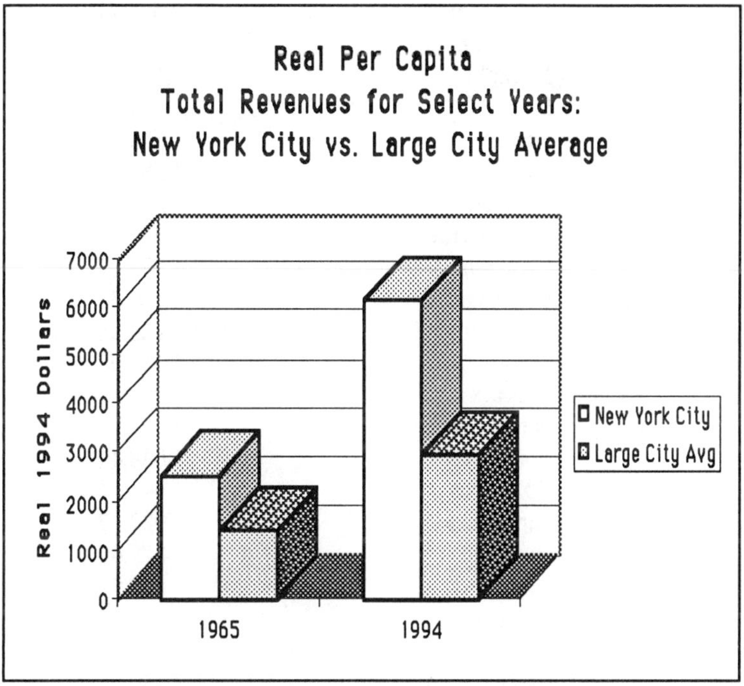


Data Source: U.S. Department of Commerce

## CITY GENERAL REVENUES: CITY RANKINGS

New York City ranked highest among the largest cities (500,000+ population) in the nation in terms of per capita city general revenues in 1994.

**Per Capita City General Revenues**

| Rank | City | Per Capita General Revenues |
|---|---|---|
| 1 | **New York City** | **$5,401.61** |
| 2 | San Francisco | 4,064.14 |
| 3 | Boston | 3,269.09 |
| 4 | Baltimore | 2,554.71 |
| 5 | Philadelphia | 2,025.95 |
| 6 | Memphis | 1,634.62 |
| 7 | Detroit | 1,604.58 |
| 8 | Seattle | 1,570.20 |
| 9 | Indianapolis | 1,386.70 |
| 10 | Chicago | 1,241.35 |
| 11 | Jacksonville | 1,218.95 |
| 12 | Cleveland | 1,178.07 |
| 13 | Los Angeles | 1,168.33 |
| 14 | Honolulu | 1,163.36 |
| 15 | Dallas | 1,119.98 |
| 16 | Phoenix | 1,093.20 |
| 17 | San Diego | 1,052.90 |
| 18 | Milwaukee | 1,038.49 |
| 19 | Columbus | 941.11 |
| 20 | San Jose | 927.47 |
| 21 | Houston | 879.40 |
| 22 | Seattle | 692.34 |
| 23 | El Paso | 572.67 |
| | Large City Average | 2,440.50 |

Note: See Part One of this book for District of Columbia.

Data Source: U.S. Department of Commerce

## CITY GENERAL REVENUES: NEW YORK CITY VS. LARGE CITY AVERAGE

In 1994, New York City's per capita city general revenues exceeded the large city average by 121.3 percent—$5,401.61 in New York City versus a large city (500,000+ population) average of $2,440.50.

Between 1965 and 1994, real per capita city revenues grew by 150.5 percent in New York City. In 1994 dollars, New York City's 1965 per capita general revenues registered $2,156.05.

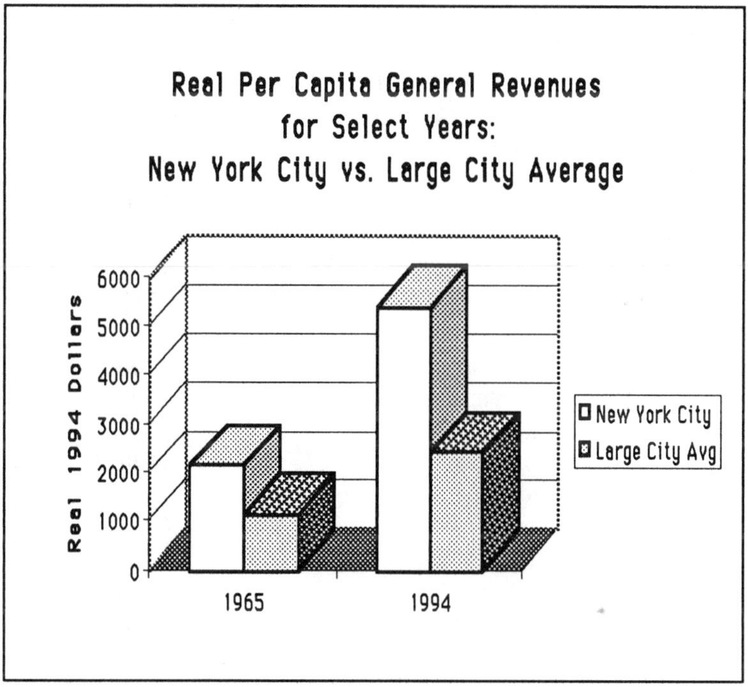


Data Source: U.S. Department of Commerce

# CITY REVENUES FROM THE FEDERAL GOVERNMENT: CITY RANKINGS

New York City ranked highest among the largest cities (500,000+ population) in the nation in terms of per capita city revenues from the federal government in 1994.

**Per Capita City Revenues from the Federal Government**

| Rank | City | Per Capita Revenues |
|---|---|---|
| 1 | **New York City** | **$201.99** |
| 2 | San Francisco | 187.73 |
| 3 | Detroit | 149.07 |
| 4 | Cleveland | 144.50 |
| 5 | Philadelphia | 138.00 |
| 6 | Jacksonville | 105.66 |
| 7 | Boston | 101.76 |
| 8 | Honolulu | 97.65 |
| 9 | Milwaukee | 96.91 |
| 10 | San Diego | 96.68 |
| 11 | Phoenix | 95.69 |
| 12 | Los Angeles | 89.48 |
| 13 | Chicago | 87.54 |
| 14 | Baltimore | 79.30 |
| 15 | Indianapolis | 69.42 |
| 16 | Dallas | 55.06 |
| 17 | Columbus | 53.14 |
| 18 | Memphis | 50.48 |
| 19 | Seattle | 49.58 |
| 20 | Houston | 39.08 |
| 21 | El Paso | 32.46 |
| 22 | San Antonio | 25.42 |
| 23 | San Jose | 18.15 |
| | Large City Average | 115.35 |

Note: See Part One of this book for District of Columbia.

Data Source: U.S. Department of Commerce

## CITY REVENUES FROM THE FEDERAL GOVERNMENT: NEW YORK CITY VS. LARGE CITY AVERAGE

In 1994, New York City's per capita city revenues from the federal government surpassed the large city (500,000+ population) average by 75.1 percent—$201.99 in New York City versus the large city average of $115.35.

Between 1965 and 1994, real per capita New York City revenues from the federal government increased by 647.0 percent. In 1994 dollars, New York City's 1965 per capita revenues from the federal government equaled $27.04.

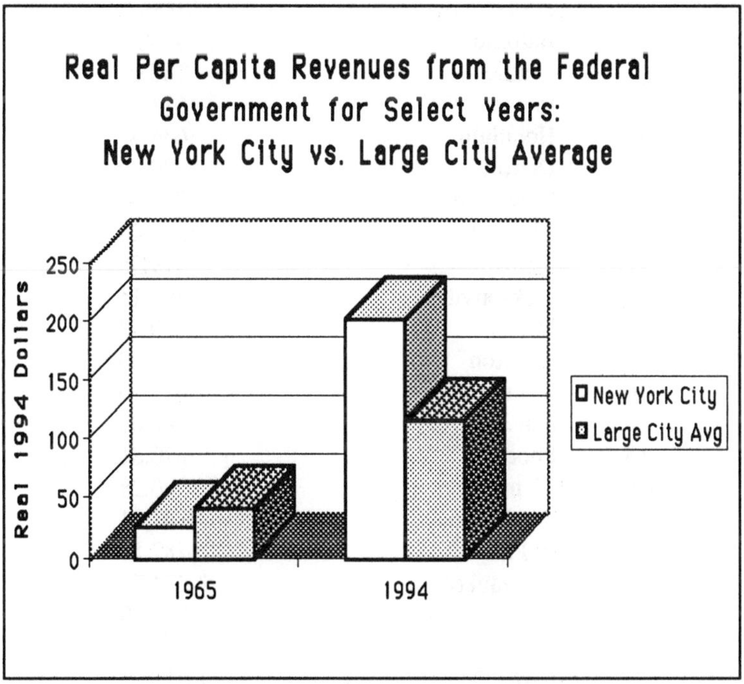


Data Source: U.S. Department of Commerce

## CITY TOTAL TAXES: CITY RANKINGS

New York City ranked the very highest among the largest cities (500,000+ population) in the nation in terms of per capita city total taxes in 1994.

**Per Capita City Total Taxes**

| Rank | City | Per Capita Total Taxes |
|---|---|---|
| **1** | **New York City** | **$2,474.00** |
| 2 | San Francisco | 1,296.09 |
| 3 | Boston | 1,270.32 |
| 4 | Philadelphia | 1,006.79 |
| 5 | Baltimore | 960.54 |
| 6 | Seattle | 780.07 |
| 7 | Indianapolis | 671.22 |
| 8 | Honolulu | 634.39 |
| 9 | Detroit | 580.79 |
| 10 | Cleveland | 572.93 |
| 11 | Chicago | 564.44 |
| 12 | Los Angeles | 519.55 |
| 13 | Jacksonville | 492.13 |
| 14 | Dallas | 490.47 |
| 15 | Houston | 470.90 |
| 16 | Columbus | 459.19 |
| 17 | San Jose | 440.05 |
| 18 | Phoenix | 370.81 |
| 19 | Memphis | 360.28 |
| 20 | San Diego | 347.21 |
| 21 | El Paso | 287.58 |
| 22 | Milwaukee | 274.71 |
| 23 | San Antonio | 262.59 |
| | Large City Average | 1,034.93 |

Note: See Part One of this book for District of Columbia.

Data Source: U.S. Department of Commerce

## CITY TOTAL TAXES: NEW YORK CITY VS. LARGE CITY AVERAGE

In 1994, New York City's per capita total taxes exceeded the large city (500,000+ population) average by 139.0 percent—$2,474.00 in New York City versus the large city average of $1,034.93.

Between 1965 and 1994, New York City's real per capita total taxes leaped by 84.3 percent. In 1994 dollars, New York City's 1965 per capita total taxes equaled $1,342.39.

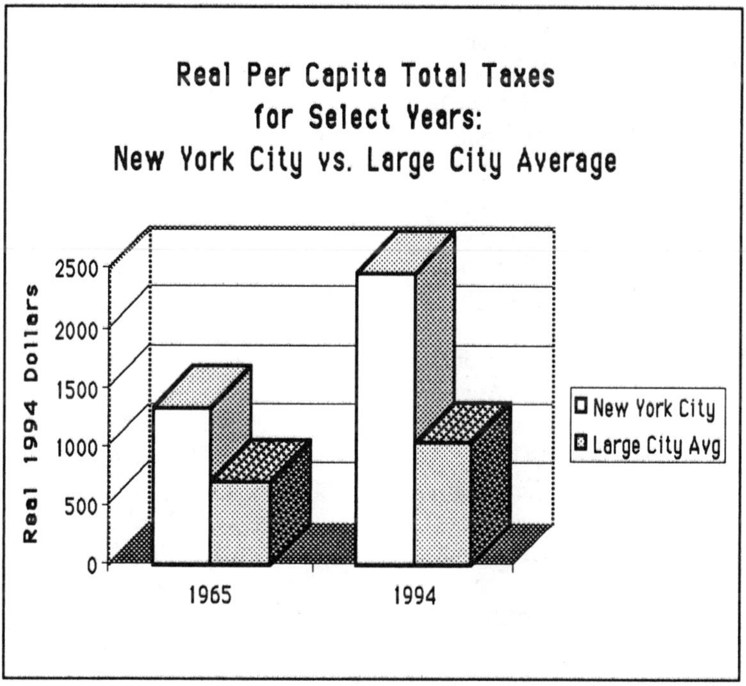


Data Source: U.S. Department of Commerce

## CITY PROPERTY TAXES: CITY RANKINGS

New York City ranked the second highest among the largest cities (500,000+ population) in the nation in terms of per capita city property taxes in 1994.

**Per Capita City Property Taxes**

| Rank | City | Per Capita Property Taxes |
|---|---|---|
| 1 | Boston | $1,186.49 |
| **2** | **New York City** | **1,076.39** |
| 3 | Baltimore | 665.88 |
| 4 | San Francisco | 650.18 |
| 5 | Indianapolis | 553.33 |
| 6 | Honolulu | 511.29 |
| 7 | Jacksonville | 313.20 |
| 8 | Memphis | 292.96 |
| 9 | Dallas | 278.68 |
| 10 | Seattle | 263.23 |
| 11 | Milwaukee | 255.41 |
| 12 | Houston | 241.36 |
| 13 | Chicago | 225.52 |
| 14 | Detroit | 223.75 |
| 15 | Philadelphia | 220.99 |
| 16 | Los Angeles | 183.90 |
| 17 | San Jose | 154.85 |
| 18 | El Paso | 150.44 |
| 19 | San Diego | 120.21 |
| 20 | Phoenix | 116.04 |
| 21 | Cleveland | 101.35 |
| 22 | San Antonio | 77.67 |
| 23 | Columbus | 37.23 |
| | Large City Average | 466.07 |

Note: See Part One of this book for District of Columbia.

Data Source: U.S. Department of Commerce

## CITY PROPERTY TAXES: NEW YORK CITY VS. LARGE CITY AVERAGE

In 1994, New York City's per capita surpassed the large city (500,000+ population) by 130.9 percent—$1,076.39 in New York City versus the large city average of $466.07.

Between 1965 and 1994, New York City's real per capita property taxes jumped by 35 percent. In 1994 dollars, New York City's 1965 per capita property taxes totaled $797.56.

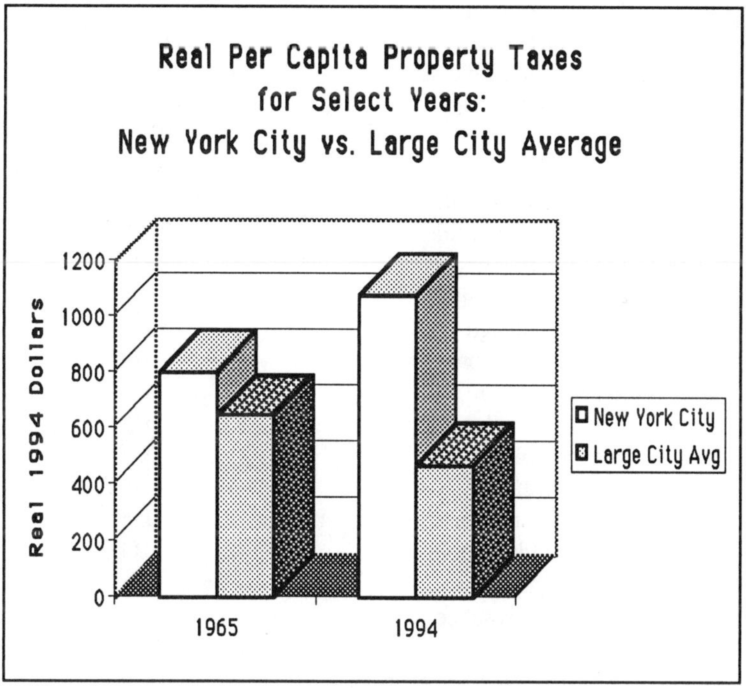


Data Source: U.S. Department of Commerce

## CITY GENERAL SALES TAXES: CITY RANKINGS

New York City ranked highest among the largest cities (500,000+ population) in the nation in terms of per capita city general sales taxes in 1994.

### Per Capita City General Sales Taxes

| Rank | City | Per Capita Sales Taxes |
|---|---|---|
| **1** | **New York City** | **$342.40** |
| 2 | Seattle | 166.90 |
| 3 | Phoenix | 152.87 |
| 4 | Houston | 133.94 |
| 5 | Dallas | 117.44 |
| 6 | San Francisco | 116.20 |
| 7 | San Diego | 109.92 |
| 8 | San Jose | 100.65 |
| 9 | El Paso | 100.60 |
| 10 | San Antonio | 83.52 |
| 11 | Jacksonville | 80.00 |
| 12 | Los Angeles | 73.84 |
| 13 | Philadelphia | 53.89 |
| 14 | Chicago | 50.65 |
| 15(t) | Baltimore | 0.00 |
| 15(t) | Boston | 0.00 |
| 15(t) | Cleveland | 0.00 |
| 15(t) | Columbus | 0.00 |
| 15(t) | Detroit | 0.00 |
| 15(t) | Honolulu | 0.00 |
| 15(t) | Indianapolis | 0.00 |
| 15(t) | Memphis | 0.00 |
| 15(t) | Milwaukee | 0.00 |
| | Large City Average | 132.75 |

Note: See Part One of this book for District of Columbia.

Data Source: U.S. Department of Commerce

## CITY GENERAL SALES TAXES: NEW YORK CITY VS. LARGE CITY AVERAGE

In 1994, New York City's per capita sales taxes topped the large city (500,000+ population) average by 157.9 percent—$342.40 in New York City versus the large city average of $132.75.

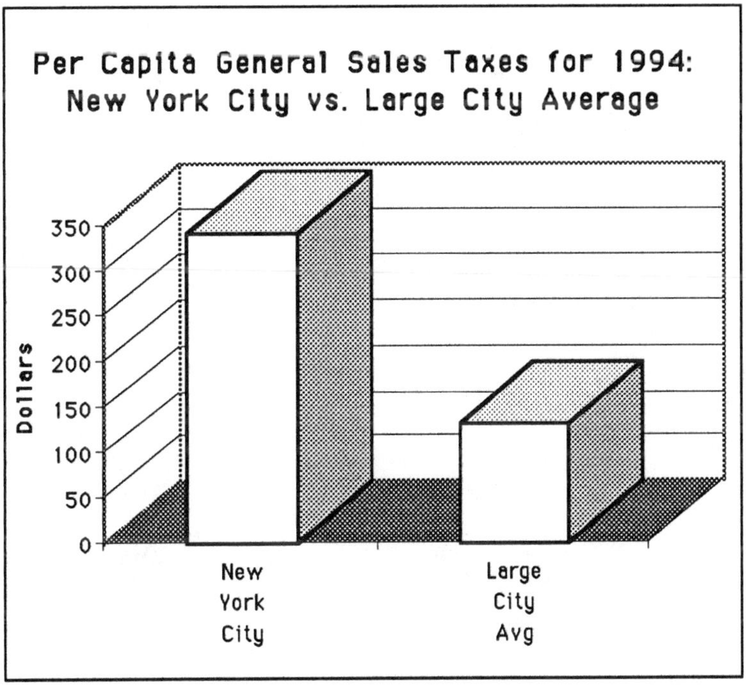


Data Source: U.S. Department of Commerce

## CITY INCOME TAXES: CITY RANKINGS

New York City ranked highest among the largest cities (500,000+ population) in the nation in terms of per capita city income taxes in 1994.

**Per Capita City Income Taxes**

| Rank | City | Per Capita Income Taxes |
|---|---|---|
| **1** | **New York City** | **$830.03** |
| 2 | Philadelphia | 529.11 |
| 3 | Cleveland | 434.54 |
| 4 | Columbus | 384.99 |
| 5 | Detroit | 289.84 |
| 6 | Baltimore | 173.36 |
| 7 | Indianapolis | 72.12 |
| 8(t) | Boston | 0.00 |
| 8(t) | Chicago | 0.00 |
| 8(t) | Dallas | 0.00 |
| 8(t) | El Paso | 0.00 |
| 8(t) | Honolulu | 0.00 |
| 8(t) | Houston | 0.00 |
| 8(t) | Jacksonville | 0.00 |
| 8(t) | Los Angeles | 0.00 |
| 8(t) | Memphis | 0.00 |
| 8(t) | Milwaukee | 0.00 |
| 8(t) | Phoenix | 0.00 |
| 8(t) | San Antonio | 0.00 |
| 8(t) | San Diego | 0.00 |
| 8(t) | San Francisco | 0.00 |
| 8(t) | San Jose | 0.00 |
| 8(t) | Seattle | 0.00 |
| | Large City Average | 257.07 |

Note: See Part One of this book for District of Columbia.

Data Source: U.S. Department of Commerce

## CITY INCOME TAXES: NEW YORK CITY VS. LARGE CITY AVERAGE

In 1994, New York City's per capita income taxes exceeded the large city (500,000+ population) average by 222.9 percent—$830.03 in New York City versus the large city average of $257.07. However, when you extract the New York City numbers from the large city average, the average falls to $76.11. The Big Apple's per capita city income taxes then top the large city average by an astounding 990.6 percent.

In fiscal year 1964-65, New York City did not levy an income tax. It was passed in 1966 and imposed in the 1966-67 fiscal year.

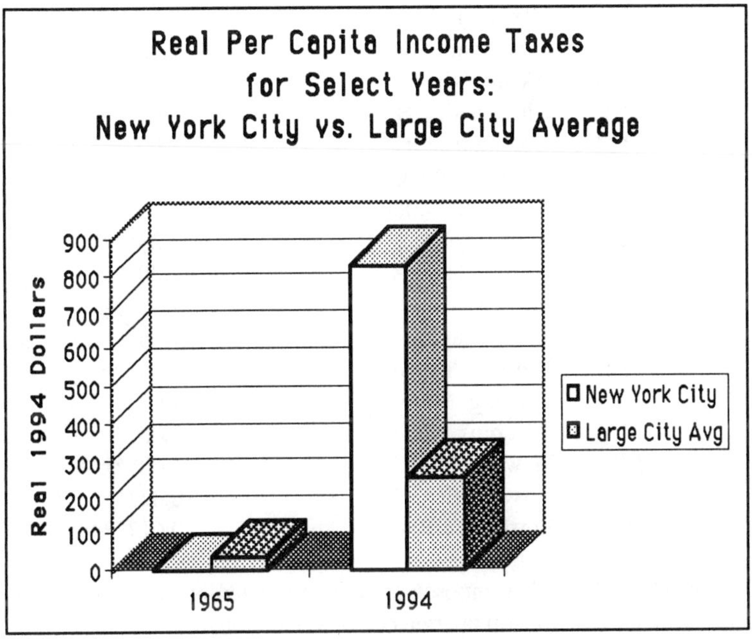


Data Source: U.S. Department of Commerce

## CITY INDIVIDUAL INCOME TAX RATES: CITY RANKINGS

In 1996, New York City claimed the highest tax rate among cities with 125,000+ population that levy their own individual income tax.

**City Individual Income Tax Rates (125,000+ population)**

| Rank | City | Top Tax Rate |
|---|---|---|
| **1** | **New York City** | **4.46%*** |
| 2 | Philadelphia, PA | 3.46** |
| 3 | Detroit, MI | 3.00 |
| 4 | Pittsburgh, PA | 2.875 |
| 5 | Baltimore, MD | 2.50 |
| 6(t) | Dayton, OH | 2.25 |
| 6(t) | Lexington, KY | 2.25 |
| 6(t) | Toledo, OH | 2.25 |
| 9 | Louisville, KY | 2.20 |
| 10 | Cincinnati, OH | 2.10 |
| 11(t) | Akron, OH | 2.00 |
| 11(t) | Cleveland, OH | 2.00 |
| 11(t) | Columbus, OH | 2.00 |
| 11(t) | Youngstown, OH | 2.00 |
| 15 | San Francisco, CA | 1.50*** |
| 16 | Yonkers, NY | 1.03**** |
| 17(t) | Birmingham, AL | 1.00 |
| 17(t) | Flint, MI | 1.00 |
| 17(t) | Grand Rapids, MI | 1.00 |
| 17(t) | Kansas City, MO | 1.00 |
| 17(t) | Lansing, MI | 1.00 |
| 17(t) | St. Louis, MO | 1.00 |
| 17(t) | Newark, NJ | 1.00***** |
| 24 | Los Angeles, CA | 0.825****** |
| 25 | Portland, OR | 0.6179******* |

* New York City also imposes an unincorporated business tax rate of 4%, which raises the top tax rate on some individuals to 8.46%.
** City income tax of 3.46%. Nonresidents pay a city income tax of 4.3125% and the Philadelphia School District levies a 4.96% tax on residents investment net income and other nonbusiness income.

Therefore, the top city and school district income tax rate equals 8.42%.
*** Payroll expense tax on employers.
**** A 15% surcharge on net state tax (using top rate of 6.85% due to be imposed in 1997, December 1995 rate equaled 7.59375%). An additional 0.5% rate is levied on wages and net earnings from self-employment—raising the combined top city income tax rate for some individuals to 1.53%.
***** Payroll tax on employers having a payroll over $2,500 per quarter.
****** Payroll expense tax of $33 per year of the first $4,000 payroll expense plus $8.25 for each additional $1,000 of payroll expense.
******* Transit district payroll tax on wages paid by employers.

Data Sources: CCH Incorporated, *State Tax Handbook December 1995* and New York City budget documents

## DEVELOPMENT OF NEW YORK CITY'S PERSONAL INCOME TAX

New York City Mayor John Lindsay imposed a city personal income tax in 1966 at a rate of 2 percent. The rate jumped to 3.5 percent in 1975, to 4.3 percent in 1976, to 4.52 percent in 1982, and hit its peak in 1983 at 4.73 percent. The city rate meandered down to 3.4 percent by 1989, but then rose again to 3.91 percent in 1990 and to 4.46 percent in 1991.

The combined state and city top income tax rate hit an economy-crushing 19.68 percent in 1976. In 1995, it stood at a still onerous rate of 12.05 percent. When state tax cuts currently scheduled to go into effect actually do so, the top combined state and city personal income tax rate in New York City will fall to 11.31 percent by 1997—an improvement but still far too burdensome.

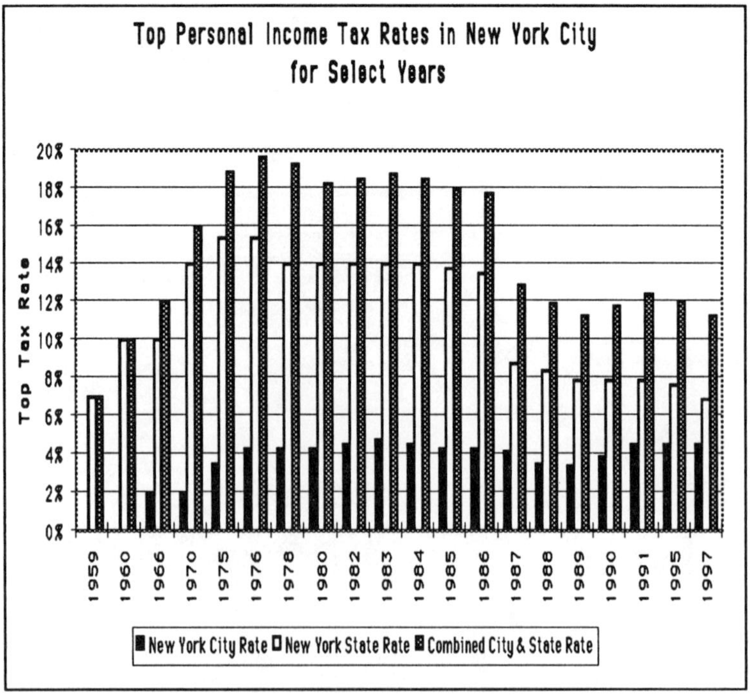


Data Source: New York City budget documents

## CITY CORPORATE INCOME TAX RATES: CITY RANKINGS

In 1996, New York City claimed the highest tax rate among cities with 125,000+ population that imposed their own corporate income taxes.

**City Corporate Income Tax Rates (125,000+ population)**

| Rank | City | Top Tax Rate |
|---|---|---|
| **1** | **New York City** | **10.38%*** |
| 2 | Portland, OR | 3.65 |
| 3(t) | Dayton, OH | 2.25 |
| 3(t) | Lexington, KY | 2.25 |
| 3(t) | Toledo, OH | 2.25 |
| 6 | Louisville, KY | 2.20 |
| 7 | Cincinnati, OH | 2.10 |
| 8(t) | Akron, OH | 2.00 |
| 8(t) | Cleveland, OH | 2.00 |
| 8(t) | Columbus, OH | 2.00 |
| 8(t) | Detroit, MI | 2.00 |
| 8(t) | Youngstown, OH | 2.00 |
| 13(t) | Flint, MI | 1.00 |
| 13(t) | Grand Rapids, MI | 1.00 |
| 13(t) | Kansas City, MO | 1.00 |
| 13(t) | Lansing, MI | 1.00 |
| 13(t) | St, Louis, MO | 1.00 |

* City corporate income tax rate of 8.85% plus a 17% transit surcharge on the state's corporate income tax (9% state rate as of mid-1996) for firms in the New York City area.

Data Sources: CCH Incorporated, *State Tax Handbook December 1995* and New York City budget documents

# DEVELOPMENT OF NEW YORK CITY'S BUSINESS INCOME TAXES

New York City Mayor John Lindsay imposed a city corporate income tax of 5.5 percent in 1966 as well as an unincorporated business income tax of 4 percent on top of the city's new personal income tax. New York City's combined state and city top tax rate on unincorporated business income reached a high of 29.18 percent in 1976. The combined state and city corporate tax rate reached a high of 22.05 percent the same year.

By 1995, the top rate on unincorporated business income stood at 16.05 percent and the top rate on corporate income was 19.91 percent. By 1997, scheduled state tax rate reductions would lower the top rate on unincorporated business income to 15.31 percent and the top corporate rate to 19.38 percent. If the state's 17 percent transit district surcharge actually was allowed to expire on schedule in 1997, the combined corporate rate would fall further to 17.85 percent. However, chances remain slim that the transit district surcharge will be allowed to expire. It has been extended numerous times since being imposed in December 1982.

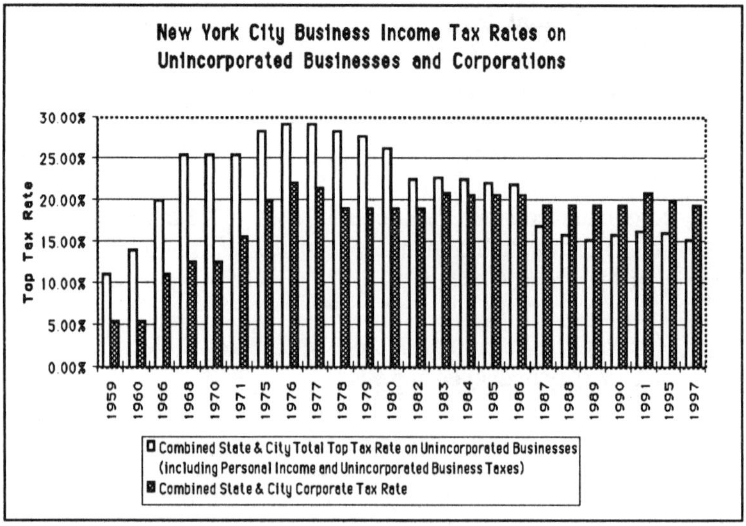


Data Source: New York City budgets documents

## NEW YORK CITY CAPITAL GAINS TAXES AND INFLATION

New York City taxes individual capital gains at the same 4.46 percent rate as general income. However, gains are not adjusted for inflation, therefore the *real* capital gains tax rate ranges much higher. As can be seen in the following chart, tax rates can jump considerably. Indeed, capital gains taxes can be paid even on real capital losses.

However, many entrepreneurs fall prey to the city's unincorporated business tax, which boosts their top tax rate to 8.46 percent. Likewise, their real capital gains tax rate jumps as well.

**New York City Real Capital Gains Tax Rates at Various Investment Returns and Rates of Inflation**

| One-Year Rate of Return | Inflation Rate | Nominal Capital Gains Tax Rate | Real Capital Gains Tax Rate |
|---|---|---|---|
| 6% | 3% | 4.46% | 8.9% |
| 6% | 4% | 4.46% | 13.4% |
| 6% | 5% | 4.46% | 26.8% |
| 8% | 3% | 4.46% | 7.1% |
| 8% | 4% | 4.46% | 8.9% |
| 8% | 5% | 4.46% | 11.9% |
| 10% | 3% | 4.46% | 6.4% |
| 10% | 4% | 4.46% | 7.4% |
| 10% | 5% | 4.46% | 8.9% |

Source: Author's calculations

**New York City Real Capital Gains Tax Rates—Including the Unincorporated Business Tax—at Various Investment Returns and Rates of Inflation**

| One-Year Rate of Return | Inflation Rate | Nominal Capital Gains Tax Rate | Real Capital Gains Tax Rate |
|---|---|---|---|
| 6% | 3% | 8.46% | 16.9% |
| 6% | 4% | 8.46% | 25.4% |
| 6% | 5% | 8.46% | 50.8% |
| 8% | 3% | 8.46% | 13.5% |
| 8% | 4% | 8.46% | 16.9% |
| 8% | 5% | 8.46% | 22.6% |
| 10% | 3% | 8.46% | 12.1% |
| 10% | 4% | 8.46% | 14.1% |
| 10% | 5% | 8.46% | 16.9% |

Source: Author's calculations

## New York City Taxes

In addition to a host of minor taxes and fees, New York City imposes the following major taxes:

- Top personal income and capital gains tax rate of 4.46 percent.

- General corporate income tax rate of 8.85 percent.

- Banking corporate income tax rate of 9 percent.

- Unincorporated business income tax rate of 4 percent, in addition to the personal income tax.

- Property tax of various rates based on assessed values.

- Sales tax of 4.25 percent.

- Commercial rent tax of 6 percent.

- Mortgage recording tax with a top rate of 1.75 percent.

- Real property transfer tax with a top rate of 2.625 percent.

- Subsidiary capital corporation tax rate of 0.075 percent.

- Utility tax of 2.35 percent of gross earnings.

- Hotel tax of 5 percent.

- Passenger motor vehicle tax of $15 per vehicle.

- Commercial motor vehicle tax applied at various rates, including $1,000 per year for medallion taxicabs and $400 per year for livery cabs and omnibuses.

- Taxicab license transfer tax of 5 percent on consideration paid.

• Beer and liquor taxes of 12 cents per gallon of beer and 26.4 cents per liter of liquor with alcohol content greater than 24 percent.

• Cigarette tax of 8 cents per pack of 20 cigarettes.

• Liquor license surcharge of 25 percent of the state license fees.

• Coin operated amusement devices tax of $175 per device.

• Horse race admissions tax of 3 percent of the price of admission.

• OTB surcharge on most bets placed at New York City OTB offices and most bets statewide on races held in New York City.

• Vault charge of $2 per foot on any sub-surface opening or structure extending from the building line into the street.

• City income tax applies to nonresident city employees.

And remember, all of New York City's taxes are levied *in addition to* New York's state-level taxes.

## CITY TOTAL EXPENDITURES: CITY RANKINGS

New York City ranked highest among the largest cities (500,000+ population) in the nation in terms of per capita city total expenditures in 1994.

### Per Capita City Total Expenditures

| Rank | City | Per Capita Total Expenditures |
|---|---|---|
| **1** | **New York City** | **$6,701.63** |
| 2 | San Francisco | 4,918.11 |
| 3 | Boston | 3,491.06 |
| 4 | Memphis | 3,139.91 |
| 5 | Philadelphia | 2,574.62 |
| 6 | Seattle | 2,558.52 |
| 7 | Jacksonville | 2,417.28 |
| 8 | Baltimore | 2,381.01 |
| 9 | Detroit | 2,045.90 |
| 10 | Los Angeles | 1,918.33 |
| 11 | Cleveland | 1,888.98 |
| 12 | Indianapolis | 1,762.47 |
| 13 | San Antonio | 1,744.41 |
| 14 | Honolulu | 1,572.96 |
| 15 | Chicago | 1,517.73 |
| 16 | Dallas | 1,504.76 |
| 17 | Phoenix | 1,320.43 |
| 18 | Milwaukee | 1,233.59 |
| 19 | Houston | 1,216.21 |
| 20 | San Diego | 1,200.82 |
| 21 | Columbus | 1,197.61 |
| 22 | San Jose | 1,056.18 |
| 23 | El Paso | 724.04 |
| | Large City Average | 3,033.19 |

Note: See Part One of this book for District of Columbia.

Data Source: U.S. Department of Commerce

## CITY TOTAL EXPENDITURES: NEW YORK CITY VS. LARGE CITY AVERAGE

In 1994, New York City's per capita total expenditures surpassed the large city (500,000+ population) average by 120.9 percent—$6,701.63 in New York City versus the large city mean of $3,033.19.

Between 1965 and 1994, New York City's real per capita total expenditures grew by 164.8 percent. In 1994 dollars, New York City's 1965 total expenditures equaled $2,530.42.

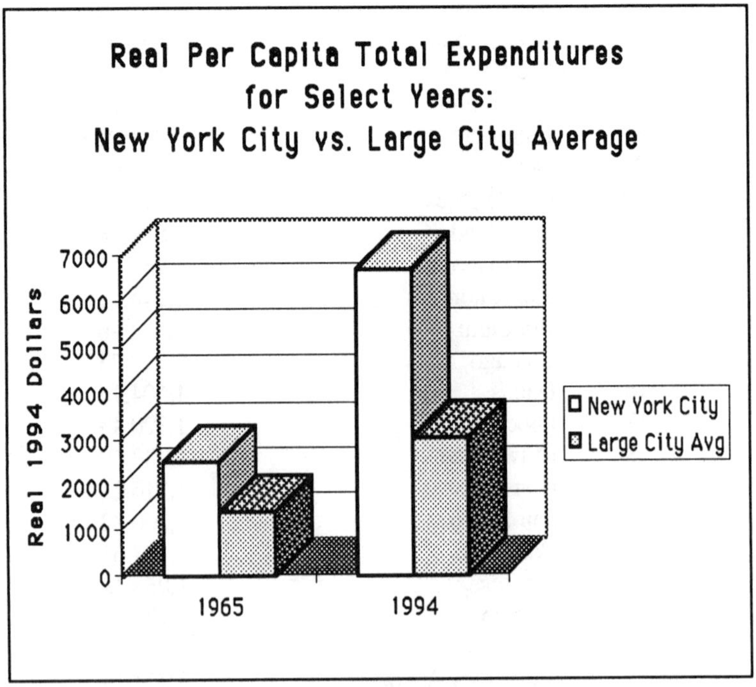


Data Source: U.S. Department of Commerce

## CITY GENERAL EXPENDITURES: CITY RANKINGS

New York City ranked highest among the largest cities (500,000+ population) in the nation in terms of per capita city general expenditures in 1994.

**Per Capita City General Expenditures**

| Rank | City | Per Capita General Expenditures |
|---|---|---|
| **1** | **New York City** | **$5,586.75** |
| 2 | San Francisco | 3,788.90 |
| 3 | Boston | 3,047.86 |
| 4 | Baltimore | 2,149.33 |
| 5 | Philadelphia | 1,903.43 |
| 6 | Indianapolis | 1,682.85 |
| 7 | Memphis | 1,616.15 |
| 8 | Chicago | 1,517.73 |
| 9 | Seattle | 1,507.35 |
| 10 | Detroit | 1,488.53 |
| 11 | Honolulu | 1,308.69 |
| 12 | Jacksonville | 1,307.70 |
| 13 | Cleveland | 1,278.46 |
| 14 | Dallas | 1,233.17 |
| 15 | Phoenix | 1,074.81 |
| 16 | Los Angeles | 1,054.97 |
| 17 | Milwaukee | 1,044.16 |
| 18 | Columbus | 1,006.77 |
| 19 | Houston | 1,004.69 |
| 20 | San Diego | 969.76 |
| 21 | San Jose | 956.31 |
| 22 | San Antonio | 789.70 |
| 23 | El Paso | 546.98 |
| | Large City Average | 2,376.49 |

Note: See Part One of this book for District of Columbia.

Data Source: U.S. Department of Commerce

## CITY GENERAL EXPENDITURES: NEW YORK CITY VS. LARGE CITY AVERAGE

In 1994, New York City's per capita general expenditures topped the large city (500,000+ population) average by 135.1 percent—$5,586.75 in New York City versus the large city average of $2,376.49.

Between 1965 and 1994, real per capita city general expenditures grew by 175.7 percent in New York City. In 1994 dollars, New York City's per capita general expenditures in 1965 registered $2,026.38.

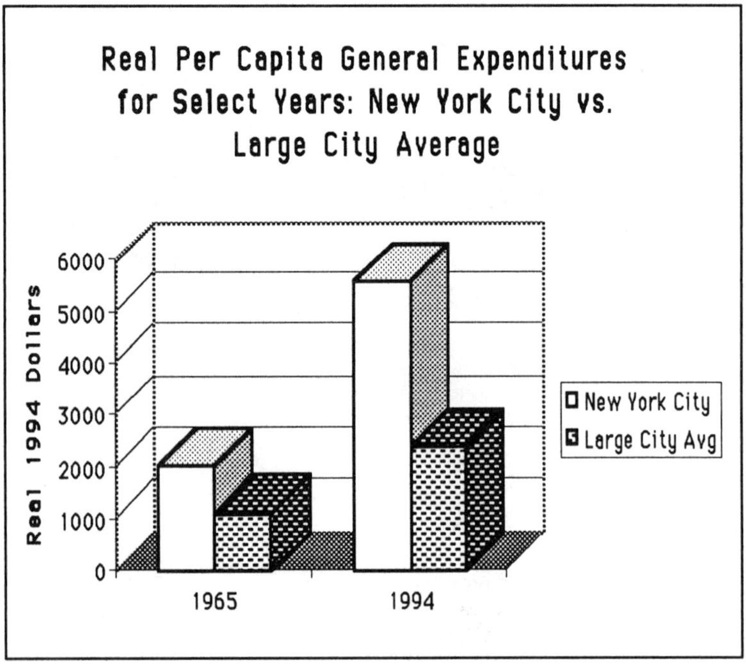


Data Source: U.S. Department of Commerce

## CITY PUBLIC WELFARE EXPENDITURES: CITY RANKINGS

New York City ranked highest among the largest cities (500,000+ population) in the nation in terms of per capita city public welfare expenditures in 1994. Indeed, New York City's per capita public welfare spending registered more than twice the amount of the number-two ranked city in the nation.

**Per Capita City Public Welfare Expenditures**

| Rank | City | Per Capita Welfare Expenditures |
|---|---|---|
| **1** | **New York City** | **$1,056.34** |
| 2 | San Francisco | 487.70 |
| 3 | Boston | 169.68 |
| 4 | Indianapolis | 118.57 |
| 5 | Chicago | 45.72 |
| 6 | San Antonio | 25.34 |
| 7 | Philadelphia | 23.72 |
| 8 | Jacksonville | 15.98 |
| 9 | Memphis | 15.59 |
| 10 | Columbus | 0.71 |
| 11 | Baltimore | 0.60 |
| 12 | El Paso | 0.05 |
| 13(t) | Cleveland | 0.04 |
| 13(t) | San Diego | 0.04 |
| 15(t) | Dallas | 0.00 |
| 15(t) | Detroit | 0.00 |
| 15(t) | Honolulu | 0.00 |
| 15(t) | Houston | 0.00 |
| 15(t) | Los Angeles | 0.00 |
| 15(t) | Milwaukee | 0.00 |
| 15(t) | Phoenix | 0.00 |
| 15(t) | San Jose | 0.00 |
| 15(t) | Seattle | 0.00 |
| | Large City Average | 285.00 |

Note: See Part One of this book for District of Columbia.
Data Source: U.S. Department of Commerce

## CITY PUBLIC WELFARE EXPENDITURES: NEW YORK CITY VS. LARGE CITY AVERAGE

In 1994, New York City's per capita public welfare spending exceeded the large city (500,000+ population) average by 270.6 percent—$1,056.34 in New York City versus the large city average of $285.00.

Between 1965 and 1994, New York City's real per capita public welfare expenditures jumped by 302.3 percent. In 1994 dollars, New York City's 1965 per capita public welfare spending stood at $262.58.

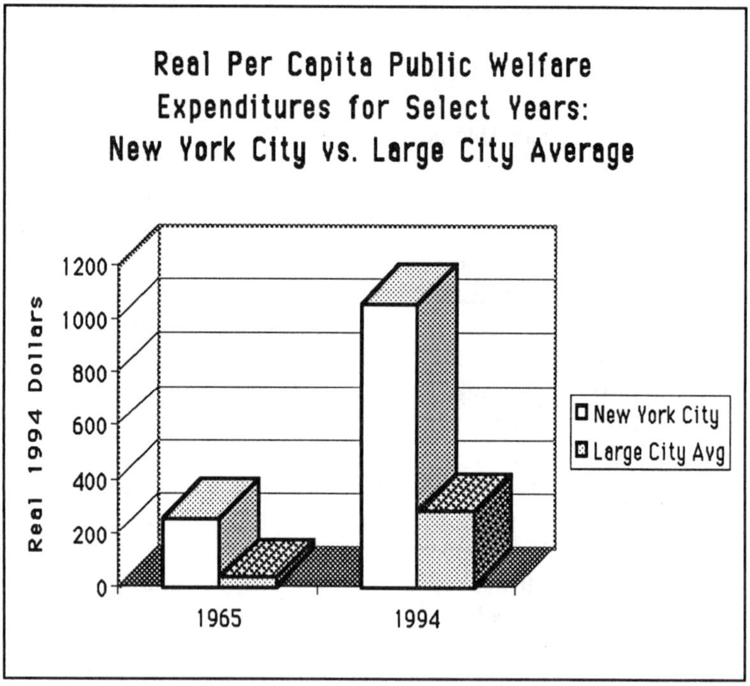


Data Source: U.S. Department of Commerce

## WAGE EQUIVALENT OF WELFARE: CITY RANKINGS

In a September 19, 1995, CATO Institute study ("The Work vs. Welfare Trade-Off: An Analysis of the Total Level of Welfare Benefits by State"), analysts Michael Tanner, Stephen Moore, and David Hartman calculated the pretax wage equivalent of total welfare benefits for each state and select cities. New York City ranked the very highest for the 16 cities analyzed. The full welfare package in New York City equals a pretax wage level of $30,700 annually, or $14.76 on an hourly basis (assuming a 2,080-hour work year).

**Wage Equivalent of Welfare**

| Rank | City | Pretax Wage Equivalent | Pretax Hourly Wage |
|---|---|---|---|
| 1 | **New York City** | **$30,700** | **$14.76** |
| 2 | Philadelphia, PA | 25,900 | 12.45 |
| 3 | Baltimore, MD | 23,600 | 11.35 |
| 4 | Detroit, MI | 22,700 | 10.91 |
| 5 | Indianapolis, IN | 21,100 | 10.14 |
| 6(t) | Akron, OH | 20,100 | 9.66 |
| 6(t) | Toledo, OH | 20,100 | 9.66 |
| 8(t) | Cleveland, OH | 20,000 | 9.62 |
| 8(t) | Pittsburgh, PA | 20,000 | 9.62 |
| 10(t) | Lexington, KY | 19,800 | 9.52 |
| 10(t) | Cincinnati, OH | 19,800 | 9.52 |
| 12 | Columbus, OH | 19,500 | 9.38 |
| 13 | Louisville, KY | 18,600 | 8.94 |
| 14 | Kansas City, MO | 17,700 | 8.51 |
| 15 | St. Louis, MO | 17,450 | 8.39 |
| 16 | Birmingham, AL | 15,300 | 7.36 |

Data Source: "The Work vs. Welfare Trade-Off: An Analysis of the Total Level of Welfare Benefits by State" by Michael Tanner, Stephen Moore, and David Hartman, CATO Institute, September 19, 1995

## INDIVIDUALS RECEIVING PUBLIC ASSISTANCE IN NEW YORK CITY

The following chart breaks down the number of persons receiving some kind of public assistance by program type in New York City during 1993.

**Individuals Receiving Public Assistance in New York City in 1993**

| Program | Persons |
|---|---|
| Aid to Families with Dependent Children | 792,263 |
| Home Relief | 293,553 |
| Emergency Assistance—Families | 36,396 |
| Emergency Assistance—Individuals | 776 |
| Medical Assistance | 1,049,783 |
| Services | 247,066 |
| Food Stamps | 1,317,012 |
| Home Energy Assistance Program | 755,841 |

Data Source: The Nelson A. Rockefeller Institute of Government, *1995 New York State Statistical Abstract*

## CITY HOSPITALS EXPENDITURES: CITY RANKINGS

New York City ranked highest among the largest cities (500,000+ population) in the nation in terms of per capita city hospitals expenditures in 1994.

**Per Capita City Hospitals Expenditures**

| Rank | City | Per Capita Hospitals Expenditures |
|---|---|---|
| 1 | **New York City** | **$489.41** |
| 2 | San Francisco | 460.63 |
| 3 | Boston | 408.05 |
| 4 | Indianapolis | 224.15 |
| 5 | Chicago | 45.72 |
| 6 | Houston | 40.53 |
| 7 | Seattle | 32.33 |
| 8 | Philadelphia | 28.87 |
| 9 | Jacksonville | 28.17 |
| 10 | Milwaukee | 23.13 |
| 11(t) | Baltimore | 0.00 |
| 11(t) | Cleveland | 0.00 |
| 11(t) | Columbus | 0.00 |
| 11(t) | Dallas | 0.00 |
| 11(t) | Detroit | 0.00 |
| 11(t) | El Paso | 0.00 |
| 11(t) | Honolulu | 0.00 |
| 11(t) | Los Angeles | 0.00 |
| 11(t) | Memphis | 0.00 |
| 11(t) | Phoenix | 0.00 |
| 11(t) | San Antonio | 0.00 |
| 11(t) | San Diego | 0.00 |
| 11(t) | San Jose | 0.00 |
| | Large City Average | 137.68 |

Note: See Part One of this book for District of Columbia.

Data Source: U.S. Department of Commerce

## CITY HOSPITALS EXPENDITURES: NEW YORK CITY VS. LARGE CITY AVERAGE

In 1994, New York City's per capita hospitals expenditures exceeded the large city (500,000+ population) average by 255.5 percent—$489.41 in New York City versus the large city average of $137.68.

Between 1965 and 1994, real per capita city hospitals expenditures increased by 140.1 percent. In 1994 dollars, New York City's 1965 per capita hospitals spending equaled $203.80.

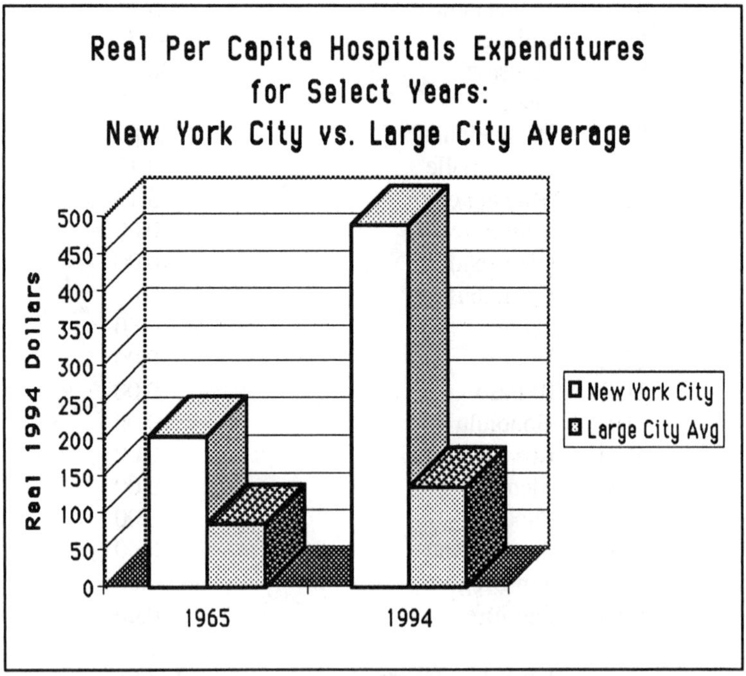


Data Source: U.S. Department of Commerce

## CITY HEALTH EXPENDITURES: CITY RANKINGS

New York City ranked fifth among the largest cities (500,000+ population) in the nation in terms of per capita city health expenditures in 1994.

**Per Capita City Health Expenditures**

| Rank | City | Per Capita Health Expenditures |
|---|---|---|
| 1 | San Francisco | $404.33 |
| 2 | Philadelphia | 211.05 |
| 3 | Detroit | 100.44 |
| 4 | Baltimore | 92.30 |
| **5** | **New York City** | **69.03** |
| 6 | Cleveland | 46.18 |
| 7 | Indianapolis | 40.65 |
| 8 | Houston | 40.53 |
| 9 | Chicago | 38.92 |
| 10 | Columbus | 38.55 |
| 11 | El Paso | 37.21 |
| 12 | Seattle | 32.33 |
| 13 | Jacksonville | 30.40 |
| 14 | Milwaukee | 23.13 |
| 15 | San Antonio | 23.01 |
| 16 | Dallas | 18.00 |
| 17 | Honolulu | 13.98 |
| 18 | Memphis | 10.94 |
| 19 | Los Angeles | 5.47 |
| 20 | San Jose | 2.56 |
| 21 | Phoenix | 1.03 |
| 22 | San Diego | 0.99 |
| 23 | Boston | 0.72 |
| | Large City Average | 55.97 |

Note: See Part One of this book for District of Columbia.

Data Source: U.S. Department of Commerce

## CITY HEALTH EXPENDITURES: NEW YORK CITY VS. LARGE CITY AVERAGE

In 1994, New York City's per capita health expenditures topped the large city average by 23.3 percent—$69.03 in New York City versus the large city average of $55.97.

Between 1965 and 1994, New York City's real per capita health expenditures increased by 83.5 percent. In 1994 dollars, New York City's 1965 per capita health spending equaled $37.61.

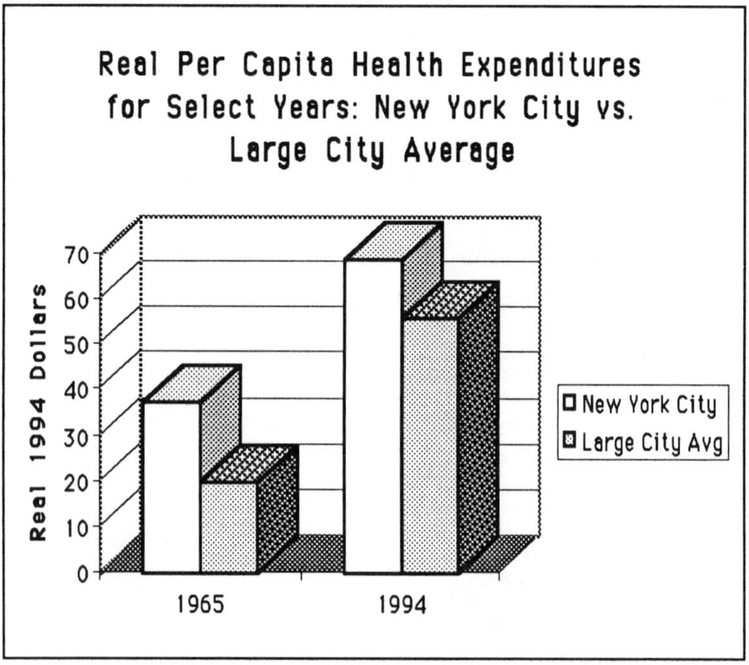


Data Source: U.S. Department of Commerce

## CITY HIGHWAY EXPENDITURES: CITY RANKINGS

New York City ranked second among the largest cities (500,000+ population) in the nation in terms of per capita city highway expenditures in 1994.

**Per Capita City Highway Expenditures**

| Rank | City | Per Capita Highway Expenditures |
|---|---|---|
| 1 | Seattle | $136.29 |
| **2** | **New York City** | **125.36** |
| 3 | Baltimore | 119.40 |
| 4 | Cleveland | 115.82 |
| 5 | Boston | 110.34 |
| 6 | Houston | 106.36 |
| 7 | Chicago | 100.25 |
| 8 | Indianapolis | 92.99 |
| 9 | Columbus | 81.72 |
| 10 | San Francisco | 80.83 |
| 11 | Milwaukee | 77.80 |
| 12 | Detroit | 74.75 |
| 13 | Phoenix | 69.77 |
| 14 | San Diego | 68.54 |
| 15 | San Antonio | 65.73 |
| 16 | Dallas | 63.38 |
| 17 | Jacksonville | 60.92 |
| 18 | San Jose | 57.39 |
| 19 | Philadelphia | 55.15 |
| 20 | Memphis | 54.51 |
| 21 | El Paso | 51.09 |
| 22 | Los Angeles | 45.48 |
| 23 | Honolulu | 35.20 |
| | Large City Average | 87.19 |

Note: See Part One of this book for District of Columbia.

Data Source: U.S. Department of Commerce

## CITY HIGHWAY EXPENDITURES: NEW YORK CITY VS. LARGE CITY AVERAGE

In 1994, New York City's per capita highway expenditures topped the large city (500,000+ population) average by 43.8 percent—$125.36 in New York City versus the large city average of $87.19.

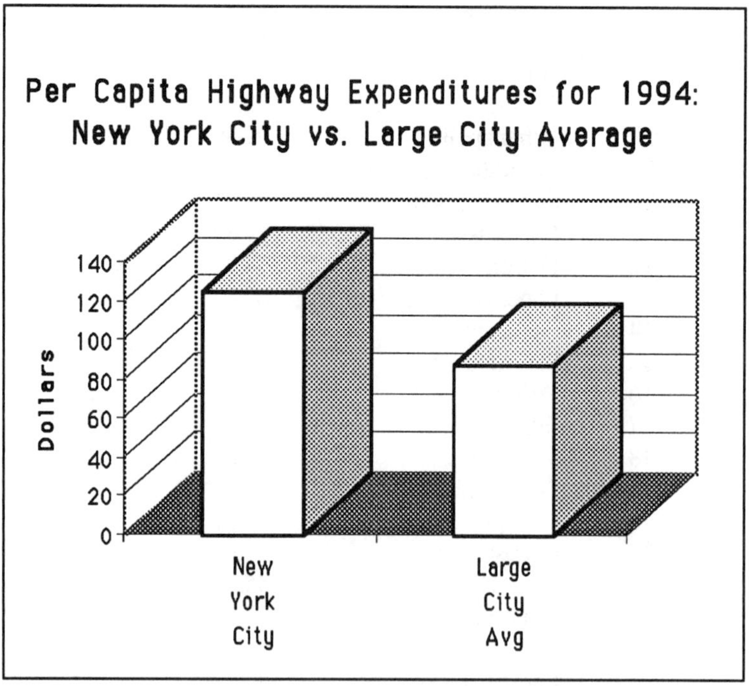


Data Source: U.S. Department of Commerce

## CITY FIRE PROTECTION EXPENDITURES: CITY RANKINGS

New York City ranked eighth among the largest cities (500,000+ population) in the nation in terms of per capita city fire protection expenditures in 1994.

**Per Capita City Fire Protection Expenditures**

| Rank | City | Per Capita Expenditures |
|---|---|---|
| 1 | San Francisco | $176.21 |
| 2 | Boston | 154.95 |
| 3 | Cleveland | 144.81 |
| 4 | Seattle | 138.02 |
| 5 | Columbus | 125.36 |
| 6 | Baltimore | 117.07 |
| 7 | Memphis | 110.70 |
| **8** | **New York City** | **107.21** |
| 9 | Milwaukee | 100.53 |
| 10 | Houston | 98.84 |
| 11 | Jacksonville | 93.49 |
| 12 | Phoenix | 92.81 |
| 13 | Chicago | 90.99 |
| 14 | Detroit | 88.12 |
| 15 | San Antonio | 78.15 |
| 16 | Philadelphia | 77.20 |
| 17 | Dallas | 77.12 |
| 18 | Los Angeles | 75.41 |
| 19 | San Jose | 75.00 |
| 20 | San Diego | 60.80 |
| 21 | Honolulu | 60.34 |
| 22 | Indianapolis | 57.06 |
| 23 | El Paso | 55.25 |
| | Large City Average | 95.00 |

Note: See Part One of this book for District of Columbia.

Data Source: U.S. Department of Commerce

## CITY FIRE PROTECTION EXPENDITURES: NEW YORK CITY VS. LARGE CITY AVERAGE

In 1994, New York City's per capita fire protection expenditures exceeded the large city (500,000+ population) average by 12.9 percent—$107.21 in New York City versus the large city average of $95.00.

Between 1965 and 1994, real per capita fire protection expenditures increased by 39.3 percent in New York City. In 1994 dollars, New York City's 1965 per capita fire protection spending equaled $76.95.

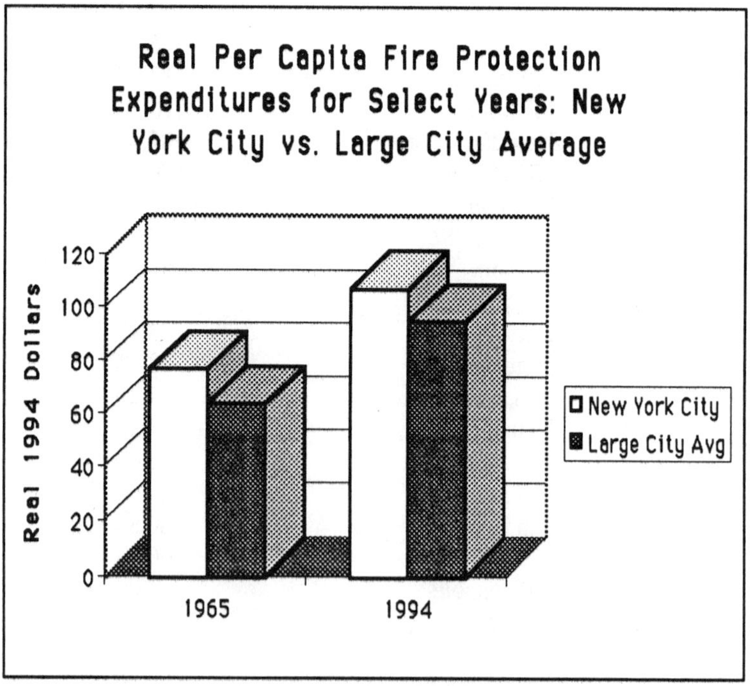


Data Source: U.S. Department of Commerce

## CITY SEWERAGE EXPENDITURES: CITY RANKINGS

New York City ranked eleventh among the largest cities (500,000+ population) in the nation in terms of per capita city sewerage expenditures in 1994.

**Per Capita City Sewerage Expenditures**

| Rank | City | Per Capita Sewerage Expenditures |
|---|---|---|
| 1 | San Francisco | $206.77 |
| 2 | Boston | 203.15 |
| 3 | San Diego | 201.09 |
| 4 | Columbus | 169.60 |
| 5 | Detroit | 167.24 |
| 6 | Seattle | 165.17 |
| 7 | Honolulu | 135.50 |
| 8 | Houston | 131.89 |
| 9 | San Jose | 125.96 |
| 10 | Baltimore | 122.70 |
| **11** | **New York City** | **115.73** |
| 12 | Dallas | 106.11 |
| 13 | Milwaukee | 105.84 |
| 14 | San Antonio | 97.09 |
| 15 | Phoenix | 87.78 |
| 16 | Philadelphia | 77.88 |
| 17 | Los Angeles | 75.64 |
| 18 | Indianapolis | 72.52 |
| 19 | El Paso | 67.76 |
| 20 | Memphis | 66.11 |
| 21 | Jacksonville | 64.39 |
| 22 | Chicago | 44.07 |
| 23 | Cleveland | 16.79 |
| | Large City Average | 107.51 |

Note: See Part One of this book for District of Columbia.

Data Source: U.S. Department of Commerce

## CITY SEWERAGE EXPENDITURES: NEW YORK CITY VS. LARGE CITY AVERAGE

In 1994, New York City's per capita sewerage spending topped the large city (500,000+ population) average by 7.6 percent—$115.73 in New York City versus the large city average of $107.51.

Between 1965 and 1994, real per capita sewerage spending increased by 222.2 percent. In 1994 dollars, New York City's 1965 per capita sewerage spending equaled $35.92.

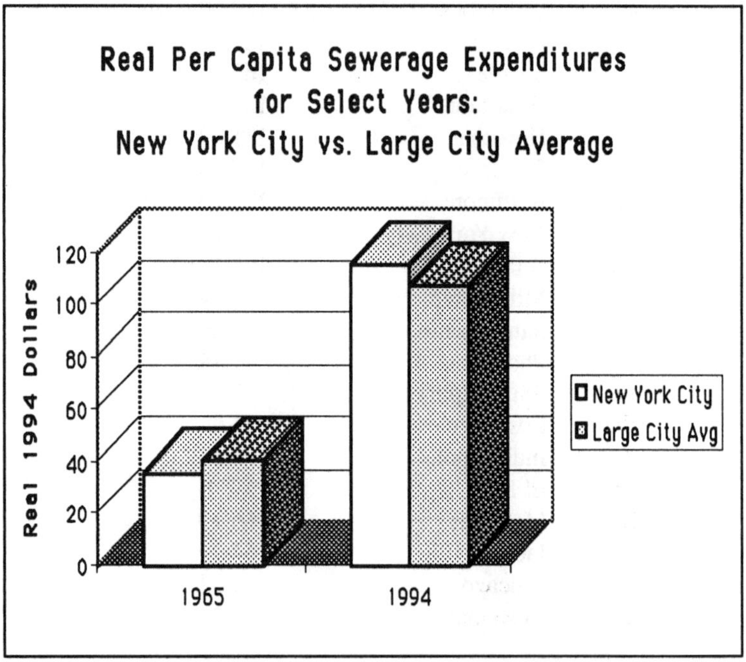


Data Source: U.S. Department of Commerce

# CITY SOLID WASTE MANAGEMENT EXPENDITURES: CITY RANKINGS

New York City ranked third highest among the largest cities (500,000+ population) in the nation in terms of per capita city solid waste management expenditures in 1994.

**Per Capita City Solid Waste Management Expenditures**

| Rank | City | Per Capita Expenditures |
|---|---|---|
| 1 | Seattle | $147.21 |
| 2 | Honolulu | 107.41 |
| **3** | **New York City** | **104.27** |
| 4 | Detroit | 92.83 |
| 5 | Philadelphia | 77.26 |
| 6 | Jacksonville | 74.93 |
| 7 | Memphis | 72.49 |
| 8 | Milwaukee | 69.04 |
| 9 | San Jose | 68.80 |
| 10 | Baltimore | 67.48 |
| 11 | Cleveland | 62.43 |
| 12 | Boston | 58.66 |
| 13 | Columbus | 55.75 |
| 14 | Indianapolis | 54.79 |
| 15 | San Diego | 53.63 |
| 16 | Chicago | 53.56 |
| 17 | Louisiana | 44.01 |
| 18 | Phoenix | 38.29 |
| 19 | Houston | 35.09 |
| 20 | El Paso | 34.97 |
| 21 | Dallas | 33.52 |
| 22 | San Antonio | 28.14 |
| 23 | San Francisco | 21.79 |
| | Large City Average | 68.35 |

Note: See Part One of this book for District of Columbia.

Data Source: U.S. Department of Commerce

## CITY SOLID WASTE MANAGEMENT EXPENDITURES: NEW YORK CITY VS. LARGE CITY AVERAGE

In 1994, New York City's per capita solid waste management expenditures outpaced the large city (500,000+ population) average by 52.6 percent—$104.27 in New York City versus the large city average of $68.35.

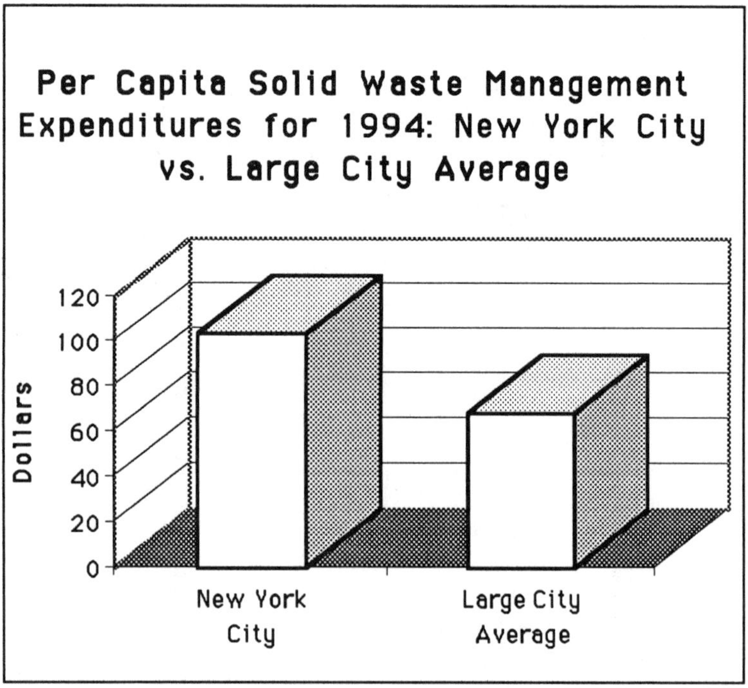


Data Source: U.S. Department of Commerce

## CITY PARKS AND RECREATION EXPENDITURES: CITY RANKINGS

New York City ranked seventeenth among the largest cities (500,000+ population) in the nation in terms of per capita city parks and recreation expenditures in 1994.

**Per Capita City Parks and Recreation Expenditures**

| Rank | City | Per Capita Expenditures |
|---|---|---|
| 1 | Indianapolis | $281.17 |
| 2 | San Francisco | 232.79 |
| 3 | Seattle | 216.10 |
| 4 | Cleveland | 133.64 |
| 5 | Phoenix | 116.23 |
| 6 | San Antonio | 112.07 |
| 7 | Memphis | 110.89 |
| 8 | Dallas | 107.79 |
| 9 | Honolulu | 102.19 |
| 10 | San Diego | 100.71 |
| 11 | Detroit | 88.31 |
| 12 | San Jose | 81.16 |
| 13 | Baltimore | 75.99 |
| 14 | Columbus | 73.78 |
| 15 | Houston | 50.85 |
| 16 | Jacksonville | 50.03 |
| **17** | **New York City** | **49.36** |
| 18 | Philadelphia | 48.48 |
| 19 | Los Angeles | 46.87 |
| 20 | El Paso | 39.39 |
| 21 | Milwaukee | 25.60 |
| 22 | Boston | 20.19 |
| 23 | Chicago | 15.76 |
| | Large City Average | 73.24 |

Note: See Part One of this book for District of Columbia.

Data Source: U.S. Department of Commerce

## CITY PARKS AND RECREATION EXPENDITURES: NEW YORK CITY VS. LARGE CITY AVERAGE

In 1994, the large city (500,000+ population) average per capita parks and recreation spending topped New York City's by 48.3 percent—$49.36 in New York City versus the large city average of $73.24.

Between 1965 and 1994, real per capita parks and recreation spending in New York City increased by 3.9 percent. In 1994 dollars, New York City's 1965 per capita parks and recreation expenditures equaled $47.51.

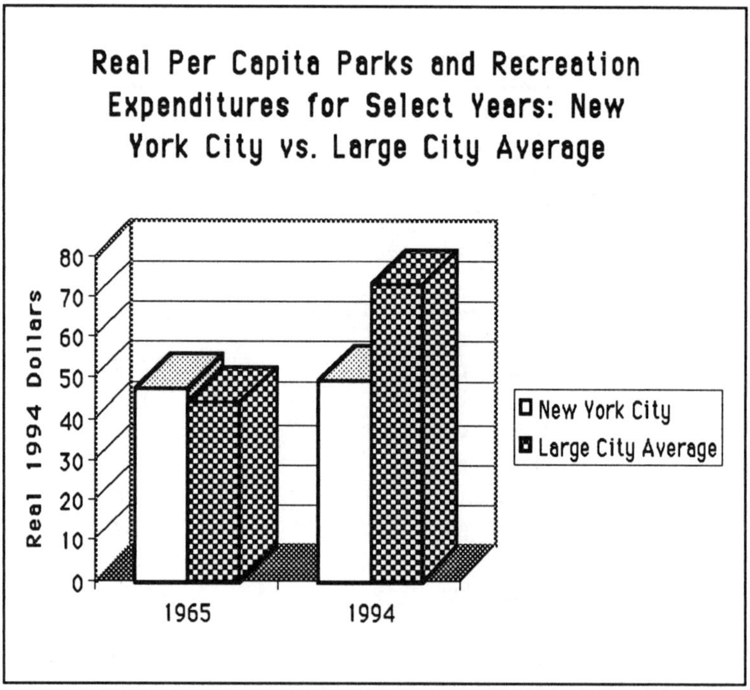


Data Source: U.S. Department of Commerce

## THE STATE OF NEW YORK CITY PARKS

According to *The Mayor's Management Report Fiscal 1995*, 86 percent of New York City parks in the spring of 1995 were rated as acceptable in terms of cleanliness, and only 43 percent acceptable in terms of "overall condition" including infrastructure.

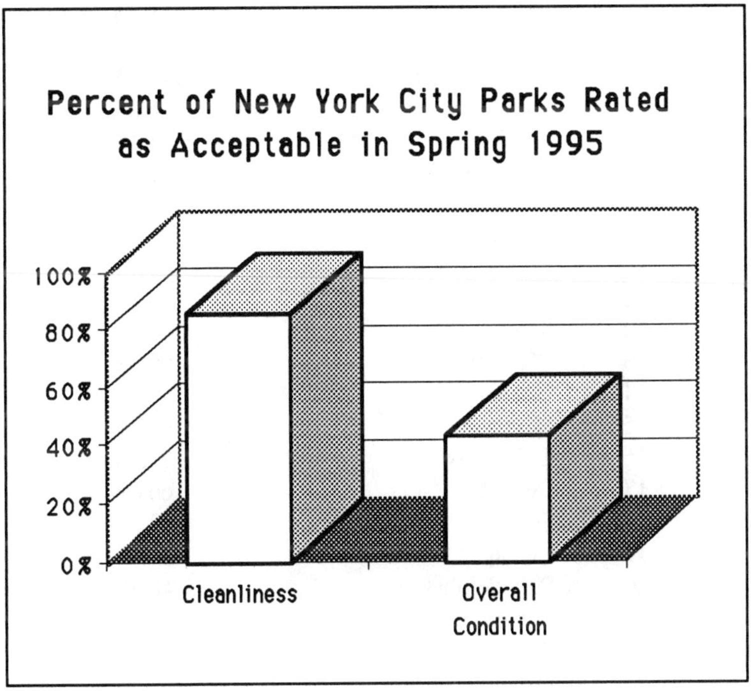

# CITY HOUSING AND COMMUNITY DEVELOPMENT EXPENDITURES: CITY RANKINGS

New York City ranked highest among the largest cities (500,000+ population) in the nation in terms of per capita city housing and community development expenditures in 1994. In fact, New York City's development spending was so high that it registered more than twice the level of the city ranking second highest in the country.

**Per Capita City Development Expenditures**

| Rank | City | Per Capita Expenditures |
|---|---|---|
| 1 | **New York City** | **$349.66** |
| 2 | Indianapolis | 156.45 |
| 3 | Honolulu | 142.32 |
| 4 | San Francisco | 117.89 |
| 5 | Phoenix | 116.23 |
| 6 | San Jose | 115.48 |
| 7 | San Antonio | 112.07 |
| 8 | Memphis | 110.89 |
| 9 | Boston | 108.68 |
| 10 | Dallas | 107.79 |
| 11 | Baltimore | 104.77 |
| 12 | San Diego | 100.71 |
| 13 | Cleveland | 99.33 |
| 14 | Jacksonville | 97.16 |
| 15 | Milwaukee | 90.78 |
| 16 | Columbus | 73.78 |
| 17 | Detroit | 66.08 |
| 18 | Seattle | 53.77 |
| 19 | Chicago | 50.79 |
| 20 | Philadelphia | 48.48 |
| 21 | Los Angeles | 46.87 |
| 22 | El Paso | 39.39 |
| 23 | Houston | 21.71 |
| | Large City Average | 135.97 |

Note: See Part One of this book for District of Columbia.
Data Source: U.S. Department of Commerce

## CITY HOUSING AND COMMUNITY DEVELOPMENT EXPENDITURES: NEW YORK CITY VS. LARGE CITY AVERAGE

In 1994, New York City's per capita housing and community development expenditures exceeded the large city (500,000+ population) average by 157.2 percent—$349.66 in New York City versus the large city average of $135.97.

Between 1965 and 1994, real per capita housing and community development spending in New York City jumped by 126.1 percent. In 1994 dollars, New York City's 1965 per capita housing and community development expenditures equaled $154.65.

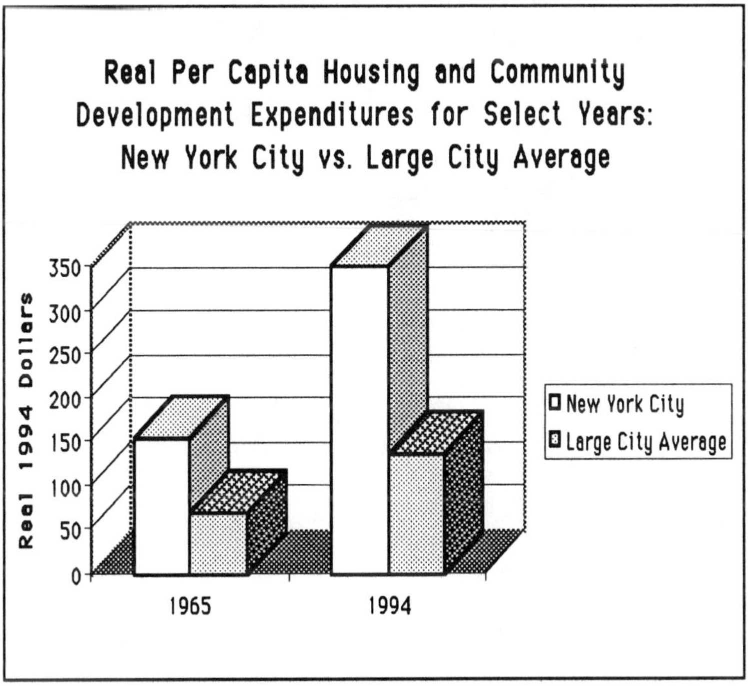


Data Source: U.S. Department of Commerce

## CITY CAPITAL OUTLAYS: CITY RANKINGS

New York City ranked second highest among the largest cities (500,000+ population) in the nation in terms of per capita city capital outlays in 1994.

### Per Capita City Capital Outlays

| Rank | City | Per Capita Capital Outlays |
|---|---|---|
| 1 | San Francisco | $546.70 |
| **2** | **New York City** | **531.84** |
| 3 | Indianapolis | 510.77 |
| 4 | Dallas | 367.30 |
| 5 | Honolulu | 358.28 |
| 6 | Phoenix | 284.79 |
| 7 | Cleveland | 272.16 |
| 8 | San Diego | 263.11 |
| 9 | Boston | 252.20 |
| 10 | Houston | 229.14 |
| 11 | Baltimore | 218.47 |
| 12 | Chicago | 203.26 |
| 13 | Seattle | 198.17 |
| 14 | San Antonio | 191.72 |
| 15 | Memphis | 190.43 |
| 16 | Milwaukee | 189.75 |
| 17 | Columbus | 189.33 |
| 18 | Jacksonville | 187.38 |
| 19 | San Jose | 187.15 |
| 20 | Los Angeles | 173.26 |
| 21 | Philadelphia | 169.72 |
| 22 | Detroit | 131.21 |
| 23 | El Paso | 124.15 |
| | Large City Average | 305.52 |

Note: See Part One of this book for District of Columbia.

Data Source: U.S. Department of Commerce

## CITY CAPITAL OUTLAYS: NEW YORK CITY VS. LARGE CITY AVERAGE

In 1994, New York City's per capita capital outlays topped the large city (500,000+ population) average by 74.1 percent—$531.84 in New York City versus the large city average of $305.52.

Between 1965 and 1994, real per capita capital outlays grew by 60.3 percent in New York City. In 1994 dollars, New York City's 1965 per capita capital outlays equaled $331.74.

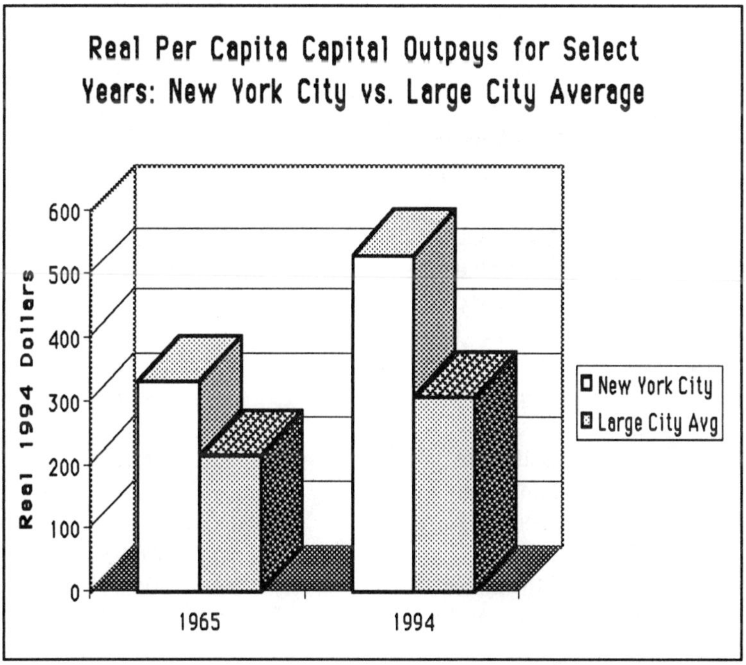


Data Source: U.S. Department of Commerce

## CITY DEBT OUTSTANDING: CITY RANKINGS

New York City ranked highest among the largest cities (500,000+ population) in the nation in terms of per capita city debt outstanding in 1994.

**Per Capita City Debt Outstanding**

| Rank | City | Per Capita Debt |
|---|---|---|
| **1** | **New York City** | **$5,510.85** |
| 2 | San Francisco | 4,832.73 |
| 3 | San Antonio | 4,424.51 |
| 4 | Dallas | 3,792.52 |
| 5 | Phoenix | 2,755.99 |
| 6 | Seattle | 2,537.45 |
| 7 | Chicago | 2,516.45 |
| 8 | Los Angeles | 2,424.34 |
| 9 | Philadelphia | 2,365.41 |
| 10 | Houston | 2,261.69 |
| 11 | Cleveland | 2,187.86 |
| 12 | Columbus | 2,126.38 |
| 13 | Indianapolis | 2,088.28 |
| 14 | Boston | 2,020.39 |
| 15 | Detroit | 1,992.22 |
| 16 | San Jose | 1,889.11 |
| 17 | Honolulu | 1,860.77 |
| 18 | Baltimore | 1,697.19 |
| 19 | San Diego | 1,572.69 |
| 20 | Memphis | 1,377.19 |
| 21 | El Paso | 1,000.95 |
| 22 | Milwaukee | 906.53 |
| 23 | Jacksonville | 725.81 |
| | Large City Average | 3,250.04 |

Note: See Part One of this book for District of Columbia.

Data Source: U.S. Department of Commerce

## CITY DEBT OUTSTANDING: NEW YORK CITY VS. LARGE CITY AVERAGE

In 1994, New York City's per capita debt outstanding outpaced the large city (500,000+ population) average by 69.6 percent—$5,510.85 in New York City versus the large city average of $3,250.04.

Between 1965 and 1994, real per capita debt outstanding grew by 22.4 percent in New York City. In 1994 dollars, New York City's 1965 per capita debt outstanding stood at $4,501.92.

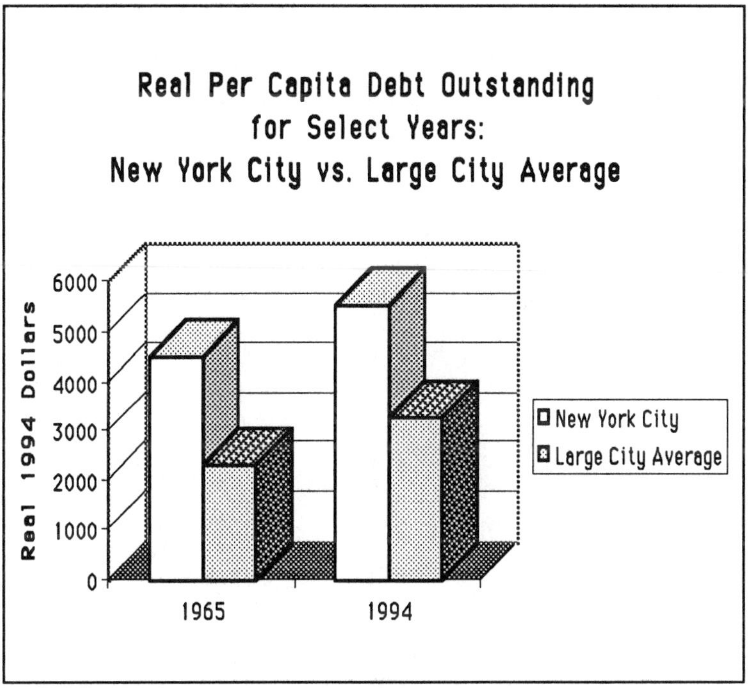


Data Source: U.S. Department of Commerce

## CITY INTEREST PAID ON DEBT: CITY RANKINGS

New York City ranked second highest among the largest cities (500,000+ population) in the nation in terms of per capita city interest paid on debt in 1994.

**Per Capita City Interest Paid on Debt**

| Rank | City | Per Capita Interest on Debt |
|---|---|---|
| 1 | Jacksonville | $279.93 |
| **2** | **New York City** | **244.31** |
| 3 | San Francisco | 233.50 |
| 4 | Dallas | 205.48 |
| 5 | Chicago | 143.06 |
| 6 | Phoenix | 135.93 |
| 7 | Honolulu | 121.68 |
| 8 | San Diego | 114.88 |
| 9 | Baltimore | 113.84 |
| 10 | Boston | 93.71 |
| 11 | Los Angeles | 92.52 |
| 12 | Houston | 91.55 |
| 13 | Detroit | 89.81 |
| 14 | Indianapolis | 78.93 |
| 15 | Columbus | 78.20 |
| 16 | San Jose | 75.15 |
| 17 | Philadelphia | 59.62 |
| 18 | San Antonio | 58.30 |
| 19 | Milwaukee | 56.82 |
| 20 | El Paso | 56.80 |
| 21 | Cleveland | 45.35 |
| 22 | Seattle | 37.88 |
| 23 | Memphis | 32.89 |
| | Large City Average | 140.43 |

Note: See Part One of this book for District of Columbia.

Data Source: U.S. Department of Commerce

## CITY INTEREST PAID ON DEBT: NEW YORK CITY VS. LARGE CITY AVERAGE

In 1994, New York City's per capita interest paid on debt outpaced the large city (500,000+ population) average by 73.9 percent—$244.31 in New York City versus the large city average of $140.43.

Between 1965 and 1994, real per capita city interest on debt increased by 213.3 percent in New York City. In 1994 dollars, New York City's 1965 per capita interest paid equaled $77.98.

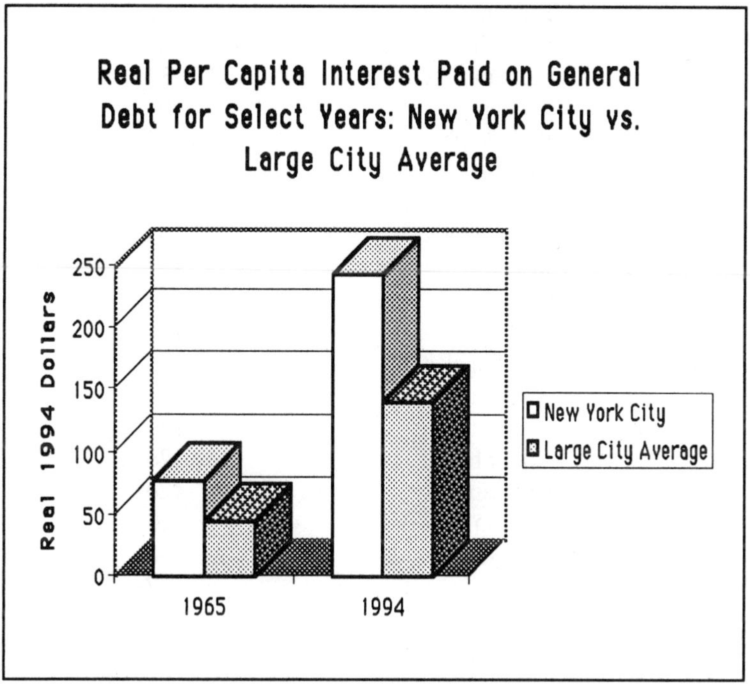


Data Source: U.S. Department of Commerce

## CITY GOVERNMENT EMPLOYMENT: CITY RANKINGS

New York City ranked highest among the largest cities (500,000+ population) in the nation in terms of the number of city employees per 10,000 population in 1993, exceeding the large city average by 85.7 percent.

**City Government Employees Per 10,000 Population**

| Rank | City | City Employees Per 10,000 pop. |
|---|---|---|
| **1** | **New York City** | **520** |
| 2 | Baltimore | 380 |
| 3 | Boston | 366 |
| 4 | Memphis | 360 |
| 5 | San Francisco | 332 |
| 6 | Seattle | 194 |
| 7 | Philadelphia | 189 |
| 8 | Detroit | 185 |
| 9 | Cleveland | 178 |
| 10 | Indianapolis | 164 |
| 11 | Jacksonville | 157 |
| 12 | Chicago | 144 |
| 13 | Dallas | 139 |
| 14 | Los Angeles | 138 |
| 15 | Houston | 135 |
| 16 | Milwaukee | 127 |
| 17 | Columbus | 126 |
| 18 | Honolulu, HI | 120 |
| 19 | El Paso | 116 |
| 20 | San Diego | 90 |
| 21 | San Jose | 77 |
| | Large City Average | 280 |

Note: Data not available for San Antonio and Phoenix.

Data Source: U.S. Department of Commerce, *Statistical Abstract of the United States 1996*

## CITY SALARIES AND WAGES: CITY RANKINGS

In 1994, New York City ranked highest among the largest cities (500,000+ population) in the nation in terms of per capita salary and wage costs.

**Per Capita Salaries and Wages**

| Rank | City | Salaries and Wages |
|---|---|---|
| **1** | **New York City** | **$2,282.41** |
| 2 | San Francisco | 1,833.09 |
| 3 | Boston | 1,492.22 |
| 4 | Baltimore | 1,114.02 |
| 5 | Memphis | 1,013.28 |
| 6 | Seattle | 826.54 |
| 7 | Philadelphia | 749.03 |
| 8 | Chicago | 631.96 |
| 9 | Los Angeles | 604.52 |
| 10 | Cleveland | 588.41 |
| 11 | Detroit | 562.14 |
| 12 | Milwaukee | 472.96 |
| 13 | Indianapolis | 469.93 |
| 14 | Honolulu | 429.90 |
| 15 | Dallas | 423.83 |
| 16 | Jacksonville | 420.39 |
| 17 | Phoenix | 413.80 |
| 18 | San Antonio | 413.70 |
| 19 | Columbus | 384.76 |
| 20 | Houston | 378.34 |
| 21 | San Diego | 361.85 |
| 22 | San Jose | 359.14 |
| 23 | El Paso | 263.85 |
| | Large City Average | 1,009.68 |

Data Source: U.S. Department of Commerce

## CITY SALARIES AND WAGES: NEW YORK CITY VS. LARGE CITY AVERAGES

In 1994, New York City per capita salary and wage costs outpaced the large city (500,000+ population) average by 126.1 percent—$2,282.41 in New York City versus the large city average of $1,009.68.

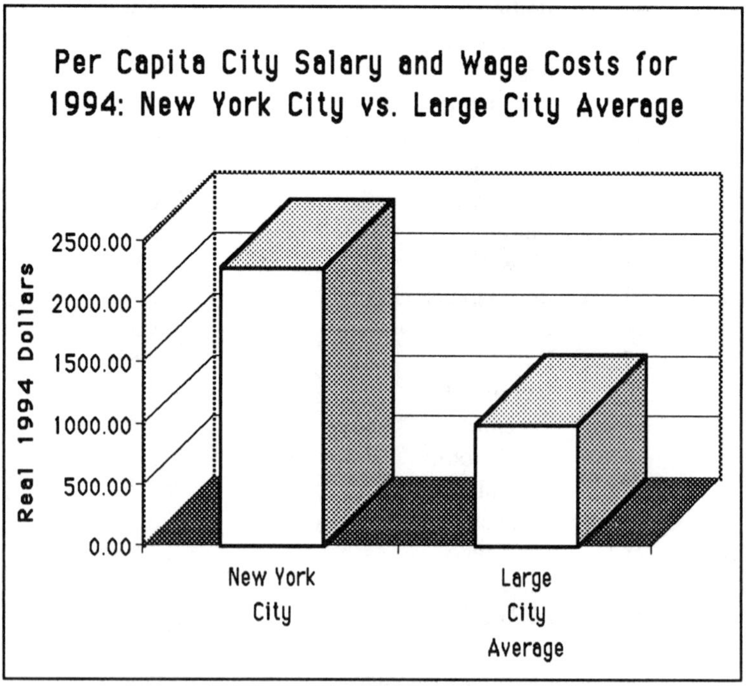


Data Source: U.S. Department of Commerce

## SALARIES OF TOP NEW YORK CITY GOVERNMENT OFFICIALS

New York City officials garner quite lucrative salaries. In December 1995, officials voted themselves sizable increases, including a $30,000 raise for the mayor, $15,500 raises for each of the 51 city council members, $28,000 raise for the city comptroller, $19,000 raises for the city's borough presidents, $10,000 for each district attorney, and $20,000 for the public advocate.

**Current Salaries of New York City's Top Officials**

| Position | Salary |
|---|---|
| Mayor | $165,000 |
| City Council Members | 70,500 |
| City Comptroller | 133,000 |
| Borough Presidents | 114,000 |
| District Attorneys | 125,000 |
| Public Advocate | 125,000 |
| Schools Chancellor | 195,000 |

Data Source: New York City budget documents

## NEW YORK CITY EXPENDITURES BY MAJOR CATEGORIES

In fiscal year 1996, New York City total expenditures totaled more than $37 billion. The chart below breaks out spending by major categories.

**New York City Expenditures by Major Category, FY 1996**

| Category | Amount (in millions) |
|---|---|
| Board of Education | $7,826 |
| Social Services | 7,175 |
| Capital Budget Expenditures | 4,367 |
| Police | 2,345 |
| Debt Service | 2,301 |
| Pensions | 1,516 |
| Health and Hospitals Corporation | 1,220 |
| Correction | 759 |
| Fire | 757 |
| Sanitation | 601 |
| Environmental Protection | 582 |
| Transportation | 527 |
| Department of General Services | 493 |
| Housing Preservation and Development | 463 |
| Health | 412 |
| City University of New York | 406 |
| Homeless Services | 397 |
| Elected Officials other than Mayor | 337 |
| Mental Health | 334 |
| General Reserve | 200 |
| Parks | 163 |
| Finance | 162 |
| Municipal Assistance Corporation | 127 |
| Mayoralty | 89 |
| Health Resources Administration | 42 |
| Other Mayoral Agencies | 1,210 |
| Miscellaneous | 3,006 |

Data Source: New York City Office of Management and Budget, *The City of New York Financial Plan Fiscal Years 1996-2000, Volume 1*

# CHAPTER EIGHT

# NEW YORK CITY: EDUCATION

- Various Expenditures
- Student Performance

# CITY ELEMENTARY AND SECONDARY EDUCATION EXPENDITURES: CITY RANKINGS

New York City ranked highest among the largest cities (500,000+ population) in the nation in terms of per capita city elementary and secondary education expenditures in 1994.

### Per Capita City Elementary and Secondary Education Expenditures

| Rank | City | Per Capita Education Expenditures |
|---|---|---|
| **1** | **New York City** | **$1,159.41** |
| 2 | Boston | 875.48 |
| 3 | Memphis | 836.78 |
| 4 | Baltimore | 825.59 |
| 5 | San Francisco | 86.67 |
| 6 | San Antonio | 14.36 |
| 7 | Detroit | 4.26 |
| 8 | Lois Angeles | 3.32 |
| 9 | Phoenix | 2.08 |
| 10 | Indianapolis | 0.99 |
| 11 | Chicago | 0.23 |
| 12(t) | Cleveland | 0.00 |
| 12(t) | Columbus | 0.00 |
| 12(t) | Dallas | 0.00 |
| 12(t) | El Paso | 0.00 |
| 12(t) | Honolulu | 0.00 |
| 12(t) | Houston | 0.00 |
| 12(t) | Jacksonville | 0.00 |
| 12(t) | Milwaukee | 0.00 |
| 12(t) | Philadelphia | 0.00 |
| 12(t) | San Diego | 0.00 |
| 12(t) | San Jose | 0.00 |
| 12(t) | Seattle | 0.00 |
| | Large City Average | 117.68 |

Note: See Part One of this book for District of Columbia.
Data Source: U.S. Department of Commerce

## CITY ELEMENTARY AND SECONDARY EDUCATION EXPENDITURES: NEW YORK CITY VS. LARGE CITY AVERAGE

In 1994, New York City's per capita elementary and secondary education expenditures topped the large city (500,000+ population) average by 885.2 percent—$1,159.41 in New York City versus the large city average of $117.68.

Between 1965 and 1994, real per capita city elementary and secondary education spending grew by 140.4 percent in New York City. In 1994 dollars, New York City's 1965 per capita elementary and secondary education expenditures equaled $482.44.

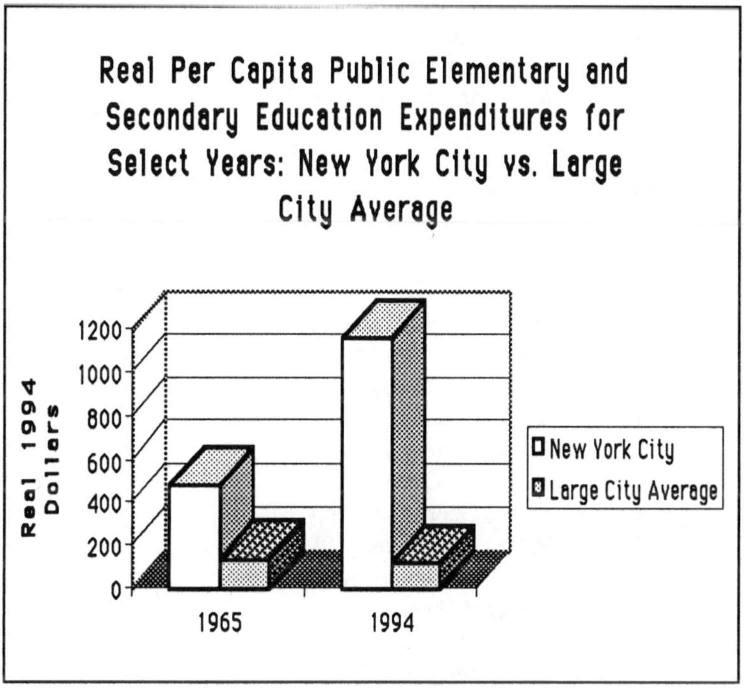


Data Source: U.S. Department of Commerce

## PER PUPIL EXPENDITURES IN PUBLIC SCHOOL DISTRICTS WITH MORE THAN 50,000 STUDENTS

New York City ranked second among the 70 largest public school school districts in the nation—50,000 or more students—in terms of per pupil current expenditures in 1992-93.

**Per Pupil Expenditures—Districts With More Than 50,000 Students**

| Rank | District | Per Pupil Expenditures |
|---|---|---|
| 1 | Washington, DC | $8,382 |
| **2** | **New York City** | **7,420** |
| 3 | Boston, MA | 7,076 |
| 4 | Milwaukee, WI | 6,873 |
| 5 | Cleveland, OH | 6,765 |
| 6 | Montgomery County, MD | 6,652 |
| 7 | Portland, OR | 6,604 |
| 8 | Philadelphia, PA | 6,470 |
| 9 | Cincinnati, OH | 6,444 |
| 10 | Atlanta, GA | 6,401 |
| 11 | Fairfax County, VA | 6,224 |
| 12 | Columbus, OH | 6,162 |
| 13 | Detroit Public Schools, MI | 5,748 |
| 14 | Los Angeles Unified, CA | 5,706 |
| 15 | Dade County, FL | 5,698 |
| 16 | Chicago, IL | 5,551 |
| 17 | Hawaii Public Schools | 5,526 |
| 18 | Baltimore County, MD | 5,462 |
| 19 | Prince George's County, MD | 5,405 |
| 20 | Palm Beach County, FL | 5,358 |
| 21 | DeKalb County, GA | 5,316 |
| 22 | Oakland Unified, CA | 5,267 |
| 23 | Broward County, FL | 5,228 |
| 24 | San Diego Unified, CA | 5,155 |
| 25 | Anne Arundel County, MD | 5,116 |
| 26 | Fulton County, GA | 5,057 |

*continued*

*continued*

| Rank | District | Per Pupil Expenditures |
|---|---|---|
| 27 | Denver, CO | 5,034 |
| 28 | Hillsborough County, FL | 4,981 |
| 29 | Fresno Unified, CA | 4,953 |
| 30 | San Antonio ISD, TX | 4,873 |
| 31 | San Francisco Unified, CA | 4,853 |
| 32 | Jefferson County, CO | 4,837 |
| 33 | Baltimore City, MD | 4,824 |
| 34 | Orange County, FL | 4,804 |
| 35 | Long Beach Unified, CA | 4,795 |
| 36 | Charlotte-Mecklenburg, NC | 4,779 |
| 37 | Pinellas County, FL | 4,750 |
| 38 | Guilford County, NC | 4,709 |
| 39 | Polk County, FL | 4,580 |
| 40 | Clark County, NV | 4,526 |
| 41 | Wake County, NC | 4,465 |
| 42 | Volusia County, FL | 4,403 |
| 43 | Brevard County, FL | 4,396 |
| 44 | Jefferson County, KY | 4,354 |
| 45 | Jefferson Parish, LA | 4,353 |
| 46 | Gwinnett County, GA | 4,348 |
| 47 | Cobb County, GA | 4,344 |
| 48 | Orleans Parish, LA | 4,341 |
| 49 | Austin ISD, TX | 4,297 |
| 50 | East Baton Rouge, LA | 4,286 |
| 51 | Fort Worth ISD, TX | 4,263 |
| 52 | Virginia Beach, VA | 4,234 |
| 53 | Duval County, FL | 4,214 |
| 54 | Nashville-Davidson County, TN | 4,199 |
| 55 | Dallas ISD, TX | 4,158 |
| 56 | El Paso ISD, TX | 4,088 |
| 57 | Greenville County, SC | 4,055 |
| 58 | Tucson Unified, AZ | 4,035 |
| 59 | Houston ISD, TX | 4,029 |
| 60 | Seminole County, FL | 3,982 |
| 61 | Memphis, TN | 3,945 |

*continued*

*continued*

| Rank | District | Per Pupil Expenditures |
|---|---|---|
| 62 | Caddo Parish, LA | 3,878 |
| 63 | Albuquerque, NM | 3,864 |
| 64 | Knox County, TN | 3,827 |
| 65 | Northside ISD, TX | 3,785 |
| 66 | Mesa Unified, AZ | 3,665 |
| 67 | Jordan, UT | 3,057 |
| 68 | Davis County, UT | 2,870 |
| 69 | Granite, UT | 2,841 |
| 70 | Mobile County, AL | 2,779 |

Data Source: U.S. Department of Education, *Digest of Education Statistics 1995*

## CITY LIBRARY EXPENDITURES: CITY RANKINGS

New York City ranked fourth among the largest cities (500,000+ population) in the nation in terms of per capita city library expenditures in 1994.

**Per Capita City Library Expenditures**

| Rank | City | Per Capita Library Expenditures |
|---|---|---|
| 1 | San Francisco | $83.75 |
| 2 | Boston | 46.99 |
| 3 | Seattle | 44.16 |
| **4** | **New York City** | **39.20** |
| 5 | Milwaukee | 35.27 |
| 6 | Philadelphia | 23.72 |
| 7 | Baltimore | 23.71 |
| 8 | Detroit | 23.33 |
| 9 | Chicago | 20.23 |
| 10 | San Jose | 19.39 |
| 11 | San Diego | 18.46 |
| 12 | Houston | 16.41 |
| 13 | Jacksonville | 16.02 |
| 14 | Memphis | 15.59 |
| 15 | Phoenix | 14.74 |
| 16 | Dallas | 14.58 |
| 17 | San Antonio | 13.72 |
| 18 | Los Angeles | 12.54 |
| 19 | El Paso | 11.15 |
| 20 | Honolulu | 0.53 |
| 21(t) | Cleveland | 0.00 |
| 21(t) | Columbus | 0.00 |
| 21(t) | Indianapolis | 0.00 |
| | Large City Average | 24.03 |

Data Source: U.S. Department of Commerce

## CITY LIBRARY EXPENDITURES: NEW YORK CITY VS. LARGE CITY AVERAGE

In 1994, New York City's per capita library expenditures outpaced the large city (500,000+ population) average by 63.1 percent—$39.20 in New York City versus the large city average of $24.03.

Between 1965 and 1994, real per capita city library expenditures increased by 68.7 percent in New York City. In 1994 dollars, New York City's 1965 per capita library spending stood at $23.24.

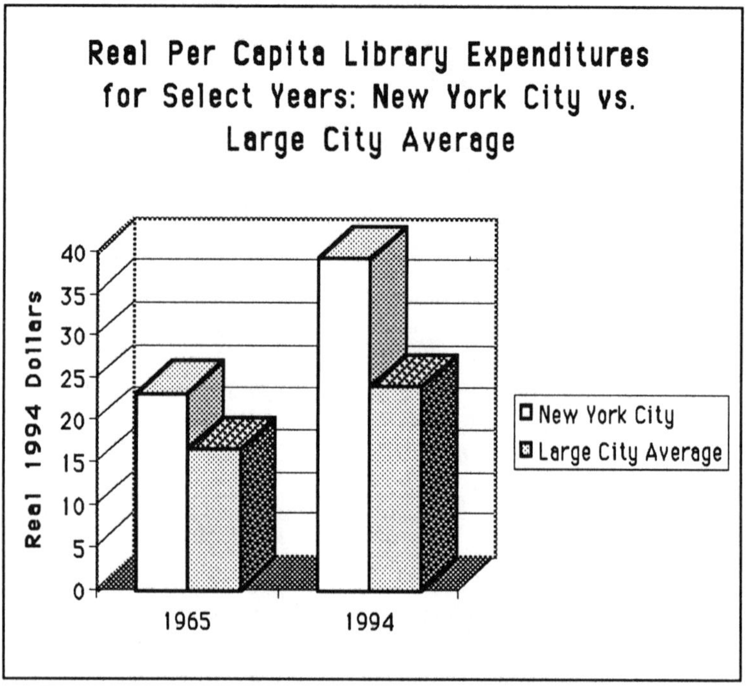


Data Source: U.S. Department of Commerce

## STUDENTS PERFORMING AT GRADE LEVEL

According to *The Mayor's Management Report Fiscal 1995*, in grades 3-8, only 53.3 percent of students performed at grade level in mathematics in 1994-95. In terms of elementary, intermediate and junior high students, only 47.5 percent performed at grade level in terms of reading in 1994-95. In 1993-94, only 45 percent of ninth-graders read at grade level and 57.2 percent of tenth-graders.

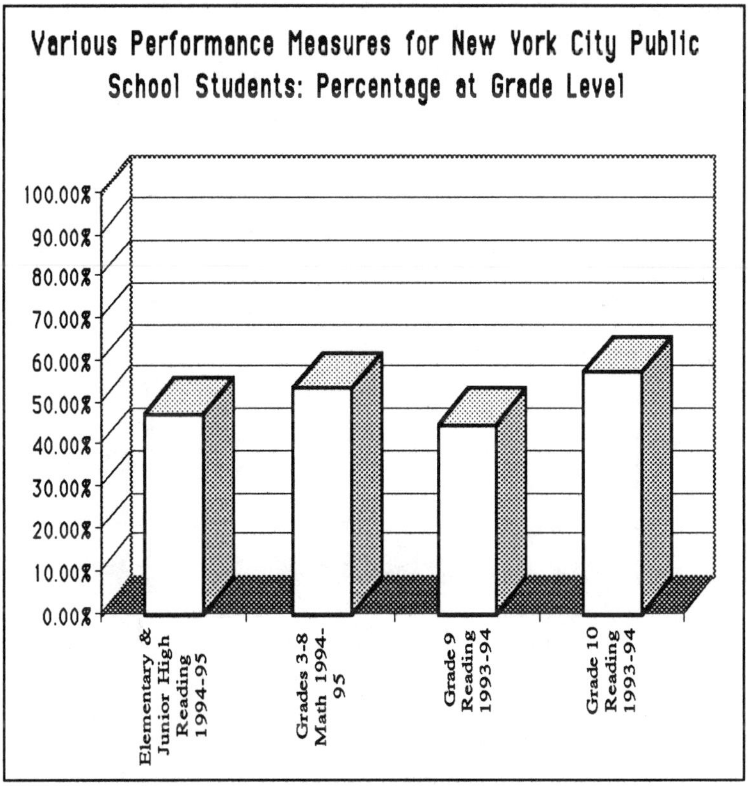

## GRADUATION RATE

In 1993-94, New York City public school on-time graduation rate equaled 51.5 percent, compared with the U.S. average of 70.2 percent.

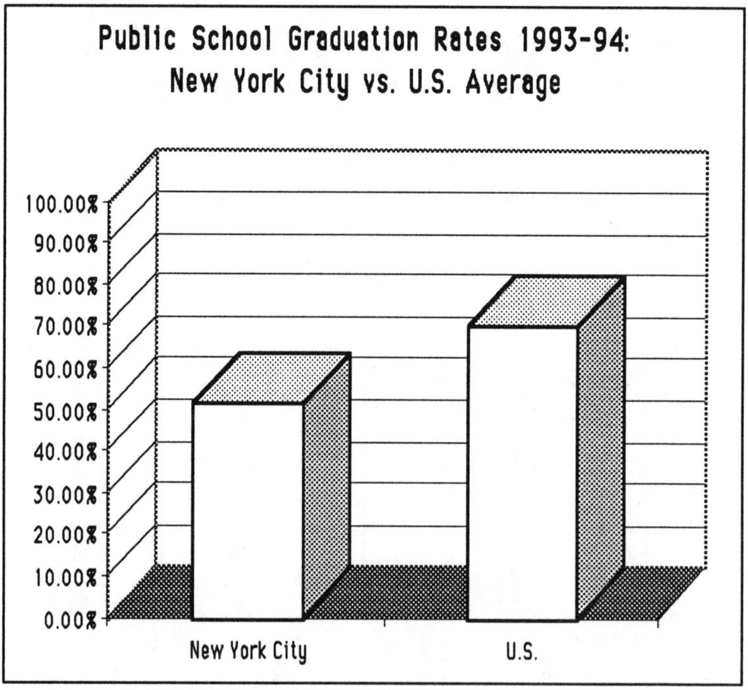


Data Sources: New York City, *The Mayor's Management Report Fiscal 1995*, and U.S. Department of Education, *Digest of Education Statistics*, annual

## EDUCATIONAL ATTAINMENT: NO HIGH SCHOOL DIPLOMA—15 LARGEST METROPOLITAN AREAS

New York City ranked fifth among the fifteen largest metropolitan areas in the nation in terms of the percentage of those 25 years of age or older without a high school diploma.

**No High School Diploma—25 Years of Age or Older**

| Rank | Metropolitan Area | Percent |
|---|---|---|
| 1 | Miami, FL | 24.6% |
| 2 | Los Angeles/Anaheim/Riverside, CA | 23.4 |
| 3 | Chicago, IL | 21.4 |
| 4 | Philadelphia, PA | 20.4 |
| **5** | **New York City** | **19.7** |
| 6(t) | Dallas, TX | 19.1 |
| 6(t) | St. Louis, MO | 19.1 |
| 8 | Detroit, MI | 18.3 |
| 9 | Pittsburgh, PA | 17.7 |
| 10 | Houston, TX | 16.7 |
| 11 | San Francisco, CA | 16.0 |
| 12 | Atlanta, GA | 15.9 |
| 13 | Cleveland, OH | 14.0 |
| 14 | Boston, MA | 13.0 |
| 15 | Washington, DC/MD/VA | 12.0 |

Data Source: U.S. Department of Education, *Digest of Education Statistics 1995*

## REGENTS DIPLOMAS: NEW YORK CITY VS. NEW YORK STATE

In 1994-95, 40 percent of New York State public high school graduates received Regents Diplomas compared with 21 percent in New York City.

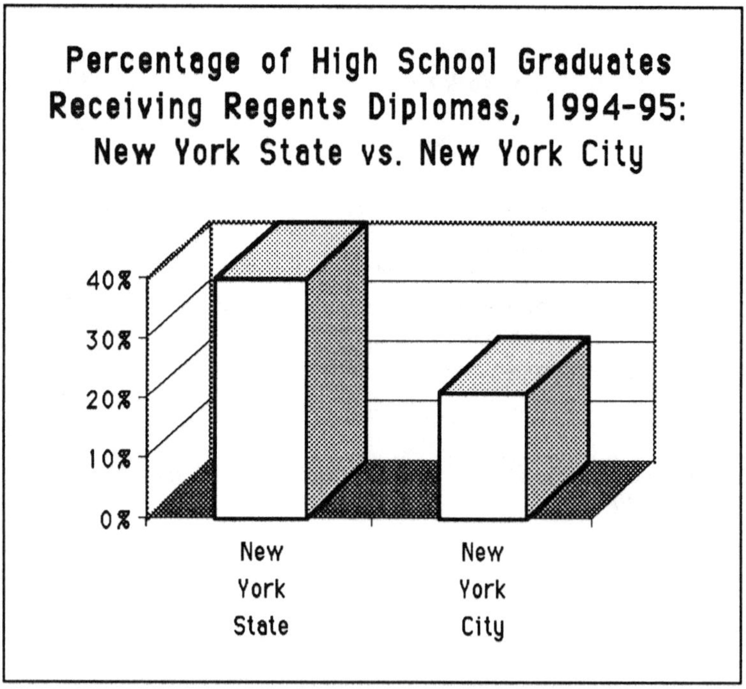


Data Source: New York State Education Department

## PUBLIC SCHOOL FREE OR REDUCED LUNCHES AND BREAKFASTS

In 1994-95, according to *The Mayor's Management Report Fiscal 1995*, 683,449 New York City public school students were eligible for free lunches and breakfasts and an additional 66,498 eligible for reduced price meals. Therefore, out of 1,036,000 enrolled students, over 72 percent qualified for free or reduced price meals each day.

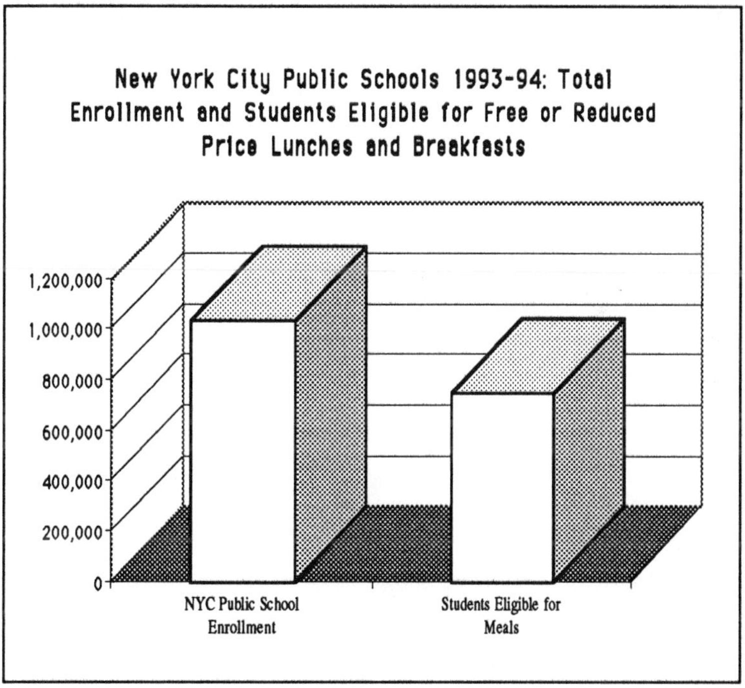

# Chapter Nine

# New York City: Crime

- Total Crime
- Murder
- Rape
- Robbery
- Aggravated Assault
- Burglary
- Larceny-Theft
- Motor Vehicle Theft
- Arson
- Law Enforcement Employees
- Police and Corrections Expenditures

## TOTAL CRIME: LARGE CITY RANKINGS

In 1995, New York City ranked a respectable forty-seventh out of the 51 largest cities (300,000+ population) in the nation in terms of its total crime index per 100,000 residents (excluding Chicago, Oakland, and Albuquerque due to incomplete data).

Buffalo, New York State's second largest city, ranked higher than New York City—twenty-second out of 51.

Total crime index takes into account the violent crimes of murder and non-negligent manslaughter, forcible rape, robbery, and aggravated assault, and the property crimes of burglary, larceny-theft, motor vehicle theft, and arson.

**Total Crime Index (Per 100,000 Inhabitants)**

| Rank | City | Total Crime Index |
|---|---|---|
| 1 | Atlanta, GA | 17,081.9 |
| 2 | St. Louis, MO | 16,101.3 |
| 3 | Miami, FL | 15,612.1 |
| 4 | Baltimore, MD | 13,322.3 |
| 5 | Washington, DC | 12,173.5 |
| 6 | Tucson, AZ | 12,156.9 |
| 7 | Portland, OR | 12,058.4 |
| 8 | Detroit, MI | 11,942.3 |
| 9 | Fresno, CA | 11,924.5 |
| 10 | Kansas City, MO | 11,788.1 |
| 11 | Minneapolis, MN | 11,536.0 |
| 12 | Oklahoma City, OK | 11,507.5 |
| 13 | New Orleans, LA | 10,964.9 |
| 14 | Phoenix, AZ | 10,877.2 |
| 15 | Nashville, TN | 10,704.2 |
| 16 | Memphis, TN | 10,512.9 |
| 17 | Seattle, WA | 10,473.0 |
| 18 | Sacramento, CA | 10,319.9 |
| 19 | Charlotte-Mecklenburg, NC | 9,579.0 |
| 20 | Boston, MA | 9,487.8 |
| 21 | Dallas, TX | 9,464.9 |

*continued*

*continued*

| Rank | City | Total Crime Index |
|---|---|---|
| 22 | Buffalo, NY | 9,217.0 |
| 23 | Columbus, OH | 9,188.6 |
| 24 | Jacksonville, FL | 9,002.8 |
| 25 | Mesa, AZ | 8,885.2 |
| 26 | Fort Worth, TX | 8,623.3 |
| 27 | Milwaukee, WI | 8,469.1 |
| 28 | Toledo, OH | 8,393.8 |
| 29 | Wichita, KS | 8,213.1 |
| 30 | San Francisco, CA | 8,194.3 |
| 31 | Austin, TX | 8,127.1 |
| 32 | San Antonio, TX | 7,993.1 |
| 33 | Omaha, NE | 7,851.7 |
| 34 | Cleveland, OH | 7,811.1 |
| 35 | Los Angeles, CA | 7,680.4 |
| 36 | Honolulu, HI | 7,630.1 |
| 37 | Houston, TX | 7,589.5 |
| 38 | Las Vegas, NV | 7,588.7 |
| 39 | Cincinnati, OH | 7,480.8 |
| 40 | Tulsa, OK | 7,380.4 |
| 41 | Philadelphia, PA | 7,077.0 |
| 42 | El Paso, TX | 7,066.4 |
| 43 | Long Beach, CA | 7,031.4 |
| 44 | Denver, CO | 6,871.3 |
| 45 | Colorado Springs, CO | 6,774.4 |
| 46 | Pittsburgh, PA | 6,126.2 |
| **47** | **New York City** | **6,075.9** |
| 48 | San Diego, CA | 5,547.1 |
| 49 | Indianapolis, IN | 4,717.9 |
| 50 | Virginia Beach, VA | 4,561.4 |
| 51 | San Jose, CA | 4,385.9 |
| | U.S. Average | 5,277.6 |

Note: Total Crime Index for Chicago, Oakland, and Albuquerque unavailable.
Data Source: Federal Bureau of Investigation, *Crime in the United States 1995*

## TOTAL CRIME: NEW YORK CITY VS. U.S.

New York City's 1995 total crime rate (per 100,000 inhabitants) surpassed the U.S. average by 15.1 percent—6,075.9 in New York City versus the U.S. average of 5,277.6. While the 1995 New York City crime rate was down significantly from the 1990 rate of 9,699, it still exceeded the 1970 rate of 5,220 by 16.4 percent.

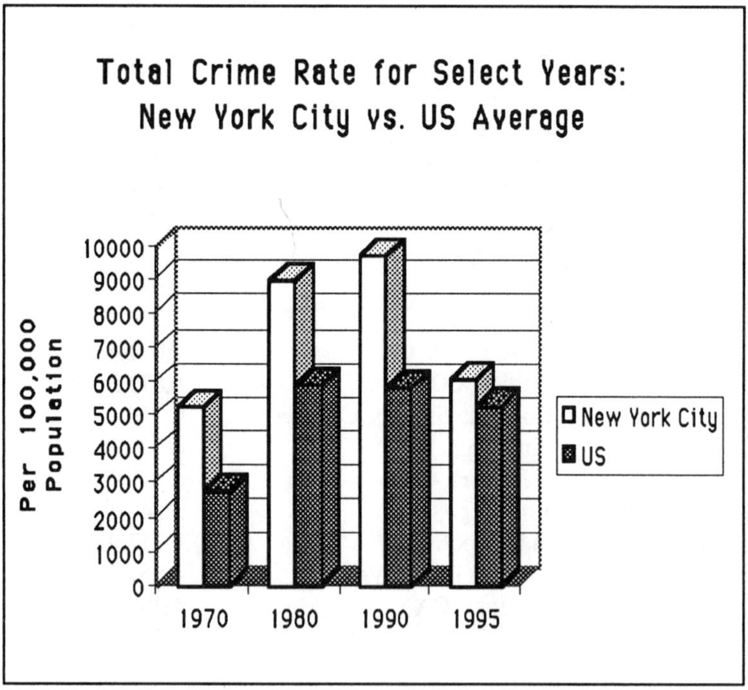


Data Sources: Federal Bureau of Investigation, *Crime in the United States*, annual, and *Statistical Abstract of the United States*, annual

# MURDER INDEX: LARGE CITY RANKINGS

In 1995, New York City ranked twenty-eighth out of the 53 largest cities (300,000+ population) in terms of its murder rate per 100,000 inhabitants.

Buffalo ranked twentieth.

The murder index includes murder and non-negligent manslaughter. According to the FBI, murder and non-negligent manslaughter is defined as the willful (non-negligent) killing of one human being by another.

**Murder Index (Per 100,000 Inhabitants)**

| Rank | City | Murder Index |
|---|---|---|
| 1 | New Orleans, LA | 74.5 |
| 2 | Washington, DC | 65.0 |
| 3 | St. Louis, MO | 55.0 |
| 4 | Oklahoma City, OK | 48.7 |
| 5 | Detroit, MI | 47.6 |
| 6 | Baltimore, MD | 45.6 |
| 7 | Atlanta, GA | 45.5 |
| 8 | Chicago, IL | 30.0 |
| 9(t) | Miami, FL | 29.0 |
| 9(t) | Memphis, TN | 29.0 |
| 11 | Philadelphia, PA | 28.2 |
| 12 | Minneapolis, MN | 26.8 |
| 13 | Dallas, TX | 26.5 |
| 14 | Cleveland, OH | 26.1 |
| 15 | Los Angeles, CA | 24.5 |
| 16 | Kansas City, MO | 24.0 |
| 17 | Fort Worth, TX | 23.5 |
| 18 | Milwaukee, WI | 22.2 |
| 19 | Nashville, TN | 20.0 |
| 20 | Buffalo, NY | 19.9 |
| 21 | Phoenix, AZ | 19.7 |
| 22(t) | Fresno, CA | 18.3 |
| 22(t) | Long Beach, CA | 18.3 |

*continued*

*continued*

| Rank | City | Murder Index |
|---|---|---|
| 24 | Houston, TX | 18.2 |
| 35 | Boston, MA | 17.4 |
| 26 | Charlotte-Mecklenburg, NC | 16.4 |
| 27 | Pittsburgh, PA | 16.3 |
| **28** | **New York City** | **16.1** |
| 29 | Denver, CO | 16.0 |
| 30 | Sacramento, CA | 15.2 |
| 31 | Las Vegas, NV | 14.9 |
| 32 | Tucson, AZ | 14.4 |
| 33 | San Antonio, TX | 14.2 |
| 34 | Cincinnati, OH | 13.9 |
| 35 | San Francisco, CA | 13.4 |
| 36 | Wichita, KS | 13.1 |
| 37 | Indianapolis, IN | 12.8 |
| 38 | Jacksonville, FL | 12.7 |
| 39 | Albuquerque, NM | 12.6 |
| 40 | Columbus, OH | 12.1 |
| 41 | Toledo, OH | 10.8 |
| 42 | Portland, OR | 9.4 |
| 43 | Austin, TX | 8.8 |
| 44 | Tulsa, OK | 8.0 |
| 45 | San Diego, CA | 7.9 |
| 46 | Omaha, NE | 7.8 |
| 47 | Seattle, WA | 7.7 |
| 48 | El Paso, TX | 6.3 |
| 49 | Colorado Springs, CO | 5.6 |
| 50 | Mesa, AZ | 5.2 |
| 51 | San Jose, CA | 4.6 |
| 52 | Honolulu, HI | 4.3 |
| 53 | Virginia Beach, VA | 3.7 |
| | U.S. Average | 8.2 |

Note: No data available for Oakland.

Data Source: Federal Bureau of Investigation, *Crime in the United States 1995*

## MURDER RATE: NEW YORK CITY VS. U.S.

New York City's 1995 murder rate (per 100,000 population) exceeded the U.S. average by 96.3 percent—16.1 in New York City as opposed to 8.2 across the nation. Between 1990 and 1995, New York City's murder rate dropped from 31 to 16.1—a decline of 48.1 percent. However, the city's crime rate in 1995 still outpaced the 1970 rate of 10.5 by 53.3 percent.

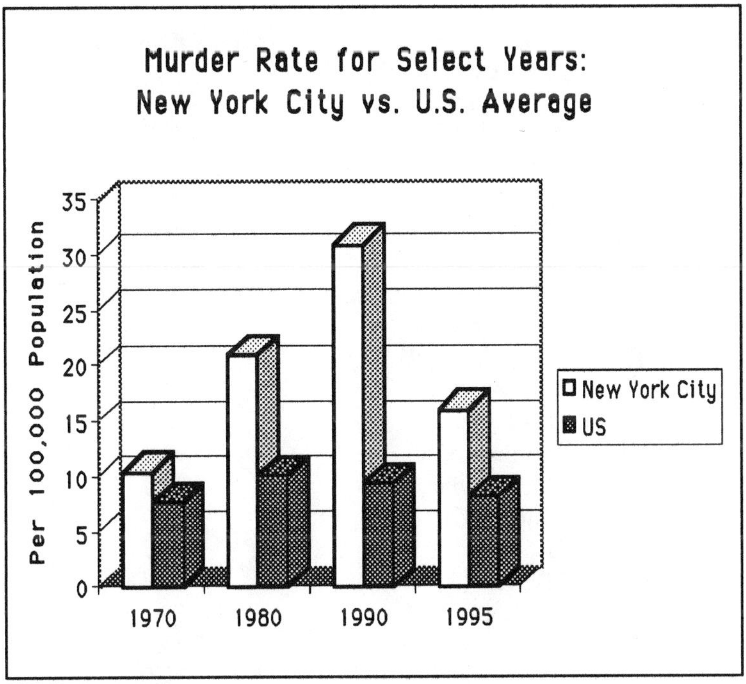


Data Sources: Federal Bureau of Investigation, *Crime in the United States*, annual, and *Statistical Abstract of the United States*, annual

## RAPES: LARGE CITY RANKINGS

In 1995, New York City ranked forty-eighth out of the 52 largest U.S. cities (300,000+ population) in terms of its rate of forcible rape per 100,000 inhabitants.

Meanwhile, Buffalo ranked sixteenth among the largest 52 cities.

As defined by the FBI, forcible rape is the carnal knowledge of a female forcibly and against her will. Assaults and attempts to commit rape also are included, but statutory rape without force and other sex offenses are not included.

**Forcible Rape Index (Per 100,000 Inhabitants)**

| Rank | City | Forcible Rape Index |
|---|---|---|
| 1 | Minneapolis, MN | 161.5 |
| 2 | Cleveland, OH | 139.2 |
| 3 | Memphis, TN | 125.8 |
| 4 | Cincinnati, OH | 113.3 |
| 5 | Detroit, MI | 110.7 |
| 6 | Atlanta, GA | 109.2 |
| 7 | Kansas City, MO | 105.4 |
| 8 | Oklahoma City, OK | 101.5 |
| 9 | New Orleans, LA | 100.0 |
| 10 | Columbus, OH | 99.5 |
| 11 | Baltimore, MD | 95.9 |
| 12 | Nashville, TN | 92.9 |
| 13 | Portland, OR | 92.8 |
| 14 | Jacksonville, FL | 92.0 |
| 15 | Toledo, OH | 85.8 |
| 16 | Buffalo, NY | 83.7 |
| 17 | Dallas, TX | 81.8 |
| 18 | St. Louis, MO | 73.6 |
| 19 | Fort Worth, TX | 72.2 |
| 20 | Las Vegas, NV | 72.0 |
| 21 | Albuquerque, NM | 70.5 |
| 22 | Boston, MA | 68.8 |
| 23 | Pittsburgh, PA | 68.5 |

*continued*

*continued*

| Rank | City | Forcible Rape Index |
|---|---|---|
| 24 | Tulsa, OK | 67.6 |
| 25 | Charlotte, NC | 67.3 |
| 26 | San Antonio, TX | 65.8 |
| 27 | Wichita, KS | 65.1 |
| 28 | Tucson, AZ | 64.9 |
| 29 | Colorado Springs, CO | 63.9 |
| 30 | Denver, CO | 63.2 |
| 31 | Milwaukee, WI | 59.5 |
| 32 | Indianapolis, IN | 59.1 |
| 33 | Austin, TX | 58.8 |
| 34 | Fresno, CA | 54.6 |
| 35 | Washington, DC | 52.7 |
| 36 | Miami, FL | 52.2 |
| 37 | Philadelphia, PA | 50.5 |
| 38 | Seattle, WA | 49.1 |
| 39 | Houston, TX | 48.3 |
| 40 | San Jose, CA | 47.0 |
| 41 | Los Angeles, CA | 45.9 |
| 42 | Sacramento, CA | 42.0 |
| 43 | San Francisco, CA | 41.2 |
| 44 | El Paso, TX | 41.0 |
| 45 | Mesa, AZ | 39.4 |
| 46 | Long Beach, CA | 39.2 |
| 47 | Phoenix, AZ | 37.8 |
| **48** | **New York City** | **32.4** |
| 49 | San Diego, CA | 29.9 |
| 50 | Honolulu, HI | 24.7 |
| 51 | Omaha, NE | 23.0 |
| 52 | Virginia Beach, VA | 22.7 |
| | U.S. Average | 37.1 |

Note: Data for Chicago and Oakland unavailable.

Data Source: Federal Bureau of Investigation, *Crime in the United States 1995*

## RAPE RATE: NEW YORK CITY VS. U.S.

The U.S. 1995 rape rate (per 100,000 population) outpaced New York City's rate by 14.5 percent—a U.S. average of 37.1 versus New York City's 32.4. New York City's 1995 rate was down from the 1990 rate of 43, however, it still exceeded the 1970 rate of 19.9 by 62.8 percent.

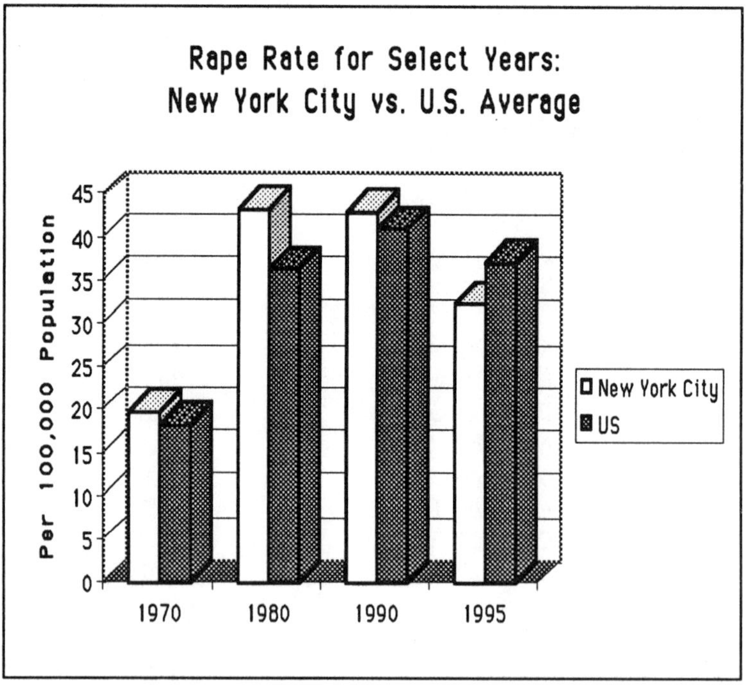


Data Sources: Federal Bureau of Investigation, *Crime in the United States*, annual, and *Statistical Abstract of the United States*, annual

## ROBBERY RATE: LARGE CITY RANKINGS

In 1995, New York City ranked sixteenth out of the 53 largest U.S. cities (300,000+ population) in terms of its rate of robberies per 100,000 inhabitants.

Meanwhile, Buffalo ranked eleventh among the largest 53 cities.

As defined by the FBI, robbery is the taking or attempted taking of value from the care, custody, or control of a person or persons by force or threat of force or violence and/or by putting the victim in fear.

**Robbery Index (Per 100,000 Inhabitants)**

| Rank | City | Robbery Index |
|---|---|---|
| 1 | Baltimore, MD | 1,594.5 |
| 2 | Miami, FL | 1,497.6 |
| 3 | St. Louis, MO | 1,384.4 |
| 4 | Atlanta, GA | 1,302.0 |
| 5 | Washington, DC | 1,239.0 |
| 6 | New Orleans, LA | 1,098.4 |
| 7 | Chicago, IL | 1,094.0 |
| 8 | Detroit, MI | 1,010.6 |
| 9 | Minneapolis, MN | 991.6 |
| 10 | Memphis, TN | 926.1 |
| 11 | Buffalo, NY | 909.0 |
| 12 | Philadelphia, PA | 889.7 |
| 13 | San Francisco, CA | 876.6 |
| 14 | Cleveland, OH | 853.3 |
| 15 | Los Angeles, CA | 840.6 |
| **16** | **New York City** | **809.8** |
| 17 | Kansas City, MO | 750.2 |
| 18 | Boston, MA | 652.8 |
| 19 | Long Beach, CA | 636.2 |
| 20 | Cincinnati, OH | 598.6 |
| 21 | Milwaukee, WI | 586.8 |
| 22 | Pittsburgh, PA | 585.1 |
| 23 | Sacramento, CA | 566.2 |
| 24 | Dallas, TX | 566.1 |

*continued*

*continued*

| Rank | City | Robbery Index |
|---|---|---|
| 25 | Fresno, CA | 558.2 |
| 26 | Charlotte-Mecklenburg, NC | 542.1 |
| 27 | Houston, TX | 531.8 |
| 28 | Columbus, OH | 521.0 |
| 29 | Nashville, TN | 510.5 |
| 30 | Portland, OR | 500.7 |
| 31 | Las Vegas, NV | 468.1 |
| 32 | Toledo, OH | 436.4 |
| 33 | Jacksonville, FL | 430.0 |
| 34 | Fort Worth, TX | 427.2 |
| 35 | Seattle, WA | 417.5 |
| 36 | Albuquerque, NM | 386.4 |
| 37 | Oklahoma City, OK | 344.0 |
| 38 | Phoenix, AZ | 340.1 |
| 39 | Indianapolis, IN | 326.4 |
| 40 | Wichita, KS | 286.9 |
| 41 | San Diego, CA | 280.1 |
| 42 | Denver, CO | 279.2 |
| 43 | Tucson, AZ | 264.9 |
| 44 | Austin, TX | 255.0 |
| 45 | Tulsa, OK | 251.2 |
| 46 | San Antonio, TX | 234.5 |
| 47 | Omaha, NE | 232.2 |
| 48 | El Paso, TX | 182.4 |
| 49 | Mesa, AZ | 156.0 |
| 50 | Honolulu, HI | 155.8 |
| 51 | San Jose, CA | 146.9 |
| 52 | Colorado Springs, CO | 128.4 |
| 53 | Virginia Beach, VA | 109.9 |
|  | U.S. Average | 220.9 |

Note: No data available for Oakland.

Data Source: Federal Bureau of Investigation, *Crime in the United States 1995*

## ROBBERY RATE: NEW YORK CITY VS. U.S.

In 1995, New York City's robbery rate (per 100,000 population) topped the U.S. average by 266.6 percent—809.8 in New York City versus the U.S. average of 220.9. Between 1990 and 1995, the city's robbery rate plummeted by 40.9 percent—from 1,370 in 1990 to 809.8. However, the 1995 rate still outpaced the 1970 New York City rate of 664.8 by 21.8 percent.

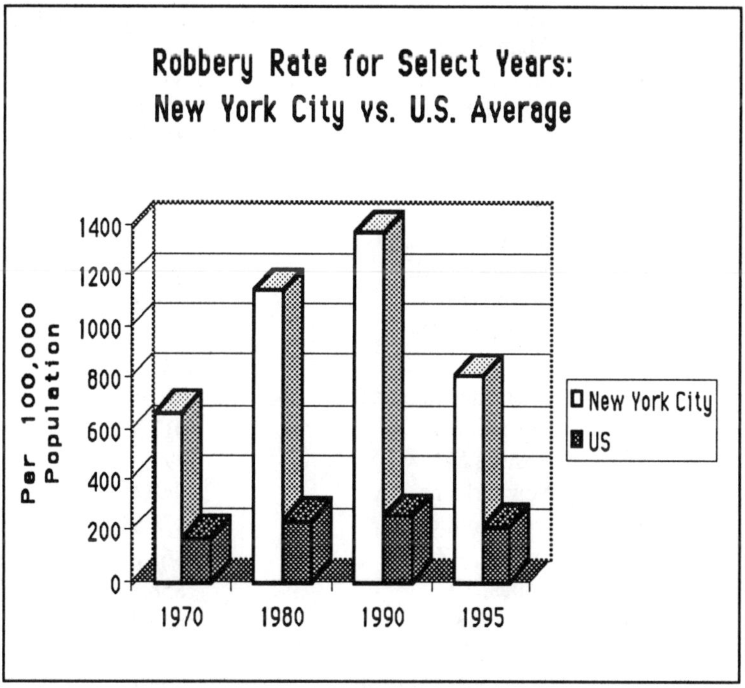


Data Sources: Federal Bureau of Investigation, *Crime in the United States*, annual, and *Statistical Abstract of the United States*, annual

## AGGRAVATED ASSAULT RATE: LARGE CITY RANKINGS

In 1995, New York City ranked twenty-fourth out of the 52 largest U.S. cities (300,000+ population) in terms of its aggravated assault rate per 100,000 inhabitants.

Meanwhile, Buffalo ranked thirteenth among the largest 52 cities.

As defined by the FBI, aggravated assault is an unlawful attack by one person upon another for the purpose of inflicting severe or aggravated bodily injury.

**Aggravated Assault Index (Per 100,000 Inhabitants)**

| Rank | City | Aggravated Assault Index |
|---|---|---|
| 1 | Atlanta, GA | 2,192.8 |
| 2 | St. Louis, MO | 1,843.4 |
| 3 | Miami, FL | 1,831.9 |
| 4 | Chicago, IL | 1,425.6 |
| 5 | Portland, OR | 1,321.6 |
| 6 | Washington, DC | 1,304.4 |
| 7 | Kansas City, MO | 1,302.9 |
| 8 | Baltimore, MD | 1,282.9 |
| 9 | Detroit, MI | 1,239.3 |
| 10 | Nashville, TN | 1,165.8 |
| 11 | Los Angeles, CA | 1,123.6 |
| 12 | Charlotte-Mecklenburg, NC | 1,070.6 |
| 13 | Buffalo, NY | 1,017.3 |
| 14 | Boston, MA | 997.6 |
| 15 | New Orleans, LA | 960.4 |
| 16 | Jacksonville, FL | 878.5 |
| 17 | Tucson, AZ | 861.8 |
| 18 | Dallas, TX | 858.2 |
| 19 | Tulsa, OK | 829.4 |
| 20 | Fresno, CA | 827.3 |
| 21 | Oklahoma City, OK | 799.1 |
| 22 | Minneapolis, MN | 796.6 |
| 23 | Omaha, NE | 767.2 |
| **24** | **New York City** | **714.8** |

*continued*

*continued*

| Rank | City | Aggravated Assault Index |
|---|---|---|
| 25 | Memphis, TN | 688.1 |
| 26 | Houston, TX | 685.4 |
| 27 | Phoenix, AZ | 669.6 |
| 28 | Las Vegas, NV | 645.9 |
| 29 | Fort Worth, TX | 638.9 |
| 30 | San Diego, CA | 638.7 |
| 31 | Cleveland, OH | 627.9 |
| 32 | Mesa, AZ | 611.1 |
| 33 | San Jose, CA | 609.4 |
| 34 | El Paso, TX | 609.0 |
| 35 | Long Beach, CA | 601.8 |
| 36 | Cincinnati, OH | 563.1 |
| 37 | San Francisco, CA | 546.2 |
| 38 | Sacramento, CA | 514.9 |
| 39 | Denver, CO | 502.6 |
| 40 | Indianapolis, IN | 470.4 |
| 41 | Philadelphia, PA | 467.6 |
| 42 | Seattle, WA | 450.9 |
| 43 | Austin, TX | 450.4 |
| 44 | Milwaukee, WI | 414.6 |
| 45 | Columbus, OH | 404.1 |
| 46 | Toledo, OH | 353.7 |
| 47 | Wichita, KS | 335.3 |
| 48 | Pittsburgh, PA | 308.7 |
| 49 | Colorado Springs, CO | 285.5 |
| 50 | San Antonio, TX | 203.3 |
| 51 | Honolulu, HI | 142.7 |
| 52 | Virginia Beach, VA | 85.8 |
| | U.S. Average | 418.3 |

Note: No data available for Oakland and Albuquerque.

Data Source: Federal Bureau of Investigation, *Crime in the United States 1995*

## AGGRAVATED ASSAULT RATE: NEW YORK CITY VS. U.S.

In 1995, New York City's aggravated assault rate (per 100,000 population) outpaced the U.S. average by 70.9 percent—714.8 in New York City versus 418.3 across the nation. The city's 1995 rate was down by 21.8 percent versus the 1990 rate of 941, but still exceeded the 1970 rate of 285.6 by 150.3 percent.

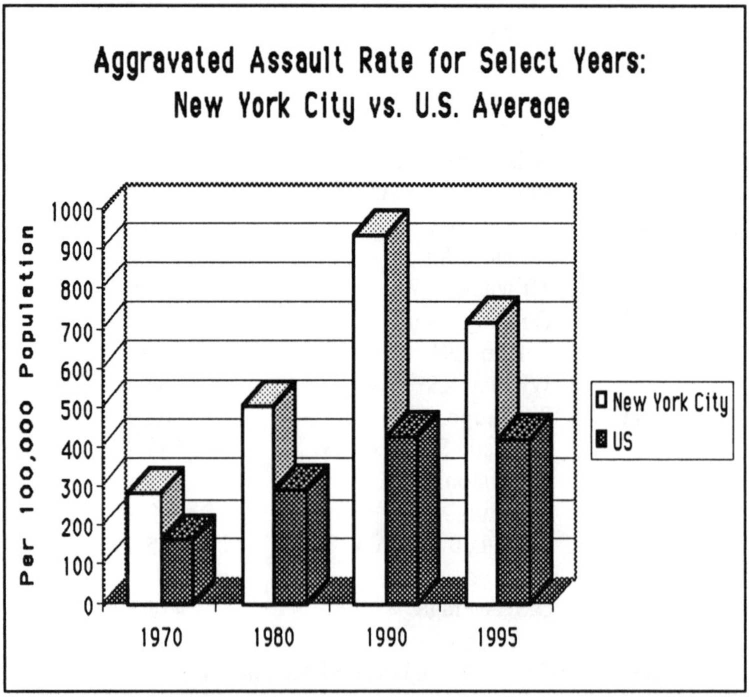


Data Sources: Federal Bureau of Investigation, *Crime in the United States*, annual, and *Statistical Abstract of the United States*, annual

## BURGLARY RATE: LARGE CITY RANKINGS

In 1995, New York City ranked a respectable forty-seventh out of the 53 largest U.S. cities (300,000+ population) in terms of its burglary rate per 100,000 inhabitants.

Buffalo ranked a dismal sixth among the largest 53 cities.

As defined by the FBI, burglary is the unlawful entry of a structure to commit a felony or a theft.

**Burglary Index (Per 100,000 Inhabitants)**

| Rank | City | Burglary Index |
|---|---|---|
| 1 | Atlanta, GA | 2,894.6 |
| 2 | St. Louis, MO | 2,881.9 |
| 3 | Miami, FL | 2,605.3 |
| 4 | Memphis, TN | 2,568.3 |
| 5 | Baltimore, MD | 2,327.1 |
| 6 | Buffalo, NY | 2,273.1 |
| 7 | Detroit, MI | 2,243.3 |
| 8 | Minneapolis, MN | 2,241.3 |
| 9 | Oklahoma City, OK | 2,236.1 |
| 10 | Kansas City, MO | 2,185.7 |
| 11 | Sacramento, CA | 2,128.5 |
| 12 | New Orleans, LA | 2,101.8 |
| 13 | Columbus, OH | 2,057.3 |
| 14 | Albuquerque, NM | 1,991.0 |
| 15 | Fresno, CA | 1,968.6 |
| 16 | Toledo, OH | 1,943.8 |
| 17 | Phoenix, AZ | 1,929.4 |
| 18 | Jacksonville, FL | 1,839.6 |
| 19 | Washington, DC | 1,838.4 |
| 20 | Charlotte-Mecklenburg, NC | 1,830.7 |
| 21 | Wichita, KS | 1,719.2 |
| 22 | Portland, OR | 1,702.2 |
| 23 | Tulsa, OK | 1,610.6 |
| 24 | Dallas, TX | 1,603.2 |
| 25 | Fort Worth, TX | 1,594.3 |

*continued*

*continued*

| Rank | City | Burglary Index |
|---|---|---|
| 26 | Nashville, TN | 1,571.8 |
| 27 | Cleveland, OH | 1,554.1 |
| 28 | Las Vegas, NV | 1,540.9 |
| 29 | Cincinnati, OH | 1,490.6 |
| 30 | Mesa, AZ | 1,465.8 |
| 31 | Denver, CO | 1,464.4 |
| 32 | Chicago, IL | 1,463.2 |
| 33 | Seattle, WA | 1,450.8 |
| 34 | Austin, TX | 1,435.3 |
| 35 | Houston, TX | 1,431.9 |
| 36 | San Antonio, TX | 1,396.1 |
| 37 | Milwaukee, WI | 1,345.0 |
| 38 | Tucson, AZ | 1,332.2 |
| 39 | Long Beach, CA | 1,279.1 |
| 40 | Boston, MA | 1,210.7 |
| 41 | Los Angeles, CA | 1,192.3 |
| 42 | Honolulu, HI | 1,150.8 |
| 43 | Omaha, NE | 1,115.8 |
| 44 | Colorado Springs, CO | 1,063.6 |
| 45 | Philadelphia, PA | 1,056.5 |
| 46 | Pittsburgh, PA | 1,013.5 |
| **47** | **New York City** | **1,009.4** |
| 48 | Indianapolis, IN | 1,008.7 |
| 49 | San Francisco, CA | 965.7 |
| 50 | San Diego, CA | 890.4 |
| 51 | Virginia Beach, VA | 668.6 |
| 52 | San Jose, CA | 665.5 |
| 53 | El Paso, TX | 648.8 |
| | U.S. Average | 987.6 |

Note: No data available for Oakland.

Data Source: Federal Bureau of Investigation, *Crime in the United States 1995*

## BURGLARY RATE: NEW YORK CITY VS. U.S.

In 1995, New York City's burglary rate (per 100,000 population) exceeded the U.S. average by 16.1 percent—1,009.4 in New York City versus the U.S. average of 987.6. Between 1980 and 1995, the city's burglary rate declined by 62.1 percent. The 1980 rate stood at 2,660.7. The 1995 rate is even down by 44.6 percent versus the 1970 rate of 1,821.

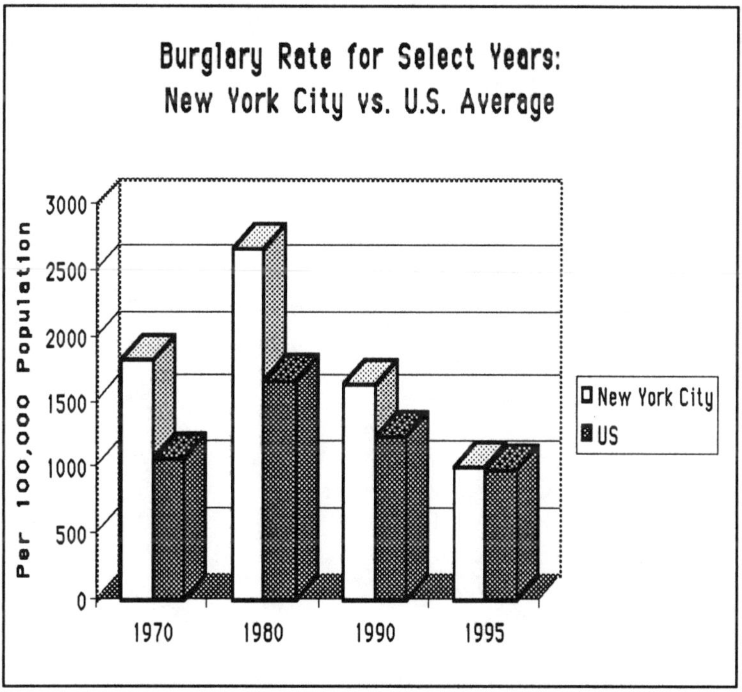


Data Sources: Federal Bureau of Investigation, *Crime in the United States*, annual, and *Statistical Abstract of the United States*, annual

## LARCENY-THEFT RATE: LARGE CITY RANKINGS

In 1995, New York City ranked an excellent fifty-first out of the 53 largest U.S. cities (300,000+ population) in terms of its larceny-theft rate per 100,000 inhabitants.

Buffalo ranked forty-first among the largest 53 cities.

As defined by the FBI, larceny-theft is the unlawful taking, carrying, leading, or riding away of property from the possession or constructive possession of another.

**Larceny-Theft Index (Per 100,000 Inhabitants)**

| Rank | City | Larceny-Theft Index |
|---|---|---|
| 1 | Atlanta, GA | 8,470.5 |
| 2 | Tucson, AZ | 8,274.4 |
| 3 | St. Louis, MO | 7,705.4 |
| 4 | Miami, FL | 7,265.7 |
| 5 | Oklahoma City, OK | 6,880.5 |
| 6 | Seattle, WA | 6,786.8 |
| 7 | Portland, OR | 6,446.4 |
| 8 | Baltimore, MD | 6,407.2 |
| 9 | Minneapolis, MN | 6,064.2 |
| 10 | Kansas City, MO | 5,897.1 |
| 11 | Washington, DC | 5,833.8 |
| 12 | Nashville, TN | 5,794.5 |
| 13 | Albuquerque, NM | 5,586.0 |
| 14 | Phoenix, AZ | 5,479.9 |
| 15 | Charlotte-Mecklenburg, NC | 5,381.1 |
| 16 | Honolulu, HI | 5,306.4 |
| 17 | Fresno, CA | 5,296.9 |
| 18 | San Antonio, TX | 5,237.0 |
| 19 | Austin, TX | 5,235.5 |
| 20 | Mesa, AZ | 5,228.0 |
| 21 | Columbus, OH | 4,993.0 |
| 22 | Wichita, KS | 4,945.2 |
| 23 | Sacramento, CA | 4,930.3 |
| 24 | El Paso, TX | 4,921.0 |

*continued*

*continued*

| Rank | City | Larceny-Theft Index |
|---|---|---|
| 25 | Jacksonville, FL | 4,905.2 |
| 26 | Fort Worth, TX | 4,810.4 |
| 27 | Colorado Springs, CO | 4,799.1 |
| 28 | Boston, MA | 4,719.1 |
| 29 | Dallas, TX | 4,709.0 |
| 30 | San Francisco, CA | 4,627.8 |
| 31 | Omaha, NE | 4,618.1 |
| 32 | New Orleans, LA | 4,610.7 |
| 33 | Toledo, OH | 4,574.4 |
| 34 | Chicago, IL | 4,417.7 |
| 35 | Detroit, MI | 4,354.6 |
| 36 | Milwaukee, WI | 4,217.2 |
| 37 | Cincinnati, OH | 4,170.0 |
| 38 | Memphis, TN | 3,957.5 |
| 39 | Las Vegas, NV | 3,839.2 |
| 40 | Houston, TX | 3,574.2 |
| 41 | Buffalo, NY | 3,565.4 |
| 42 | Denver, CO | 3,510.1 |
| 43 | Virginia Beach, VA | 3,496.3 |
| 44 | Tulsa, OK | 3,445.9 |
| 45 | Long Beach, CA | 3,213.5 |
| 46 | Pittsburgh, PA | 3,180.0 |
| 47 | Los Angeles, CA | 3,120.3 |
| 48 | Philadelphia, PA | 3,028.2 |
| 49 | Cleveland, OH | 2,780.6 |
| 50 | San Diego, CA | 2,634.3 |
| **51** | **New York City** | **2,500.5** |
| 52 | San Jose, CA | 2,399.1 |
| 53 | Indianapolis, IN | 2,062.2 |
| | U.S. Average | 3,044.9 |

Note: No data available for Oakland.

Data Source: Federal Bureau of Investigation, *Crime in the United States 1995*

## LARCENY-THEFT RATE: NEW YORK CITY VS. U.S.

In 1995, the U.S. larceny-theft rate (per 100,000 population) outpaced the New York City rate by 21.8 percent—2,500.5 in New York City versus the U.S. rate of 3,044.9. New York City's 1995 rate was down by 31.8 percent versus its 1990 rate of 3,668. However, the 1995 rate outpaced the 1970 rate of 1,471.2 by 70 percent.

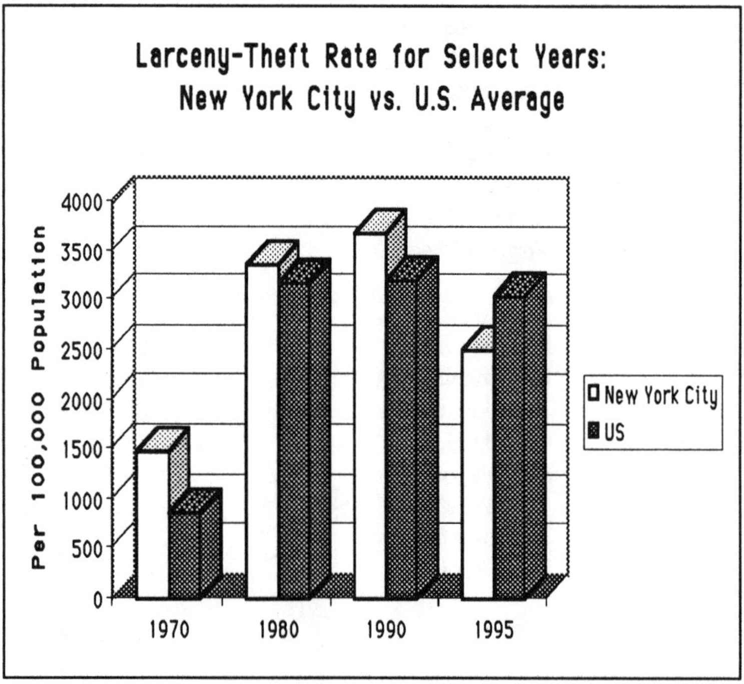


Data Sources: Federal Bureau of Investigation, *Crime in the United States*, annual, and *Statistical Abstract of the United States*, annual

## MOTOR VEHICLE THEFT RATE: LARGE CITY RANKINGS

In 1994, New York City ranked thirty-ninth out of the 53 largest U.S. cities (300,000+ population) in terms of its motor vehicle theft rate per 100,000 inhabitants.

Meanwhile, Buffalo ranked far worse—twenty-first among the largest 53 cities.

As defined by the FBI, obviously, motor vehicle theft is the theft or attempted theft of a motor vehicle.

**Motor Vehicle Theft Index (Per 100,000 Inhabitants)**

| Rank | City | Motor Vehicle Theft Index |
|---|---|---|
| 1 | Fresno, CA | 3,200.5 |
| 2 | Detroit, MI | 2,936.1 |
| 3 | Miami, FL | 2,330.3 |
| 4 | Memphis, TN | 2,217.5 |
| 5 | St. Louis, MO | 2,157.7 |
| 6 | Phoenix, AZ | 2,132.7 |
| 7 | Sacramento, CA | 2,122.9 |
| 8 | Atlanta, GA | 2,067.3 |
| 9 | New Orleans, LA | 2,019.1 |
| 10 | Portland, OR | 1,985.4 |
| 11 | Washington, DC | 1,839.9 |
| 12 | Cleveland, OH | 1,829.9 |
| 13 | Milwaukee, WI | 1,824.0 |
| 14 | Boston, MA | 1,821.4 |
| 15 | Dallas, TX | 1,620.2 |
| 16 | Baltimore, MD | 1,569.1 |
| 17 | Philadelphia, PA | 1,556.1 |
| 18 | Nashville, TN | 1,548.7 |
| 19 | Kansas City, MO | 1,522.9 |
| 20 | Mesa, AZ | 1,379.7 |
| 21 | Buffalo, NY | 1,348.7 |
| 22 | Tucson, AZ | 1,344.2 |
| 23 | Los Angeles, CA | 1,333.1 |
| 24 | Chicago, IL | 1,316.3 |

*continued*

*continued*

| Rank | City | Motor Vehicle Theft Index |
|---|---|---|
| 25 | Seattle, WA | 1,310.2 |
| 26 | Houston, TX | 1,299.7 |
| 27 | Minneapolis, MN | 1,253.9 |
| 28 | Long Beach, CA | 1,243.1 |
| 29 | Albuquerque, NM | 1,189.3 |
| 30 | Tulsa, OK | 1,167.6 |
| 31 | San Francisco, CA | 1,123.4 |
| 32 | Columbus, OH | 1,101.7 |
| 33 | Oklahoma City, OK | 1,097.6 |
| 34 | Omaha, NE | 1,087.6 |
| 35 | San Diego, CA | 1,065.8 |
| 36 | Fort Worth, TX | 1,056.7 |
| 37 | Denver, CO | 1,035.8 |
| 38 | Las Vegas, NV | 1,007.7 |
| **39** | **New York City** | **992.9** |
| 40 | Toledo, OH | 988.9 |
| 41 | Pittsburgh, PA | 954.1 |
| 42 | Wichita, KS | 848.4 |
| 43 | Honolulu, HI | 845.5 |
| 44 | Jacksonville, FL | 844.8 |
| 45 | San Antonio, TX | 842.2 |
| 46 | Indianapolis, IN | 778.3 |
| 47 | Austin, TX | 683.4 |
| 48 | Charlotte-Mecklenburg, NC | 671.0 |
| 49 | El Paso, TX | 658.0 |
| 50 | Cincinnati, OH | 531.4 |
| 51 | San Jose, CA | 513.4 |
| 52 | Colorado Springs, CO | 428.4 |
| 53 | Virginia Beach, VA | 264.4 |
| | U.S. Average | 560.5 |

Note: No data available for Oakland.

Data Source: Federal Bureau of Investigation, *Crime in the United States 1995*

## MOTOR VEHICLE THEFT RATE: NEW YORK CITY VS. U.S.

In 1995, New York City's motor vehicle theft rate (per 100,000 population) of 992.9 surpassed the U.S. rate of 560.5 by 77.1 percent. The city's motor vehicle theft rate for 1995 was down by 50.6 percent versus the 1990 rate of 2,009, and down by 32.5 percent versus the 1970 rate of 1,471.2.

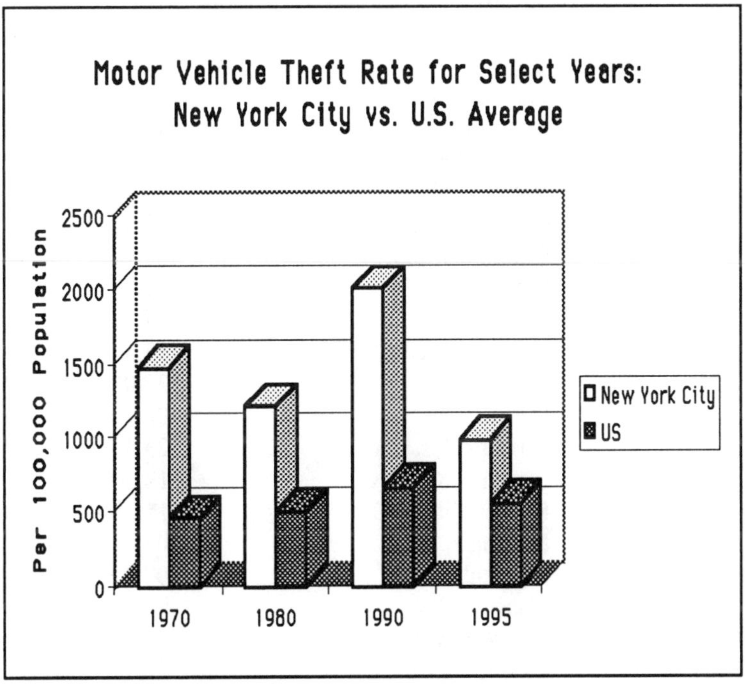


Data Sources: Federal Bureau of Investigation, *Crime in the United States*, annual, and *Statistical Abstract of the United States*, annual

## ARSON RATE: LARGE CITY RANKINGS

In 1995, New York City ranked twenty-ninth out of the 49 largest U.S. cities (300,000+ population) in terms of its arson rate per 100,000 inhabitants. (Arson numbers for 1995 for New York City were unavailable.)

Meanwhile, Buffalo ranked fourth among the largest cities.

As defined by the FBI, arson is any willful or malicious burning or attempted burning, with or without attempt to defraud, a dwelling house, public building, motor vehicle or aircraft, personal property of another, etc.

**Arson Index (Per 100,000 Inhabitants)**

| Rank | City | Arson Index |
|---|---|---|
| 1 | Fresno, CA | 231.1 |
| 2 | St. Louis, MO | 219.0 |
| 3 | Toledo, OH | 163.9 |
| 4 | Buffalo, NY | 160.5 |
| 5 | Philadelphia, PA | 160.3 |
| 6 | Columbus, OH | 159.7 |
| 7 | Cleveland, OH | 152.0 |
| 8 | Boston, MA | 144.3 |
| 9 | Cincinnati, OH | 133.5 |
| 10 | Portland, OR | 132.0 |
| 11 | Dallas, TX | 128.7 |
| 12 | Los Angeles, CA | 123.3 |
| 13 | Austin, TX | 118.6 |
| 14 | Kansas City, MO | 115.7 |
| 15 | Memphis, TN | 102.4 |
| 16 | Milwaukee, WI | 100.3 |
| 17 | Houston, TX | 90.4 |
| 18 | Fort Worth, TX | 87.1 |
| 19 | Oklahoma City, OK | 86.8 |
| 20 | San Antonio, TX | 86.5 |
| 21 | Detroit, MI | 82.7 |
| 22 | Denver, CO | 82.0 |

*continued*

*continued*

| Rank | City | Arson Index |
|---|---|---|
| 23 | Baltimore, MD | 81.1 |
| 24 | Charlotte, NC | 79.7 |
| 25 | Oakland, CA | 78.2 |
| 26 | Tulsa, OK | 75.1 |
| 27 | Pittsburgh, PA | 74.0 |
| 28 | El Paso, TX | 70.1 |
| **29** | **New York City** | **67.1** |
| 30 | Omaha, NE | 62.6 |
| 31 | Jacksonville, FL | 61.4 |
| 32 | San Francisco, CA | 58.8 |
| 33 | Miami, FL | 58.7 |
| 34 | San Jose, CA | 58.2 |
| 35 | Chicago. IL | 58.0 |
| 36 | Seattle, WA | 55.9 |
| 37 | Las Vegas, NV | 53.9 |
| 38 | Atlanta, GA | 49.1 |
| 39 | Virginia Beach, VA | 46.6 |
| 40 | Long Beach, CA | 46.4 |
| 41 | Indianapolis, IN | 45.6 |
| 42 | Sacramento, CA | 40.6 |
| 43 | Honolulu, HI | 37.6 |
| 44 | Colorado Springs, CO | 38.5 |
| 45 | Washington, DC | 36.1 |
| 46 | Mesa, AZ | 33.3 |
| 47 | Tucson, AZ | 29.0 |
| 48 | Phoenix, AZ | 26.1 |
| 49 | San Diego, CA | 18.5 |

Note: No data available for Albuquerque, NM; Wichita, KS; New Orleans, LA; Minneapolis, MN; and Nashville, TN.

Source: Federal Bureau of Investigation, *Crime in the United States 1994*

## LAW ENFORCEMENT EMPLOYEES BY LARGE CITIES

In 1994, New York City ranked third among the largest cities (300,000+ population) in terms of the number of full-time law-enforcement employees per 10,000 inhabitants.

**Full-Time Law-Enforcement Employees (Per 10,000 Inhabitants)**

| Rank | City | Employees per 10,000 pop. |
|---|---|---|
| 1 | Washington, DC | 83.9 |
| 2 | St. Louis, MO | 57.1 |
| **3** | **New York City** | **54.5** |
| 4 | Chicago, IL | 54.3 |
| 5 | Baltimore, MD | 49.2 |
| 6 | Atlanta, GA | 48.0 |
| 7 | Boston, MA | 47.6 |
| 8 | Philadelphia, PA | 44.7 |
| 9 | Detroit, MI | 42.9 |
| 10 | Milwaukee, WI | 39.9 |
| 11 | Houston, TX | 39.8 |
| 12 | Cleveland, OH | 38.8 |
| 13 | Kansas City, MO | 38.5 |
| 14 | New Orleans, LA | 37.8 |
| 15 | Miami, FL | 36.0 |
| 16 | Cincinnati, OH | 32.8 |
| 17 | Jacksonville, FL | 32.7 |
| 18 | Seattle, WA | 32.5 |
| 19 | Pittsburgh, PA | 32.4 |
| 20 | Dallas, TX | 32.3 |
| 21 | Denver, CO | 30.7 |
| 22 | Los Angeles, CA | 30.3 |
| 23 | San Francisco, CA | 30.1 |
| 24 | Las Vegas, NV | 29.6 |
| 25 | Fort Worth, TX | 29.1 |
| 26(t) | Columbus, OH | 28.9 |
| 26(t) | Nashville, TN | 28.9 |
| 28 | Charlotte, NC | 28.7 |

*continued*

*continued*

| Rank | City | Employees per 10,000 pop. |
|---|---|---|
| 29 | Oklahoma City, OK | 28.5 |
| 30 | Memphis, TN | 28.3 |
| 31(t) | Minneapolis, MN | 27.5 |
| 31(t) | Albuquerque, NM | 27.5 |
| 33 | Portland, OR | 27.4 |
| 34 | Oakland, CA | 26.5 |
| 35 | Phoenix, AZ | 26.4 |
| 36 | Honolulu, HI | 25.8 |
| 37(t) | Austin, TX | 25.0 |
| 37(t) | Long Beach, CA | 25.0 |
| 39 | Mesa, AZ | 23.7 |
| 40 | Sacramento, CA | 23.4 |
| 41(t) | Omaha, NE | 23.3 |
| 41(t) | Toledo, OH | 23.3 |
| 43 | Tucson, AZ | 23.1 |
| 44 | San Diego, CA | 22.6 |
| 45 | Tulsa, OK | 22.3 |
| 46 | Wichita, KS | 21.9 |
| 47 | Colorado Springs, CO | 21.4 |
| 48 | El Paso, TX | 21.3 |
| 49 | Virginia Beach, VA | 20.9 |
| 50 | San Antonio, TX | 20.8 |
| 51 | San Jose, CA | 19.5 |
| 52 | Fresno, CA | 18.5 |
| 53 | Indianapolis, IN | 17.4 |

Note: No data available for Buffalo, NY, and number for Albuquerque, NM is based on population estimate for 1994.

Data Source: Federal Bureau of Investigation, *Crime in the United States 1994*

# CITY POLICE PROTECTION EXPENDITURES: CITY RANKINGS

New York City ranked second highest among the largest cities (500,000+ population) in the nation in terms of per capita city police protection expenditures in 1994.

**Per Capita City Police Protection Expenditures**

| Rank | City | Per Capita Police Expenditures |
|---|---|---|
| 1 | Detroit | $283.43 |
| **2** | **New York City** | **281.07** |
| 3 | Cleveland | 268.87 |
| 4 | Boston | 266.47 |
| 5 | San Francisco | 265.55 |
| 6 | Chicago | 263.94 |
| 7 | Baltimore | 231.00 |
| 8 | Milwaukee | 216.42 |
| 9 | Seattle | 215.42 |
| 10 | Philadelphia | 215.04 |
| 11 | Los Angeles | 198.42 |
| 12 | Columbus | 194.88 |
| 13 | Houston | 189.66 |
| 14 | Dallas | 166.48 |
| 15 | Phoenix | 166.04 |
| 16 | San Diego | 151.02 |
| 17 | San Jose | 148.52 |
| 18 | Honolulu | 142.04 |
| 19 | Memphis | 141.36 |
| 20 | Jacksonville | 136.91 |
| 21 | Indianapolis | 125.03 |
| 22 | San Antonio | 117.39 |
| 23 | El Paso | 97.70 |
| | Large City Average | 217.28 |

Note: See Part One of this book for District of Columbia.

Data Source: U.S. Department of Commerce

## CITY POLICE PROTECTION EXPENDITURES: NEW YORK CITY VS. LARGE CITY AVERAGE

In 1994, New York City's per capita police protection spending exceeded the large city (500,000+ population) average by 29.4 percent—$281.07 in New York City versus the large city average of $217.28.

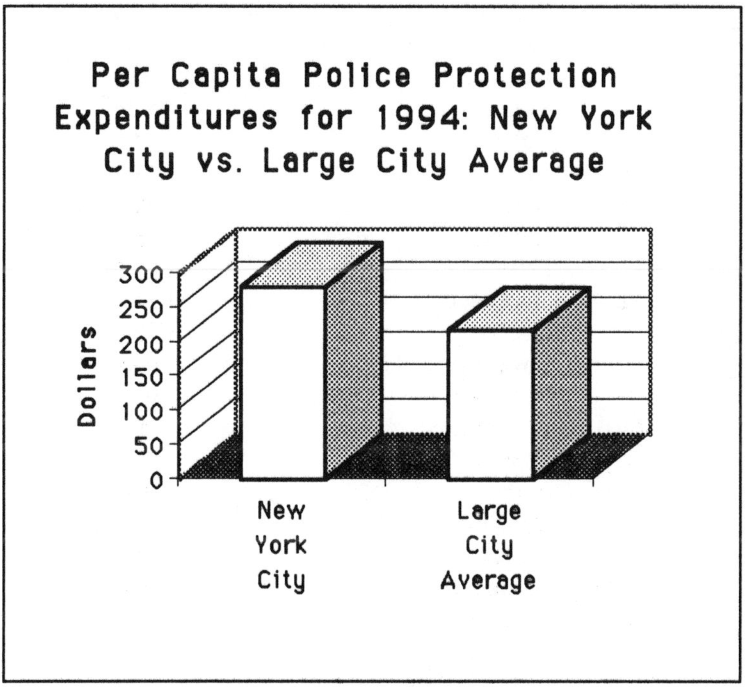


Data Source: U.S. Department of Commerce

## CITY CORRECTIONS EXPENDITURES: CITY RANKINGS

New York City ranked highest among the largest cities (500,000+ population) in the nation in terms of per capita city corrections expenditures in 1994.

**Per Capita City Corrections Expenditures**

| Rank | City | Per Capita Corrections Expenditures |
|---|---|---|
| 1 | **New York City** | **$152.55** |
| 2 | Philadelphia | 124.51 |
| 3 | San Francisco | 100.53 |
| 4 | Boston | 95.43 |
| 5 | Jacksonville | 55.38 |
| 6 | Indianapolis | 40.07 |
| 7 | Seattle | 15.86 |
| 8 | Columbus | 15.06 |
| 9 | Cleveland | 11.05 |
| 10 | Houston | 8.33 |
| 11 | Dallas | 5.14 |
| 12 | Phoenix | 4.56 |
| 13 | San Diego | 3.90 |
| 14 | Detroit | 1.43 |
| 15 | Los Angeles | 0.84 |
| 16 | San Antonio | 0.66 |
| 17(t) | Baltimore | 0.00 |
| 17(t) | Chicago | 0.00 |
| 17(t) | El Paso | 0.00 |
| 17(t) | Honolulu | 0.00 |
| 17(t) | Memphis | 0.00 |
| 17(t) | Milwaukee | 0.00 |
| 17(t) | San Jose | 0.00 |
| | Large City Average | 51.18 |

Note: See Part One of this book for District of Columbia.

Data Source: U.S. Department of Commerce

## CITY CORRECTIONS EXPENDITURES: NEW YORK CITY VS. LARGE CITY AVERAGE

In 1994, New York City's per capita corrections expenditures topped the large city (500,000+ population) average by 198.1 percent—$152.55 in New York City versus the large city average of $51.18.

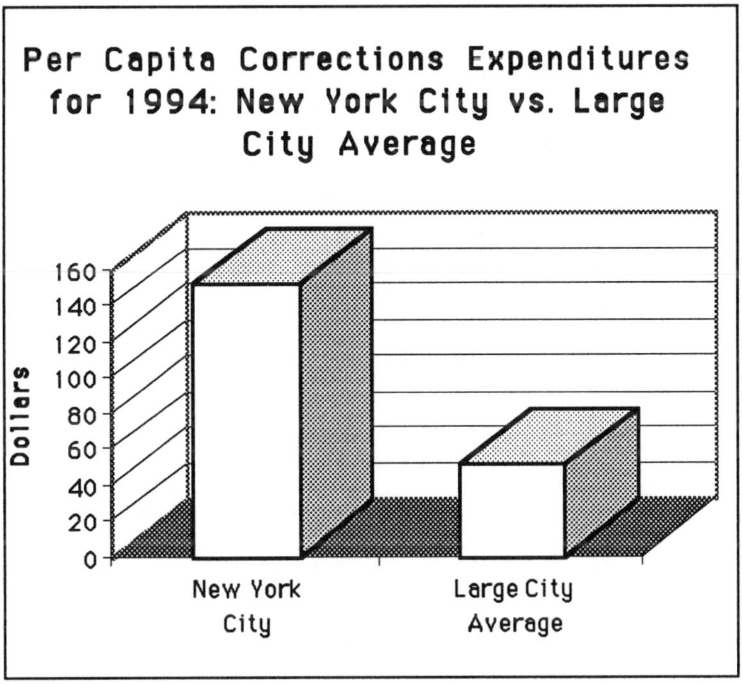


Data Source: U.S. Department of Commerce

# Chapter Ten

# New York City: The Economy

- Total Employment
- Private-Sector Employment
- Population

## TOTAL EMPLOYMENT: NEW YORK CITY VS. U.S.

Since the late 1950s, New York City total employment growth has been abysmal. In fact, no growth has occurred at all. Instead, New York City's total employment between 1958 and 1995 actually *declined* by 4.6 percent, compared with total U.S. employment *growth* of 111.4 percent. From the city's total employment peak in 1969 to 1995, total employment *declined* by 12.6 percent, compared with U.S. *growth* of 63.5 percent. On an annual basis, the city's rate of job creation only outpaced the U.S. rate in three out of 36 years—1980, 1981, and 1982.

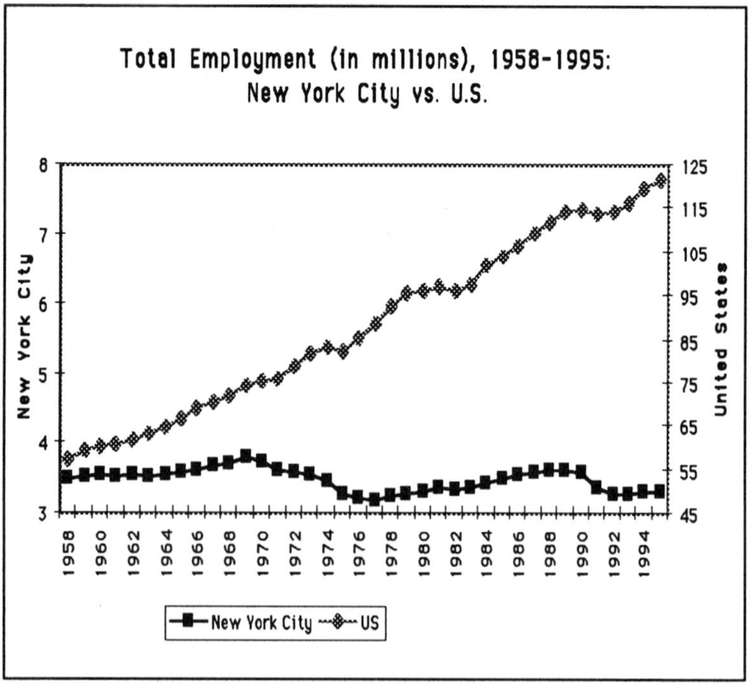


Data Sources: U.S. Department of Labor and the New York State Department of Labor

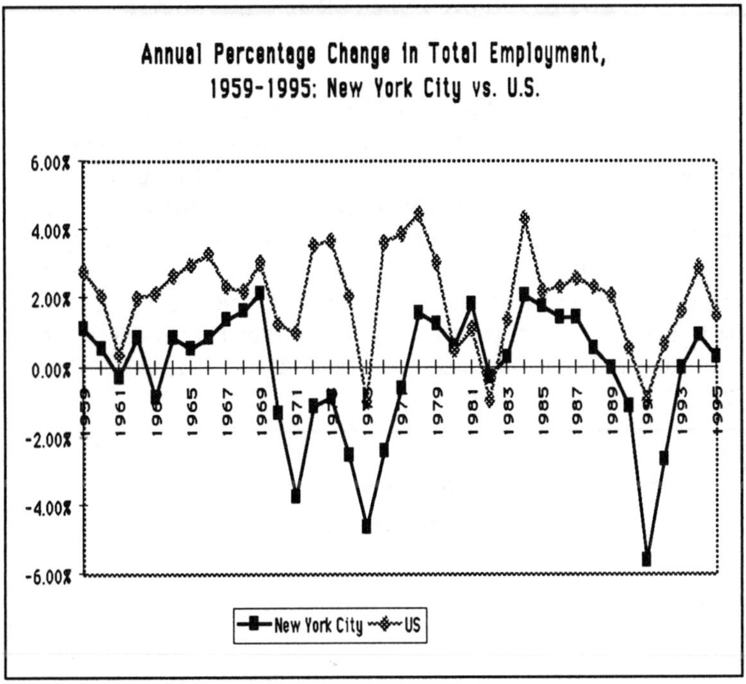


Data Sources: U.S. Department of Labor and the New York State Department of Labor

## TOTAL PRIVATE SECTOR EMPLOYMENT: NEW YORK CITY VS. U.S.

Since the late 1950s, New York City total private sector employment growth has been nonexistent. In fact, total private sector employment has declined. Between 1958 and 1995, New York City private sector employment actually *declined* by 9.7 percent, compared with total U.S. employment *growth* of 106 percent. From the city's total employment peak in 1969 to 1995, total private sector employment *declined* by 14.5 percent, compared with U.S. *growth* of 64.5 percent. On an annual basis, the city's rate of private sector job creation only managed to outpace the U.S. rate in three out of 36 years—1980, 1981, and 1982.

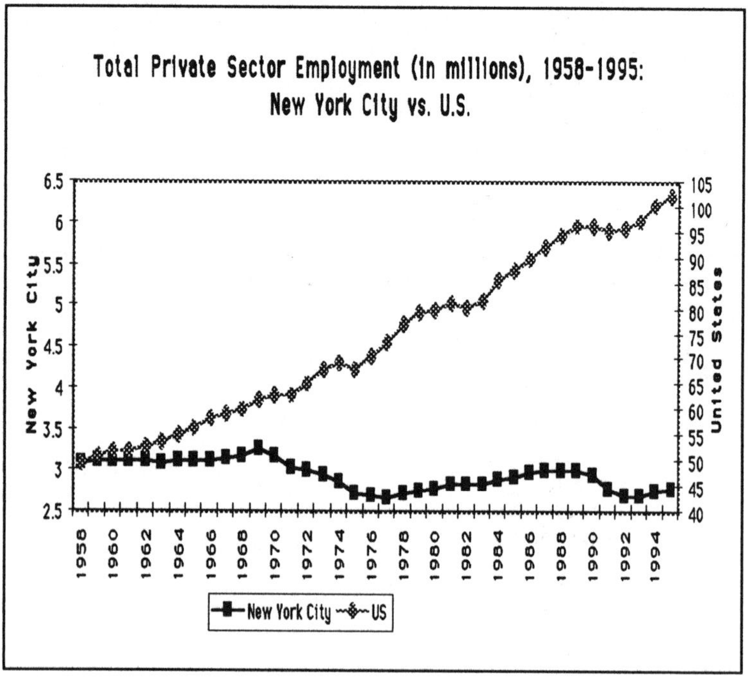


Data Sources: U.S. Department of Labor and the New York State Department of Labor

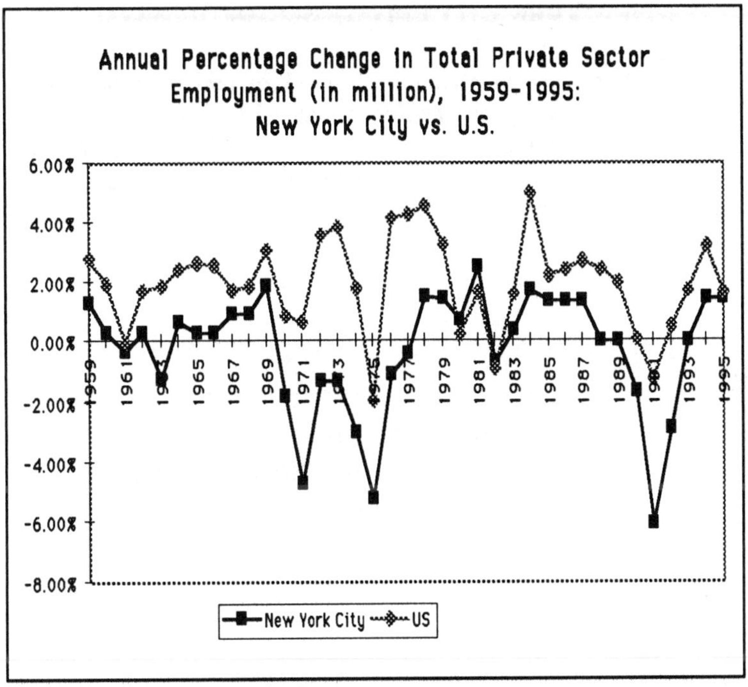


Data Sources: U.S. Department of Labor and the New York State Department of Labor

## NEW YORK CITY PRIVATE SECTOR JOBS GAP

If New York City only had managed to keep pace with the national rate of private sector job creation between 1958 and 1995, the city would have laid claim to 6.34 million jobs in 1995 versus the actual total of 2.78 million. The New York City jobs gap over this period amounted to 3.56 million jobs.

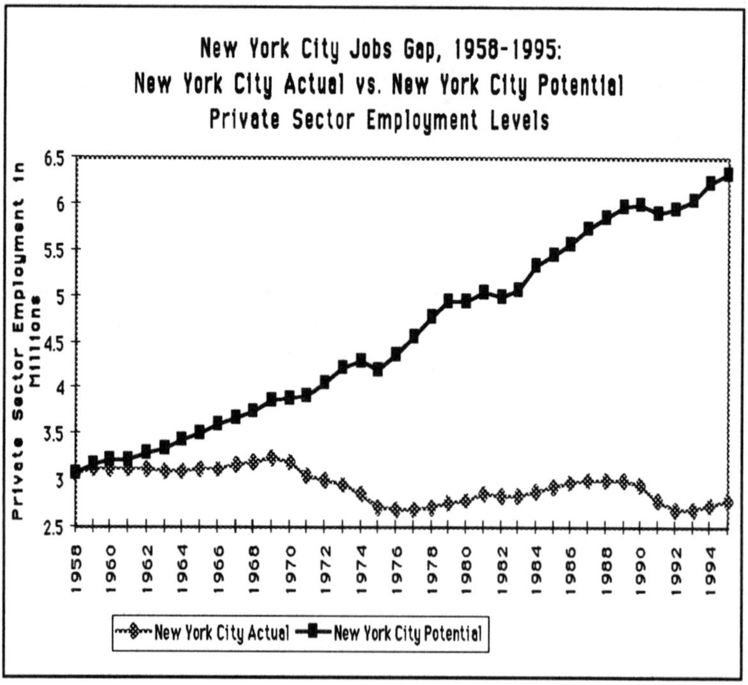


Data Source: Author's calculations

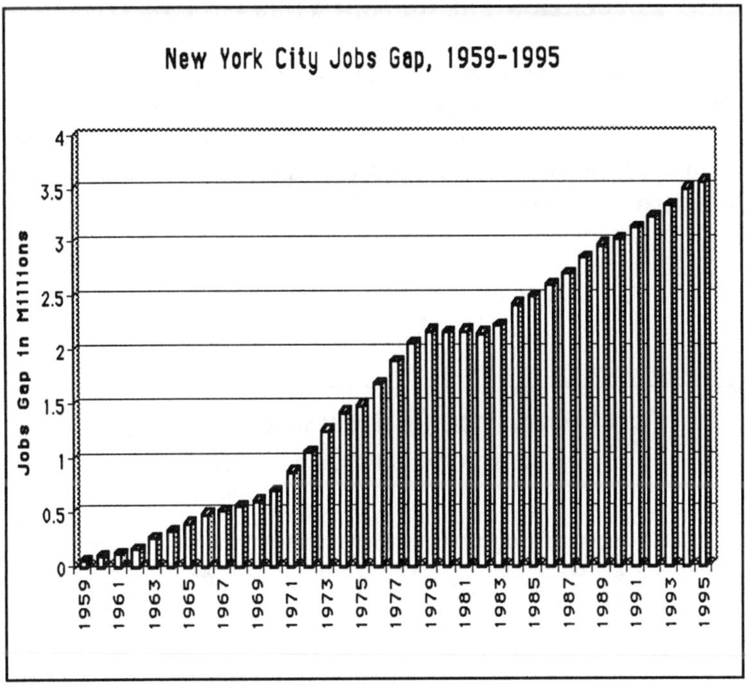


Data Source: Author's calculations

## POPULATION TREND: NEW YORK CITY VS. U.S.

New York City population growth far outpaced total U.S. growth in the 1920s and 1930s, roughly equaled the U.S. rate in the 1940s, and ever since has lagged way behind U.S. growth. Indeed, the city suffered a population loss in the 1950s, a substantial loss in the 1970s, and witnessed a small decline between 1990 and 1992.

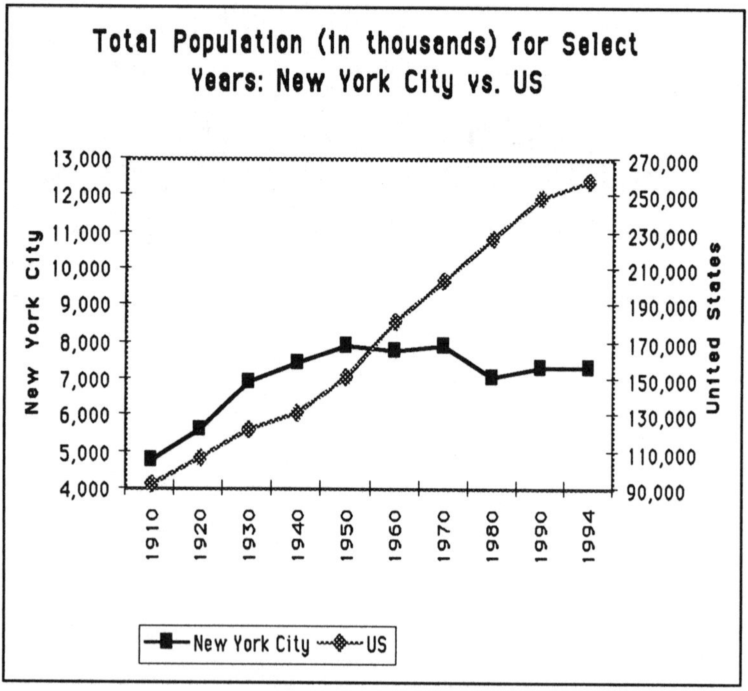


Data Sources: U.S. Department of Commerce, *Statistical Abstract of the United States 1996*, and The Nelson Rockefeller Institute of Government, *1995 New York State Statistical Yearbook*

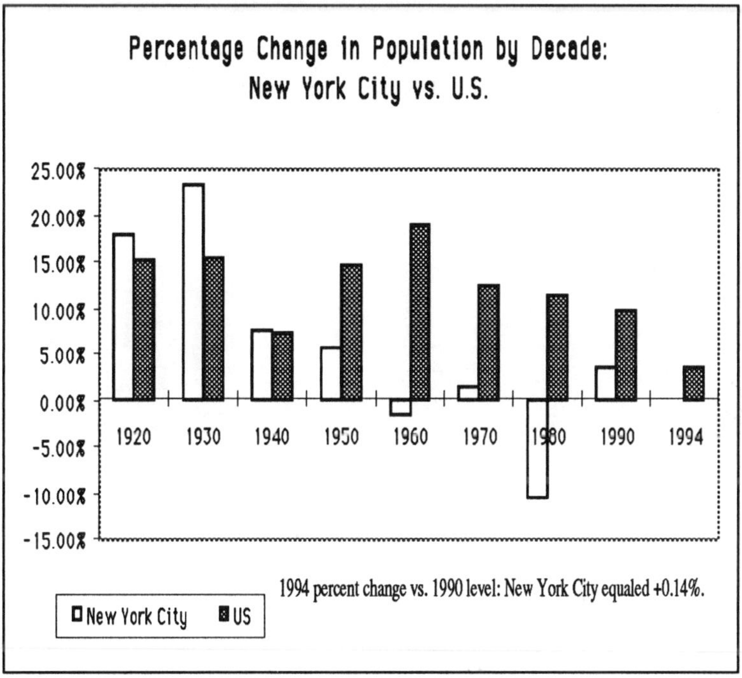
Percentage Change in Population by Decade:
New York City vs. U.S.
25.00%
20.00%
15.00%
10.00%
5.00%
0.00%
-5.00%
-10.00%
-15.00%
1920
1930
1940
1950
1960
1970
1980
1990
1994
New York City
US
1994 percent change vs. 1990 level: New York City equaled +0.14%.

# Part Three: New York in the Twenty-First Century

# Chapter Eleven

# The Road to Revitalization

One of three possible roads will pave New York's way into the twenty-first century. The first road has been well traveled by both New York State and New York City for at least the latter half of the twentieth century. It is the big-government road.

As described in the numerous rankings, charts, and graphs in the preceding pages, spending, debt, and taxes in both the state and city ballooned in recent decades and have come to rank among the most burdensome in the nation. The results for the economy and society in general in New York have been predictably dismal. Continuing down the road of activist government ensures that New York's long decline will continue and likely accelerate.

The second road seems to be where New York rides today. It is the path of least resistance—straddling between stewardship of the status quo and small reform steps.

For all the discussion and comments regarding his vision for the future of New York and the nation, Mario Cuomo seemed content to manage New York's decline during his years as governor. He failed to make the *monstrous* errors of the Rockefeller years, though Cuomo made many significant mistakes. For example he imposed eight new taxes—the business tax surcharge, natural gas tax, lubricating oil tax, petroleum business tax, real property gains tax, container tax, hotel occupancy tax, and the auto rental tax—hiked the state's capital gains tax, and at the same time, either opposed or was the last to embrace the few, minimal positive initiatives others proposed during his 12 years in the Governor's Mansion. And in the 1990s, Cuomo reneged on promised, already-legislated tax cuts year after year.

Cuomo's successor, Governor George Pataki, thus far largely tinkers at the margins. Whether tinkering is a reflection of Pataki's actual desires, or mere submission to the political reality of a State Assembly enamored with the activist government philosophy and a State Senate guided by no prevailing government philosophy whatsoever, remains an open question. The New York State Senate largely blows with the political winds. For example, during state budget negotiations in 1995, State Senate Republicans stood fairly firm in favor of spending restraint and tax cuts. The following year witnessed the Senate GOP majority abandoning Pataki's efforts to keep spending under control and joining Assembly Democrats in pushing for higher spending. Overall under Pataki, small steps have been taken toward lower taxes and state spending restraint. In the opposite direction, though, substantial spending cuts have not occurred (in fact, overall state spending increased in 1996-97), ground continues to be lost on the property rights front as federal, state and local government acquire and regulate more land in New York, and corporate welfare continues to flourish.

Unfortunately, New York City manages to produce even fewer truly positive reforms. Status-quo stewardship seems the overall rule for the city. For example, while progress on crime and some spending restraint have come about in the last few years, much more is required on these fronts. As for taxes, reductions have been minimal, verging on nonexistent. Indeed, some recent slippage back to the city's old fiscal shenanigans can be detected. In April and early May of 1996, for example, Mayor Rudy Giuliani proposed a new public authority—the New York City Infrastructure Financing Authority—for public school and other capital costs to avoid city constitutional borrowing limits (the state's constitution limits New York City's outstanding debt to no more than 10 percent of the city's full taxable value of real estate). Giuliani also advocated spending more than a billion dollars on a new stadium for the New York Yankees, along with another $100-plus million toward a new ballpark for the crosstown Mets. Worst of all, Giuliani reneged on his support for allowing the city's income tax surcharge finally to expire at the end of 1996. Instead, his 1996-97 budget plan called for a *four-year* extension of the surcharge.

Mayor Giuliani's limited understanding of the depths of New York City's continuing woes perhaps was best captured by his quote at the opening of *The City of New York Financial Plan Fiscal Years 1996-2000*: "In the past two years New York City has done more downsizing, privatization and restructuring than any city in America. But there is a point beyond which we cannot go in downsizing in any one year without destroying the city." In fact, New York City's efforts at downsizing and privatization amount to nothing more than a good *start*, and the city's destruction—which has been going on for decades—will continue unless this process is greatly accelerated.

The third road is the one least traveled in both New York State and New York City. In fact, it is a road that has remained desolate throughout this century. It is the road, however, that leads to vigorous economic growth and a vital, healthy society—paved with low taxes, small government, and sound moral principles.

This third road remains the only choice that leads to the revitalization of both New Yorks—state and city. It calls for a dramatic change in how government is thought about in New York, with increased recognition of the vast limits and inefficiencies of government and how government creates perverse incentives.

The following pages outline a new agenda for both New York State and New York City—New York's "road to revitalization." Critics of these ideas will range from those who simply possess a stake in the current system—generally classified as "special interests"—to those who recognize the merits of such steps but believe them to be not feasible politically.

One expects nothing less from special interests. As for political infeasibility, these ideas have to be injected into the public-policy mix, debated, and discussed, in order to enter the realm of feasibility and eventually to be implemented. Rejecting such ideas as infeasible merely ensures that they remain infeasible. New York policymakers and politicians who acknowledge the merits of the following initiatives behind closed doors, but then fail to push them publicly, are nothing more than political cowards—not worthy of respect or elected office.

The time has come to muster the political courage to advance the ideas that will revitalize New York State and New York City.

## Supply-Side Tax Cuts

### New York State

The state of New York needs to cut taxes, and cut them deeply. The focus of tax reduction should be on those levies that present the greatest obstacles to economic growth, that is, those taxes that directly raise the costs of working, saving, investing, and risk taking in New York.

Every tax, though, creates inefficiencies by removing resources from the private sector, from individual decision-making, and from the disciplines of the marketplace; and transferring them to government, to political and bureaucratic decision-making, and freeing them from almost any disciplines whatsoever. The following is a four-step tax program for New York's revitalization:

• *Step One: Eliminate the state's capital gains tax.* Taxing the returns on investing and entrepreneurship makes no economic sense whatsoever. In 1997, New York's top tax rate on capital gains is scheduled to decline to 6.85 percent—still 27 percent higher than its most recent low of 5.4 percent in 1986 and almost double the 1958 rate of 3.5 percent. In addition, as explained earlier, capital gains are not indexed for inflation, therefore the real capital gains tax rate is much higher than the stated rate of 6.85 percent.

As the first major step on the road to revitalization, New York State officials should eliminate the state's capital gains taxes. Based on the latest figures available from the state's Department of Taxation and Finance (1992), eliminating the capital gains tax for individuals would translate into a *static* (i.e., based on the absurd assumption that individuals do not change their economic activity and decisions when tax rates change) annual revenue loss of roughly $400 million to $450 million. The *actual* revenue loss to the state would be far less, as higher economic growth feeds additional revenues back to the state through other levies.

So, absolutely no downside exists to eliminating the state's capital gains tax. Revenue loss to the state would be minimal, while the boost to economic growth would be substantial—greatly enhancing incentives to invest and take risks in the Empire State.

• *Step Two: Eliminate the state's estate tax.* Contrary to popular belief, the estate tax stands as perhaps the most unfair of taxes, while also being counter-productive from an economics standpoint.

The estate tax amounts to nothing more than a hostile government takeover of a business and/or assets at the owner's death. Individuals and businesses pay taxes throughout their lifetimes, but both New York State and the federal government come knocking for even more at death. The estate tax is a tax on assets, not just on earnings.

As was also the case with the income tax, the estate tax was borne out of pure envy. Envy always makes for bad economics. The estate tax diminishes incentives for investing in and expanding businesses, and deprives businesses of precious capital at a critical juncture, such as when a transfer of ownership occurs.

A rather generous federal tax credit is offered for state-level estate taxes. Of course, New York stands as one of the very few states where the estate tax reaches beyond the level of the federal credit, giving business owners and families additional reasons to leave New York. New York's estate tax raised an estimated $706 million in 1995-96. As we shall see later, such an amount can be offset by spending cuts, not to mention by a more robust New York economy.

New York officials should be working on two fronts. At the state level, New York's estate tax should be eliminated, and the state's congressional delegation should be pushing for elimination of the federal estate tax. The result will be the continued existence of businesses in New York that otherwise would have moved elsewhere or simply died, and additional capital left will be in the private sector for investment, business expansion, and job creation.

• *Step Three: Cut and eventually eliminate the state's personal income tax.* When initially imposed in 1919, New York State personal income tax was levied at rates of 1 percent, 2 percent, and 3 percent. The upper rates of 2 percent and 3 percent did not take hold until $87,719 and $438,596, respectively, in 1995 dollars. This compares with the scheduled 1997 personal income tax structure with rates ranging from 4 percent up to 6.85 percent, with the lowest rate applying to incomes up to $16,000 and the top rate taking hold at $40,000.

At the very least, New York State should look to the state's original top personal income tax rate of 3 percent and implement it as a modified flat tax. Eliminating all tax deductions, but allowing for some standard exemptions for individuals, spouses, and children—in the neighborhood of $20,000 for a married couple and $5,000 per child (all indexed for inflation)—and a 3 percent flat tax on all subsequent income would give a real boost to pro-growth incentives in New York.

In the end, however, New York should eliminate the personal income tax. Again, incentives to live, work, invest, and take risks in New York would be enhanced greatly. The economy and job creation would flourish. In fact, states which do not levy a personal income/capital gains tax generally perform better in terms of job creation than the rest of the nation. States without a personal income/capital gains tax increased employment by 30 percent between 1980 and 1995, for example, while states with the tax saw employment rise by 24 percent. Incidentally, New York's employment level over this period increased by a meager 8 percent.

The main obstacle in eliminating New York's personal income tax, obviously, is the loss of revenues to state government. The state's total personal income tax siphoned off an estimated $16.9 billion from the private sector in 1995-96. Most of this revenue loss could be offset by spending cuts (see below). If necessary, after all possible spending cut options were exhausted, a small increase in the state sales tax could be instituted. Such a sales tax hike would present its own set of problems, of course, but would be far less harmful to New York's economy than the continuance of the personal income tax.

The retail sales tax has two distinct advantages when compared with the income tax: 1) income taxes *directly* raise the costs of working, saving, investing, and risk taking—the supply-side engines of economic growth; and 2) a retail sales tax reveals the cost of government to individuals each time they make a purchase—it is not hidden.

• *Step Four: Cut the corporate income tax.* In 1996, New York State's corporate income tax rate dropped back to 9 percent with the final phase-out of the business tax surcharge. Nine percent remains too high—64 percent higher than the 5.5 percent rate in place prior to the Rockefeller era of government expansion in New York.

Returning the rate to its pre-Rockefeller rate of 5.5 percent makes sense. Cutting the rate in half—to 4.5 percent—makes even more sense. The corporate rate would then rest well below the national state average, improving the state's competitive position. New York would keep and even attract businesses—something that has not occurred on a significant basis in decades.

New York State has so much to offer families and individuals—from the beaches of Long Island, to the arts, entertainment, and great private universities of New York City, to the beauty of the Catskill and Adirondack Mountains and Niagara Falls, to the Baseball Hall of Fame ... the list goes on. Unfortunately, government gone awry in New York repels these same families and individuals, not to mention entrepreneurs and businesses. This four-step tax program would help launch New York's economy into the twenty-first century. Private-sector opportunities would abound. Such opportunities make it much easier for New York to implement another critical aspect of this program—

massive government downsizing.

## New York City

*Any* New York State tax cut benefits New York City more than any other part of the state. One might be surprised by such a statement given the fact that city officials regularly and vehemently attack any efforts to cut taxes at the state level. The most glaring recent example was Mayor Giuliani's attack on then-gubernatorial candidate George Pataki's plan to cut income taxes. Giuliani, a Republican, supported Mario Cuomo, a Democrat, for re-election in 1994. Giuliani attacked the Pataki tax cut plan largely on the basis that it would result in fewer state-aid dollars finding their way to New York City. In Giuliani's perverse political and economic calculus, government-to-government aid serves the economy better than allowing individuals to keep more of what they earn.

A more rational economic, and even political, calculus shows that since New York City levies the highest local tax burden in the state, a state tax cut would reap its greatest rewards in the city. No city or locality in all of New York—and perhaps in all of the nation —is more in need of tax relief than New York City.

For New York City, the three-step program outlined below is based exclusively on the idea that in order to compete and prosper, New York City has to remove three horrendous taxes that few other cities actually impose.

• *Step One: Eliminate the unincorporated business tax.* As noted earlier, New York City imposes a 4 percent unincorporated business income tax—levied in addition to the city's personal income tax with a top rate of 4.46 percent. In 1995-96 the unincorporated business tax directly drains almost $500 million from the city's economy—not counting the total economic costs of lost entrepreneurship and jobs.

The city's unincorporated business tax acts as a "Detour" sign, diverting entrepreneurs away from the hazards of New York City to more hospitable economic climates elsewhere. Especially in this era of vast economic decentralization, where more and more people are opting or being forced to dive into the entrepreneurial waters, this tax is simply absurd. Indeed, even after tax-rate reductions at the state level since 1976, nonincorporated entrepreneurs in New York City face a top state and city combined marginal income tax rate of 15.31 percent.

Step one in bringing New York City back to economic life is to begin to lower barriers to entrepreneurship. That means eliminating the unincorporated business tax. It is a modest step that even New York State decided to take in the late 1970s, as the state unincorporated business tax was phased out by 1981. This simple act of eliminating a major state tax set Hugh Carey's years as governor apart from his immediate predecessors—Nelson Rockefeller and Malcolm Wilson—and his successor—Mario Cuomo. City officials need to learn from Carey's example regarding the unincorporated business tax.

• *Step Two: Eliminate the city's personal income and capital gains taxes.* In 1996, New York City's top individual tax rate on personal income and capital gains stood at 4.46 percent. Add this rate to New York State's scheduled 1997 tax rate of 6.85 percent, and the top rate on personal income and capital gains for individuals registers 11.31 percent (again, reaching 15.31 percent for some entrepreneurs). And since capital gains are not adjusted to account for inflation, the city's real capital gains tax rate reaches much higher.

Few cities in America impose their own personal income levies, and of those that do, none present such a severe structure as New York City. The two that come close—the District of Columbia and Philadelphia—possess economic woes similar to New York City's.

New York City needs to eliminate its personal income tax, which drains the city's economy for an estimated $3.5-4.0 billion annually—again, not counting the total economic costs. The city economy would receive a much-needed jolt if incentives for living, working, investing, and risk taking were enhanced and if city government was forced to downsize.

• *Step Three: Eliminate the city's corporate income tax.* Imposing a city corporate income tax stands as an even rarer burden in U.S. cities. Of course, New York City levies a formidable rate of 8.85 percent. Again, this is on top of a 9 percent state rate and a 17 percent state metropolitan transit district surcharge—making for a combined state and city corporate tax rate of 19.38 percent in New York City.

Once again, the signal to corporations shines brightly—please take your business elsewhere. Just as clear are the benefits that would result from eliminating the city's corporate income tax—more businesses in New York City and more jobs.

Make no mistake, while New York City's economy was in relative decline since the 1930s, it went into economic free fall after the city imposed three of its own income taxes—personal income/capital gains, corporate income, and unincorporated business income. These taxes, I argue, are the true sources of New York City's economic and commensurate fiscal woes. Other taxes cry out to be reduced—in particular the city's property tax—but these income-based taxes shriek to be killed off completely. Eliminating New York City's income taxes and vastly downsizing city government (see below) stand as *necessary* means to New York City's revitalization.

## Smaller, More Accountable Government

Speak of minor cuts in government spending in New York and the cries of "blood in the streets" and accusations of attacking the old and disabled reach deafening levels. Some will even irresponsibly hurl accusations of racism. After all, one New York congressman recently declared that calls for tax cuts were simply thinly veiled examples of racism. Indeed, vitriolic attacks have been launched in recent years against mere spending restraint proposed by Governor Pataki and New York City Mayor Giuliani.

Actually *cutting* the size of government in New York remains a Herculean task, opposed by a well-financed army of special interests. However, without deep reductions in the size of government in New York, both state and city will continue to move in and out of fiscal crises, and the New York economy will continue its long, steady decline. The massive tax cuts called for above will, indeed, be "paid for" in part through economic growth, but also require deep government spending reductions.

The spending reductions outlined below will appear monumental and unrealistic to New Yorker's familiar with the state and city political scenes. But as I argued earlier, the usual tinkerings at the margin by New York State and New York City officials remain unrealistic if one is serious about revitalizing the New York economy. New York rising, once again, as an international center of entrepreneurship, economic growth, and opportunity requires that government be cut not with a scalpel, but with a meat ax.

The meat ax approach follows.

## New York State

Opportunities for taxpayer savings abound in New York State government. Department eliminations, program cutbacks, program reforms, competitive contracting alternatives (where private sector enterprises compete to provide services—on average creating savings of 25-30 percent[21]), and privatization (where assets and services are completely shifted to the private sector with no further government involvement) can all contribute to state government downsizing. What follows is a substantial, *but by no means exhaustive* list of savings opportunities in the New York State budget (all expenditure numbers reflect 1995-96 appropriation levels).

• *As a first step, cut total state spending across the board by 25 percent.* Per capita total state spending in New York tops the U.S. average by 41 percent. Cutting all programs in the state budget by 25 percent across the board would bring New York more in line with other U.S. states in terms of expenditures, though it would still leave New York's per capita state spending *above* the national average. Savings to state and federal taxpayers would equal about $16 billion annually.

• *Cut the salaries and staff of state officials by 50 percent.* It costs about $10.5 million to run the executive chamber and $177 million for the state legislature. The state legislature's budget breaks down to roughly $1.3 million per State Senate office and $633,000 per State Assembly office. Much room exists for downsizing.

• *Eliminate the Department of Economic Development with its more than $50 million budget.* Growth and development occur through the private sector, not through the strategies, subsidies, productivity assessments, and other actions taken by government economic development bureaucrats.

• *Cut the business and economic development initiatives in the state's Department of Agriculture and Markets—accounting for more than 75 percent of the department's $87.8 million budget.* The agriculture industry in New York is more than able to look after its own interests without government assistance.

• *Eliminate the Empire State Development Corporation (formerly the Urban Development Corporation) with its total budget topping $92 million.* Again, economic growth occurs through private sector investment, innovation, invention, efficiencies, and entrepreneurship. Government loans, subsidies, and assistance programs merely distort this process, diverting resources from their best economic uses determined through the disciplines of the marketplace, to endeavors decided by politics.

• *Eliminate the Energy Research and Development Authority with a budget of more than $36 million.* As one might have thought, this agency was created in 1975 (though its forerunner—the New York State Atomic Research and Space Development Authority—was created in 1962), in the middle of the "energy crisis" and amid great fanfare regarding government's ability to control energy markets. Such programs long ago proved ineffective. Indeed, when untouched by government intervention and mistaken policies, energy markets work quite well.

• *Savings opportunities in the Department of Environmental Conservation.* The state's Department of Environmental Conservation (DEC) has a budget of about $600 million. Significant savings can be culled by privatizing the Belleayre Mountain Ski Center, privatizing the state's 12 fish hatcheries and two game farms, privatizing state-owned lands (the DEC manages more than 4 million acres of state land), privatizing or contracting out operations of state recreational and camping facilities (including 260 boat launching and fishing access sites, 50 campgrounds, and 23 day-use areas), eliminating all grants to localities for land acquisitions, reducing the department's 3,800-plus workforce, and much more.

• *Eliminate the Division of Housing and Community Renewal with its budget of more than $180 million, along with the Affordable Housing Corporation ($25 million), the Housing Finance Agency ($2.8 million), the Housing Trust Fund Corporation ($41 million), and the State of New York Mortgage Agency ($97 million).* It is time to get New York State out of the housing business. All public housing projects should be privatized, and subsidy and loan programs terminated. The only way to ensure affordable low- and moderate-income housing—the Division of Housing and Community Renewal's very reason for being—is to build more housing. Government need only get out of the way—that is, deregulate (roll back zoning, rent controls, etc.) and cut taxes—to ensure that this process occurs. The Division of Housing and Community Renewal is just another hapless, inefficient, and ultimately counter-productive state agency with a nice name.

• *Eliminate the Olympic Regional Development Authority with a budget of almost $8 million.* All of the operations of the Olympic Regional Development Authority should be privatized, including the state's other two ski facilities, Whiteface Mountain and Gore Mountain, the Olympic Ice Center, and the Mount Van Hoevenberg Complex (including bobsled and luge runs, cross-country ski trials, and a biathlon range).

• *Savings opportunities in the Office of Parks, Recreation and Historic Preservation.* Privatization and competitive contracting opportunities are numerous in the Office of Parks, Recreation and Historic Preservation. For example, park operations could be contracted out for competitive bidding on a regular basis. In addition, the state should privatize the 17 golf courses (seven of which actually *lost* money over the three-year period of 1989-90 though 1991-92, according to a 1993 state comptroller's report) and the several marinas it owns.

• *Eliminate the New York State Science and Technology Foundation with its budget of about $34 million.* The foundation's mission is to identify, promote, and invest in new high technology enterprises and to foster the transfer of technologies from the realm of research to commercial markets. In essence, this is using taxpayer dollars for venture capital investments—an undertaking that government bureaucrats remain ill-equipped to pursue and for which taxpayers should not be forced to pay. As history consistently shows, government lacks the proper incentives, knowledge, and experience to be picking the winning industries, firms, and ideas of the future.

• *Eliminate the Council on the Arts with a budget of $36 million.* One might have been able to justify government funding of the arts in medieval times, where wealth was not abundant and much of daily life was caught up in mere survival. Today, however, we live in a wealthy society where abundant private dollars exist for the arts. Government funding of the arts amounts to nothing more than welfare for the elite.

• *Eliminate the Council on Children and Families.* How could anyone advocate eliminating a department named for children and families? Isn't this the height of conservative, free-market insensitivity? No, it is not. It is mere recognition that this council amounts to nothing more than another layer in the state's burgeoning public welfare bureaucracy. Children and families would benefit far more from new jobs and rising incomes that result from substantive tax and regulatory relief.

• *Phase out the City University of New York and the State University of New York and replace them with a tuition voucher "college choice" program for the needy.* New York lays claim to *two* of the *three* largest public university systems in the United States. The State University of New York (SUNY) ranks as the largest with an amazing 64 separate campuses, and the City University of New York (CUNY) ranks third largest with 19 schools. From the start, SUNY and CUNY were bad ideas. They were destined to become large, bureaucratic monstrosities —exactly what they are today. CUNY's total budget equaled $2.2 billion and SUNY's hits $3.6 billion in 1995-96. The per full-time-equivalent student costs of running the complete SUNY system registers about $22,700 annually and $23,000 for CUNY.

New York, obviously, is not unique in having a public university system. However, the idea of state and city governments running their own colleges and universities when a vibrant private college and university system has long existed in this nation is another case of government assistance gone awry. Rather than building and operating large universities, *if* government is going to venture into the higher education waters at all, it should limit itself to aiding those who wish to and are capable of continuing their schooling but don't possess the resources. A higher education voucher for the needy makes sense; large, public university systems do not.

Shifting gradually from a public university system in New York State and New York City would save huge amounts of money (in the billions annually), present tremendous privatization opportunities, and introduce "college choice" to financially poor students.

• *Savings opportunities in the Department of Social Services.* In 1995-96, 2.1 million individuals in New York received public assistance through Aid to Families with Dependent Children (AFDC), Supplemental Security Income (SSI), and Home Relief (HR), with tens of thousands more receiving aid through other programs. Such programs assume that individuals cannot provide for themselves and their families, and that private charity is not up to helping those in true need. These paternalistic and dangerous assumptions have created an unhealthy dependency upon government, and helped to destroy the family unit primarily by supplanting government for fathers. Compared with private charity, government possesses few incentives to move individuals off the public dole and into productive economic roles.

In addition, incentives for recipients to move off of welfare are prohibitive when one combines the loss of benefits with the tax rate on earned income. The stigma of welfare also has diminished in recent years. Therefore, embarrassment, self-respect, and public and private disapproval of being on welfare play a much smaller role in pushing people to get off of welfare. Lastly, as already noted, the total welfare package remains quite lucrative in both New York State and New York City. Allowing individuals to demand before they supply a marketable good or service makes no sense and damages the economy. Production starts the economic process.

Workfare programs and soft time limits do nothing to cure such ills. New York desperately needs some serious "tough love" on the public welfare front. That means ending the state's home relief program, placing hard time limits on all other forms of public welfare assistance (such as six months or a year and you are off welfare altogether), and providing no additional funds to single mothers who have additional children. In addition, the total level of welfare benefits in New York needs to be reduced so that working pays off. Despite all the hoopla, the new federal welfare reforms represent but a tiny step in this direction. And even Governor Pataki's recent proposal to "end" the state's home relief welfare program for able-bodied, childless adults only replaces cash benefits with assorted vouchers. Home relief would continue, just under a different name and with no time limits.

True compassion—defined as moving individuals from government dependency to self-sufficiency—means that New York's federal, state, city, and local officials should be dismantling the current welfare morass.

• *Savings opportunities in the Department of Correctional Services.* New York State operates 70 correctional facilities with 30,000 employees and roughly 69,000 inmates at a total budget of $1.87 billion. That translates into $27,152 per inmate annually, and one employee per 2.3 inmates.

Contracting out prison services has provided savings in other parts of the country. For example, the Reason Foundation reports that private prison bids in Florida must offer more vocational and educational training and cost 10 percent less than comparable state-run facilities.[22] Reason notes that such cost savings requirements are common in private prison contracts, and that profit margins at private prisons have ranged about 8-10 percent annually.

Contracting out prison services to the private sector is a growth trend that makes sense. The *New York Times* reported on August 19, 1995, that the number of inmates in privately managed or owned prisons increased from 1,345 in 1985 to 65,000 in 1995.

• *Savings opportunities in the Department of Health with a budget of $20 billion.* Government's role in health care needs to be completely overhauled and reduced, not only in New York but across the nation. Third-party payments—both by government and private insurance—have allowed costs to skyrocket. Buyers and sellers in the health care marketplace do not care about costs because someone else is paying the bill—usually either an employer-provided health insurance plan or the government. And when government does try to rein in costs, it usually fails in dollar terms and raises costs in terms of lost quality (e.g., health-care rationing).

Medicaid and other health programs should be replaced with a system for the very needy made up of medical savings accounts and catastrophic health insurance. No one loses under such a system—patients have incentives to be concerned about costs and services, a catastrophic insurance plan covers large and/or unforeseen costs (the true purpose of insurance), and in the long run, tax dollars are saved. This is the direction that New York's elected officials should be pushing health care in the state and across the nation.

• *Eliminate the Temporary State Commission on Investigation with a budget of $1.9 million.* This "temporary" commission has been around since 1958. The time has come to give meaning once again to the word "temporary" and leave this commission's duties regarding organized crime, racketeering, and the conduct of public officials to law enforcement officials.

• *Eliminate the Office of Alcoholism and Substance Abuse Services with a budget of $419 million.* If any role exists for government to be involved in the treatment of alcoholism and drug abuse, it should be left to the localities to decide. Otherwise, responsibility lies with private charities and groups, churches, and individuals.

• *Savings opportunities in the Department of Motor Vehicles with a budget of $198 million.* Few other departments in government are better known for inefficiency than the Department of Motor Vehicles. Competitive contracting can only lead to savings and better service.

• *Savings opportunities in the Department of Transportation with a budget of $4.6 billion.* The Department of Transportation (DOT) serves as a common stop on the state's "pork express." Year after year, the *state* DOT budget is crammed full of spending items on *local* transportation issues—roads, sidewalks, curbs, trains, subways, etc. Such local transportation issues should be left to local government, or to the private sector where appropriate. The state DOT should concern itself solely with state-level transportation needs. And some state highways, roads, and bridges can and should be privatized or their servicing put out to competitive bidding. Annual state taxpayer savings would run into billions of dollars.

• *Eliminate the Consumer Protection Board with a budget of $2.6 million.* The Consumer Protection Board's mission clearly overlaps with the state attorney general. All duties, therefore, should be shifted to the attorney general's office.

The savings opportunities listed above for New York State government run into the tens of billions of dollars annually and do not amount to an exhaustive list. Similar opportunities to cut back programs, eliminate departments, privatize services and assets, and open government services to competitive contracting abound at the local level in New York as well (some specifics in terms of New York City are provided below). Additional state, city, and local taxpayer savings are spelled out in the following sections on deregulation and primary and secondary education.

In addition to downsizing government in New York State, greater accountability is needed as well. While a host of reforms present themselves in this area, I believe that two stand out most prominently:

term limits and the elimination of off-budget public authorities.

• *Term limits.* Arrogant, bloated government largely springs from the actions of career-minded politicians. Make government your life's work, and incentives to expand the size and power of government are clear. Salaries and benefits mount, as do staffs. And of course, all of these people need to justify their existence, so government meddling in the economy greatly expands. Taxes, regulations, departments, and programs multiply like rabbits -- big, fat rabbits, that is.

New York State needs a deliberative government and a citizen legislature. I suggest term limits of two four-year terms for

**A Sample of New York State Public Authorities**

- Buffalo and Fort Erie Public Bridge Authority
- New York State Bridge Authority
- Thousand Islands Bridge Authority
- Triborough Bridge and Tunnel Authority
- New York State Thruway Authority
- Battery City Park Authority
- Development Authority of the North Country
- United Nations Development Corporation
- Empire State Development Authority
- New York State Energy Research and Development Authority
- Environmental Facilities Corporation
- Long Island Power Authority
- New York Power Authority
- Dormitory Authority
- Housing Finance Agency
- Local Government Assistance Corporation
- State of New York Mortgage Agency
- Municipal Assistance Corporation for the City of New York
- Municipal Assistance Corporation for the City of Troy
- Municipal Bond Bank Agency
- Project Finance Agency
- Albany Port District Commission
- Ogdensburg Bridge and Port Authority
- Port Authority of New York and New Jersey
- Port of Oswego Authority
- Capital District Transportation Authority
- Central New York Regional Transportation Authority
- Metropolitan Transportation Authority
- Niagara Frontier Transportation Authority
- Rochester-Genessee Regional Transportation Authority

governor and four two-year terms for state legislators.

In 1993, New York City voters approved, with 60 percent of the vote, terms limits for city officials of two four-year terms. City council members have been trying to find ways to rebuke this vote of the people ever since. They failed at the ballot box in November 1996.

• *Put an end to New York's public authorities.* New York has 30 debt-issuing public authorities that operate free from direct oversight by the voters and elected officials (see box on the previous page). Other authorities created over the years offer rather striking titles that clearly call into question the so-called imperative for their existence: American Museum of National History Planetarium, Industrial Exhibit Authority, New York State World War Memorial Authority, the Brooklyn Sports Center Authority, and the infamous New York State Atomic Research and Space Development Authority. Apparently even gravity could not hold back Nelson Rockefeller's ambitions for expanding New York State government.

Indeed, as noted earlier, public authorities are used to evade the state constitutional requirement that voters approve incurrence of long-term debt, a requirement in place since 1846 when New Yorkers realized that some additional limits were needed on government officials. The public authorities farce began in 1921, but was perfected by Rockefeller in the 1960s and 1970s.

Always a sham, the public authorities game received a new twist in 1990, as explained by economist Edwin Rubenstein in the winter 1992 issue of the *City Journal*:

> The politicization of state authorities reached a new peak in June 1990, when the Legislature instructed UDC [the Urban Development Corporation] to "buy" Attica prison from the state. The proceeds were to help close a $2 billion budget gap. To raise the cash UDC sold $241.7 million worth of thirty year bonds. The bonds were discounted by $10.7 million, so the authority sold them for $231 million. The state pocketed $200 million, the "purchase price" of Attica.

As off-budget "public benefit corporations," state taxpayers theoretically have no responsibility for authority debt. However, as we learned with the Urban Development Corporation during the fiscal crisis of the 1970s, this distinction is a complete fiction. If a state public authority gets into trouble, the state's overall fiscal health is placed in jeopardy and taxpayer dollars will be used in a bailout. In addition, the fees collected by these authorities are *government* fees. Reclassifying state departments and moving them off budget merely gives elected officials immunity when fees are levied and increased.

In the end, public authorities spend more than $12 billion annually; receive more than $1.4 billion in taxpayer subsidies through the official state budget; and claim more than $35 billion in outstanding debt. Authorities certainly are not private businesses subject to the disciplines of the marketplace. Public authorities effectively are departments of state government not under the direct control of elected officials.

Accountability and gaining an honest assessment of the total size of government dictate that the public authority scam come to an end. New York's public authorities should be eliminated, and their various undertakings either terminated or moved back under the New York State budget umbrella. If public authorities continue in existence, their debt—like all other long-term New York State debt—should be subject to voter approval.

## New York City

Allow me to place once again the size of New York City government in perspective: if per capita New York City total spending were cut in *half*, it would still outpace the U.S. large-city (500,000+ population) average by more than 10 percent. When combined with state actions, New York City carries the largest governmental burden in the entire nation.

Opportunities to downsize government and save taxpayer dollars are so numerous that it is difficult to comprehend. However, the obstacles to cutting government stand more ominous than at the state level or in any other city or locality in New York. In a city of about 7.3 million people, where roughly 2 million receive some kind of public assistance and total city government employment registers more than 400,000, a formidable foundation exists to oppose any and all efforts to downsize government.

Nonetheless, mere tinkering at the edges will get New York City absolutely no where. Mayor Rudy Giuliani, for example, has instituted some spending restraint, but the city's long decline continues. Giuliani wound up reneging on a promise to allow the city's personal income tax surcharge to expire at the end of 1996 (which would have dropped the top tax rate from 4.46 percent to 3.91 percent). No one has mustered the courage to do what needs to be done in New York City—slash government dramatically, and institute deep cuts in taxes and regulations.

The spending cuts listed below (numbers reflect 1995-96 budget levels) stand as a substantial, but by no means complete, list of savings opportunities in the New York City budget.

• *As a first step, an across-the-board cut in total city spending.* As shown throughout much of this book, and noted again above, New York City spending is completely out of sync with economic and societal realities, as well as with other cities. An across-the-board cut of 25 percent in city total spending will save taxpayers—city, state, and federal—roughly $9 billion annually.

Will "city services" suffer? In the sense that many things city government does now and will not do later, or will transfer to the private sector, then the answer to this question is "yes." Will city employees receive pay cuts, and many lose their government jobs and be forced to seek productive, private-sector employment? Absolutely—all to the long-run benefit of all New Yorkers.

• *Eliminate the city borough presidents with a total budget of more than $28 million.* Citizens of New York are represented by the mayor and city council members. Borough presidents are just another layer of unnecessary government.

• *Eliminate the city's public advocate with his budget of $2.4 million.* Again, the citizens' "advocates" are the mayor and city council members. The public advocate is just another layer in a deeply stratified city government.

• *Slash top city officials salaries—those for the mayor, city council members, city comptroller, and schools chancellor—by 70 percent.* In cutting the size of government, top officials should lead by example. As described earlier, current New York City salaries for all of these positions are completely beyond the realm of sanity. A 70 percent cut still leaves these officials well compensated for their work. Government is a public service, not a path to growing rich at taxpayer expense.

• *Likewise, cut the mayoralty budget by 70 percent.* The mayor's office claimed a $90 million budget in 1996. Though substantially lower than the 1995 level of $114 million—a good step in the right direction—much, much more can and should be cut. Reducing the mayoralty budget to about $27 million seems quite reasonable. Indeed, such levels still leave room for greater savings down the road.

• *Opportunities for savings in the Department of Correction with a total budget exceeding $1 billion.* The per inmate annual cost of New York City's Department of Correction for 1996 registered about $55,400. (This translates into a per day cost of $152—more expensive than many hotels.) This is an astounding number—more than twice the cost of New York State prisons. The city's ratio of corrections employees to inmates equaled one employee to 1.5 inmates, compared with the state's ratio of one employee per 2.3 inmates.

Cutting the number of Correction's employees by 35 percent, and cutting total expenditures by half would bring New York City's Department of Correction's budget and personnel at least more in line with New York State's—saving taxpayers more than $500 million annually. Further savings are available beyond that point as well, particularly through competitive contracting.

• *Opportunities for savings in the Department of Social Services with a budget of $7.5 billion.* The Department of Social Services claims a massive portion of the city budget. I have already explained the paternalistic assumptions underlying a massive welfare state and the perverse incentives created.

The solutions are outlined above in the New York State section: hard time limits on public assistance, reduced benefits, the replacement of Medicaid with a medical savings account/catastrophic insurance system, and far greater reliance on private charity. Implementation of such changes in New York City would save billions annually for city, state, and federal taxpayers, and be of greater help to the individuals currently ensnared in New York's public welfare web.

• *Eliminate the Department of Homeless Services with a budget of $440 million.* The city has saved an estimated $5.6 million by contracting out seven adult shelters, and should be commended for such steps. However, New York City's focus on assisting the homeless needs a dramatic shift in order to see any real, positive results. For homeless individuals who possess the wherewithal to support themselves, city homeless services should be phased out, with those in need of assistance guided to private charities and churches.

• *Opportunities for savings in the Department of Sanitation with a total budget of more than $800 million.* New York City has contracted out the removal of abandoned vehicles from city streets and property—deserving kudos. However, all of the major undertakings of the Department of Sanitation—garbage pickup, street cleaning, and snow removal—can and should be put up for regular competitive bidding. Assuming that the city would experience similar savings as those seen on average under competitive contracting (25-30 percent), taxpayers benefit to the tune of between $200 to $250 million annually. In the long run, no reason exists why garbage pickup should not be completely privatized.

• *Opportunities for savings in the Department of Parks and Recreation with a budget of almost $340 million.* Competitive contracting and privatization opportunities clearly present themselves. Park maintenance should be put out to regular competitive bidding, and city-owned golf courses (operations were contracted out a few years ago), stadiums, skating rinks, and zoos should be privatized. Indeed, instead of building new stadiums for the Yankees and Mets, Yankee and Shea Stadiums should be privatized and the city should leave stadium ownership and operation to the private sector.

• *Opportunities for savings in the Department of Infrastructure Management and Transit with its total budget of almost $1.3 billion.* Privatization opportunities overflow in the Department of Infrastructure and Transit, including toll bridges and tunnels, parking facilities, ferries, and buses. City government should pull out of owning and operating such enterprises. The sale of such assets could be applied to retiring some of the city's debt, services would improve, and taxpayers would save money.

• *Eliminate the Department of Housing Preservation and Development with its total budget of more than $850 million.* Government plays no positive role in the housing industry. Public housing has been an abysmal failure. New York City's surest route to replenishing and expanding its housing stock is to cease production of all new public housing, privatize all current city-owned housing units (give it away if you have to), and lift the heavy hand of government on the housing industry (taxes and regulations) so that incentives to build new housing are enhanced.

The taxpayers would save hundreds of millions of dollars annually, and New York City's housing stock would return to the vigorous growth levels of decades gone by.

• *Eliminate the Department of Business Services and the Economic Development Corporation with a total budget of $345 million ($39 million operating expenses and $346 million in capital commitments).* New York City government can best service business and the economy by slashing taxes and regulations, not with business and economic development programs staffed by bureaucrats who are spending and/or placing at risk taxpayer dollars.

The city's Corporate Retention program is one of the biggest shams ever perpetrated by government. The city hikes taxes and regulations to prohibitive levels, and then sets up a program to cut deals with particular firms deemed worthy of being kept in the city by politicians and bureaucrats.

• *Eliminate the Department of Cultural Affairs with a total budget of more than $225 million.* No doubt, New York City is a mecca of the arts. It is one of New York's great advantages. However, the question needs to be asked: Why is New York City government involved in the arts business—especially to the tune of $225 million in 1996?

According to Mayor Giuliani's 1997 budget proposal, this total expenditure level will drop by about 40 percent—very commendable. Over the longer haul, however, New York City should pull itself out of what one might call the "market for culture." In the late twentieth century, more than enough private capital exists to fund the arts, and taxpayers in general should not be asked to bear the burden of "arts welfare" for largely middle- and upper-income earners.

New York City's sale of the WNYC television station—for a reported selling price of $207 million—serves as an excellent example of what can be accomplished through privatization in the area of the arts and culture.

• *Privatize New York City hospitals.* The Health and Hospitals Corporation operates 11 acute care hospitals, five long-term care facilities, and a network of neighborhood health centers. Privatization is the path to be taken here, and New York City already has begun the process of privatizing three of these hospitals—Coney Island, Elmhurst, and Queens. If accomplished, this will be a monumental achievement for the city. In the long term, all of these patient facilities should be privatized and the HHC doors closed.

• *Savings opportunities for New York City Transit.* Two major reforms should be considered for New York City Transit: 1) stop running the subway system 24 hours a day—closing it down in the wee hours of the morning would save money and reduce crime; 2) privatize bus lines and subway lines.

• *Phasing out the City University of New York.* New York City also would save money (more than $400 million annually) with the phase-out of the City University of New York system, as suggested earlier in the New York State section.

These savings—running well into the billions of dollars annually—for New York City will strike the city's big-government advocates as mad. They mistakenly believe that government is what keeps New York City and its residents afloat. In reality, big government in New York City effectively has acted like an enemy attack submarine, stealthily bombarding the city with destructive torpedoes for decades. And make no mistake, New York City started taking on water after the first few shots.

For New York City's sinking taxpayers and economy, these savings—*and much more*—are desperately needed. The bottom line remains that no avenue other than dramatically reducing the size of city government exists to allow New York City to put an end to its ongoing crises and actually restore itself as a great city of opportunity and growth.

In terms of governmental accountability, a greatly downsized and simplified city government structure, focusing on more traditional government services, will allow voters to more easily assess the performance of elected officials. In addition, the approval of term limits of two four-year terms for city elected officials in 1993 was a dramatic step forward on the government accountability front in New York City. Voters need to stand vigilant against current city officials who will continue with attempts to weaken or reverse this grand accomplishment.

## Deregulation

Ask any business owner and he or she will tell you that regulations are just as costly as taxes—if not more so. For example, at the federal level, total regulations cost the U.S. economy more than $600 billion annually, about the same amount of money collected by the federal government through the personal income tax. While overall state and local level regulatory costs remain difficult to quantify, both New York State and New York City have earned reputations for imposing weighty regulatory burdens on businesses.

The Public Policy Institute of New York—a business-financed think tank—recently offered a glimpse of New York State's regulatory morass.[23] The following are just a few major points raised:

• 37 or so state agencies possess the authority to issue permits and licenses to engage in business in New York.

• Roughly 1,100 different business activities require a state permit or filing.

• According to a 1985 study by Patty D. Renfrow, regulations were then coming fast and furious, with 1,100 pages of new regulations being added each year.

• Various laws and rules require a total of 899 posters and notices in various New York places of employment.

• Even charities in New York are sucked into the regulatory mess, as they need to file identical information on complex, separate forms for two different state agencies on an annual basis.

• Hospitals surely are not immune either—having to deal with 15 different state agencies.

• The state drives up the costs of health insurance by mandating various specific services be covered at the urgings of special interests.

• The Public Policy Institute noted other woes regarding New York State's regulatory process:

> Agencies can, and do, bypass the normal statutory requirements for public comment on proposed new rules by declaring that the issue is an "emergency"—even if the only emergency is that they wish they had acted sooner. Agencies often appear to give only cursory review to the comments they receive before adopting regulations even on a non-emergency basis. There is no comprehensive procedure for systematically reviewing existing regulations to see if they have become outdated, or if they overlap with, or are superseded by, some new state or federal rules—and employers cannot legally petition for review of an outmoded regulation. Even in cases in which new rules seem clearly to go beyond the legal authority granted to regulating agencies, the affected parties can find it difficult to appeal to a higher authority or to seek relief in court. Appeals from agency decisions are often made to administrative law judges who themselves work for the agencies involved. And there are no comprehensive requirements that agencies must act on permits requested by employers within a set time period—indeed, agencies get to pocket the fee for the permit as soon as the application is filed, however long it takes them to actually issue the permit.[24]

New York City residents, entrepreneurs, and businesses obviously are impacted by the state's regulatory quagmire *plus* New York City's own regulatory mess—added permits, licenses, paperwork, rules, and regulations. In the autumn 1992 issue of the *City Journal*, William Tucker observed regarding regulation in New York City: "Small businessmen complain not only that there are too many regulations, but also that they are so complicated and overlapping that conflicts between them often cannot be resolved. Moreover, the city often uses regulations as a way of collecting even more revenues in the form of fines."

Rules and regulations run the gauntlet from obscure and annoying to massive and destructive. Among the most destructive are zoning regulations that have long stymied dynamic change in the city's economy and rent controls that simply have destroyed much of the city's housing stock. In an article ("Why Laws Backfire") in the August 1996 issue of the *Freeman*, Marisa Manley, president of Manhattan-based Commercial Tenant Real Estate Representation Ltd., noted:

> Before the 1942 imposition of rent control, New York City had a housing market one planner called the "envy of the world." Responding to market demand, developers produced more than

> 90,000 new units a year. Today, after five decades of rent control, there is little construction of new housing. The city owns 6,645 buildings. An estimated 76,000 dwellings have been abandoned because the owners found this more profitable than paying costs imposed by the city.

Such developments perhaps were best illustrated and explained by William Tucker in his seminal work *The Excluded Americans: Homelessness and Housing Policies.* Interestingly, Tucker found that higher home prices (of which exclusionary zoning is a major cause) and rent control serve as the best predictors of homelessness. As Tucker pointed out, the private housing industry is more than capable of building housing for all different levels of income earners. And in the end, "affordable" housing only can be achieved when one allows developers to build more housing. Tucker declared simply: "The best strategy for improving the overall housing stock is to build new housing and let it circulate," that is, new homes are built, people leave older housing for the new homes, freeing up older housing for former renters, and so on. This process of circulation proceeds through the entire system.

A plethora of other counterproductive rules and regulations hamper entrepreneurship and economic growth in New York City. A recent report by the Institute for Justice offered just a few examples, including:[25]

• Van drivers face enormous obstacles in actually gaining a license and then are severely restricted and face considerable fines if they try to compete against the city's public buses.

• Hairbraiders are shut down unless they take five months of state-mandated classes that have absolutely nothing to do with hairbraiding.

• The city arbitrarily limits the number of permits for street vendors. It is estimated that there are three to four times as many vendors operating in New York City than there are permits. The study's author, William H. Mellor, notes: "The city's Office of Consumer Affairs sets the number of permits it issues so low that it will not even give out the permit application, so it is unlikely that one of the legal permits will become available."[26]

• The city places another artificial ceiling on the number of taxi medallions which allow drivers to pick up passengers on the street. The price for a medallion in the private marketplace has reached $175,000, and if a car service driver without a medallion is caught picking up a passenger hailing a cab on the street, they face discipline from the city's Taxi and Limousine Commission.

• In-home food preparation businesses are prohibited, forcing would-be entrepreneurial cooks into leasing commercial kitchen space or going out of business.

• Under an April 1994 law, manicurists must take 250 hours of training in order to operate legally.

As a result of taxes and regulations, economic activity is pushed underground, beyond the reach of regulators, bureaucrats, and tax officials. Mellor notes that the underground economy in New York City has probably grown to as much as 20 percent of the city's $50 billion economy. Moving such a substantial portion of the economy underground has grave consequences, as Mellor observed:

> Restrictive laws, whatever their justification, force entrepreneurs underground. Once underground, these entrepreneurs have little hope of growing their business or obtaining necessary capital as they would in the formal economy. Enormous resources, human capital and energy must be devoted to avoidance of enforcement. When they seek to operate within the above-ground economy, they face time-consuming credentialing or paperwork they are ill-equipped to handle. The cumulative effect of such an environment suppresses the very dynamic of initiative, self-help, and economic growth most needed in New York's low income communities today.[27]

The following are just a few steps needed to be taken along the road to easing regulatory burdens in both New York State and New York City:

• *Eliminate all rent controls and rent regulations in New York City (as well as in the few other areas in New York State that impose some kind of rent regulations—localities in the counties of Albany, Erie, Nassau, Rockland, Schenectady, Rennsselaer, and Westchester).* The only accomplishment of rent control is the destruction of New York City's housing stock. Landlords either abandon rent-controlled buildings or allow them to deteriorate because it makes no economic sense to maintain and upgrade them.

• *The elimination of rent control presents another good reason—among many—to eliminate zoning restrictions in New York City as well as elsewhere in New York State.* Zoning regulations are an affront to individual liberty and have the quite predictable result of hiking the price of housing for individuals, families, and businesses.

Zoning generally has its origins in "quality of life" and NIMBY-ism (not in my backyard) trends that supposedly benefit those already settled in a community over those seeking housing. However, the NIMBYists often shoot themselves in the foot, if not in the head. Exclusionary zoning results in higher taxes (due to a smaller tax base) and higher housing prices—sending individuals, families, and businesses to areas where such costs are much lower. Zoning must go.

• *Sunset all regulations and rules.* All government regulations should be set to expire in a certain amount of time—preferably no more than three years. Sunsetting at least would provide the opportunity to review the effectiveness, costs, and other consequences of each regulation, creating a system whereby burdensome, wrongheaded regulations and rules can be terminated.

• *Require substantive, science-based risk assessment and cost-benefit analysis of each regulation and rule before implemented.* One might be tempted to assume that before implementing a new regulation or rule, government officials ask two key questions: 1) Does an actual risk exist which this regulation seeks to ameliorate?, and 2) Do the actual benefits of this regulation truly outweigh the total costs? Unfortunately, you would be quite wrong to make such an assumption in New York, or at the federal level for that matter. Such questions and the required analysis, if they occur at all, remain the gross exception rather than the rule. The regulatory process in New York would gain at least some sanity and common sense by instituting thorough risk assessment and cost-benefit analysis requirements for new regulations and rules being promulgated at the state, city, and local levels.

• *Require that all new rules and regulations be approved by elected officials before being implemented.* Too often, politicians will point fingers at regulatory bodies when confronted with stupid rules and regulations, saying they have little control over regulators. New York State needs to require that rules, regulations, permits, licenses, and fees, all be approved by elected officials before being imposed or increased.

• *Eliminate unfunded state mandates in New York.* Regulations not only affect the private sector, but can be imposed on other governments as well. State government in New York is notorious for imposing costly mandates on localities.

The incentives for state legislators to impose mandates on localities are quite clear. They can take credit for implementing programs, but do not have to partake in the unsavory and unpopular business of raising revenues to pay for such programs. That task is left to local officials and, in turn, local taxpayers. New York State needs to implement one major reform to deal with the mandate issue: pass a state constitutional amendment prohibiting state unfunded mandates. New unfunded mandates would be immediately prohibited, while existing mandates would be either eliminated or state financing phased in.

## Choice in Education

The woes of public education across New York were illustrated in the preceding pages. In summary, costs are high, while results are relatively poor. The question remains: how do we turn things around?

A host of proposals regularly make appearances in the education debate. For example, school district and school consolidations often are suggested as cost-saving measures. Local income taxes are proposed as a counter to burdensome school property taxes. Local public schools call for reducing state education mandates. Others suggest lengthening the school day or the school year as an answer to declining student performance measures. Tougher state education standards have been a cause celeb for some time and were recently implemented with all New York high school graduates being required early in the next decade to pass Regents exams. The list grows quite lengthy.

Unfortunately, none of these proposals will help our failing, expensive public school system. School and school district consolidations have been going on throughout this century in New York and across the nation. Some short-term savings can result from such actions. In the long run, though, larger schools and districts merely create larger bureaucracies. As explained earlier, rather than decreasing, costs actually rise.

Perhaps the most ridiculous proposal to ease New York's heavy school property tax burden is the implementation of local income taxes or a state income tax surcharge. Supported by various Democrats and Republicans in New York, such a proposal merely replaces one onerous tax with an even more onerous tax.

As governor, Mario Cuomo proposed such a plan. Cuomo didn't suggest replacing the school property tax altogether with an income tax. Cuomo's plan called for an income tax add-on, so property taxes would remain in place—at current levels or slightly reduced levels—and localities would be allowed to add on an income tax. The Cuomo plan called for capping property and income levies. However, New York's history is replete with promised tax caps being violated—usually obliterated. Inevitably, both local property taxes and local income taxes would have been poised for increases under the Cuomo plan.

Unfortunately, the local income tax or state income tax surcharge idea for funding public schools—whether in part or in whole—failed to depart the political scene with Mario Cuomo. The local income tax idea represents New York politics at its most cowardly. Few muster the courage to deal with the source of burdensome school property taxes—runaway public school spending—so they divert attention by suggesting alternative tax structures. And worst of all, they suggest adopting the most destructive tax known to man—the income tax.

As for state education mandates, as called for above, unfunded state mandates should be prohibited through the state constitution. Local schools certainly would experience savings. However, leaders and taxpayers need to understand that the vast majority of school expenses are controlled at the local level. Salaries represent the bulk of school spending and remain completely within the control of local school officials. State mandate relief will help in the effort to reduce school costs, but the power to implement deep, substantive cost reductions exists right now at the local level.

Suggestions for longer school days and school years make no sense either. Public schools are failing with the time they have students within their grasp now; extending that time will likely only extend the schools' failures. Right now, many New York City public schools regularly show movies during the school day—not educational movies, mind you. No Shakespeare to be found here. Instead, they are the standard mindless movies one finds at the local video rental store.

These schools can't even manage to fill up today's school days.

Longer school days or school years are not needed. In fact, if quality education were the rule, you could probably shorten the school year!

Tougher standards actually do make sense. One problem, however, is that tougher standards may not actually turn out to be tougher standards in the end. Curriculum has been softened and infiltrated with political correctness. Throughout this century, the quality or difficulty of standard exams, for example, has deteriorated. Changes in the SAT in 1995 and 1996—which coincided with an increase in SAT scores—raised serious questions as to the new test's degree of difficulty. In particular, the antonym section on the verbal exam was eliminated. In addition, public school administrators, teachers, and education unions will exert great pressure to hike school spending, arguing that additional resources are needed to help meet new standards.

None of the answers to our current education woes offered by the education establishment are the correct answers. The true answer to today's education mess is replacing a government monopoly with a more market-driven system based on choice and competition.

Public schools amount to little more than a government monopoly. But for upper income earners, including mayors of New York City, few parents can afford to send their children to private schools—religious or secular. They are confronted with a government monopoly that tells them where and how their children will be educated. If public schools are to be salvaged at all in New York, then they must be exposed to the outside forces of competition, which will stir public education to make dramatic changes.

Substantial changes are needed. For example, the public education profession needs to be "de-unionized" and tenure terminated. These reforms would give greater weight to merit and performance when it comes to employment and compensation decisions, resulting in greater rewards for excellence and fewer benefits for poor-to-mediocre teachers.

Some argue that full (public and private) school choice will mean the end of public schools in New York. In fact, in the long run that may be the case. Government, however, should not be in the business of protecting a failed government school system. Instead, it should making sure that a high-quality education is available to all students. If public schools fade away in a more competitive market, that means they were not meeting the needs of parents and children and they should fade away.

Others argue that school choice will only leave troubled or special education children in public schools. I have not seen any hard evidence presented that such a scenario would result; just sweeping accusations by public school special interests. There is no reason to believe that the private sector could not adequately respond to the needs of troubled or special education children. Indeed, the private sector stands more likely to come up with innovative ways to help such children. In fact, according to Janet Beales at the Reason Foundation, an estimated 10,000 special education students learn in private schools that are contracted by their public school districts.

But let's go through a thought experiment for a moment. If we accept—only for the purposes of this thought experiment—the idea that public schools will be left with the hard cases, the question then becomes: So what? This would mean that market failure exists when it comes to educating hard cases, and therefore, government action is justified in this instance. Government's role in primary and secondary education largely would be limited to the hard cases, with others choosing among various private schools. After all, under this hypothetical example, no reason exists to bring all children into government schools.

A full school choice plan could work several ways in New York. For example, local school districts could vote to opt in or opt out of private/public school choice. Or, choice could be implemented statewide.

This latter idea presents the opportunity for the most significant overhaul. For example, New York State could distribute vouchers worth roughly $4,000 to the parents or guardians of all school-age children across the state to be used at any public or private (secular or religious) school. This $4,000 per student amount approximately equals the State Education Department's current budget.

Two additional cost-saving measures should accompany a shift to vouchers. First, the voucher amount would be indexed each year for inflation—larger increases would not be allowed.

Second, parents and guardians should be provided with incentives to shop around for the best quality at the best price. Any savings a parent or guardian finds—for example, paying tuition of just $2,500 a year with a $4,000 voucher—should be allowed to accrue in the child's education savings account (ESA). These funds could be used for any additional education expenses or saved for college.

Another savings option would be to means test vouchers, with the amount of the voucher declining above certain income levels. State taxpayers would reap added savings. Vouchers also eliminate the need for much of today's massive State Education Department and its thousands of bureaucrats.

In turn, under such a state voucher plan, local school property taxes could be eliminated. And since school taxes make up about 70 percent of the average property tax bill, taxpayers would see a real 70 percent cut in property taxes. This would be a boon to the New York economy.

In order to compete, as noted above, public schools would finally have to confront and deal with exorbitant costs and stagnating or declining quality. Many entrepreneurial teachers and administrators long frustrated by the public school system would have an opportunity to raise capital and start their own schools. Indeed, small, responsive, entrepreneurial schools would become the rule in such a competitive, choice-based system, as opposed to today's large, unresponsive, bureaucratic public schools. Parents would be free to choose schools based on a host of factors, including quality of teachers, class size, values, curriculum, religious teachings, etc.

However, some people fear that private schools could be regulated extensively under a government voucher program, losing independence and many of the features that allow them to provide a high quality education. Such fears certainly carry merit, and any voucher program would have to be carefully constructed to avoid such pitfalls.

Many market advocates in education believe that government-supplied vouchers will inevitably hurt private education, no matter how carefully crafted. For them, school choice in New York would be better advanced by a tax abatement plan. Some local tax and education activists have been pushing the idea in New York State. Generally, such plans allow individuals and businesses to take a school property tax abatement up to a certain amount—say, $1,000 or $2,000—for each local student for which they pay tuition and other education expenses (e.g., books) at a private school. Under such a plan, choice is enhanced, and expanded government involvement in private schools perhaps better avoided. As more and more children move from public to private schools, beyond some break-even point, state and local taxpayers accrue significant savings based on the different per pupil costs (i.e., lower costs for the private school students versus higher costs for the public schools). Unfortunately, government could slap various restrictions and requirements on the use of such tax abatements as well, thereby *de facto* regulating private schools. In the end, any school choice plan must be carefully crafted so that private schools are not neutered by government regulation. I believe vouchers are the best course.

The only real losers under either full school choice system are those individuals working in public schools who grew fat and lazy over the years, and education unions who did the same.

## A Choice for Life

Abortion is more prevalent in New York State than anywhere else in the nation with the exception of Washington, D.C.

Unfortunately, the pro-choice position has grown some in recent years among self-proclaimed conservatives and libertarians. They argue to get the government out of this decision, along with all of the other areas from which government should be banished, such as the economy. However, the fundamental function of government that conservatives, libertarians, and even liberals agree upon remains the protection of life, limb, and property. Protection of the unborn life fits quite neatly into this straightforward framework. After all, to enjoy liberty—a right near and dear to conservatives and libertarians—one must first have a chance at life.

## Re-Birth of the Civil, Opportunity Society in New York

Over the past several decades, the quality of life in New York has declined. Where before economic opportunity abounded, today such opportunity remains quite sparse. Where before quality, values-based education was the rule, today it is the exception. Where before taking responsibility for one's actions was expected, today excuses absolve responsibility. Where before private, individual charity helped people back onto their feet, today government welfare programs knock people off their feet—many times permanently so. Where before crime was harshly punished, today the criminal often gains status of victim. Where before innocent life was valued, today it is considered expendable.

The numbers, graphs, and rankings in this book bear out such an interpretation. Of course, New York is by no means alone in suffering from such woes, but it certainly leads the way. Government action has been the catalyst for much of this decline. New York adopted all of the bad ideas implemented by the federal government over the years, took them several steps further, and added many of their own dismal notions as well—with New York City going farthest.

Government in New York played the primary role in destroying economic opportunity, quality education, individual responsibility, the benefits of private charity, public safety, and innocent life. In this concluding chapter, I have outlined a few reform measures to begin turning around the economy and education, and boosting individual responsibility in New York State and New York City. Measures are needed on other fronts as well, including getting even tougher on criminals (e.g., ending parole and extending the reach of New York's new death penalty law), supporting innocent life by bringing abortion to an end, and respecting and protecting individual property rights.

New York has created an uncivil, dependent society. Again, some of the destructive effects of such a society have been captured in the preceding pages through charts and graphs. Most of the grim effects cannot be captured by numbers, however, like people giving up, believing they can't succeed, and losing their moral bearings.

New York needs to return to a civil, opportunity society. Civility comes with individual responsibility, and opportunity springs from man's ability to create and innovate—free from the shackles of high taxes, onerous regulations, and bloated government.

New York's perpetual state of crisis can come to an end, but only if state and city social engineers are fired and forced to find productive, private-sector employment. This change will only come about at the ballot box. Unfortunately, though, New York State and New York City suffer on both the demand-side and on the supply-side of politics. The demand for change has only begun to percolate over the past five or six years. On the supply-side, few free-market, conservative reformers come forth to run for political office in New York. Just as there is a dearth of much-needed entrepreneurship on the supply-side of New York's economy, a dearth of pro-growth, conservative ideas exists on the supply-side of New York politics as well.

While they will not succeed initially, New York desperately needs articulate people willing to run for office on a platform of truly smaller government, lower taxes, less regulation, school choice, and individual responsibility. These ideas need to be introduced—or supplied—in the political mix in New York. After all, according to Say's Law, supply creates demand.

## End Notes

1. Norman Ture, "Supply Side Analysis and Public Policy," in *Essays in Supply-Side Economics*, edited by David G. Raboy (Institute for Research on the Economics of Taxation), 11.
2. Jean-Baptiste Say, *A Treatise on Political Economy* (New York: Augustus M. Kelley Publishers, 1971), 133.
3. Say, *A Treatise on Political Economy*, 161.
4. Say, *A Treatise on Political Economy*, 139.
5. George Gilder, *Microcosm* (New York: Touchstone, 1989), 61-62.
6. Ture, "Supply Side Analysis," 13.
7. George Gilder, *Recapturing the Spirit of Enterprise* (San Francisco: ICS Press, 1992), 165.
8. Paul Craig Roberts, "The Breakdown of the Keynesian Model," in *Keeping the Tablets: Modern American Conservative Thought*, edited by William F. Buckley, Jr. and Charles R. Kesler (New York: Harper & Row, 1988), 229.
9. Richard Vedder, "State and Local Taxation and Economic Growth: Lessons for Federal Tax Reform," Joint Economic Committee of the United States Congress, Washington, D.C. (December 1995).
10. Fred Siegel and Bruce Bender, "The Decline of the Empire State," *The New Democrat* (November 1994).
11. Adam Smith, *An Inquiry into the Nature and Causes of the Wealth of Nations*, Volume II (Chicago: University of Chicago Press, 1976), 389-390.
12. Ray B. Smith, *History of New York State: Political and Governmental*, Volume IV, 1896-1920 (Syracuse, N.Y.: The Syracuse Press, Inc., 1922), 316.
13. Mario Cuomo, *The New York Idea: An Experiment in Democracy* (New York: Crown Publishers, Inc., 1994), 42.
14. Ron Chernow, *The House of Morgan: An American Banking Dynasty and the Rise of Modern Finance* (New York: Atlantic Monthly Press, 1990), 126.

15. Chernow, *House of Morgan*, 225.
16. *The Wall Street Journal*, "Personal Income Tax for New York City Called 'Last Resort'" (November 30, 1965).
17. Dennis P. Doyle, "Lessons in Hypocrisy" (*The Wall Street Journal*, June 13, 1995).
18. Jane Jacobs, *The Economy of Cities* (New York: Vintage Books, 1970), (originally in 1969), 95.
19. Jane Jacobs, *Cities and the Wealth of Nations* (New York: Vintage Books, 1985), (originally in 1984), 179.
20. Smith, *History of New York State*, 316.
21. E.S. Savas, "Privatization," in *Encyclopedia of Government and Politics*, Volume 2, edited by Mary Hawkesworth and Maurice Kogan (Routledge), 830.
22. The Reason Foundation; *Privatization '94* (Los Angeles: The Reason Foundation, 1994), 18.
23. David F. Shaffer and Robert B. Ward, *The Comeback State* (New York: The Public Policy Institute of New York State, Inc., January 1994), 66-73.
24. Shaffer and Ward, *The Comeback State*, 72-73.
25. William H. Mellor, "Is New York City Killing Entrepreneurship?" Institute for Justice, Washington, D.C. (1996).
26. Mellor, "Is New York City Killing Entrepreneurship?", 3.
27. Mellor, "Is New York City Killing Entrepreneurship?", 3-4.

# Index

## About the Author

Raymond J. Keating serves as chief economist with the Small Business Survival Foundation, a research and education organization focusing on public policy issues impacting entrepreneurs and the economy, and with the Small Business Survival Committee, a small-business advocacy group with more than 40,000 members across the nation. Keating also is a principal with Capital Hill Research—a political and economic research service for the investment community. In addition, Keating is a regular contributor to *Newsday* and co-writes a weekly syndicated column, "Carolan & Keating," on New York issues with Matthew Carolan of *National Review*.

Keating's first book, *D.C. by the Numbers: A State of Failure*, was published by University Press of America in January 1995. He contributed an essay to *Private Means, Public Ends: Voluntarism vs. Coercion* published by the Foundation for Economic Education in 1996. Keating also has written hundreds of policy studies and articles, published in such periodicals as *The Wall Street Journal, The New York Times, National Review, Newsday, Investor's Business Daily, The Journal of Commerce, The Washington Times, New York Post, Daily News, Times Union* (Albany, N.Y.), *Record* (Troy, N.Y.), *Buffalo News, Insight, The Freeman, Human Events, The City Journal,* and many more. His areas of expertise include taxation; federal, state and city budget issues; monetary policy; regulation; supply-side economics; the economics of sports stadiums and arenas; the U.S. economy; and a host of small-business issues.

Previously, Keating served as director of New York Citizens for a Sound Economy.

Keating holds an MA in economics from New York University, an MBA in banking and finance from Hofstra University, and a BS in business administration and economics from St. Joseph's College.

Keating resides on Long Island with his wife, Beth, and their son, David.